AFRICA

2002

© NASA—Africa from Apollo 17

Editor: Les de Villiers

A publication of
The Corporate Council on Africa
and
Business Books International

Cover picture

Bororo maiden adorned for a yaake dance   © *Victor Englebert*

Library of Congress Catalog Card Number 2001 130668

AFRICA 2002
Africa - Reference - Business
Politics - Geography - History

ISBN 0-916673-10-3
ISSN 1536-1454

The information in this book is furnished for informational use only and should not be construed as recommendations on investment and business transactions. It was developed largely on the basis of review of both secondary resources and first-hand advice and contains subjective opinion. While efforts were made to include the most recent and reliable sources of information, the accuracy of the content cannot be guaranteed. Investment and business decisions should only be made after proper further investigation and due diligence on the part of the reader.

AFRICA TODAY

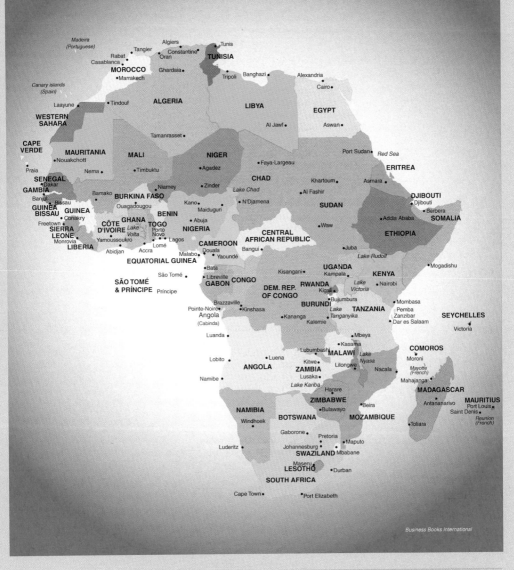

Business Books International

Size	11,709,908 sq miles/30,328,662 sq. km	Island nations	Six, with Equatorial Guinea part landbased
	Second largest continent after Asia		Madagascar is world's 4th largest island
Distance	North-South 5,000 miles/8,000 km	Population	At 800 million 13% of world total
	East-West 4,700 miles/7,560 km		Speak more than 1,000 languages
Mountains	Highest: Mt. Kilimanjaro 19,340 ft/5,895 m	Density	Average of 26 people per sq. km
	Ranks sixteenth worldwide		Well below Asia's 116 and Europe's 102
Lakes	Lake Victoria is world's 3rd largest	Resources	8.2 % of world's oil, 7.7% of its natural gas
	Lake Tanganyika is 7th largest		11% to 45% of world's strategic minerals
Rivers	Longest: Nile is 4,180 miles/6,690 km	Economy	Average 4% growth in output from 1994-1998
	World's longest river		Per capita income $315—one-third Asia's
Countries	53 countries of which 15 landlocked	Investment	Return on US investment in 1997 was 25.3%
	Largest: Sudan, Algeria & DR of Congo		Exceeded 16.2% in Asia and 12.3% worldwide

CONTENTS

STOMPING

GROUNDS

Jump on one of our jumbos to Africa,
and enjoy all the advantages that come
with the territory. Like daily nonstops from
New York and Atlanta. Award-winning
in-flight service. And a continental
network with convenient connections
to over 22 major African cities. No one
in Africa is better connected.

*For reservations call your travel agent
or 1-800-722-9675 or visit www.flysaa.com*

SOUTH AFRICAN
Fly the South African Dream

CONTENTS CONTINUED

HSBC Equator

Member HSBC *Group*

FOREWORD

The Corporate Council on Africa (CCA) is honored to cooperate with Business Books International to bring to you AFRICA 2002, the second edition of CCA's comprehensive guide for American individuals and businesses seeking to learn more about doing business with the nations of Africa.

Americans are increasingly turning to Africa as a critical new market that includes nearly a billion people. CCA member companies represent more than 80 percent of all U.S. private sector investment in Africa. There remains ample space for more American businesses to explore the many rewarding opportunities that are today's Africa. For example:

Africa is the last great economic frontier on Earth. Currently, there is no greater return on investment in the world than that available in many nations of Africa. Two-way trade between Africa's 53 independent nations and the United States totals almost $40 billion and this figure is growing. The U.S. already conducts more business with Africa than it does with Russia, the Newly Independent States and Eastern Europe combined.

Experts estimate that Africa will supply 20 percent of American oil and natural gas needs by 2010. And although the bulk of U.S. trade with Africa has traditionally been oil and gas-related, investments in agribusiness, infrastructure, telecommunications, textiles and other sectors have registered significant increases in recent years.

More investment in Africa will help the American economy as much as it will assist in the development of Africa. For me, Africa represents our common future, where the economic health of a nation depends upon its ability to promote and sustain international trade. As Africa's economy moves forward, so will we as a global civilization.

I invite you to join us in discovering the opportunities, challenges and rewards of Africa.

Stephen Hayes
President
The Corporate Council on Africa
Washington, D.C.

PUBLISHER'S NOTE

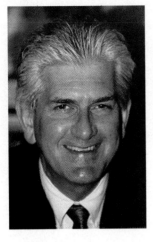

In this book we have tried to meet the demands not only of business but the academic community and general public as well.

The first edition has found a ready demand in libraries where there has long been a need for a comprehensive reference to the continent and its 53 nations.

Like Shakespeare in Henry IV we speak here about "Africa and its golden joys." But we do not ignore its sorrows.

On one hand there is the beauty of this vast continent of contrasts and great promise as new leaders forge ahead with plans to make the African Renaissance become a reality. On the other, there are continuing wars, famine and HIV/AIDS. We try to cover it all in a fair and balanced way.

The response to our first edition was very encouraging. We have received numerous editorial suggestions, many of which were incorporated. That is the convenience of producing an annual reference: it affords the opportunity to improve and expand—and correct.

We will, however, never reach the stage where we could claim absolute accuracy. Even though we relied largely on UN and World Bank statistics, there are instances where we were obliged to seek answers elsewhere and found ourselves caught in conflicting numbers. Unsettled borders and territorial claims further complicated our task.

Without the support of the Corporate Council on Africa and its membership, as well as a number of other prominent US and African corporations, this book would not have been possible. A special word of gratitude goes to the president of the Corporate Council, Steve Hayes, and his colleagues.

Readers are invited to send comments and suggestions regarding editorial to us at Business Books Intl., P.O. Box 1587, New Canaan, CT 06840, or by email to editor@businessbooksusa.com. Additional copies may be purchased by logging on to www.businessbooksusa.com.

Dr. Les de Villiers
Publisher/Editor

Business is done
a little differently here.

When doing business in South Africa, travel with a company that knows the destination. From Johannesburg to Cape Town, African Travel can provide thorough knowledge, advice and expertise.

We offer competitive rates on South African Airways, touring, hotel & lodge accommodations. Contact African Travel today for all your business travel needs.

African Travel, Inc.

Live the Dream

1-800-722-7755
www.africantravelinc.com

SOUTH AFRICA

CST: 20-51877

African milestones[1]

BC

5,000,000	*Australapithecus africanus*—fossils found in eastern and southern Africa.
2,200,000	*Homo habilis* (emergent man and first toolmaker)—fossils found in East Africa.
1,600,000	*Homo erectus* (middle-period man)—expansion into Eurasia.
500,000	*Homo sapiens.*
100,000	Middle Stone Age (Neolithic era).
20,000	Late stone age and early agriculture.
4000	Stone and copper age. Settlement of the Nile Valley. Settlements in the Sahara.
3200	King Menes unites the kingdoms of the Delta and the Nile. Egypt invades Nubia.
2700	King Zoser, Imhotep and Step Pyramid at Sakara.
2600	Khufu (Cheops) and Great Pyramid at Giza.
2500	Egypt sends expeditions to land of Punt and into Sahara area.
2280	Old Kingdom ends. First Intermediate Period in Egypt.
2100	Middle Kingdom begins with Mentuhotep. Egypt expands southward into Nubia.
2000	Amenemhet I, founder of new Dynasty.
1780	Second Intermediate Period; Egypt has fifty rulers in slightly over a century.
1660	Asiatic invaders (Hyksos) conquer Lower and Middle Egypt.
1557	Ahmose I drives Hyksos out of Egypt and establishes XVIII Dynasty.
1511	Thutmose I reconquers Nubia. Egypt expands into Asia and Kush area.
1400	Amenophis III. Queen Tiy.
1360	Amarna Period in Egypt. Akhnaten, the heretic Pharaoh.
1340	Pharaoh Tutankhamen.
1300	Time of Moses. First horses in Africa.
1230	Exodus of Israelites from Egypt.
1000	Makeda of Axum (Queen of Sheba) visits Solomon.
751	Kush King Kashta conquers Upper Egypt. Piankhi conquers all of Egypt.
690	Pharaoh Taharqa.
650	Assyrians under Assurbanipal conquer Egypt. Capital of Kush moved to Meroë.
600	Greeks establish colony at Cyrene.
525	Persians, under Cambyses, conquer Egypt.
500	Axum begins to develop.
450	Herodotus visits Egypt and Kush. Earliest construction at Zimbabwe.
332	Alexander the Great conquers Egypt.
304	Ptolemy I establishes dynasty.
200	Height of Nok culture.
150	Cities of Zanj established.
100	Bantu introduce iron working into the area south of the Sudan.
146	Carthage conquered and razed by Rome.
46	Cleopatra becomes mistress of Augustus Caesar.
42	Cleopatra wins affection of Marc Antony.
31	Augustus Caesar conquers Egypt.

AD

1	Beginning of east African city states.
30	Lion Temple built in Kush.
100	Axum becomes capital of the major state of Eritrea.
200	Nok culture fades away; Ghana begins.
200	Roman Emperor Septimus Severus fortifies frontier in North Africa.
238	Revolt in Africa against Roman rule.
300-400	Bantu cereal cultivators begin to herd cattle.
333	King Ezana of Axum becomes a Christian.
350	Kingdom of Axum supercedes Kush.
354	St. Augustine born at Carthage.
429	Vandals invade North Africa.

1. *Some dates and events in the early years remain in dispute among scholars.*

African milestones (ctd)

534	Justinian's Byzantine expedition conquers North Africa.
571	Yoruba migration from Upper Egypt.
550	Nubians in Sudan become Christian.
600	Muslims start conquering North Africa.
640	Caliph Omar, successor to Mohammed as Islamic leader, conquers Egypt.
652	Christian Nubians and Arabs agree on Aswan as border on Nile.
700	So tribes settle Kanem (Lake Chad). Bantu peoples spread out.
788	Idris, Arab chief, ruler in Morocco.
790	First dynasty established in Benin. Ghana at its peak.
800s	Christian empire in Ethiopia continues after decline of Aksum.
800s	Arabs and Persians establish trading posts in East Africa.
950	Kilwa established. University of Cairo founded.
1000	Igbo-Ukwu culture thrives in Nigeria.
1100	Bantu-speaking peoples move into Southern Africa.
1054	Almoravid Moslems invade Ghana.
1061	Beni Halil Moslems invade North Africa.
1173	Muslim warrior Saladin becomes sultan of Egypt.
1200	King Lalibela of Ethiopia establishes churches cut from rock.
1220	City state of Kilwa in Tanzania prospers.
1235	Warrior Sun Diata founds Mali empire.
1250	Kanem kingdom in Lake Chad disintegrates; Mamelukes seize power in Egypt.
1300	Ife culture of West Africa produces famous brass objects.
1324	Emperor Mansa Musa of Mali travels on pilgrimage from Timbuktu to Mecca.
1348	Egypt devastated by Black Death plague.
1380	Kongo kingdom at river mouth.
1400	Mombasa becomes Swahili city state.
1445	Portuguese start slave trade on West Coast of Africa.
1450	Great Zimbabwe at its height; Oyo Empire is created.
1460	Songhai Empire established.
1479	Portuguese build Elmina Castle on West African coast.
1482	Portuguese explore Congo river estuary.
1488	Portuguese explorer Bartholomeu Dias sails around the southern tip of Africa.
1491	Ruler of Kongo kingdom baptized as Christian by Portuguese.
1497	Portuguese explorer Vasco da Gama sails around Africa to India.
1500	Songhai empire expands in West Africa. Hausa states grow through trade.
1502	First African slaves sent to the New World.
1505	Portuguese capture Sofala and settle in Mozambique on east coast.
1517	Ottomans defeat Mamelukes in Egypt.
1528	Portuguese capture Mombasa.
1529	Muslims defeat Ethiopian Christians.
1530	Beginning of trans-Atlantic slave trade by Portuguese.
1543	Portuguese help Christian Ethiopians to defeat Muslims.
1562	Sir John Hawkins starts English slave trade from West Africa to Americas.
1575	Portuguese start colonizing Angola.
1598	First Dutch trade posts on Guinea coast.
1619	First slaves arrive in colony of Virginia.
1640	Beginning of large-scale selling of slaves to Caribbean and Americas.
1650	Ethiopian ruler expels Portuguese missionaries.
1652	Dutch establish a settlement at the Cape of Good Hope.
1670	French settle in Senegal.
1680	Ashanti Kingdom is formed.
1686	Louis XIV of France officially annexes Madagascar.
1689	French Huguenots arrive at the Cape.
1701	Osei Tutu creates free Ashanti nation in West Africa.
1705	Bey Husain ibn Ali founds Tunis dynasty.
1727	Death of Mulai Ismail followed by 30 years of anarchy in Morocco.
1740	The Lunda create new kingdom.
1746	Mazrui dynasty in Mombasa becomes independent from Oman.
1750	Buganda becomes the leading Lake Kingdom.

African milestones (ctd)

1755	First outbreak of smallpox at Cape by sailors, decimating Khoisan tribesmen.
1768	Scottish explorer James Bruce travels to Ethiopia.
1770	Tukulor kingdom emerges in former Songhai region of West Africa.
1777	Sidi Mohammed, ruler of Morocco, abolishes slavery of Christians.
1779	First war between the Bantu and Boers in Cape border areas
1784	Yoruba civil wars.
1785	Omani rulers reassert rule over Zanzibar.
1787	British settlers, including slaves, establish colony at Sierra Leone.
1789	Spain opens slave trade to Cuba.
1794	French National Convention emancipates French colonial slaves.
1795	British occupy Dutch Cape Colony to preempt French until 1803.
1796	Scottish explorer Mungo Park reaches Niger.
1798	Napoleon takes Egypt.
1801	French troops withdraw after defeat by British at Alexandria.
1805	Mohammad Ali conquers Egypt.
1806	British wrest Cape Colony from Dutch.
1807	British parliament bans slave trade.
1807	Britain converts Sierra Leone into a crown colony.
1810	British negotiate elimination of slave trade in South Atlantic with Portugal.
1814	Cape colony finally ceded to Britain by Netherlands.
1815	British pressure Netherlands, Spain, Portugal and France to end slavery.
1816	Gambia occupied by British after French withdrawal.
1816-28	Shaka Zulu dominates eastern part of South Africa.
1817	American Colonization Society encourages return of slaves to Africa.
1820	Mohammad Ali captures Sudan in search of slaves and gold.
1820	British settlers land at Cape Colony.
1821	American Colonization Society establishes colony at Cape Mesurado—Liberia.
1822	Ex-slaves from America settle in Liberia.
1828	Egyptians found city of Khartoum in Sudan.
1830	French capture Algiers.
1832-47	Abd-al-Kadir directs resistance against French in Algeria.
1834-36	Great Trek begins in Cape as Boers migrate north away from British authority.
1838	Boers defeat Zulu leader Dingaan at Blood River in Natal.
1845	British annex Natal.
1847	Liberia declares itself an independent state.
1852	Independent Boer Transvaal Republic established.
1854	Independent Boer Republic of Orange Free State founded.
1852	Tukolor leader al-Hajj Umar launches Jihad along Niger and Senegal rivers.
1853-56	Livingstone discovers Victoria Falls.
1858-59	Burton and Speke discover Lake Tanganyika and Speke, Lake Victoria.
1858-61	Livingstone discovers Lake Nyasa.
1860	Speke identifies Lake Victoria as source of the White Nile.
1861	US recognizes the new state of Liberia founded by freed American slaves.
1862	US President Lincoln grants freedom to slaves after rebellion in the South.
1863	Al Hajj Umar captures Timbuktu.
1863	French establish protectorate over Porto Novo on coast of Dahomey.
1865	Slavery in the US abolished under the 13th Amendment to the Constitution.
1865-68	Wars between Orange Free State Republic and Basuto people.
1866	French establish posts on Guinea coast.
1867	Diamonds discovered at Hopetown in Cape colony of South Africa.
1868	French sign protectorate treaties for Ivory Coast.
1868	Britain annexes Basutoland at request of Basuto King Mosweshwe.
1870	Diamond rush starts at Kimberley South Africa.
1871	Stanley meets Livingstone at Ujiji and resupplies him.
1873	Livingstone dies at Chitambo's village, Ilala.
1879	Stanley begins operations in Congo on behalf of King Leopold.
1879	British defeated by Zulu at Ulundi in Natal.
1874	Britain occupies former Dutch colony of Gold Coast.
1880	Brazza signs treaty with King Makoko and establishes Brazzaville.

African milestones (ctd)

1881	Transvaal Republic defeats British in First Boer War.
1881-7	Stanley signs treaties with Congo chiefs and founds Leopoldville.
1881	French army invades Tunisia from Algeria and imposes protectorate.
1883	French establish protectorate over Dahomey.
1883	Paul Kruger elected president of Transvaal.
1884	German protectorate declared over Angra Pequena.
1884	Nachtigal takes over Togo on behalf of Bismarck.
1884	Carl Peters signs treaties with mainland chiefs in Zanzibar region.
1884	Britain signs protectorate treaties with Niger and Oil River chiefs.
1884	With assistance from Bismarck, Leopold gets recognition for Congo claims.
1885	Mahdi captures Khartoum and massacres Gordon and the British garrison.
1885	Bismarck declares German protectorate over part of East Africa.
1885	European powers divide Africa at the Berlin Conference.
1886	Gold discovered in the Transvaal.
1887	Britain signs conditional agreement with Turkey to withdraw from Egypt.
1887	British incorporate Zululand into Natal.
1888	Cecil Rhodes gets mining rights from Lobenguela north of Transvaal.
1888	Britain gives royal charter to Rhodes' British South Africa (BSA) in new region.
1889	France declares protectorate over Ivory Coast.
1889	Emperor Yohannes of Ethiopia killed by Menelik—supported by Italy.
1890	British-French agreement recognizes their respective interests in West Africa.
1890	Peters extends German influence in Uganda by treaty with Kabaka Mwanga.
1891	British recognize Italian protectorate over Ethiopia.
1891	Britain recognizes Rhodes BSA Company's control over Rhodesia.
1892	French defeat King Behanzin of Dahomey and extend protectorate.
1891-2	Harry Johnston secures British influence over Nyasaland.
1893	Guinea and Ivory Coast colonies established by France.
1894	French set up protectorate in Dahomey (Benin).
1895	Britain secures control over Uganda.
1895	Italians start invasion of Ethiopia from Eritrea.
1896-8	Kitchener and Anglo-Egyptian army recapture Sudan.
1896	British defeat Ashanti in West Africa.
1896	Menelik defeats Italians but allows them to keep Eritrea.
1897	Britain signs treaty with Ethiopia and concedes part of Somaliland.
1897	Slavery is banned in Zanzibar.
1899	British and Egyptian governments create condominium rule over Sudan.
1899	Anglo-Boer War starts.
1901	British add Ashanti to Gold Coast.
1902	In treaty with Anglo-Egyptian authority Menelik abandons claims to Upper Nile.
1902	Boer Republics sign away independence in peace treaty with Britain.
1903-1905	Exposure of atrocities in the Belgian and French Congo by Morel and Brazza.
1904	France creates the Federation of French West Africa.
1910	Union of South Africa granted independence by Britain.
1916	South African leader Jan Smuts leads fight against Germans in East Africa.
1922	Egypt gains sovereignty from British under King Fuad.
1930	Ras Tafari crowned emperor of Ethiopia as Haile Selassie.
1931	First trans-African railroad from Angola to Mozambique completed.
1935-36	Italians under Mussolini invade and annex Ethiopia.
1936	Native Representation Act denies black South Africans chance of equality.
1939	South Africa under Smuts declares war against Germany.
1941	German army under Rommel campaigns in North Africa.
1941	Ethiopia liberated from Italy by South African and British troops.
1942	British Commonwealth troops defeat German army at El Alamein in Egypt.
1942	Germany and Italy driven from North Africa.
1948	National Party comes to power in South Africa and adopts apartheid.
1951	Libya gains independence under King Idris.
1952-59	Mau-Mau guerillas led by Kenyatta fight British in Kenya.
1952	King Farouk forced to abdicate by Colonel Naguib.
1954-62	War for independence in Algeria.
1954	Colonel Abdul Nasser succeeds Naguib and exiles King Farouk.

African milestones (ctd)

1956	Sudan receives independence from Egypt.
1956	Suez crisis erupts and British and French lose control of the canal.
1956	Morocco gains freedom from France and additional territory from Spain.
1956	Tunisia gains freedom from France.
1957	Ghana (former Gold Coast) granted independence by Britain.
1958	Guinea gains freedom from France.
1960	South Africa becomes Republic outside British Commonwealth.
1960	Civil war starts in South Sudan.
1960	Independence for Benin (former Dahomey), Burkina Faso (former Upper Volta).
1960	Central African Republic, Chad, Congo (Brazzaville), Côte d'Ivoire independent.
1960	Gabon, Madagascar, Mali, Mauritania, Niger, Senegal, and Togo independent.
1960	French Cameroon and part of British Cameroon form new nation of Cameroon.
1960	Belgian Congo becomes independent and civil war starts.
1960	Colonel Mobutu establishes rule over Zaire (former Belgian Congo).
1960	Nigeria gains independence from Britain.
1960	Former British and Italian Somaliland form independent Somalia.
1961	Sharpeville uprising in South Africa results in death of 69 black protesters.
1961	Sierra Leone independent from Britain.
1961	Tanzania (Tanganyika) gains independence from Britain.
1962	Algeria gains independence from France.
1962	Rwanda and Burundi (former Ruanda-Urundi) gain freedom from Belgium.
1962	Uganda becomes independent from Britain.
1963	Kenya gains independence from Britain.
1963	Organization of African Unity formed.
1964	Malawi (former Nyasaland) gains independence from Britain.
1964	United Republic of Tanzania and Zanzibar established.
1964	Zambia (Northern Rhodesia) gains independence from Britain.
1965	The Gambia granted independence by Britain.
1965	White-ruled Rhodesia declares unilateral independence from Britain.
1964	Nelson Mandela and other ANC leaders jailed at Robben Island, South Africa.
1966	Botswana (Bechuanaland) and Lesotho (Basutoland) independent from Britain.
1967-70	Biafran War in Nigeria.
1968	Equatorial Guinea granted independence by Spain.
1968	Mauritius gains freedom from Britain.
1968	Kingdom of Swaziland gains independence from Britain.
1968	Cape Town surgeon Christiaan Barndard performs world's first heart transplant.
1969	Muammar Qaddafi seizes power after coup in Libya.
1973	Guinea-Bissau granted freedom by Portugal.
1975	Angola, Mozambique, and Cape Verde independent from Portugal.
1975	São Tomé & Príncipe granted independence by Portugal.
1975	Comoros receives independence from France.
1976	Seychelles gains independence from Britain.
1976	Soweto uprising results in calls for further sanctions against South Africa.
1977	Former French Somaliland becomes independent Djibouti.
1980	Zimbabwe (Rhodesia) gains independence from Britain under Robert Mugabe.
1986	US Congress passes law requiring sanctions against South Africa.
1990	President FW de Klerk of South Africa starts dismantling apartheid.
1990	Nelson Mandela freed from jail.
1990	Namibia (former South West Africa) gains freedom from South Africa.
1991	Eritrea wins freedom from Ethiopia.
1992	All sanctions against South Africa lifted.
1994	ANC wins first multiracial election in South Africa.
1994	Nelson Mandela sworn in as president of South Africa.
1997	Mobutu of Zaire overthrown by Laurent Kabila.
1997	Democratic Republic of Congo replaces Zaire.
1997	Ghanaian diplomat Kofi Annan elected UN Secretary General.
1998	Border war starts between Eritrea and Ethiopia.
2000	Peace accord signed between Ethiopia and Eritrea.
2001	Organization of Africa Union disbanded in favor of new African Union.
2001	Kofi Annan reelected UN Secretary General.

Africa's mountains

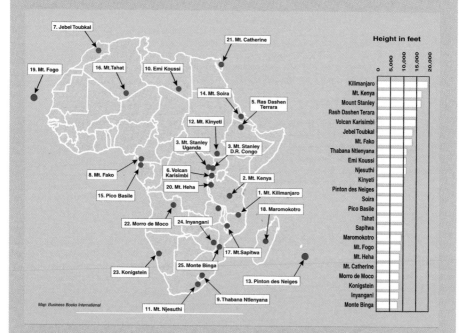

Map: Business Books International

Country	Peak/Mountain	Feet	Meters	Rank Africa	Rank World
Tanzania	Kilimanjaro	19340	5895	1	16
Kenya	Mount Kenya	17057	5199	2	22
Congo, Dem. Rep.	Mt. Stanley	16765	5110	3	25
Uganda	Mount Stanley	16765	5110	3	26
Ethiopia	Ras Dashen Terara	15157	4620	5	33
Rwanda	Volcan Karisimbi	14826	4519	6	34
Morocco	Jebel Toubkal	13665	4165	7	40
Cameroon	Fako	13435	4095	8	42
Lesotho	Thabana Ntlenyana	11424	3482	9	53
Chad	Emi Koussi	11204	3415	10	55
South Africa	Njesuthi	11181	3408	11	56
Sudan	Kinyeti	10456	3187	12	57
Reunion	Pinton des Neiges	10069	3069	13	63
Eritrea	Soira	9901	3018	14	64
Equatorial Guinea	Pico Basile	9869	3008	15	66
Algeria	Tahat	9852	3003	16	67
Malawi	Sapitwa	9849	3002	17	68
Madagascar	Maromokotro	9436	2876	18	76
Cape Verde	Mt.Fogo	9281	2829	19	80
Burundi	Mount Heha	8760	2670	20	89
Egypt	Mt. Catherine	8625	2629	21	92
Angola	Morro de Moco	8596	2620	22	93
Namibia	Konigstein	8550	2606	23	94
Zimbabwe	Inyangani	8504	2592	24	96
Mozambique	Mt. Binga	7992	2436	25	104

Chapter 1

The African Continent

With a land mass of 11,709,908 sq. miles (30,328,662 sq. km), Africa is the second largest continent. The farthest point north—Ras ben Sekka, near Bizerte in Tunisia, and the southernmost point, Cape Agulhas in South Africa—are almost equidistant from the equator at around 2,500 miles (4,000 km). The farthest eastern extremity, Ras Hafun Peninsula in Somalia, and the westernmost point, Cape Verde in Senegal—are about 4,700 miles (7,560 km) apart. The Sahara Desert (3,250,000 sq. miles or 8,417,500 sq. km) is the world's largest and at 19,340 ft. (5,895 m) Mt. Kilimanjaro in Tanzania is Africa's highest peak. The Nile river flowing northwards over a distance of 4,160 miles (6,695 km) to the Mediterranean sea, is the world's longest. Madagascar is the world's 4th largest island after Greenland, New Guinea and Borneo. Africa's three largest countries— Sudan, Algeria and the Democratic Republic of Congo—form 25% of the total land area. Fifteen are landlocked.

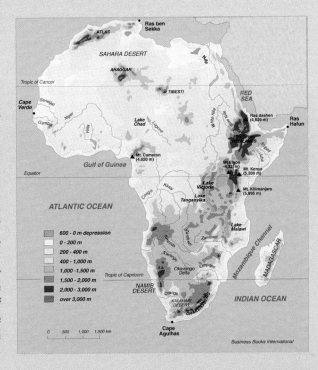

Business Books International

Topography

Africa is basically one enormous plateau modified in part by erosion and earth movements. It resembles, in the words of explorer David Livingstone, "a wide awake hat with the crown a little depressed." Another explorer, John Speke, described it as "a dish turned upside down." Africa consists of three major regions: the Northern Plateau, the Central and Southern Plateau, and the Eastern Highlands. Elevation increases across the continent from the northwest to southeast reaching an average of 1,900 ft (600 m). The main feature of the Northern Plateau is the Sahara desert, which occupies more than one-quarter of the continent. At the fringes of the Northern Plateau are the Atlas Mountains, which extend from Morocco into Tunisia. The higher Central and Southern Plateaus contain several major depressions, notably the Congo River Basin and the Kalahari Desert, as well as the peaks of the Drakensberg mountains. The Eastern Highlands, extending from the Red Sea to the Zambezi River, averages more than 5,000 ft (2,000 m) and reaches 15,157 ft (4,620 m) at Ras Dashen in northern Ethiopia. South of the Ethiopian Plateau are a number of towering volcanic peaks, including Kilimanjaro, Mount Kenya, and Mount Elgon. A distinctive feature of the Eastern Highlands is the Great Rift Valley—a vast geologic fault system.

Climate

With three-quarters of its landmass situated between the Tropic of Cancer and Capricorn Africa is mostly tropical—hot summers and brief, mild winters. In some regions altitude has a moderating influence, and mountains near the equator such as Mt.

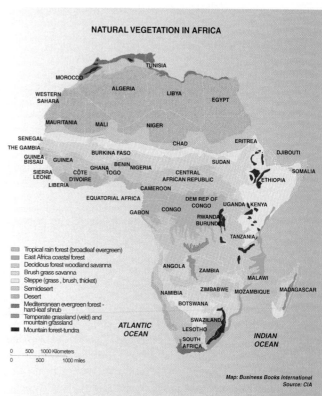

NATURAL VEGETATION IN AFRICA

- Tropical rain forest (broadleaf evergreen)
- East Africa coastal forest
- Deciduous forest woodland savanna
- Brush grass savanna
- Steppe (grass , brush, thicket)
- Semidesert
- Desert
- Mediterranean evergreen forest - hard-leaf shrub
- Temperate grassland (veld) and mountain grassland
- Mountain forest-tundra

0   500   1000 Kilometers
0   500   1000 miles

Map: Business Books International
Source: CIA

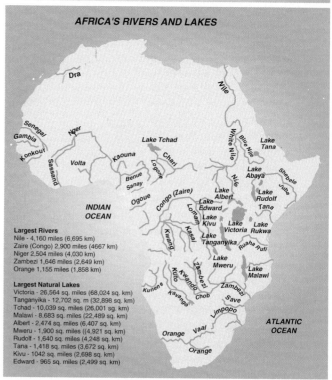

AFRICA'S RIVERS AND LAKES

Largest Rivers
Nile - 4,160 miles (6,695 km)
Zaire (Congo) 2,900 miles (4667 km)
Niger 2,504 miles (4,030 km)
Zambezi 1,646 miles (2,649 km)
Orange 1,155 miles (1,858 km)

Largest Natural Lakes
Victoria - 26,564 sq. miles (68,024 sq. km)
Tanganyika - 12,702 sq. m (32,898 sq. km)
Tchad - 10,039 sq. miles (26,001 sq. km)
Malawi - 8,683 sq. miles (22,489 sq. km)
Albert - 2,474 sq. miles (6,407 sq. km)
Mweru - 1,900 sq. miles ((4,921 sq. km)
Rudolf - 1,640 sq. miles (4,248 sq. km)
Tana - 1,418 sq. miles (3,672 sq. km)
Kivu - 1042 sq. miles (2,698 sq. km)
Edward - 965 sq. miles (2,499 sq. km)

The mapping of Africa

Geographers in Africa maps
With Savage-Pictures fill their Gaps:
And o'er unhabitable Downs
Place Elephants for want of Towns.
                    Dean Swift

This old limerick summed up the efforts of early European cartographers to portray Africa. They depended on hearsay and fancy and the drawings of Claudius Ptolomy, who lived in Alexandria around 150 A.D. Referred to as the Aristotle of map-making, Ptolomy's influence extended well into the 16th Century.

First printed Africa map, Milan, Italy - 1508

The first printed map of Africa dates back to Milan in 1508 but it was Sebastian Munster who gained fame for his rendition of the Dark continent in 1540. Inspired by Ptolomy and the tales of Arab and Portuguese explorers, he drew an imaginary mountain range roping north Africa off from the rest and the Niger flowing in the wrong direction. And, of course, the elephant in the southern interior where both fact and fancy fell short.

When Munster drew his map, discoveries by Portuguese seafarers Dias (1486) and Da Gama (1497) had already dispelled the original notion of an Africa and Asia joined at the hip and enclosing the Indian ocean between them. Regular sea traffic around Africa brought new knowledge about the coastline but large portions of the interior remained a mystery for years to come.

Lack of information about the African interior obliged cartographers to innovate. Maps of Africa were often as ornate as they were inaccurate. French cartographer Bourguignon D'Anville was the exception. In the 18th Century he introduced—with limited success—the novel notion that unless there were reliable evidence, imaginary mountains and hypothetical lakes should be left out. His stark rendition of Africa stuck out like a sore thumb in a profession where aesthetics ruled over mathematics.

Today the works of men like Ortelius, Bleau, Moll, Merian, Ogilby, Jaillot, Hondius, Visscher, Speed, Sandrart, and Seutter grace our walls not to enlighten but to entertain—as works of art instead of representations of reality.

At the close of the 19th Century D'Anville finally prevailed. After extensive journeys by the likes of Livingstone and Stanley the *Encyclopaedia Brittanica* proudly introduced what it confidently proclaimed to be a true and final map of Africa. Little did it know how many borders and names would change in the next century.

Sebastian Munster - 1540

Kilimanjaro and Mt. Kenya are covered with snow. Beyond the equatorial zone rainfall is unreliable and large parts of the continent are prone to droughts. Some 40 per cent of Africa is classified as desert or semidesert. Even in high rainfall areas, downpours are strictly seasonal and unpredictable in both volume and timing, making farming a gamble. Both the Namib and Sahara Desert get less than 2 inches (50 mm) of rain per year.

Vegetation

With its average annual rainfall of more than 50 inches (1,300 mm), Africa's tropical rain forest is densely covered tropical hardwood trees, oil palms and a thick undergrowth of shrubs, ferns, and mosses. In the mountain forest zones of Cameroon, Angola, eastern Africa, and parts of Ethiopia, where the rainfall average is only slightly less, a ground covering of shrubs gives way to oil palms, hardwood trees, and primitive conifers. The savanna woodland zone, with an annual rainfall of 35 to 55 inches (900 to 1,400 mm), consists of deciduous and leguminous fire-resistant trees and undergrowth of grass and shrubs. The savanna grassland zone, with an annual rainfall of 20 to 35 inches (500 to 900 mm), is covered with low grass and shrubs and widely spaced, small deciduous trees. The so-called thornbush zone with its annual rainfall of 12 to 20 inches (300 to 500 mm), has a sparser grass covering and scattered succulent and semi-succulent trees. The sub-desert scrub zone, with an annual rainfall of 5 to 12 inches (130 to 300 mm) is covered with grasses and scattered low shrubs. In the desert zones, with an annual rainfall of less than 5 inches (130 mm), vegetation varies from sparse to none.

Rivers and Lakes

Even though Africa's 4,160 mile long (6,695 km) Nile is the world's longest river, it is hardly a continent known for abundant navigable rivers. Africa offers few reliable waterways to and from the interior. Some rivers are very short and have no outlet to the sea. Many are dependent on seasonal rains that transform dry riverbeds into raging torrents for a short while. Sandbars and muddy deltas at their mouths and cataracts and falls further inland complicate navigation on the Nile, Niger, and Zambezi. Some rivers such as the Sudd in the Upper Nile region lose themselves in swamps while others terminate in enclosed pools. Despite these complications the Senegal, Gambia, Zambezi, Niger and the mighty Nile serve not only as major water sources for communities along their banks but as traffic routes for a variety of craft. Several major lakes are situated in the Great Rift region of East Africa, including Turkana, Albert, Tanganyika, and Nyasa (Malawi). Lake Victoria—the largest lake in Africa and the third largest in the world—is not part of this system but occupies a shallow depression in the Eastern Highlands.

Peoples & languages

In 2000, some 13% of the world's population lived in 53 African countries. Africa tops the world not only with the number of countries within one continent but also the diversity of its 800 million peoples and the number of languages spoken. Rural cultures where foods, religions, lifestyles, dress and daily life have remained unchanged for hundreds of years, continue to thrive despite the rapid intrusion of bustling modern cities. More than 1,000 languages and dialects are spoken. Arabic in northern Africa, Mandinke, Igbo, Yoruba and Hausa in western Africa, Swahili in eastern Africa, Amharic and Oromo in the Horn of Africa, and Zulu, Sotho and Xhosa in southern Africa, are spoken by millions. Most of Africa's languages are, however, spoken by less than a million people and some, such as Kw'adza in Tanzania used by only a few older people, are close to extinction. Many countries have selected the languages of former colonial powers for official and business purposes. Arabic is the official language in 12 countries, English in 20, and French

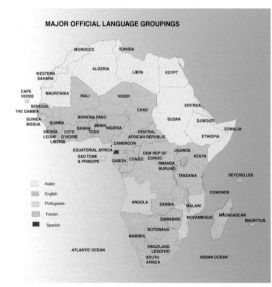

MAJOR OFFICIAL LANGUAGE GROUPINGS

in 21. Cameroon and Mauritius have both English and French as official languages. Portuguese is official in five countries and Spanish and French enjoy equal status in Equatorial Guinea. Spanish is spoken in Morocco and some Italian in Libya, Eritrea and Somalia.

Religions

Christianity at its very beginning spread from the north to Nubia (northern Sudan) and Ethiopia. Much later it was introduced elsewhere by Portu-

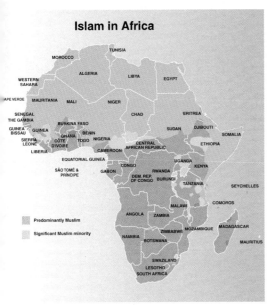

Islam in Africa

Predominantly Muslim

Significant Muslim minority

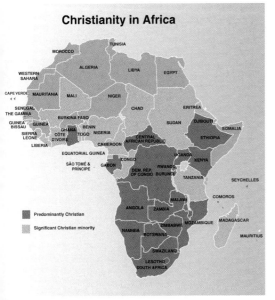

Christianity in Africa

Predominantly Christian

Significant Christian minority

guese and other seafarers, early Dutch settlers at the Cape and 19th Century missionaries. Islam spread from the Arabian Peninsula through Northern Africa in the course of the 17th Century. Today, Christianity dominates in 19 countries, Islam in 13 countries, and the Hindu faith in one (Mauritius). In the rest, ethnic beliefs still largely prevail and other faiths remain in the minority. Even though there is no single unifying and distinct religious code set out in a Koran or a Bible, indigenous religions continue to exert a strong influence on family life, rulers and the justice system in parts of the continent. What ethnologists refer to as Naturism, Animism, and Fetishism are all aspects of a deep-seated belief in a Creator that defies definition. Indigenous African religions—practiced under the guidance of priests, elders, rainmakers, diviners and prophets—are concerned with the origin of tribes and their cultures, the nature of society, the relationship of men and women and of the living and dead. Social values are frequently expounded in myths, legends, folktales, and riddles are passed along by word-of-mouth. Voodoo (juju) and other forms of witchcraft have, however, come to represent in the minds of foreigners the essence of African religion—a subject as complex and varied as Africa's multitude of nations and tribal groupings.

Early history

Several scientific discoveries of the remains of what seems to be early man in South Africa's Sterkfontein area and Tanzania's Olduvai Gorge lend strong support to Africa's claim of being the cradle of mankind. Less contentious is Egypt's claim to be among the world's first civilizations. A number of city states in the lower Nile Valley were united some 5,000 years ago under Menes, the first pharaoh. To the south in the Nubian desert (today's northern Sudan) another kingdom developed some 3,000 years ago that equalled Egypt in both splendor and achievement. The Semitic Phoenicians became the first colonizers of Africa when they set out from today's Lebanon to establish the city state of Carthage along the Mediterranean in what eventually became Tunis. Centuries of struggle in North Africa involving Romans and Germanic Vandals, and Christians and Muslims, left the rest of the continent largely free from outside influences. It was only about 1,000 AD that black Africans from the Sahel region, on the fringe of the Sahara desert, first entered the North African theater—even though the kingdoms of Ghana, Mali, and Kanem (on the eastern shores of Lake Chad) had existed for many centuries. Inhabitants of the tropical forest regions originated in the north and were exclusively Negroid. More than 2,000 years ago some of them migrated from West Africa to settle around the great lakes and on the savannah plains in East Africa and the Congo Basin. Classified as Bantu-speaking, they were crop cultivators and livestock breeders. To the north of Lake Victoria (in today's Uganda) the Nilotes (or Nilotic people), who migrated from the north, ruled for centuries over various Bantu-speaking groups. Some Bantu-speakers moved south and reached today's South Africa about 1,500 years ago.

First Europeans

Toward the end of the 15th Century Portugal had established trade relations with the kingdoms of Benin and Kongo and built a fort at Elmina (Ghana). Barter items included gold, palm oil, cocoa, ivory and human cargo—consisting of slaves supplied by African kingdoms to a ready market in the Americas and elsewhere. In their search for a sea route to the Far East, Portuguese explorers rounded the Cape and extended trade to the east coast where the Arabs were already active. The Dutch, English, French and Spanish soon followed and for the next four centuries established spheres of influence along the coast of Africa.

Slavery

For most of the 18th Century the relationship between Europe and Africa was dominated by the slave trade. Before the middle of the 19th Century, the slave trade had been declared illegal in the northern hemisphere by all the the former European and North American slave-trading nations. That did not completely deter profit seekers from moving human cargo in bondage wherever the opportunity presented itself, and at towards the end of the 19th Century explorer David Livingstone still encountered a flourishing slave trade on his exploration routes.

First settlement

In 1652 the Dutch established a small settlement at the southern tip of the African continent. Originally intended as a supply station for its ships enroute to the Far East, the Cape settlement soon developed into a full-fledged colony. After the British took over, the Dutch descendants (Boers) trekked north to establish independent republics in the 1850s. The Cape was, however, the excep-

tion. Until the latter part of the 19th Century European powers had no desire for colonial possessions in Africa. Instead, they were content with mere trading stations. The British had enclaves

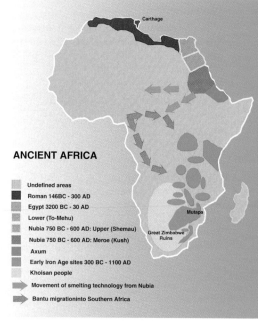

ANCIENT AFRICA

	Undefined areas
	Roman 146BC - 300 AD
	Egypt 3200 BC - 30 AD
	Lower (To-Mehu)
	Nubia 750 BC - 600 AD: Upper (Shemau)
	Nubia 750 BC - 600 AD: Meroe (Kush)
	Axum
	Early Iron Age sites 300 BC - 1100 AD
	Khoisan people
	Movement of smelting technology from Nubia
	Bantu migration into Southern Africa

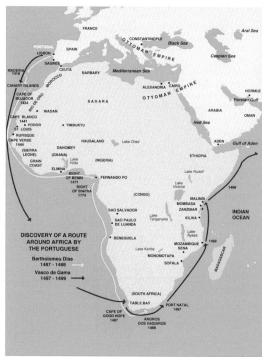

The African diaspora

In 1977 more than 80 million Americans tuned in to an eight-part ABC-TV miniseries on slavery. *Roots*, based on a book by African American author Alex Haley traced his family history back to his enslaved ancestors in Africa. This stark depiction of the suffering inflicted on these unfortunate souls came as a shock to many.

Haley was not the first to take up this theme. As early as 1852 New Englander Harriet Beecher Stowe wrote *Uncle Tom's Cabin*. This sentimental work about an escaped slave was based on her superficial, brief encounter with life on a Kentucky plantation. It was seen in the South as an attack on their constitutional rights and hailed in the north as a timely exposure of a cancer in the body of the United States. During the Civil War, President Lincoln described Mrs. Stowe as "the little woman who made this Great War."

Roots - ABC-TV

Exactly how many men, women and children were sent in slavery from Africa across the Atlantic to the Caribbean islands and North and South America will never be known. Estimates vary, but there seems general agreement that there might have been as many as ten million who were shipped from the western shores of Africa and reached the markets while another 5 million perished during the arduous journey in cramped and unhygienic quarters.

Even though the abolition of slavery by the British—largely as a result of the efforts of William Wilberforce and his friend William Pitt—might have reduced the numbers, it did not stop the trade altogether. At the same time it made the journey more perilous as smugglers hid their human cargo in the even more unaccommodating holds of small, new craft, fast enough to outrun the British naval patrol ships along the African coast. When in danger of capture, these smugglers would readily jettison their contraband human cargo to prevent their expensive craft from being confiscated. Slaves were cheaper to replace than these new craft. Records show slaves selling at about two for the price of three lengths of woolen cloth or at an exchange of 3 muskets for one young robust male slave. The illegal trade to markets such as Brazil and Cuba continued well into the nineteenth century and did not come to a total end until the 1860s.

Most of the slaves who were sold into the United States came directly from the West African region stretching from the Senegal River through the Congo region. About a tenth arrived via the West Indies, after a "seasoning" period. The first "shipments" arrived in the American Colonies during the early 1600s.

The bulk of the slaves sold in the United States were settled in the South where they worked on rice, tobacco, sugar cane, and eventually, cotton plantations. The invention of the cotton gin by Eli Whitney of Massachusetts in 1793 caused a rapid expansion in the Southern cotton industry and a rising demand for plantation slaves. Others were craft workers, messengers, and servants.

Slaves at times resorted to mutiny and, after their arrival, to armed rebellion. In 1839 mutineers aboard the *Amistad*, off the coast of Cuba, diverted the vessel to New York where they won their freedom. Sixty people died in a revolt led by slave preacher Nat Turner in 1831 in Virginia.

Today, the African Diaspora in the New World numbers close to 80 million. African Americans represent more than 12 percent of the total population of the United States and thirty percent of Brazil are descendants of slaves. In both these countries, and the Caribbean, the descendants of African slaves have reached prominence in all professions and count among their ranks celebrities in the arts, politics and sports. Many of them have, like Haley, created a greater awareness of Africa among fellow Americans.

along the West African coastline to protect the palm oil trade. They also maintained a presence in Freetown, Sierra Leone, established in 1787 as a haven for freed slaves. The French had a modest toehold in Libreville (Gabon) and freed American slaves settled in Liberia in 1822. The Portuguese had occupied the coast of Mozambique and the Arabs continued to pursue the slave trade in the East African interior.

Colonialism

Encouraged by explorers such as Livingstone, Burton, De Brazza, Nachtigal and Stanley, and spurred on by the growing need for raw materials and new markets, the Europeans started their scramble for Africa in the 1870s. It was Livingstone's vision of bringing Christianity, Civilization and Commerce to Africa that prompted Belgium's King Leopold to establish a personal colony in the Congo basin. Soon the European superpowers were tripping over each other in their quest for colonies all over Africa. The Berlin Conference of 1884-1885, convened by the German government to determine the fate of Leopold's Congo and to set the rules of the game, further turned up the heat. The Germans established enclaves in Togo, Cameroon, German West Africa (Namibia) and German East Africa (Tanzania) while the French expanded their territorial holdings inland from Senegal and Gabon across West Africa and parts of Equatorial Africa. Britain spread its rule over Nigeria, Ghana and Sierra Leone and retained The Gambia. Its major focus was, however, on Egypt and South Africa. At the turn of the century, Cecil John Rhodes' dream of a British Africa from the Cape to Cairo was well underway with Rhodesia, Nyasaland (Malawi), Kenya, and Uganda flying the Union Jack. Portugal acquired two major overseas possessions, Angola and Portuguese East Africa (Mozambique), which it ran as provinces. The scramble for Africa—completed in under 30 years—repainted the continent in bright colonial colors without any consideration for the peoples or their homelands. Italy and Spain had their own designs in North Africa. In one celebrated instance Queen Victoria decided to indent the straight border drawn between British East Africa and German East Africa (today's Kenya and Tanzania) to make a detour around Mt. Kilimanjaro so her German cousin King Wilhelm could have the mountain. "Willie likes big things," she explained.

Decolonization

After the First World War Germany was stripped of all its African possessions, which were then given to those who fought on the winning side. In the wake of a Second World War (fought

Dr. Livingstone, I presume?

Ask anyone to name an explorer and the name David Livingstone jumps to the fore. Even that other famous explorer, Henry Stanley, was in such awe when he caught up with the famous Scottish missionary at Ujiji in darkest Africa that he lost his eloquence and merely muttered: "Dr. Livingstone, I presume?"

But few know that it was Verney Lovett Cameron who first crossed the continent from east to west.

David Livingstone

This accomplished British officer was doomed to obscurity much in the same way as Norwegian Roald Amundsen who beat Captain Robert Scott to the South Pole.

Before Livingstone there were Scottish, English, French and German explorers such as Brue, Bruce, Park, Clapperton, Caillie, Krapf and Rebmann, and after him came the Grants and Brazzas. Few were humanitarians such as David Livingstone. Most were in it for fame and other more selfish reasons. There was Baker the hunter, Burton the intellectual and writer, and Henry Stanley, writer-adventurer and colonial agent.

Even though the search for the source of the Nile and the course of the Niger were major themes for early exploration, Africa is hardly a continent of waterways.

With the exception of these two major rivers and a few other partly navigable ones such as the Senegal, Gambia, and Zambezi, most consist of forbidding swamps or seasonal swirling waters.

Few explorers could claim that they "discovered" new territory. Friendly local folks often served as guides and facilitators while hostile tribesmen at times added to the dangers already posed by wildlife and debilitating tropical diseases.

But by "ripping Africa open," as Englishman John Speke dramatically described the process, these explorers sparked an interest in Europe that turned into a scramble for land and the stripping of Africa's newly-discovered wealth. Some explorers actually became agents of imperialism. Stanley was employed by Belgian King Leopold as his agent in the Congo while De Brazza helped found the French Congo, and Karl Peters helped launch the German Protectorate of East Africa.

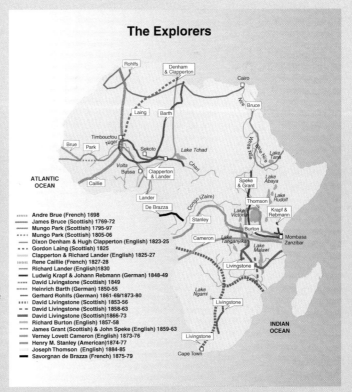

The Explorers

Rohlfs
Denham & Clapperton
Cairo
Nile
Bruce
Laing
Barth
Timbouctou
Niger
Brue
Park
Sekoto
Lake Tchad
White Nile
Blue Nile
Lake Tana
Volta
Bussa
Clapperton & Lander
Chari
ATLANTIC OCEAN
Caillie
Speke & Grant
Lake Abaya
Lander
Congo (Zaire)
Lake Rudolf
De Brazza
Thomson
Krapf & Rebmann
Stanley
Lake Victoria
Cameron
Lake Tanganyika
Burton
Mombasa
Zanzibar
Lake Malawi
Livingstone
Lake Ngami
Livingstone
INDIAN OCEAN
Livingstone
Cape Town

:::::: Andre Brue (French) 1698
— James Bruce (Scottish) 1769-72
— Mungo Park (Scottish) 1795-97
···· Mungo Park (Scottish) 1805-06
:::::: Dixon Denham & Hugh Clapperton (English) 1823-25
– – – Gordon Laing (Scottish) 1825
:::::: Clapperton & Richard Lander (English) 1825-27
:::::: Rene Caillie (French) 1827-28
— Richard Lander (English)1830
— Ludwig Krapf & Johann Rebmann (German) 1848-49
:::::: David Livingstone (Scottish) 1849
:::::: Heinrich Barth (German) 1850-55
— Gerhard Rohlfs (German) 1861-69/1873-80
:::::: David Livingstone (Scottish) 1853-56
– – David Livingstone (Scottish) 1858-63
— David Livingstone (Scottish)1866-73
— Richard Burton (English) 1857-58
:::::: James Grant (Scottish) & John Speke (English) 1859-63
— Verney Lovett Cameron (English) 1873-76
:::::: Henry M. Stanley (American)1874-77
— Joseph Thomson (English) 1884-85
— Savorgnan de Brazza (French) 1875-79

with the help of thousands of African soldiers in colonial armies) came a revulsion against colonial rule that led to armed uprisings in many of the colonies. This "wind of change" swept across Africa, forcing first Belgium and Britain, then France, and eventually Portugal to grant freedom to all their former colonies. In some cases the departure of the former colonial rulers had some dignity and style while in others it was more like a frantic scramble to escape the consequences of mismanagement. The initial euphoria of the 1960s soon made way for pessimism and despair as military rulers and despots took the place of former colonial rulers. In many instances, the root of the problem happened to be the artificially drawn colonial borders that grouped diverse peoples together who had never been at peace with each other. By using Africa as a surrogate battleground the new superpowers, the United States and the Soviet Union added fuel to the fire. Oppressive dictatorships were tolerated and supported from both sides in a struggle for ideological supremacy in Africa. For many years, South Africa, despite its apartheid policies, received the support of the US and its allies because of its strategic importance at the tip of the continent and supplies of strategic minerals.

Reform & Hope

Coinciding with the collapse of the Soviet bloc and the end of the Cold War, a wave of democratic reform swept over Africa in the early 1990s. A new breed of leaders came to the fore intent on arresting the decline in living standards by introducing true democratic rule and far-reaching economic reforms. These leaders are no longer driven by ideological conflict at the behest of outside powers but by the imperatives set by internal economic and so-

cial conditions. South Africa, which abandoned apartheid in 1994, has given new impetus to this era of liberation, which many believe will lead to a renaissance as the continent attracts from abroad true business partnership instead of colonial exploitation. Despite ongoing unrest and frequent warfare between ethnic groups boxed into entities created in 19th Century Europe, there has been enough growth and development in recent years to raise hopes of a resurgent Africa in the new millennium. The World Bank and IMF, and governments such as the US, Britain, Germany, Japan, France, Canada, Norway, Denmark and Sweden have placed Africa high on their priority list. Numerous foreign firms have joined the ranks of multinationals with long-standing interests on the continent, making profits and contributing to much-needed growth in countries where prosperity is the key to peace and democracy.

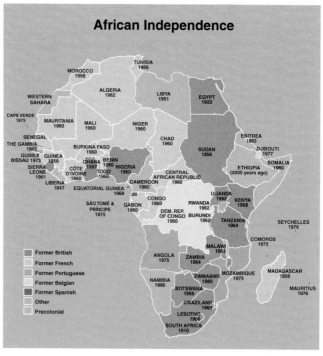

*In 1951, **Libya** was granted independence by France and Britain which were in joint control after Italy's defeat during World War II; in 1960, when the French (former German) Cameroun received its independence, part of British **Cameroon** joined in while the rest merged with Nigeria; in 1960, the former Italian (then under French control) and British Somalia joined to become independent **Somalia**; incorporated into Ethiopia after World War II, the former Italian colony of **Eritrea** gained its freedom in 1991; a mandate under South African control since the end of World War I, the former German colony of South West Africa gained its independence as **Namibia** in 1990; administered by Morocco since 1976, Western Sahara is still an area under dispute, awaiting a final UN referendum.*

"Rumours of Timbuctou"

In 1825 when nineteen year old Oxford student-poet Alfred Tennyson was assigned the task of comparing Timbuktu with the legendary lost civilizations of Atlantis and El Dorado, he asked, rhetorically:

Is the rumour of thy Timbuctou

A dream as frail as those of ancient Time?

His following lines suggested a place with *"low-built, mudwall'd barbarian settlement."*

Tennyson took his cue from French explorer Rene Caillie who had just returned from Timbuktu to debunk the wondrous tales of a city built on gold. Instead, he found a mud-walled town whose glory had largely faded.

It was a distinguished Moroccan traveler, Leo Africanus, who first stimulated European interest in Timbuktu with the appearance of his *History and Description of Africa* in 1525—translated into English in 1600. Africanus spoke of a rich king who possessed great treasures in gold with some ingots weighing as much as 1,300 pounds. He found in the city many men of learning and a treasure of books.

By the late fifteenth century Timbuktu or, as some called it, the Queen of the Sudan, had become the educational and commercial center of Western Sudan.

In 1618 a company was formed in London with the expressed purpose of establishing a gold trade with Timbuktu. The first expedition ended in the massacre of all its members along the Gambia River and the second lost its way.

Of the almost fifty Europeans who braved the Sahara desert in an attempt to reach this legendary city in Mali, Englishman Gordon Lang was the first to succeed. He did not survive, however, to tell his story. On his way back he was murdered.

So Caillie was the one to bring back the disappointing tale. In pursuing his goal to reach Timbuktu—that had become "the continual object of all my thoughts"—Caillie traveled as a Muslim to evade the wrath of religious fanatics encountered by other European explorers.

Other explorers followed, including Dr. Heinrich Barth, the scholarly German contemporary and friend of David Livingstone. Barth's accounts of his journey to Timbuktu form part of a five volume set of books (600 pages each) on his *Travels in Central Africa*. Apart from contributing further to the knowledge of Timbuktu, Barth also lays claim to having "discovered" Agades, a sister city which, in his words, has by "mere accident" not attracted as much attention as Timbuktu.

In its glory days during the fifteenth and sixteenth century, Timbuktu was seen by some as the "gateway to the Sahara desert " and by others as "the most distant place on earth." While the first image rapidly faded as Caillie and others dismantled the golden tales of the past, the second appellation stuck until today. How often do we still hear this expression whenever someone plans to travel to far and remote places: "I am going to Timbuktu."

Caravan approaching Timbuktu - German engraving - 1853 (Barth, Travels in Central Africa, 1857)

The mighty Nile

The Nile is the longest river in the world and its fertile basin covers one-tenth of the African continent. But the Nile is much more than merely a source of water, food, electric power, and tourism and trade revenues. It is the umbilical cord to world's oldest civilization. Starting at about 5,000 BC, the Egyptian pharaohs spread their influence south along the river as far as northern Sudan, leaving along its banks magnificent edifices in the form of pyramids, temples and burial sites.

Greek historian Herodotus saw Egypt as "the gift of the River Nile." The Nile derives its current name from the Greek word *Neilos* (valley or river) but originally the Egyptians called it *Ar* or *Aur* (black) after the seasonal deposits of fertile black sediment along its banks. This is where the art of agriculture was perfected in ancient times with the first use of the hand plow. Today, tourists relaxing on the decks of river boats on the Nile can still observe farmers plying or plowing their craft in Biblical-type settings.

The actual length of the Nile remains in dispute, depending on where the starting point is drawn. It measures 3,470 miles (5,584 km) from its principal source, Lake Victoria, and 4,180 miles (6,690 km) from its remotest headstream in Burundi—a branch of the Kagera River that feeds into the lake. Indeed, it was the search for the origin of the Nile that lured 19th Century explorers such as Baker, Speke, Burton, Livingstone and Stanley, who in turn whetted the appetite of European powers for acquisitions in the region. Much of the tumultuous colonial period involved the independent nations that today feed off the Nile and its tributaries—Tanzania, Burundi, Rwanda, Democratic Republic of Congo, Kenya, Uganda, Ethiopia, Sudan, and Egypt.

The terrain along the Nile and its tributaries changes from rain forests and mountains in the south to savanna and swamps halfway, and ultimately to desert along its northern section. Starting in the mountains of Burundi, the waters flow via Lake Victoria into the Victoria Nile in Uganda and follow a northwest course for about 300 miles (500 km) through Lake Kyoga and across rapids and the famous Murchison Falls before entering Lake Albert. Continuing northwards as the Albert Nile, it becomes the Bahr al Jabal in Sudan and slows down in the As Sudd swamps, changing its name once again to the White Nile. At Sudan's capital, Khartoum, the White Nile is joined by the Blue Nile that originates 850 miles (1,370 km) southeast at Lake Tana in the Ethiopian highlands. Now known as the Nile, this river is joined further north by the Atbara River before it takes an S-shape turn through the Nubian desert. After passing through five cataracts in Sudan and one in Egypt, near Aswan, the Nile takes a course past Cairo, splitting into the Rosetta and Dalmietta branches before entering the Mediterranean Sea along a 160 mile (250 km)—wide delta.

Irrigation from the river supports large-scale cultivation of cotton, wheat, sorghum, citrus fruit, sugar, dates and a variety of legumes along the Nile River Basin. An abundance of Nile perch and tilapia underpins commercial fishing. Tourism, concentrated around the river with its historical sites and interesting wildlife, is a major revenue source. The river is navigable in parts. Major river ports include Cairo, Luxor and Aswan in Egypt, and Wai Halfa, Kusti, Malakal and Juba in Sudan.

During the 20th Century several dams were built to control the flow of the Nile and to generate power. Egypt's Aswan Dam was completed in 1902 and further extended in 1936. In 1919, Sudan built the Sennar Dam to supply water for its cotton industry. The Jabal Aulia Dam on Sudan's White Nile (1937), Owen Falls on Uganda's Victoria Nile (1954), Roseires Dam on the

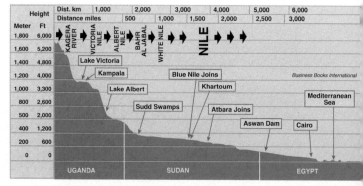

Sudanese Blue Nile (1962) and Egypt's High Aswan Dam (1970) generate hydroelectricity. While most experts agree that the pros of these dam projects far outweigh the cons, critics are not slow to point out the negatives. Controlling and reducing the flow of the river deny farmers deposits of fertile sediment along the river banks that came with summer floods. A decrease in flow towards the ocean has caused a greater salt content in the delta region. Lake Nasser, formed upstream from High Aswan Dam, submerged several once thriving communities and historical sites.

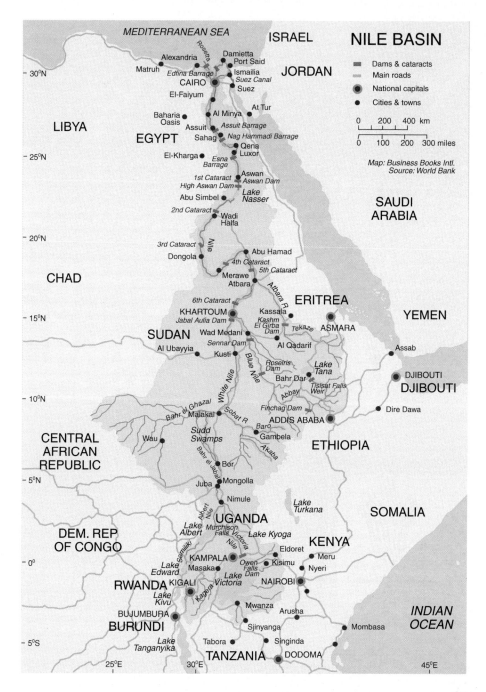

DBSA
Development Bank
of Southern Africa

Southern Africa's
leading change agent
for socio-economic development

Chapter 2

The Economy of Africa

Despite some slippage in recent years agriculture still accounts for one third of Africa's GDP, two-thirds of its employment and 40% of its export revenues. Most foreign economic activity is, however, concentrated in the exploration and exploitation of the continent's abundant mineral resources. Multinationals are prominent in petroleum and gas and minerals extraction ranging from gold and diamonds to copper, uranium, manganese and phosphate rock to platinum and bauxite. Increasingly, however, foreign investors have engaged in manufacturing for both local and regional as well as international markets where African nations often enjoy special duty free status. There is growing interest among foreign investors and traders as privatization and infrastructure projects—including transport, power generation and telecommunications—create a need for venture capital, materials and services.

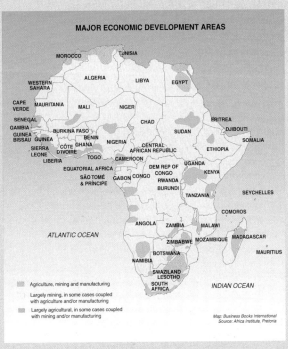

MAJOR ECONOMIC DEVELOPMENT AREAS

Agriculture, mining and manufacturing

Largely mining, in some cases coupled with agriculture and/or manufacturing

Largely agricultural, in some cases coupled with mining and/or manufacturing

Map: Business Books International
Source: Africa Institute, Pretoria

Economy

The Africa that emerged after the Second World War as the winds of change swept away colonial rule was largely unprepared for new economic challenges. Belgian, British, French, Portuguese, Spanish, German and Italian possessions primarily served the interests of their colonial masters, not local populations. Education, training and local development—inadequate as they were—were there to satisfy imperialistic greed, not local need. Euphoria soon made way for chaos and despair as ill-equipped independent governments failed to sustain multi-ethnic states with artificial borders drawn in 19th Century imperial Europe. Newly independent states were left short of both administrative and entrepreneurial skills. Africa at large earned the reputation for coups, corruption and chaos. As the Cold War expanded into Africa, Marxist-driven policies further served to erode free market practices and drive economies and infrastructures into a state of disrepair.

In a recent World Bank publication—*Can Africa Claim the 21st Century?*—an expert group sponsored by several agencies observed: "Explaining Africa's slow growth in the second half of the 20th Century remains a major challenge to economists and other analysts." There is no simple answer as to why a continent that stood at roughly one-third of Europe's income level at the beginning of the 19th Century fell so far behind and was totally eclipsed by Asia. In the 1960s, Gunnar Myrdal saw an Africa poised for steady growth in contrast to an Asia doomed to stagnation. The opposite happened. South Korea, for example, starting out far behind Ghana in 1957, had an economy six times its size by the 1990s. Indonesia, setting out even with Nigeria in 1965, had an output in 1993 three times that of its West African counterpart.

Structural Adjustment

During the 1970s and the 1980s, the IMF and the World Bank extended loans to African countries in terms of structural adjustment programs (SAPs) conditioned on balanced budgets, devaluation of currencies, a cutback in state employment and privatization of state enterprises. While these programs in most cases played a positive role in arresting economic decline and increasing economic growth, in some instances they also had negative side effects on the population. Even though in the 1980s countries with SAPs in place showed growth rates double those of nonparticipants, the austere and at times harsh conditions remained contentious.

Debt and aid

Equally heated has been the debate on foreign debt and aid. In 1997, Africa's foreign debt stood at $311 billion, representing a reduction of $22 billion since 1995. Sub-Saharan Africa accounted for 71% of the total. Debt on average represented 80% of GNP—varying from 16% in Botswana to 427% in Mozambique. Little of this borrowed money found its way into real development and productive programs. The bulk was used to cover budget deficits and imports, often in the case of bilatral loans, from the lending countries. An undetermined amount found its way into the private foreign bank accounts of government leaders. The search continues for the best way to restructure or write off debts owed by HIPCs (Highly Indebted Poor Countries). During the Cold War, aid to Africa was quite often driven not by development considerations but by ideology. Today, even though political considerations still play a role, aid is by and large

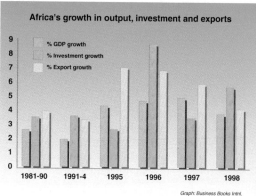

Africa's growth in output, investment and exports

% GDP growth
% Investment growth
% Export growth

1981-90   1991-4   1995   1996   1997   1998

Graph: Business Books Intnl.
Source: World Bank

driven by a genuine effort to stimulate real growth instead of buying favors from rulers. Despite criticisms, USAID and other programs have had many successes to show in Africa where they funded health, educational, agricultural, infrastructural and manufacturing projects, in many instances in cooperation of non-governmental organizations. The consensus is that Africa will need significant aid until at least 2015 to attain certain preset development goals. With Africa no longer the ideological battleground it once was, political support for aid is on the wane in the US and elsewhere. Also, the former members of the Soviet bloc have now become rivals for aid. Since 1990, US foreign aid has dropped by 20% despite massive post-Cold War military budget cuts.

New leadership

More significant than foreign assistance or economic discipline imposed from abroad has been the emergence in Africa in the mid-1990s of a new breed of leaders imbued with a determination to make the so-called African renaissance a reality. Often obscured by continuing headlines about crises and conflicts, disease and disaster, are the accomplishments of this cadre of new professionals in building democratic rule, developing sound macro-economic policies and opening their economies to international markets and influences. From 1994-1998 the growth in output in a typical African country increased by 4.3%. Exports showed rapid growth and foreign investment improved significantly as the international business community responded favorably to far-reaching reforms that offered partnerships in privatized or restructured state-owned enterprises, greater access to foreign products and wide-ranging investment incentives. At the end of the 1990s more than 3,000 transactions totalling $6.5 billion had been completed. Private enterprise has been granted a significant role in areas such as telecommunications, and railways and harbors— fields hitherto regarded as the exclusive domain of government and state-owned entities. After two decades of serious economic decline, Africa seems to have reversed the trend and entered the new millennium with greater confidence and better prospects. There is confident talk about a renaissance in the making and newcontinent-wide development plans have been laid in terms of a Millennium African Recovery Plan (MAP) and the formation of an African Union.

Fast facts

▶ Africa is largely dependent on agriculture for employment and exports.

▶ Foreign direct investment is heavily concentrated in minerals and mining but there is a growing involvement in food processing, infrastructure development and tourism and other service sectors.

▶ There are more foreign banks involved in Africa than in any other region of the world.

▶ During the past 40 years Africa's population increased from 280 million to about 800 million and it is expected to double itself every 25 years, reaching a billion at the end of the 21st Century.

▶ At an average of 26 persons per sq km Africa's population density is well below the world's average of 42, Asia's 116 and Europe's 102.

▶ Africa is the world's least urbanized region. It has 60 urban areas with a population of more than a half million, including 30 cities with more than one million people.

▶ In 2000 Africa's total external debt stood at $231 billion with Sub-Saharan Africa accounting for the major share. This represents a debt reduction of some $100 billion since 1995.

▶ In 1999 the average income in Africa stood at $677—and in Sub-Sharan Africa at $492.

▶ From 1994 to 1998 the average annual growth in output in a typical African country rose by 4.3%, largely as a result of far-reaching reforms introduced by new market-oriented leaders.

▶ Restructuring or privatization has opened up large chunks of Africa's previously state-run economies to competition and participation from both the domestic and foreign private sectors. At the end of the 1990s, more than 3,000 transactions totalling $6.5 billion had been completed.

Challenges

Serious challenges remain. In 1999 the average income in Africa stood at $677. In terms of PPP or purchasing power parity (taking into account the higher costs and prices on the continent) average income in Africa was less than one-third that of South Asia, making it the poorest region in the world. Sadly, dramatic improvement in life expectancy in Africa up to 1990 came to a halt as a result of HIV/AIDS—a disease of pandemic proportions threatening communities on the continent with extinction. In more than 21 countries on the continent at least 7% of all adults suffer from AIDS. In some countries the figure rises to as high as 25%. The full impact of this disease on the economies of Africa has yet to be determined but it has already become abundantly clear that unless the spread of this disease can be arrested or contained, hopes of economic resurgence might well become a dream deferred.

Resources

Originally the Europeans were lured to Africa with tales of gold. Today foreign investors are still mostly drawn to.the continent by its vast reserves of mineral resources, ranging from gold and diamonds to platinum, chrome, cobalt, copper and a host of other precious, strategic and base metals. While South Africa has long been the focus of major mining houses, the World Bank has identified 25 other African nations with a vast potential for future mineral exploration, with Ghana, Angola, Namibia and Congo (Kinshasa) topping the list. For more than a century, foreign mining companies have been active in Africa both as independent operators and in partnership. Foreign oil and energy companies are involved in the extraction of oil and natural gas in countries such as Algeria, Nigeria, Gabon, Angola and Mozambique.

Agriculture

Despite the importance of minerals, Africa's people remain largely dependent on farming for jobs and survival. On an average, agriculture accounts for one-third of all Africa's gross domestic product (GDP) and provides two-thirds of all employment. In Sub-Saharan Africa, agriculture represents 40% of GDP. Major food crops include cassava, maze, millet, rice and sorghum. Prime exports are cocoa and coffee beans, palm oil, groundnuts, cotton, tea, sisal and tobacco. With food production steadily falling behind population growth during the past 30 years, Africa has become a net importer of food. Even though cattle herds in Ethiopia, Sudan and Nigeria exceed its own, South Africa has traditionally been the largest meat producer. Fishing is an important sector in several countries, serving both local needs and as a foreign exchange earner.

Manufacturing

Apart from South Africa, which ranks among the world's twenty-six industrialized nations, manufacturing in Africa is relatively undeveloped. Other countries where manufacturing, mining and agriculture all contribute significantly to the overall economic activity are Zimbabwe, Morocco,

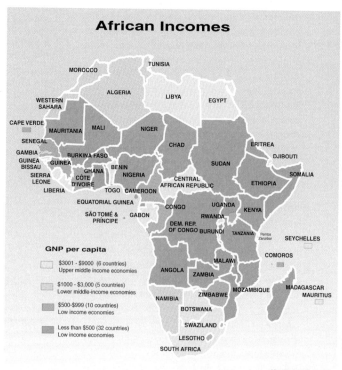

African Incomes

GNP per capita

- $3001 - $9000 (6 countries) Upper middle income economies
- $1000 - $3,000 (5 countries) Lower middle-income economies
- $500-$999 (10 countries) Low income economies
- Less than $500 (32 countries) Low income economies

Map: Business Books Intl.
Source: Africa Institute, Pretoria
World Bank classification

Algeria and Egypt. Apart from a few food processing and mineral beneficiation plants, however, most manufacturing activity in Africa is limited to import-substitution of consumer items such as clothes, footwear, soap, cigarettes, liquor, soft drinks and basic tools. Manufacturing's share of GDP on the continent stood at slightly more than 15% towards the end of the 1990s.

Services

As in most other parts of the world, the service sector—comprising banking, insurance and other financial services, as well as wholesale and retail trade, tourism, transport and communications—is the single largest contributor to the African economy. Foreign financial institutions have been particularly active in recent times.

Foreign banks

According to the World Bank, Africa has the highest penetration by foreign banks of any region. Despite this foreign involvement and widespread restructuring of state services, governments still play an inordinately large role in many countries. Reforms continue, however, to open up not only state utilities in telecommunications and power generation but to make it possible for local and foreign entrepreneurs to become partners in air, road and rail transport and shipping.

Population

During the past 40 years Africa's total population increased from 280 million to about 800 million, representing an average annual growth rate of almost 3%. At this rate the population of the continent is expected to double itself every 25 years, reaching a billion towards the end of this century. There are indications, however, that the continent's population growth might have peaked. The high incidence of HIV/AIDS may also prompt futurists to revise drastically their forecasts.

Density

At an average of 26 persons per sq km, Africa has a population density well below the world average of 42 per sq km. (It runs as high as 116 in Asia and 102 in Europe). Although there has been a move towards the cities, Africa is still the world's least urbanized continent. At latest count there were more than 60 urban areas with a population of more than a half a million, including 30 cities with more than one million. Cairo and its surrounding suburbs form a mega-metropolis of 12 million inhabitants, making it the fifteenth largest city in the world. It is expected to be overtaken within a matter of a few years by the Lagos metropolis, which stood at 10 million toward the end of the 1990s. Africa's single most affluent urbanized region is, the Pretoria/Witwatersrand/Vereeniging or PWV complex around Johannes-burg, South Africa, with more than 7 million people. In the 5 million plus range are Kinshasa/Brazzaville spanning across the Congo River and the Casablanca/Rabat complex in Morocco. Next in line at 3.5 million is the Durban/Pietermaritzburg complex in South Africa, and the city of Algiers. The Cape Peninsula leads in the 2 million plus league, which includes Maputo, Zambia's Copperbelt region, Luanda, Abidjan, Khartoum, Addis Ababa, Tripoli, Nairobi, and Dar es Salaam.

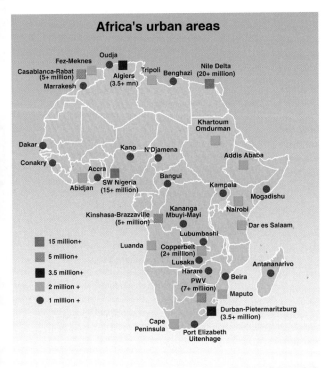

Africa's urban areas

- 15 million+
- 5 million+
- 3.5 million+
- 2 million +
- 1 million +

Oudja
Fez-Meknes
Casablanca-Rabat (5+ million)
Marrakesh
Algiers (3.5+ mn)
Tripoli
Benghazi
Nile Delta (20+ million)
Khartoum Omdurman
Dakar
Kano
N'Djamena
Addis Ababa
Conakry
Accra
Bangui
Kampala
Abidjan
SW Nigeria (15+ million)
Mogadishu
Kananga Mbuyi-Mayi
Nairobi
Kinshasa-Brazzaville (5+ million)
Dar es Salaam
Lubumbashi
Luanda
Copperbelt (2+ million)
Lusaka
Antananarivo
Harare
Beira
PWV (7+ million)
Maputo
Durban-Pietermaritzburg (3.5+ million)
Cape Peninsula
Port Elizabeth Uitenhage

Map: Business Books International
Source: Africa Institute, Pretoria

37

International and regional links

The United Nations has been a valuable forum for African nations in their struggle to end colonialism and apartheid on the continent. Today, Africa's 53 nations play a strong role not only in the world organization itself but in most of the organizations and agencies within the UN System. Encouraged by the World Bank, the IMF and other international agencies, there has been a concerted effort in Africa to establish economic regions able to compete more effectively in world markets. While groupings such as ECOWAS, COMESA, SADC, UDEAC, UAM and SACU are determined by geographical factors, common currency and historical ties, there has been a tendency of late to be more pragmatic. One recently formed grouping, IOARC, aims at promoting trade and economic cooperation among African, Arab, Asian and Australasian nations along the rim of the Indian Ocean. Both France and Britain have maintained a formal relationship with their former colonies in the Franc Zone and Commonwealth, respectively. The European Union has cultivated a special trade relationship with African, Caribbean and Pacific nations under the Lomé Convention—recently revitalized and rearranged under the Cotonou accord. The US has special bilateral relationships with South Africa, Egypt and Nigeria and is in the process of forging stronger economic ties with Sub-Saharan Africa through its African Growth and Opportunity Act. Japan, China and Taiwan have become active players on the continent, both as investors and traders. The Arab nations have expanded their involvement beyond North Africa into Sub-Saharan Africa.

UN SYSTEM

United Nations (UN)
United Nations
New York NY 10017, USA
Tel: [1] (212) 963 1234
Fax: [1] (212) 963 4879
Established on 26 June 1945, and starting operations on October 1945, the United Nations has witnessed the growth of a formidable and active African bloc since the sixties.

Economic Commission for Africa (ECA)
P. O. Box 3001-3005
Addis Ababa, Ethiopia
Tel: [251] (1) 51 72 00 Fax: [251] (1) 51 44 16
Web: *www.un.org/depts/eca/*
Established on 29 April 1958 to promote economic development as a regional commission of the UN's Economic and Social Council. All African nations are members. France and Britain serve as associate members.

Food and Agriculture Organization (FAO)
Viale delle Terme di Caracalla
00100 Rome, Italy
Tel: [39] (6) 57051 Fax:[39] (6) 5705 3152
Web: *www.fao.org*
Established on 16 October 1945 to raise living standards and increase availability of agricultural products.

International Atomic Energy Agency (IAEA)
Wagramerstrasse 5
P. O. Box 100
A-1400 , Vienna, Austria
Tel: [43] (1) 26000
Fax: [43] (1) 26007
Established on 26 October 1956, and operating since 29 July 1957, to promote peaceful uses of atomic energy among 129 members, including 25 from Africa: Algeria, Benin, Burkina Faso, Cameroon, Democratic Republic of Congo, Cote d'Ivoire, Egypt, Gabon, Kenya, Liberia, Libya, Madagascar, Mali, Mauritius, Morocco, Namibia, Niger, Nigeria, Senegal, Sierra Leone, South Africa, Tanzania, Uganda, Zambia, Zimbabwe.

International Development Association (IDA)
1818 H Street NW
Washington DC 20433
Tel: [1] (202) 477 1234
Fax: [1] (202) 477 6391
Established on 26 January 1960, as a specialized UN agency and part of the World Bank affiliate to provide financing on highly concessionary terms to low countries among its 160 members. South Africa is classified among the 26 developed countries and the rest of the continent among less developed countries.

International Finance Corporation (IFC)
2121 Pennsylvania Avenue NW
Washington, DC 20433, USA
Tel: [1] (202) 477 1234
Fax: [1] (202) 974 4384
Established on 25 May 1955, and starting operations on 24 July 1956, as a support mechanism for private enterprise in international economic development. It is a UN specialized agency and World Bank affiliate. All African countries are members by virtue of their Wolrd Bank membership.

AFRICAN MEMBERSHIPS

	ACP	AfDB	ABEDA	AMU	BDEAC	CWLTH	CCC	EADB	ECA
ALGERIA		☑	☑	☑			☑		☑
ANGOLA	☑	☑					☑		☑
BENIN	☑	☑							☑
BOTSWANA	☑	☑				☑	☑		☑
BURKINA FASO	☑	☑					☑		☑
BURUNDI	☑	☑							☑
CAMEROON	☑	☑			☑		☑		☑
CAPE VERDE	☑	☑							☑
CENTRAL AFRICAN REP.	☑	☑			☑		☑		☑
CHAD	☑	☑			☑				☑
COMOROS	☑	☑					☑		☑
CONGO (BRAZZAVILLE)	☑	☑			☑		☑		☑
CONGO (KINSHASA)	☑	☑					☑		☑
CÔTE D'IVOIRE	☑	☑					☑		☑
DJIBOUTI	☑	☑							☑
EGYPT		☑	☑				☑		☑
EQUATORIAL GUINEA	☑	☑			☑				☑
ERITREA	☑	☑					☑		☑
ETHIOPIA	☑	☑					☑		☑
GABON	☑	☑			☑		☑		☑
GAMBIA,THE	☑	☑				☑	☑		☑
GHANA	☑	☑				☑	☑		☑
GUINEA	☑	☑					☑		☑
GUINEA-BISSAU	☑	☑							☑
KENYA	☑	☑				☑	☑	☑	☑
LESOTHO	☑	☑				☑	☑		☑
LIBERIA	☑	☑					☑		☑
LIBYA		☑	☑	☑			☑		☑
MADAGASCAR	☑	☑					☑		☑
MALAWI	☑	☑				☑	☑		☑
MALI	☑	☑					☑		☑
MAURITANIA	☑	☑	☑	☑			☑		☑
MAURITIUS	☑	☑				☑	☑		☑
MOROCCO		☑	☑	☑			☑		☑
MOZAMBIQUE	☑	☑				☑	☑		☑
NAMIBIA	☑	☑				☑	☑		☑
NIGER	☑	☑					☑		☑
NIGERIA	☑	☑				☑	☑		☑
RWANDA	☑	☑					☑		☑
SÃO TOMÉ & PRÍNCIPE	☑	☑							☑
SENEGAL	☑	☑					☑		☑
SEYCHELLES	☑	☑				☑			☑
SIERRA LEONE	☑	☑				☑	☑		☑
SOMALIA	☑	☑							☑
SOUTH AFRICA	☑	☑				☑			☑
SUDAN	☑	☑	☑				☑		☑
SWAZILAND	☑	☑				☑	☑		☑
TANZANIA	☑	☑				☑	☑	☑	☑
TOGO	☑	☑					☑		☑
TUNISIA	☑	☑	☑	☑			☑		☑
UGANDA	☑	☑				☑		☑	☑
ZAMBIA	☑	☑				☑	☑		☑
ZIMBABWE	☑	☑				☑	☑		☑

☑ Full member ✓ Associate/Observer Status

Sources: UN, CIA Fact Book, OAU

AFRICAN MEMBERSHIPS

	CEEAC	CEPGL	COMESA	ECOWAS	ICC	ICFTU	INTERPOL	INMARSAT	IFC
ALGERIA						☑	☑	☑	☑
ANGOLA	☑		☑				☑		☑
BENIN				☑		☑	☑		☑
BOTSWANA						☑	☑		☑
BURKINA FASO				☑	☑	☑	☑		☑
BURUNDI	☑	☑	☑				☑		☑
CAMEROON	☑				☑	☑	☑		☑
CAPE VERDE				☑		☑	☑		☑
CENTRAL AFRICAN REP.	☑					☑	☑		☑
CHAD	☑					☑	☑		☑
COMOROS			☑				☑		☑
CONGO (BRAZZAVILLE)	☑						☑		☑
CONGO (KINSHASA)	☑	☑	☑			☑	☑		☑
CÔTE D'IVOIRE				☑	☑	☑	☑		☑
DJIBOUTI			☑			☑	☑		☑
EGYPT					☑		☑	☑	☑
EQUATORIAL GUINEA	☑						☑		☑
ERITREA			☑			☑			☑
ETHIOPIA			☑				☑		☑
GABON	☑					☑	☑	☑	☑
GAMBIA,THE				☑		☑	☑		☑
GHANA				☑		☑	☑	☑	☑
GUINEA				☑		☑	☑		☑
GUINEA-BISSAU				☑		☑	☑		☑
KENYA			☑			☑	☑	☑	☑
LESOTHO							☑		☑
LIBERIA				☑		☑	☑	☑	☑
LIBYA							☑		☑
MADAGASCAR			☑		☑	☑	☑		☑
MALAWI			☑			☑	☑		☑
MALI				☑		☑	☑		☑
MAURITANIA				☑			☑		☑
MAURITIUS			☑			☑	☑	☑	☑
MOROCCO					☑	☑	☑		☑
MOZAMBIQUE						☑	☑	☑	☑
NAMIBIA			☑				☑		☑
NIGER				☑			☑		☑
NIGERIA				☑	☑		☑	☑	☑
RWANDA	☑	☑	☑			☑	☑		☑
SÃO TOMÉ & PRÍNCIPE	☑						☑		☑
SENEGAL				☑	☑	☑	☑	☑	☑
SEYCHELLES			☑			☑	☑		☑
SIERRA LEONE				☑		☑	☑		☑
SOMALIA			☑				☑		☑
SOUTH AFRICA					☑	☑	☑	☑	☑
SUDAN			☑				☑		☑
SWAZILAND			☑			☑	☑		☑
TANZANIA			☑			☑	☑	☑	☑
TOGO				☑	☑	☑	☑		☑
TUNISIA					☑	☑	☑		☑
UGANDA			☑			☑	☑		☑
ZAMBIA			☑			☑	☑		☑
ZIMBABWE			☑			☑	☑		☑

☑ Full member   ✓ Associate/Observer Status

Sources: UN, CIA Fact Book, OAU

AFRICAN MEMBERSHIPS

	ILO	IOM	IMO	IMARSAT	IMF	ISO	ICRM	INTELSAT	OAU¹
ALGERIA	☑	✓	☑	☑	☑	☑	☑	☑	☑
ANGOLA	☑	☑	☑		☑		☑	☑	☑
BENIN	☑		☑		☑	✓	☑	☑	☑
BOTSWANA	☑				☑	☑	☑	☑	☑
BURKINA FASO	☑				☑		☑	☑	☑
BURUNDI	☑				☑		☑	✓	☑
CAMEROON	☑		☑		☑		☑	☑	☑
CAPE VERDE	☑	✓	☑		☑		☑	☑	☑
CENTRAL AFRICAN REP.	☑				☑		☑	☑	☑
CHAD	☑				☑		☑	☑	☑
COMOROS	☑				☑			☑	☑
CONGO (BRAZZAVILLE)	☑	✓	☑		☑		☑	☑	☑
CONGO (KINSHASA)	☑		☑		☑	✓	☑	☑	☑
CÔTE D'IVOIRE	☑	✓	☑		☑	✓	☑	✓	☑
DJIBOUTI	☑		☑		☑		☑	☑	☑
EGYPT	☑	☑	☑	☑	☑	☑	☑	☑	☑
EQUATORIAL GUINEA	☑		☑		☑		☑	☑	☑
ERITREA	☑		☑		☑			✓	☑
ETHIOPIA	☑	✓	☑		☑	☑	☑	☑	☑
GABON	☑		☑	☑	☑			☑	☑
GAMBIA,THE	☑		☑		☑		☑	✓	☑
GHANA	☑	✓	☑	☑	☑	☑	☑	☑	☑
GUINEA	☑	✓	☑		☑	✓	☑	☑	☑
GUINEA-BISSAU	☑	☑	☑		☑		☑	✓	☑
KENYA	☑	☑	☑		☑	☑	☑	✓	☑
LESOTHO	☑				☑		☑	✓	☑
LIBERIA	☑		☑	☑	☑		☑	✓	☑
LIBYA	☑		☑		☑	☑	☑	☑	☑
MADAGASCAR	☑	✓	☑		☑	✓	☑	☑	☑
MALAWI	☑		☑		☑	✓	☑	☑	☑
MALI	☑	☑			☑		☑	☑	☑
MAURITANIA	☑		☑		☑		☑	☑	☑
MAURITIUS	☑		☑	☑	☑	☑	☑	☑	☑
MOROCCO	☑	☑	☑		☑	☑	☑	☑	☑
MOZAMBIQUE	☑	✓	☑	☑	☑	✓	☑	☑	☑
NAMIBIA	☑	✓	☑		☑		☑	☑	☑
NIGER	☑				☑		☑	☑	☑
NIGERIA	☑		☑	☑	☑	☑	☑	☑	☑
RWANDA	☑	✓			☑		☑	☑	☑
SÃO TOMÉ & PRÍNCIPE	☑	✓	☑		☑		☑	✓	☑
SENEGAL	☑	☑	☑	☑	☑		☑	☑	☑
SEYCHELLES	☑		☑		☑	✓	☑	✓	☑
SIERRA LEONE	☑		☑		☑		☑	☑	☑
SOMALIA	☑	✓	☑		☑		☑	☑	☑
SOUTH AFRICA	☑	☑	☑	☑	☑	✓	☑	☑	☑
SUDAN	☑	☑	☑		☑		☑	☑	☑
SWAZILAND	☑				☑		☑	☑	☑
TANZANIA	☑	☑	☑	☑	☑	☑	☑	☑	☑
TOGO	☑		☑		☑		☑	☑	☑
TUNISIA	☑	☑	☑		☑	☑	☑	☑	☑
UGANDA	☑	☑			☑	✓	☑	☑	☑
ZAMBIA	☑	☑			☑		☑	☑	☑
ZIMBABWE	☑	✓			☑	☑	☑	☑	☑

☑ Full member ✓ Associate/Observer/Correspondent/Non-member User status 1. To be superceded by an African Union.

AFRICAN MEMBERSHIPS

	OPEC	SACU	SADC	WCL	WBANK	WFTU	WIPO	WToO[1]	WTO[2]
ALGERIA	☑			☑	☑		☑	☑	
ANGOLA			☑	☑	☑	☑	☑	☑	☑
BENIN				☑	☑	☑	☑	☑	☑
BOTSWANA		☑	☑	☑	☑	☑	☑	☑	☑
BURKINA FASO				☑	☑	☑	☑	☑	☑
BURUNDI					☑		☑	☑	☑
CAMEROON				☑	☑	☑	☑	☑	☑
CAPE VERDE				☑	☑		☑		⊙
CENTRAL AFRICAN REP.				☑	☑		☑	☑	☑
CHAD				☑	☑		☑	☑	☑
COMOROS					☑		☑		⊙
CONGO (BRAZZAVILLE)					☑	☑	☑	☑	☑
CONGO (KINSHASA)			☑	☑	☑	☑	☑	☑	☑
CÔTE D'IVOIRE				☑	☑	☑	☑	☑	☑
DJIBOUTI					☑	☑	☑	☑	☑
EGYPT					☑	☑	☑	☑	☑
EQUATORIAL GUINEA					☑		☑	☑	⊙
ERITREA					☑	☑	☑		
ETHIOPIA					☑	☑	☑	☑	
GABON				☑	☑		☑	☑	☑
GAMBIA,THE				☑	☑	☑	☑	☑	☑
GHANA				☑	☑	☑	☑	☑	☑
GUINEA					☑	☑	☑	☑	☑
GUINEA-BISSAU					☑	☑	☑	☑	☑
KENYA				☑	☑		☑	☑	☑
LESOTHO		☑	☑	☑	☑	☑	☑	☑	
LIBERIA				☑	☑	☑	☑		☑
LIBYA	☑				☑	☑	☑		
MADAGASCAR				☑	☑	☑	☑	☑	☑
MALAWI			☑		☑	☑	☑	☑	☑
MALI				☑	☑	☑	☑	☑	☑
MAURITANIA					☑		☑	☑	☑
MAURITIUS			☑	☑	☑	☑	☑	☑	☑
MOROCCO					☑		☑	☑	☑
MOZAMBIQUE			☑		☑	☑	☑	☑	☑
NAMIBIA		☑	☑	☑	☑		☑	☑	☑
NIGER				☑	☑	☑	☑	☑	☑
NIGERIA	☑			☑	☑	☑	☑	☑	☑
RWANDA				☑	☑		☑	☑	☑
SÃO TOMÉ & PRÍNCIPE					☑		☑	☑	⊙
SENEGAL				☑	☑	☑	☑	☑	☑
SEYCHELLES			☑	☑	☑		☑	☑	⊙
SIERRA LEONE				☑	☑	☑	☑	☑	☑
SOMALIA					☑	☑	☑		✓
SOUTH AFRICA		☑	☑	☑	☑	☑	☑	☑	☑
SUDAN					☑	☑	☑	☑	✓
SWAZILAND		☑	☑		☑		☑		☑
TANZANIA			☑	☑	☑	☑	☑	☑	☑
TOGO					☑	☑	☑	☑	☑
TUNISIA					☑	☑	☑	☑	☑
UGANDA				☑	☑	☑	☑	☑	☑
ZAMBIA			☑	☑	☑		☑	☑	☑
ZIMBABWE			☑	☑	☑	☑	☑	☑	☑

1. World Tourism Organization 2. World Trade Organization

☑ Full member ✓ Associate/Observer/Correspondent/Non-member User status ⊙ Applicants   Sources: UN, CIA Fact Book, OAU

AFRICAN MEMBERSHIPS

	UNHCR	WADB	WAEMU
ALGERIA	☑		
ANGOLA			
BENIN		☑	☑
BOTSWANA			
BURKINA FASO		☑	☑
BURUNDI			
CAMEROON			
CAPE VERDE			
CENTRAL AFRICAN REP.			
CHAD			
COMOROS			
CONGO (BRAZZAVILLE)			
CONGO (KINSHASA)	☑		
CÔTE D'IVOIRE		☑	☑
DJIBOUTI			
EGYPT			
EQUATORIAL GUINEA			
ERITREA			
ETHIOPIA	☑		
GABON			
GAMBIA,THE			
GHANA			
GUINEA			
GUINEA-BISSAU		☑	☑
KENYA			
LESOTHO	☑		
LIBERIA			
LIBYA			
MADAGASCAR	☑		
MALAWI			
MALI		☑	☑
MAURITANIA			
MAURITIUS			
MOROCCO	☑		
MOZAMBIQUE			
NAMIBIA	☑		
NIGER		☑	☑
NIGERIA	☑		
RWANDA			
SÃO TOMÉ & PRÍNCIPE			
SENEGAL		☑	☑
SEYCHELLES			
SIERRA LEONE			
SOMALIA	☑		
SOUTH AFRICA	☑		
SUDAN	☑		
SWAZILAND			
TANZANIA	☑		
TOGO		☑	☑
TUNISIA			
UGANDA	☑		
ZAMBIA			
ZIMBABWE			

☑ Full member   *Sources: UN, CIA Fact Book, OAU*

International Fund for Agricultural Development (IFAD)
Via del Serafico 107
I-00142 Rome
Italy
Tel: [39] (6) 54591 Fax:[39] (6) 5043463
Web: *www.ifad.org*
Established in December 1977 to promote agricultural development.

International Labour Organization (ILO)
4 route des Morillons
CH-1211 Geneva 22
Switzerland
Tel: [41] (22) 799 61 11
Fax: [41] (22) 798 86 85
Web: *www.ilo.org*
The ILO seeks the promotion of social justice and internationally recognized human and labour rights. It was founded in 1919 and is the only surviving major creation of the Treaty of Versailles which brought the League of Nations into being and it became the first specialized agency of the UN in 1946. The ILO formulates international labor standards in the form of Conventions and Recommendations and set minimum standards of basic labor rights: freedom of association, the right to organize, collective bargaining, abolition of forced labour, equality of opportunity and treatment, and other standards regulating conditions across the entire spectrum of work related issues. Within the UN system, the ILO has a unique tripartite structure with workers and employers participating as equal partners with governments. All African nations and other UN members belong.

International Maritime Organization (IMO)
4 Albert Embankment
London SE1 7SR, UK
Tel: [44] (171) 735 7611
Fax: [44] (171) 587 3210
Web: *www.imo.org*
Established on 6 March 1948, as the Intergovernmental Maritime Consultative Organization (IMCO) and changed to the IMO on 22 May 1982, this specialized UN agency deals with international maritime affairs. Its 157 members include 39 African countries: Algeria, Angola, Benin, Cameroon, Cape Verde, Democratic Republic of Congo, Republic of the Congo, Côte d'Ivoire, Djibouti, Egypt, Equatorial Guinea, Eritrea, Ethiopia, Gabon, The Gambia, Ghana, Guinea, Guinea-Bissau, Kenya, Liberia, Libya, Madagascar, Malawi, Mauritania, Mauritius, Morocco, Mozambique, Namibia, Nigeria, São Tomé & Príncipe, Senegal, Seychelles, Sierra Leone, Somalia, South Africa, Sudan, Tanzania, Togo, Tunisia.

International Monetary Fund (IMF)
700 19th Street NW
Washington DC 20431, USA
Tel: [1] (202) 623 7000 Fax: [1] (202) 623 4661
Web: *www.imf.org*
Established on 22 July 1944, and operative since 27 December 1945, the IMF, a specialized UN agency, works towards world monetary stability and economic development. All African countries are represented in the 182-member organization.

International Telecommunication Union (ITU)
Place des Nations
CH-1211 Geneva 20, Switzerland
Tel: [41] (22) 730 5111
Fax: [41] (22) 733 7256
Web: www.itu.int
Established on17 May 1865 and affiliated with the UN since 1947, the ITU handles world telecommunications issues among members.

United Nations Conference on Trade and Development (UNCTAD)
Palais des Nations
CH-1211 Geneva 10, Switzerland
Tel: [41] (22) 907 12 34 Fax: [41] (22) 907 00 57
Web: www.unctad.org
Established on 30 December 1964 to facilitate the integration of developing countries into the world economy and international trading system.

United Nations Educational, Scientific, and Cultural Organization (UNESCO)
7 place de Fontenoy
F-75352 Paris 07SP, France
Tel: [33] (1) 45 68 10 00
Fax: [33] (1) 45 67 16 90
Web: www.unseco.org
Established on in 1946 to promote cooperation in education, science, and culture among UN members.

United Nations High Commissioner for Refugees (UNHCR)
Case Postale 2500 Depot
CH-1211 Geneva 2, Switzerland
Tel: [41] (22) 739 81 11
Fax: [41] (22) 731 95 46
Web: www.unhcr.ch
Established on in1951, UNHCR seeks to ensure the humanitarian treatment of refugees and to find permanent solutions to refugee problems. A significant part of its operations, which now aid internally-displaced persons as well as cross-border refugees, is in Africa.

United Nations Industrial Development Organization (UNIDO)
Vienna International Center
PO Box 300
A-1400 Vienna, Austria
Tel: [43] (1) 260 260 Fax:[43] (1) 269 2669
Web: www.unido.org
Established in 1966, to promote industrial development among UN member nations.

Universal Postal Union (UPU)
Bureau International de l'UPU
Weltpoststrasse 4
CH-3000 Berne 15
Switzerland
Tel: [41] (31) 350 31 11
Fax: [41] (31) 350 31 10
Established in 1874, and became a UN specialized agency in 1948, Its role is to promote international postal cooperation among UN member states.

World Bank
[A.k.a. the International Bank
for Reconstruction
and Development or IBRD)
1818 H Street NW
Washington DC 20433
Tel: [1] (202) 477 1234
Fax: [1] (202) 477 6391
Web: www.worldbank.org
Established on 22 July 1944 and operative since 27 December 1945, this UN specialized agency provides economic development loans to its membership of 181 members, including all 53 African countries. It is an active key participant in development programs geared to stimulate growth in Africa.

World Health Organization (WHO)
20, Avenue Appia
CH-1211 , Geneva 27, Switzerland
Tel: [41] (22) 791 21 11 Fax: [41] (22) 791 07 46
Web: www.who.org
Established on 22 July 1946, as a specialized UN agency and started on 7 April 1948, to deal with health matters worldwide.

World Intellectual Property Organization (WIPO)
34 Chemin des Colombettes
CH-1211 Geneva 20, Switzerland
Tel: [41] (22) 338 9111
Fax: [41] (22) 733 5428
Web: www.wipo.int
Established on 14 July 1967 and operative since 26 April 1970, WIPO as a specialized UN agency furnishes protection for literary, artistic, and scientific works. Its 171 members include all 53 African countries.

World Meteorological Organization (WMO)
41 Avenue Giuseppe-Motta
CH-1211 Geneva 2, Switzerland
Tel: [41] (22) 730 81 11
Fax: [41] (22) 734 23 26
Web: www.wmo.ch
Established in 1947 and became a UN specialized agency in 1951. Its aims at providing authoritative scientific meterological information on a global basis.

World Tourism Organization (WTO)
Calle Capitan Haya 42
28020 Madrid, Spain
Tel: [34] (1) 567 81 00
Fax: [34] (1) 571 37 33
Established on 2 January 1975, to promote tourism as a means of contributing to economic development, international understanding, and peace. Its 131 members include 47 African countries: Algeria, Angola, Benin, Botswana, Burkina Faso, Burundi, Cameroon, Central African Republic, Chad, Democratic Republic of the Congo, Republic of Congo, Côte d'Ivoire, Djibouti, Egypt, Equatorial Guinea, Ethiopia, Gabon, The Gambia, Ghana, Guinea, Guinea-Bissau, Kenya, Lesotho, Libya, Madagascar, Malawi, Mali, Mauritania, Mauritius, Morocco,Mozambique, Namibia, Niger, Nigeria, Rwanda,

São Tomé & Príncipe, Senegal, Seychelles, Sierra Leone, South Africa, Sudan, Tanzania, Togo, Tunisia, Uganda, Zambia, Zimbabwe.

WorldTrade Organization (WTO)
Centre William Rappard
154 Rue de Lausanne
CH-1211 Geneva 21, Switzerland
Tel :[41] (22) 739 51 11
Fax: [41] (22) 739 54 58
Web: *www.wto.org*
Established on 15 April 1994, and operating since 1 January 1995, as a successor to the General Agreement on Tariff and Trade (GATT), the WTO provides the mechanism to resolve trade conflicts between members and to carry on negotiations with the goal of further lowering and/or eliminating tariffs and other trade barriers. Its 140 members include 41 African members: Angola, Benin, Botswana, Burkina Faso, Burundi, Cameroon, Central African Republic, Chad, Democratic Republic of the Congo, Republic of Congo, Côte d'Ivoire, Djibouti, Egypt, Gabon,

The Gambia, Ghana, Guinea, Guinea-Bissau, Kenya, Lesotho, Madagascar, Malawi, Mali, Mauritania, Mauritius, Morocco, Mozambique, Namibia, Niger, Nigeria, Rwanda, Senegal, Sierra Leone, South Africa, Swaziland, Tanzania, Togo, Tunisia, Uganda, Zambia, Zimbabwe. Two African nations have observer status: Somalia, Sudan. Another five have applications pending: Cape Verde, Comoros, Equatorial Guinea, São Tomé & Príncipe, and Seychelles.

OTHER ORGANIZATIONS

Following are other significant world and regional organizations to which all or some of Africa's nations belong:

African, Caribbean, and Pacific Group of States (ACP Group)
Avenue Georges Henri 451
B-1200 Brussels, Belgium
Tel: [32] (2) 743 06 00
Fax [32] (2) 735 55 73
Established on 6 June 1975 to manage preferential economic and aid relationships with the EU. All Sub-Saharan African countries belong to the group of 71 less-developed African, Caribbean and Pacific (ACP) countries associated with the European Union (EU) under the Lomé Convention. Under this treaty the EU grants ACP exports access to its markets on either a low or zero tariff basis. The EU also provides financial and technical aid to Lomé signatories, including the Stabex and Sysmin stabilization funds. The Stabex scheme was designed to compensate the ACP countries for fluctuations in the price of their agricultural exports. Similarly, Sysmin safeguards exports of minerals. Four Conventions have been concluded since 1975 when the first treaty was signed in Lomé, the capital of Togo. When it became a signatory in 1997, South Africa did not qualify for all the provisions of the convention as it was considered too highly developed for full membership. Other African member states are Angola, Benin, Botswana, Burkina Faso, Burundi, Cameroon, Cape Verde, Central African Republic, Chad, Comoros, Democratic Republic of the Congo, Republic of the Congo, Côte d'Ivoire, Djibouti, Equatorial Guinea, Eritrea, Ethiopia, Gabon, The Gambia, Ghana, Guinea, Guinea-Bissau, Kenya, Lesotho, Liberia, Madagascar, Malawi, Mali, Mauritania, Mauritius, Mozambique, Namibia, Niger, Nigeria, Rwanda, São Tomé & Príncipe, Senegal, Seychelles, Sierra Leone, Somalia, Sudan, Swaziland, Tanzania, Togo, Uganda, Zambia, Zimbabwe. The Cotonou Agreement, signed in Benin in June 2000, replaces the Lomé agreement. Discussions are underway to thrash out details among the 15 European signatories and the African and other ACP member nations. Taken into consideration are not only changed circumstances in Europe and Africa but WTO requirements.

African Development Bank (ADB)
[A.k.a.*Banque Africaine de Developpement*or BAD]
01 BP 1387
Abidjan 01
Côte d'Ivoire
Tel: [225] 20 44 44
Fax: [225] 21 77 53
Established on 4 August 1963 to promote economic and social development in Africa. All African countries are are regional members regional members. There are 25 non-regional members: Argentina, Austria, Belgium, Brazil, Canada, China, Denmark, Finland, France, Germany, India, Italy, Japan, South Korea, Kuwait, Netherlands, Norway, Portugal, Saudi Arabia, Spain, Sweden, Switzerland, UAE, UK, US.

Arab Bank for Economic Development in Africa (ABEDA)
[A.k.a. Banque Arabe de Developpement Economique en Afrique or BADEA]
Abdel Rahman El Mahdi Avenue
P. O. Box 2640
Khartoum, Sudan
Tel: [249] (11) 770498
Fax: [249] (11) 770600
Established on 18 February 1974, and started operations on 16 September 1974, to promote economic development. Its 17 members include: Algeria, Egypt, Libya, Mauritania, Morocco, Sudan, Tunisia. Other Arab members: Bahrain, Iraq, Jordan, Kuwait, Lebanon, Oman, Qatar, Saudi Arabia, Syria, UAE.

Arab Maghreb Union (AMU)
27 Avenue Okba Agdal
Rabat, Morocco
Tel: [212] (7) 77 26 82
Fax: [212] (7) 77 26 93
Established on 17 February 1989, to promote cooperation and integration among the Arab states of northern Africa. A.k.a. the Union of the Arab Maghreb (UAM) or Union du Maghreb Arabe (UMA), aims at safeguarding

the region's economic interests, fostering and promoting economic and cultural cooperation, and intensifying mutual commercial exchanges as a precursor for integration and the creation of a North African Common Market (also referred to as Maghreb Economic Space). The secretariat is based in Rabat, Morocco. It has a membership of 5: Algeria, Libya, Mauritania, Morocco, Tunisia.

Central African States Development Bank (BDEAC)

[Acronym for *Banque de Developpement des Etats de l'Afrique Centrale*]
Place du Gouvernement
BP 1177, Brazzaville
Republic of the Congo
Tel: [242] 81 18 85
Fax: [242] 81 18 80
Established on 3 December 1975, to provide loans for economic development in African countries. The BDEAC's African members are Cameroon, Central African Republic, Chad, Republic of Congo, Equatorial Guinea, and Gabon. Other members are France, Germany, and Kuwait.

Commonwealth (CWLTH)

[A.k.a. Commonwealth of Nations]
Commonwealth Secretariat
Marlborough House
Pall Mall
London SW1Y 5HX
United Kingdom
Tel: [44] (171) 839 3411, 747 6535
Fax: [44] (171) 930 0827, 839 9081
The Commonwealth was established on 31 December 1931 as a voluntary association evolving from the British Empire, to foster multinational cooperation and provide assistance to members where needed. The Commonwealth functions as an association of independent states—most of them, but not all, former British colonies. More affluent members such as Australia, Canada, New Zealand and the United Kingdom channel a substantial portion of their foreign aid into less developed fellow Commonwealth nations. There are also special trade and investment agreements in place. Links between governments are complemented by the activities of a large number of non-governmental Commonwealth organizations active in a variety of community building and social projects. Its current membership of 53 includes 18 from Africa: Botswana, Cameroon, The Gambia, Ghana, Kenya, Lesotho, Malawi, Mauritius, Mozambique, Namibia, Nigeria, Seychelles, Sierra Leone, South Africa, Swaziland, Tanzania, Uganda, Zambia, Zimbabwe. The other members are: Antigua and Barbuda, Australia, The Bahamas, Bangladesh, Barbados, Belize, Brunei, Canada,

Cyprus, Dominica, Fiji, Grenada, Guyana, India, Jamaica, Kiribati, Malaysia, Maldives, Malta, Nauru, New Zealand, Pakistan, Papua New Guinea, Saint Kitts and Nevis, Saint Lucia, Saint Vincent and the Grenadines, Samoa, Singapore, Solomon Islands, Tonga, Trinidad and Tobago, Sri Lanka, United Kingdom, Vanuatu.

Common Market for Eastern and Southern Africa (COMESA)

Tel: [260] 1 229-726
Fax: [260] 1 225-107
PO Box 30051
Lusaka 10101, Zambia
In November 1993, the member states of the Preferential Trade Area for Eastern and Southern Africa (PTA) signed a treaty transforming the PTA into the Common Market for Eastern and Southern Africa (COMESA). The goal are a fully integrated free trade area, a customs union with a common external tariff, free movement of capital and finance, a payments union, and free movement of people. It also aims at promoting cooperation in the development and rationalization of basic and strategic industries, agricultural development, the improvement of transport links, and the development of technical and professional skills. COMESA has 21 members: Angola, Burundi,Comoros, Djibouti, Eritrea, Ethiopia, Kenya, Madagascar, Ma-lawi, Mauritius, Namibia, Rwanda, Seychelles, Somalia, Sudan, Swaziland, Tanzania, Uganda, Democratic Republic of Congo, Zambia and Zimbabwe.

Customs and Economic Union of Central Africa (CEMAC)

[Acronym for *Communauté économique et monétaire en Afrique Centrale*].
Bangui, Central African Republic
Tel: [237] 21 44 15
Fax: [237] 21 44 88
Established in 1966 under the Brazzaville Treaty of 1964 as a customs union, the *Union douanière et économique de l'Afnique Centrale* (UDEAC) allowed duty-free trade between French- and Spanish-speaking countries in Central Africa. A common external tariff applied to imports from third countries. In 1994 the members of UDEAC entered into a second agreement, the Economic and Monetary Community in Central Africa or *Communauté économique et monétaire en Afrique Centrale* (CEMAC), replacing the UDEAC. Members

are: Cameroon, Central African Republic, Chad, Congo, Equatorial Guinea and Gabon. CEMAC's secretariat is in Bangui, Central African Republic. CEMAC members share as a central bank the *Banque des états de l'Afrique centrale (BEAC)* in Yaoundé, Cameroon.

Customs Cooperation Council (CCC)

[A.k.a. World Customs Organization (WCO)]
Rue du Marche 30
B-1210, Brussels, Belgium
Tel: [32] (2) 209 92 11
Fax: [32] (2) 109 92 92
Established on15 December 1950 to promote international cooperation in customs matters. Its 145 signatories include 44 African nations: Algeria, Angola, Botswana, Burkina Faso, Burundi, Cameroon, Cape Verde, Central African Republic, Comoros, Democratic Republic of Congo, Republic of the Congo, Côte d'Ivoire, Egypt, Eritrea, Ethiopia, Gabon, The Gambia, Ghana, Guinea, Kenya, Lesotho, Liberia, Libya, Madagascar, Malawi, Mali, Mauritania, Mauritius, Morocco, Mozambique, Namibia, Niger, Nigeria, Rwanda, Senegal, Sierra Leone, South Africa, Sudan, Swaziland, Tanzania, Togo, Tunisia, Zambia, Zimbabwe.

Commission for East African Co-operation (EAC)

P.O. Box 1096
Arusha, Tanzania
Tel: [225] 57 4253/8
Fax: [225] 57 4255
The Tripartite Commission for East African Cooperation (EAC) was formed by Kenya, Tanzania and Uganda in July 1999. It aims at eliminating all tariff rates between the member states and issuing a single passport for the region. Both Rwanda and Burundi are expected to join.

East African Development Bank (EADB)

4 Nile Avenue
P. O. Box 7128
Kampala
Uganda
Tel: [256] (41) 230021, 230825
Fax: [256] (41) 259763
Established on 6 June 1967, and started operations on 1 December 1967, promoting economic development among its three members—Kenya, Tanzania, and Uganda.

Economic Community of Central African States (CEEAC)

[Acronym derived from
*Communaute Economique
des Etats de l'Afrique Centrale*]
BP 2112
Libreville
Gabon
Tel: [241] 73 35 47, 73 35 48
Established on 18 October 1983, to promote regional economic cooperation and develop a Central African Common Market. Its eleven members are: Angola, Burundi, Cameroon, Central African Republic, Chad, Democratic Republic of Congo, Republic of the Congo, Equatorial Guinea, Gabon, Rwanda, São Tomé & Príncipe.

Economic Community of the Great Lakes Countries (CEPGL)

[Acronym—CEPGL—derived from *Communaute Economique des Pays des Grands Lacs*]
BP 91, Gitega
Burundi
Established on 20 September 1976, to promote regional economic cooperation and integration of its 3 members: Burundi, Democratic Republic of Congo, Rwanda.

Economic Community of West African States (ECOWAS)

6 King George V Road
PMB 12745, Lagos, Nigeria
Tel: [234] (1) 636839, 636841, 636064, 630398
Fax: [234] (1) 636822
Established in May 1975, the Economic Community of West African States (ECOWAS) is a common market striving towards uniform lower tariff rates. Poorer members are to be compensated from a common fund. ECOWAS also promotes the free movement of people, services and capital, harmonization of agricultural policies, joint development of economic and industrial policies, common monetary policies, and the elimination of disparities in levels of development. It has a membership of 16: Benin, Burkina Faso, Cape Verde, Côte d'Ivoire, The Gambia, Ghana, Guinea, Guinea-Bissau, Liberia, Mali, Mauritania, Niger, Nigeria, Senegal, Sierra Leone and Togo.

Franc Zone (CFA)

[*Officially known as the* Communauté
Financière Africaine or CFA]
Direction Generale des Service
Etrangers (Service de la Zone Franc)
Banque de France
Paris, France
Tel: [33] 42 92 31 26
Established in December 1945, the Franc Zone is a union of African countries with currencies linked to the French franc at a fixed rate of exchange. The *Communauté Financière Africaine* (CFA) franc is ensured by the French Treasury, and remains readily convertible. In 1994, the exchange rate parity was reduced by 50 percent to a fixed parity of 100 CFA francs to one French franc. Under mutual agreement members hold their reserves mainly in French francs and undertake to exchange them on the French market. With the exception of Guinea and Mauritania, all former members of French West Africa and French Equatorial Africa joined this monetary union. So did the former French island possession of Comoros. Equatorial Guinea, a former Spanish colony, joined in 1985, and in 1997, Guinea Bissau, a former Portuguese Guinea, in 1997. There are two Franc Zone groupings, one in Western

and one in Central Africa. A separate agreement applies to Comoros. Apart from Guinea and Mauritania, other African francophone nations who opted not to join the monetary union are Madagascar, Djibouti, the Democratic Republic of Congo, Rwanda and Burundi. The CFA franc has been useful in facilitating international payments and foreign trade. Francophone countries received assistance from France in the form of development and technical, budget and military support, as well as subsidies on commodity exports.

International Chamber of Commerce (ICC)

38 Cours Albert 1st
F-75008 Paris, France
Tel: [33] (1) 49 53 28 28
Fax: [33] (1) 49 53 29 42
Established in 1919 to promote free trade and private enterprise and to represent business interests at national and international levels. The 62 national councils represented include 11 from African countries: Burkina Faso, Cameroon, Côte d'Ivoire, Egypt, Madagascar, Morocco, Nigeria, Senegal, South Africa, Togo, Tunisia.

International Confederation of Free Trade Unions (ICFTU)

International Trade Union House
Boulevard Emile Jacqmain 155
B-1210 , Brussels, Belgium
Tel: [32] (2) 224 02 11
Fax: [32] (2) 201 58 15, 203 07 56
Established in December 1949, to promote trade union movements. More than 200 organizations representing 141 countries, are affiliated. Movements from 38 African countries are represented: Algeria, Benin, Botswana, Burkina Faso, Cameroon, Cape Verde, Central African Republic, Chad, Democratic Republic of the Congo, Republic of Congo, Côte d'Ivoire, Djibouti, Eritrea, Gabon, The Gambia, Ghana, Guinea, Guinea-Bissau, Kenya, Liberia, Madagascar, Malawi, Mali, Mauritius, Morocco, Mozambique, Rwanda, Senegal, Seychelles, Sierra Leone, South Africa, Swaziland, Tanzania, Togo, Tunisia, Uganda, Zambia, Zimbabwe.

International Criminal Police Organization (Interpol)

BP 6041, F-69411
Lyon CEDEX 06, France
Tel: [33] (4) 72 44 70 00
Fax: [33] (4) 72 44 71 63
Established in 1923 as the International Criminal Police Commission and modified on 13 June 1956, under its current name to promote international cooperation among police authorities in combating crime. Among its 177 members, 51 African countries are represented: Algeria, Angola, Benin, Botswana, Burkina Faso, Burundi, Cameroon, Cape Verde, Central African Republic, Chad, Democratic Republic of the Congo, Republic of the Congo, Côte d'Ivoire, Djibouti, Egypt, Equatorial Guinea, Ethiopia, Gabon, The Gambia, Ghana, Guinea, Guinea-Bissau, Kenya, Lesotho, Liberia, Libya, Madagascar, Malawi, Mali, Mauritania, Mauritius, Morocco, Mozambique, Namibia, Niger, Nigeria, Rwanda, São Tomé & Príncipe, Senegal, Seychelles, Sierra Leone, Somalia, South Africa, Sudan, Swaziland, Tanzania, Togo, Tunisia, Uganda, Zambia, Zimbabwe.

Intergovernmental Authority for Development (IGAD)

BP 2653, Djibouti
Djibouti
Tel : [253] 354050, (253) 352880
Fax : [253] 356994
Signatories to the Intergovernmental Authority on Development (IGAD) are Djibouti, Eritrea, Ethiopia, Kenya, Somalia and Uganda. The group focuses on economic cooperation and regional integration to combat the effects of drought and to help solve regional conflicts. The focus has also been on transportation and communications infrastructure building. There is a possibility that in the long term, the membership could increase as countries such as Egypt might join.

International Organization for Migration (IOM)

17 route des Morillons CP 71
CH-1211 Geneva 19, Switzerland
Tel: [41] (22) 717 91 11
Fax: [41] (22) 798 61 50
Established on 5 December 1951, to facilitate orderly international emigration and immigration. Among its 69 members are the following 13 African countries: Angola, Egypt, Guinea-Bissau, Kenya, Mali, Morocco, Senegal, South Africa, Sudan, Tanzania, Tunisia, Uganda, Zambia. Fourteen African countries are among the 47 hat have observer status: Algeria, Cape Verde, Democratic Republic of Congo, Republic of the Congo, Ethiopia, Ghana, Guinea, Madagascar, Mozambique, Namibia, Rwanda, São Tomé & Príncipe, Somalia, Zimbabwe.

International Mobile Satellite Organization (Inmarsat)

99 City Road
London EC1Y 1AX, UK
Tel: [44] (171) 728 1000 Fax: [44] (171) 728 1044
Established on 3 September 1976 as the International Maritime Satellite Organization, the renamed Inmarsat, it promotes cooperation in worldwide communications for commercial, distress, and safety applications at sea, in the air, and on land. Its membership of 86 includes 12 from Africa: Algeria, Egypt, Gabon, Ghana, Kenya, Liberia, Mauritius, Mozambique, Nigeria, Senegal, South Africa, Tanzania.

Indian Ocean Commission (IOC)

Commission de l'Océan Indien
Q4 Avenue Sir Guy Forget
Quatre Bornes
Ile Maurice
Fax: [230] 425.12.09
The Indian Ocean Commission (IOC) was formed by Comoros, Madagascar, Mauritius, Seychelles and France (Reunion), in 1999 to represent members' interests in other regional and international organizations. It also aims at tariff reduction among members and joint trade promotion.

International Organization for Standardization (ISO)

CP 56, 1 Rue de Varembe
CH-1211 Geneva 20
Switzerland
Tel: [41] (22) 749 01 11
Fax:- [41] (22) 733 34 30

Established in February 1947, to further the development of international standards in the exchange of goods and services and to develop cooperation in the sphere of intellectual, scientific, technological and economic activity among members. There are 14 African countries among the 88 members: Algeria, Botswana, Egypt, Ethiopia, Ghana, Kenya, Libya, Mauritius, Morocco, Nigeria, South Africa, Tanzania, Tunisia, Zimbabwe. Eleven African nations are among the 44 correspondent and subscriber members: Benin, Democratic Republic of Congo, Côte d'Ivoire, Guinea, Madagascar, Malawi, Mozambique, Namibia, Seychelles, Sudan, Uganda.

International Telecommunications Satellite Organization (Intelsat)

3400 International Drive NW
Washington
DC 20008-3098
Tel: [1] (202) 944 7500
Fax: [1] (202) 944 7890

Esyablished on 20 August 1964, as the Telecommunications Satellite Consortium and changed to Intelsat on 12 February 1973, the International Telecommunications Satellite Organization aims at developing and operating a global commercial telecommunications satellite system. Forty- three of its 143 members are African: Algeria, Angola, Benin, Botswana, Burkina Faso, Cameroon, Cape Verde, Central African Republic, Chad, Comoros, Democratic Republic of Congo, Republic of the Congo, Côte d'Ivoire, Egypt, Equatorial Guinea, Ethiopia, Gabon, Ghana, Guinea, Kenya, Libya, Madagascar, Malawi, Mali, Mauritania, Mauritius, Morocco, Mozambique, Namibia, Niger, Nigeria, Rwanda, Senegal, Somalia, South Africa, Sudan, Swaziland, Tanzania, Togo, Tunisia, Uganda, Zambia, Zimbabwe. A further 10 African countries are among the non-signatory users: Burundi, Djibouti, Eritrea, The Gambia, Guinea-Bissau, Lesotho, Liberia, São Tomé & Príncipe, Seychelles, Sierra Leone.

Indian Ocean Rim Association for Regional Cooperation (IOR-ARC)

Secretariat
Port Louis, Mauritius

Launched in Mauritius in March 1997, the Indian Ocean Rim Organization for Regional Cooperation aspires to be a regional economic grouping such as ASEAN and APEC. It involves the business community, academia and governments in the promotion of wide-ranging cooperation among member states. Similar trading blocs elsewhere prompted a movement towards closer economic ties among some 30 countries bordering the Indian Ocean. The focus is on trade and investment and the exchange of technical know-how, research and training. In 1997 the following 14 countries became signatories: Australia, India, Indonesia, Kenya, Madagascar, Malaysia, Mauritius, Mozambique, Oman, Singapore, South Africa, Sri Lanka, Tanzania and Yemen. They have a combined population of more than 1.3 billion, or 23% of the world's population—with India and Indonesia accounting for 85% of the Indian Ocean Rim Association's total population. In 1997 the Association represented a GNP of $1,184 billion or 4% of the world total. Its leading members are Australia, India, Indonesia, South Africa, Singapore and Malaysia. The GNP per capita for the region as a whole amounted to about $892 in 1995, which qualified it as lower middle income area in terms of the World Bank's classification. At the beginning of 2000 a Working Group on Trade and Investment (WGTI) met formally for the first time in Muscat to formulate formulate an Action Plan to liberalize trade and promote investment in the Indian Ocean Rim Region.

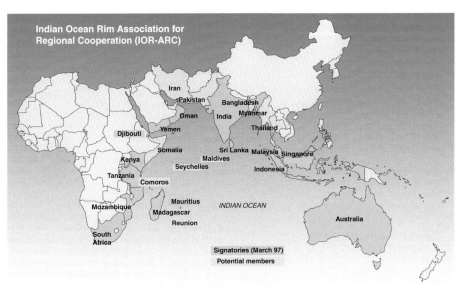

Indian Ocean Rim Association for Regional Cooperation (IOR-ARC)

Signatories (March 97)
Potential members

49

International Red Cross and Red Crescent Movement (ICRM)
International Conference of the Red Cross
19 Avenue de la Paix
CH-1202 Geneva
Switzerland
Tel: [41] (22) 734 60 01
Fax: [41] (22) 733 20 57
Established in 1928 to promote worldwide humanitarian aid through the International Committee of the Red Cross (ICRC) in wartime, and in peacetime through the International Federation of Red Cross and Red Crescent Societies (IFRCS). Of the 175 national societies 50 African: Algeria, Angola, Benin, Botswana, Burkina Faso, Burundi, Cameroon, Cape Verde, Central African Republic, Chad, Democratic Republic of the Congo, Republic of Congo, Côte d'Ivoire, Djibouti, Egypt, Equatorial Guinea, Ethiopia, The Gambia, Ghana, Guinea, Guinea-Bissau, Kenya, Lesotho, Liberia, Libya, Madagascar, Malawi, Mali, Mauritania, Mauritius, Morocco, Mozambique, Namibia, Niger, Nigeria, Rwanda, São Tomé & Príncipe, Senegal, Seychelles, Sierra Leone, Somalia, South Africa, Sudan, Swaziland, Tanzania, Togo, Tunisia, Uganda, Zambia, Zimbabwe.

Organization of African Unity (OAU)
PO Box 3243
Addis Ababa, Ethiopia
Tel: [251] (1) 517700
Fax: [251] (1) 512622, 517844
The OAU was established on 25 May 1963, to promote unity and cooperation among African states. All 53 African nations are members and the so-called Saharan Arab Democratic Republic, which lays claim to Western Sahara, has been given the 54th seat. The OAU held its last full meeting in June 2001, when it was announced that it will make way for an African Union, modeled after the European Union. The declared intent is to have closer cooperation between African states—even to the point of establishing a common currency.

Organization of Petroleum Exporting Countries (OPEC)
Obere Donaustrasse 93
A-1020 Vienna
Austria
Tel: [43] (1) 21 11 20
Fax: [43] (1) 216 43 20
Established on 14 September 1960 to coordinate petroleum policies among major oil producers. Algeria, Libya and Nigeria are members of the eleven-member body. Other members include Indonesia, Iran, Iraq, Kuwait, Qatar, Saudi Arabia, UAE, Venezuela.

Southern African Customs Union (SACU)
Director of Customs and Excise
Ministry of Finance
Private Bag 13295
Windhoek
Namibia
A Southern African Customs Union (SACU) was established in 1969 between South Africa, Botswana, Lesotho and Swaziland. Namibia became a member in 1990. Goods move freely between members, unhampered by tariffs or quantitative constraints, and there is a common customs tariff on goods imported from outside. All duties are paid into a common pool administered and disbursed annually by the South African Reserve Bank. Smaller countries receive a 42 percent allowance to compensate for the disadvantage of sharing with the much larger South Africa. Except for Botswana, all members of the Southern African Customs Union are also in a common monetary area arrangement (CMA), under which the currencies of Lesotho, Namibia and Swaziland are backed by the South African rand.

Southern African Development Community (SADC)
Private Bag 0095
Gaborone
Botswana
Tel: [267] (31) 351863
Fax: [267] (31) 372848
The Southern African Development Community (SADC) is an outgrowth of the Southern African Development Coordination Conference (SADCC). It established in July 1979 by 11 nations in an effort to reduce the region's economic dependence on apartheid-ruled South Africa. On 17 August 1992, ten SADCC member states signed a treaty establishing the Southern African Development Community (SADC) with South Africa as the eleventh member. Mauritius joined in 1995, followed by the Democratic Republic of Congo and the Seychelles in 1997. All the members of the SADC—with the exception of Botswana, South Africa, Lesotho and Mozambique—are also members of COMESA. The Southern African Development Community promotes cross-border economic cooperation, investment and trade, and freer movement of goods and services, free enterprise, competitiveness, democracy and good governance, respect for the rule of law and human rights, popular participation and the alleviation of poverty. A tribunal was established to arbitrate disputes between member states arising from the treaty. To avoid an unwieldy bureaucracy at the SADC secretariat in Gaborone, Botswana, organizational responsibilities are shared by the various member states: Angola—energy; Botswana—economic affairs, agricultural research, animal disease control and livestock production; Lesotho—tourism, environment and land management; Malawi—inland fisheries, wildlife and forestry; Mozambique—transport and communication, culture and information; Namibia—marine fisheries and resources; Swaziland—human resources development; Tanzania—trade and industry; Zambia—mining; Zimbabwe—food security. When South Africa became the eleventh member in August

1994, it was given responsibility for finance and investment. The sector for tourism was allocated to Mauritius after the island nation it joined the Southern African Development Community in August 1995.

World Confederation of Labor (WCL)
Rue de Treves 33
B-1040 Brussels
Belgium
Tel: [32] (2) 230 62 95
FAX - [32] (2) 230 87 22
Established on 19 June 1920, as the International Federation of Christian Trade Unions (IFCTU) and renamed on 4 October 1968, the WCL promotes trade union activity among its 99 members of whom 31 are African: Algeria, Angola, Benin, Botswana, Burkina Faso, Cameroon, Cape Verde, Central African Republic, Chad, Democratic Republic of Congo, Côte d'Ivoire, Gabon, The Gambia, Ghana, Guinea, Kenya, Lesotho, Liberia, Madagascar, Mali, Mauritius, Namibia, Niger, Nigeria, Rwanda, Senegal, Seychelles, Sierra Leone, Tanzania, Zambia, Zimbabwe.

World Federation of Trade Unions (WFTU)
Branicka 112
14701 Prague 4
Czech Republic
Tel: [42] (2) 44 46 21 40
Fax: [42] (2) 44 46 13 78
Established on 3 October 1945, to promote the trade union movement among its 125 members, including 36 African countries: Angola, Benin, Botswana, Burkina Faso, Cameroon, Democratic Republic of the Congo, Republic of Congo, Côte d'Ivoire, Djibouti, Egypt, Eritrea, Ethiopia, The Gambia, Ghana, Guinea, Guinea-Bissau, Lesotho, Liberia, Libya, Madagascar, Malawi, Mali, Mauritius, Mozambique, Niger, Nigeria, Senegal, Sierra Leone, Somalia, South Africa, Sudan, Tanzania, Togo, Tunisia, Uganda, Zimbabwe.

West African Development Bank (WADB)
[A.k.a. Banque Ouest-Africaine de Developpement or BOAD]
68 Avenue de la Liberation
BP 1172 Lome
Togo
Tel: [228] 21 59 06, 21 42 44
Fax: [228] 21 52 67, 21 72 69
Established on 14 November 1973, as a financial institution of WAEMU, the WADB promotes regional economic development and integration among its 8 regional members: Benin, Burkina Faso, Cote d'Ivoire, Guinea-Bissau, Mali, Niger, Senegal, and Togo. Also represented are 5 international/nonregional members: African Development Bank, Belgium, European Investment Bank, France, and Germany.

West African Economic and Monetary Union (WAEMU)
[A.k.a. Union Economique et Monetaire Ouest Africaine or UEMOA]
Commission de l'UEMOA
01 BP 543
Ouadgadougou
Burkina Faso
Tel: [226] 31 88 73
Fax: - [226] 31 88 72
Established on 1 August 1994, to increase the competitiveness of its 8 members' economic markets. The West African Economic and Monetary Union (WAEMU) promotes closer cooperation between West African states, the establishment of a common market and coordination of monetary policies. Tariff reduction is high on the priority list. Members are: Benin, Burkina Faso, Côte d'Ivoire, Guinea Bissau, Mali, Niger, Senegal and Togo. A secretariat is planned at Bamako in Mali.

MAP to the future?

In July 2001, at the 37th and final ordinary session of the Organization of African Unity in Lusaka, Zambia, delegates voted to replace the OAU with a new African Union, loosely modeled on the European Union. A new pan-African parliament and judiciary may follow, although some African leaders have their reservations. Underlying this new Union is MAP, the Millennium Africa Recovery Program, brainchild of the leaders of Nigeria, Algeria and South Africa. MAP is intended to encourage peace, democracy and development and aims at consensus on liberalizing economic policies. The plan places emphasis on "economic governance" and views regional trade as the key to greater industrial diversification in countries which are still relying largely on the exportation of commodities. Like the European Union, the aim will be to create bigger regional markets which could conceivably lead to a fully-fledged economic union, and even a single currency.

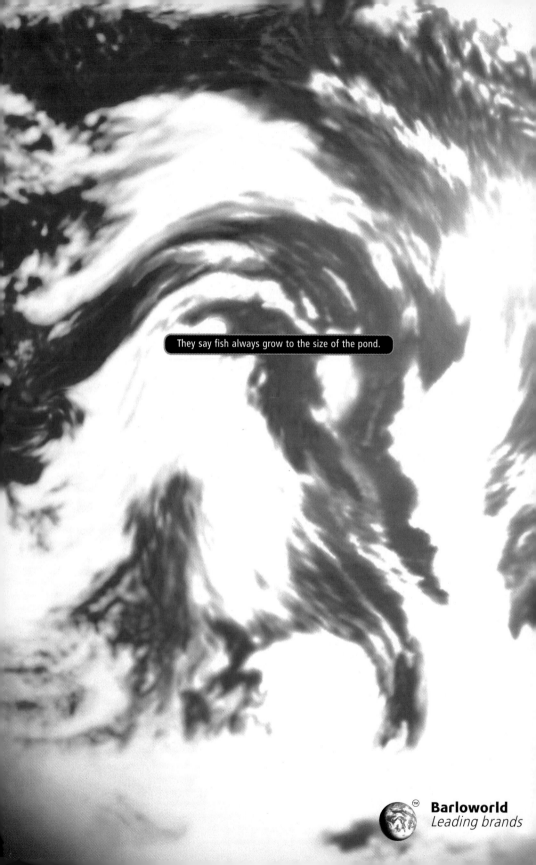

They say fish always grow to the size of the pond.

Barloworld
Leading brands

Chapter 3

Trade and Investment

Even though Africa represents only 2% of the world's total, its trade rose by 12.5% during 2000—twice the average for the past decade. Fuel-rich nations posted an export growth of between 25% and 50%. Currently the continent relies heavily on petroleum and other natural resources such as gold, diamonds and a whole range of strategically important minerals, including chrome, platinum and manganese. The trend is, however, towards diversification and expectations are that Africa will increasingly become a source for manufactured goods and more sophisticated equipment. The nineties saw foreign direct investment reach new highs on the continent. The largest recipients were South Africa, Nigeria, Egypt, Tunisia and Angola where privatization of large state-owned telecommunications, manufacturing and transport facilities lured sizeable investments from abroad. Rates of return on US FDI in Africa, averaging between 25 and 35 percent in recent years, far outstrip profits elsewhere in the world. Still, Africa represents at best only 3% of the total FDI in the emerging markets.

Approaching Cape Town harbor © Safmarine

Trade

In 2000, according to the WTO, Africa was among the regions that recorded a strong growth in trade. The value of world merchandise trade rose by 12.5% in 2000, wice the average for the last decade. Regions with a large share of fuels in their merchandise exports (including parts of Africa) posted an export growth of between 25% and 50%. Still, Africa, with almost a third of all WTO members (41 out of 140), still accounts for only 2% of the world's total trade.

While the continent still relies heavily on its rich natural resources, including gold, diamonds, petroleum and a whole range of strategic minerals, foreign firms have found that trade preferences for African-made products and a growing number of export free zones on the continent make it profitable to move factories there. Textile exports from Mauritius and automobiles and other sophisticated equipment from South Africa to the rest of the world are part of this trend.

US trade

Total US trade with Africa was $26.4 billion in 1999, with Egypt ($3 billion) the biggest purchaser of American goods, and Nigeria ($4.4 billion) the largest supplier, mostly of petroleum and energy related products. In total trade South Africa led the way with $5.7 billion. Petroleum and energy-related products and minerals and metals form the bulk of US imports from the African continent. Its largest single manufactured import from Africa is steel mill products (largely from South Africa) with steel pipes and tubes accounting for 90%. US agricultural products find a ready market in most of Africa, with Egypt, Algeria, Morocco, Nigeria, South Africa and Ghana among the biggest buyers. There is a limited market for forest products. The sale of US chemicals and related products averages a billion dollars per year, consisting primarily of miscellaneous organic chemicals used as feedstock, downstream specialty chemicals and pharmaceuticals, plastics in primary and semi-primary forms, and various fin-

ished chemical products such as soaps, detergents, and cosmetics and toiletries. US imports of chemicals and related products from Africa consist largely of miscellaneous organic and inorganic chemicals. In recent times the strongest growth in US exports to Africa was in electronic products as improvement of telecommunications and computer networks created an ongoing need for a whole range of sophisticated equipment. There is also a growing demand for US transportation equipment, consisting of construction and mining equipment, general aviation aircraft, motor vehicles, and automotive parts. In 1998 the US recorded an annual average services trade surplus of more than a billion dollars, with South Africa accounting for almost 30 percent of US services exports and imports during these years. In Africa as a whole 60% of US trade earnings was in services, compared to a worldwide average of 50%. Services included tourism (inbound to the US), construction, freight forwarding, royalties and licensing fees, and professional consulting, accounting and legal services.

Tariffs

High tariffs and duties on imports aimed at protecting domestic industry, corrupt practices, inadequate transport and marketing facilities, relatively small markets and low consumer bases have hampered trade in some parts of the continent. Lack of infrastructure has left valuable mineral and other natural resources untouched in countries that are in great need of additional revenues. There are no major navigable rivers that can be used to carry ocean-going trade all the way from the source to the sea. Fifteen countries are landlocked, paying a premium on transport. Duty reduction and other reforms, a move towards greater transparency, the creation of free trade zones and the formation of regional trade groupings have addressed some of these concerns. Massive infrastructural projects including road, rail and pipeline construction, airport improvement and the expansion of air links and telecommunications, widening use of radio and television and the Internet, and the refurbishing of harbors and expansion of shipping links are underway in several corners of the continent. Not only will these developments place Africa closer to the trading lanes of the world but they provide good opportunities for foreign participation in construction and the provision of services and equipment.

AFRICAN TRADE FIGURES - 1999

	Exports goods non factor serv. US$m	Imports goods non factor serv. US$m	Exports of total services US$m	Imports of total services US$m
Algeria	13,917	12,379	940	5,070
Angola	3,203	3,465	160	4,197
Benin	724	864	151	229
Botswana	2,448	2,044	917	1,369
Burkina Faso	395	875	52	187
Burundi	208	311	8	44
Cameroon	3,249	2,571	575	1,274
Cape Verde	145	314	107	119
Central African Republic	367	289	43	133
Chad	337	602	54	237
Comoros	53	101	28	21
Congo, Dem. Rep. of	2,404	1,838	83	1,257
Congo, Republic of	1,726	1,312	69	1,507
Côte d'Ivoire	5,351	4,299	835	2,197
Djibouti	..	..	..	..
Egypt	14,152	19,520	11,015	5,069
Equatorial Guinea	520	437	7	410
Eritrea	70	587	61	112
Ethiopia	1,029	2,047	460	398
Gabon	2,698	1,920	261	1,663
Gambia, The	198	257	82	79
Ghana	2,885	4,267	483	760
Guinea	953	949	112	470
Guinea-Bissau	58	100	5	45
Kenya	2,382	3,279	873	894
Lesotho	313	1,211	357	144
Liberia	..	..	..	..
Libya	..	..	..	..
Madagascar	1,037	1,319	335	524
Malawi	529	838	53	140
Mali	880	1,145	99	417
Mauritania	469	605	42	205
Mauritius	3,113	3,216	1,132	1,091
Morocco	7,060	12,236	3,323	3,171
Mozambique	614	1,492	353	628
Namibia	1,871	2,081	565	644
Niger	394	428	38	165
Nigeria	12,969	16,176	1,219	7,622
Rwanda	144	483	56	207
São Tomé and Principe	19	44	13	23
Senegal	1,782	2,188	600	660
Seychelles	394	521	306	178
Sierra Leone	187	181	28	78
Somalia	..	..	..	..
South Africa	40,933	36,298	6,371	9,659
Sudan	..	..	101	1,692
Swaziland	1,213	898	394	347
Tanzania	1,098	1,503	672	911
Togo	438	718	161	289
Tunisia	9,648	10,412	3,009	2,212
Uganda	1,265	1,465	227	521
Zambia	1,754	1,473	116	483
Zimbabwe	3,785	3,833	656	993
ALL AFRICA	167,232	175,108	41,482	63,634

Source: Wolrd Bank Data 2001

Africa's share of total world trade

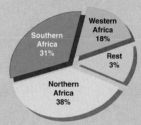

Developed world 71%

Africa 2.9%

Developing world 26.7%

Regional share of Africa's trade with the rest of world

Western Africa 18%

Southern Africa 31%

Rest 3%

Northern Africa 38%

US Imports 1999

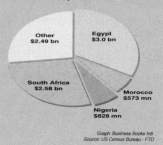

Algeria $1.8 bn

Other $3.3 bn

Angola $2.4 bn

South Africa $3.2 bn

Gabon $1.5 bn

Nigeria $4.3 bn

US Exports - 1999

Other $2.49 bn

Egypt $3.0 bn

South Africa $2.58 bn

Morocco $573 mn

Nigeria $628 mn

Graph: Business Books Intl
Source: US Census Bureau - FTD

AFRICA'S COMMODITY TRADE

	Exports		Imports	
	Main products	**Main partners**	**Main products**	**Main partners**
Algeria	Petroleum and natural gas	Italy, US, France, Spain, Germany	Capital goods, food and beverages, consumer goods	France, Spain, Italy, US, Germany
Angola	Crude oil, diamonds, refined petroleum products, gas, coffee, sisal, fish and fish products, timber, cotton	US, EU, China	Machinery and electrical equipment, vehicles and spare parts; medicines, food, textiles and clothing; substantial military goods	Portugal, US, France, South Africa
Benin	Cotton, crude oil, palm products, cocoa	Brazil, Portugal, Morocco, Libya, France	Foodstuffs, beverages, tobacco, petroleum products, intermediate goods, capital goods, light consumer goods	France, UK, Thailand, Hong Kong, China
Botswana	Diamonds, copper, nickel, meat	EU, Southern African Customs Union (SACU), Zimbabwe	Foodstuffs, vehicles and transport equipment, textiles, petroleum products	Southern African Customs Union (SACU), Europe, Zimbabwe
Burkina Faso	Cotton, animal products, gold	Côte d'Ivoire, France, Italy, Mali	Machinery, food products, petroleum	Côte d'Ivoire, France, Togo, Nigeria
Burundi	Coffee, tea, cotton, hides	UK, Germany, Benelux, Switzerland	Capital goods, petroleum products, foodstuffs, consumer goods	Benelux, France, Germany, Japan
Cameroon	Crude oil and petroleum products, lumber, cocoa beans, aluminum, coffee, cotton	Italy, Spain, France, Netherlands	Machines and electrical equipment, transport equipment, fuel, food	France, Nigeria, US, Germany
Cape Verde	Shoes, garments, fish, bananas, hides	Portugal, Germany, Spain, France, UK, Malaysia	Foodstuffs, consumer goods, industrial products, transport equipment, fuels	Portugal, Netherlands, France, UK, Spain, US
Central African Republic	Diamonds, timber, cotton, coffee, tobacco	Belgium-Luxembourg, Côte d'Ivoire, Spain, Egypt, France	Food, textiles, petroleum products, machinery, electrical equipment, motor vehicles, chemicals, pharmaceuticals, consumer goods, industrial products	France, Côte d'Ivoire, Cameroon, Germany, Japan
Chad	Cotton, cattle, textiles	Portugal , Germany, Thailand, Costa Rica, South Africa, France	Machinery and transportation equipment, industrial goods, petroleum products, foodstuffs, textiles	France, Nigeria, Cameroon, India
Comoros	Vanilla, ylang-ylang, cloves, perfume oil, copra	France, US, Germany	Rice and other foodstuffs, consumer goods; petroleum products, cement, transport equipment	France, South Africa, Kenya
Congo, Rep. (Brazzaville)	Diamonds, copper, coffee, cobalt, crude oil	Benelux, US, South Africa, France, Germany, Italy, UK, Japan	Consumer goods, foodstuffs, mining and other machinery, transport equipment, fuels	South Africa, Benelux, China, Netherlands, US, France, Germany, Italy, Japan, UK
Congo, Dem. Rep. of (Kinshasa)	Petroleum, lumber, plywood, sugar, cocoa, coffee, diamonds	US, Belgium-Luxembourg, Taiwan, China	Intermediate manufactures, capital equipment, construction materials, foodstuffs, petroleum products	France, Italy, US, UK
Côte d'Ivoire	Cocoa, coffee, tropical woods, petroleum, cotton, bananas, pineapples, palm oil, cotton, fish	Netherlands, France, Germany, US, Italy	Food, consumer goods; capital goods, fuel, transport equipment	France, Nigeria, US, Italy, Germany
Djibouti	Hides and skins, coffee (in transit)	Ethiopia, Somalia, Yemen, Saudi Arabia	Foods, beverages, transport equipment, chemicals, petroleum products	France, Ethiopia, Italy, Saudi Arabia, Thailand

AFRICA'S COMMODITY TRADE

	Exports		Imports	
	Main products	Main partners	Main products	Main partners
Egypt	Crude oil and petroleum products, cotton yarn, raw cotton, textiles, metal products, chemicals	EU, US, Japan	Machinery and equipment, foods, fertilizers, wood products, durable consumer goods, capital goods	US, EU, Japan
Equatorial Guinea	Petroleum, timber, cocoa	US, Japan, Spain, China, Nigeria	Petroleum, food, beverages, clothing, machinery	Cameroon, Spain, France, US
Eritrea	Livestock, sorghum, textiles, food, small manufactures	Ethiopia, Sudan, US, Italy, Saudi Arabia, Yemen	Processed goods, machinery, petroleum products	Ethiopia, Saudi Arabia, Italy, United Arab Emirates
Ethiopia	Coffee, leather products, gold, oilseeds	Germany, Japan, Italy, UK, Djibouti, Saudi Arabia	Food and live animals, petroleum and petroleum products, chemicals, machinery, motor vehicles and aircraft	Italy, US, Germany, Saudi Arabia
Gabon	Crude oil, timber, manganese, uranium	US, China, France, Japan	Machinery and equipment, foodstuffs, chemicals, petroleum products, construction materials	France, US, Cameroon, Netherlands, Côte d'Ivoire, Japan
Gambia, The	Peanuts and peanut products, fish, cotton lint, palm kernels	Belgium, Japan, Senegal, Hong Kong, France, Switzerland, UK, US, Indonesia	Foodstuffs, manufactures, raw materials, fuel, machinery and transport equipment	Côte d'Ivoire, Hong Kong, UK, Germany, Netherlands, France, Belgium
Ghana	Gold, cocoa, timber, tuna, bauxite, aluminum, manganese ore, and diamonds	UK, Germany, US, Netherlands, Japan, Nigeria	Capital equipment, petroleum, consumer goods, foods, intermediate goods	UK, Nigeria, US, Germany, Japan, Netherlands
Guinea	Bauxite, alumina, diamonds, gold, coffee, fish, agricultural products	Russia, US, Belgium, Ukraine, Ireland, Spain	Petroleum products, metals, machinery, transport equipment, textiles, grain and other foodstuffs	France, Côte d'Ivoire, US, Belgium, Hong Kong
Guinea-Bissau	Cashews, fish, peanuts, palm kernels, sawn lumber	Spain, India, Thailand, Italy	Foodstuffs, transport equipment, petroleum products, machinery and equipment	Portugal, Thailand, Netherlands, US
Kenya	Tea, coffee, petroleum products	Uganda, Tanzania, UK, Germany	Machinery and transportation equipment, consumer goods, petroleum products	UK, UAE, South Africa, Germany
Lesotho	Manufactures (clothing, footwear, road vehicles), wool and mohair, food and live animals	South African Customs Union, North America, EU	Food; building materials, vehicles, machinery, medicines, petroleum products	South African Customs Union, Asia, EU
Liberia	Diamonds, iron ore, rubber, timber, coffee	Belgium, Norway, Ukraine, Singapore	Fuels, chemicals, machinery, transportation equipment, manufactured goods; rice and other foodstuffs	South Korea, Japan, Italy, Singapore
Libya	Crude oil, refined petroleum products, natural gas	Italy, Germany, Spain, France, Turkey, Greece, Egypt	Machinery, transport equipment, food, manufactured goods	Italy, Germany, UK, France, Spain, Turkey, Tunisia, Eastern Europe
Madagascar	Coffee, vanilla, cloves, shellfish, sugar, petroleum products	France, Japan, Germany, Reunion	Intermediate manufactures, capital goods, petroleum, consumer goods, food	France, Iran, South Africa, Japan, US
Malawi	Tobacco, tea, sugar, coffee, peanuts, wood products	US, South Africa, Germany, Japan	Food, petroleum products, semimanufactures, consumer goods, transportation equipment	South Africa, Zimbabwe, Japan, US, UK, Germany

AFRICA'S COMMODITY TRADE

	Exports		Imports	
	Main products	**Main partners**	**Main products**	**Main partners**
Mali	Cotton, gold, livestock	Thailand, Italy, China, Brazil, franc zone	Machinery and equipment, construction materials, petroleum, foodstuffs, textiles	Côte d'Ivoire, France, other franc zone and EU countries
Mauritania	Fish and fish products, iron ore, gold	Japan, Italy, France	Foodstuffs, consumer goods, petroleum products, capital goods	France, Algeria, Spain, China, US
Mauritius	Clothing and textiles, sugar	UK, France, US, Germany, Italy	Manufactured goods , capital equipment, foodstuffs , petroleum products, chemicals	South Africa, France, India, UK, Germany
Morocco	Food and beverages, semiprocessed goods, consumer goods, phosphates	EU, Japan, India, US, Libya	Semiprocessed goods, capital goods, food and beverages, fuel and lubricants, consumer goods, raw materials	EU, US, Saudi Arabia, Brazil
Mozambique	Shrimp, cashews, cotton, sugar, copra, citrus	Spain, South Africa, Portugal, US, Japan, Malawi, India, Zimbabwe	Food, clothing, farm equipment, petroleum	South Africa, Zimbabwe, Saudi Arabia, Portugal, US, Japan, India
Namibia	Diamonds, copper, gold, zinc, lead, uranium; cattle, processed fish, karakul skins	UK, South Africa, Spain, Japan	Foodstuffs; petroleum products and fuel, machinery and equipment, chemicals	South Africa, Germany, US, Japan
Niger	Uranium ore, livestock products, cowpeas, onions	Greece, Canada, France, Nigeria	Consumer goods, primary materials, machinery, vehicles and parts, petroleum, cereals	France, Côte d'Ivoire, US, Belgium-Luxembourg, Nigeria
Nigeria	Petroleum and petroleum products, cocoa, rubber	US, Spain, Italy, France	Machinery, chemicals, transportation equipment, manufactured goods, food and animals	US, UK, Germany, France, Netherlands
Rwanda	Coffee, tea, hides, tin ore	Brazil, Germany, US, Netherlands, UK	Foodstuffs, machinery and equipment, steel, petroleum products, cement and construction material	Italy, Kenya, Tanzania, US, Belgium-Luxembourg
São Tomé & Príncipe	Cocoa, copra, coffee, palm oil	Netherlands, Germany, Portugal	Machinery and electrical equipment, food products, petroleum products	Portugal , France, Angola, Belgium, Japan
Senegal	Fish, ground nuts (peanuts), petroleum products, phosphates, cotton	France, other EU countries, India, Côte d'Ivoire, Mali	Foods and beverages, consumer goods, capital goods, petroleum products	France, other EU countries, Nigeria, Cameroon, Côte d'Ivoire, Algeria, US, China, Japan
Seychelles	Fish, cinnamon bark, copra, petroleum products (re-exports)	France, UK, China, Germany, Japan	Manufactured goods, food, petroleum products, tobacco, beverages, machinery and transportation equipment	China, Singapore, South Africa, UK
Sierra Leone	Diamonds, rutile, cocoa, coffee, fish	Belgium, Spain, US, UK	Foodstuffs, machinery and equipment, fuels and lubricants	UK, US, Cote d'Ivoire, Belgium-Luxembourg
Somalia	Livestock, bananas, hides, fish	Saudi Arabia, Yemen, Italy, UAE, US	Manufactures, petroleum products, foodstuffs, construction materials	Kenya, Djibouti, Brazil, Pakistan
South Africa	Gold, other minerals and metals, food, chemicals, manufactured goods	UK, Italy, Japan, US, Germany	Machinery, transport equipment, chemicals, petroleum products, textiles, scientific instruments	Germany, US, UK, Japan

AFRICA'S COMMODITY TRADE

| | Exports | | Imports | |
	Main products	Main partners	Main products	Main partners
Sudan	Cotton, sesame, livestock/meat, gum arabic	Saudi Arabia, UK, China, Italy	Foodstuffs, petroleum products, manufactured goods, machinery and equipment, medicines and chemicals, textiles	Saudi Arabia, South Korea, Germany, Egypt
Swaziland	Soft drink concentrates, sugar, wood pulp, cotton yarn, citrus and canned fruit	South Africa, EU, Mozambique, North Korea	Motor vehicles, machinery, transport equipment, foodstuffs, petroleum products, chemicals	South Africa, Japan, UK, Singapore
Tanzania	Coffee, manufactured goods, cotton, cashew nuts, minerals, tobacco, sisal	India, Germany, Japan, Malaysia, Rwanda, Netherlands	Consumer goods, machinery and transportation equipment, industrial raw materials, crude oil	South Africa, Kenya, UK, Saudi Arabia, Japan, China
Togo	Cotton, phosphates, coffee, cocoa	France, Canada, Taiwan, Nigeria, South Africa	Machinery and equipment, consumer goods, petroleum products	Ghana, France, China, Cameroon
Tunisia	Hydrocarbons, textiles, agricultural products, phosphates and chemicals	EU, North African countries, Asia, US	Industrial goods and equipment, hydrocarbons, food, consumer goods	EU countries, North African countries, Asia, US
Uganda	Coffee, gold, fish and fish products, cotton, tea, corn	Spain, Germany, Netherlands, France, Italy	Transportation equipment, petroleum, medical supplies, iron and steel	Kenya, UK, Japan, India, South Africa
Zambia	Copper, cobalt, zinc, lead, tobacco	Japan, South Africa, US, Saudi Arabia, India, Thailand, Malaysia	Machinery, transportation equipment, foodstuffs, fuels, petroleum products, electricity, fertilizer	South Africa, Saudi Arabia, UK, Zimbabwe
Zimbabwe	Tobacco, gold, ferroalloys, cotton	South Africa, UK, Germany, Japan, US	Machinery and transport equipment, other manufactures, chemicals, fuels	South Africa, UK, US, Japan

Liberalization

Until 1990, when reforms started, much of Africa was closed to trade except in minerals, oil and other natural resource exports. In the past decade, however, Africa has become part of the process of globalization, offering ample opportunity for both exporters of products ranging from consumer goods to high technology equipment and importers not only of minerals, oil and raw materials, but food, textiles and other manufactures. African governments through a variety of tax incentives and lowered tariffs encourage both trade and investment. Export Processing Zones (EPZs) have become a convenient springboard for foreign manufacturers taking advantage of special trade quotas and privileges for African goods in other parts of the world.

Regional markets

The growing tendency in Africa to bolster markets by combining individual countries into regional groupings has been a boon to foreign exporters in recent years. By lowering or eliminating tariffs among the member states, these economic groupings facilitate crossborder marketing and distribution to an extended market. The Southern African Development Community (SADC), the Common Market for Eastern and Southern Africa (COMESA), and the Economic Community of West African States (ECOWAS) are all in the process of becoming common markets.

Africa Act

The passage by the US Congress in 2000 of the Africa Growth and Opportunity Act as part of an omnibus trade bill is intended to stimulate further trade between the US and the continent. Similar moves are underway in the European Union and Japan while the WTO and the UN Conference on Trade and Development and other agencies are developing plans to hasten Africa's full integration into the world markets.

Direct Investment

The nineties saw foreign direct investment (FDI) reach new highs. By and large, however, Africa has been bypassed by this surge of investment money. In the late 1990s, Africa's share of world FDI stood at a mere 1.4% and its portion of direct investment earmarked for emerging markets was never higher than 3%. In 1997, when total flows of FDI topped $400 billion, Africa's share was a mere $4.7 billion—comparable to the inflows into a single Asian developing economy, Malaysia. The largest recipients in Africa were South Africa, Nigeria, Egypt, Morocco, Tunisia and Angola—together accounting for well over two-thirds of all FDI flows to Africa. Most of the capital flowing to Africa went into petroleum projects. More than 39% of the continent's total FDI in 1997 went to North Africa.

Principal investors in Africa from 1982 until 1996 were transnational corporations from the United States, Britain, France, Germany, Japan, the Netherlands, Italy and Switzerland. FDI has since increased significantly from Asian economies such as Malaysia, South Korea and Taiwan.

Assistance

UNCTAD undertakes investment policy reviews in African countries and, together with International Chamber of Commerce (ICC) launched a project on investment guidelines and capacity-building. The World Bank's Multilateral Investment Guarantee Agency (MIGA) carries out assessments for a number of investment promotion agencies (IPAs) and, primarily through its Promote Africa field functions, assists them in formulating effective strategies to attract FDI.

Sectors

From 1989 until 1996, 40% of all FDI in Africa went into the primary sector with the rest evenly split between manufacturing and services. In the case of the United States, there has been a shift towards food and related products, primary and fabricated metals and other manufacturing activities. Tertiary investments from the US are also on the rise in Africa as governments liberalize their banking and insurance sectors. HSBC Equator Bank has, for example, been active in opening offices from Angola to Uganda.

Framework

Africa seems set to attract larger amounts of FDI in the new millennium. Flows of capital to North Africa have already shown a sharp increase and Sub-Saharan Africa seems to be at the beginning of a similar trend. In its 1998 *World Investment Report,* UNCTAD identifies—in conjunction with the World Economic Forum (WEF)—the following factors that led to this increased interest in Africa: political stability; predictability and reliability of the policy and regulatory framework af-

Rates of return on US FDI in Africa %									
Region	1989	1990	1991	1992	1993	1994	1995	1996	1997[1]
Africa[2]	17.4	24.2	30.6	28.4	25.8	24.6	35.3	34.2	25.3
Primary[3]	13.0	22.8	35.4	29.1	26.1	23.9	34.2	36.9	.....
Manufacturing[3]	15.4	20.4	16.0	18.9	30.5	30.0	42.8	21.3	.....
Tertiary[3]	N/A	23.8	N/A	22.2	23.5	21.7	21.6	23.1	.....
Other	N/A	48.0	28.4	40/8	13.5	44.1	35.0	17.4	.....
Asia[4]	23.3	27.6	23.8	22.6	20.7	18.4	20.2	19.3	16.2
Latin America	15.7	13.0	12.1	14.3	14.9	15.3	13.1	12.8	12.5
Developing countries	17.8	17.2	15.9	17.2	16.9	16.5	15.8	15.3	14.0
All countries	14.8	14.3	11.6	10.4	11.1	11.7	13.3	12.5	12.3

The % rate of return is calculated as the net income of US foreign affiliates in a given year divided by the average beginning-of-year and year-end FDI stock. 1. The stock data for 1997 used in the calculation are estimates by the US Department of Commerce. 2. Excluding South Africa. 3. Including South Africa. 4. Including West Asia, South, east and Southeast Asia and the Pacific, excluding Australia, Israel, Japan and New Zealand.

Source: UNCTAD, US Department of Commerce

fecting business, such as taxes; transparency and efficiency in decision-making; less corruption; and effective investment promotion. Forty seven of Africa's 53 countries have adjusted laws governing FDI to make it easier for foreigners to invest. A recent survey conducted by UNCTAD showed that only six of the 29 least developed countries in Africa for which data could be found still had restrictive regimes as far as repatriation of dividends and capital were concerned. Most of these countries have expanded their list of industries open to foreign investors.

Natural resources

Natural resources are bound to continue to be the most important investment asset in Africa. Most of the current front-runners in luring new investment are countries with economies dominated by primary products. FDI in Equatorial Guinea is almost exclusively devoted to the exploitation of its rich oil and gas reserves. Botswana and Namibia received significant FDI in mining, especially diamonds. Ghana attracts FDI mostly in mining, and Gabon, Tunisia, Chad, Cameroon and Algeria in petroleum-related fields.

Profit

Profit ultimately drives foreign direct investment. Africa has rewarded investors handsomely. During the period from 1980 to 1997 there was only one year (1986) that the rate of return for US investors dipped below 10%. From 1990, the returns on US investment in Africa averaged 29% and from 1991 it topped that of any other region. Net income of British FDI is reported to have increased by 60% between 1989 and 1995. Japanese companies also did much better in Africa than elsewhere, returning 6% on FDI in Africa in 1995 compared with a world average of 2%.

Privatization

In recent years privatization of significant state enterprises in sectors such as telecommunications and transport, as well as government-run monopolies in manufacturing, food processing, agricultural projects, oil production and refining, and mining has boosted FDI. More than 20 governments have already privatized all or part of their holdings.

Survey

Since 1990, overall FDI inflows have been increasing but they still represent only about 5% of the total FDI flows to developing countries. A

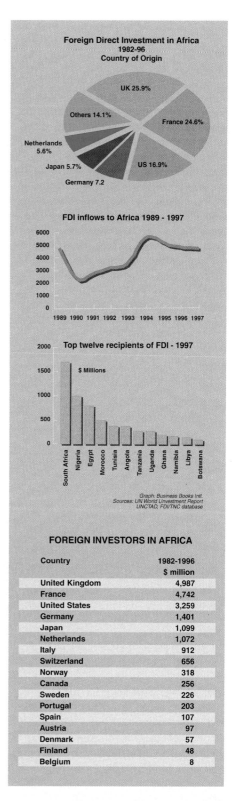

Foreign Direct Investment in Africa
1982-96
Country of Origin

UK 25.9%
Others 14.1%
France 24.6%
Netherlands 5.6%
Japan 5.7%
US 16.9%
Germany 7.2

FDI inflows to Africa 1989 - 1997

Top twelve recipients of FDI - 1997

$ Millions

South Africa, Nigeria, Egypt, Morocco, Tunisia, Angola, Tanzania, Uganda, Ghana, Namibia, Libya, Botswana

Graph: Business Books Intl.
Sources: UN World Unvestment Report
UNCTAD, FDI/TNC database

FOREIGN INVESTORS IN AFRICA

Country	1982-1996 $ million
United Kingdom	4,987
France	4,742
United States	3,259
Germany	1,401
Japan	1,099
Netherlands	1,072
Italy	912
Switzerland	656
Norway	318
Canada	256
Sweden	226
Portugal	203
Spain	107
Austria	97
Denmark	57
Finland	48
Belgium	8

1999 UNCTAD survey of 44 African IPAs indicated expectations of better prospects for FDI in the period 2000-2003. Among these, South Africa, Nigeria, Botswana, Côte d'Ivoire and Tunisia stood out as countries most frequently mentioned as the most attractive destinations. The most attractive sectors for FDI from1996 to 1998 were telecommunications, food and beverages, tourism, mining and quarrying and textile and leather. Agriculture and mining and quarrying ranked in fifth and sixth positions. As factors likely to have a positive impact on foreign investors, profitability, the regulatory and legal framework and the political and economic outlook were cited most frequently. Access to regional markets (and to a lesser extent global markets), trade policy, the tax regime as well as access to low-cost skilled labor were also mentioned by most investment agencies as positive factors. However, only half of the participating agencies considered access to low-cost unskilled labor and the relative low cost of doing business as important. The most frequently mentioned negative influence was extortion and bribery. Other negative factors mentioned include high administrative costs of doing business, the lack of skilled labor, and problems in obtaining finance for investment.

Promotion

In an effort to attract investment, smaller nations and economies in Africa have joined forces with larger neighbors in a number of regional groups. These provide foreign investors with a larger domestic market for their manufactures and preferential trade access to industrial markets abroad.

In the 1990s, regulatory and other reforms have been introduced by a number of governments to make their economies more attractive to foreign investors. Today, the regulatory conditions established in many African countries are on a par with those in other developing countries.

Not only larger nations such as South Africa, Egypt, Morocco and Nigeria have shown promising growth

in FDI. When adjusted for market size (FDI per US$1,000 GDP) a number of small countries have also performed well. Figures show that even least developed countries (LDCs), such as Mozambique, Tanzania and Uganda can be attractive to foreign investors despite their very low income levels.

Outward investment

Several African companies—especially in South Africa—have become outward investors, with FDI flowing into other parts of the continent and abroad in mining and the manufacturing of paper, beer and a whole range of other commodities, as well as the expansion of information technology.

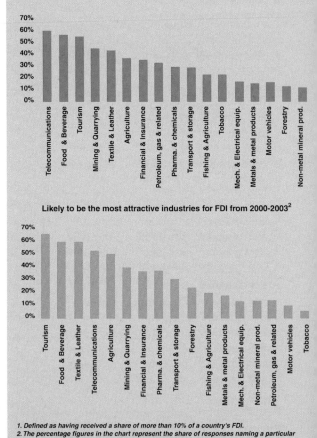

African Industries that received considerable FDI inflows - 1996-1998[1]

Likely to be the most attractive industries for FDI from 2000-2003[2]

1. Defined as having received a share of more than 10% of a country's FDI.
2. The percentage figures in the chart represent the share of responses naming a particular industry in the total of responses received from African IPAs

Source: UNCTAD, (based on results of a survey of African investment promotion agencies, 1999

Indirect Investment

A number of new exchanges have sprung up in Africa to join the well established bourses in South Africa, Egypt and Zimbabwe. The Cairo Exchange was founded in 1883 and the Johannesburg Securities Exchange in 1887 while Zimbabwe's exchange dates back to 1896. Newcomers with full trading facilities are Botswana, Côte d'Ivoire, Ghana, Kenya, Malawi, Mauritius, Morocco, Namibia, Nigeria, Tanzania, Tunisia, and Zambia.

The SADC Committee of Stock Exchanges was formed in January 1997 with South Africa, Namibia, Botswana, Mauritius, Swaziland, Tanzania, Malawi, Zambia and Zimbabwe as members. These exchanges have to agreed adopt the JSE Securities Exchange's (JSE) listing requirements. The ultimate aim is to have an integrated real-time network among all the exchanges in the region by 2006, each offering automated trading in a wide range of financial instruments from a single desktop workstation with settlement and central depository facilities conforming to international standards.

ASEA

The African Stock Exchange Association (ASEA) was formed in 1993 to provide a formal framework for co-operation between all African stock exchanges. In 1998 the Abidjan Stock Exchange in Côte d'Ivoire was replaced by the first regional exchange, *Bourse Régionale des Valeurs Mobilières* (BRVM), serving the members of the WAEMU—Benin, Burkina Faso, Côte d'Ivoire, Guinea Bissau, Mali, Niger, Senegal and Togo. It opened with a listing of 35 companies. A second exchange is planned for Cameroon, Central African Republic, Chad, Republic of Congo, Equatorial Guinea and Gabon, which all share the CFA franc currency and a central bank. A separate exchange is also under consideration for Gabon. All of these exchanges are, however, small by world standards with the exception of the JSE Securities Exchange.

FDI Climate

Among the steps to improve the FDI climate taken by African governments are:

☑ **Improved environment**
Trade liberalization, strengthening of the rule of law, improved legal and support institutions, better governance, improved transparency and better transport and telecommunications have helped make it easier to do business in many African countries. Over 40 African countries are now members of the WTO, with more in the process of joining.

☑ **Economic reforms**
Many African countries have stabilized their economies by the devaluation of overvalued currencies, reducing inflation rates and cutting budget deficits. Others are raising educational standards and upgrading their human resources.

☑ **Private sector encouragement**
A growing number have broad-based privatization programs in place. More than twenty Sub-Saharan countries have transferred all or part of their telecommunications ownership from the state to the private sector.

☑ **Better FDI regulatory framework**
Most countries have substantially improved their FDI regulatory frameworks by allowing profits to be repatriated freely, and offering tax incentives and similar inducements to foreign investors. Many African countries have investment promotion agencies (IPAs), to assist investors.

☑ **Foreign treaties**
At the international level, 37 African States are now members of the Multilateral Investment Guarantee Agency (MIGA), 42 are signatories to the Convention on Investment Disputes between States and Nationals of Other States, and 26 to the Convention on Recognition and Enforcement of Foreign Arbitral Awards. Fifty countries have concluded bilateral investment treaties aimed at protecting and promoting FDI, and 41 have signed double taxation treaties.

JSE

The total value of equity capital raised on the primary share market by companies listed on the JSE Securities Exchange (JSE) increased to R74 billion in 2000—almost twice as much as in 1999. Volatile price movements throughout 2000 boosted trading activity in the secondary share market with shares to the value of R537 billion traded—20 percent more than the previous record set in 1999. While South Africa enjoys the benefit of large foreign trading in its share, bond and futures markets, it is also more susceptible to volatility in world financial markets. During 2000 exchange rate concerns dampened enthusiasm for the usually popular rand-denominated bonds. The JSE offers screen trading through its Johannesburg Equities Trading (JET) system. Its Share TRAnsactions Totally Electronic (STRATE) system eliminates paper transactions by making settlement and the transfer of ownership of scrip possible through electronic book entry. The JSE accounts for more than 93% of the total portfolio equity flows into Sub-Saharan Africa.

CASE

In May 2000, the Cairo & Alexandria Stock Exchange (CASE) (a.k.a. Egyptian Stock Exchange or ESE) launched its fully-automated and integrated trading, clearing and settlement system (ATS), increasing its capacity in daily trades tenfold. CASE aims at increasing the number of local individual investors from a half a million to 5 million by 2005.

Returns

During the mid-1990s African stock exchanges produced attractive returns, averaging around 40%. Nigeria's stock exchange rose 144%, the Côte d'Ivoire index was up 57%, and averages on the exchanges in Namibia and Zimbabwe rose more than 50%. Towards the end of the 1990s African markets—with the exception of Ghana where a gain of 63.1% was still recorded in 1998—turned in less impressive results. Still, in 2000 Sub-Saharan African markets achieved an average return of 1.5%, outstripping the Dow, FTSE and NASDAQ, despite surprisingly disappointing returns in dollar terms from South Africa due to a further weakening of the rand. The governments of South Africa, Morocco, Egypt and Ghana have all on occasion utilized their respective stock markets to privatize state-owned enterprises through IPOs.

Analysis

Apart from South Africa where local brokerage houses maintain sophisticated research teams and foreign banks have a strong presence, authoritative and reliable analysis of African investment prospects is hard to obtain. In the process, many good opportunities slip by those investors without insufficient first-hand knowledge.

ADRs

While the mechanics of cross-border investment flows are often complex, American Depositary Receipts (ADRs) and Global Depositary

African Stock Exchanges

COUNTRY	EXCHANGE	CITY	TELEPHONE	FACSIMILE
BOTSWANA	Botswana Stock Exchange	GABERONE	(267) 37-4078	(267) 37-4079
CÔTE D'IVOIRE	BRVM (REGIONAL)[1]	ABIDJAN	(225) 32-66-85	(225) 32-66-84
EGYPT	Cairo & Alexandria SE	CAIRO	(202) 392-1447	(202) 392-4214
GHANA	Ghana Stock Exchange	ACCRA	(233) 21-669-908	(233) 21-669-913
KENYA	Nairobi Stock Exchange	NAIROBI	(254) 2-23-0692	(254) 2-22-4200
MALAWI	Malawi Stock Exchange	BLANTYRE	(092) 65-624-233	(092) 65-623-636
MAURITIUS	Mauritius Stock Exchange	PORT LOUIS	(230) 212-9541	(230) 208-8409
MOROCCO	Casablanca Stock Exchange	CASABLANCA	(212) 2-20-0366	(212) 2 20-0365
NAMIBIA	Namibian Stock Exchange	WINDHOEK	(264) 61-227-647	(264) 61-248-531
NIGERIA	Nigerian Stock Exchange	LAGOS	(234) 1-266-0287	(234) 1-266-8724
SOUTH AFRICA	JSE Securities Exchange	JOHANNESBURG	(27) 11-520-7000	(27) 11-520-8608
SWAZILAND	Swaziland Stock Exchange	MBABANE	(268) 404-1829	(268) 404-9493
TANZANIA	Dar-es-Salaam Exchange	DAR-ES-SALAAM	(255) 51-133659	(255) 51-113846
UGANDA	Kampala Stock Exchange	KAMPALA	(256) 41-343-2977	(256) 41-342-841
ZAMBIA	Lusaka Stock Exchange	LUSAKA	(260) 1-22-8391	(260) 1-22-5969
ZIMBABWE	Zimbabwe Stock Exchange	HARARE	(263) 4-73-6861	(263) 4-79-1045

1. Bourse Régionale des Valuers Mobiliéres (BRVM)

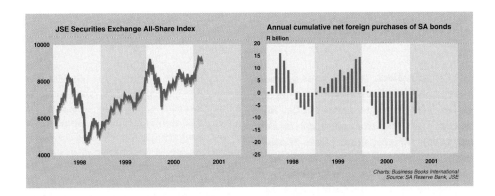

Charts: Business Books International
Source: SA Reserve Bank, JSE

Receipts (GDRs) offer a convenient way for Americans who wish to invest in about 100 African companies listed by major US banks and institutions. All but four—Ashanti Goldfields of Ghana (now listed on the NYSE), Botswana RST Ltd., Mangura Copper Mines and Nigeria's United Bank for Africa PLC—are South African companies. An ADR is a negotiable certificate held in a US bank representing a specific number of shares of a foreign stock traded on an American stock exchange. The widespread availability of dollar-denominated price information, lower transaction costs, and timely dividend distributions, make many American investors opt for ADRs. Several South African companies—including Sappi, SA Breweries, Sasol, Old Mutual and Anglo-American—are listed on the London, Frankfurt and New York Exchanges.

Africa Funds

Few of the world's more than 1300 emerging market equity funds focus on Africa. Recent political and economic and structural reforms (including the lifting of exchange controls, currency reforms and privatization) in several African countries, especially in post-apartheid South Africa, and the shrinking gains from more mature emerging markets have stimulated new interest among American and other foreign investors. The number of Africa-specific funds has also mushroomed. At least 12 Africa funds with a combined worth of US$1 billion have been established over the past six years. The Overseas Private Investment Corporation (OPIC) currently has several privately-managed investment funds that support investment in Sub-Saharan Africa.

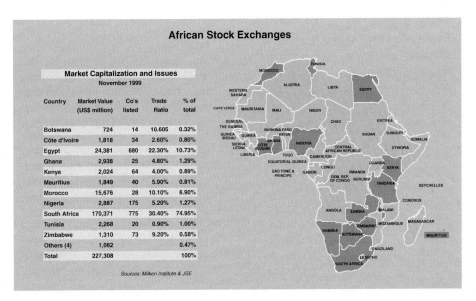

African Stock Exchanges

Market Capitalization and Issues
November 1999

Country	Market Value (US$ million)	Co's listed	Trade Ratio	% of total
Botswana	724	14	10.605	0.32%
Côte d'Ivoire	1,818	34	2.60%	0.80%
Egypt	24,381	680	22.30%	10.73%
Ghana	2,938	25	4.80%	1.29%
Kenya	2,024	64	4.00%	0.89%
Mauritius	1,849	40	5.90%	0.81%
Morocco	15,676	28	10.10%	6.90%
Nigeria	2,887	175	5.20%	1.27%
South Africa	170,371	775	30.40%	74.95%
Tunisia	2,268	20	0.90%	1.00%
Zimbabwe	1,310	73	9.20%	0.58%
Others (4)	1,062			0.47%
Total	227,308			100%

Sources: Milken Institute & JSE

Privatization

Privatization, which first gained acceptance and popularity in conservative Britain in the early 1980s, has become an inextricable part of the economic development plans of most African nations. Although still a mere mantra for some, most of them are set on selling off or liquidating state assets in a variety of sectors ranging from power utilities to railroads, telecoms, hotels and factories. Privatization comes in a variety of configurations, ranging from outright sales to partial minority share-holdings and joint venture ownership. Some African governments still seem reluctant to release control altogether, while others find it politically expedient to restructure in stages. In South Africa, where the government is committed to rectify the racial injustices of the past, a certain percentage of the shareholding in restructured state-owned enterprises is usually reserved for black investors and employees.

By the end of 2000 the World Bank had documented more than 3,529 privatizations in Africa. Examples include water distribution in Angola; agro-industries, transport, mining, beverages, and tourism in Cameroon; more than a hundred private firms established in the two Congos; palm oil industries in Côte d'Ivoire: electricity and water in Gabon; breweries, mines, resorts, and land in Mozambique; game reserves, breweries, tour operations, and hotels in Tanzania; retail stores, flour mills and pharmaceutical companies in Lesotho; and telecommunications, hotels, airlines, banks, and coffee marketing in Uganda. Major multi-million dollar deals include South Africa's sale of a 30 percent share in its huge telecommunications monopoly, Telkom, to US and Malaysian investors; Morocco's sale of a 30 percent stake in its state refinery, SAMIR, to Swedish investors; Ghana's sale of its gold mining company, Ashanti Goldfields, through an international placement of shares; and Kenya and South Africa's partial sale of their respective national airlines.

The **objectives** are usually one or more of the following: 1) raising revenue for the state; 2) raising investment capital for the industry or company being privatized; 3) reducing government's role in the economy; 4) promoting wider share ownership; 5) increasing efficiency; 6) introducing greater competition; and 7) exposing firms to market discipline.

Privatization came to South Africa first. It started in the eighties with the highly successful sale of Sasol's assets on the Johannesburg Stock Exchange and broadened in the post-apartheid era to include state-owned iron, steel industries, toll roads, agricultural marketing, transport, broadcasting and telecommunications. Not only South Africa but other governments in Africa frequently experience opposition from some quarters who see it simply as the transfer of state monopolies to private conglomerates, thereby enriching a small elite class at the expense of the masses. Another recurring concern on the part of organized labor is that it will result in job retrenchment as the private sector tries to accomplish greater efficiency and profitability with fewer people.

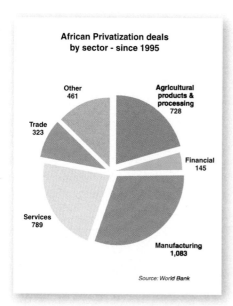

African Privatization deals by sector - since 1995

Other 461

Agricultural products & processing 728

Trade 323

Financial 145

Services 789

Manufacturing 1,083

Source: World Bank

Privatization of Public Enterprises in Africa

	Total no of deals	Total sales value US$m	Transactions completed					
			Pre 1995	1995	1996	1997	1998	1999
Algeria	..	..	..	..	..	..	..	..
Angola	331	25	..	..	56	..	..	..
Benin	46	63	39	5	..	..	..	..
Botswana	40	..	..	..	..	..	..	..
Burkina Faso	..	24	17	3	6	..	2	4
Burundi	42	11	26	..	13	3	..	..
Cameroon	48	72	13	3	23	5	4	..
Cape Verde	46	172	13	9	10	9	..	..
Cent. Afr.Rep.	35	0	35	..	..	..	..	..
Chad	31	6	12	13	6	..	..	..
Comoros	4	0	..	..	..	..	..	..
Congo DR of	61	50	2	44	15	..	..	..
Congo, R of	21	0	16	2	3	..	..	..
Côte d'Ivoire	105	811	21	27	21	15	11	6
Djibouti	..	..	..	..	..	..	..	..
Egypt	54	307	..	5	10	8	31	..
Eq. Guinea	3	0	..	..	..	..	..	..
Eritrea	..	..	..	..	..	..	..	..
Ethiopia	125	203	..	9	..	..	1	..
Gabon	26	0	..	..	..	1	..	..
Gambia, The	34	10	31	..	..	..	1	1
Ghana	233	674	146	23	20	27	4	8
Guinea	117	9	112	4	..	1	..	..
Guin.-Bissau	29	1	18	11	..	..	..	..
Kenya	188	248	66	69	22	27	4	..
Lesotho	21	24	2	7	..	1	4	6
Liberia	..	..	..	..	..	..	..	..
Libya	..	..	..	..	..	..	..	..
Madagascar	86	43	60	24	..	..	..	1
Malawi	68	57	35	..	8	5	5	12
Mali	65	32	60	..	..	..	..	..
Mauritania	56	10	29	6	..	..	..	2
Mauritius	..	..	..	..	..	..	..	..
Morocco	52	259	..	12	17	16	6	1
Mozambique	579	217	398	112	38	31	..	..
Namibia	..	..	..	..	..	..	..	..
Niger	34	3	32	2	..	..	..	..
Nigeria	81	207	81	..	..	..	..	..
Rwanda	2	0	..	..	..	..	..	..
São Tomé Pr.	9	0	8	1	..	..	..	..
Senegal	61	412	37	1	11	4	4	1
Seychelles	..	..	..	..	..	..	..	..
Sierra Leone	10	0	7	1	..	1	..	..
Somalia	..	..	..	..	..	..	..	..
South Africa	13	2,461	3	..	1	2	3	3
Sudan	32	0	32	..	..	..	..	..
Swaziland	..	..	..	..	..	..	..	..
Tanzania	283	246	86	22	46	40	64	23
Togo	57	39	25	1	18	9	2	1
Tunisia	36	29	27	..	..	6	3	..
Uganda	91	149	44	23	18	2	..	3
Zambia	268	906	30	60	91	55	16	10
Zimbabwe	6	166	2	..	..	3	..	1
ALL AFRICA	**3,529**	**7,946**	**1,565**	**499**	**453**	**271**	**165**	**83**

Source: World Bank Database, 20001

Privatization terms and methods

"Privatization" has been defined in a number of ways. Most observers, however, see it simply as the reduction of the role of government or increasing the role of the private sector through the sale of part or all of a state enterprise. As such "privatization" is the opposite of "nationalization," where governments take over the ownership of private enterprise, with or without payment or compensation. Other terms often found in the privatization stable are *devolution, corporatization, commercialization, deregulation and restructuring of state assets.* The removal of a state subsidy can also be viewed as a form of privatization. *Privatization can be implemented in varying degrees.* It could be comprehensive—with the private investors taking over a major portion of the state entity—or partial. Private participation comes in many forms: the purchase of a shareholding, directly or in a competitive bid, or via preemptory rights or a public offering; the purchase of assets, directly or through a competitive bid or in a liquidation procedure; through a debt/equity swap; leasing; joint venture; a management or employee buyout; management contract; or a trusteeship arrangement. It can be a combination of several of these. One innovative financing method growing in popularity in Africa involves a foreign investor who builds and operates a plant for a prescribed period, and then transfers it to the host company or country (BOOT). This has been a popular means of encouraging foreign investment in power projects. In some African countries foreign investment commitments have been restricted to a joint venture with a domestic company, especially in strategic industries. As indicated overleaf, Africa has utilized most of these methods.

Privatization methods used in Africa until 1999

	Sales of shares				Sale of assets			Other methods							
	Compet. sale	Direct Sale	Pre-empt rights	Public flot.	Liqui-dation	Compet. sale	Direct sale	Debt/Equity swaps	Leases	Joint vent.	Mgmt./empl. buyout	Mgmt. contracts	Trustee	Restit-ution	Other
Algeria	..	..	..	..	..	..	..	..	..	..	..	..	..	..	..
Angola	..	..	..	..	..	57	..	..	..	..	..	..	..	..	274
Benin	1	2	..	..	23	12	3	..	2	..	..	2	..	1	..
Botswana	..	..	..	..	..	..	..	..	..	..	..	..	..	..	..
Burk. Faso	15	3	..	..	14	..	..	..	1	..	..	1	1	1	4
Burundi	11	3	..	..	13	5	..	..	..	..	1	9	..	..	..
Cameroon	20	..	..	..	18	..	..	..	..	..	..	..	..	..	10
Cape Verde	20	2	5	..	10	1	1	..	..	..	6	1	..	..	..
CAR	..	..	..	..	26	..	..	..	1	1	..	1	..	..	6
Chad	12	2	..	..	11	..	..	..	..	..	..	5	..	..	1
Comoros	..	..	..	..	..	..	..	..	..	..	..	..	..	..	4
Congo, DR	1	..	..	..	15	..	..	..	..	..	..	5	..	..	..
Congo, Rep.	1	..	..	..	53	..	..	..	..	..	..	2	..	..	5
Côte d'Ivoire	15	2	23	22	2	25	8	..	3	1	..	..	..	..	4
Djibouti	..	..	..	..	..	..	..	..	..	..	..	..	..	..	..
Egypt	..	..	..	..	..	..	..	..	..	..	..	..	..	..	..
Eq. Guinea	..	..	..	..	..	..	..	..	..	..	..	..	..	..	3
Eritrea	..	..	..	..	..	..	..	..	..	..	..	..	..	..	..
Ethiopia	..	..	..	..	..	10	..	..	..	..	..	..	..	..	115
Gabon	..	..	..	..	..	..	..	..	..	..	..	..	..	..	26
Gambia, The	13	7	..	..	3	1	..	..	5	1	1	1	..	..	2
Ghana	8	11	19	13	56	76	12	2	5	13	..	1	..	..	5
Guinea	42	1	..	..	67	1	..	..	4	..	..	2	..	..	..
Guin.-Bissau	7	2	..	..	8	2	..	..	2	1	..	7	..	12	..
Kenya	13	..	96	16	36	17	4	1	..	..	1	1	..	..	3
Lesotho	5	3	..	..	7	2	..	..	1	..	..	..	..	..	3
Liberia	..	..	..	..	..	..	..	..	..	..	..	..	..	..	..
Libya	..	..	..	..	..	..	..	..	..	..	..	..	..	..	..
Madagascar	6	14	..	..	29	15	6	..	1	1	..	3	..	8	3
Malawi	22	5	..	2	..	13	..	1	..	..	..	..	3	..	22
Mali	14	1	..	..	30	11	..	..	1	..	..	1	3	..	4
Mauritania	25	..	..	..	17	3	..	..	..	..	..	1	3	..	7
Mauritius	..	..	..	..	..	..	..	..	..	..	..	..	..	..	..
Morocco	..	..	..	..	..	..	..	..	..	..	..	..	..	..	..
Mozambique	509	..	..	..	..	22	..	..	37	10	..	1	..	..	..
Namibia	..	..	..	..	..	..	..	..	..	..	..	..	..	..	..
Niger	13	..	..	..	17	..	..	..	..	..	..	2	..	..	2
Nigeria	5	5	..	37	2	29	..	..	..	..	1	..	2	..	..
Rwanda	..	..	..	..	..	..	..	..	..	..	..	..	..	..	2
São Tomé & P.	..	1	..	..	6	..	..	..	..	..	1	1	..	..	..
Senegal	26	1	1	2	23	1	..	1	3	1	..	1	2	..	1
Seychelles	..	..	..	..	..	..	..	..	..	..	..	..	..	..	..
Sierra Leone	..	..	..	..	1	..	..	..	5	..	..	3	..	..	1
Somalia	..	..	..	..	..	..	..	..	..	..	..	..	..	..	..
South Africa	9	..	..	1	..	1	..	..	..	..	..	..	..	..	2
Sudan	7	..	..	..	..	15	..	5	1	..	..	..	..	..	4
Swaziland	..	..	..	..	..	..	..	..	..	..	..	..	..	..	..
Tanzania	61	4	13	1	84	70	3	1	25	3	6	3	..	2	5
Togo	8	7	..	..	20	13	1	..	6	..	..	2	..	..	..
Tunisia	..	..	..	..	..	..	..	..	..	..	..	..	..	..	..
Uganda	10	..	6	1	18	24	..	2	1	4	1	..	5	11	8
Zambia	37	6	14	4	22	109	2	..	38	1	17	..	..	16	2
Zimbabwe	1	1	..	4	..	..	..	..	..	..	..	..	..	..	..
ALL AFRICA	937	83	177	103	631	535	40	13	142	37	35	56	19	51	528

Source: World Bank Database, 2001

Chapter 4

Key Sectors in Africa

Over many years coffee, cocoa and cotton and a whole range of other cash crops from the continent have made millionaires out of foreign investors and traders. Then came gold and diamonds and a slew of high priced strategic minerals. This was followed by major oil discoveries beyond the traditional North African fields in West Africa and more recently as far south as Angola. With more than 8.2% of the world's proven oil reserves, close to 8% of its gas, more than 6% of its coal supply and a full range of strategic minerals, oil extraction and mining are major areas of foreign involvement in Africa. In recent times, however, restructuring and reform have opened up lucrative new avenues for overseas entrepreneurs in exciting new areas such as telecommunications, transport, tourism, health services and banking. Africa is also seen by information technology companies as the last lucrative frontier where annual spending on products and services is estimated to double within the next two years from its current $18 billion level.

Courtesy Satour

Africa's abundant energy products are major sources of export revenues and the engine for local development and growth in a number of countries. With close to 8.2% of the world's proven oil reserves, 7.7% of its natural gas reserves and more than 6% of its coal supply, the continent is a significant player in the field of energy exports. Participation of major overseas firms in partnership with governments and domestic firms in the exploration and exploitation of these assets has had considerable spin-offs aside from earning much-needed foreign revenues. Companies such as ExxonMobil and Chevron have been active participants in infrastructure development, education and training, housing and, lately, AIDS prevention programs. Two gigantic newly-announced pipeline projects by these firms are destined to introduce poor backwater communities in West Africa to the benefits of the 21st Century.

At 1.5 million barrels per day, Africa is the third largest crude oil exporter to the US, supplying 16.36% of its import needs—compared to 23% from the Persian Gulf region. ExxonMobil and Chevron lead a number of US and other foreign companies involved in oil and gas exploration and extraction. In the process they have developed opportunities for engineering and construction firms such as Kellogg Brown and Root. Several US-based firms have plans to expand existing investments in Africa's energy sectors. In May 1999, Chevron announced plans to invest $12 billion in its African operations over the next five years. It is the project manager for the West Af-

rican Gas Pipeline (WAGP) that will connect Nigeria's gas reserves to markets in Benin, Togo, and Ghana. ExxonMobil is leading the development of the Chad Export Project (CEP) to produce and transport oil from southern Chad through neighboring Cameroon to the Atlantic coast for export to world markets, including the US.

Leaders

The countries with the largest proven crude oil reserves are Libya (29.5 billion barrels), Nigeria (22.5), Algeria (9.2), and Angola (5.4). In 1999, Nigeria was the continent's largest producer (2,030 barrels per day—bbl/d), followed by Libya (1,425), Algeria (1,340), Egypt (835) and Angola (780). Africa also has abundant natural gas reserves—Algeria leads with 4.52 trillion cubic meters (Tcm), followed by Nigeria (3.51), Libya (1.31) and Egypt (1).

MAJOR PRODUCERS

Petroleum and other energy products are major contributors to the economies of several African nations. In 1999 Algeria's oil and gas export revenues accounted for at least 90% of its total export revenues, and more than half of total fiscal revenues. Oil export revenues account for about 98% of Libya's hard currency earnings and half its fiscal receipts. Crude oil exports generate over 90% of Nigeria's foreign exchange earnings. Although Chad is not on the charts at this time, it is expected to join the list of major oil revenue recipients once the Chad-Cameroon Pipeline is completed. Of special significance is South Africa which has developed into a major player in the energy field despite its hitherto limited proven reserves of oil and gas. To compensate, South Africa in the 1950s created Sasol to extract oil from coal. First as a state-run operation and subsequently as a privatized undertaking, Sasol is not only the world's

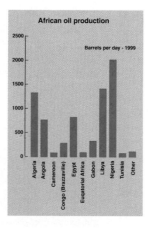

African oil production

Barrels per day - 1999

foremost producer of synfuels but a major producer and exporter of chemicals, polymers and plastics.

Algeria

A member of OPEC and an important energy source of oil for Europe, Algeria should see a sharp increase in crude oil exports over the next few years due to a rapid shift towards domestic natural gas consumption and planned increases in oil production by state-owned Sonatrach and its foreign partners. Approximately 90% of Algeria's crude oil exports go to Western Europe. Algeria's Saharan Blend oil, 45% API with 0.05% sulfur and negligible metal content, is among the best in the world. Unlike most OPEC producers, Algeria opened its oil sector to foreign investment more than a decade ago. At the start of 1999, there were 25 foreign firms from 19 countries operating in Algeria such as Exxon-Mobil, Anadarko, BP (Beyond Petroleum), Phillips Petroleum, Lasmo, Burlington Resources and Occidental Petroleum Corporation. There are four oil refineries capable of meeting most of the country's domestic requirements. Algeria's 4.52 Tcm of proven natural gas reserves place it among the top 10 worldwide. It provides about 25% of Europe's needs. In 1964, Algeria became the world's first producer of liquefied natural gas (LNG).

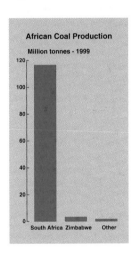

African Coal Production
Million tonnes - 1999

Angola

Angola, sub-Saharan, Africa's second largest oil producer after Nigeria and the sixth largest supplier to the US, is not a member of OPEC. Although reserves have been located north of Luanda, most of its crude production is in the Cabinda exclave. The oil sector accounts for over 40% of GDP and four-fifths of Angola's revenues. Arrangements between the state-owned Sonangol and foreign companies are either joint ventures (JVs) with investment costs and production divided according shareholding in the venture, or production sharing agreements (PSAs) with the foreign partners acting as contractors, financing all investment costs, and recovering their investment when production begins. A Chevron subsidiary, Cabinda Gulf Oil Company (CABGOC), is the main foreign operator in offshore Cabinda with a 39.2% share in a joint venture including Sonangol (41%), Elf Aquitaine (Elf 10%) and ENI-Agip (Agip 9.8%). Gas reserves are estimated at 1.6 trillion cubic feet (Tcf). Angola's largest individual hydroelectric project is the $2 billion 520-megawatt Capanda facility.

Cameroon

As Africa's fifth largest oil producer, Cameroon averaged crude oil production of 95,000 bbl/d in 1999. Petroleum products constitute more than half of its exports. ExxonMobil, Shell, Elf Aquitaine, Texaco and Total are major foreign participants. Both Cameroon and Nigeria have laid claims to the 1,000 sq km oil-rich Bakassi Peninsula in the Gulf of Guinea. Development of several discoveries is on hold awaiting a ruling by the International Court of Justice (ICJ). In the meantime Cameroon will gain largely from the construction of a 1,050- kilometer oil pipeline to be built by a consortium led by ExxonMobil from landlocked neighboring Chad to offshore export facilities near Kribi. Cameroon's gas reserves top 3.9 Tcf. The state-owned Société Nationale de Raffinage (SONARA) refinery in Limbé supplies the local market. Along with the Democratic Republic of Congo (DROC), Cameroon has the best potential for hydroelectric power in Africa. Over 110 possible sites have been identified, with a combined potential capacity of 500,000 megawatts (MW) that could make the country a net electricity exporter.

Chad

In 2000, plans were finalized for the construction of a $3.7 billion pipeline to Kribi in Cameroon which will transport oil from Chad's Doba fields that remained dormant for 30 years. The economy of landlocked, relatively poor, Chad is expected to improve drastically as a result of the so-called Chad Export Project undertaken by ExxonMobil in partnership with several other oil companies and the governments of Cameroon and Chad, supported by the World Bank. Chad's revenues are anticipated to increase by between 45 percent and 50 percent per year in the next four years.

Congo

The Republic of Congo (Brazzaville) is sub-Saharan Africa's fourth largest oil producer and the 15th largest supplier to the US. Most of its crude is located offshore. With support from the French government, Elf Aquitaine (Elf) maintains a dominant position. The official Société Nationale des Pétroles du Congo (SNPC) prefers production-sharing agreements (PSAs) with foreign firms which carry out exploration and development within a pre-determined time (usually three years for each phase), finance all investment costs and recover their investments when production begins. Congo's premier field, N'Kossa, represents Elf's largest single investment in oil production worldwide. It has partnered with Chevron (30%), SNPC (15%), and Energy Africa (Engen) (4%) in a recent expansion project. Other firms involved are the US independent CMS Nomeco (offshore Yombo field) and Shell and ExxonMobil (Mer Profonde Nord). A single refinery, Société Congolaise de Raffinage (CORAF), operates in Pointe Noire. Congo is, after Nigeria and Cameroon, the third largest gas resource base in Sub-Saharan Africa. Most of the reserves are found with oil and vented or flared. There is vast potential for hydro power.

Côte d'Ivoire

Côte d'Ivoire is self-sufficient in refined petroleum products and a major supplier to the West African region. During the twenty-year period from 1970 to 1990, over 100 wells were drilled offshore Côte d'Ivoire, and several commercial oil and gas fields were discovered. Two fields were operated by Phillips Petroleum until 1988 when they became uneconomical. US-based Apachi and Santa Fe Energy Resources, as well as Ocean, Shell and Petroci are involved in current exploration. There were recent significant offshore discoveries of oil and gas off the coastline in the Gulf of

Guinea. The *Société Ivoirienne Raffinage* (SIR) refinery and an adjacent Abidjan asphalt plant (*Société Multinationale des Bitumes*—SMB) rely in part on crude from Nigeria. ENI-Agip, Elf Aquitaine, ExxonMobil, Texaco, Total and Shell dominate the downstream retail sector.

Egypt

Egypt is a significant oil producer and a rapidly growing gas producer. Oil companies which began active exploration for natural gas in Egypt in the early 1990s found a series of significant deposits in the Nile Delta and the Western Desert. The Suez Canal and Sumed Pipeline are strategic routes for Persian Gulf oil shipments. There are eight refineries and plans were approved to build five new ones. Major foreign companies involved in gas exploration and production in Egypt include British Gas, Beyond Petroleum, ENI-Agip, and Shell. Currently, Egypt consumes all the gas it produces but there are plans to export. Around 84% of Egypt's electrical power is thermal (gas turbines), with the remaining 16% hydroelectric, mostly from the Aswan High Dam. Egypt is planning to add power plants through Build, Own, Operate, and Transfer (BOOT) arrangements with foreign firms. Coal production started in 1995 at the El-Maghara mine

Equatorial Guinea

Equatorial Guinea's recent emergence as an important oil producer has not been without controversy. Regional relations between Cameroon, São Tomé & Príncipe, and Nigeria have been strained over maritime border demarcation in the Gulf of Guinea. Nigeria's border claims against Cameroon are awaiting a decision at the International Court of Justice. The outcome of this case will also affect Equatorial Guinea's offshore oil interests as the Nigerian government has questioned Equatorial Guinea's sole ownership of certain offshore properties. Offshore petroleum reserves were pinpointed in 1991 by the Spanish firm CEPSA, followed by ExxonMobil discoveries in the Zafiro field, northwest of the island province of Bioko, and approximately 36 km south of Nigeria's Edop field, also operated by ExxonMobil. A partnership between Samedan Oil and CMS Energy and Equatorial Guinea's government—Atlantic Methanol Production Company—is building a new methanol plant on Bioko Island to manufacture chemicals, solvents, fuel additives, and building materials from existing gas production.

African gas, oil and coal

Oil

Country	Reserves Barrels billion	Share world total	Production Barrels thousand per day	Share world total
Algeria	9.2	0.9%	1,340	1.6%
Angola	5.4	0.5%	780	1.1%
Cameroon	0.4	#	95	0.1%
Congo (Brazzaville)	1.5	0.1%	295	0.4%
Egypt	2.9	0.3%	835	1.2%
Equatorial Guinea	#	#	100	0.1%
Gabon	2.5	0.2%	340	0.5%
Libya	29.5	2.9%	1,425	2.0%
Nigeria	22.5	2.25%	2,030	2.9%
Tunisia	0.3	#	85	0.1%
Other Africa	0.6	0.1%	120	0.2%
AFRICA TOTAL	74.9	8.2%	7,445	10.2%

Coal

Country	Reserves Million tonnes	Share world total	Production Million tonnes	Share world total
South Africa	55,333	5.6%	116.7	5.5%
Zimbabwe	734	0.1%	3.5	0.2%
Other Africa	5,345	0.5%	1.9	0.1%
Middle East	193	##	0.8	##
AFRICA & M/E	61,605	6.2%	122.9	5.8%

 # Less than 0.05%

Source: BP Amoco

Natural gas

Country	Reserves Trillion cubic meters	Share world total	Production Billion cubic meters	Share world total
Algeria	4.52	3.1%	82.2	3.5%
Egypt	1.00	0.7%	14.7	0.6%
Libya	1.31	0.9%	5.9	0.3%
Nigeria	3.51	2.4%	5.7	0.3%
Other Africa	0.82	0.6%	5.2	0.2%
AFRICA TOTAL	11.16	7.7%	113.7	4.9%

Principal producers

Proven reserves at the end of 2000

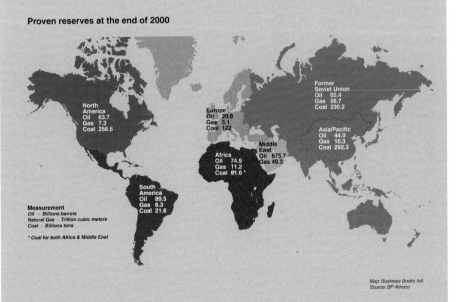

North America
Oil 63.7
Gas 7.3
Coal 256.5

Europe
Oil 20.6
Gas 5.1
Coal 122

Former Soviet Union
Oil 65.4
Gas 56.7
Coal 230.2

Asia/Pacific
Oil 44.0
Gas 10.3
Coal 292.3

Middle East
Oil 675.7
Gas 49.3

Africa
Oil 74.9
Gas 11.2
Coal 61.6 *

South America
Oil 89.5
Gas 6.3
Coal 21.6

Measurement
Oil - Billions barrels
Natural Gas - Trillion cubic meters
Coal - Billions tons

* Coal for both Africa & Middle East

Map: Business Books Intl.
Source: BP Amoco

Gabon

Gabon is sub-Saharan Africa's third largest producer and exporter of crude oil, which accounts for about 80% of total export revenues, 60% of government revenues, and over 40% of GDP. France's Elf Aquitaine is a major participant, but in recent years other oil companies, particularly from North America, have increasingly invested in Gabon's oil sector. Newcomers include Santa Fe Energy Resources of Gabon (a subsidiary of US-based Santa Fe Snyder Corporation), Total, Unocal, Vanco Energy, KerrMcGee, Eni, and Amerada Hess. In July 1998, South Africa's Sasol Petroleum International and Vaalco Energy announced an offshore crude oil discovery. Sogara refinery at Port Gentil is the only refinery. In 1998, the state-run *Société d'Electricité et d'Eau du Gabon* (SEEG) became the first sub-Saharan water and electric utility to be privatized.

Ghana

In the seventies discoveries were made offshore near western and central Ghana by US-based companies Santa Fe Energy Resources, Hunt Oil and Nuevo Energy, as well Yukong of South Korea and United Kingdom's Dana Petroleum and Seafield Resources. Significant gas reserves were considered commercially non-viable and relinquished. Ghana's estimated 16.5 million barrels of recoverable oil reserves are located in five sedimentary basins. The Ghana National Petroleum Company (GNPC) produces 6,000 bbl/d. The Tema Oil Refinery (TOR) near Accra primarily processes imported Bonny Light/Brass River crude from Nigeria for domestic consumption and export. ExxonMobil and other foreign firms are involved in the distribution and marketing of refined products. Ghana is the proposed terminus of the West African Gas Pipeline, which will deliver natural gas from Nigeria to markets in Benin, Togo and Ghana.

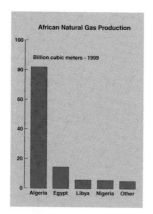

African Natural Gas Production

Billion cubic meters - 1999

Algeria Egypt Libya Nigeria Other

Libya

Libya , an OPEC member, has Africa's largest proven oil reserves and is a major oil exporter to Europe of high-quality, low-sulphur crude oil. Oil export revenues, which account for about 95% of Libya's hard currency earnings, declined as a result of US and UN sanctions. While UN sanctions were suspended after the recent extradition of two suspects in the 1988 bombing of Pan Am flight 103 over Lockerbie, Scotland, US sanctions remain. Their ultimate lifting is awaited by US companies eager to reclaim properties which they have abandoned. Two US oil companies (Exxon and Mobil) withdrew from Libya in 1982, following a US trade embargo that began in 1981 but five others (Amarada Hess, Conoco, Grace Petroleum, Marathon, and Occidental) remained until 1986, when President Reagan ordered them to cease all activity. Since 1968, Libya's oil industry has been run by the state-owned National Oil Corporation (NOC) together with several foreign firms, including Italy's Agip-ENI, which has been operating in the country since 1959. There are three refineries with a combined capacity nearly twice domestic oil consumption. Libya distributes refined products in Italy, Germany, Switzerland, and Egypt. Expansion of gas production is encouraged both for domestic use and export. In 1971, Libya became the second country in the world (after Algeria in 1964) to export liquefied natural gas (LNG).

Morocco

Although it has only a small supply of natural gas, Morocco is a major transit center for Algerian gas exports across the Strait of Gibraltar to Spain via the Maghreb-Europe Gas (MEG) pipeline. Despite efforts to attract foreign investors to explore for oil and gas, only a few companies signed agreements including Saudi Aramco, Australia's ROC, Sweden's Taurus, and US-based Skidmore. Morocco produces small volumes of natural gas from the Gharb Basin in the north, and appears to have a considerable gas field at Meskala. Coal from its one mine at Jerada is insufficient and has to be augmented with imports from the US, Colombia, and South Africa.

Mozambique

Enron has concluded an agreement to develop the Pande gas field in the central region and construct a 610 km pipeline to Maputo. Hidroelectrica de Cahora Bassa (HCB)—a joint-venture between Portugal and Electricidade de Mocambique (EDM)—has restored the connections between its Cahora Bassa dam and South Africa, replacing over 2,000 pylons damaged during the civil war. Cahora Bassa, with a nominal capacity of 2000 MW, also supplies power to neighboring Zimbabwe.

Nigeria

Nigeria, a member of OPEC, is one of the world's largest oil exporters and fifth largest supplier of crude oil to the US . Oil accounts for nearly 50% of its GDP and 95% of the country's foreign exchange earnings. Nigeria's proven oil reserves of 22.5 billion barrels place it second in Africa after Libya. Most reserves are found along the coastal Niger River Delta. ExxonMobil, Chevron, Shell, ENI/Agip (Agip) and Elf Aquitaine (Elf) have long-standing presences. Foreign participation in offshore exploration and production activities is usually through joint ventures (JVs), while deepwater exploration is on a basis of production-sharing contracts (PSCs). In a typical PSC the operator covers all exploration and development costs and pays tax and royalties to the government once production commences. Cameroon and Nigeria are in litigation at the World Court over the Bakassi Peninsula in the Gulf of Guinea, believed to contain significant oil reserves. Nigeria's four refineries have a combined capacity of over 438,750 bbl/d, but in the past sabotage, fire, poor management and lack of turn-

around maintenance (TAM) sharply decreased actual output. ExxonMobil and the Nigerian National Petroleum Corporation (NNPC) produce NGLs (natural gas liquids) and Chevron, together with Sasol— the South African energy, synfuels and petrochemicals company—will construct a 20,000 bbl/d gas-to-liquids (GTL) plant to turn natural gas to synthetic crude oil and refined petroleum products such as sulfur-free diesel. The government aims to increase foreign participation in the electric power sector by offering Build, Own, and Operate (BOO) projects. Both Exxon Mobil and Enron are already involved.

South Africa

With the exception of offshore gas reserves in Mossel Bay, South Africa has yet to show meaningful reserves of oil and natural gas. The parastatal, Soekor, is concentrating its exploration efforts on South Africa's West and South coasts. The Oribi gas field 140 km off the Mossel Bay coast produces 25,000 bbl/d through a liquefaction process run by Mossgas. The first privatization in South Africa's gas distribution sector was completed in December 1999, when a consortium led by the US-based Cinergy acquired Johannesburg's Metro Gas Company. South Africa is one of the major refining nations in Africa with a total refining capacity (excluding synfuel) of 466,547 bbl/d. A Sasol/Total joint venture announced in August 1999 involves a $123 million expansion project of the Natref refinery. Multinational companies (including BP, Shell, Caltex, and Total) are major participants in South Africa's downstream petroleum markets. Parastatal Eskom, one of the largest utilities in the world, generates nearly all South Africa's electricity. Its plants are mostly coal fired. Koeberg, the only nuclear-fired electricity plant on the African continent, accounts for 7.1% of the total. Eskom exports power to Botswana, Lesotho, Mozambique, Namibia, Swaziland and Zimbabwe. With proven reserves of more than 555 billion tons, South Africa compensates for the lack of oil and gas with coal. It is the third biggest coal exporter in the world and uses substantial quantities to produce synfuel. In the fifties the government established the South African Coal and Gas Corporation (Sasol) to develop the world's first and largest commercially viable oil-from-coal extraction operation. Coal is first gasified, then turned into a range of liquid fuels and petrochemical feedstocks. Today Sasol, privatized two decades ago, is a diversi-

PIPELINE PROJECTS

TUNISIA
MOROCCO
ALGERIA   LIBYA   EGYPT
Muglad - Red Sea Pipeline
CHAD
Chad Export Project Pipeline   SUDAN
TOGO   BENIN
CÔTE   GHANA   NIGERIA
D'IVOIRE
West African Gas Pipeline (WAGP)   CAMEROON   ETHIOPIA
GULF OF GUINEA
EQUATORIAL   UGANDA
GUINEA
GABON   DEM. REP.
CONGO   OF CONGO
TANZANIA
ATLANTIC
OCEAN   ANGOLA   MOZAMBIQUE
Pande-Maputo Gas Pipeline
LESOTHO   INDIAN
OCEAN
SOUTH AFRICA

Business Books International

New projects

- ☑ The $3.7 billion Chad Export Project (CEP) provides for the extraction and transport of 250,000 barrels of oil per day from southern Chad to Kribi in Cameroon for export. ExxonMobil leads the consortium that will undertake the project. It will generate billions in revenues for Chad and Cameroon and bring new development to the whole region.

- ☑ The $400 million West African Gas Pipeline Project (WAGP) under leadership of Chevron will connect Nigeria's gas reserves to markets in Benin, Togo, and Ghana for electricity generation and manufacturing.

- ☑ Dallas-based Triton Energy allocated $191 million for an exploration and appraisal activity in Equatorial Guinea.

- ☑ Sicor and Ethiopia formed a $1.4 billion joint venture, Gasoil Ethiopia Project (GEP), to develop a gas field in the eastern part of the country and build a pipeline.

- ☑ Enron concluded a power purchase agreement to supply emergency electricity to state-owned power utility Nigerian Electric Power Authority (NEPA). It is negotiating with Mozambique to construct a pipeline from the Pande gasfield to Maputo.

- ☑ Chevron combined with Sasol, the South African energy, synfuels and petrochemicals company, to construct a gas-to-liquids (GTL) plant in Nigeria to turn natural gas into synthetic crude oil and refined petroleum products.

- ☑ AES Nile Power (AESNP)—a joint venture between AES and Madhvani International of Uganda—was formed to build a 250 MW hydroelectric plant at Bujagali Falls.

- ☑ CMS Energy Corporation and its Ghanaian partner Volta River Authority took over commercial operation and announced expansion plans for the Takoradi Thermal Power plant near Aboadze, Ghana.

fied private oil and chemical enterprise with extensive international business base and is active in the US, Europe and Africa.

Sudan

In 1999 Sudan became a net oil exporter when it opened a 1,500 km pipeline from the oil fields of the Muglad Basin in southern Sudan to an export terminal on the Red Sea. This pipeline is an undertaking of the Greater Nile Petroleum Operating Company (GNPOC), consisting of the China National Petroleum Corporation (CNPC)(40%), Petronas of Malaysia (30%), Sudanese national firm Sudapet (5%), and Canadian-based Arakis (25%). Hydropower accounts for more than 70% of Sudan's electricity.

Tunisia

Tunisia produces modest volumes of oil and gas, expected to increase with sufficient investment. New projects worth $400 million have been announced, including one in the Gulf of Gabes. Houston-based Nuevo Energy is involved in the region while a Tunisian-Libyan joint venture is exploring an oilfield straddling the border Tunisian and Libyan territorial waters. Tunisia has 2.8 trillion cubic feet (Tcf) of proven natural gas reserves and British Gas (the largest investor in Tunisia's energy sector) is planning a $450 million expansion in the southeastern region.

Other sources

The Inga hydroelectric facility in the Democratic Republic of Congo supplies power to the Congo power grid. Other interconnections are currently underway or planned, including a $500-million Angola-Namibia Kunene River hydroelectric project that will supply power to Angola, Namibia, and South Africa. Tanzania is the only nation in the Lake Victoria region with proven natural gas reserves and significant coal reserves. After South Africa, Zimbabwe is Africa's major producer of coal. The Lesotho Highlands Water Project provides for a 274 MW of hydroelectric generating capacity. In Mauritius, bagasse (biomass refuse from the processing of sugar cane) is used to generate power and Zimbabwe will utilize solar power to electrify over 500 districts. South Africa plans to install 2,500 photovoltaic systems in rural areas with the help of US Department of Energy laboratories. Zambia is acquiring solar energy and using ethanol as an alternative transport fuel.

Electricity

Together North and Southern Africa account for 82 percent of total power generating capacity on the continent. The Democratic Republic of Congo (Central), Kenya (East), and Nigeria (West) are leading in power generation elsewhere. South Africa's utility, Eskom, is not only Africa's biggest, but the world's fifth largest utility both in terms of electricity sales and generating capacity. Eskom also operates Africa's only nuclear power generation facility at Koeberg, near Cape Town. South Africa with 6.6 terawatthours (Twh) of power, Zambia with 1.2 Twh and Ghana with 0.3 Twh are the three largest net exporters of electricity in Africa. But globally, Africa lags far behind both in terms of production and consumption of electricity. At the end of the nineties Africa's total electricity generating capacity of 94 gigawatts represented about 3 percent of the world total. Even though commercial energy production in Africa has nearly doubled since 1970, and is expected to increase another 68% by 2020, its share of the world's total remained at 7%. The continent's share of world commercial energy consumption is also small due to low per capita incomes, low levels of industrialization and ownership of electric appliances. Underdeveloped commercial energy resources and insufficient energy delivery systems, coupled with widespread and severe poverty, force rural populations to rely heavily on biomass. Firewood and charcoal is both the most common and the most environmentally detrimental biomass energy source. The resulting deforestation has become one of the most pressing environmental problems faced by African nations. In many countries three-quarters of the forest cover has already been depleted.

NASA's composite picture of the world at night depicts an Africa that appears dark against the festive lights of Europe, North America, Asia and even Latin America. Africa's energy sector has, however, begun to light up the radar screens of international investors. While still modest, interest is growing in new construction projects and a growing number of privatization prospects. The World Bank is helping to accelerate the privatization process and to build overseas investor confidence. Even utilities that are expected to remain state-owned have been targeted for overhaul with the help of private expertise.

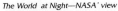

The World at Night—NASA' view

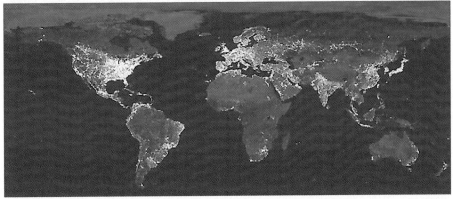

In its latest report, the US Energy Information Administration summarizes recent developments in electricity generation in Africa as follows:

North Africa

A newly constructed Hamma 450-megawatt (MW) natural gas-fired facility provides power to **Algeria**'s capital city, Algiers. Several IPP projects are planned, including a 1,200-MW plant near Tipasa, the 2X600-MW Terga plant near Oran Tipasa and a 2X600-MW plant near Annaba. InterGen plans to have **Egypt**'s first Build Own Operate Transfer (BOOT) power project operational by the beginning of 2002. The complex, Sidi Kerir 3 and 4, will consist of two 325-MW gas-fired units which will form the largest private power station in North Africa and the Middle East. The Egyptian Electric Authority (EEA) has signed two additional BOOT agreements with Electricite de France (EDF) for 650-MW gas-fired facilities at each end of Egypt's Suez Canal at an estimated total cost of $900 million. **Morocco**'s state-owned

Office Nationale d'Electricite (ONE) plans to invest $900 million in the country's power generation sector. Planned additions to generating capacity include the Kouida al Baida 50-MW wind farm overlooking the Strait of Gibraltar, a 470-MW station located near Tangiers at Tahaddart, a 200-MW hydroelectric facility at Dchar el Oued, and a 300-MW pumped storage hydroelectric facility near Afourar. Morocco also plans to add two 330-MW units on a build-operate-transfer (BOT) basis to the Jorf Lasfar plant. Another $200-million 180-MW hybrid solar-gas power plant is expected to be built in the northeastern Jerada province. Morocco plans to raise the rate of electrification in rural areas to 60% in 2003 from 21% in 1994 by electrifying 550,000 rural households at an annual estimated cost of $153 million. The US-based PSEG is leading a consortium developing **Tunisia**'s first privately-run generating facility. The 470-MW combined cycle gas-fired plant, Rades II, will be located outside the capital of Tunis.

Central Africa

A Canadian firm, Ocelot Energy, and the Societe Nationale des Hydrocarbures (SNH), **Cameroon**'s state-owned oil firm, signed a memorandum of understanding for the construction of a 175-MW gas-powered facility utilizing the Sanaga Sud field in offshore southern Cameroon. The **Democratic Republic of Congo** announced plans to expand the Inga hydroelectric facility on the Congo River. The combined capacity of the 2,000-MW Inga II plant and the 40,000-MW Grand Inga facility is almost as large as all of Southern Africa's current

installed capacity. Three firms—EEF (Switzerland), Infra-Consult (Germany) and Medis (Belgium)—have signed an agreement to rehabilitate the DRC's Societe Nationale d'Electricite (SNEL) electricity system, including work on generating facilities in Kinshasa and production and distribution in the North and South Kivu provinces. In **Equatorial Guinea** the diesel plant on the island of Bioko is being replaced with a 6-MW to 8-MW thermal power plant that will utilize flared gas from the Alba field.

East Africa

Electricite de **Djibouti** (EDD) increased its generating capacity by 20 MW with the purchase of four 5-MW diesel-powered generators with assistance from the Kuwaiti Fund. EDD also has plans to construct an 18-MW facility in Marabout. Studies are underway to evaluate the geothermal potential of **Eritrea**'s Alid region. Initial results indicated that temperature and permeability conditions were favorable for an electrical-grade geothermal resource. Djibouti and Uganda are also exploring the possibility of utilizing geothermal resources for power generation. The **Ethiopian** Electric Power Corporation (EEPC) increased the country's electric generating capac-

ity with the upgrading of facilities on the Koka and Tis Abay rivers and the completion of a 34-MW hydroelectric plant on the Fincha river in its western region. The EEPC is also constructing hydroelectric facilities on Ethiopia's Gilgel-Gibe (184 MW) and Blue Nile (73 MW) rivers. A 150-MW hydroelectric facility on the Gojeb river is expected to become operational by 2003. Additional hydroelectric facilities are planned on the Tekeze, Tana, Beles, and Halele

Africa's Electricity Industry

Region	Capacity			Net Generation 1997		
	Total[1] (GW)[2]	Hydro (%)	Thermal (%)	Total[1] (BKWh)[3]	Hydro (%)	Thermal (%)
Central Africa	4.3	91%	9%	10.8	95%	5%
East Africa	2.8	64%	34%	10.4	78%	17%
North Africa	33.0	12%	88%	111.6	12%	88%
Southern Africa	43.8	15%	81%	217.6	7%	87%
West Africa	9.6	48%	52%	24.8	52%	48%

1. Approximately 5% of East Africa's generation was from geothermal and 6% of Southern Africa's generatioin was from nuclear.
2. GW = Gigawatt (1 million kilowatts)
3. BKHWh = Billion Kilowatthours

Source: US Energy Information Administration

Werabisa rivers. **Kenya** has several independent power projects (IPPs) underway. Recently completed are coal-fired plants at Nairobi South and the 75-MW Kipevu II. **Kenya** plans to generate 25% of its electricity from geothermal energy by 2017 as the Olkaria III project enters its second phase. This country already has the highest penetration rate of photovoltaic systems in the world, with over 80,000 systems in place and annual sales of another 20,000. Two Chinese firms, the International Water and Electric Company and the Machinery Export and Import Company, have agreed to finance 75% of the Kajbar hydroelectric facility in northern **Sudan**. The $200 million project will be located on the Nile, and will have a generating capacity of 300 MW. The 180-MW Owens Falls hydroelectric facility, located in southern **Uganda** on the Nile, is being expanded to provide an additional 200 MW of generating capacity. US-based AES plans to develop the 250-MW Bujagali Falls hydroelectric facility on the Nile. The $450-$500 million project, which could be operational by the end of 2002, is the largest of several hydroelectric IPP projects currently being developed in Uganda. Norway's Norpak is heading a consortium that plans to build the 180-MW Karuma Falls hydroelectric project in northwestern Uganda and a smaller facility (10-12 MW), financed by the Commonwealth Development Corporation, is planned for the Muzizi River.

West Africa

US-based firms Enron and Abacan negotiated with the government of **Benin** to develop, construct and operate an 80-MW power generation facility. The proposed project includes building a 20-mile (30-kilometer) pipeline to feed natural gas to a plant south of Porto Novo. **Côte d'Ivoire's** Compagnie Ivoirienne de Production d'Electricite (CIPREL) project was one of the first to be undertaken in Sub-Saharan Africa. The 210 MW gas-fired plant is a joint-development of the French firms EDF and Saur-Bouygues (SAUR). The Cinergy consortium won a 23-year BOOT concession to build a thermal power plant at Azito outside of Abidjan, Côte d'Ivoire. Plans called for a $223-million, 420-MW gas-fired facility. Cinergy comprises the Swiss-based Asea Brown Boveri (ABB), Industrial Promotion Services (IPS) and EDF. The government of **Burkina Faso** plans to electrify 48 of the estimated 350 communities in the country by 2010. **Ghana** has developed plans for an additional hydroelectric facility to be located on the Black Volta River at Bui with a generating capacity of 400 MW for exporting to Burkina Faso, Côte d'Ivoire and Mali. A consortium of American and Japanese firms participated in the construction of a 220-MW power station in Tema, Ghana. The Ghanaian government is committed to bringing electric service to every community of 500 or more people by the year 2020. The 75-MW Garafi hydroelectric facility was inaugurated in **Guinea** in July 1999. It is the country's largest hydroelectric facility and will supply power to Conakry, Guinea's capital. **Nigeria** is developing two IPP projects. ExxonMobil will  generate power from a 350-MW, gas-fired facility located at Bonny in southeastern Rivers State for the state-owned National Electric Power Authority (NEPA), while Enron has signed an agreement for the construction of a 540-MW power plant. Nigeria plans to spend an estimated $144 million on the rehabilitation of six generating facilities. **Senegal**'s SENELEC plans to electrify over 150 rural towns bringing electricity to all villages with a population of 3,000 or more.

Southern Africa

The Southern African Power Pool (SAPP) was created in 1995 by the 12 countries in the Southern African Development Community (SADC). Participating utilities include Angola's ENE, the Botswana Power Corporation (BPC), the Democratic Republic of Congo's SNEL, Lesotho Elec-

Energy briefs

☑ Oil accounts for 63% of Africa's commercial energy production, coal 19%, natural gas 15%, hydroelectricity 2.3%, and nuclear power 0.5%.

☑ Africa's share of the world's commercial energy production has remained at 7% since 1970. The continent accounts for 3% of the world's commercial energy consumption.

☑ Oil production (including crude oil and natural gas liquids) is concentrated in five countries—Algeria, Angola, Egypt, Libya, and Nigeria—together accounting for 88% of the continent's total oil output.

☑ Close to 96% of the continent's coal comes from South Africa, the only country to produce coal-based synthetic fuels in its Sasol plants on a commercial basis.

☑ Natural gas is concentrated in 5 countries—Algeria, Egypt, Libya, Nigeria, and Tunisia—accounting for 96% of Africa's output.

☑ Africa's net energy exports have been rising rapidly since 1997 and are expected to double by 2020.

☑ Five African countries—South Africa, Egypt, Algeria, Nigeria, and Libya—account for 78% of the continent's total energy consumption and 84% of its production.

☑ Africa is a heavy user of traditional (non-commercial) fuels, primarily biomass which makes up 65% of Africa's total energy consumption.

☑ Geothermal generating plants make up only about 0.1% of the total electric generating capacity in Africa with Ethiopia and Kenya accounting for most of it.

☑ Only South Africa has nuclear power production.

tricity Corporation (LEC), Malawi's Electricity Supply Commission (ESCOM), Mozambique's EDM, Namibia's Nampower, South Africa's Eskom, Swaziland Electricity Board (SEB), Tanzania Electric Supply Company (TANESCO), Zambia's ZESCO and Zimbabwe's ZESA. The power grids of Angola, Malawi and Tanzania are in the process of being connected. **Angola**'s generation capacity doubled with the completion of the 520-MW Capanda hydroelectric facility. Its state-owned utility, Empresa Nacional de Electricidade (ENE), plans to construct an oil-fired power plant in the city of Lubango. The **Lesotho** Highlands Water Project, involving the construction of dams, tunnels and pipelines, will have a power generating capacity of 274 MW. The first phase of the 80-MW Muela hydro facility came online in 1999. The Compagnie Thermique de Belle Vue (CTBV), a joint-venture between Harel Freres (51%) of **Mauritius**, France's Cidec (27%), the  Sugar Investment Trust of Mauritius (14%) and the State Investment Fund (8%), constructed a 70-MW IPP facility north of the Mauritian capital of Port Louis. The CTBV plant utilizes bagasse (biomass refuse from the processing of sugar cane) as its primary fuel. Electricidade de Mocambique (EDM), **Mozambique**'s state utility, and Hidro-electrica de Cahora Bassa (HCB)—a joint venture between Portugal and EDM—have restored the link between the Cahora Bassa dam and **South Africa**, by replacing over 2,000 pylons that were damaged during the civil war. Cahora Bassa, with a nominal capacity of 2,000 MW, also supplies power to neighboring Zimbabwe. There are plans for a second dam on the Zambezi River, with capacity of 2,000-2,500 MW. The **Zambia** Electricity Supply Corporation (ZESCO) plans to rehabilitate the generation facilities at Victoria Falls. ZESCO also began rehabilitation work on its main generation facility, the Kafue Gorge hydroelectric station, in 1999. National Power of Britain, in conjunction with the **Zimbabwe** Electricity Supply Authority (ZESA), plans to develop a 1,400-MW coal-fired plant at Gowke North to supply one-third of Zimbabwe's electricity requirements. The government has commited itself to bringing solar power with a capacity of between 100 KW and 500 KW to 500 districts and rural service points.

Minerals & Mining

Africa is not only one of the world's major sources of hydrocarbon fuels but also of hard minerals. It ranks first or second in terms of concentration of world reserves of gold, antimony, bauxite, chromite, cobalt, diamonds, fluorspar, hafnium, manganese, phosphate rock, the platinum group, titanium, vanadium, vermiculite, and zirconium. The continent accounts for between 1% to 6% of the world's supplies of aluminum, cement, coal, copper, graphite, iron ore, lead, steel, and zinc; from 11% to 31% of the total global supplies of bauxite, cobalt, gold, manganese, phosphate, and uranium; and from 50% to 57% of the world's chromium and diamonds. South Africa alone accounts for 76% of the world supply of vermiculite, 62% of vanadium, 59% of its alumino–silicates (andalusite and kyanite), 43% of its platinum-group of metals, 26% of the world's supply of total zirconium minerals, and 23% of all titanium minerals.

These natural resources continue to be vital to the economies of African nations as earners of foreign exchange, providers of employment and stimulants for the development of transportation, energy and other infrastructure projects. Trade in both fuel and hard minerals in countries such as Algeria, Angola, Botswana, Gabon, Guinea, Libya, Namibia, Niger, Nigeria, Zaire, and Zambia accounts for between 50% and 95% of their export earnings, and between 50% and 66% of the export earnings of South Africa, Ghana and Egypt. West and North Africa dominate in oil and gas and subequatorial Africa (especially the southern portion) leads in the production of hard minerals.

Key

Mining is seen as key to economic development and attaining an international competitive advantage in a mineral-rich Africa. Mining operators, who are often pioneer foreign investors in African countries, generate substantial amounts of foreign exchange that significantly boost government revenues. Unlike other infrastructural projects, the immediate foreign exchange earnings of mines minimizes currency risk, one of the main bugbears of investment in Africa. Mining, unlike manufacturing, does not bring the same level of competition from other low-wage countries. In recent years, mining transformed the economies of several countries. Botswana's earnings from its diamond mining industry enabled it to post impressive growth rates. Foreign direct investment (FDI) of more than $800 million in Zambia's copper mines revived a stagnant sector and the economy at large while in Zimbabwe foreign mining investment totaling $544 million gave a shot in the arm to a sagging economy in 1998. Mozambique's economic revival was greatly accelerated by a $1 billion aluminum smelter and renewed exploration interest. FDI totalling $297 million in Tanzania's mining sector during 1995-1999, and further likely investments following the discovery of promising gold ore bodies, are bound to stimulate growth in other sectors as well. Mining's contribution to these economies involves not only mining operations themselves but also upstream and downstream activities.

South Africa

In South Africa—Africa's and the world's foremost mineral giant—mining still accounts for

South Africa Reserves & Production of Key Minerals

Production
Reserves
1999

Zinc, Iron Ore, Uranium, Nickel, Coal, Diamonds, Fluorspar, Zirconium, Vermiculite, Gold, Vanadium, PGM's, Chromium, Manganese

Percentage of world total: 0 20% 40% 60% 80%

Graph: Business Books International
Source: SA Chamber of Mines

Mineral briefs

☑ Africa is a major supplier of strategic minerals to the United States and other world markets.

☑ There has been a resurgence in mineral exploration in recent years involving major and medium-sized US, Canadian and South African mining companies. *The Metals and Economics Group* of Halifax, Canada, estimated an exploration outlay of some $418 million by 223 firms in various parts of the continent.

☑ The World Bank's Multilateral Investment Guarantee Agency (MIGA) has worked with many African countries to develop more progressive mining and foreign ivetsment laws to lure foreign capital and technology.

☑ Recent changes in the political climate made it possible to resume exploration in countries such as Mozambique and Angola.

☑ With the lifting of sanctions the mining giants of post-apartheid South Africa have been able to spread their wings over the rest of Africa, frequently in profitable partnership with other foreign entrepreneurs.

☑ Economic reforms in countries such as Ghana and Zambia have widened the scope for private enterprise and led to greater efficiency and profitability in privatized former state mining enterprises.

☑ There is a high probability that much of Africa's mineral wealth still lies hidden in remote and high risk regions. As infrastructures improve and governments stabilize, these new opportunities are bound to attract mineral seekers from abroad.

half of all exports and continues to be the single most important earner of foreign exchange. Despite the contraction in gold mining output and the decline in the weighting of the mining industry on the JSE Securities Exchange, the country's other major minerals have experienced impressive growth. Numerous large-scale investment projects are at varying stages of design and implementation. Sectors such as coal, platinum group metals (PGM) and chrome have doubled in size since 1980, while iron ore production has increased by more than half. Major projects were launched in ferrochrome, zinc and other minerals and new investment in mines and smelters has grown at a rate of 5-7 per cent per year. Since the 1990s there has been modernization at several levels: mining house, mining company and workplace. Emerging is a leaner, more focused, more competitive and internationally active mining industry with world-class mining companies in gold, platinum, diamonds, coal, ferrochrome and base metals. There are also world-class engineering and other companies that serve the industry. The mining industry provides the base for the country's competitive advantage in electricity, chemicals and related industries.

Development

Post-apartheid South Africa has become a prime driving force for mining development in Africa and the world at large. South African mining companies are leading the resurgence of mining activity on the continent, frequently in partnership with foreign mining operations. Anglo American, Randgold, Gencor and JCI have invested heavily in exploration. Billiton is building an aluminum smelter in Mozambique and Anglo American and Gold Fields are involved in gold projects in West Africa. Both Anglo American and Anglovaal Mining have invested in copper/cobalt operations in Zambia. Johannesburg is in the process of becoming the global center for mining technology, specialist services and supplies. South African firms are among world leaders in mining explosives, drilling equipment and abrasives, metallurgical processes and plants, and delivering knowledge-based services to mines everywhere. AECI and Sasol lead as suppliers of mining explosives; Boart International is a world leader in abrasives; and two South African firms, SRK and Bateman, are among the foremost mining consultancies in the world.

African minerals

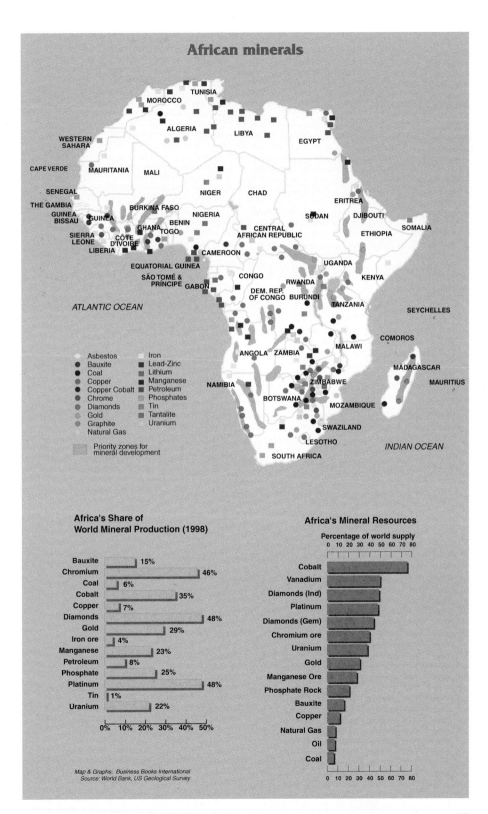

TUNISIA
MOROCCO
ALGERIA
LIBYA
EGYPT
WESTERN SAHARA
CAPE VERDE
MAURITANIA
MALI
SENEGAL
THE GAMBIA
GUINEA BISSAU
GUINEA
BURKINA FASO
NIGER
CHAD
ERITREA
DJIBOUTI
SOMALIA
SIERRA LEONE
CÔTE D'IVOIRE
GHANA
TOGO
BENIN
NIGERIA
CENTRAL AFRICAN REPUBLIC
SUDAN
ETHIOPIA
LIBERIA
CAMEROON
EQUATORIAL GUINEA
SÃO TOMÉ & PRÍNCIPE
GABON
CONGO
DEM. REP. OF CONGO
RWANDA
BURUNDI
UGANDA
KENYA
TANZANIA
SEYCHELLES
ATLANTIC OCEAN
COMOROS
MALAWI
ANGOLA
ZAMBIA
MADAGASCAR
MAURITIUS
NAMIBIA
ZIMBABWE
BOTSWANA
MOZAMBIQUE
SWAZILAND
LESOTHO
INDIAN OCEAN
SOUTH AFRICA

Legend:
- ○ Asbestos
- ● Bauxite
- ● Coal
- ● Copper
- ● Copper Cobalt
- ● Chrome
- ● Diamonds
- ○ Gold
- ● Graphite
- Natural Gas
- ▫ Iron
- ■ Lead-Zinc
- ■ Lithium
- ■ Manganese
- ■ Petroleum
- Phosphates
- ■ Tin
- ■ Tantalite
- ■ Uranium

Priority zones for mineral development

Africa's Share of World Mineral Production (1998)

Bauxite	15%
Chromium	46%
Coal	6%
Cobalt	35%
Copper	7%
Diamonds	48%
Gold	29%
Iron ore	4%
Manganese	23%
Petroleum	8%
Phosphate	25%
Platinum	48%
Tin	1%
Uranium	22%

0%   10%   20%   30%   40%   50%

Africa's Mineral Resources

Percentage of world supply
0 10 20 30 40 50 60 70 80

- Cobalt
- Vanadium
- Diamonds (Ind)
- Platinum
- Diamonds (Gem)
- Chromium ore
- Uranium
- Gold
- Manganese Ore
- Phosphate Rock
- Bauxite
- Copper
- Natural Gas
- Oil
- Coal

0 10 20 30 40 50 60 70 80

Map & Graphs: Business Books International
Source: World Bank, US Geological Survey

AFRICAN PRODUCTION OF SELECTED MINERAL COMMODITIES 1998
(Thousand metric tons gross weight unless otherwise specified)

Country	Diamonds (thousand carats)	Gold[e] (kilogram)	Manganese ore	Phosphate rock[e]	Uranium concentrate[3] (mt. tons)	Bauxite	Chromite	Aluminum	Cobalt mt. tons
Algeria	--	--	--	1,155[1]	--	--	--	--	--
Angola	2,764[1]	--	--	--	--	--	--	--	--
Botswana	19,772[1]	1[1]	--	--	--	--	--	--	335[1]
Burkina Faso	--	1,100	1[1]	--	--	--	--	--	--
Burundi	--	5	--	--	--	--	--	--	--
Cameroon	--	1,000	--	--	--	--	--	88	--
Central African Republic	530	100	--	--	--	--	--	--	--
Congo Rep. of	--	10	--	--	--	--	--	--	--
Congo Dem. Rep. of	24,500	134	--	--	--	--	--	--	1,500
Côte d'Ivoire	310	1,500	--	--	--	--	--	--	--
Egypt	--	--	10	1,050[1]	--	--	--	230[1]	--
Eritrea	--	573	--	--	--	--	--	--	--
Ethiopia	--	2,500	--	--	--	--	--	--	--
Gabon	500	70	2,092	--	862	--	--	--	--
Ghana	809[1]	72,541[1]	537	--	--	650	--	56[1]	--
Guinea	400	14,000	--	--	--	15,000	--	--	--
Kenya	--	388[1]	--	--	--	--	--	--	--
Liberia	300	800	--	--	--	--	--	--	--
Madagascar	--	50	--	--	--	--	150[p]	--	--
Mali	--	25,000	--	--	--	--	--	--	--
Morocco	--	450	28	23,587[2]	--	--	--	--	230[1]
Mozambique	--	17[1]	--	--	--	6	--	--	--
Namibia	1,467[1]	1,882[1]	--	--	3,257	--	--	--	--
Niger	--	1,000	--	--	4,400	--	--	--	--
Nigeria	--	10	--	--	--	--	--	20	--
Rwanda	--	26	--	--	--	--	--	--	--
Senegal	--	--	--	1,320	--	--	--	--	--
Sierra Leone	250	15	--	--	--	--	--	--	--
Somalia	--	--	--	--	--	--	--	--	--
South Africa	10,756[1]	464,216[1]	3,044	2,739	1,134	--	6,480	693[1]	435
Sudan	--	5,000	--	--	--	--	20[e]	--	--
Swaziland	70	--	--	--	--	--	--	--	--
Tanzania	93	720	--	2	--	--	--	--	--
Togo	--	--	--	1,900	--	--	--	--	--
Tunisia	--	--	--	7,901[1]	--	--	--	--	--
Uganda	--	2,500	--	--	--	--	--	--	--
Zambia	--	25,175[1]	--	--	--	--	--	--	5,011
Zimbabwe	29[1]	634	--	91	--	--	605[e]	--	137
TOTAL AFRICA[4]	62,550	621,548	5,712	39,745	9,653	15,656	7,246	1,089	7,648
TOTAL WORLD	114,938	2,480,000	18,700	145,000	40,016	122,000	13,503	22,100	26,300
AFRICA SHARE	54%	25%	31%	27%	24%	13%	54%	5%	29%

1. Reported figure.
2. Includes production from Western Sahara.
3. U_3O_8 Source Uranium Institute, London, England.
4. Rounded figures.
e. Estimated.
p. Preliminary.

Telecommunications

With 12 per cent of the world's population, Africa has only 2 per cent of its telephones. The continent has fewer telephones available for its 800 million people than either New York or Tokyo. The average waiting time for the installation of a telephone in Africa is five years and fewer than one in 50 Africans has direct telephone access. Africa has a teledensity of 2—calculated on the basis of the number of telephones per 100 inhabitants—compared with a world average of 30. The number of Internet users in Europe and North America is estimated at one in six. In all of Africa the figure is one per thousand. Excluding South Africa, its is one in five thousand. Africans in general have negligible access to basic e-mail services and other new digital services that require an ever expanding broadband capacity, such as telemedicine, distance learning, e-commerce, Integrated Services Digital Network (ISDN), and video conferencing.

Africans pay much more than Americans and Europeans for both telephone services and access to the Internet. International calls within Africa are often routed via Europe, adding an estimated US $600 million to the continent's annual phone bill.

Information gap

United Nations Secretary General Kofi Annan called on the international community to help Africa "bridge the information gap." Some look at this digital divide between Africa and the developed world as too deep and wide to bridge while others see it as an opportunity. In recent years foreign private entrepreneurs, together with world organizations and state telecoms, have been making remarkable progress in getting Africa plugged into the world by constructing cable, satellite, and cellular links.

Realizing that it is key to their future economic development, many African countries have made information and communication technology (ICT) development a national priority by allocating substantial sums to digitalization, fiber optics and the latest in cellular and mobile phone technology. In the 1990s mobile cellular services have expanded from 6 countries to 42, serving an estimated five million Africans, a figure that is expected to grow to 32 million within five years. In digital switching Africa has managed to come close to the world average of 79% but its average of 116 faults per year per line still compares poorly with a world's 22.

With the participation of a number of foreign telecommunications companies, Africa has not only made significant progress in fixed line installation and technology but a variety of economic, low risk developments in cellular services, trunk radio technology, very small aperture terminals (VSATs) and value-added services, including the Internet. By restructuring former monopolistic, and inefficient state-owned telecommunications companies, entering into strategic partnerships with foreign entrepreneurs, and allowing others to compete, several African governments have indeed succeeded in narrowing the gap.

Organizations

International organizations involved in the coordination and promotion of telecommunications development in Africa range from the Inter-

Ten largest African markets for US Telecommunications Exports

150 — $ Million

South Africa | Egypt | Nigeria | Algeria | Angola | Tanzania | Morocco | Kenya | Ghana | Uganda

Graph: Business Books Intl
Source: US Department of Commerce

national Telecommunications Union (ITU) and the African Telecommunications Union (ATU) to the World Bank and the recently established African Connection Program. The ATU was created in December 1999 by the Organization of African Unity as a successor to the Pan African Telecommunications Union (PATU) to coordinate African telecommunications policy, establish a regulatory framework, and help arrange the financing of development programs. The World Bank has been assisting in telecommunication development in 25 African countries and expects to be heavily involved in sector reforms and privatization over the next few years. The African Connection Program (ACP) was launched by African Ministers of Communication in October 2000 to fill the need for an African-led, regionally-focused, unified program. The ACP secretariat is situated at the offices of the Development Bank of Southern Africa in South Africa.

Regional initiatives such as Pan-African Telecommunications (Panaftel)—covering some 39,000 kilometers of radio-relay systems, about 39 international telephone switches and 8,000 kilometers of submarine cable—aim at eliminating cross-border interconnection problems, such as those experienced between Kenya and Malawi; Kenya, Ethiopia and Djibouti; and Cameroon and Chad. Resulting tariff restructuring should benefit major customers. The Common Market for Eastern and Southern Africa (COMESA) contemplates a regional telecommunications network to be built and managed by COMTEL Communications Ltd., a private company. The East African Community Digital Transmission Project involves Kenya, Uganda and Tanzania and aims at linking capital cities and major towns in the three countries by optical fiber cable. The Regional African Satellite Communications (RASCOM) project envisages the creation of a regional satellite system that will be cheaper than the existing International Telecommunications Satellite Organization circuits.

Privatization

More than 35 countries in Africa are in the process of privatizing telecommunications services. Proceeds to date top $1.7 billion with roll-out obligations by participating private investors totaling 3.8 million lines at a further estimated $4 to $6 billion. The rapidly-growing, largely private, cellular market already comprises about 20% of the total market. Deregulation, privatization, and regulatory reform are creating a robust telecommunications environment that stimulates demand for new services, especially on the Internet.

Thirteen African countries have sold significant shareholdings in state telecommunications operations to private investors, mostly foreigners: Cape Verde, Central African Republic, Chad, Côte d'Ivoire, Equatorial Guinea, Gabon, Ghana, Guinea Bissau, Guinea, São Tomé & Príncipe, South Africa, Sudan and Uganda. Ten countries have indicated plans to sell off part of their state telecommunications corporations to the private sector: Benin, Burundi, Cameroon, Egypt, Kenya, Mauritius, Nigeria, Senegal, Seychelles, and Tunisia. Seventeen countries licensed cellular service providers on a wholly-owned private basis or in partnership with state telecoms: Benin, Botswana, Burundi, Central African Republic, Congo (Brazzaville), Egypt, Ghana, Madagascar, Malawi, Mauritius, Mozambique, Rwanda, South Africa, Tanzania, Uganda, Zambia, and Zimbabwe.

To date the single biggest privatization deal involving an African telecom was the purchase in 1997 of a 30% share in South Africa's Telkom by the American giant SBC and Telekom Malaysia for $1,260 million and a commitment to spend more than that amount on future expansion. This year, Telkom will make an initial public offering on both the Johannesburg and New York Stock Exchanges to complete the privatization of the continent's largest telecom . Analysts anticipate Telkom to remain the dominant force in South Africa and an engine for development elsewhere in the region, even after its fixed line monopoly expires in 2002.

Morocco accomplished the largest privatization deal in the Arab world when it transformed

Telecommunications privatization

Country	Year	Sales $ million	Share sold %
Cape Verde	1995	20	89
Guinea	1995	45	60
Ghana	1996	38	30
Côte d'Ivoire	1997	210	51
South Africa	1997	1,260	30
Senegal	1997	191	60

Source: ITU, World Bank

COMMUNICATIONS IN AFRICA

	Telephone main lines per 1,000 persons	Waiting List for telephones thousands	Av. call cost in $ per 3 min. local call	Mobile phones per 1,000 persons	Radios per 1,000 persons	Television sets per 1,000 persons	Computers per 1,000 persons
Algeria	42	732	0.02	1	241	105	3.4
Angola	5	..	0.14	1	54	14	N/A
Benin	5	3	0.12	1	108	10	N/A
Botswana	41	12	0.03	15	156	20	6.7
Burkina Faso	3	..	0.1	0	33	9	N/A
Burundi	3	5	0.03	0	71	4	N/A
Cameroon	5	45	0.06	0	163	32	N/A
Cape Verde	56	10	0.04	3	180	5	N/A
Central African Republic	2	0	0.2	0	83	5	N/A
Chad	1	1	0.17	0	242	1	N/A
Comoros	9	..	0.17	0	138	4	N/A
Congo, Dem. Rep. of	1	6	..	0	375	135	N/A
Congo, Rep. of	8	1	0.12	1	124	12	N/A
Côte d'Ivoire	9	82	0.11	6	164	70	1.4
Djibouti	13	0	0.19	0	84	45	1.7
Egypt	9	12	0.06	1	121	122	5.8
Eq. Guinea	6	..	..	1	429	162	N/A
Eritrea	5	42	0.03	0	91	14	N/A
Ethiopia	3	207	0.03	0	195	5	N/A
Gabon	29	10	0.15	8	183	55	4.5
Gambia, The	18	22	0.32	4	168	3	N/A
Ghana	4	28	0.09	1	238	99	1.2
Guinea	2	2	0.1	3	47	41	0.3
Guinea-Bissau	9	1	0.14	0	44	..	N/A
Kenya	9	77	0.05	0	104	21	1.6
Lesotho	9	9	0.03	5	49	25	N/A
Liberia	..	2	..	0	274	24	N/A
Libya	14	109	0.03	4	93	126	N/A
Madagascar	2	10	0.09	1	192	21	N/A
Malawi	3	31	0.03	1	249	2	N/A
Mali	2	..	0.14	0	54	12	N/A
Mauritania	4	1	0.1	0	151	91	N/A
Mauritius	132	23	0.04	53	368	226	31.9
Morocco	42	732	0.02	1	241	160	1.7
Mozambique	4	17	0.04	0	40	5	0.8
Namibia	51	7	0.05	12	144	37	12.7
Niger	1	1	0.15	0	69	27	N/A
Nigeria	4	98	0.26	0	223	66	4.1
Rwanda	2	..	0.04	1	102	0	N/A
São Tomé & Principe	19	1	0.02	0	275	227	N/A
Senegal	10	17	0.13	2	142	41	N/A
Seychelles	176	2	0.16	49	545	149	N/A
Sierra Leone	4	14	0.04	0	253	13	N/A
Somalia	2	..	..	0	46	13	N/A
South Africa	100	116	0.07	56	317	125	37.7
Sudan	3	320	0.02	0	271	87	0.7
Swaziland	22	15	0.14	5	164	111	N/A
Tanzania	3	37	0.09	1	279	21	N/A
Togo	5	13	0.1	2	218	18	N/A
Tunisia	47	1,310	0.01	1	324	198	6.7
Uganda	2	6	0.18	1	128	27	0.5
Zambia	9	12	0.06	1	121	137	N/A
Zimbabwe	14	109	0.03	4	93	30	6.7
ALL AFRICA	18	2,338	..	5	212	66	..

Sources: World Bank Database, 2001, UNESCO

The Big Cell

✓ Nine years ago, only 6 African countries had cellular networks. Today there are some 78 networks in 42 countries. The ITU predicts that 40 million Africans will have cell phones by 2003.

✓ With the recent sharp growth in pre-paid cellular services, the number of mobile users is already overtaking fixed-line subscribers in South Africa, Uganda, and Botswana.

✓ At the end of 2000, Vodacom, the leading cellular operator in South Africa, announced that it had more than four million subscribers. When it started operations in 1994, it had hoped to sign on 250,000 customers within ten years. It now expects to have ten million subscribers, or forty times as many as it originally predicted, within the next five years.

✓ There are more than 8.8 million cellular phone numbers in use in South Africa, a nation of 43 million people.

✓ Industry analysts predict that the number of cell phone users in Tunisia will increase from 100,000 to 400,000 by the end of this year.

✓ Morocco currently has the fastest cellular phone growth in the world. The number of mobile phones has soared from 200,000 to 1.26 million since 1999. Experts forecast that Morocco will have up to 10 million mobile phones within five years.

✓ MobiNile, Egypt's largest mobile phone provider, has doubled its subscriber base to 1.2 million in 2000.

✓ Following a competitive bid process, Nigeria decided to sell instead of granting a cellular license to three bidders at $285 million each. The reason? Within 5 years, the subscriber base is expected to reach nine million.

the state-owned ONPT into Itissalat Al Maghrib (IAM) and sold shares on the Casablanca Stock Exchange. Benin offered privatization with a new twist when it entered into a $60 million BOT agreement with Alcatel and Titan to establish a cellular network, digitize central exchanges and install fiber optic.

Business potential

Foreign telecommunications firms are not only involved as partners in privatized former state telecoms but as independent new operators and suppliers of hardware, software, services and expertise. In many instances, the operation of cellular networks is licensed to local private operators with overseas partners. With the rapidly expanding use of the Internet as an educational and business tool, e-commerce is expected to become an important part of doing business with various parts of the continent beyond South Africa where it has already been firmly established.

In its latest World Investment Report, the United Nations Conference on Trade and Development (UNCTAD) cited telecommunications as one of the sectors in Africa with the greatest potential for foreigners. The International Telecommunications Union (ITU) estimates that this sector will grow by 40 percent over the next ten years. The African Telecommunications Union (ATU) believes there is sufficient demand to support an additional 60 million lines on the continent, which, at an installation cost of $1,000 per line, would result in a business opportunity of $60 billion for equipment manufacturers and vendors. Telecom engineering and equipment firm Siemens AG projects a growth of at least 25 percent per year in Sub-Saharan Africa's telecommunications business as markets open up to competition and governments issue new mobile licenses.

The need in Africa for improved telecommunications and computing power—both industries where the US leads the world— is expected to spur a growth in US exports to the continent. In 1998, US telecommunications equipment sales to technologically-advanced South Africa accounted for 75.9% of all the ADP machines, 75.7% of the telephone and telegraph equipment, 49.3% of the radio apparatus, and 97.3% of the optical fiber and cables exported to Sub-Saharan Africa.

Bridging the divide

Experts believe that with a combination of state-of-the-art technologies Africa might be able

Cell phone growth					
	Cellular subscribers regional		Annual growth %	Per 100 persons	% of total users
	1998	1999	1998-99	1999	1999
South Africa	2,600,000	5,269,000	102.7	13.21	49.0
Africa	3,498,600	7,092,400	103.0	0.95	28.9
Oceania	6,174,100	7,437,400	20.6	29.89	38.4
Americas	96,156,800	134,125,200	39.5	16.40	33.5
Asia	108,163,600	157,339,400	45.5	4.44	35.7
Europe	105,115,400	174,627,500	66.1	21.86	36.4
World	319,108,400	480,622,000	50.6	75.3	8.1

Source: ITU

to integrate itself fully into the global communications network. Plain old telephone services (POTS)—requiring land-based copper cables, telephone poles and switches—are too costly and slow to install and subject to high maintenance. It has been suggested that Africa should opt for a "wireless weave" consisting of land-based infrastructure (copper and fiber optic cables) together with "very small aperture terminals" (VSAT) satellite systems, digital cellular phone systems and cheap point-to-multipoint rural radio systems. Wireless systems offer far more rapid roll out times, greater reliability, lower maintenance costs and better security. Cellular technologies have gained great acceptance not only among mobile but fixed users in areas where the local telecommunication infrastructure is poor. Over 35 African countries have developed cellular telephone services and at one stage South Africa was the fastest growing cellular market in the world. Lucent is currently working with Telkom South Africa to deploy telephone services in rural areas where there is little or no infrastructure, using wireless technology with Digital Enhanced Cordless Telecommunications (DECT) and Time Division Multiple Access (TDMA) systems. In a recent development, TranXactive and Nokia have introduced the first Wireless Application Protocol or WAP-based, portal in Africa to provide Internet access for small hand-held devices such as mobile phones and personal digital assistants (PDAs).

Networking

A promising development was the entry into the market of PACONET. With the backing of the American International Group (AIG) Infrastructure Fund a Mauritius company, Pan African Communications Network (PACONET), is in the process of establishing a network based on intra-continental connectivity bandwith utilizing capacity leased from geostationary satellite operators. This satellite network uses a combined point-to-multipoint architecture by deploying a combined "star" and "mesh" configuration. It allows for individualized offerings to African nations.

PACONET's network aims at eliminating the need for African countries to rely on North American or European switches to route data traffic, even with neighboring countries. According to the company this system makes it a speedier and more economical for Africa to integrate than traditional terrestrial-based solutions. The company has been steadily signing up African countries that are anxious to tap into an efficient, lower cost entrance ramp to the global information highway.

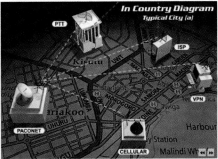

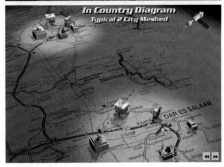

INTERNET IN AFRICA - SEP. 2000

COUNTRY	POPULATION MILLION	DENSITY USER/POP[1]	TELEPH. LINES	INTERNET POPs[2]	TOTAL ISPs[3]	INTERNET CLIENTS[4]
Algeria	30.08	15,040	1,619	4	4	2,000
Angola	12.09	3,023	82	5	4	4,000
Benin	5.78	1,445	44	2	2	4,000
Botswana	1.57	105	109	3	3	15,000
Burkina Faso	11.31	3,770	44	1	3	3,000
Burundi	6.46	43,067	19	1	2	159
Cameroon	14.31	5,724	79	2	3	2,500
Cape Verde	0.41	228	41	1	1	1,800
Central African Republic	3.48	17,400	11	1	1	200
Chad	7.27	24,233	10	1	1	300
Comoros	0.66	3,300	6	1	1	200
Congo Rep. of	2.79	13,950	25	2	1	200
Congo Dem. Rep. of	49.3	82,167	30	4	3	600
Côte d'Ivoire	14.29	1,786	261	2	4	8,000
Djibouti	0.62	2,480	8	1	1	250
Egypt	65.98	660	4,063	14	50	100,000
Equatorial Guinea	0.43	2,150	6	1	1	200
Eritrea	3.58	11,933	24	1	1	300
Ethiopia	59.65	23,860	164	1	1	2,500
Gabon	1.17	780	47	2	2	1,500
Gambia	1.23	2,460	31	1	1	500
Ghana	19.16	2,395	166	7	4	8,000
Guinea	7.71	25,700	59	3	2	300
Guinea Bissau	1.13	4,520	30	1	1	250
Kenya	29.01	967	277	6	34	30,000
Lesotho	2.06	8,240	30	1	2	250
Liberia	2.67	35,600	16	1	0	75
Libya	5.98	11,960	520	1	1	500
Madagascar	16.36	8,180	60	4	3	2,000
Malawi	10.75	4,479	47	2	2	2,400
Mali	10.69	10,690	31	1	3	1,000
Mauritania	2.53	4,600	19	2	5	550
Mauritius	1.15	88	305	1	1	13,000
Morocco	27.87	372	1,631	10	250	75,000
Mozambique	18.88	3,147	82	4	5	6,000
Namibia	1.66	553	134	11	3	3,000
Niger	10.08	28,800	19	1	1	350
Nigeria	106.41	10,641	428	5	12	10,000
Rwanda	6.6	33,000	26	1	1	200
São Tomé & Príncipe	0.14	700	18	1	1	200
Senegal	9.0	2,250	162	1	8	4,000
Seychelles	0.08	40	23	1	1	2,000
Sierra Leone	4.57	30,467	21	1	1	150
Somalia	10.63	141,733	15	0	0	75
South Africa	44.31	68	7,575	100	75	650,000
Sudan	28.29	14,145	171	1	1	2,000
Swaziland	0.95	792	34	2	2	1,200
Tanzania	32.1	7,133	160	2	5	4,500
Togo	4.4	2,588	39	1	2	1,700
Tunisia	9.34	584	791	7	5	16,000
Uganda	20.55	5,138	87	1	3	4,000
Zambia	8.78	1,351	83	3	3	6,500
Zimbabwe	12.68	634	267	4	8	20,000

1. Number of people per Internet user. 2. POPs: Local points of presence—number of cities. 3. ISPs: Internet Service Providers. 4. Internet service subscribers. (Source: AISI , ECA, Mike Jensen)

The Internet

In 1996, only 11 African countries had Internet access. Less than four years later, all 53 nations have established permanent connectivity and full service dialup Internet Service Providers (ISPs). With the exception of South Africa, where some 100 cities and towns have points of presence (POPs), the Internet in Africa is largely limited to major cities. In some 16 countries, however, national telecom operators offer nationwide Internet access through a special 'area-code' charged at local call tariffs. In January 2001 the total number of subscribers in Africa was estimated at one million—650,000 in South Africa and about 200 000 in North Africa with the remaining 150 000 spread over 47 African countries. Each subscriber, according to the UN Economic Commission for Africa (ECA), supports an average of three users. This translates into a total of 3 million users, with about 1 million of them outside South Africa.

Africa has one Internet user for every 250 people, compared to a world average of one user for every 35 people, and a North American and European average of one for every 3 people. According to a UNDP World Development Report, the average number of users for other developing areas are as follows: 1 in 125 for Latin America and the Caribbean, 1 in 200 for South East Asia and the Pacific, 1 in 250 for East Asia, 1 in 500 for the Arab States and 1 in 2,500 for South Asia.

Cost

The growth of the Internet in Africa at large has been inhibited by low incomes and the relatively steep cost of both computers and connectivity. In the late nineties, according to the UNDP report, monthly usage fees and telephone time (excluding telephone rental charges) in Africa averaged $50 for 5 hours. At $200 for 20 hours per month, the cost in Africa is much higher than $29 for the same access in the US (including telephone rental charges) or Germany ($74), France ($52), Britain ($65) and Italy ($53)—all countries with per capita incomes at least 10 times the African average.

Other inhibiting factors in most African countries, according to Africa Internet expert Mike Jensen (www3.wn.apc.org/Africa), are high international tariffs, lack of circuit capacity, and insufficient international bandwidth for delivering web pages over the Internet. Currently only 24 countries have 512Kps or more, and 15 have outgoing links of 1Mbps or more: Botswana, Egypt, Ghana, Kenya, Libya, Madagascar, Mauritius, Morocco, Mozambique, Namibia, Nigeria, Senegal, South Africa, Tanzania and Tunisia. Excluding South Africa, the total international outgoing Internet bandwidth installed in Africa is about 60Mbps, which means that on average about 6 dialup users must share each 1Kbps of international bandwidth, making for slow connections to remote sites. As a result, Jensen points out, a growing number of African Internet sites are hosted on servers in Europe or the US.

Email

In response to the high cost of full Internet-based services lower-cost email-only services have been launched by many African ISPs. A large number of African email users have resorted to free US and other overseas services such as Hotmail, Yahoo or Excite. There is also a rapidly-growing market for kiosks, cyber cafes and other forms of public Internet access. PCs have been installed for public use in phone shops, schools, police stations and clinics. Most hotels and business centers across the continent provide convenient Internet access for visitors. (In a recent study the UNDP points out that a 40-page document can be sent from Madagascar to Côte d'Ivoire by five-day courier for $75, by 30-minute fax for $45 or by two-minute email for less than 20 cents—and the email can go to hundreds of additional people at no extra cost). A study by the Economic Commission for Africa (ECA) puts the average level of Internet use per account in Africa at about one incoming and one outgoing email per day, averaging 3 to 4 pages in communications, mostly with correspondents abroad. Surveys also indicated that about 25 percent of the email traffic is in replacement of faxes, while 10 percent is instead of phone calls and the other 65 percent new communications.

Circuits

With the exception of ISPs in South Africa, most of the international Internet circuits in Africa connect to the USA, the United Kingdom, Italy and France. However, ISPs in South Africa's neighboring countries benefit from the low tariff policies instituted by its international telecom operator. South Africa therefore acts as a hub for countries such as Lesotho, Namibia, and Swazi-land. Major international Internet suppliers to Africa are AT&T, BT, Global One/Sprint, UUNET/AlterNet, MCI, NSN, BBN, Teleglobe, Verio and France Telecom/FCR. Roaming dialup Internet access is available to travellers in most African countries through the commercial division of the airline operative SITA-SCITOR, recently renamed Equant. It operates dialup points of presence in 40 African countries. South Africa is the only country on the continent with X.400 service while ISDN services are also available in Egypt, Tunisia, Morocco, and the Seychelles. The American Registry for Internet Numbers (ARIN) administers Internet IP address space for Africa (along with North America, South America, and the Caribbean). A proposal for an Africa Network Information Centre (NIC) has been under discussion.

Users

According to Jensen, most of the users surveyed belong to non-governmental organizations (NGOs), private companies and universities while the ratio of nationals to non-nationals varies sharply between countries. In Zambia, for example, 44 percent of the users surveyed were nationals, compared to 90 percent in Ghana. Most users are male— 86 percent in Ethiopia, 83 percent in Senegal, and 64 percent in Zambia. The large majority of users are well educated—87 percent in Zambia and 98 percent of the respondents in Ethiopia had university degrees. A recent South African survey showed similar results: an average user that is male, 26 to 30, spoke English, and had a high-school or university-level education.

Importance

The importance to Africa of larger connectivity to the Internet has frequently been emphasized by both its own leaders and international organizations. It goes way beyond faster and more convenient personal and business connections by email. E-commerce, the availability of data and instant exchanges between African and overseas government policymakers, academics, and medical and other professionals, are vital in the promotion of trade, investment, good governance, better education and health services. The Small Islands Developing States Network, or SIDSNet, enables 42 countries from Malta to Mauritius to Cuba and the Comoros to share data on common concerns ranging from energy options and sustainable tourism to coastal and marine resources and biodiversity. PEOPLink, for example, links more than 130,000 artisans selling crafts across 14 countries in Africa, Asian and Latin America. As an example of the value of networking in the medical field, UNDP cites HealthNet which supports health care workers in more than 30 developing countries, including 22 in Africa. Using radio and telephone-based computer networks, this network provides summaries of the latest medical research, email connectivity and access to medical libraries. It was used in 1995 to share information on the outbreak of the Ebola virus. Burn surgeons in Mozambique, Tanzania and Uganda utilized the network for consultation on reconstructive surgery techniques while malaria researchers at remote regions in Ghana used it in daily communications with colleagues in London.

Development

UN Economic Commission for Africa has launched several initiatives to upgrade Africa's information and communication technology (ICT) capability. A framework document, the African Information Society Initiative (AISI), calls for the formulation and development of a national information and communication infrastructure (NICI) plan in every African country, driven by national development priorities, and proposes closer regional co-operation. Countries that have started developing in-depth national information infrastructure and communication development plans include Benin, Burkina Faso, Cameroon, Comoros, Ethiopia, Lesotho, Namibia, Mozambique, Rwanda, South Africa and Uganda. Efforts by the ITU and other members of the international community aim at giving rural areas better access to ICT via shared public access facilities. The UN Secretary General has launched a System-Wide Initiative on Africa while the USAID's Leland Initiative develops Internet connectivity in African countries in return for allowing 3rd party Internet service providers and an unrestricted flow of information. The World Bank assists telecommunication and ICT development in some 25 countries in Sub-Saharan Africa.

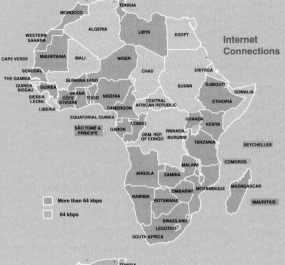

Internet Connections

More than 64 kbps

64 kbps

INTERNET USE

	Internet users as percentage of population
United States	26.3%
OECD (excl. US)	6.9%
Latin America & Caribbean	0.8%
South-East Asia & Pacific	0.5%
East Asia	0.4%
Eastern Europe & the CIS	0.4%
Arab States[1]	0.2%
Sub-Saharan Africa	0.1%
South Asia	0.04%
World	2.4%

1. Algeria, Egypt, Libya, Morocco and Tunisia included under Arab States.

Sources: NUA, UNDP, Network Wizards 1999

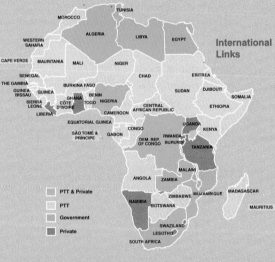

International Links

PTT & Private

PTT

Government

Private

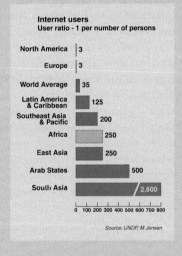

Internet users
User ratio - 1 per number of persons

North America	3
Europe	3
World Average	35
Latin America & Caribbean	125
Southeast Asia & Pacific	200
Africa	250
East Asia	250
Arab States	500
South Asia	2,500

0 100 200 300 400 500 600 700 800

Source: UNDP, M Jensen

Retail Sector

PTT & Private

PTT

Government

Private

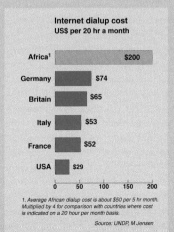

Internet dialup cost
US$ per 20 hr a month

Africa[1]	$200
Germany	$74
Britain	$65
Italy	$53
France	$52
USA	$29

0 50 100 150 200

1. Average African dialup cost is about $50 per 5 hr month. Multiplied by 4 for comparison with countries where cost is indicated on a 20 hour per month basis.

Source: UNDP, M Jensen

Maps: Business Books International
Sources: AISI, Mike Jensen

Transport

Africa is a vast, sparsely populated continent with only 19% of its people within 100 kilometers of the coast. With the exception of the Nile, Niger and a few others, most of Africa's rivers are seasonal or not navigable. There are few natural harbors. Challenging terrain, varying from deserts to mountain ranges, has posed special challenges in rail and road construction to both the colonial powers and the leadership of independent Africa. In recent years, fiscal shortfalls and other priorities have led to the decay of existing roads and railways and, in most parts, the cessation of new construction. Colonial fragmentation and lack of regional coordination has left some adjoining states with incompatible rail widths. Only 16% of all roads are paved. While more than 80% of the unpaved roads are in fair or reasonable condition, 85% of rural feed roads are in a poor state.

Although Africa fares better than East or South Asia in the length of roads per capita, it is worse off in terms of road density per square kilometer of land. Poor transport is considered one of the main reasons for Africa's low competitiveness. The continent's reasonably well developed ports, railroads and roads need repair and better utilization. Both road and maritime transport costs top those of any other region. In recent years, for example, freight costs for imported goods shipped to West and East Africa were 70% higher and, to landlocked countries in Africa, twice as high as to Asian destinations. The cost of air freight between destinations in Africa (where such services are available) runs as

much as two to four times the rate for equivalent distances across the Atlantic. Some experts have concluded that in many parts of Africa, transport costs are more of a barrier to free trade than tariffs. Lack of adequate transport has been cited by firms as a major stumbling block to doing business with Africa. High transport costs and the possibility of being cut off from supply sources at critical times have prompted some buyers of high value crops to go elsewhere.

Roads

Despite attempts in colonial times to link regions by rail, roads remain Africa's principal mode of moving people and freight—accounting for 80% of the total in almost every country. After heavy construction projects in the 1960s and 1970s on top of networks left by former colonial powers, Africa had nearly 2 million km of roads in the early 1990s, much of it in a state of neglect due to shortages in budgets for post-construction maintenance.

Rail, Air & Sea

Railroads, harbors and airports suffered the same fate. With few exceptions—notably South Africa where links are well maintained—much of Africa's rail transport needs upgrading. Many har-

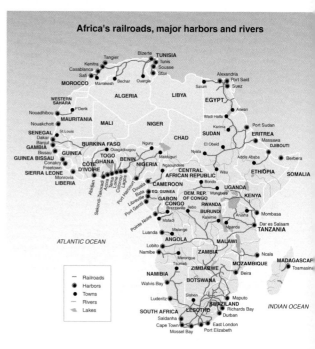

Africa's railroads, major harbors and rivers

bors and airports need to be enlarged and modernized to cope with larger freight demands. Southern Africa—where a sophisticated network of railroads and highways as well as efficient harbors and state-of-the-art airports support a rapidly expanding trade that benefits both South Africa and its neighbors—serves as a model for the continent as it moves towards globalization in the new millennium.

Recovery

In recent years the focus in several countries has been on road and rail building and repair, harbor refurbishing and streamlining of air connections and airport facilities. Since the late 1980s some nations have had the benefit of a Road Maintenance Initiative (RMI), introduced by the UN Economic Commission for Africa (ECA) and administered by the World Bank's Africa Technical Department. Financing came largely from the EU and Japan. More recently, the US Overseas Private Investment Corporation (OPIC) underwrote a $350 infrastructure fund to promote development in Africa. This is seen as a catalytic effort, contributing together with other private equity funds $1 billion towards the estimated $100 billion required for African infrastructural development over the next twenty years, with road building comprising 43% of the total, sanitation 34%, and telecommunications and electricity the rest. (For example, putting an all-weather road within 20 km reach of most of Ethiopia's population, will cost an estimated $4 billion). At the same time, these funds targeting Africa's infrastructural needs offer investors long-term appreciation in equity.

Privatization

Several African governments have responded to the need of getting the private sector involved in the construction and maintenance of road, rail and air links. They have allowed private firms to build, own and operate (BOO) toll roads, transferred airports and harbors to domestic and overseas management, and privatized state-owned railroad companies, airlines and shipping lines. These public-private partnerships (PPPs) take many forms but most have resulted in more efficient and less costly services to consumers. The continent's largest single transport utility, South Africa's Transnet is being primed for restructuring while its national airline, South African Airways, has already been sold in part to Swissair. A further shareholding in the airline is expected to be

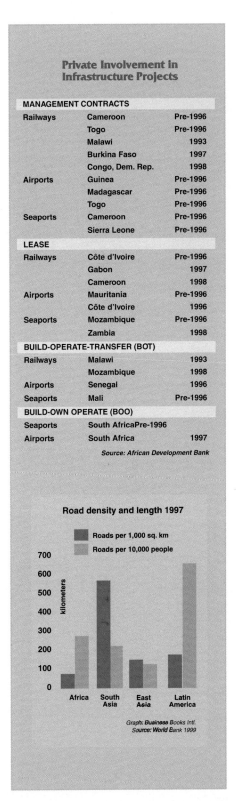

Private Involvement in Infrastructure Projects

MANAGEMENT CONTRACTS		
Railways	Cameroon	Pre-1996
	Togo	Pre-1996
	Malawi	1993
	Burkina Faso	1997
	Congo, Dem. Rep.	1998
Airports	Guinea	Pre-1996
	Madagascar	Pre-1996
	Togo	Pre-1996
Seaports	Cameroon	Pre-1996
	Sierra Leone	Pre-1996
LEASE		
Railways	Côte d'Ivoire	Pre-1996
	Gabon	1997
	Cameroon	1998
Airports	Mauritania	Pre-1996
	Côte d'Ivoire	1996
Seaports	Mozambique	Pre-1996
	Zambia	1998
BUILD-OPERATE-TRANSFER (BOT)		
Railways	Malawi	1993
	Mozambique	1998
Airports	Senegal	1996
Seaports	Mali	Pre-1996
BUILD-OWN OPERATE (BOO)		
Seaports	South Africa	Pre-1996
Airports	South Africa	1997

Source: African Development Bank

Road density and length 1997

- Roads per 1,000 sq. km
- Roads per 10,000 people

Graph: Business Books Intl.
Source: World Bank 1999

95

TRANSPORT FACILITIES IN AFRICA

	Total Area (sq km)	Coastline (km)	Railroads (km) - total	Highways (km) Total	Paved Road	Unpaved or Gravel	Inland Water-ways (km)	Marine Ports	Runway Total
ALGERIA	2,381,740	998	4,733	95,576	57,346	38,230		13	139
ANGOLA	1,246,700	1,600	3,189	73,828	8,577	65,251	1,295	8	289
BENIN	112,620	121	578	8,432	1,038	7,397		2	7
BOTSWANA	600,370	LL	888	11,514	1,600	9,914		0	100
BURKINA FASO	274,200	LL	620	16,500	1,300	15,200		0	48
BURUNDI	27,830	LL	0	5,900	640	5,260		1	4
CAMEROON	475,440	402	1,111	65,000	2,682	60,318	2,090	5	60
CAPE VERDE	4,030	965	0	1,100	680	420		3	6
CENTRAL AFRICAN REP.	622,980	LL	0	22,000	458	21,542	800	2	61
CHAD	1,284,000	LL	0	31,322	263	31,059	2,000	0	66
COMOROS	2,545	525	0	792	228	564		4	5
CONGO (BRAZZAVILLE)	342,000	169	797	11,960	560	11,400	1,120	5	41
CONGO (KINSHASA)	2,345,410	37	5,138	146,500	2,800	143,700	15,000	11	270
CÔTE D'IVOIRE	322,460	515	660	46,600	3,600	43,300	980	4	40
DJIBOUTI	22,000	314	97	2,900	280	2,620		1	13
EGYPT	1,001,450	2,450	4,895	47,387	34,593	12,794	3,500	9	91
EQUATORIAL GUINEA	28,050	296	0	2,760	NA	NA		3	3
ERITREA	121,320	2,234	307	3,845	807	1,796		2	20
ETHIOPIA	1,127,127	LL	681	24,127	3,289	20,838		0	98
GABON	267,670	885	649	7,500	560	6,940	1,600	6	69
GAMBIA,THE	11,300	80	0	3,083	431	2,652	400	1	1
GHANA	238,540	539	953	32,250	6,084	26,166	1,293	2	12
GUINEA	245,860	320	1,048	30,100	1,145	23,455	1,295	3	15
GUINEA-BISSAU	36,120	350	0	3,218	2,698	520		1	32
KENYA	582,650	536	2,650	64,540	7,000	4,150		3	246
LESOTHO	30,350	LL	2.6	7,215	572	6,643		0	29
LIBERIA	111,370	579	490	10,087	603	9,484		4	59
LIBYA	1,759,540	1,770	0	19,300	10,800	8,500	0	9	146
MADAGASCAR	587,040	4,828	1,020	40,000	4,694	35,306		5	138
MALAWI	118,480	LL	789	13,135	2,364	10,771	144	4	47
MALI	1,240,000	LL	642	15,700	1,670	14,030	1,815	1	33
MAURITANIA	1,030,700	754	690	7,525	1,685	5,840		5	28
MAURITIUS	1,860	177	0	1,800	1,640	160		1	5
MOROCCO	446,550	1,835	1,893	59,474	29,440	30,034		12	74
MOZAMBIQUE	801,590	2,470	3,288	26,498	4,593	21,905	3,750	5	192
NAMIBIA	825,418	1,572	2,341	54,500	4,080	50,420		2	135
NIGER	1,267,000	LL	0	39,970	3,170	36,800	300	0	29
NIGERIA	923,770	853	3,567	107,990	30,019	77,971	8,575	6	80
RWANDA	26,340	LL	0	4,885	880	4,005		3	7
SÃO TOMÉ & PRÍNCIPE	960	209	0	300	200	100		2	2
SENEGAL	196,190	531	905	14,007	3,777	10,230	897	7	24
SEYCHELLES	455	491	0	260	160	100		1	14
SIERRA LEONE	71,740	402	84	7,400	1,150	6,250	800	3	11
SOMALIA	637,660	3,025	0	22,500	2,700	19,800		5	76
SOUTH AFRICA	1,219,912	2,798	20,638	188,309	54,013	134,296		7	853
SUDAN	2,505,810	853	5,516	20,703	2,000	18,703	5,310	7	70
SWAZILAND	17,360	LL	297	2,853	510	2,343		0	18
TANZANIA	945,090	1,424	2,600	81,900	3,600	78,300		11	108
TOGO	56,790	56	532	6,462	1,762	4,700	50	2	9
TUNISIA	163,610	1,148	2,260	29,183	17,510	11,673		7	31
UGANDA	236,040	LL	1,300	26,200	1,970	24,230		3	29
ZAMBIA	752,610	LL	1,273	36,370	6,500	29,870	2,250	1	113
ZIMBABWE	390,580	LL	2,745	85,237	15,800	69,437		2	471

LL: Landlocked

Source: US Department of Transport - World Directory of Transport

offered in the near future. Also Kenya Airways and a number of other African national carriers are heading towards privatization. Not only in South Africa but elsewhere on the continent airports and harbors have been entrusted to private management with immediate results. South Africa's Safmarine is one of the major carriers on shipping routes between the United States and Africa and on routes to and from the Far East and Europe. Its fleet of some 40 owned and chartered ships transports a diverse range of commodities. In 1995, Côte d'Ivoire's failed state-owned shipping line, SITRAM, was liquidated and replaced by a new carrier, COMARCO, with private Ivorians as majority shareholders. This private carrier is not only better run but the demise of the state-run shipping line enabled the government to liberalize all non-conference traffic, lowering import prices for consumers and shipping costs for exporters of vital commodities such as bananas, pineapples and palm oil. A major new highway from Witbank in South Africa to Maputo in Mozambique is being built and will be operated as a toll road for profit by a private consortium. An American firm was contracted to construct an international air cargo freight facility and an industrial park at Zimbabwe's Harare International Airport that will enhance the ability of regional agricultural producers to sell and ship their products overseas.

Funds

Learning from the mistakes of the past, several nations have established road funds for maintenance purposes. Financing is largely through user charges such as fuel levies and vehicle licensing fees. Several of these funds are controlled by public-private boards. In a matter of two years in Ghana, for example, these new revenues helped double the funds available for maintenance.

Regional cooperation

Coordination within regional groupings—actively encouraged by ECA—has resulted in more efficient and economical transport links benefiting several member states. The Maputo Corridor between Mozambique and South Africa will not only profit these two countries but provide other members of the Southern African Development Community (SADC) with better and more economical access to the outside world. Towards the end of 1999, 23 West and Central African nations agreed to liberalize air transport in their region and make it more competitive. In road and rail transport, efforts are being made to eliminate long bureaucratic border delays and overcome challenges posed by adjoining incompatible gauge rail lines inherited from the colonial era. There has been a concerted campaign—both on a regional and individual country basis—to eliminate pilfering and theft at harbors and airports, corruption in customs services and other extortionary practices. In many instances this is being done with the help of official and private foreign security expertise. The US government and several American companies are involved. The US Department of Transport recently launched a Safe Skies project—involving some ten African nations—to upgrade airports and assist their airlines to meet IATA safety requirements. The ultimate goal is not only to provide greater access to the US for African airlines but to build the necessary infrastructure or platform for American airlines to extend their services into Africa. While countries such as Egypt, South Africa, Nigeria and Kenya have built up extensive overseas air links many African countries remain isolated. Codesharing agreements between American and African carriers are seen as a preliminary step to full involvement as cross-Atlantic trade and tourism grows.

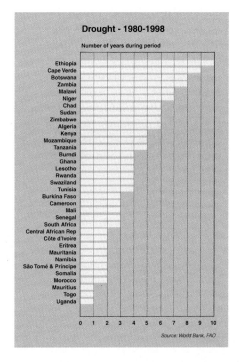

Drought - 1980-1998

Number of years during period

Ethiopia
Cape Verde
Botswana
Zambia
Malawi
Niger
Chad
Sudan
Zimbabwe
Algeria
Kenya
Mozambique
Tanzania
Burndi
Ghana
Lesotho
Rwanda
Swaziland
Tunisia
Burkina Faso
Cameroon
Mali
Senegal
South Africa
Central African Rep
Côte d'Ivoire
Eritrea
Mauritania
Namibia
São Tomé & Príncipe
Somalia
Morocco
Mauritius
Togo
Uganda

0 1 2 3 4 5 6 7 8 9 10

Source: World Bank, FAO

97

Agriculture

Africa has traditionally been seen as the continent of coffee, cocoa and cotton. Commercial and subsistence farming on average contribute between 30% and 35% of GDP and provide employment for some 70% of the continent's work force. Despite its importance, agriculture has been allowed to slip far below its potential. Less than 7% of the crop-growing areas are irrigated, inputs are limited and mechanization often lacking. Most of the continent is vulnerable to droughts and there is little access to irrigation. Six countries—Egypt, Madagascar, Morocco, Nigeria, South Africa and Sudan—account for nearly 75 percent of the total irrigated land in Africa. HIV/AIDS further undermines agricultural systems and threatens the food security of rural families. Global projections of food production show that although the world population growth rate will be matched by similar growth in food production and that food prices will continue to decline, Africa as a region will continue to be unable to meet its own food demand. The total annual shortfall is estimated to reach 150 million tons of grain by 2020.

With some notable exceptions where nations actually manage not only to feed themselves but earn valuable foreign exchange through exports, agriculture in Africa at large has for centuries been plagued by poor policies and institutional failures. In many parts of the continent not only heavy state control but under-capitalization, inadequate infrastructures and antiquated farming methods have inhibited growth. Still, the UN Food and Agri-culture Organization (FAO) maintains that sub-Saharan Africa has the potential to increase agricultural production and become self-reliant. World Bank and IMF-inspired programs encourage research and new strategies to raise productivity. In its analysis of the agricultural crisis in Sub-Saharan Africa, the FAO identified arable land expansion, increased yields and increased cropping intensity as potential sources of increased production. Biotechnology has shown that it can increase crop yields.

Opportunities

There is an ongoing market for food purchases abroad as a decline in the production of wheat, rice and corn in some areas necessitates substantial imports. In recent years, however, as government reforms opened up the sector, foreign entrepreneurs have become increasingly involved in large-scale commercial farming and food processing. Several countries that have recently moved away from constrictions in the production, processing and marketing of agricultural products have managed to increase productivity and attract outside investors. There is a continuing need for foreign agricultural inputs such as fertilizer and machinery.

AFRICA'S SHARE OF WORLD AGRICULTURAL PRODUCTION

Food	% Share of world	Leading producers in Africa Percentage of total African production
Cassava	52%	Nigeria 37%, DROC 21%
Maize	8%	South Africa 24%, Nigeria 13%, Egypt 12%
Millet	44%	Nigeria 44%, Niger 14%, Mali 5%
Rice	3%	Egypt 30%, Nigeria 20%, Madagascar 16%
Sorghum	30%	Nigeria 34%, Sudan 20%, Ethiopia 10%
Wheat	4%	Morocco 26%, Egypt 25%, Algeria 12%
Fish catch	5%	Morocco 15%, South Africa 11%, Tanzania 7%
Fresh fruit	13%	Uganda 19%, Nigeria 13%, Egypt 10%
Meat	4%	South Africa 13%, Nigeria 11%, Egypt 10%
Cash crops		
Cocoa beans	65%	Côte d'Ivoire 66%, Ghana 18%, Nigeria 8%
Coffee beans	19%	Uganda 22%, Ethiopia 20%, Côte d'Ivoire 14%
Cotton lint	9%	Egypt 21%, Mali 10%, Nigeria 7%, Sudan 6%
Groundnuts	21%	Nigeria 28%, Senegal 13%, Sudan 7%
Palm oil	10%	Nigeria 44%, Côte d'Ivoire 15%, DROC 10%
Sisal	29%	Kenya 37%, Tanzania 35%
Sugar cane	7%	South Africa 28%, Egypt 18%, Mauritius 7%, Sudan 7
Tea leaves	13%	Kenya 66%, Malawi 10%, Tanzania 6%
Tobacco leaves	6%	Zimbabwe 42%, Malawi 29%, Tanzania 6%
Roundwood	16%	Nigeria 19%, DROC 8%, Kenya 7%

Source: Africa Institute, 1994

AFRICAN AGRICULTURE

	Cereal prod. Thousands Metric tons 1999	Agricltural exports $ million 1997	Fertilizer use 000 mt. 1998	Fertilizer imports 000 mt 1998	Hectares under major crops - 000 1998	Food prod. per capita index[1] 1999
Algeria	1,540	91	96	90	7,661	109
Angola	550	6	5	5	3,000	105
Benin	890	198	38	38	1,700	121
Botswana	20	115	4	4	343	79
Burkina Faso	2,662	119	50	50	3,400	106
Burundi	265	82	2	2	770	76
Cameroon	1,455	504	40	40	5,960	99
Cape Verde	10	0	0	0	39	113
Central African Republic	173	33	1	1	1,930	112
Chad	1,153	135	17	17	3,520	119
Comoros	21	4	0	0	78	92
Congo, Democratic Rep. of	1,649	95	0	0	6,700	68
Congo, Republic of	2	15	5	5	173	92
Côte d'Ivoire	1,832	2,001	113	157	2,950	104
Djibouti	0	0	0	0	..	71
Egypt	18,677	442	1,113	139	2,834	127
Equatorial Guinea	..	4	0	0	130	80
Eritrea	270	2	7	7	498	99
Ethiopia	8,406	526	164	176	9,950	97
Gabon	32	10	0	0	325	90
Gambia, The	144	12	2	3	195	93
Ghana	1,686	616	15	15	3,600	128
Guinea	971	48	3	3	885	112
Guinea-Bissau	191	22	1	1	300	98
Kenya	2,514	1,157	128	128	4,000	83
Lesotho	174	9	6	6	325	83
Liberia	210	20	0	0	190	..
Libya	251	0	50	42	1,815	132
Madagascar	2,829	92	9	9	2,565	84
Malawi	2,655	359	50	50	1,875	140
Mali	2,952	271	53	53	4,606	104
Mauritania	196	40	2	2	488	83
Mauritius	0	405	33	34	100	77
Morocco	3,860	832	350	193	9,033	83
Mozambique	1,821	50	5	5	3,120	104
Namibia	76	201	..	..	816	77
Niger	2,823	45	1	1	4,994	103
Nigeria	22,405	522	188	153	28,200	123
Rwanda	179	38	0	0	820	87
São Tomé and Principe	1	3	..	..	2	134
Senegal	963	58	27	34	2,230	96
Seychelles	..	2	0	0	1	122
Sierra Leone	280	14	3	3	484	69
Somalia	207	76	1	1	1,040	..
South Africa	9,861	2,464	783	287	14,791	88
Sudan	3,097	556	38	38	16,700	128
Swaziland	114	300	6	6	168	69
Tanzania	3,977	400	28	30	3,750	83
Togo	761	128	17	17	2,200	112
Tunisia	1,819	530	121	13	2,900	113
Uganda	1,874	405	2	2	5,060	91
Zambia	1,057	50	40	38	5,260	83
Zimbabwe	1,987	1,157	174	67	3,220	92
AFRICA	111,542	15,263	3,789	1,962	177,694	97

1. Food production index (1981-1991=100)

Source: World Bank Africa Database 2001

Manufacturing

Africa's share of global manufactured products is almost zero. With the exception of South Africa, which offers a broad range of manufactured goods, most other African countries that are currently relying on industry for more than one third of their GDP are in urgent need of diversification. In many instances, industrial activity is based almost solely on the extraction of a single product such as oil or diamonds or, as one economist put it, indus-trialization is likely to be linked to natural resource endowments rather than "foot loose" industries. There is a concerted effort on the part of African nations to attract expertise and funding from abroad. The emphasis is on labor-intensive activity in rural regions and export-oriented manufacturing in free trade zones. Incentives range from tax holidays to subsidized training programs and facilities on government-sponsored sites and in state-owned buildings. In resource-rich countries there is increasingly an insistence on local beneficiation of minerals and fuels to create jobs and much-needed value-added income. Southern Africa—with South Africa at its hub—has the continent's strongest industrial base. In countries such as Mauritius, Swaziland, Zambia and Zimbabwe, manufacturing accounts for well over 20% and in South Africa more than 30% of GDP.

The sophistication of its manufacturing industry places South Africa in the company of the world's 30 top industrial nations. In 1999, manufacturing, electricity, gas, water and construction constituted almost a third of the nations' total GDP compared to agriculture's 4.5% and mining's 7.8%. Some import substitution industries that were started during the sanctions era grew rapidly with the help of large infusions of foreign capital and the opening up of foreign markets since 1994. Manufacturing and assembly in this country involves most of the larger multinationals in North America, Europe and the Far East and products ranging from autos and parts, to chemicals, textiles, machinery and pulp and paper. South African-made foreign brand cars and trucks are exported to South America, Australasia and China. Automotive parts from Johannesburg are sold to Detroit. Since 1994 South Africa has also been a significant outward investor in manufacturing and mining in other parts of the continent and abroad.

Flying geese

Africa has begun to experience what became known in the Far East as the "flying geese" phenomenon, with some of its more advanced countries opting for manufacturing in neighboring countries where wages are lower and incentives higher. Not only South Africa but even smaller nations such as Mauritius have, for economic reasons, shifted their manufacturing of garments and other textiles, hand-made toys and other labor-intensive operations to less developed nations in Africa, thus duplicating the process with which Asia has become so familiar in recent years.

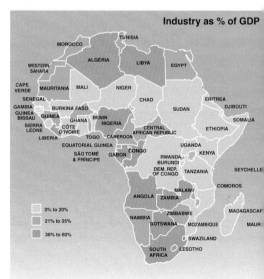

Industry as % of GDP

Development Bank

In 1986, the African Development Bank (AfDB), the International Finance Corporation (IFC), the United Nations Development Programme (UNDP) and 15 other donor countries jointly established the Africa Project Development Facility (APDF) to assist African entrepreneurs. APDF's objective is to accelerate the development of productive private enterprises sponsored and owned by African entrepreneurs as a means of stimulating sustainable economic growth and productive employment in sub-Saharan Africa. The Johannesburg-based Development Bank of Southern Africa (DBSA) has played a significant role in stimulating growth of industries in the SADC region.

Opportunities

Foreign direct investment in Africa is no longer concentrated in the traditional natural resources sector; manufacturing and services industries have received considerable amounts in recent years. Multinational textile and apparel manufacturers have been establishing themselves in African nations to take advantage of trade preferences and quotas in European and North American markets. Other light industries are now following their example by setting up plants in free trade zones across the continent from Mauritius to Cape Verde. With the passage of the US African Growth and Opportunity Act (AGOA), the textile industry is expected to expand further. Several countries have already geared up to take advantage of the new opportunities presented by this legislation not only for textiles but a variety of other basic products in the world's most affluent market. In coming years the adoption of the AGOA might prove to be a watershed event in the development of the manufacturing industry in Africa. In South Africa, Zimbabwe, Nigeria, Egypt and several other countries the emphasis is already on higher technology and heavy industry items.

IDC

The Industrial Development Corporation of South Africa Limited (IDC) continues to be a key facilitator of new manufacturing not only in South Africa but several neighboring nations. Through loan financing up to 50 percent of the startup cost as well as technical expertise and marketing and export assistance, the IDC has helped create a whole slate of major industries since its inception some fifty years ago.

African giants

☑ Unleashed in the early 1990s when sanctions were scrapped, several of post-apartheid's South Africa's industrial giants have gone on a takeover spree in Africa and abroad.

☑ Starting with a dramatic takeover of the US-based Warren in 1994, South Africa's Sappi has grown into the world's leading producer of coated fine paper. With manufacturing operations in eight countries and on three continents, and sales in more than 125 countries, it has a 24% share of the US market, 22% in Europe and more than 60% in Africa. It also leads the world in the production of dissolving pulp, used in viscose textiles.

☑ South Africa's synthetic oil giant, Sasol, has consolidated its position as a world leader in the commercial production of liquid fuels and chemicals from coal and crude oil. In partnership with US oil giants it has expanded operations and markets into Africa and the United States.

☑ Anglogold and Billiton have established themselves as leading mining companies in Africa, Europe and Australasia, while De Beers has long been the biggest player in diamonds around the world.

☑ South African Breweries expanded its brewing operations across Africa, where it has established operations in 17 countries, and Eastern Europe into the Far East, moving into fifth position worldwide.

☑ While only one African company— Anglo American with revenues of $11.5 billion—made the Fortune 500 list of the world's biggest corporations, eight of the top ten in this list are heavily involved on the continent, General Motors, Exxon-Mobil, Ford Motor, Daimler Chrysler, Mitsubishi, Toyota Motor and General Electric.

Banking

In several parts of the continent banking has been strengthened by financial liberalization, restructuring, and other reforms, and became more competitive and more transparent. There is an ongoing process of consolidation through mergers, privatization and liquidations. Foreign banks are allowed in countries where until recently banking was tightly controlled and all overseas competition excluded. In countries where public sector institutions are the largest users of banking services, reforms are allowing them to decide whether to bank with public, local private or foreign banks. But apart from South Africa and a few other countries such as Egypt, Morocco, Zimbabwe, Mauritius, Kenya and Botswana, the continent is still lagging behind in services. Some of the least developed countries rely on poorly run state banks. However, the current trend is towards restructuring even though insufficient capital remains a problem in several regions.

In the immediate post-colonial era most African governments interfered in their financial sectors by nationalizing existing institutions and creating state-owned banks. Credit was curtailed and strict exchange controls introduced. In the 1980s when it finally became apparent that this approach failed miserably, a new wave of reform spread across the continent. The transformation to freer financial markets did not happen without cost. In many instances the larger spread between lending and deposit rates led to higher local interest rates. Some governments still cling to failing state banks and a number of undercapitalized institutions spawned in the process of reform are experiencing problems. In general, however, the freer financial environment has been a boon to both domestic and foreign investors.

North Africa

In North Africa countries such as Egypt, Morocco, Tunisia and Algeria have gone through major structural adjustments in recent years. In Morocco, which has led the way in both reform and privatization in the region, Wafa Bank, with 12 per cent of total Moroccan deposits, is a prime example of successful diversification. The same trend is evident in Tunisia, albeit at a slower pace due to a higher degree of state ownership of banks and a paternalistic political system. Challenges in both Morocco and Tunisia are much less severe than those faced in Algeria where the state-run banking sector has had a difficult time adapting to economic reforms. Egyptian banking has undergone substantial liberalization in the past decade. Even though the privatization of Egypt's "big four" state banks was delayed, private banks such as Commercial International Bank (CIB), Misr International Bank (MIBank) and Egyptian American Bank (EAB) have made great strides in gaining market share. Today the private sector accounts for some 20% of the total and is by far the most profitable with a return on equity (ROE) ranging between 19% and 30%.

Foreign Banks

Foreign banks have provided know-how and much-needed support to African financial systems in need of a fresh inflow of capital to buttress economic reforms. They have been useful catalysts for inward investment and trading by offering financing and expertise and, in some cases, acting as go-betweens to clinch deals. Often foreigners prefer the comfort zone of a familiar bank when dealing with remote and unfamiliar countries. US,

	Ranking	
World ranking of African banks		
Bank	**1997**	**1998**
ABSA (South Africa)	170	195
Stanbic (South Africa)	181	158
Nedcor (South Africa)	282	215
FNB (South Africa)	285	252
Investec (South Africa)	375	296
Credit Populaire du Maroc	—	466
NBS Boland (South Africa)	510	297
Banque Commerciale du Maroc	—	618
Banque Morocaine du Commerce	—	633
Banque Nationale Agricole (Tunisia)	—	704
Wafabank (Morocco)	—	802
First Bank of Nigeria	—	879
United Bank for Africa (Nigeria)	—	880
Mauritius Commercial Bank	—	905

Source: The Banker, The Top 1000

French and British banks are prominent on the continent. HSBC Equator Bank was founded as a subsidiary of the powerful HSBC group, to pursue trade and finance opportunities in sub-Saharan Africa. With Africa as its sole market, HSBC Equator has developed a unique knowledge of the region and developed strong relationships with both the private and public sectors. It provides a full slate of services ranging from institutional banking to equity management, structured trade financing and investment banking. It has been a significant player in privatization and mergers and acquisitions on the continent. Its network of strategically-located offices enables it to provide full services in 26 countries ranging from Ethiopia and Eritrea in the north to Senegal and Nigeria on the west coast, Kenya and Tanzania on the east coast, and Zimbabwe and South Africa in the south.

South Africa

Banking and financial services in South Africa are not only state-of-the-art by any world standard but actually lead in some respects. Several of South Africa's top banks have in recent years established themselves overseas to offer their extensive services in Southern Africa to prospective investors and traders as well. Most foreign banking institutions setting their sights on Africa start in South Africa where a sophisticated $9 billion financial market presents no surprises and minimum risk. However, to make serious inroads in this market foreign enterprises have to spend substantial sums as opposed to relatively small outlays elsewhere on the continent. With 30 local banking institutions (five of them ranking among the top 300 worldwide), 24 foreign-controlled banks and another 30 foreign bank representatives, the competition is tough. It is therefore not surprising that both foreign and South African banks such as ABSA and Stanbic are seeking new opportunities elsewhere on the continent where widespread reform in the financial sector has opened up the field in recent times. In a review of the African banking scene, the World Bank concluded that Africa already has the highest penetration by foreign banks of any region.

Regional

Crossborder cooperation and greater cohesiveness in banking, insurance and stock market activity within groupings such as the Southern African Development Community (SADC), the Common Market for eastern and Southern Africa (COMESA) and the Economic Community of West African States (ECOWAS) should make the market more attractive for prospective foreign participants.

ADB

African Development Bank (www.afdb.org —rated AA+ with a stable outlook by Standard & Poor's and triple A by Moody's) has its focus on rural development, human capital development (health and education) and the private sector. It also aims at incorporating gender, the environment and regional integration into its projects, and to take a lead on promoting good governance.

DBSA

The Johannesburg-based Development Bank of Southern Africa (www.dbsa.org—rated Baa3 by Moody's) has become a major facilitator of development programs in the region. It operates in all the provinces of South Africa as well as in the other 13 countries of the Southern African Development Community (SADC). In the past year the DBSA approved more than R2 billion in investment loans for projects with a total capital value of R6.3 billion, most of them involving infrastructure development. Its loan portfolio to date totals R21 billion with leverage funding at a rate of R2.17 for every R1 invested. The bank's team of development experts also provides technical assistance and policy analysis. In South Africa alone, projects funded by the DBSA are estimated to have benefited 1.1 million households and 5.5 million individuals. The bank works with overseas donors and other partners on international, national and provincial levels. It recently introduced a development fund to finance capacity building in clients not currently creditworthy.

	South Africa's largest banks				
Rnk	Bank	Total Assets R m	Rnk	Bank	Capital & Reserves R m
1	ABSA Bank	10,772	1	ABSA Bank	152,460
2	Standard Bank	9,025	2	Standard Bank	137,530
3	Nedcor	8,509	3	First National	124,209
4	First National Bank	8,273	4	Nedcor	123,266
5	BoE Bank Ltd	5,341	5	BoE Bank Ltd	49,472

Source: Financial Mail - 2000 Survey

Behind the masks

"If sculpture is the projection of one's thoughts into three dimensions, then the African continent has produced many of the greatest sculptors of all time, even though no single name has ever been passed down," writes art critic Claude Rilly "The African mask is not an *objet d'art* in itself, but neither is it a simple cultural or theatrical accessory. At the same time, the sculptor is not an 'artist,' but his function goes much further than that of a simple craftsman."

From the beginning of civilization, masks have been part of tribal life—not only in Africa but in most other parts of the world. In Africa masks can instruct, discipline, warn, honor, protect and entertain. They depict deities, mythological beings, good and evil spirits, the spirits of ancestors and the dead, animal spirits, and a variety of other beings believed to have supernatural powers.

Vuvi

They are used in fertility and initiation rites, religious and funeral celebrations. And even when utilized as props in dramas and comedies they remain linked to ethnic myths. Sometimes a mask bestows on the wearer a certain social status or membership to closed societies or cults.

Most masks made for royalty were destroyed after the death of the emperor. Idia's mask is an exception. Carved from ivory, this 16th Century masterpiece represents Idia—mother of Oba Esigie, then king of Benin. The mask was worn by him at ceremonies commemorating his mother and eventually made its way to New York's Metropolitan Museum of Art via the Nelson D.

Ngady aMwaash

Kpeliyehe

Rockefeller private art collection. This ivory pendant mask is one of a pair of nearly identical works; its counterpart is on exhibit at the British Museum in London.

African royalty has also left behind masks sculpted from gold, brass and copper, but most were carved from wood and sometimes decorated with shells, beads, animal skins and raffia. They vary in size, from the 6 inch (15 cm) lukwakongo masks of the Lega people to the 3 ft.

Idia

(almost 1 meter) high kakuunga half-helmet mask of the Suku tribe. The Vuvi people in the Gabon region are masters of abstraction and simplicity as exemplified in a painted wooden mask from the collection of the Detroit Institute of Arts.

Much more elaborate is a Ngady aMwaash mask from the Peabody Museum at Harvard University. Originating with the Kuba tribe in Central Africa this mask—consisting of wood, raffia cloth, beads and cowrie shells—symbolizes links between the royal family and mythic characters.

Nigil

The Nigil hardwood dance mask from the Fang tribe, on display in Geneva's Musée Barbier-Mueller, is intended to intimidate and enforce obedience. The same collection shows a Kpeliyehe mask made from brass, used by the Senufo people in West Africa for rituals inspired by jungle spirits. Also housed in the Musée Barbier-Mueller is a specimen of the elaborate Mwaash aMbooy masks made for royalty from vegetable fibers adorned with beads and cowries as a symbol of wisdom and authority.

Mwaash aMbooy

The Harlemm Network

Tourism

Considering its wealth of wildlife, ancient civilizations, cultural diversity, superb scenery, magnificent beaches, and sunny climate, Africa should be getting a lion's share of the world's growing tourist traffic. The continent's apparent inability to pull in larger numbers of visitors have been ascribed to a variety of factors including lack of promotion, insufficient infrastructure, remoteness and real and unfounded perceptions of a continent rife with disease, war and crime. Sophisticated and discerning tourists who will never entertain the thought of cancelling a visit to France or Germany because of a war in the Balkans often eschew all of Africa when war breaks out in an area thousands of miles away from the country which they intended to visit. At the same time there are encouraging signs of increased investment from abroad in infrastructure and other tourist-related aminities that should increase Africa's competitiveness.

Statistics released by the World Tourism Organization show that Africa was largely left out of a world tourism boom in 2000. Despite an en-couraging increase in the number of visitors to countries such as Egypt, Kenya, Zambia, Mauritius and Morocco, the continent's 2% average growth falls short of the world's 7.4% and is well below East Asia's of 14.5% and Europe's 6.2%.

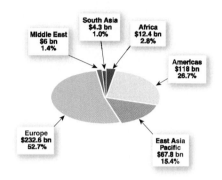

SHARE OF INTERNATIONAL TOURISM RECEIPTS
1998 - TOTAL $441.1 BILLION

Graph: Business Books International
Source: World Tourism Organization

An impressive growth of nearly 15% in Egypt and 30% in Kenya during 2000 was countered by flat numbers in the continent's foremost tourist market, South Africa. Another major tourist destination, Zimbabwe, showed a massive decline of almost 60% as a result of political upheaval.

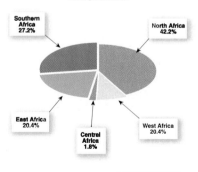

REGIONAL SHARE OF AFRICA'S
INTERNATIONAL TOURISM RECEIPTS
TOTAL $12.4 BILLION

Graph: Business Books International
Source: World Tourism Organization

TOP DESTINATIONS IN AFRICA

Country	Arrivals in 2000	% change
South Africa	6,108,000	+1.4
Egypt	5,150,000	+14.7
Tunisia	5,057,000	+4.7
Morocco	4,100,000	+7.4
Kenya	1,226,000	+30.0
Algeria	859,000	+13.8
Zimbabwe	840,000	-60.0
Mauritius	636,000	+10.1
Zambia	574,000	+25.9

Source: WToO

There is, however, little doubt on the part of both economists and travel experts that Africa is destined to reap as much benefit from this natural resource as it has in the past from metals, minerals.

INTERNATIONAL TOURISM TO AFRICA

		INTERNATIONAL TOURIST ARRIVALS					INTL. TOURISM RECEIPTS	
			Market share in		Growth		US$	Growth
	1000		Africa (%)		rate (%)		million	Rate (%)
	1998	1999	1998	1999	1997/8	1998/9	1998	1997/98
AFRICA	28,163	31,326			7.5[2]	7.6[2]	12,421	4.9[2]
NORTH AFRICA	11,870	13,941	42.1	44.5	8.5[2]	8.9[2]	24	14.9[2]
Algeria	678	755	2.4	2.4	6.8	11.4	24	300.0
Egypt[1]	3,213	4,489	11.4	14.3	-12.1	39.7	2,564	-31.2
Morocco	3,242	3,824	11.5	12.2	5.5	18.0	1,712	18.2
Sudan	39		0.1		30.0		8	100.0
Tunisia	4,718	4,832	16.7	15.42	10.7	2.4	1,557	10.1
WEST AFRICA	2,390	2,628	8.4	8.3	11.5	10.0	945	9.6
Benin	152		0.5		2.7		33	6.5
Burkina Faso	160	218	0.5	0.7	15.9	36.3	42	7.7
Cape Verde	52		0.2		15.6		20	33.3
Côte d'Ivoire	301		1.0		9.9		108	13.7
Gambia	91		0.3		7.1		33	3.1
Ghana	348	373	1.23	1.2	7.1	7.2	284	2.9
Guinea	23	27	0.08	0.09	35.3	17.4	1	600.0
Mali	83		0.3		10.7		50.0	92.3
Mauritania							21	0.0
Niger	20	39	0.07	0.1	5.3	95.0	18	16.7
Nigeria	739		2.6		20.9		142	20.3
Senegal	352	369	1.2	1.2	12.1	4.8	178	16.3
Sierra Leone								
Togo	69	99	0.2	0.3	-25.0	43.5	15	15.4
CENTRAL AFRICA	480	523	1.7	1.6	11.1	9.0	88	3.5
Angola	52	45	0.2	0.1	15.6	-13.5	8	62.5
Cameroon	135		0.5		1.5		40	2.6
Centr. Afr. Republic	7	10	0.02	0.03	-58.8	42.9	6	20.0
Chad	11	43	0.04	0.1	22.2	290.9	10	11.1
Congo (Brazzaville)	25		0.08		-3.8		10	0.0
Congo (Kinshasa)	53		0.2		76.7		2	0.0
Equatorial Guinea							2	0.0
Gabon	192	194	0.7	0.6	15.0	1.0	8	14.3
São Tomé & Príncipe	5		0.02		0.0		2	0.0
EAST AFRICA	5,736	6,078	20.36	19.4	9.1	6.0	2,267	-1.8
Burundi	15		0.05		36.4		1	0.0
Comoros	27	24	0.1	0.08	3.8	-11.1	16	-38.5
Djibouti	21		0.07		5.0		4	0.0
Eritrea	188	57	0.7	0.2	-54.1	-69.7	34	-62.2
Ethiopia	91		0.3		-20.9		11	-69.4
Kenya	857	943	3.0	3.0	-5.5	10.0	233	-35.5
Madagascar	121	138	0.4	0.4	19.8	14.0	91	23.0
Malawi	178	150	0.6	0.5	-13.6	-15.7	15	36.4
Mauritius	558	578	2.0	1.8	4.1	3.6	503	3.7
Reunion	400	402	1.4	1.3	7.0	0.5	265	6.4
Rwanda	2		0.0		100		19	0.0
Seychelles	128	125	0.5	0.4	-1.5	-2.3	111	9.0
Somalia	10		0.04		0.0			
Tanzania	450		1.6		29.7		570	45.4
Uganda	238		0.8		4.8		142	5.2
Zambia	362	456	1.3	1.5	6.2	26.0	75	0.0
Zimbabwe	2,090	2,328	7.4	7.4	39.8	11.4	177	-23.0
SOUTHERN AFRICA	7,667	8,155	27.2	26.0	4.0	6.4	3,256	-1.3
Botswana	740		2.6		0.8		175	28.7
Lesotho	150	186	0.5	0.6	4.2	24.0	18	-18.2
Namibia	560		2.0		116		288	-13.5
South Africa	5,898	6,253	20.9	20.0	4.3	6.0	2,738	-1.1
Swaziland	319		1.1		-6.2		37	-5.1

1. Although Egypt is included in Middle East by WTO it is factored in here as it forms part to African continent.   2. Egypt excluded.
Source: World Tourism Organization

Africa's golden joys

In Henry IV, Shakespeare spoke of *"Africa and golden joys,"* and two thousand years ago, Pliny the Elder recorded those famous words in Latin: *"Ex Africa semper aliquid novi"*— *"Out of Africa always something new." Since then many have journeyed to Africa in search of its golden joys and to experience the new. They came from all corners of the world. The writers and the visionaries, the presidents and the princes, the rich and the regulars, the famous and the not so familiar. The went as individuals and in groups. First in hundreds and then in thousands. Lately in millions.*

Still, Africa remains surprisingly under-travelled. For a continent with all its offerings and charm, according to the experts, it should be getting a much larger chunk of the world's tourist traffic. Many countries on the continent stand to gain almost as much from tourism as they did in past years by exploiting other natural resources such as oil, gas, gold, platinum and a host of other precious and strategic minerals.

There is in the far north the mighty Nile, quietly flowing through the world's oldest civilization, and at the southern tip majestic Table Mountain that so impressed the world 's leading seafarers since the days of Vasco da Gama and Francis Drake. And in-between there are the likes of Lake Victoria, Victoria Falls, Mount Kilimanjaro and The Ngorongoro Crater. There are the Atlas mountains in the northeast, bordering the Sahara Desert, and there is a strip on the southwest coast aptly called the Skeleton Coast. There are tens of major animal kingdoms and literally hundreds of smaller wildlife estates where the exotic animals of the ark roam free for all to see.

Experts such as Dave Herbert, president of African Travel sees the African continent's biodiversity, ranging from desert to tropical jungle, from snow-capped volcanic mountains to glimmering beaches, as major assets. Africa, he insists, is not merely a destination but a life experience. Many of his clients repeat after they have made that first trip.

What is it that have, since the time of Pliny and Leo Africanus, turned so many foreigners into Africa addicts? Writing under the pen name Isak Dinesen, Karen Blixen in *Out of Africa* summed up her own experience as follows: "Now, looking back on my life in Africa, I feel that it might altogether be described as the existence of a person who had come from a rushed and noisy world, into a still country."

In *A Glimpse of Eden,* Evelyn James declares: "Nothing can really prepare you for Africa. It is too full of extremes and contrasts, too immense, a spectrum of creation so much wider and more vivid than anywhere else that it seems to require a new set of senses, or the rediscovery of lost ones."

Pres. Theodore Roosevelt, who spent considerable time on the continent, wrote from Khartoum on March 15, 1910: "There are no words that can tell the hidden spirit of the wilderness, that can reveal its mystery, its melancholy, and its charm." It is something in your blood, says Chris McBride, author of *The White Lions of Timbavati*. "A combination of the climate, the landscape, the wildlife, the whole atmosphere"

Pictures: Les de Villiers

Going there

☑ *Air services* to and within Africa are provided by a number of international and domestic airlines. South African Airways (www. flysaa.com/800-722-9675) has, however, established itself as the premier carrier to and from the continent and on routes within Africa. It utilizes the latest long-haul aircraft on its direct and non-stop services between the US, Europe, the Far East, Australasia and Africa.

☑ *Travel arrangements* to Africa are offered by several agencies, with African Travel (www.africantravelinc.com/ 800-421-8907) among the most experienced and well-established—offering trips ranging from economy to upscale, customized and individualized to packed group tours.

☑ *Visa and health requirements* differ vastly between Africa's 53 countries and travelers who are making their own travel arrangements should contact the respective embassies beforehand to ensure that they comply.

☑ *Customs* vary on a vast continent where literally thousands of cultures coexist, and all the major religions plus some indigenous beliefs hold sway. It makes for interesting travel but also could lead to uncomfortable experiences if ignored. Some background reading is needed not only for business travelers who wish to avoid costly mistakes but for vacationers who wish to avoid embarrassment and, in the worst cases, official disapproval.

that makes "you somehow feel that you're missing everything when you're not there."

Among those who fell prey to the quiet charm of the mighty Nile was author Vivienne de Wateville. In *Out of The Blue* she mused upon this river that "stands as a symbol of time itself, running down through the ages" and the patience of those who live along its banks. "There, perhaps, lay the solution. Africa is too mighty for anything so brittle as impatience, and one's strength lies not in pitting oneself against it, but in ranging oneself upon the same side."

In 1550, a Moor by the adopted name of Joannes Leo Africanus—his real name was Al-Hassan Ibn Mohammed Al-Wezaz Al-Fasi—recorded his impressions of Africa. Originally written in Italian, it was later published in old English as *The History and Description of Africa and the Notable Things Therein Contained* .

Here are some of his impressions: *"The Hippopotamus or water-horse is somewhat tawnie, of the colour of a lion; in the night he comes on lands to feed upon the grasse, and keepeth in the water all the day time...the Zebra or Zabra of this country being about the bignes of a mule, is a beast of incomparable swiftnes, straked about the body, legges, eares, and other parts, with blacke, white and browne circles of three fingers broad; which do make a pleasant shew... Also here are infinite store of elephants of such monstrous bignes, that by the report of sundrie credible persons, some of their teeth do weigh two hundred pounds, at sixteene ounces the pound: upon the plaines this beast is swifter than any horse, by reason of his long steps; onely he cannot turne with such celeritie. Trees he overturneth with the strength of his backe, or breaketh them between his teeth; or standeth upright upon his hinder feete to browse upon the leaves and tender sprigs. The she elephants beare their brood in their wombes two years before they bring foorth yoong ones. This creature is saide to live 150 yeeres; hee is of a gentle disposition, and relying upon his great strength, he hurteth none but such as do him injurie; only he will in a sporting maner gently heave up with his snowte such persons as he meeteth."*

They are still all there for visitors to behold thanks to timely intervention of Africa-based and foreign conservationists. So are hundreds of other species, protected in pristine land set aside by African governments.

Cultures of Africa

In *Long Walk to Freedom* Nelson Mandela vividly recalls the Xhosa circumcision ceremony at age sixteen that signalled his entry into manhood. Even though this *abakwetha, performed by an elder (ingcibi)* with a spear or assegai and without any anaesthetic, caused excruciating pain, no one was to show any outward emotion. "A boy may cry; a man conceals pain," Mandela explains. "I had now taken the essential step in the life of every Xhosa man. Now I might marry, set up my own home and plough my own field."

Until this day the *abakwetha* is performed in the Xhosa region of South Africa. So are numerous other unique ceremonies across the face of Africa, designed to build character and honor, solidify marriages and strengthen family and community ties. Everyone of these ceremonies—even those that might seem as bizarre to foreigners as certain customs in their world might appear to the Africans—have a definite purpose and a deeper meaning.

Today much of the travel to Africa is inspired by a desire to learn more about the cultures and customs of this continent with its many hundreds of diverse peoples. African-American author Henry Louis Gates has done much to educate the outside world about the hidden *Wonders of Africa* in a television series, revealing its rich cultures and ancient civilizations unknown to many in the Western world.

In Delgo, Gates was invited to participate in a traditional Nubian wedding, in Ethiopia he mingled with Christians whose faith predated that of England by several hundred years and whose icons were all in black, and in Dogon he was allowed a glimpse of the circumcision cave with its fascinating wall paintings—an area totally closed to women.

But it took two enterprising women to produce what could arguably be described as the most extensive and impressive photographic record of Africa's ceremonies. Accomplished Africanists and photographers Carol Beckwith and Angela Fisher collaborated in the production of a dramatic two volume presentation of *African Ceremonies,* published by Henry M. Abrams Inc., New York. (www.abrams books.com).

"Living in traditional African societies has made us aware of the value that rites of passage have for the individual and the community. Ceremonies that mark the stages of life from birth to death provide clear definitions of what is expected of the individual and give him or her a sense of identity and belonging," write Beckwith and Fisher. "Each rite begins with a gift or an offering and nothing is taken from the land without giving something back to it. Survival depends on this basic principle."

While no one can truly expect to experience more than a fraction of the numerous magnificent rites, rituals and ceremonies which took Beckwith and Fisher ten years and patient trust-building to record, a mere sampling of these magnificent color photographs is bound to wet the appetite for travel to Africa.

Brides of Africa

Himba, Namibia

Ashanti, Ghana

Masaai, Kenya

Fulani, Mali

© Carol Beckwith & Angela Fisher

AFRICA'S MAJOR GAME RESERVES

Courtesy www.africantravelinc.com

Major safari destinations such as Botswana, Kenya, Malawi, Namibia, South Africa, Uganda, Zambia and Zimbabwe, offer opportunities in national parks and game reserves, as well as a growing number of private game parks. Around South Africa's Kruger National Park numerous private game parks have sprung up where accommodations and services are tailored to suit the taste of the most demanding visitors. While some might complain about too much luxury in the wilds, others obviously want it. The owner of one of the private game parks explains as follows: "To view the animals you don't have to live like one." But for those who long for something more closely resembling the experience of Livingstone and other pioneers there is still ample opportunity to rough it, usually—but not always—at lower rates.

Foreign interest is, however, not only in the enjoyment of the offerings but in the supply side as well. In recent years investors from abroad have increasingly become involved in the development of new private game parks and the upgrading of existing ones. Several governments have privatized parks and are actively seeking partners in both the development and management of facilities. There are no shortage of takers who anticipate a massive expansion in ecotourism to the world's foremost wildlife region in the coming years.

Following are the major national parks (NP), game parks (GP), and game reserves (GR) in Africa. Smaller private game parks are not listed:

BOTSWANA:

Chobe National Park
At 4,247 sq. miles (11,000 sq km), this is Botswana's second largest park with varied wildlife including Africa's largest elephant population.

Okavango Delta
Referred to as *The Jewel of the Kalahari,* it covers an area of 6,178 sq. miles (16,000 sq. km). It is the largest inland delta in the world and home to abundant wildlife such as crocodile, hippo, water buck.

Moremi Game Reserve
The Moremi Game Reserve lies within the Okavango Delta, covers an area of over 1,351 sq. miles (3,500

Botswana

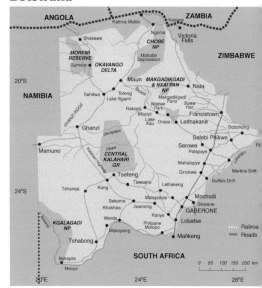

sq.km) and has a wide variety of wildlife, including elephant, buffalo, giraffe, lion, leopard, cheetah, wild dog, hyena, jackal and antelope.

Central Kalahari Game Reserve

This is Africa's largest wildlife conservation area, covering an area of over 20,080 sq. miles (52,000 sq km). It is home to a wide variety of antelope including eland, gemsbok, kudu, red hartebees and springbok as well as giraffe, lion, cheetah, leopard, wild dog and brown hyena.

Kgalagadi National Park

This is the first official *transfrontier* park, managed jointly by the Botswana and South African governments. Kagalagadi covers an area of 10,850 sq. miles (28,105 sq. km) and has abundant wildlife including lion, leopard, cheetah, wildebeest, eland, hartebeest, gemsbok and springbok.

KENYA:

Aberdare National Park

Part of the Aberdare Mountain Range with wildlife that includes elephant, lion, black rhino, waterbuck, gazelle, giant forest hog, genet cats, leopard, buffalo and rare spiral-horned antelope known as bongo.

Amboseli National Park

Relatively small at approx 153 sq. miles (395 sq. km), Amboseli is one of Kenya's most popular game parks

with views of Mount Kilimanjaro and a wide variety of game, including large herds of elephants.

Lake Nakuru National Park

The main attraction is Lake Nakuru, a shallow alkaline, soda lake set beneath the high cliffs of the eastern Rift Valley, offering a spectacular view of up to 2 million flamingos at the same time (during the season) along with hundreds of other bird species.

Marsabit National Park

This park was famous for it's large tusker elephants before the poachers slaughtered most of the large ones. Elephants are, however, still present along with large herds of kudu and many birds of prey.

Masai Mara Game Reserve

This is Kenya's most popular game reserve. From July to September it experiences the annual influx of over a million wildebeest and zebra, migrating from the Serengeti across the Mara River. Masai Mara is also populated by lion, hippo, crocodile, elephant, cheetah, baboon, gazelle, giraffe, jackal, leopards, hyena, water buffalo, and antelope.

Meru National Park

This was the setting for Joy Adamson's book, *Born Free.* Meru offers varied scenery on the slopes of the Nyambeni Mountain Range and game ranging from lion, cheetah, leopard, elephant, antelope, and buffalo to hippo and crocodile.

Mount Kenya National Park

Mount Kenya is an extinct volcano on the equator and a favorite of both botanists and game viewers in search of unique plants and species such as the bongo and Black and White colobus and Sykes monkeys. Mt. Kenya park also has bushbuck, buffalo, elephant, baboon, black rhino, and leopard.

Nairobi National Park

Within easy distance from Kenya's capital, this park is inhabited by leopard, lion, buffalo, rhino, giraffe, hippo, crocodile, antelope, wildebeest, eland, zebra and Thompson's gazelle.

Sambura Game Reserve

This is a semi-desert region with a large concentration of game including rare species such as the oryx, gerenuk, reticulated giraffe and Grevy's zebra.

Shaba Game Reserve

This semidesert region is the natural habitat for the Grevy zebra, reticulated giraffe, and gerenuk—unique to this part of Kenya. It also has elephants, lions, cheetah, crocodile, and hundreds of bird species.

Sibiloi National Park

Kenya's most remote national park. It is hot, dry and windswept, features a petrified forest and has a large variety of wildlife including Grevy's zebra, ostrich, gerenuk, oryx, tiang and a large population of Nile crocodile.

111

Tsavo National Park

This is Kenya's oldest and largest park with parts still inaccessible to the public. The southern region spans across the Kanderi Swamp and the Aruba Dam on the Voi river and has a large concentration of game, including hippo, crocodile, lion, leopard, waterbuck, kudu, zebra, ostrich, and the largest herd of elephant in the country.

Tsavo West National Park

Three rivers—the Galana, the Athi and the Tsavo—attract large concentrations of game including buffalo, rhino, giraffe, zebra, lion, leopard, cheetah, crocodile and many varieties of antelope.

MALAWI

Nyika National Park

At 1,158 sq. miles (3,000 sq. km) and with an average elevation of 5,906 ft. (1,800m) it is the largest and highest of Malawi's parks—settled by a few Aphoka people and populated by large herds of zebra, eland, roan antelope, sable, hartebeest, kudu reedbuck, bushbuck, duiker, and warthog, as well as 300 bird species.

Vwaza Marsh Game Reserve

This reserve contains large herds of buffalo and elephant, and a great variety of antelope, including roan, greater kudu, Liechtenstein's hartebees, eland and impala, as well as abundant birdlife.

Kasungu National Park

At 772 sq. miles (2,000 sq. km), this is Malawi's second largest park. Kasungu is known for its elephants and hippo—resident in several rivers that flow through the park—as well as sable, roan, kudu, impala and and predators such as hyena, wild dog and serval.

Nkhotakota Game Reserve

The oldest established reserve in Malawi with elephant, buffalo, lion, leopard, hyena and 300 species of birds.

Lake Malawi Marine Park

This park is the most important freshwater fish sanctuary in Africa and the first worldwide to protect to the marine life of in tropical deep freshwater.

Liwonde National Park

On the banks of the Upper Shire River, vegetation ranges from swamps, lagoons and reed-beds to dense woodland. It is home to Malawi's largest elephant population, as well as sable antelope, kudu, duiker, oribi, hippos and lion. Birds are abundant.

Majete Game Reserve

Known for the Kapichira Falls in the Shire River, and its abundant bird life.

Lengwe National Park

Known for its nyala antelope and bushbuck, impala, duiker and kudu, warthogs, monkeys and baboons.

Mwabvu Game Reserve

At 135 sq. miles (350 sq. km), Malawi's smallest park with rugged terrain and various kinds of antelope, lion, baboons, monkeys, and a variety of birdlife.

NAMIBIA

Daan Viljoen Game Park

A small park close to Windhoek with kudu, red hartebees, springbok, klipspringer, steenbok, eland, oryx, baboons, blouwildebees, and giraffe, as well as 200 bird species.

Etosha National Park

Covering an area of 8,880 sq. miles (23,000 sq. km), Etosha is one of Africa's largest game reserves. It is home to elephant, zebra, giraffe, lion, leopard, black rhinoceros, red hartebees, wildebees, cheetah, hyena, eland, kudu, springbok, gemsbok, black-faced impala and many other types of antelope, as well as over 340 species of birds.

Fish River Canyon NP

The Grand Canyon of Southern Africa, situated on the lower parts of the Fish River near the southern border of Namibia. Its hiking trails are closed in summer when temperatures reach highs of 122°F (50°C).

Khaudom Game Reserve

This is a remote, medium-sized park situated in the Kalahari region, at the bottom of the Capriri strip, accessible only with a convoy of four wheel drive vehicles. It offers a wide variety of wildlife including lion and hyena.

Mahango Game Reserve

This smallish park at the western end of the Capriri strip along the gateway to Botswana's Okavango Delta, offers a wide range of wildlife.

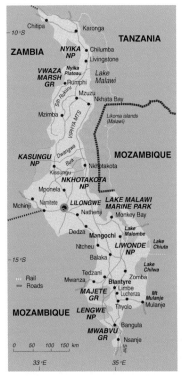

Malawi

ZAMBIA
TANZANIA
MOZAMBIQUE

Chitipa
Karonga
-10°S
NYIKA NP
Chilumba
Livingstone
VWAZA MARSH GR
Nyika Plateau
Rumphi
Lake Malawi
Mzuzu
Nkhata Bay
Mzimba
Likoma islands (Malawi)
VIPHYA MTS
S.R. Rukuru
KASUNGU NP
Dwangwa
Bua
Kasungu
Nkhotakota
Mponela
NKHOTAKOTA NP
Mchinji
Namitete
Namitenji
LILONGWE
LAKE MALAWI MARINE PARK
Nathenji
Monkey Bay
Dedza
Mangochi
Lake Malombe
Ntcheu
LIWONDE NP
Lake Chiuta
-15°S
Balaka
Lake Chilwa
Rail
Roads
Tedzani
Mwanza
Zomba
Blantyre
MAJETE GR
Limbe
Luchenza
Mt Mulanje
Thyolo
Mulanje
MOZAMBIQUE
LENGWE NP
Bangula
MWABVU GR
Nsanje
0   50   100 150 km
Shire
33°E
35°E

112

Picturing wildlife

US President Teddy Roosevelt started out as a big game hunter and trophy collector, then became an avid conservationist and wildlife photographer. Following in his footsteps were a host of other prominent personae picturing wildlife. Among these notables was George Eastman, founder of the of Eastman Kodak Company, whose product has helped millions to record and preserve memorable African moments over the past 75 years.

Teddy clicks

During the forties and the fifties Hollywood gave its own interpretation of Africa in productions such as *African Queen, The Macomber Affair,* the *Snows of Kilimanjaro* and *King Solomon's Mines* and more recently, *Gorillas in the Mist* and *Out of Africa.* Set against the backdrop of Africa these dramas—some based on the lives of real people like Karen Blixen and others on the fancy of writers such as Rider Haggard and Ernest Hemingway—create an awareness abroad of the joys of Africa.

Inspired by such fascinating footage on television and the movies and intriguing images in magazines, hundreds of thousands of visitors set out to Africa every year with still and video camera in hand to hunt for pictures of their own. Even though theirs rarely rise to the same heights as the ones turned out by the professionals, they proudly show them off to their to their friends and hang onto them as memories of the journey. Quite often, the fun is not in the end result on film but in the process of tracking animals and experiencing the wilds of Africa.

© *Nigel Dennis (nigeldennis.com)*

Maxwell, in *Stalking Big Game with a Camera in Equatorial Africa,* sees the "chief aim of the camera hunter" as obtaining "a result that will be of value alike to the naturalist, to the sculptor, and to the painter."

This daunting task has been performed by a host of outstanding professional photographers who spend endless hours waiting patiently for nature to take its course and present them with that unique moment when everything comes together, resulting in unforgettable images.

These pictures are a sampling from the work of the renowned South African wildlife and nature photographer Nigel Dennis who has travelled and photographed in southern Africa for the past 15 years. His work has appeared in magazines, books, calendars and advertisements in over 25 countries and his pictures are sold both to commercial enterprises and individuals with an interest in wildlife. Nigel Dennis (*nigeldennis.com*) has produced twelve wildlife books,

Mamili & Mudumu National Park

Referred to as the mini-Okavango Delta, the flooded marshy terrain of Mamili and Mudumu is accessible only in four wheel drive vehicles. It contains some of Namibia's most abundant wildlife, including large numbers of water buffalo and hippo.

Namib-Naukluft National Park

Interaction between the hot Namibian desert and the cold Atlantic ocean along a 1200 mile (1,930 km) strip of land provides a breeding ground for lizards, snakes, beetles and other intriguing wildlife.

Skeleton Coast Park

Associated with famous shipwrecks and sailors who died in search of food and water and the topic of many an adventure novel, parts of the Skeleton Coast Park are inhabited by springbok, oryx, hyena, ostrich, the rare Desert Elephant, black rhino, lion and giraffe.

SOUTH AFRICA

Addo Elephant Park

This small park, near the harbor city of Port Elizabeth, was established to protect the huge herds of elephants that once roamed the area.

Augrabies Falls National Park

Features the Augrabies Falls, where the Orange River drops 56 meters into a solid granite ravine, and small mammals including klipspringer antelope, squirrel, rock dassie, as well as black rhino, eland, springbok and kudu.

Bontebok Park

Established to protect the bontebok from extinction and provides shelter for other antelope thriving on fynbos such as grey rhebok, grysbok, red hartebeest and Cape mountain zebra.

Drakensberg National Park

The Afrikaans word, Drakensberge, means Dragon Mountains. The peaks of this mountain range are covered with snow in winter and heavy clouds in summer. The lush slopes with a variety of African flora are home to grey rheebok, oribi, eland and a variety of large birds such as the lammergeyer.

Kalahari Gemsbok National Park

A semi-desert inhabited by the big-horned gemsbok, springbok and the Kalahari lion as well as a variety of birds, reptiles and small mammals.

Karoo National Park

A semidesert with 60 species of mammal, including the dassie and bat-eared fox.

Kruger National Park

Established in 1898 by President Paul Kruger, this well-known park is home to a wealth of wildlife, including 147 species of mammals, 500 types of bird and 33 amphibian types. The flora is equally diverse. There are 300 difference types of trees. All the big game can be found here including lion, leopard, cheetah, elephant, hippo, giraffe, rhino and buffalo.

Namibia

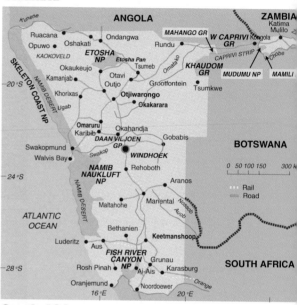

South Africa

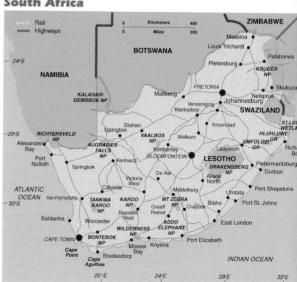

Mountain Zebra NP

This small park protects one of the rarest animals in the world, the mountain zebra, and is also home to other antelope.

St. Lucia Wetland

A lagoon separated from the sea by a chain of dunes with swamp forests and mangroves, inhabited by seabirds, crocodiles and hippo.

Tankwa Karoo Park

An arid region with natural springs and succulent vegetation, small mammals, birds and a variety of reptiles.

Blouwildebees migration   Courtesy: www.africantravelinc.com

Umfolozi & Hluhluwe GR

A hilly savannah landscape, covering 425 sq. miles (1,100 sq km), with large herds of rhinos as well as elephants, buffalo, lion, leopard, and giraffe.

Vaalbos National Park

Situated along the Vaal River in a former alluvial diamond digging area near Kimberley, this park's wildlife includes black rhino, white rhino, buffalo, eland, red hartebees and tsessebe .

TANZANIA

Arusha National Park

Contains a diverse population of herbivores, primates and predators, including black and white colobus monkey, baboon, elephant, giraffe, buffalo, hippo, leopard, hyena, waterbuck and other antelope.

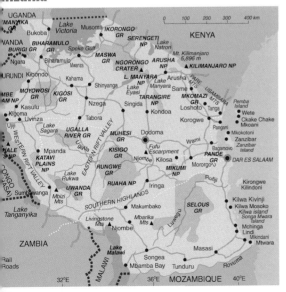

Gombe Stream National Park

Among Tanzania's smallest parks, with a total area of 20 sq. miles (52 sq.km), Gombe Stream is also one of the most popular. It is known for chimpanzees in their natural habitat. The park is also home to several species of monkey including the red colobus, red-tail and blue monkey, as well as grey duiker, bushbuck and bushpig and numerous bird species.

Katavi National Park

With an area of 870 sq. miles (2,253 sq km) Katavi is considered one the most natural sanctuaries in Africa, with minimal human interference. It has abundant wildlife, including big mammals.

Lake Manyara National Park

An area consisting of forest, woodland, grasslands, and swamps situated at the base of the Great Rift Valley escarpment with abundant wildlife including gazelle, impala, buffalo, wildebeest, tree climbing lions, hyena, baboon, giraffe, hippo, a great number of smaller mammals and 350 bird species.

Mikumi National Park

Its wildlife includes giraffe, zebra, buffalo, hartebeest, wildebees, elephant, wild dog and tree climbing lions, as well as smaller mammals and reptiles. The park is home to more than 300 species of birds.

Mkomazi Game Reserve

Together with Tsavo, Mkomazi forms part of one of East Africa's most important savannah ecosystems, characterized by the semi-arid climatic conditions of the Sahel. Most of the large mammal species found in Tsavo are also resident in Mkomazi or migrate here from the Kenyan game park. Wildlife includes lion, cheetah, elephant, giraffe, buffalo, zebra, impala, and leopard.

Mt. Kilimanjaro National Park

The area surrounding Africa's highest mountain has been a game reserve since 1921 and was desig-

115

Zebra   Courtesy: www.africantravelinc.com

Tarangire National Park

During the dry season from June to October this park has a high concentration of wildlife, crowding along the Tarangire River. It has more than 300 bird species.

Uwanda Game Reserve

Its dominant feature is Lake Rukwa, a shallow alkaline lake with an extensive floodplain that attracts large herds after the rains. Mammals include the rare puku and albino giraffe.

UGANDA

nated a national park in 1973. The rainforest is home to many species of animals and birds including leopard, rhino, elephant, buffalo. There are six different routes up the mountain with varying degrees of difficulty.

Mahale Mts. National Park

This remote park can only be reached by air or boat. It has chimpanzees still living in their natural habitat along with elephant, buffalo, antelope, giraffe, leopard and lion.

Ngorongoro Crater Conservation Area

This conservation area in the world's largest intact crater is a blend of landscapes and wildlife and contains Africa's main archaeological site. It teems with wildlife such as zebra, wildebeest, black rhino, antelope, elephants, giraffe, buffalo, lion, cheetah, and leopard. Thousands of flamingos are to be found in the shallows the lake area.

Ruaha National Park

This is Tanzania's second largest park, covering an area of over 5,019 sq. miles (13,000 sq km). It is the world's largest elephant sanctuary. Wildlife includes elephant, buffalo, giraffe, cheetah, lion, leopard, a wide variety of antelope. There are 465 bird species.

Selous Game Reserve

Africa's largest game reserve and one of the largest protected wildlife areas in the world. With more than 120,000 elephants, 160,000 buffaloes and about 2,000 rhinos, Selous also tops the world in big game. It has the greatest concentration of hippo, crocodile and wild dogs.

Serengeti National Park

Tanzania's most popular game reserve. Named after the Masai word *Serengeti*, which means *endless plain*, the park consists of flat, treeless plains and offers one of the highest concentrations of wildlife in Africa. Virtually every species in Africa can be found here but the park is known for its vast herds of wildebeest, zebra and antelope, and the *Serengeti lions*.

Bwindi National Park

Known for its mountain gorilla, it is also home to over 120 other species of mammals, including chimpanzee, black and white colobus, blue monkey, bushpig, duiker, leopard, jackal and elephant in the south east region of the park. There are over 350 bird species.

Kibale Forest National Park

Represents the vast diversity of wildlife and flora typical of a tropical rainforest. The park has the largest population of forest elephants in Uganda and is inhabited by the red-tailed money, blue monkey, olive baboon, chimpanzee, black, white and red colobus.

Kipedo Valley National Park

A mountainous region bordering Sudan with wildlife ranging from giraffe, ostrich, elephant, cheetah, and leopard, to kudu, zebra, and buffalo.

Lake Mburo National Park

Its terrain consists of savannah and includes four lakes that are frequented by large herds of elephants,

Uganda

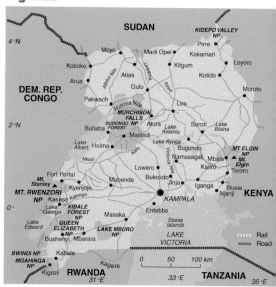

buffalo, leopard, hyena, hippo and a variety of antelope and birds.

Mgahinga National Park

Uganda's smallest park, covering an area 13 sq. miles (34 sq km) on the Congolese border, Mgahinga is one of the last remaining habitats of the mountain gorilla along the slopes of the Virunga Mountains. Three extinct volcanos rise within the park—Mt. Muhuvura, Mt. Gahinga and Mt. Sabinyo.

Mt Rwenzori National Park

The mist-shrouded, snow-capped Rwenzori mountain peaks have been referred to as the *Mountains of the Moon*. At the center of the range is Africa's third highest mountain, Mt. Stanley at 16,765 ft. (5,110 m). Wildlife includes elephant, genet, Vervet monkey, Rwenzori colobus, chimpanzee and duiker.

Mt Elgon National Park

The park at Mt. Elgon, an extinct volcano, offers a variety of vegetation and wildlife including, duiker, hyena, leopard, chimpanzee, buffalo and elephant, as well as numerous species of birdlife.

Murchison Falls National Park

This is the largest park in Uganda. It covers an area of over 1,483 sq. miles (3,840 sq km) and is known for its scenic beauty, spectacular falls and varied wildlife. The Nile river that divides the park into the northern and southern sections, attracts large numbers of game including elephant, giraffe, hippo, lion, leopard, buffalo, Nile crocodiles, monkeys, and over 450 species of birds.

Queen Elizabeth National Park

This game area covers almost 772 sq. miles (2,000 sq. km) and is known for hippo, as well as elephant, buffalo, Uganda kob, antelope, baboons and chimpanzees, and tree-climbing lions. There are more than 500 different bird species.

ZAMBIA

Kafue National Park

The third largest park in Africa with over 40 species of wildlife including elephant, buffalo, zebra, kudu, sable, roan antelope, lion, leopard, hyena, hippo and crocodile. It is home to the rare lechwe antelope and has more than 400 varieties of bird life.

Kasanka National Park

This small park on the edge of the vast wetlands of Lake Bangweulu is privately managed. Its mammals include elephant, hippo, warthog, bushpig, baboon, leopard, leopard, and the rare blue monkey.

Liuwa Plain National Park

The Luambimba and Luanginga rivers run through the region and are flanked by a grass-covered flood plain in this remote park. It has large herds of blouwildebees, buffalo, and zebra. It also has red lechwe, oribi, steenbok, duiker, tsessebe, roan, jackal, serval, wildcat, wild dog, and hyena. Massive flocks of birds migrate through the park.

Lochinvar National Park

A small park with a wide variety of game including large herds of the lechwe antelope, buffalo, zebra, blouwildebees, orbi, bushbuck, kudu, hippo and over 420 bird species.

Lower Zambezi National Park

A recently established area of over 1,544 sq. miles (4,000 sq. km) on the northern bank of the Zambezi river, downstream from the Victoria Falls. The river attracts wildlife including elephant, hippo, buffalo, zebra, lion, cheetah, leopard, various antelope species, and a large variety of birds.

Mosi-Oa-Tunya National Park

The country's smallest national park, with a name that means *the smoke that thunders*, it has as a centerpiece, the famous Victoria Falls, and offers game viewing along the riverbank. It is best known for its giraffe, but also contains sizeable numbers of sable, eland, wildebeest, lechwe, impala, warthog, baboon and monkey.

Nsumbu National Park

Situated in the remote north of Zambia, Nsumbu had to be restocked after severe poaching drastically reduced its animal population. Once it again offers a diverse range of wildlife including large herds of elephant, bushbuck, warthog, puku, roan antelope, sable, eland, hartebees, buffalo and zebra.

North Luangwa National Park

Primarily a woodland area known for its huge herds of buffalo as well as leopard, wildcat, el-

mbia

ephant, hyena, and blouwildebees as well as oribi, hartebeest, reedbuck and eland.

South Luangwa National Park
The park covers an area over 3,494 sq. miles (9,050 sq. km) and is considered one of the prime sanctuaries in Zambia. Its wildlife include elephant, hippo, buffalo, black rhino, zebra, blouwildebees, leopard, lion, and a wide variety of antelope as well as numerous bird species.

ZIMBABWE PARKS

Chimanimani National Park
A region for botanists, the area has orchids, hibiscus, lobelia, heather aloes and many species of meadow wildflowers. Animal life includes baboon, antelope, blue duiker, klipspringer and waterbuck as well as bird species such as Gurney's sugarbird and the malachite sunbird.

Chizarira National Park
Remote, wild, and rich in wildlife, with mammals including elephant, leopards, lions, warthog and numerous species of antelope. Chizarira consists of three regions—the Zambezi Escarpment, the Uplands and the Bush Valley.

Gonarezhou National Park
In Shona, the name of the park means *abode of elephants*, but poaching has unfortunately taken its toll. Apart from elephant, the area contains buffalo, hippopotamus, hartebeest, zebra, giraffe, nyala and roan antelope, and black rhinoceros. Among the rich birdlife are species such as the hooded vulture, fishing owl, and Mashona and yellow-bellied sunbird.

Hwange National Park
As Zimbabwe's largest national park, covering 5,598 sq. miles (14,500 sq. km), it has the country's biggest variety of animals, including elephant, giraffe, zebra, buffalo, hyena, lion, leopard, cheetah, and antelope. Situated at the ragged edge of the Kalahari Sands, it was once home to nomadic San people. Hwange National Park was named after an early Ndebele chief.

Lake Kariba
This man-made lake, covering an area of over 2,510 sq. miles (6,500 sq. km), does not only provide hydropower and irrigation but has become an important water playground and game region. Surrounding the lake is a conservation area, rich both in game and bird life. After the construction of the dam when the water started rising, a rescue mission—dubbed Operation Noah—managed to save thousands of animals trapped on islands, from drowning.

Mana Pools National Park
The name *Mana* means four to indicate the number of pools situated around the park's headquarters. Mana Pools Park is wild and remote and has been designated a World Heritage site. Its animal population includes elephant, buffalo, zebra, kudu, waterbuck, hippos and crocodile.

Matopos National Park
Matopos or Matobo offers a combination of history, scenery and wildlife. British empire builder Cecil John Rhodes was buried at the top of Malindidzimu Mountain, to which he referred to as *View of the World*. A million years ago the first hunting and gathering societies appeared around the Matobo Hills. Evidence of these early inhabitants is preserved in the form of rock paintings in caves, and under rock shelters and overhangs throughout the region.

Matusadona National Park
Situated on Lake Kariba's southern shore, two-thirds of this 579 sq. miles (1,500 km) park is only accessible on foot. It has herds of buffalo and elephants and varied birdlife. Matusadona is a melodic word for *constant dripping of dung,* in reference to the huge elephant population which took to these high grounds after they were rescued from Kariba's rising waters under Operation Noah.

Victoria Falls Park
Considered one of the world's most spectacular natural wonders, Victoria Falls is surrounded by a fair amount of wildlife including warthog, hippo, crocodile, antelope, elephants and buffalo.

Zambezi National Park
Game found within the park includes of hippo, elephant, giraffe, sable and other species of antelope, zebra, and buffalo.

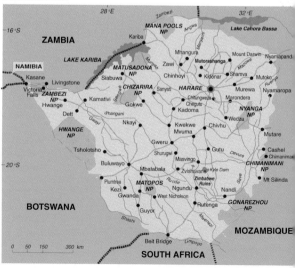

118

The Safari Experience

"Safari" in Kiswahili simply means "journey" but in the foreign mind it conjures up images of adventurous stalking of animals in the wilds of Africa. Safari-goers get a close look at Africa's diverse wildlife under protection of expert game rangers. With it comes an array of extras in the form of exotic accommodations, campfire entertainment and culinary treats. It is this total experience that draws foreigners by their tens of thousands to the southern and southeastern parts of the continent.

At first there is the burning desire to track down every member of the so-called big five—elephant, lion, buffalo, leopard and rhinocerus. But soon one discovers that there is much more to the experience than viewing and photographing animals. It is what some might call the Africa mystique. That is what gets to people and makes them come back again and again.

Some safari lovers have gone one step further. They have become facilitators in the lion kingdom and on elephant estates. There were the William Holdens of yesteryear and there are the Richard Bransons of today. Not all of them are household names but everyone has a the same purpose: having fun making money, preserving the environment, providing jobs and income for underdeveloped regions, and giving immense pleasure to ecotourists.

My most recent destination was Impalila, a small 18 sq. km (7 sq. mile) island right on the spot where Zambia, Zimbabwe, Botswana and Namibia meet. Squeezed between the Chobe and Zambezi rivers Impalila and its sister island, Susuwe, are two exotic estuaries in a riverene animal-rich area that also comprises the Kwando, Linyati and Okavango rivers—five in all.

In 1996, several enterprising and detail-driven ecologists constructed a lodge and eight chalets on the lush water edge at Impalila Island—managing a perfect blend between luxury and raw nature. There is boating on the Chobe River where elephants, hippos, crocodiles and a large variety of birds compete for attention. There is angling in the Zambezi where sharp-toothed tiger fish present a special challenge. *[My catch weighed 7.5 kilos or 16.5 lbs. but I have no trophy to show, only the picture. In line with their strict ecotourist practices, the lodge owners insist on 'catch and release').* There are walks on the island or climbing a two thousand year old baobab tree. And there is the calming glide on the Zambezi waters with a *makoro*—chiseled from the trunk of an indigenous tree. There are great culinary moments in unusual settings.

Life on the river banks at Impalila
www.islandsinafrica.com

The owners have not only provided a unique experience for safari-thirsty foreigners but created jobs and built a clinic and other facilities on the island. Working closely with the folks of the WWF they have managed to make conservationists out of the inhabitants. Ecotourism has made an island which was once in desperate need of aid, largely self-sufficient.

The creators of Impalila Lodge *(www.islandsinafrica.com)* have expanded onto Susuwe Island in northeast Namibia where they have chiselled out another environmentally friendly luxury hideout in lion, elephant, hippo and leopard country—and, once again, stimulated new growth and jobs at a unique destination for safari-goers in search of the unusual. —*Editor*

Trying to put the pieces together

There is nothing new about the concept. Towards the close of the 19th Century, Empire builder Cecil John Rhodes envisioned an Africa united under the British flag from Cape to Cairo. In the 1950s, newly-independent Ghana's first president, Kwame Nkrumah, dreamed of a Pan African union of free and independent countries. Both failed. But Nkrumah had the satisfaction of being a co-founder of the Organization of African Unity in 1963 with the expressed purpose to promote solidarity in the struggle to eradicate colonialism and apartheid. In the nineties, after seeing both these goals accomplished and its membership expanding from 31 to 53, the OAU seemed ready for new challenges. Foremost among those who felt that the OAU was ripe for retirement and replacement by something new was Col. Muammar Qadaffi of Libya, who pushed for the creation of United States of Africa. Despite initial skepticism, the required number of member states ratified the formation of a new African Union to replace the OAU at its Addis Ababa headquarters in May 2002. There is talk about the establishment of an European Union-type parliament, central bank and common currency. The skeptics believe this all to amount to little more than a name change despite the ambitious goals. Others, including the United States, question the plan on the basis of its originator.

In the meantime South African President, Thabo Mbeki, has been doing the rounds selling the Millennium African Recovery Program (MAP). Aimed at accomplishing the African Renaissance, which Mbeki has made a priority task, MAP was introduced with the endorsement of two other heavyweights on the continent—President Olusegun Obesanjo of Nigeria and President Abdelaziz Bouteflika of Algeria. The plan requires Africa's political leadership to make a firm commitment "to take ownership and responsibility for the sustainable economic development of the continent." It lays out a strategy needed for Africa "to break out of the mould of being producers and exporters of raw materials" and to become competitive in all other areas. "We march into the new era of the African century as Africans who have made the determination that this century will be a hundred years in which we cease to be victims of our circumstances but victors," Mbeki declared. "Through our own actions we will ensure that poverty gives way to prosperity." His message and his plan met with a good response abroad. MAP was endorsed by the President of the United States, the Prime Minister of Britain, the Chancellor of Germany and several other world leaders.

Chapter 5

Challenges of Africa

While African leaders might at times be justified in their complaint that the world press focuses too much on the negative and ignores the positive, there is no denying that the continent has more than its fair share of problems. The reed-thin refugees from famine and fierce factional fighting that appear on TV screens and feature in newsprint are real. So are the growing millions of HIV/AIDS infected Africans that make the malaria epidemics of the past look like an outbreak of the common cold. And so are the coups and wars that persist in places despite admirable efforts by the new leadership intent on responsible and transparent market-friendly governance. Africa is carrying a heavy debt burden and corruption still prevails in parts. As elsewhere in the world the outlook in Africa can described in terms of partly cloudy or partly sunny—depending on individual preference.

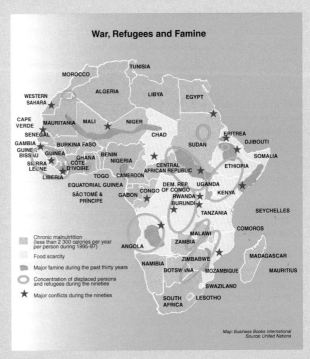

War, Refugees and Famine

Chronic malnutrition
(less than 2 300 calories per year
per person during 1995-97)

Food scarcity

Major famine during the past thirty years

Concentration of displaced persons
and refugees during the nineties

Major conflicts during the nineties

Map: Business Books International
Source: United Nations

Wars & Refugees

According to the United Nations more than 30 wars have been fought in Africa since 1970, most of them internal struggles. In 1996, the worst single year, 14 of the continent's 53 countries were affected by armed conflict, accounting for more than half of all war-related deaths worldwide and resulting in more than 8 million refugees, returnees and displaced persons. Deaths as the result of a 16-year civil war in the Sudan are estimated at 2 million while 500,000 have died in Angola over the past 25-years and a million in Rwanda over a six year period. While Africa as a whole has made significant economic and political strides in recent years, substantial portions continue to be devastated by armed conflict and unrest. Almost all of these conflicts involve power struggles within countries. Wars between states are rare.

According to the UN High Commissioner for Refugees (UNHCR) there were 20 million refugees and 25 million internally displaced people throughout the world in the mid-nineties. The UNHCR provided the following detailed breakdown of refugees and internally displaced persons in different parts of Africa at the end of December 1999. While there are no precise statistics, the UNHCR believes that women and children constitute the majority of these refugee and displaced populations:

WESTERN SAHARA CONFLICT
Algeria: 165,000 refugees tha crossed over from Western Sahara.

CIVIL WAR IN LIBERIA AND UNREST IN SIERRA LEONE
1,976,680 refugees
Sierra Leone: 10,000 refugees from Liberia and 670,000 of its own citizens displaced in the interior.
Guinea: 411,500 refugees from Liberia and Sierra Leone.
Ghana: 12,600 refugees from Liberia.
Côte d'Ivoire: 119,200 refugees from Sierra Leone and Liberia.
Liberia: 103,00 refugees from Sierra Leone and 251,000 displaced citizens.

ANGOLAN WAR
312,200 refugees
Zambia: 149,800 Angolan refugees.
Dem. Rep. of the Congo: 137,000 Angolan refugees.
Namibia: 2,500 refugees from Angola.
France/Brazil: 2,900 Angolan refugees.

CONFLICT IN THE GREAT LAKES REGION
1,700,660 refugees
Rwanda: 32,300 refugees from Congo (Kinshasa) and 625,000 displaced persons in the interior;
Burundi: 23,000 refugees from the Congo (Kinshasa) and 100,00 displaced in the interior.
Tanzania: 532,100 refugees from Burundi and the Congo (Kinshasa).
Congo (Kinshasa): 55,000 refugees from Rwanda and Burundi.

WARS IN THE HORN OF AFRICA
1,465,990 refugees
Sudan: 342,300 refugees from Eritrea.
Uganda: 189,800 refugees from Sudan.
Ethiopia: 254,000 refugees from Somalia and Sudan.
Yemen: 57,400 refugees from Somalia.
Congo (Kinshasa): 31,200 refugees from Sudan.
Kenya: 212,900 refugees from Somalia and Sundan.
Somalia: 155,240 refugees—some returned to Somalia but remain under UNHCR protection.

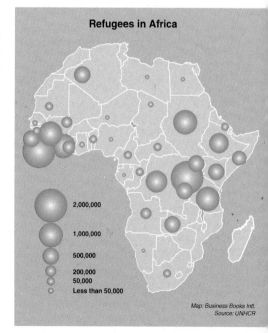

Refugees in Africa

2,000,000
1,000,000
500,000
200,000
50,000
Less than 50,000

Map: Business Books Intl.
Source: UNHCR

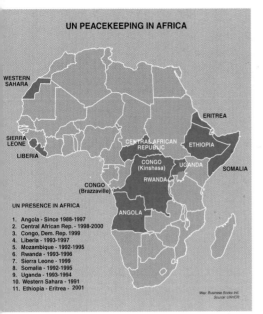

UN PEACEKEEPING IN AFRICA

WESTERN SAHARA

ERITREA

SIERRA LEONE

LIBERIA

CENTRAL AFRICAN REPUBLIC

ETHIOPIA

CONGO (Kinshasa)

UGANDA

SOMALIA

CONGO (Brazzaville)

RWANDA

ANGOLA

UN PRESENCE IN AFRICA

1. Angola - Since 1988-1997
2. Central African Rep. - 1998-2000
3. Congo, Dem. Rep. 1999
4. Liberia - 1993-1997
5. Mozambique - 1992-1995
6. Rwanda - 1993-1996
7. Sierra Leone - 1999
8. Somalia - 1992-1995
9. Uganda - 1993-1994
10. Western Sahara - 1991
11. Ethiopia - Eritrea - 2001

Map: Business Books Intl.
Source: UNHCR

Causes

The legacy left by the Berlin Conference in 1885 when Africa was partitioned by European colonial powers without any regard for populations is undoubtedly a contributing factor. Some states accomplished a remarkable degree of peace and national unity among diverse peoples within their arbitrary borders. Others, however, are having a hard time to cope not only with internal divisions but attempts from people divided by these artificial borders to reunite with their kinsmen.

While ethnic wars continue to plague the continent and account for most casualties, other reasons advanced are greed, grievance against leadership, and desperation born out of poverty and hunger. One cynical view is that rebellion and war might in some instances be the only job opportunity. The warlords and the international arms merchants who gain handsomely from these small but devastating wars-for-profit have little interest in stopping the conflict. According UN Secretary General Kofi Annan in a special report on the causes of war in Africa, Liberia was a prime example where the control of diamonds, timber and other raw materials are major objectives, and in Sierra Leone the object was as much the plunder of natural resources and looting of Central Bank reserves as it was political control.

UN Peacekeeping

Despite criticism that the United Nations has been derelict in its duty in Africa, the world body has deployed more of its peacekeeping operations in Africa than in any other region. Of the 32 operations launched by the UN from 1989 until 1998, 13 were in Africa. However, since the debacle in Somalia the international community has been reluctant to get involved in Africa. There are moves afoot to have Africa's leading nations develop a peacekeeping capability of their own, involving offers of training and equipment from Britain, France and the United States.

Following are significant recent UN peacekeeping presences in Africa:

United Nations Angola
Verification Mission (UNAVEM III)
Successor to original UNAVEM and UNAVEM II, established on 20 December 1988, and renewed for third time in February 1995 to assist the parties in restoring peace and achieving national reconciliation in Angola on the basis of the Lusaka Protocol. Members: Bangladesh, Brazil, Bulgaria, Egypt, Fiji, Guinea-Bissau, Hungary, India, Jordan, Mongolia, Mali, Morocco, Netherlands, Nigeria, Portugal, Sweden, Tanzania, Uruguay, Zambia, Zimbabwe. Disbanded on 30 June 1997.

United Nations Assistance
Mission for Rwanda (UNAMIR)
Established in October 1993, to support and provide safe conditions for displaced persons through human rights monitors, and to assist in training a new national police force. Members: Argentina, Australia, Austria, Bangladesh, Canada, Chad, Republic of the Congo, Djibouti, Fiji, Germany, Ghana, Guinea, Guinea-Bissau, India, Jordan, Malawi, Mali, Niger, Nigeria, Pakistan, Russia, Senegal, Switzerland, Tunisia, Uruguay, Zambia, Zimbabwe. Terminated 8 March 1996.

United Nations Mission
for the Referendum in Western
Sahara (MINURSO)
Established in April 1991, to supervise a cease-fire and conduct a referendum in Western Sahara. Members: Argentina, Austria, Bangladesh, Canada, China, Egypt, El Salvador, France, Ghana, Greece, Guinea, Honduras, India, Ireland, Italy, Kenya, South Korea, Malaysia, Nigeria, Norway, Pakistan, Poland, Portugal, Russia, Sweden, Togo, US, Uruguay, Venezuela.

United Nations Mission in the
Central African Republic (MINURCA)
Established in April 1998 to provide security in its capital while the government implements the necessary reforms to provide for its own security by training civilian police. Members: Benin, Burkina Faso,

123

Cameroon Canada, Chad, Côte d'Ivoire, Egypt, France, Gabon, Mali, Portugal, Senegal, Togo, Tunisia. Disbanded on 15 February 2000.

United Nations Mission in Sierra Leone (UNAMSIL)

Established in October 1999 to cooperate with the Government of Sierra Leone and the other parties and implement the peace agreement; to monitor the military and security situation, to disarm and demobilize combatants and members of the Civil Defense Forces (CFD); and to assist in promoting respect for international humanitarian law. Bangladesh, Bolivia, Canada, Croatia, Czech Republic, Denmark, Egypt, France, The Gambia, Ghana, India, Indonesia, Jordan, Kenya, Kyrgyzstan, Malaysia, Namibia, Nepal, NZ, Nigeria, Norway, Pakistan, Russia, Slovakia, Sweden, Thailand, Tanzania, UK, Uruguay, Zambia.

United Nations Observer Mission in Liberia (UNOMIL)

Established in September 1993, to assist in the implementation of the peace agreement. Members: Bangladesh, Egypt, India, Kenya, Malaysia, Pakistan. Disbanded in September 1997.

United Nations Observer Mission Uganda-Rwanda(UNOMUR)

Established 1993 for six months to monitor the Uganda/Rwanda border and verify that no military assistance reaches Rwanda across the border. Members: Bangladesh, Botswana, Brazil, Hungary, Netherlands, Senegal, Slovakia, Zimbabwe. Replaced by UNAMIR.

United Nations Operation in Mozambique (UNOMOZ)

Established in December 1992 to supervise the cease-fire between the government and Renamo. Members: Argentina, Austria, Bangladesh, Botswana, Brazil, Canada, Cape Verde, China, Czech Republic, Egypt, Guinea-Bissau, Hungary, India, Ireland, Italy, Japan, Jordan, Malaysia, Netherlands, Norway, Portugal, Russia, Spain, Sweden, US, Uruguay, Zambia. Shut down its operations in January 1995.

United Nations Operation in Somalia (UNOSOM)

Established in April 1992 to facilitate an immediate cessation of hostilities, to maintain a cease-fire, promote a political settlement, and to provide urgent humanitarian assistance. Members: Australia, Bangladesh, Botswana, Canada, Egypt, India, Ireland, Malaysia, Nepal, New Zealand, Nigeria, Pakistan, Romania, Zimbabwe. UN peacekeepers left Somalia on 1 March 1995, but some UN personnel remain in Somalia engaged in humanitarian work.

United Nations Organization Mission in the Democratic Republic of the Congo (MONUC)

Established in November 1999 to establish contacts with the signatories to the cease-fire agreement and to plan for the observation of the cease-fire and dis-

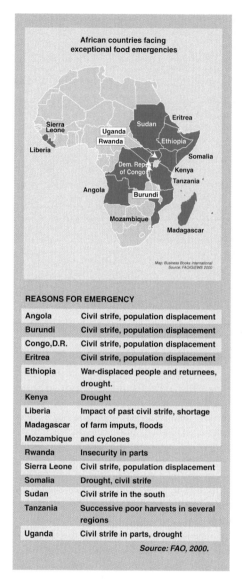

African countries facing exceptional food emergencies

Map: Business Books International
Source: FAO/GIEWS 2000

REASONS FOR EMERGENCY

Angola	Civil strife, population displacement
Burundi	Civil strife, population displacement
Congo,D.R.	Civil strife, population displacement
Eritrea	Civil strife, population displacement
Ethiopia	War-displaced people and returnees, drought.
Kenya	Drought
Liberia	Impact of past civil strife, shortage
Madagascar	of farm imputs, floods
Mozambique	and cyclones
Rwanda	Insecurity in parts
Sierra Leone	Civil strife, population displacement
Somalia	Drought, civil strife
Sudan	Civil strife in the south
Tanzania	Successive poor harvests in several regions
Uganda	Civil strife in parts, drought

Source: FAO, 2000.

engagement of forces. Members: Algeria, Bangladesh, Benin, Bolivia, Canada, Egypt, France, Ghana, India, Italy, Kenya, Libya, Mali, Nepal, Pakistan, Poland, Romania, Russia, South Africa, Sweden, UK, Tanzania, Uruguay, Zambia.

United Nations Mission in Ethiopia and Eritrea (UNMEE)

Established after Ethiopia and Eritrea signed a cease fire in December 2000 to guard a buffer zone between the two armies. Representing 71 countries, UN personnel are being deployed at key points along the 620 mile (1,000 km) frontier. Their task is to keep the peace until the border dispute is finally resolved. An unique mission insofar as having the United Nations keep the troops of sovereign nations apart.

Famine in Africa

Famine is not a problem peculiar to Africa. In 1958, between 20 and 30 million Chinese died in the worst famine of the twentieth century. Famine and malnutrition, however, present major challenges in Africa with its large expanse of arid land. Drought, conflict, natural disasters, overpopulation, overgrazing and inadequate farming methods have all been identified as contributing factors to recurring famine in Africa. Famine is the result of both warfare and weather.

The Brussels-based Center for Research on Epidemiology of Disasters (CRED) put the number of people affected by drought and famine in Africa since 1960 at over 245 million with nearly 2 million dying as a direct result. At the end of the nineties 36 African countries were affected by drought. Sometimes prolonged and extreme droughts are followed by equally extreme flood events, as witnessed in Mozambique in recent times. Roughly 2 billion hectares or 65 percent of Africa's total land area, inhabited by more than half of the continent's total population, is arid land—one third of it hyper-arid and the rest consisting of arid, semi-arid and dry land. Nineteen

African countries are among 25 in the world identified as having the highest percentage of their population without access to drinking water. Precipitation ranges from almost zero over the Horn of Africa and the Namibian Desert to more than 158 inches (4,000 mm) in the equatorial region but most of Africa's semi-arid landmass depends on between 8 and 16 inches (200-800 mm) per year. Due to inadequate infrastructure, only 4% of an estimated 5.2 trillion cubic yards (4 trillion cubic m) of Africa's renewable water is exploited. There is a lack of regional cooperation between countries in the development and exploitation of water resources offered by the Nile, Zambezi, Volta, and Niger rivers and Lake Victoria.

FOOD AID IN 1999	
Food Aid Recipients	**Mill.Tons**
Sub-Saharan Africa	2.8
Asia	4.9
North Africa & Middle East	0.5
Latin America & Caribbean	1.0
Europe and CIS	5.3

Source: World Food Program

Vegetation and soil degradation as a result of overgrazing, deforestation, and overcultivation, coupled with inappropriate agricultural technology, have also been identified as major problems. According to the World Bank about 90 percent of Africa's soils are deficient in phosphorus and low in organic matter. There is low water infiltration and retention due to surface crusting.

Between 1980 and 1990 Africa's rain forests shrunk from 569 million to 530 million hectares—averaging an annual deforestation rate of 0.7 percent. Commercial logging, clearance for agricultural reasons and wood fuel are all contributing to the problem. In Sub-Saharan Africa, 70 percent of the total consumed and 90 percent of household energy are derived from wood fuel. The average African family uses an estimated 7 metric tons of wood per year.

There is the fear that unless properly developed and managed on a regional basis, Africa's available water resources might trigger conflicts at local, national and regional levels as the demand increases. The prevention of river or water wars are as much a consideration for developers in Africa and abroad as the fight against famine.

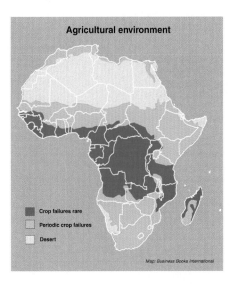

Agricultural environment

Crop failures rare

Periodic crop failures

Desert

Map: Business Books International

125

Tropical diseases

HIV/AIDS, TB and malaria are the leading killer diseases in developing regions, including Africa. Between them these three affect 300 million people and each year cause some 5 million deaths worlwide. Apart from human suffering the affected countries pay a heavy economic toll. Some experts claim that Africa would have been $100 billion better off today if malaria had been eliminated years ago. Others claim that any African nation with an HIV infection rate of more than 20% could expect a GDP decline of 1% per year.

With the public focus on HIV/AIDS not only malaria, but also a host of other deadly and costly tropics-related diseases have been largely ignored in recent years. Africans seem to be less prone to suffer from heart disease and cancer but they are exposed to a number of deadly and crippling tropical and subtropical diseases.

Malaria

While malaria is endemic in 101 countries and regions, Africa is most seriously affected. More than 90 percent of all malaria cases are on the African continent. Many millions on the African continent have this debilitating disease, transmitted by the *Anopheles* mosquito. Malaria is by far the world's most important tropical parasitic disease. It kills more people than any other communicable disease with the exception of tuberculosis. Deaths as a result of malaria are estimated at over 1 million per year, mostly among African youth. The disease also exacts an enormous toll in medical costs and in labor days.

The geographical area affected by malaria has shrunk considerably over the past fifty years but control is becoming more difficult and gains

are being eroded by the emergence of multi-drug resistant strains of the parasite and increased international travel. UN estimates in 1997 put the direct and indirect cost of malaria in sub-Saharan Africa at more than $2 billion. According to UNICEF, the average cost for each nation in Africa to implement malaria control programs is estimated to be at least $300,000 a year. This amounts to about six US cents ($.06) per person for a country of 5 million people.

Mapping Malaria Risk in Africa (MARA) in conjunction with *Atlas du Risque de la Malaria en Afrique (ARMA)* undertook extensive studies on the incidence of malaria across the African continent. The map below is based on MARA/ARMA data in which endemic regions are defined as "areas with significant annual transmission, be it seasonal or perennial" and epidemic regions as "areas prone to distinct inter-annual variation, in some years with no transmission taking place at all."

The *Multilateral Initiative on Malaria (MIM)* was launched in Dakar in January 1997, when a number of institutions (from both the public and private sectors) joined forces with the World Bank, WHO and UNDP to promote malaria research in Africa.

Malaria Risk in Africa

Legend:
- No population
- No malaria
- Epidemic malaria
- Endemic malaria
- Countries excluded

Map: Business Books International
Source: MARA/ARMA

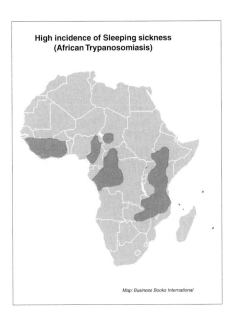

High incidence of Sleeping sickness (African Trypanosomiasis)

Map: Business Books International

Sleeping sickness

Sleeping sickness *(African trypanosomiasis)* was first identified at the beginning of the twentieth century when an epidemic left half a million dead. The disease is caused by *trypanosomes* or *protozoan* parasites transmitted to humans through the bite of the *Glossina* tsetse fly. Through persistent research and with new tools and improved field strategies, the endemic disease was slowly brought under control but not eradicated. When a person becomes infected, the *trypanosome* multiplies in the blood and lymph glands, crossing the blood-brain barrier to invade the central nervous system, where it provokes major neurological disorders. Without treatment, the disease is fatal. Sleeping sickness is a daily threat to more than 60 million men, women and children in 36 countries of sub-Saharan Africa. With an estimated 300,000 to 500,000 people infected the disease has a major impact on the labor force. In parts of Angola, Democratic Republic of Congo or Sudan an infection rate of more than 20% has been reported.

Ebola

Originating in the jungles of Africa and Asia, Ebola Haemorrhagic Fever (EHF)is one of the most virulent viral diseases known to humankind, causing death in 50% to 90% of all reported cases. The Ebola virus is transmitted by direct contact with the blood, secretions, and organs or semen of infected persons. Transmission of the Ebola virus has also occurred by handling sick or dead infected chimpanzees, as was documented in Côte d'Ivoire and Gabon. Health care workers have frequently been infected while attending patients. In the 1976 epidemic in Zaire, every person who contracted Ebola through contaminated syringes and needles, died. No specific treatment or vaccine exists. The Ebola virus was first identified in 1976 after significant epidemics in northern Zaire (Democratic Republic of Congo) and Nzara, in southern Sudan. Ebola-related filoviruses were also isolated from *cynomolgus* monkeys (*Macacca fascicularis*), imported into the United States from the Philippines in 1989. At the end of the nineties 1 100 Ebola virus cases, that resulted in over 800 deaths, have been documented.

Yellow fever

During the past four centuries there have been large epidemics of yellow fever and even though it is largely associated with the tropics of Africa and the Americas, it has, until the beginning of the 20th Century, occurred in Europe and North America. The "yellow" in the name denotes jaundice that affects some patients. Although a safe and effective vaccine has been available for 60 years, the virus is still constantly present with low levels of infection (i.e. endemic) in the African and South American tropical areas. Thirty-three countries, within a band from 15°N to 10°S of the equator with a combined population of 468 million, are at risk in Africa. The virus is spread among animals and humans by mosquitos and to their offspring through infected eggs. There is no specific treatment for yellow fever and vaccination is the single most important measure for preventing yellow fever.

Dengue

Dengue is another mosquito-borne infection found in tropical and sub-tropical regions around the world which became a major international public health concern in recent years. The disease is now endemic in more than 100 countries in Africa, the Americas, the Eastern Mediterranean, South-East Asia and the Western Pacific. South-East Asia and the Western Pacific are most seriously affected. WHO estimates there may be as many as 50 million cases of dengue infection worldwide every year. The Dengue virus is transmitted to humans by infected female *Aedes* mosquitoes. It causes a flu-like illness, which affects

127

HIV/AIDS:
Stark statistics

✓ In the past decade, 12 million people in Sub-Saharan Africa have died of AIDS—one-quarter of them children—and each day AIDS buries another 5,500 men, women and children.

✓ In 1998, AIDS was the largest killer and accounted for 1.8 million deaths in sub-Saharan Africa, nearly double the 1 million deaths from malaria, and eight times the 209,000 deaths from tuberculosis.

✓ By 2005, the daily death toll is expected reach 13,000, with nearly 5 million HIV/AIDS deaths in that year alone.

✓ In Sub-Saharan Africa, more than 22 million adults and 1 million children are currently living with HIV. Every day, 11,000 additional people are infected— one every 8 seconds.

✓ Sub-Saharan Africa continues to bear the brunt of HIV and AIDS, with close to 70% of the world's total HIV-positive people. Most will die in the next 10 years, joining the 13.7 million Africans already claimed by the epidemic.

✓ Life expectancy at birth in southern Africa, which rose from 44 years in the early 1950s to 59 in the early 1990s, is set to drop to just 45 between 2005 and 2010 because of AIDS.

These statements are based on the information currently available from UNAIDS and WHO and is provisional. These agencies, together with experts from national AIDS programs and research institutions, keep these estimates under constant review with a view to updating them as improved knowledge about the epidemic becomes available and as advances are made in the methods for compiling more accurate estimates.

infants, young children and adults, but rarely causes death. Vaccine development for dengue and DHF is difficult because any of four different viruses may cause the disease, and at present the only method of controlling or preventing Dengue and DHF is to combat the vector mosquitoes.

River blindness

Although also present in the Arabian Peninsula and the Americas, river blindness *(Onchocerciasis)* is most closely associated with Africa where it has become a public health problem and constitutes a serious obstacle to socio-economic development. Of the 36 countries where the disease is endemic, 30 are in Sub-Saharan Africa and six are in the Americas. Close to 99 percent of the 18 million people infected are in Africa. Among those infected 6.5 million suffer from severe itching or dermatitis and 270,000 are blind. *Onchocerciasis* is caused by *Onchocerca volvulus*, a parasitic worm that lives in the human body for up to 14 years. Each adult female worm, thin but more than 1/2 meter in length, produces millions of *microfilariae* (microscopic larvae) carried from one human to another by the blackfly (*Simulium damnosum*). An *Onchocerciasis* Control Programme (OCP), sponsored by the UNDP, WHO, World Bank and FAO, was launched in Africa in the seventies, is estimated to have prevented almost 300,000 cases of blindness in 11 countries.

Bilharziasis

Among human parasitic diseases, *schistosomiasis* (sometimes called *bilharziasis*) is second only to malaria as a public health threat in the world's tropical and subtropical areas. The disease is endemic in 74 developing countries, infecting more than 200 million people in rural agricultural and peri-urban areas. *Schistosomes* enter the body through contact with infested surface water, mainly among people engaged in agriculture and fishing. With the rise in "off-track" travel more tourists are prone to contract the disease by exposing themselves to infected waters. Three drugs—*praziquantel,oxamniquine and metrifonate*—are included in the WHO list of essential ways of treating the disease.

HIV/Aids

HIV/AIDS (human immunodeficiency virus/acquired immune deficiency syndrome) is now the number one killer in Africa and among the greatest threats to the continent's social and economic development. The epidemic has spread beyond all predictions and threatens the future of the continent, where it has already personally affected one quarter of all Africans. In the hard-hit countries, where up to a quarter of all adults are infected, AIDS is wiping out development gains achieved over many decades.

Africa continues to dwarf the rest of the world on the HIV/AIDS charts. According to UNAIDS and WHO estimates, in 1998 seven out of ten people who are newly infected with the HIV virus lived in sub-Saharan Africa—and of all AIDS-related deaths since the epidemic started,

83% were in the region. While sub-Saharan Africa accounts for only one-tenth of the global population, it currently carries the burden of more than 80% of AIDS deaths worldwide. In Botswana, Namibia, Swaziland and Zimbabwe, estimates show that more than one person in five between the ages of 15 and 49 is living with HIV or AIDS. In South Africa, Malawi, Mozambique, Rwanda

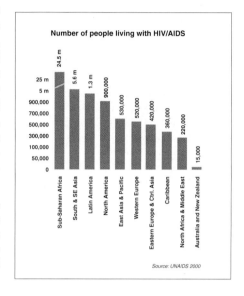

and Zambia infection among adults ranges from one in seven to one in nine. In Central African Republic, Côte d'Ivoire, Djibouti and Kenya, at least one out of every ten adults is HIV-infected.

HIV/AIDS in Sub-Saharan Africa, notes the United Nations, is the "worst infectious disease catastrophe since the bubonic plague." Deaths due to AIDS in the region, the UN predicts, will soon surpass the 20 million people in Europe who perished during the plague of 1347 and the more than 20 million people worldwide who died in the influenza epidemic of 1917. Over the next decade, AIDS is expected to kill more people in Sub-Saharan Africa than the total number of lives lost in all wars during the 20th Century.

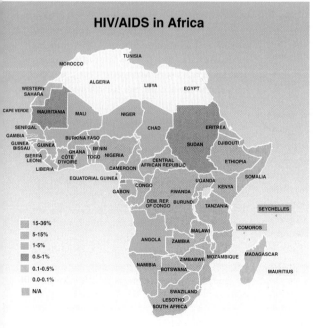

HIV/AIDS in Africa

Map: Business Books International
Source: UNAids

Development crisis

Given the scale of the epidemic, it is no longer just a public health problem. It is a development crisis. And it has been in the making for at least 10 years. HIV/AIDS has already reversed 30 years of hard-won social progress in some countries. A has impacted on every level from the micro- to the macroeconomic.

Companies have begun to realize that HIV/AIDS poses a genuine threat to the workforce and the marketplace. Alarming new costs are showing up on balance sheets. This is especially the case in Africa, where the private sector is feeling the cumulative impact of a severe, long-standing and still-emerging epidemic. Many businesses have started prevention programs at the workplace to try to protect their investment in human capital. They provide information and condoms to workers, often through peer education programmes. Forward-thinking companies in high HIV/AIDS-prone countries, however, are looking beyond prevention to the inevitable dent that the disease will make in their workforce and their profits.

Employee turnover related to the disease increases training and recruitment costs. The effect of HIV/AIDS on the macro-level is hard to judge but expert studies point to a likely loss of real GDP growth in some African countries in the order of one to two percent. The Southern Africa AIDS Information Dissemination Service estimates that over the next 20 years HIV/AIDS might reduce the some economies in sub-Saharan Africa by a fourth.

The disease undermines agricultural systems and threatens the food security of rural families. The UN Food and Agriculture Administration (FAO) has estimated that in the 25 most-affected African countries, AIDS has killed seven million agricultural workers since 1985. Rural communities bear a higher burden of the cost of the disease as urban dwellers and migrant laborers return to their village of origin when they fall ill. Household expenditures rise to meet medical bills and funeral expenses.

Increased cost

In Africa, the disease attacks educated urban professionals—the backbone of economic expansion—first. The loss of these people can rob the continent of much of its potential. The damage is immeasurable, economists say, because it appears in ways that cannot be seen—businesses that will never be founded, ideas that will never be pitched, university departments that will never be created. In eastern and southern Africa, where the epidemic is worst, the economically strongest countries—South Africa, Botswana, Zimbabwe, Kenya, Uganda and Zambia—have infection rates of between 10 percent and 25 percent. Virtually all of those infected will die within 10 years. West Africa's strongest economies such as Nigeria, Ghana and the Ivory Coast, have lower, but still alarming, infection rates.

Increased benefits and training costs, and the disruption of regular production due to sick and bereavement leave, are seriously affecting both the private and public sectors. A study in South Africa found that at current levels of benefits per employee, these costs might rise from 7% of salaries and wages in 1995 to 19% by 2005 as a result of HIV/AIDS. A study carried out in a number of African countries by American researchers, Matthew Roberts and Bill Rau for AIDSCAP, in Arlington, Virginia, found that absenteeism accounted for 52 percent of the additional labor costs as a result of HIV/AIDS. [The chart on the opposite page is based on their extensive study, *African Workplace Profiles: Private Sector AIDS Policy*].

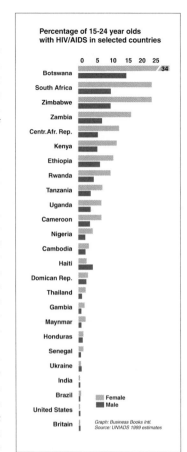

Percentage of 15-24 year olds with HIV/AIDS in selected countries

Graph: Business Books Intl.
Source: UNIADS 1999 estimates

Projects

Between 1986 and early 1999, the World Bank committed over US$750 million for more than 75 HIV/AIDS projects worldwide. Most of the resources were provided on highly concessional terms through the International Development Association. Private corporations, too, are beginning to play a critical role in this battle by providing premises for HIV education, by giving protection and support to their employees, and by taking a lead within the wider community. Several multinational corporations have shown that HIV/AIDS need not be a deterrent to doing business on the continent and that there are ways and means to cope with the problem. In Nigeria, for example, the Chevron oil company has taken an imaginative and tenacious approach to HIV/AIDS prevention, working to protect the wider community as well as its own workforce. In South Africa, the electricity-generating company Eskom, which has over 37,000 employees, has made HIV/AIDS one of its strategic priorities. As a result, it can now guarantee benefits to employees with AIDS and their families. It has funded clinics that offer tests, immune-system monitoring, and medical support. In Zimbabwe, Rio Tinto has taken steps to protect its skilled workforce. It has formed AIDS action

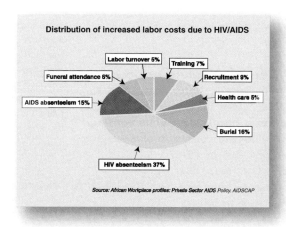

Distribution of increased labor costs due to HIV/AIDS

- Labor turnover 5%
- Training 7%
- Funeral attendance 6%
- Recruitment 9%
- AIDS absenteeism 15%
- Health care 5%
- Burial 16%
- HIV absenteeism 37%

Source: African Workplace profiles: Private Sector AIDS Policy. AIDSCAP

groups, led by volunteer employees, to act as counsellors and lead education campaigns among their colleagues. And it is providing condoms to the largely male staff in its mining camps, many of whom face long periods of separation from their wives. In South Africa Bristol-Myers Squibb and Merck & Co. have slashed the prices of their AIDS drugs and an Indian firm, Cipla Ltd. of Bombay, offered generic AIDS drugs to African nations at competitive prices. The battle against HIV/AIDS is continuing on both official and unofficial levels with increasing cooperation between the two. The Corporate Council on Africa has formed an HIV/AIDS task force to coordinate efforts among its influential membership and help devise a strategy for the future.

REGIONAL HIV/AIDS STATISTICS AND FEATURES - END 2000

	Adults & children living with HIV/AIDS	Adults & children newly infected with HIV	Adult prevalence rate[1]	% HIV positive women	Main mode(s) of transmission for those living with HIV/AIDS[2]
Sub-Saharan Africa	25.3 million	3.8 million	8.8%	55%	Hetero
North Africa & Middle East	400,000	80,000	0.2%	40%	Hetero, IDU
South & Southeast Asia	5.8 million	780,000	0.56%	35%	Hetero, IDU
East Asia & Pacific	640,000	130,000	0.07%	13%	IDU, Hetero, MSM
Latin America	1.4 million	150,000	0.5%	25%	MSM, IDU, Hetero
Caribbean	390,000	60,000	2.3%	35%	Hetero, MSM
Eastern Europe & Centr. Asia	700,000	250,000	0.35%	25%	IDU
Western Europe	540,000	30,000	0.24%	25%	MSM, IDU
North America	920,000	45,000	0.6%	20%	MSM, IDU, Hetero
Australia & New Zealand	15,000	500	0.13%	10%	MSM, IDU
TOTAL	36.1 million	5.3 million	1.1%	47%	

1. The proportion of adults (15 to 49 years of age) living with HIV/AIDS, using 2000 population numbers.
2. Hetero—heterosexual transmission; IDU—transmission through injecting drug use; MSM—homosexual transmission between men.

Source: WHO, UNAIDS—December 2000

Corruption

Recent scandals in Germany, France, Britain, Italy, Japan and the United States have shown that corruption is hardly a problem confined to developing countries or emerging markets. But in Africa, the poorest continent, the effect of corrupt practices is especially harmful. Corruption not only siphons off funds that could have been utilized for infrastructure and human development. It also inflates the cost of doing business and scares off foreign investors. Billions of dollars diverted into secret foreign bank accounts represent a significant share of the continent's stock of flight capital, totaling, according to the UN Economic Commission for Africa, around $148 billion. Economists estimate that in a few African countries bribes, sales "commissions" and the diversion of funds add between 10% and 20% to the cost of development projects.

The World Bank and the IMF have become actively engaged in the war on corruption in Africa and the rest of the world. They have developed plans to eliminate corruption from their own lending programs and to encourage governments to act against the malady. "Let's not mince words," World Bank President James Wolfensohn declared, "we need to deal with the cancer of corruption." No one believes that corruption, one of the world's oldest and most persistent sins, can be stamped out altogether in Africa or elsewhere. But serious efforts are needed in Africa to facilitate a business climate that is more conducive to foreign participation.

The Berlin-based Transparency International (TI) leads a number of NGOs and think-tanks intent on quantifying global corruption and pressuring UN agencies and governments to take remedial action. In its latest *Corruption Perceptions Index* (CPI) Transparency International ranks six African countries among the top fifty nations with the least corruption. At the same time 5 African countries occupied spots in the bottom ten of a total of 90 countries surveyed. (A perfect 10 indicates a country that is totally non-corrupt while a zero denotes a completely corrupt country). While TI's CPI focuses on officials in recipient countries, its Bribe Payers Index (BPI) concerns bribe paying governments and corporations seeking to win business and other favors abroad. It was discovered that in some industrialized countries governments not only turned a blind eye to corrupt practices in the foreign dealings of their nationals but encouraged bribery and pay-offs by making it tax deductible.

In 1999 the Organization for Economic Cooperation and Development (OECD) adopted its own Convention on Combating Bribery, based on the US Foreign Corrupt Practices Act. Most industrialized nations have signed on and several African states have pledged to take further constructive steps to combat corruption.

Corruption Perceptions Index		
Rank	Country	CPI
-1	Finland	10.0
0	Denmark	9.8
1	New Zealand	9.4
1	Sweden	9.4
3	Canada	9.2
4	Iceland	9.1
4	Norway	9.1
4	Singapore	9.1
7	Netherlands	8.9
8	United Kingdom	8.7
9	Luxembourg	8.6
9	Switzerland	8.6
11	Australia	8.3
12	USA	7.8
13	Austria	7.7
13	Hong Kong	7.7
15	Germany	7.6
16	Chile	7.4
17	Ireland	7.2
18	Spain	7.0
19	France	6.7
20	Israel	6.6
21	Japan	6.4
21	Portugal	6.4
23	Belgium	6.1
24	Botswana	6.0
25	Estonia	5.7
26	Slovenia	5.5
26	Taiwan	5.5
28	Costa Rica	5.4
28	Namibia	5.4
30	Hungary	5.2
30	Tunisia	5.2
32	South Africa	5.0
33	Greece	4.9
34	Malaysia	4.8
35	Mauritius	4.7
35	Morocco	4.7
37	Italy	4.6
37	Jordan	4.6
39	Peru	4.4
40	Czech Republic	4.3
41	Belarus	4.1
41	El Salvador	4.1
41	Lithuania	4.1
41	Malawi	4.1
41	Poland	4.1
46	South Korea	4.0
47	Brazil	3.9
48	Turkey	3.8

Source: Transparency Intl.

Debt burden

The $231 billion that Africa owes foreign creditors—amounting to $406 for every man, woman and child on the continent—represents a crippling burden. Africa carries 11% of the developing world's debt with only 5% of its income. In the past 17 years, Africa's total debt rose by 350%. In many African countries up to 40% of government revenue is being allocated to servicing foreign debt, to the detriment of health, education and other essential social services. Sub-Saharan Africa spends over twice as much on debt service as it does on basic health care. In the past decade total debt service has risen by 39%, from $10.9 billion to $15.2 billion.

Debt is not only an African problem and not all the continent's countries are affected equally severely. Still, 33 of the 41 countries identified by the World Bank as "Heavily Indebted Poor Countries" (HIPC) are in Africa and even some countries in North Africa (none of which has been labeled as an HIPC country) are spending almost one-fourth of their export earnings on interest and debt repayments. Development aid, which has been in steep decline in recent years, does not close the gap. For example, Sub-Saharan African countries are paying $1.51 on debt service for every $1 received in grant aid from foreign donors.

Causes

In the 1960s and 1970s, international lenders readily pushed a high volume of loans on many African states. Neither the lenders nor the borrowers anticipated these to balloon due to exchange rate fluctuation and interest hikes. Other factors contributing to the debt crisis in Africa include poor government economic management, deteriorating terms of trade, shrinking market shares for major exports, and the boom and bust cycles of the recent years.

HIPC Initiative

In 1996, the World Bank, the International Monetary Fund, and major creditor nations adopted the HIPC (Heavily Indebted Poor Countries) initiative that entitled 40 developing countries to assistance beyond mere rescheduling of debt. To qualify, debtor nations had to have a GNP per capita of US$695 or less in 1993, and a present value of debt to exports higher than 220%, or a present value of debt to GNP higher than 80%. The program envisages the cancellation of as much 80% of external debt—one third of which is owed to multilateral institutions. With the adoption of the Enhanced HIPC program in October 1999, the international community agreed to make the Initiative broader, deeper and faster by increasing the number of eligible countries, raising the amount of debt relief, and speeding up the process. The Enhanced HIPC initiative will be provided on top of

Debt reduction and Relief for 22 Decision Point Countries
Status at end February 2001

Debt reduction is measured by the common factor. This refers to the percentage by which each creditor needs to reduce its debt stock at the decision point to enable the country to reach its debt sustainability target. The calculation is based on net present value (NPV) information.
For Bolivia, Burkina Faso, Guyana, Mali, Mozambique and Uganda assistance under the original and enhanced frameworks is combined.
Chart: Business Books Intl.   Source: IMF, World Bank

AFRICA'S EXTERNAL DEBT STRUCTURE $ MILLION

| | BILATERAL | | | | MULTILATERAL | | | |
| | Concessional | | Nonconcessional | | Concessional | | Nonconcessional | |
	1980	1998	1980	1998	1980	1998	1980	1998
Algeria	1,255	2,892	1,956	12,132	14	385	270	4,005
Angola	..	2,527	..	1,011	..	212	..	67
Benin	82	429	31	106	84	904	20	28
Botswana	28	102	23	11	32	194	53	178
Burkina Faso	89	122	30	8	133	1,053	9	47
Burundi	49	157	1	0	55	891	5	30
Cameroon	663	3,724	142	2,506	210	835	222	652
Cape Verde	..	29	..	17	..	164	..	16
Central African Republic	17	138	28	48	42	613	12	15
Chad	97	95	34	78	75	778	0	37
Comoros	21	28	0	0	21	152	0	9
Congo, Democratic Rep. of	667	1,806	1,620	4,213	194	1,601	127	681
Congo, Republic of	355	1,643	132	1,169	49	243	69	382
Côte d'Ivoire	369	3,232	355	1,579	69	1,711	454	1,780
Djibouti	14	119	5	0	1	144	1	1
Egypt	6,230	21,300	3,767	1,253	1,885	2,167	741	2,028
Equatorial Guinea	30	56	13	47	2	88	1	10
Eritrea	..	68	..	2	..	72	..	5
Ethiopia	281	6,422	18	216	282	2,391	58	239
Gabon	103	916	173	2,238	10	32	30	522
Gambia, The	33	86	0	0	36	331	5	16
Ghana	636	1,275	119	157	139	3,345	140	218
Guinea	615	1,200	116	208	63	1,448	67	240
Guinea-Bissau	58	303	5	161	29	399	5	15
Kenya	414	1,539	159	516	270	2,584	364	415
Lesotho	4	83	2	24	40	401	0	98
Liberia	179	398	50	77	33	200	98	218
Libya	..	..	..	..	..	..	..	..
Madagascar	319	1,221	71	1,062	148	1,692	34	89
Malawi	111	284	112	16	147	1,900	72	90
Mali	451	1,218	6	37	163	1,545	9	28
Mauritania	420	1,008	38	189	106	835	18	161
Mauritius	39	294	37	27	25	60	53	201
Morocco	2,638	5,540	158	2,224	79	879	644	5,577
Mozambique	..	2,268	..	1,810	..	1,798	..	96
Namibia	..	..	..	..	..	..	..	..
Niger	42	238	70	247	112	930	30	36
Nigeria	401	919	21	12,677	38	663	533	3,419
Rwanda	51	155	1	4	91	959	0	0
São Tomé and Principe	9	70	4	2	11	166	0	1
Senegal	221	838	169	454	179	1,762	84	194
Seychelles	16	49	4	7	3	22	2	37
Sierra Leone	136	276	47	139	39	504	23	32
Somalia	400	808	9	302	147	723	13	18
South Africa	..	0	..	0	..	0	..	0
Sudan	1,361	2,865	1,298	2,750	368	1,839	266	212
Swaziland	69	74	34	0	17	69	45	79
Tanzania	2,388	2,480	88	581	305	3,049	261	93
Togo	155	253	210	250	90	775	26	24
Tunisia	1,311	2,076	218	1,440	75	421	357	3,123
Uganda	191	815	23	149	63	2,377	16	67
Zambia	778	1,617	314	1,348	19	2,031	374	211
Zimbabwe	15	961	83	238	0	532	3	1,183
SUB-SAHARAN AFRICA	12,374	45,208	5,695	36,680	3,936	45,015	3,601	12,188
NORTH AFRICA	11,435	31,809	6,098	17,048	2,053	3,852	2,013	14,733
ALL AFRICA	23,809	77,017	11,793	53,729	5,989	48,867	5,613	26,921

PRIVATE		SHORT-TERM		IMF	
1980	1998	1980	1998	1980	1998
13,545	9,054	2,325	186	0	2,011
..	5,696	..	1,710	0	0
118	4	73	86	16	94
8	24	4	7	0	0
20	4	35	59	15	112
8	1	12	20	36	20
1,014	659	278	1,398	59	156
..	11	..	6	0	0
48	33	25	60	24	18
54	17	12	23	14	64
0	0	1	12	0	3
1,462	899	329	3,565	373	423
652	814	247	834	22	34
5,091	4,330	1,059	1,576	65	644
5	0	6	15	0	9
2,070	957	4,027	4,260	411	0
7	15	7	79	16	11
..	0	..	5	..	0
49	350	57	626	79	107
955	125	228	478	15	113
24	0	23	15	16	10
131	838	131	716	105	334
159	30	80	293	35	127
36	1	5	76	1	15
1,286	834	640	858	254	197
11	55	8	8	6	24
156	199	81	694	89	317
..	..	..	..	..	..
346	41	244	230	87	58
192	20	116	32	80	102
36	0	24	188	39	187
131	22	65	265	62	110
165	1,327	47	573	102	0
4,505	6,155	778	116	457	0
..	1,770	..	365	0	207
..	..	..	..	..	..
432	72	159	63	16	76
4,376	6,061	3,553	6,575	0	0
8	1	26	50	14	56
0	0	0	12	0	0
461	33	219	273	140	293
0	31	59	42	0	0
111	7	53	108	59	191
28	35	47	591	18	158
..	13,268	..	11,444	0	0
854	2,055	598	6,349	431	772
24	0	15	28	6	0
339	263	1,770	900	171	268
415	0	120	52	33	95
1,429	2,621	136	1,040	0	129
244	74	63	135	89	398
726	141	586	329	447	1,188
594	619	90	768	0	407
20,778	40,779	11,195	42,593	3,033	7,396
21,549	18,788	7,266	5,602	868	2,140
42,327	59,567	18,461	48,195	3,901	9,536

Source: World Bank Africa Database 2001

traditional debt relief mechanisms such as the Paris Club debt rescheduling on the recently adopted Naples terms.

Two stages

Eligible countries qualify for debt relief in two stages. During the first stage, before reaching the so-called decision point—usually after three years—the debtor country needs to establish a satisfactory track record in terms of IMF and (International Development Agency (IDA) supported programs. During the second stage, after reaching the decision point, the country is required to implement a full-fledged poverty reduction strategy. During this stage, the IMF and IDA, the Paris Club creditors and others, are expected to grant interim relief. At the end of the second stage, when the floating completion point has been reached, the IMF and IDA will provide the remainder of the committed debt relief while Paris Club creditors will enter into a highly concessional stock-of-debt operation with the country involved. Other multilateral and bilateral creditors will be required to contribute to the debt relief on comparable terms.

Countries

The World Bank Group provided debt relief to Uganda and Mozambique in 1998 and 1999, respectively, under the original HIPC framework. At the end of 2000 the African Development Bank approved further debt relief under the Enhanced HIPC initiative to assist with poverty reduction in countries such as Benin, Burkina Faso and Senegal—increasing the number of countries receiving debt relief to 22 at a total cost of more than US$30 billion. While the World Bank and the IMF declared themselves satisfied with this process, criticism persists over the speed of its implementation and the sums involved. Few disagree, however, that the process has gained momentum during 2000.

Opinions

"Africa is one of the most exciting continents we are working in at the moment, and despite its complexities, we see it as one of the fastest growing regions that Microsoft is currently operating in. The Internet is the single most important tool that will open Africa up to the rest of the world. It is the future of communication worldwide and Africa is not as far behind as some people believe."

Bill Gates, CEO, Microsoft

"The prevailing misconception and negative images concerning Africa are responsible for many an excellent investment opportunity being overlooked by the investment community. Lurking behind the sensational headlines focused on bloody conflicts that have infected parts of Africa are thriving enclaves of peace, steady economic growth, and high returns on investment."

Milliken Institute

"We have almost 35 million citizens of African descent. Last year, the total US-African trade approached $30 billion, and America is Africa's largest single market. The United States is the leading foreign investor in Africa. Over 30,000 Africans are studying in the United States today. Our pasts, our presents and our futures are closely intertwined, and as America's 65th Secretary of State and her only African-American Secretary of State so far, I will enthusiastically engage with Africa on behalf of the American people."

Colin Powell, US Secretary of State

136

Chapter 6

Advice and Assistance

The old adage, Dark Continent, refuses to go away. It bespeaks the state of mind abroad whenever Africa is mentioned. Sadly, Africa still too often conjures up Hollywood images of Tarzan and other wild and adventurous tales. Even in otherwise well-informed business and academic circles there is frequently a disturbing lack of depth when it comes to discussing Africa. Some observers remain totally fixated on war, famine, and HIV/AIDS. Others are bent on going the opposite direction—ignoring all that is negative in an effort to counter the so-called Afropessimists with an overdose of optimism. Few strike a balance between the positive and the negative, breaking Africa up in   parts, as they should, before weighing the pit-   falls against the prospects.

This is the analysis needed by foreign governments to shape sound strategy and for corporations to profit from the prospects. In recent years, the Internet has greatly contributed to spreading information about Africa while a number of non-governmental organizations promote an awareness of the complex issues. Businesses are also able to rely on the reports of rating agencies and specialized consultants in the capitals of the industrial world. The real Africa is slowly emerging.

Advice

There was a time when the outside world could blame its ignorance about the real Africa on a lack of solid sources. That is no longer the case. Students, investors, entrepreneurs and travelers looking for data and detail on all aspects of the continent have a wealth of information at their disposal. Those with access to the Internet would conceivably resort to their favorite search engine which will at the entry of the word "Africa" spit out quite a few thousand suggested sites—and hundreds in response to more refined key phrases. There are numerous non-governmental organizations in Washington and other world capitals that are dedicated to African causes and countries and able to assist members in their search for information. Several universities have developed Africa-related databases. World organizations such as the United Nations and its specialized agencies, the World Bank and the International Monetary Fund, all maintain extensive, authoritative databases on Africa. But at the end of the day, business executives who are considering investment or serious dealings with any of Africa's 53 nations, usually go to experienced and trustworthy consultants to help them analyze and evaluate prospects.

Since the early nineties decision makers in Washington, London, Paris, and the other capitals of the world started focusing on the long-forgotten and neglected African continent. This sudden interest in Africa was no mere coincidence. It followed in the wake of reform and change that swept across the continent after Communism crumbled in Eastern Europe.

South Africa, which was isolated from the rest of the continent and shunned by the world, finally shed apartheid and became an engine for regional growth. Not only in Europe but in Africa a wind of change blew across the continent. Former autocrats who built a power base on the support of one of the superpowers in the Cold War and on their opposition to apartheid were obliged to take note of the needs of their own citizens instead. Several were ousted by enlightened leaders and others remained and reformed. In the process, aggregate per capita incomes rose in 31 of the 48 Sub-Saharan African countries, reliance on the state as the engine for development declined, market economies started taking form, exchange rates were liberalized, budget deficits were reduced, protectionist trade policies gave way to liberalized trade. Some 21 countries achieved growth rates exceeding 5 percent. With ample justification some of Africa's leaders are today talking confidently about an African Renaissance in the making.

Ignorance

Despite heightened interest from abroad and the proliferation of sources, South African President Thabo Mbeki still had cause to complain in a recent speech about an foreigner who, he says, wanted to know whether he might know a friend in Morocco because he also lives in Africa. This continent, it seems, still has a long way to go before outsiders really get to know it. Despite the formidable presence of Fortune 500 companies and a growing number of small and medium-sized enterprises, the international business community at large remains blissfully unaware of the untapped potential for profit awaiting enterprising entrepreneurs.

Corporate Council

The premier non-governmental organization for US and other multinational and medium-sized corporations is the Washington-based Corporate Council on Africa *(www.africacncl.org)*. Since 1992 the Corporate has acted as a catalyst for business by introducing American firms not only to potential top-level partners in Africa but to like-minded firms in the United States with a view of partnering in new ventures. Over the past ten years it has hosted a large number of African heads of state in the US and organized trade missions to various parts of the continent. It has an ongoing African business development series that reaches into every facet of deal-making and maintains a database for its corporate membership, representing more than 80 percent of the total US investment on the continent. The Council's latest biannual Africa Summit in Philadelphia during September 2001 attracted close to a thousand prominent business leaders and was attended by a dozen African heads of state and several top decision makers from the US.

Media

As is to be expected, overseas media usually cover only what could be termed as sensationally significant with little space devoted for in-depth analysis. Africa-specific magazines such as *the Business in Africa (www.businessinafrica.co.za)* are geared to fill this vacuum on a monthly basis while country-specific newspapers and magazines in both English and French are available in print and often on the Internet as well. A very useful single source to stay abreast of developments across the continent on a daily basis is the comprehensive online news service provided by *www.allafrica.com.*

Analysis

Serious investors get their information from international banks such as HSBC Equator Bank that have extensive operations on the continent, as well as a number of local banks and private consultants who offer specialized services. In Washington there are several seasoned former top government officials who offer years of inside experience and high level contact with Africa, such as Cohen and Woods. They assist clients with market analysis and deal-making, and offer expert liaison with African decision makers and business leaders. Foreign portfolio investors have the choice of either working through their local brokers or in the case of South Africa, where most of the foreign equity and bond buying takes place, employ the services of any of a number of sophisticated Johannesburg-based brokerage houses.

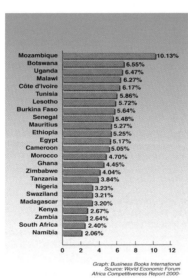

Mozambique	10.13%
Botswana	6.55%
Uganda	6.47%
Malawi	6.27%
Côte d'Ivoire	6.17%
Tunisia	5.86%
Lesotho	5.72%
Burkina Faso	5.64%
Senegal	5.48%
Mauritius	5.27%
Ethiopia	5.25%
Egypt	5.17%
Cameroon	5.05%
Morocco	4.70%
Ghana	4.45%
Zimbabwe	4.04%
Tanzania	3.84%
Nigeria	3.23%
Swaziland	3.21%
Madagascar	3.20%
Kenya	2.67%
Zambia	2.64%
South Africa	2.40%
Namibia	2.06%

Graph: Business Books International
Source: World Economic Forum
Africa Competitiveness Report 2000-

Assistance

Within the World Bank Group there are several divisions that have aid and loan programs specifically for Africa, while in the United States Eximbank, OPIC, USAID, FAS and TDA are among the agencies that offer programs aimed at expanding US business involvement on the continent. Several infrastructural and other development projects of interest to US contractors are funded by the African Development Bank, the World Bank or country donors. These programs provide opportunities not only for multinational or transnational giants but also small and medium-sized firms looking for the first time at the possibility of doing business with Africa.

International

Africa has claimed an increasing share of funds allocated for special programs by major World Bank and United Nations development agencies. In 1998 the World Bank's IFC—the largest multilateral source of loan and equity financing for private sector projects in developing countries—allocated close to $1 billion out of its $9.0 billion budget to Africa. This represented a jump of 22% over the previous year. Other international agencies involved in funding and underwriting African projects include IDA, UNIDO and UNDP. MIGA helps to minimize risk by providing investment guarantees and technical assistance in member African countries. Especially in countries where foreigners are uncertain about their legal rights reliance on the ICSIP arbitration center is a good option.

US agencies

American entrepreneurs who wish to do business with Africa have an array of possible sources of assistance in official Washington. These agencies are geared to give all possible assistance to help American businesses establish themselves in Africa. No project is too small or too big to run by these agencies. Eximbank, for example, works as enthusiastically on the sale of a few used US trucks to a small African client as it does on a major deal involving several billion dollars worth of aircraft to a major foreign airline. The Small Business Administration has been an active promoter of business between small and medium-sized US enterprises and their counterparts in Africa. Even though the Trade and Development Agency works on a small budget, its impact on expansion of business in Africa has been significant. Several of the feasibility studies which it funded eventually led to major projects financed by other agencies.

Following are some of the key international and US agencies involved in Africa:

INTERNATIONAL

**The African
Development Bank (ADB)**
01 BP 1387Abidjan 01
Côte d'Ivoire
Tel: (225) 20.20.44.44
Fax: (225) 20.20.40.06
Website: www.afdb.org
The ADB was established in the 1960s to make loans and equity investments for economic and social advancement in its 53 member countries. Its capital exceeds $23 billion and it has among its shareholders 24 countries in the Americas, Europe and Asia. The African Development Fund provides development finance on concessional terms to low-income countries unable to borrow on the non-concessional terms. As the largest non-African shareholder the US has weighted voting rights in regard to loans.

WORLD BANK GROUP

**International Development
Association (IDA)**
1818 H Street NW
Washington DC 20433
Tel: 202-477-1234
Fax: 202-477-6391
Website: www.worldbank.org/ida
The International Development Association (IDA) is the World Bank Group's concessional lending window. Half of its active projects are in Africa amounting to over $1 billion a year. The TDA's objective is to assist economic reform and create an investor-friendly environment.

**International Finance
Corporation (IFC)**
2121 Pennsylvania Avenue NW
Washington DC 20433
Tel: 202-473-7711
Fax: 202-974-4384
Website: www.if.org
Since its creation in 1989, the IFC's African Enterprise Fund (AEF) has provided a total of $206 million for 309 projects in 30 African countries. Projects are appraised, processed, and supervised by IFC representatives in Africa. North African countries are included in the IFC's Central Asia,Middle East and North Africa Department (CAMENA).

**Multilateral Insurance
Guarantee Agency (MIGA)**
1800 K Street NW (Suite 1200)
Washington DC 20433
Tel: 202-473-6167
Fax: 202-522-2630
Website: www.miga.org
MIGA's mandate is to encourage the flow of foreign direct investment to developing and other member countries. Through its guarantee program it offers insurance to mitigate political risk and provides promotional and advisory services to member countries to help attract and retain direct investment.

**International Center for
Settlement of Investment Disputes (ICSID)**
1818 H Street N W
Washington DC 20433
Tel: 202-458-1534
Fax: 202-522-2615
Website: www.worldbank.org/icsid
ICSID was established in 1966 as an autonomous international organization but maintains close links with the World Bank. All its members are also members of the Bank. It provides facilities for the conciliation and arbitration of disputes between member countries and foreign investors. Recourse to ICSID arbitration is voluntary.

UNITED NATIONS

**UN Industrial Development
Organization (UNIDO)**
Vienna International Center
A-1400 Vienna
Austria
Tel: (43) 1-26026
Fax: (43) 1-269-2269
Website: www.unido.org
UNIDO promotes and accelerates industrialization in developing countries by contracting with international consultants to provide technical assistance to local companies and organizations. Consultancy projects range from general surveys to transfer of manufacturing technology and the establishment of pilot plants. UNIDO has developed a range of special programs to attract foreign partners and financiers for industrial projects in developing countries.

UN Development Program (UNDP)
Bureau for Development Policy
United Nations, New York
Tel: 212-906-5200
Fax: 212-906-5857
Website: www.undp.org
The UNDP is the world's largest multilateral grant development and assistance organization with offices in 124 countries and drawing on the expertise of 40 specialized and technical UN agencies. It also works extensively with non-governmental organizations and the business sector. At any given time the UNDP handles some 6,000 projects valued at more than $7 billion, a large portion of it in Africa.

US AGENCIES

Export-Import Bank of the US (Eximbank)
811 Vermont Ave NW
Washington DC 20571T
oll free: 800-565-3946
Tel: 202-565-3946
Fax: 202-565-3380
Website: www.exim.gov
The Eximbank is an independent government agency that assists in the sale of US. goods and services overseas by providing loans and other credit measures. Eximbank's loans, guarantees and insurance supported more than $150 million in US exports to Sub-Saharan Africa in the first half of 1999. The bank is open to consider project finance business in every African country with the exclusion of Sudan and Libya. Financing is available for projects that do not rely on typical export credit security but need long-term cash flow financing.

Foreign Agricultural Service (FAS)
Department of Agriculture, Africa & Middle East
Washington DC 20250-1000
Tel: 202-720-3222
Website: www.fas.usda.gov
FAS assists in the development and expansion of US agricultural exports to Africa and other regions. Assistance includes Export Credit Guarantee Programs (GSM-102 and GSM-103) to underwrite private bank credit for three or ten years, a Supplier Credit Guarantee Program (SCGP) that extends short term guarantees up to 180 days, and the Facility Guarantee Program (FGP) that provides payment guarantees to improve or establish agriculture-related facilities in emerging markets.

Overseas Private Investment Corporation (OPIC)
1100 New York Avenue
Washington DC 20527
Tel: 202-336-8799
Fax: 202-408-9859
Website: www.opic.gov
OPIC is a self-sustaining government agency that provides investment information, financing, and political risk insurance for US investors in African and other developing countries. It currently has four privately managed funds that support investment in Sub-Saharan Africa: the $120 million New Africa Opportunity Fund for Southern Africa, the $150 million Modern Africa Growth and Investment Fund, the $120 million Global Environment Emerging Markets Fund II, and the $300 million Aqua International Partners Fund.

Trade Information Center (TIC)
International Trade Administration
US Department of Commerce
Washington DC 20230
Tel: 1-800-USA-TRADE
Fax: 202-482-4473
Website: www.ita.doc.gov
The TIC, operated by the International Trade Administration of the US Department of Commerce for the 20 federal agencies comprising the Trade Promotion Coordinating Committee (TPCC), is the first stop for US exporters seeking government advice and assistance. It provides country-specific export counseling and assistance for Africa, including trade leads and suggestions on potential sources for export financing.

US Agency for International Aid and Development (USAID)
Ronald Reagan Building
Washington DC 20523-0016
Tel: 202-712-4320
Fax: 202-216-3524
Website: www.usaid.gov
USAID implements government foreign economic assistance programs ranging from health, education, economic growth, population, democracy, environment, and crisis prevention. In most of these programs the US private sector has an opportunity to participate. Regional programs offered by USAID include the following: the Leland Initiative, the Greater Horn of Africa Initiative (GHAI), the Initiative for Southern Africa (ISA), the Africa Food Security Initiative (AFSI), and the Africa Trade and Investment Policy (ATRIP). The Leland Initiative seeks to bring the benefits of the global information revolution to the people of Africa.

US Small Business Administration (SBA)
409 3rd Street SW
Washington DC 20416
Tel: 800-U-ASK-SBA
Website: www.sba.gov
The SBA has taken an active role in promoting American small business ventures in Africa. SBA's Export Working Capital Program (EWCP) provides short-term loans to small businesses for export-related transactions. Its International Trade (IT) Loan Program offers a combination of woring capital and fixed asset financing to help small businesses compete more effectively in export markets. The SBA can guarantee up to $1 million for fixed assets and $750,000 for working capital.

US Trade and Development Agency (TDA)
1621 North Kent Street
Arlington VA 22209
Tel: 703-875-4357
Fax: 703-875-4009
Website: www.tda.gov
The TDA helps US businesses by funding feasibility studies, orientation visits, specialized training grants, business workshops, and various forms of technical assistance, enabling them to compete for infrastructure and industrial projects in Africa and other middle-income and developing regions. Overall TDA funding for projects related to the Africa/Middle East was $8.2 million out of a total budget of $41 million in 1998. The time lag between funding project planning activities and the identification of actual export sales associated with projects varies.

Rating Africa

Mindful of the important role that credit ratings play in the global capital markets, an increasing number of African countries are subjecting themselves to assessments by the world's leading rating agencies. So far eight African nations and the African Development Bank (ADB) have been rated by one or more of these agencies.

Moody's *(www.moodys.com)* concedes that credit ratings are by their very nature subjective as they rely on the judgment of a diverse group of credit risk professionals weighing a number of pertinent factors. Moody's issues country ceiling ratings for foreign-currency bonds and notes (both long- and short-term), and country ceilings for foreign currency bank deposits (both long- and short-term). Using an Aaa-through-C rating, an Aaa signifies the best quality with the smallest degree of investment risk and is generally referred to as "gilt edged." Aa signifies high quality by all standards while A implies favorable investment at an upper-medium-grade level. Baa is considered as medium-grade, Ba has speculative elements, B generally lacks the characteristics of the desirable investment, Caa denotes poor standing, Ca is speculative to a high degree, and C shows extremely poor prospects of ever attaining investment grading. Moody's applies numerical modifiers 1, 2, and 3 in each generic rating classification from Aa through Caa. The modifier 1 indicates that the obligation ranks in the higher end of its generic rating category; a 2 indicates a mid-range ranking; and a 3 stipulates a ranking in the lower end of a specific category.

Standard & Poor's *(www. standardpoor. com)* cautions against interpretation of its sovereign ratings as "country ratings." Instead, it suggests that a sovereign credit rating should be seen as an assessment of a government's capacity and willingness to repay debt according to its terms. Sovereign ratings address the credit risks of national governments and is not a recommendation to invest, according to S&P. An AAA rating, the highest assigned by Standard & Poor's, indicates an *extremely strong capacity* to meet financial commitments. An AA shows a *very strong capacity* to meet obligations and an A rating *a strong capacity* to meet financial commitments. A BBB is assigned to those judged to have an *adequate capacity* to meet their commitments but with a greater likelihood being affected by adverse economic conditions. Sovereign debt rated BB, B, CCC, and CC are all seen as having *significant speculative* characteristics. The ratings from AA through CCC may be modified by the addition of a plus or minus sign to show relative gradings within the major rating categories.

Fitch, ICBA, Duff & Phelps *(www.dcrco. com)* draws for its sovereign rating on recent instances of default and near-default to establish a range of key leading indicators of distress. This information is incorporated in a risk model that gives a percentage score to sovereign borrowers, which is used in turn to determine the long-term rating. Sovereign borrowers usually enjoy the highest credit standing for obligations in their own currency. There is the risk, however, that a country may service its debt through excessive money creation, effectively eroding the value of its obligations through inflation. On the other hand, when a sovereign nation borrows in a foreign currency there is the even more serious risk of outright default since the sovereign borrower cannot print the means of servicing the debt. In *long-term obligations,* an AAA rating indicates the *highest credit quality and lowest expectation of credit risk* and is highly unlikely to be adversely affected by foreseeable events. AA denotes *very high credit quality and very low expectation of credit risk.* An A rating indicates *high credit quality and a low expectation of credit risk.* BBB assigns *good credit quality and low current expectation of credit risk.* This is the lowest investment-grade category. For its *short-term ratings* Fitch uses F1 as the *highest credit quality* and the strongest capacity for timely payment of financial commitments. A plus sign may be added to denote exceptionally strong credit. F2 denotes *good credit quality* and a satisfactory capacity for timely payment of financial commitments, but with a lower margin of safety. F3 means *fair credit quality* and adequate capacity for timely payment of financial commitments with the possibility that near-term adverse changes could result in downgrading to below investment grade. While a B rating is *speculative,* C indicates *high default risk* and D *actual or imminent payment default.*

African ratings - 2001

AFRICAN DEVELOPMENT BANK

Moody's Investors Service June 2001
Senior Long-term	Aaa
Subordinate Long-term	Aa1

Standard & Poor's - June 2001
Senior unsecured long-term	AA+/Stable
Subordinated debt	AA-/Stable
Short-term Issuer Credit	A-1/Stable

BOTSWANA

Moody's Investors Service - June 2001
Govt. Bonds For. Cur. Long-term	A2[1]
Govt. Bonds Dom. Cur. Long-term	A1[1]
Bank deposits long-term[2]	A2
Bank deposits short-term[2]	P-1

Standard & Poor's - June 2001
Domestic currency long-term	A+/Stable
Domestic currency short-term	A-1/Stable
Foreign currency long-term	A/Stable
Foreign currency short-term	A-1/Stable

EGYPT

Moody's Investors Service - June 2001
Govt. Bonds For. Cur. Long-term	Ba1[1]
Govt. Bonds Dom. Cur. Long-term	Baa1[1]
Bank deposits long-term[2]	Ba2
Bank deposits short-term[2]	NP

Standard & Poor's - June 2001
Domestic currency long-term	A-/Negative
Domestic currency short-term	A-1/Negative
Foreign currency long-term	BBB-/Negative
Foreign currency short-term	A-3/Negative

Fitch, ICBA, Duff & Phelps - June 2001
Foreign currency long-term	BBB-
Foreign currency short-term	F3

MAURITIUS

Moody's Investors Service - June 2001
Govt. Bonds For. Cur. Long-term	Baa2[1]
Govt. Bonds Dom. Cur. Long-term	A2[1]
Bank deposits long-term[2]	Baa2
Bank deposits short-term[2]	P-2

MOROCCO

Moody's Investors Service - June 2001
Govt. Bonds For. Cur. Long-term	Ba1
Govt. Bonds Dom. Cur. Long-term	—
Bank deposits long-term[2]	Ba2
Bank deposits short-term[2]	NP

Standard & Poor's - June 2001
Domestic currency long-term	BBB/Stable
Domestic currency short-term	A-3/Stable
Foreign currency long-term	BB/Stable
Foreign currency short-term	B/Stable

MOROCCO

Moody's Investors Service - June 2001
Govt. Bonds For. Cur. Long-term	Ba1
Govt. Bonds Dom. Cur. Long-term	—
Bank deposits long-term[2]	Ba2
Bank deposits short-term[2]	NP

Standard & Poor's - June 2001
Domestic currency long-term	BBB/Stable
Domestic currency short-term	A-3/Stable
Foreign currency long-term	BB/Stable
Foreign currency short-term	B/Stable

SENEGAL

Standard & Poor's - June 2001
Domestic currency long-term	B+/Stable
Domestic currency short-term	B/Stable
Foreign currency long-term	B+/Stable
Foreign currency short-term	B/Stable

SOUTH AFRICA

Moody's Investors Service - June 2001
Govt. Bonds For. Cur. Long-term	Baa3
Govt. Bonds Dom. Cur. Long-term	Baa1
Bank deposits long-term[2]	Ba1
Bank deposits short-term[2]	NP

Standard & Poor's - June 2001
Domestic currency long-term	A-/Stable
Domestic currency short-term	A-2/Stable
Foreign currency long-term	BBB-/Stable
Foreign currency short-term	A-3/Stable

Fitch, ICBA, Duff & Phelps - June 2001
Foreign currency long-term	BBB-
Foreign currency short-term	F3

TUNISIA

Moody's Investors Service - June 2001
Govt. Bonds For. Cur. Long-term	—
Govt. Bonds Dom. Cur. Long-term	Baa2[1]
Bank deposits long-term[2]	Ba1
Bank deposits short-term[2]	NP

Standard & Poor's - June 2001
Domestic currency long-term	A/Stable
Domestic currency short-term	A-1/Stable
Foreign currency long-term	AAA/Stable
Foreign currency short-term	A-3/Stable

Fitch, ICBA, Duff & Phelps - June 2001
Foreign currency long-term	BBB-
Foreign currency short-term	F3

1. Issuer rating
2. Country ceilings for foreign currency
3. Non-Prime

African websites

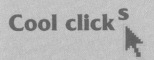
African web-space is expanding and most countries have some form of local or internationally hosted web server, unofficially or officially representing the country—some of them sponsored by international development agencies. Due to the small number of Internet users in Africa at large, most of these websites are aimed at foreign audiences. South Africa is the exception. Not only has it kept pace but in some instances outstripped many developed countries in the sophistication and scope of its electronic data services and ecommerce offerings. Outside South Africa and Egypt, French-speaking African countries have maintained a higher profile on the Web and greater institutional connectivity than the rest—due to the strong assistance provided by the various Francophone support agencies and the Canadian and French governments. International organizations such as the UN, World Bank and IMF as well as regional groupings such as the ADB, CEDEAO, COMESA, ECA, IGAD and SADC all offer useful Africa-related data. With the exception of South Africa, Egypt and Kenya, most African sites are hosted off-shore. There has been a proliferation of Africa-related web-sites in Britain and the US, offering anything from the ultimate safari to traditional foods, news, data and investment services. Any phrase with the word Africa entered on a search engine brings up hundreds—often thousands—of website addresses. Our selection of websites does not imply an endorsement or recommendation but merely signifies a high degree of usefulness.

BUSINESS
www.africacncl.org
Premier site for companies interested in Africa.

CURRENCIES
www.xe.com
Latest exchange rates for African currencies.

COUNTRY REPORTS
www.state.gov
Country reports on most African nations.
www.cia.gov
World Fact Book provides profiles of African nations.

DATA
www.worldbank.org
Extensive data about all African countries.
www.imf.org
African country information and projections.

NEWS
www.allafrica.com
Daily news coverage of events across Africa.

TRAVEL
www.africantravelinc.com
Offers travel arrangements from Cape to Cairo
www.flysaa.com
Direct flights to Africa from US, Europe, Australia & Far East
www.worldtravelguide.net
Visa and other requirements and travel tips for visitors to specific African countries.

WEATHER
www.usatoday.com/weather
Up-to-date forecasts of weather in cities and towns across Africa.

BOOK ORDERS
www.businessbooksusa.com
To order copies of AFRICA 2002 online.

Statistical sources

Statistics on Africa are not difficult to obtain. To verify the accuracy of these figures is another matter. In this book we have relied largely on figures provided by the World Bank, the IMF, UNCTAD and other international agencies—and in a few instances on individual government sources. Not infrequently data on the same topic from different sources vary. Instead of trying to adjudicate we have left these discrepancies unchanged. Although we drew our data from sources thought to be the most authoritative they remain subject to margins of error. According to the World Bank substantial data gaps remain. Strengthening the statistical capacity in African countries is an ongoing process. The World Bank also points out that differing statistical methods, coverage, practices, and definitions further complicate the task of standardizing and harmonizing related data sets and cautions that indicators must be interpreted with care. The Bank, the IMF, and other agencies by their own admission have to make estimates on the basis of available secondary information to fill critical gaps in reporting where data cannot be readily produced by national statistical sources. In some instances data gaps remain and some countries are covered only sporadically. Those in search of basic data on most issues relating to Africa are well served by visiting the World Bank's website or obtaining its Africa Database—available both in book form or on a CD. Most African countries have their own statistical departments with some of them providing statistical data online:

WORLD BANK
1818 H Street NW, Washington DC 20433
Fax: 202-477-2977
Web: www.worldbank.org/afr/stats

ALGERIA
Office National des Statistiques
8,10 Rue des moussebilines, Alger Algérie
Tel : (213) 21- 74-41-41 Fax:(213) 21- 743839
E-mail: ons@onssiege.ons.dz

ANGOLA
Insituto Nacional de Estatistica (INE)
Rua Ho-Chi-Min, Edificio INE, Luanda
Tel: (244) 320 430 or 322 757 Fax: (244) 320 430

BENIN
Institut National de la Statistique
et de l'Analyse Economique, BP 323, Cotonou
Tel (229) 31.34.31 Fax (229) 31.34.31
Email insae-ci@planben.intnet.bj
Web: http://planben.intnet.bj/13a/benin.htm

BOTSWANA
Central Statistics Office
Office P/B 0024, Gaborone, Botswana
Tel 267-352200 Fax 267-352201
Email: csobots@gov.bw
Web: www.cso.gov.bw

BURKINA FASO
Institut National de la Statistique
et de la Démographie (INSD)
01 BP 374 , Ouagadougou
Tel: (226) 32 42 69 Fax: (226) 32 42 69
Email: insd@cenatrin.bf

BURUNDI
Institut de la Statistique et des Etudes
Economiques du Burundi (ISTEEBU)
BP 1156, Bujumbura
Tel: (257) 22 67 29 or 21 67 35 Fax: (257) 22 26 35
Email isteebu@cbinf.com

CAMEROON
Direction de la Statistique et
de la Comptabilité Nationale, Yaoundé
Tel: (237) 22 04 45 Fax: (237) 23 24 37

CAPE VERDE
Instituto Nacional de Estatistica (INE)
Avenida Amilcar Cabral, C.P. 116 Praia
Tel (238) 61 39 60 or 61 38 27
Email: ine@ine.gov.cv
Web://www.ine.cv

CENTRAL AFRICAN REPUBLIC
Division des Statistiques et
des Etudes Economiques, BP 696, Bangui
Tel: (236) 61 45 74 or 61 72 69 Fax: (236) 61 03 90

CHAD
Direction de la Statistique des Etudes
Economiques et Démographiques
BP 453, N'Djaména
Tel: (235) 52 31 64 Fax: (235) 51 51 85

COMOROS
Direction de la Statistique, BP 131, Moroni
Tel (269) 74 42 34

CONGO
Centre National de la
Statistique et des Etudes Economiques
BP 64, Brazzaville
Tel: (242) 81 08 58

CÔTE D'IVOIRE
Institut National de la Statistique (INS)
01 BP V55, Abidjan 01
Tel: (225) (22) 21 05 38 Fax: (225) (22) 21 44 01
Email: ensea@ensea.ed.ci

DJIBOUTI
Direction Nationale de la
Statistique (DINAS), BP 1846, Djibouti
Tel: (253) 35 16 82

EQUATORIAL GUINEA
Direction Générale des Statistiques
A.C. 607, Malabo
Tel: (240) 9 2884

ERITREA
National Statistics Office
2 Wollo Street, P.O. Box 5838, Asmara
Tel: (291) 1-12 00 91 Fax: (291) 1-12 80 34

ETHIOPIA
Central Statistical Authority
PO Box 1143, Addis Ababa
Tel: (251) (1) 11 51 31 Fax: (251) (1) 55 03 34
Email: csa@telecom.net.et

GABON
Direction Générale de la Statistique
et des Etudes Economiques
BP 2119, Libreville
Tel: (241) 76 06 71 Fax: (241) 72 04 57

GAMBIA
Central Statistics Department
32 Buckle Street, Banjul
Tel: (220) 22.83.64 Fax: (220) 22.96.83
Email: gamcens@qanet.gm

GHANA
Ghana Statistical Service (GSS)
PO Box 1098, Accra, Ghana
Tel: (233) (21) 68 26 92 Fax: (233) (21) 67 17 31

GUINEA
Direction Nationale
de la Statistique
BP 221 Conakry
Tel: (224) 41 41 36 Fax: (224) 41 45 67

GUINEA-BISSAU
Instituto Nacional de
Estatistica e Censos
CP 6, Bissau
Tel: (245) 22 20 54 Fax: (245) 22 21 22

KENYA
Central Bureau of Statistics
PO Box 30266, Nairobi
Tel: (254) (2) 33 39 70 Fax: (254) (2) 33 30 30
Email: cbs@clubinternetk.com

LESOTHO
Bureau of Statistics, PO Box 455, Maseru
Tel: (266) 32 38 52 Fax: (266) 31 017

MADAGASCAR
Institut National de la Statistique
BP 485, Antananarivo 101
Tel: (261) (20) 22 357 03 Fax: (261) (20) 22 332 50
EMail: dginstat@dts.mg

MALAWI
National Statistical Office
P.O Box 333,
Zomba
Tel: 265 524111 Fax: 265 525130
EMail: enquiries@statistics.gov.mw
Web: www.nso.malawi.net

MALI
Direction Nationale de la Statistique et de
l'Informatique, BP 12, Bamako
Tel: (223) 22 24 55 Fax: (223) 22 71 45

MAURITANIA
Office National de la Statistique
BP 240, Nouakchott
Tel: (222) 25 50 31 Fax: (222) 25 51 70
Email dg-ons@iiardd.mr
Web: www.ons.mr

MAURITIUS
Central Statistical Office
President John Kennedy St.
Port Louis
Tel (230) 212 2316 Fax (230) 211 4150
Email cso@intnet.mu
Web: ncb.intnet.mu/cso.htm

MOROCCO
Direction de la statistique
Avenue Al Haj Ahmed Cherkaoui
Agdal - BP. 826, 10004 Rabat

MOZAMBIQUE
Instituto Nacional de Estatística
Av.Ahmed Sekou Touré, nº 21, CP 493 Maputo
Tel: (258) (1) 49 10 54 / 5 Fax: (258) (1) 49 17 44
Web: www.ine.gov.mz

NAMIBIA
Central Bureau of Statistics
Private Bag 13356, Windhoek
Tel: (264) (61) 283-4111Fax: (264) (61) 239-377

NIGER
Direction de la Statistique
et des Comptes Nationaux, BP 862, Niamey
Tel: (227) 72 35 60 Fax: (227) 72 22 89

NIGERIA
Federal Office of Statistics
PO Box 52724, Falomo PO, Ikoyi, Lagos
Tel: (234) (1) 264 72 58 Fax: (234) (1) 263 50 77
Email: fos@infoweb.abs.net

RWANDA
Direction de la Statistique
BP 46, Kigali
Tel: (250) 78 937 Fax: (250) 78 488

SAO TOME AND PRINCIPE
Instituto Nacional de Estatistica
Ministério do Planeamento
Tel: (239) (12) 21 313 Fax: (239) (12) 21 982

SENEGAL
Direction de la Prévision et
de la Statistique (DPS), BP 116, Dakar
Tel: (221) 824 03 01 Fax: (221) 825 07 43
Email: asdily@telecom-plus.sn

SEYCHELLES
Management and Information
Systems Division
Ministry of Information Technology
PO Box 206, Victoria
Tel : (248) 38 31 81
Fax: 248 22 53 39
Web: www.seychelles.net/misdstat

SIERRA LEONE
Central Statistics Office
Tower Hill, Box 595, Freetown
Tel: (232) (22) 22-3287
Fax: (232) (22) 22-3897
Email: cso@sierratel.sl

SOUTH AFRICA
Central Statistics Service (CSS)
PB X44
Pretoria 0001
Tel: (27) (12) 310-8911
Fax: (27) (12) 310-8500/1/2/3
Email: info@statssa.pwv.gov.za
Web: www.statssa.gov.za

SUDAN
Central Bureau of Statistics
Khartoum
Tel: (249) (11) 77 003
Fax: (249) (11) 77 05 76

SWAZILAND
Central Statistics Office
PO Box 456
Mbabane
Tel: (268) 42 151
Fax: (268) 43 300

TANZANIA
Bureau of Statistics
PO Box 9242
Dar-es-Salaam
Tel: (255) (51) 11 26 81/82/83
Fax: (255) (51) 13 17 23
Email: nbs.dg@raha.com

TOGO
Direction de la Statistique
BP 118, Lomé
Tel: (228) 21 27 75
Fax: (228) 21 37 53
Email: edst2@cafe.tg

UGANDA
Uganda Bureau of Statistics (UBOS)
Plot 10/11 Airport Road
P.O. Box 13
Entebbe, Uganda
Tel: (256) 041-320165 / 320741 / 32164
Fax: (256) 041-320147 / 321643
Web: www.ubos.org

ZAMBIA
Central Statistical Office
PO Box 31908
Lusaka
Tel: (260) (1) 25 34 68
Fax: (260) (1) 25 25 75
Email: dpucso@zamnet.zm

ZIMBABWE
Central Statistical Office
Box CY 342, Causeway
Harare
Tel: (263) (4) 70 66 81 to 88
Fax: (263) (4) 70 88 54 or 72 85 29

Chapter 7

The nations of Africa

Diversity should be expected in a continent of 800 million people speaking 2,000 languages in 53 countries and conducting business in English, French, Arabic, Portuguese, Spanish and Swahili. At the turn of the 19th Century, European powers drew and redrew the map of Africa to suit their own whims and desires with little consideration for the people who lived there. Certain borders remain unsettled and a few regions have been plagued by skirmishes, civil strife and outright war. While some of these border and ethnic clashes have been resolved in recent years, others persist. Despite these strikes against it, Africa has managed to attain a remarkable degree of stability and cohesiveness within nations. Real reform and economic progress followed the end of the Cold War as these nations became free to choose their partners on a basis of business instead of political ideology. There is—with good reason—talk of an African Renaissance that could make this continent one of the prime areas for investment in the new millennium.

THE 53 NATIONS OF AFRICA

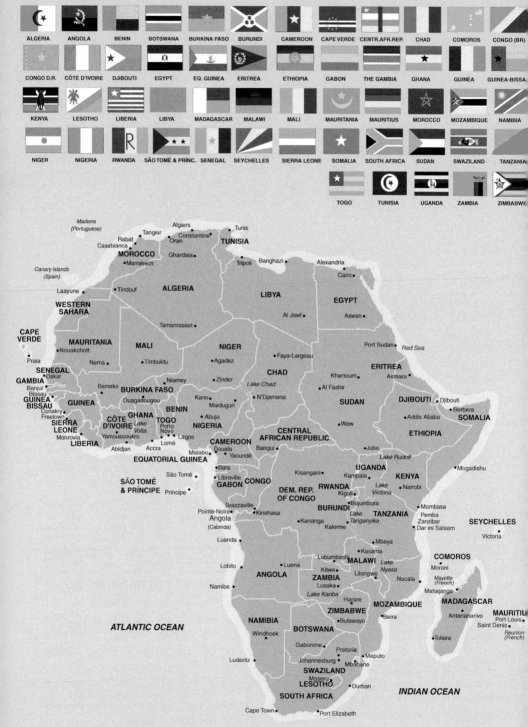

Country profiles

Profiling political and economic conditions in 53 diverse countries spanning across the African continent and an array of adjoining islands would have been impossible without the kind cooperation of several institutions—including the World Bank, the International Monetary Fund, the UN Economic Commission for Africa, and a number of other Africa-related organizations.

In assessing the business opportunities in specific countries, we are indebted to the US State Department *(www.state.gov)* and the US Department of Commerce *(www.ita.doc.gov)* and we strongly recommend that entrepreneurs who are seriously interested in conducting business in any of these countries consult with these departments.

Data

While every effort was made to cross-check statistics and to provide the most recent data available, there will no doubt be areas of dispute. In some cases where even the IMF, World Bank and a number of other UN agencies were unable to extract useful data or even make an educated guess, we simply resigned ourselves to N/A (not available).

Maps

Our maps follow the official borders recognized by the United Nations. It is not within our power to adjudicate in border disputes and adjust maps to suit the preferences of either party in contested cases.

PPP

Apart from real GDP statistics based on current official dollar exchange rates, figures are also published based on purchasing power parity (PPP). The PPP method, considered by many economists as a more accurate measure of economic strength, weighs incomes against domestic costs and prices in specific countries. Exchange rates may suddenly go up or down by 10% or more as a result of market forces or official decisions while real output remains unchanged. On 12 January 1994, for example, the 14 countries of the *Communauté Financière Africaine*, or CFA, (whose currencies are tied to the French franc) devalued by 50%. This did not, however, cut the real output of these countries by half as real GDP based on exchange rates would indicate. While PPP estimates for OECD countries are quite specific, the same estimates for developing countries are often mere approximations.

The nations

1. Administered by Morocco

ECONOMIC INDICATORS - AFRICA - 1999

COUNTRY	GDP US$ M[1]	% GDP GROWTH	GNP[2] PER CAP	% GROSS[3] DOM. SAV	EXPORTS US$ M[4]	IMPORTS US$ M[4]
Algeria	46,995	3.3	1,550	31.7	13,233	11,176
Angola	6,422	2.7	270	53.3	8,334	6,540
Benin	2,458	4.9	380	7.5	516	748
Botswana	5,893	4.5	3,240	14.2	1,650	1,982
Burkina Faso	2,936	5.8	240	9.8	292	759
Burundi	955	-1.0	120	-0.4	63	131
Cameroon	9,640	4.4	600	18.9	2,243	2,289
Cape Verde	625	8.0	1,330	10.4	135	292
Central African Republic	1,228	3.4	290	7.2	178	253
Chad	1,631	-0.7	210	-3.0	260	465
Comoros	211	-1.4	350	-5.6	50	78
Congo Dem. Rep. of	6,589	8.0	N/A	11.1	1,937	1,902
Congo Rep. of	2,402	-3.0	550	48.3	1,728	1,563
Côte d'Ivoire	12,235	2.8	710	23.1	4,967	4,204
Djibouti	471	N/A	790	N/A	N/A	N/A
Egypt	74,610	6.0	1,390	14.4	14,258	21,734
Equatorial Guinea	509	15.1	1,170	57.9	712	597
Eritrea	692	0.8	200	-21.3	66	509
Ethiopia	7,045	6.2	100	2.7	894	1,883
Gabon	5,279	-6.2	3,300	34.8	1,964	1,669
Gambia, The	457	6.4	330	1.7	199	262
Ghana	7,693	4.4	390	6.2	2,606	3,923
Guinea	4,406	3.2	510	15.2	763	828
Guinea Bissau	217	7.8	160	-2.2	56	96
Kenya	9,900	1.3	360	6.8	2,600	3,313
Lesotho	1,079	2.5	550	-28.0	222	891
Liberia	N/A	N/A	N/A	N/A	N/A	N/A
Libya	N/A	N/A	N/A	N/A	N/A	N/A
Madagascar	3,641	4.7	250	4.6	921	1,215
Malawi	1,688	4.0	180	-0.6	490	770
Mali	2,964	5.5	240	10.1	650	939
Mauritania	1,252	4.3	390	7.2	370	471
Mauritius	4,838	3.4	3,550	22.7	2,708	2,923
Morocco	38,387	-0.7	1,190	15.3	6,588	9,699
Mozambique	3,417	7.3	220	6.4	465	1,494
Namibia	3,568	3.1	1,890	9.3	1,620	1,954
Niger	2,194	-0.6	190	3.8	322	452
Nigeria	30,958	1.0	260	18.4	12,796	14,832
Rwanda	1,952	6.1	250	-0.1	109	414
São Tomé & Príncipe	49	2.5	270	-9.3	16	40
Senegal	5,487	5.1	510	12.4	1,534	1,842
Seychelles	574	1.5	6,540	19.9	386	483
Sierra Leone	837	-8.1	130	-6.0	93	135
Somalia	N/A	N/A	N/A	N/A	N/A	N/A
South Africa	164,369	1.2	3,170	18.2	33,321	30,009
Sudan	9,161	5.2	330	N/A	N/A	N/A
Swaziland	1,421	2.0	1,360	21.1	1,305	1,205
Tanzania	6,197	4.7	260	2.2	1,163	2,457
Togo	1,493	2.1	310	3.6	425	563
Tunisia	22,600	6.2	2,090	N/A	8,780	9,237
Uganda	7,458	7.4	320	4.9	726	1,467
Zambia	3,841	2.4	330	-1.1	701	1,287
Zimbabwe	8,366	0.1	530	11.0	2,537	2,560

1. Real in millions of dollars, constant 1995 prices. 2. US dollars, Atlas method. 3. Percentage of GDP.
4. Preliminary data. Nominal. Current prices.   (Source: World Bank Africa Database 2001).

 # Algeria

With 30 million inhabitants, ample oil resources and an economy in transition, formerly socialist Algeria offers great potential for foreign investment. Responding to IMF and the World Bank programs, Algeria has made remarkable economic and financial progress, improving its trade and budget balances, reducing inflation and foreign debt and bolstering foreign currency reserves. Currently the main focus of foreign investors is on oil and gas, but as privatization progresses, this is likely to change.

Country profile

The Democratic and Popular Republic of Algeria (*Al Jumhuriyah al Jaza'iriyah ad Dimuqratiyah ash Shabiyah*) is the largest of the countries in the northwestern corner of Africa, known as the Maghreb. It is, after Sudan, the second largest country on the continent. Regions vary from coastal plains along the Mediterranean, to high plateaus, mountains and the Sahara Desert—with large reserves of oil and natural gas that are so important to the economy. About 80% of the predominantly Muslim population speak Arabic. Berbers, Kabyles, and the Tuaregs are major ethnic groups. A medium ranking on the United Nations Human Development Index reflects the comparatively high levels attained in education and health.

History

The Arab culture and Islam were introduced to the predominantly Berber peoples of Algeria in the 7th Century. It survived subsequent invasions by the Turks and the French, who came in 1830 and stayed until 1962 when the Algerians won their independence after a protracted war against France. President Achmed Ben Bella and his successor, General Houari Boumedienne, introduced various socialist reforms but failed to get the economy going. In 1988 widespread strikes led to rioting and the killing of hundreds in Algiers and other cities. It also gave rise to the Islamic Salvation Front (FIS), an extremist fundamentalist movement bent on eradicating "European" influence in Algeria. With the FIS on its way to victory in the 1990 elections, the rulers suspended the process and resorted to authoritarian rule under a High Council of State (HCS). In 1994 General Liamine Zeroual was appointed president to replace the HSC. By mid-1994 some 4,000 Algerians and more than 30 foreigners had been killed by

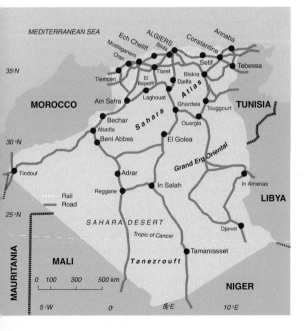

153

Fast facts

the FIS. Attempts by Zeroual to reach agreement with the FIS failed and it was excluded from the 1997 election, which the *Rassemblement national démocratique* (RND) won. Following President Zeroual's resignation in 1999, Abdelaziz Bouteflika was elected as Algeria's first civilian president after an 11th hour boycott by the other candidates. After an amnesty agreement in 1999 with some of the armed Islamic fundamentalist groups, violence and fear have diminished considerably. A referendum in September 1999 passed this peace plan with a 98% vote.

Government

In the June 1997 National Assembly elections, a voter turnout of 66% favored the *Rassemblement nationale democratique (RND)*. It gained 156 seats while 69 seats went to the Harakat Mousthama Silim (HMS), a moderate fundamentalist party in favor of religious freedom. The former ruling party, the *Front de libération nationale* (FLN), won 62 seats. The government exercised its constitutional right to exclude the more extreme Islamic fundamentalists, such as the FIS, from participating in the election.

Economic policy

In the first two decades after independence Algeria, heavily influenced by socialism, maintained an inflexible government-controlled economy. The petroleum industry was nationalized and collective ownership introduced in the agricultural sector. Heavily indebted Algeria was forced to negotiate a standby agreement with the IMF in 1989. Legislation allowing foreign-owned companies to become involved in the "reconstruction" of the national economy was adopted the following year and several reforms were introduced since. During the past five years government regulatory pricing was relaxed and more liberal tax policies introduced as part of an ongoing reform program.

Sectors

Algeria has one of Africa's more advanced economies based on oil and natural gas. The oil is of a high quality with a low sulphur content. Production is kept below full capacity to lengthen the life of the reserves, while utilization of the huge natural gas deposits is encouraged. Algeria's gas deposits are the fourth largest in the world. The key player in this sector is the state oil company, SONATRACH, which has been courting overseas investors in recent years. There are four oil refineries and four natural gas liquefaction plants. Agriculture is confined to the Mediterranean coastal region where crops such as wheat, barley, vegetables, citrus fruits, dates, olives, peas, beans, lentils, tobacco and sugar beet are grown. Wine is the main agricultural export. Other mineral resources include iron ore, uranium, zinc, phosphates, gold, antimony, bituminous coal, tungsten, manganese, lead, mercury, gypsum and salt. Manufacturing largely consists of heavy industries such as iron and steel, and fertilizer and cement plants, but the emphasis is shifting towards textiles and the processing of food, tobacco and cigarettes.

Privatization

The government has privatized or liquidated 1000 state enterprises since 1996. Insurance and banking have also been deregulated. In July, 1999 the Algiers Stock Exchange opened. There are plans for additional privatization as Algeria moves away from a centralized to a market economy. Currently the private sector accounts for 100% of the activity in agriculture, has minority representation in hydrocarbons, and leads the way in services (78%) and commerce (77%). Its share in transportation and communications has increased to 44%.

Trade

About 95 percent of Algeria's export revenues come from oil and natural gas exports. Major buyers are Spain, Portugal and Morocco. The government ran a budget surplus in 1997 as a result of increased revenues from hydrocarbon exports, which normally account for about 60 percent of fiscal revenues and 95 percent of export earnings. Algeria produces only about one-third of its food requirements and relies heavily on imports from the US and Europe.

Investment

Following the example of the state-owned petroleum corporation, SONATRACH, various sectors in Algeria have been courting foreign investors in recent years. American interest has mainly been in the petroleum sector and at the end of 1998 total US investment stood at $2.1 billion. Other significant entrants were Coca-Cola and Pepsi Cola. It is expected that in the next few years others will follow in the service, food processing and mining sectors.

Financial sector

The Bank of Algeria controls monetary growth by setting bank lending limits. Interest rates are adjusted on a weekly basis by a government board. In 1998 the central bank opened a secondary market for government debt. Still, the lack of a modern financial services sector restricts growth of the private sector and has impeded foreign investment in Algeria. Reform efforts in the state-owned banking sector overall have progressed slowly. A few foreign banks, such as Citibank, have opened representational offices since the promulgation of the currency and credit law.

Taxes & tariffs

The government reformed its tax code in 1998 to encourage business development, cutting rates in several categories as part of the 1999 budget. The new law reduces corporate tax rates from 38 to 30 percent, and going as low as 18 percent if profits are reinvested in the company. The law also excludes from taxation for five years profits on stock and bond sales. In 1996, the government modified its import duty schedule so that eight different rates cover all foodstuffs, semi-finished, and finished products, with a top rate of 45 percent.

Business activity

AGRICULTURE
Wheat, barley, oats, grapes, citrus, fruit, olives, livestock.

INDUSTRIES
Petroleum, natural gas, light industries, mining, electrical, petrochemical, food processing.

NATURAL RESOURCES
Petroleum, natural gas, iron ore, phosphates, uranium, lead, zinc.

EXPORTS
$13.2 billion (1999 est.): petroleum and natural gas (97%).

IMPORTS
$11.25 billion (1999 est.): capital goods, food and beverages, consumer goods.

MAJOR TRADING PARTNERS
Italy, US, France, Spain, Germany

Doing Business with Algeria

▶ Investment

Algeria, with its large proven oil and gas reserves and potential for new discoveries, offers significant commercial opportunities to foreign investors. Investments in the hydrocarbon sector involve a minority partnership with the state-owned SONATRACH . The same rules apply in telecommunications and national transportation, but in all other sectors foreign investors have unlimited scope. Repatriation of profits, interest, dividends or any other form of revenue is permitted.

▶ Trade

Machinery for the exploration and exploitation of oil and gas offers the best potential for US exports. As the world's fifth largest and Africa's largest importer of wheat, this commodity, as well as other foodstuffs, present good opportunities. There is a strong demand for housing materials, consumer products, and equipment for water projects and telecommunications. Import licenses are no longer required for most of these items, but the government stipulates that imported products, particularly consumer goods, must be labeled in Arabic. Distribution is largely in private hands and can be done through legally authorized dealers or wholesalers.

▶ Trade finance

Eximbank programs apply to Algeria. The World Bank has assisted with loans for purchases relating to housing, water and sewage, and urban transport. The US-based Agricultural Mutual Bank, in partnership with a major insurance company and the private Union Bank, established a leasing corporation for agricultural equipment. Algerian state corporations have the reputation of honoring their purchase obligations, even though there may sometimes be bureaucratic delays.

▶ Selling to the government

Direct negotiation for contracts is only permitted in a few special cases. Tenders for primary raw materials, agricultural products, and construction are frequently limited to known suppliers. Public tenders are advertised in the dailies, the official weekly contract bulletin of the public agency (BOMOP) and sometimes in the international press. Algerian organizations rarely buy at the tendered price as further negotiation usually takes place with a short list of bidders. It is customary for companies to visit the state organizations beforehand and introduce their products and their company's capabilities. The use of agents or other intermediaries is strictly prohibited.

▶ Exchange controls

A government board manages a float for the dinar, which is convertible for all current account transactions. Private and public importers may buy foreign exchange from five commercial banks for transactions on proof that they can pay for hard currency in dinars.

▶ Partnership

The Algerian government is looking for outside resources to modernize its plants and encourages foreign investors to enter into joint ventures. In their search for partners Algerian companies usually look for technical expertise and financial assistance. Recent legislation gave foreign banks the freedom to establish in Algeria, paving the way for partnerships in the financial sector. Other state sectors are trying to emulate the success that the state-owned petroleum giant, SONATRACH, had in striking partnerships with major foreign investors both in the exploration and downstream processing of its oil and gas.

▶ Establishing a presence

To open a liaison office, foreign firms apply for an office leasing agreement at the Algerian Ministry of Commerce. They have to ppoint a director and submit bank guarantee of $20,000.

▶ Labor

Trade unions are allowed. The law mandates a 40-hour work week and the government has set a guaranteed monthly minimum wage of 6,000 Algerian dinars ($100). A decree regulates occupational and health standards. Working conditions are largely left at the discretion of employers in consultation with employees.

▶ Legal rights

Even though Algeria is a member of the Paris Industrial Property Convention and the 1952 Convention on Copyrights, its protection of intellectual property is less than satisfactory. There is recourse to international arbitration to settle possible legal disputes with investors.

▶ Business climate

Algerian organizations usually deal only with foreign partners who have developed their trust by personal visits, follow-up, and who have shown ability to honor commitments. It is sometimes necessary to spend large amounts on market development, especially when the contracts are substantial.

156

Angola

Rich in oil and diamonds and other natural resources, Angola is a sparsely populated country roughly the combined size of Texas and California. Since independence in 1975, it has suffered severe social and political disruption as a result of a prolonged civil war. Despite Angola's great economic potential its people are among the world's poorest—a situation that is likely to be rectified once the war has ended and economic reforms have taken effect. In the meantime, major foreign investors have not been slow in picking up on business opportunities in this former Portuguese colony.

Country profile

The Republic of Angola is slightly larger than South Africa and the combined size of Texas and California. The climate varies from tropical in the north to subtropical in the south. Major rivers are the Kunene, Zambezi and the Kwanza (after which the country's currency was named). The Bantu-speaking Ovimbundu, Kimbundu and

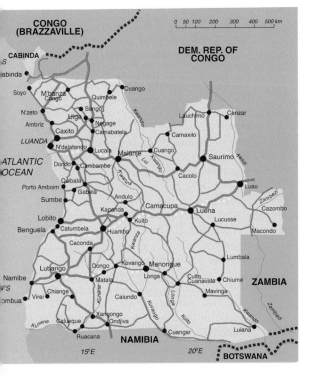

Bakongo peoples are in the majority. Fifty-three percent of the population are Christians (mostly Roman Catholic) and the rest adhere to indigenous beliefs.

History

In the 16th Century, Portuguese interest in the region focused on the slave trade to supply the needs of its newfound colony, Brazil. Portuguese influence remained centered around Luanda (founded in 1575) and the kingdom of Ndongo ruled by chiefs referred to as *ngola*—which eventually served as an inspiration when naming independent Angola. It was not until the 1920s that Portugal managed to extend its influence to the borders of Angola, as defined by European treaties in the 1880s and 1890s. A protracted anti-colonial insurgent war ended in when Portugal granted independence to Angola in 1974 after army officers toppled the Salazar regime in Lisbon. Three movements were involved in the freedom struggle, largely divided on a regional and ethnic basis: The Popular Movement for the Liberation of Angola (MPLA) (receiving support from Cuba and the Soviet Union), the National Front for the Liberation of Angola (FNLA) and the National Union for the Total Independence of Angola

Fast facts

(UNITA) (receiving assistance from the US and South Africa). On 11 November 1975, MPLA leader Agostinho Neto was sworn in as the first president of an independent Angola under Marxist one-party rule. Both FNLA and UNITA turned their offensive against the new rulers. Even though US backing and South African support were eventually withdrawn, UNITA leader Jonas Savimbi continued the war. Dr. Neto died in 1979 and was succeeded as president by the new leader of the MPLA, José Eduardo dos Santos.

Government

In 1992 President dos Santos received a plurality of votes in Angola's first round of elections, declared free and fair by UN observers. The second round never took place as UNITA repudiated the first as fraudulent. In 1994 the MPLA and UNITA signed the Lusaka Protocol in an effort to end 20 years of civil war and in April 1997, UNITA joined MPLA and 10 smaller opposition parties in a Government of Unity and National Reconciliation (GURN). UNITA took up the 70 seats won in the 220-member National Assembly during the 1992 election. Four ministers and seven deputies from UNITA ranks were included in the 78 member cabinet. In the second half of 1998, however, UNITA pulled out and resumed the war.

Economic policy

Angola operated a Soviet-style centrally planned economy until 1991, but has since been making a transition to a market-based system. The government, however, still intervenes in the markets, fixing prices, mandating the quantity and mix of imports, setting a fixed exchange rate, and owning or directing much of the non-petroleum industrial sector. In its latest strategic plan, the government listed as priorities the guaranteeing of minimum consumption levels for foodstuffs and other essential goods; ensuring minimum levels of sustained economic growth; reduction of the deficits in the country's domestic and foreign accounts; controlling inflation; decreasing unemployment; reduction of red tape; and the creation of a favorable climate for foreign investment. At the beginning of 2000, steps were underway to reach agreement with the IMF on full-fledged financing and debt rescheduling.

Privatization

A privatization program has been developed but a weak private sector in Angola seems to lack the financial and/or administrative capacity to pick up on offers. A few smaller state-run enterprises have been sold but some have turned out to be economically nonviable. Most large enterprises such as telecommunications firms, insurance companies, and banks, remain government monopolies.

Sectors

Real gross domestic product (GDP) grew by 5.7 percent in 1997, driven by the petroleum sector. Oil accounts for 56 percent of GDP. Apart from significant diamond mining, the country also has deposits of iron ore, phosphates, copper, feldspar, gold, bauxite and uranium. Agricultural production continues to suffer from a degraded infrastructure, lack of funds for investment, and, in certain areas, political instability and the presence of minefields. Production is expected to increase once the infrastructure is repaired and upgraded. The ports of Luanda, Lobito, and Namibe are all operational, but require significant improvements.

Trading

With a daily production of approximately 1 million barrels of crude, oil accounts for 93 percent of Angola's export revenues. Refined petroleum, natural gas, and raw timber are also important export items. Diamonds are another major export with sales estimated at $400-600 million per year, much of it through nonofficial channels. Angola imports most consumer items, capital goods, and transport equipment. The US, South Africa, Germany, and Belgium are major partners. The US buys 75% of Angola's oil exports. Since October 1997, UN Security Council sanctions have been applied against UNITA for failing to comply with its Lusaka Protocol obligations.

Investment

Precise foreign direct investment statistics are not available, but estimates place current US FDI at over $4 billion. Annual foreign investment exceeds $1 billion, mostly in the petroleum exploration and production sector. The pace has picked up dramatically in the last three years in the wake of large offshore oil discoveries.

Financial sector

Owned and operated by the Ministry of Finance, the *Caixa de Credito Agro-Pecuaria e Pescas* (CAP) in 1996 took over all commercial operations from *Banco National de Angola* (BNA). CAP loans, often on concessionary and sometimes interest-free terms, have been used by the government to provide off-budget financing for parastatal entities. The *Banco de Comercio e Industria* (BCI) is a semiprivate bank, with 40 percent of its shares owned by the government. It extends short- and medium-term debt. The *Banco Africano de Investimentos* (BAI) is the only investment bank in Angola and the *Banco de Poupanca e Credito* (BPC) extends 80 percent of its credit to small and medium enterprises (primarily in the trade sector) and 20 percent to large enterprises (principally construction). HSBC Equator Bank provides services. Angola is already America's third largest trading partner in Sub-Saharan Africa and the US has become its number one investor. Several major US petroleum exploration, production and service, as well as mining, banking, consulting and transport firms, are involved.

Business activity

AGRICULTURE
Bananas, sugar cane, coffee, sisal, corn, cotton, manioc, tobacco, vegetables, plantains, livestock.

INDUSTRIES
Petroleum, diamonds, iron ore, phosphates, feldspar, bauxite, uranium, gold, cement, basic metal products, fish processing, food processing, brewing, tobacco products, sugar, textiles.

NATURAL RESOURCES
Petroleum, diamonds, iron ore, phosphates, copper, feldspar, gold, bauxite, uranium.

EXPORTS
$8.3 billion (1999 est.): crude oil, diamonds, refined petroleum products, timber, cotton.

IMPORTS
$6.5 billion (f1999 est.): machinery and electrical equipment, vehicles and spare parts, medicines, food, textiles and clothing, substantial military supplies.

MAJOR TRADING PARTNERS
US, EU, China, Portugal, France, South Africa.

Doing Business with Angola

▶ **Investment**

The Foreign Investment Institute is the point of contact for investors and the Foreign Investment Code gurantees equal treatment for overseas entrepreneurs who are subject to the same tax regime as locals. Repatriation of profits is guaranteed, and prompt indemnification promised in cases of nationalization or expropriation. The country's rich resources—oil, diamonds and several other strategic minerals—have lured big foreign firms. Petroleum-related investments dominate but once the war ends, rebuilding and repair of roads and railways are expected to offer further opportunities, as will agribusiness and telecommunications.

▶ **Trade**

The best prospects for exports are in oil-field machinery and equipment, computers and parts, used clothing, cars and trucks, generators and parts, ships, and aircraft. Product distribution can be problematic as a result of poor infrastructure. Foreign companies may chose to sell through an established importer in Angola, by winning a tender, through investment, or by opening an office.

▶ **Trade finance**

In 1999 the US Eximbank resumed financing for US trade deals with Angola. Angola has in recent years been a recipient of US Department of Agriculture PL-480 Title I program foodstuffs.

▶ **Selling to the government**

The Angolan authorities solicit supplies and services in local and international publications. Bid documents are obtained from a specific government ministry, department or agency at a nonrefundable fee.

▶ **Exchange controls**

The government sets the official rate and has imposed limits on foreign exchange transactions. There are no restrictions on the total amount of foreign currency brought into Angola but it must be declared within 24 hours at an authorized agency. No national currency can be exported from Angola. It is legal to maintain accounts in dollars. All import payments must be made through the central bank, even if foreign exchange is held in another bank.

▶ **Partnerships**

Joint ventures are sanctioned under the foreign investment law, which also regulates the amount and form of capital invested. If an investment is valued at more than $50 million or involves

activities that can only be carried out by concession (such as oil and diamond exploration and production), a contract must be established defining the project's objectives, the tax benefits and incentives to be granted, and providing for government monitoring. Such contracts are subject to the approval of the Ministry of Planning, the Prime Minister, and the Council of Ministers. Joint ventures must also be licensed by the Ministry of Commerce.

▶ **Establishing a presence**

A local attorney is needed to prepare the "Articles of Association" before registering a company and to conduct due diligence investigations prior to the conclusion of any purchase or other contractual agreement. The authorities assist foreign businesses interested in establishing agency, franchise, joint venture, or licensing relationships.

▶ **Project financing**

The country is experiencing difficulty in securing financing for projects other than those guaranteed by oil production. Under the Cabinda Trust arrangement, projects in the petroleum sector can receive financing secured by future oil production. Non-Cabinda Trust loans are often short term and at high interest rates.

▶ **Labor**

Labor is plentiful, but skills are scarce. The average level of education is sixth grade. There are two significant labor organizations in Angola.

▶ **Legal rights**

Under Angola's Foreign Investment Code all overseas investments are guaranteed protection and, in the event of expropriation, prompt compensation. Angola is a member of the World Intellectual Property Organization and makes use of its international classification of patents and products and services.

▶ **Business climate**

The ongoing conflict between the government and UNITA has an unsettling influence on the business climate. Despite the war, however, several petroleum companies and other major foreign firms involved in mining, banking and the service industry continue to function. Both domestic and international telecommunications are problematic and the cellular phone system oversubscribed. Many large international corporations rely on high frequency radio transmissions for routine communication.

160

 # Benin

In 1990 Benin, formerly known as Dahomey, turned away from a centrally planned economy under one-party Marxist-Leninist rule. The new democratically-elected government adopted reforms proposed by the World Bank and International Monetary Fund aimed at developing a free market economy in this small West African country. After several structural adjustment programs (SAPs), Benin has managed a recovery that has caught the attention of US and European investors and traders. Political and economic relations with the capitalist world—once marred by Benin's hardline Marxism—are close and cordial.

Country profile

The Republic of Benin (formerly Dahomey) extends about 650 km north from the Bight of Benin (part of the Gulf of Guinea) to the Niger River.

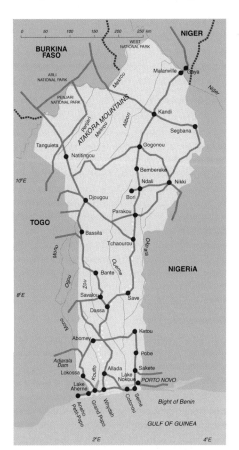

The southern equatorial region is covered with moist woodland savanna and oil palm trees along the coast. The poorer soil on the northern plateau is used for large-scale cotton cultivation and livestock. Along its borders with Niger and Burkina Faso, Benin maintains several national parks which constitute West Africa's premier wildlife conservation area. Most Beninese are related to peoples in neighboring countries. The Fon are closely related to the Ewe in Togo and the Yoruba are related to one of Nigeria's major ethnic groups. Also the Bariba (Borgu), Somba, Fulani, Dendi and Busa (Bussa) have relatives across the various borders. French is the official language and is spoken by groups of mixed descent and expatriates in the coastal towns and cities. Benin is one of only a few African countries where ethnic beliefs still hold sway over the Muslim and Christian faiths, with 70 percent adhering to indigenous beliefs and the rest evenly split between Christianity and Islam. The coastal regions of Benin and Togo practice voodoo (*vodun* or *juju*), a tribal ritual that spread to the Caribbean and the Americas during the slave trade era.

History

The Abomey kingdom of the Dahomey or Fon peoples was established in 1625. Its rich cultural life found expression in wooden masks, bronze statues, tapestries and pottery that have gained world reknown in recent years. The Portuguese and the Dutch conducted slave trade from Porto Novo until the mid-19th Century before the

Fast facts

French, with the approval of Britain and Germany, appropriated a colony extending from the Niger to the sea and named it Dahomey. Early in the 20th Century it became part of French West Africa and on 1 August 1960, was one of 14 former French African colonies granted independence. Several coups led to the assumption of power by Major Mathieu Kérékou in 1974. During his 17-year rule Kérékou turned Dahomey into the People's Republic of Benin under a Marxist dictatorship. In 1989, President Kérékou was forced by widespread opposition to his failed centralized economy to renounce Marxism-Leninism and implement a major privatization program. His cuts in the government payroll and reduction of social services promoted student and labor unrest. Fearing revolution Kérékou agreed to a new constitution and free elections in 1991. He lost to Nicéphore Soglo, who introduced economic reforms but failed to win reelection in 1996 when Kérékou made a dramatic comeback. Thus Benin became not only the first one-party state in Africa to vote an incumbent ruler out of office but also to return the same former authoritarian ruler to the presidency by popular vote. In the March 2001 presidential election Kérékou scored a comfortable victory over 16 opponents.

Government

Under a Constitution adopted in 1990 by national referendum, an executive President is elected for a 5-year term, renewable once. The President appoints the Council of Ministers. The unicameral 83-member National Assembly is elected for four years. Coalition politics is common as any of more than 30 splinter parties might swing the balance for any of the main contenders in close elections. The main players are the *Parti de la Renaissance du Benin* (PRB), the *Parti du Renouveau Democratique* (PRD) and the FARD-Alafia. For administrative purposes the country is divided into 12 departments—six in the south and six in the north.

Economic policy

Since 1989 Benin has implemented far-reaching changes in accordance with a structural adjustment program (SAP) sponsored by the World Bank and the IMF. This program aims at stabilizing public finances, reducing inflation, increasing domestic savings, and attracting investments. Marked progress has been made in all these areas and in July 2000 the World Bank and

IMF announced that Benin has qualified for $460 million in debt relief under the Heavily Indebted Poor Countries Initiative. (HIPC)

Privatization

Despite opposition from the unions, the government has proceeded with the sale of state-owned companies. Apart from selling state-owned enterprises such as SONACOP (oil company), *Société Sucrière de Save* (a sugar refinery), *Société des Ciments d'Onigbolo* (cement company), SONICOG (vegetable oil refineries), and SONAR and IARD (national insurance companies), the government has liquidated several other failing enterprises. In some cases foreign buyers are obliged to partner with Beninese nationals.

Sectors

Agriculture employs three-quarters of the population and accounts for 37% of GDP. Benin produces cotton, palm oil and kernels, coffee, and cocoa for export. It is generally self-sufficient in food production, though large quantities of foodstuffs, especially rice, are imported. Main food crops are millet, sorghum, maize, and root and tuber crops, such as cassava and yams. Livestock farming is important in the drier areas to the north. Fishing is popular in the rivers, lakes and lagoons. Timber production is negligible, but plans are underway to exploit the country's potential for forestry. Offshore oil is produced near Seme and further exploration is being undertaken. There are known deposits of phosphate, iron ore, chromium, gold and marble awaiting exploitation. Extensive limestone deposits are utilized for cement production. Manufacturing centers around the processing of agricultural products and consumer goods and construction materials. Tourism is a growing industry.

Trading

A substantial part of Benin's trade consists of goods smuggled across its border with Nigeria and therefore not accounted for in official trade statistics. Oil and cotton are major export items while food, fuel, energy and capital goods top the list of import items. Exports are mainly to Portugal, Morocco and the United States while France, Thailand and China supply in most of Benin's needs.

Investment

Major foreign investors in Benin are France, Germany, and Canada, but US firms have become increasingly involved in the petroleum sector. Other recent foreign investment came through acquisition of state-owned enterprises in textiles, tobacco, cement, beer brewing, petroleum and public transportation.

Financial sector

In 1989 five major commercial banks were established after the state-owned banking system failed, causing a serious liquidity crisis. With foreign assistance and guidance from the World Bank and IMF, Benin took measures to attract foreign banks back. The present financial system includes the Credit Promotion Benin (CCB), the postal checking accounts (CCP), the Savings Bank (CNE) and the Sonar, a state-owned insurance company.

Taxes and tariffs

Tax reforms were introduced in recent years to attract investors. In September 1994, Benin adopted one of the most open trade regimes in Africa, reducing the maximum tariff rate from 63% to 20%.

Links

Relations between the US and Benin have been warm since the early 1990s. The United States has supported Benin's move towards democracy with several human rights fund grants. Both the USAID and Peace Corps are represented and the US offered military training to the Beninese armed forces.

Business activity

AGRICULTURE
Corn, sorghum, cassava (tapioca), yams, beans, rice, cotton, palm oil, peanuts, poultry, livestock.

INDUSTRIES
Textiles, cigarettes, beverages, food, construction materials, petroleum.

EXPORTS
$516 million (1999 est.): cotton, crude oil, palm products, cocoa.

IMPORTS
$748 million (1999 est.): petroleum products, intermediate goods, capital goods, light consumer goods.

MAJOR TRADING PARTNERS
Brazil, Portugal, Morocco, Libya, France, UK, Thailand, Hong Kong, China.

Doing Business with Benin

▶ **Investment**

Good investment opportunities stem from the privatization process, with the oil sector offering the best potential for foreign investors. The government is slowly, but not entirely, disengaging itself from the this sector. Further scope is offered by Benin's efforts to improve the infrastructure for telecommunications, electricity and roads. The country also holds potential for those who are able to offer modern techniques for cold storage, canning, and packing. Saltwater fishing is another area where foreign involvement is sought. Considerable cotton production and privatization of the textile industry open up further prospects.

▶ **Trade**

Agricultural products, food processing machinery, consumer goods and gas powered turbines for electricity generation are good prospects. Large foreign firms often enter into exclusive contracts with an agent/distributor. Overseas firms are cautioned to deal only with Beninese companies that are registered with the government. Among the long-established distributors of consumer goods are French firms and Lebanese and Indian traders. The main types of outlets are open-air markets, street displays and street vendors, and European-style supermarkets and convenience stores with a wide range of local and imported products.

▶ **Trade finance**

Eximbank operates programs in support of US capital goods and services. With properly documented trade transactions, authorization for overseas payments is easily obtained. There is, however, no protection against currency fluctuations. Several banks have reliable and efficient correspondent relationships with overseas banks.

▶ **Selling to the government**

There has been a concerted effort on the part of the authorities to promote transparency and eliminate favoritism when considering bids. Bureaucratic red tape remains a problem.

▶ **Exchange controls**

Any enterprise engaged in a commercial, industrial, agricultural, or artisan activity, or that provides services, is entitled to transfer capital, profits and dividends.

▶ **Establishing a presence**

A limited company (Inc.) is the most common form of entry. Its establishment is speedy and simple. Establishing of a company normally requires authorization by the relevant ministry after completion of specific forms. Some industrial firms may opt for preferential schemes under the Investment Code, offered by the Technical Investment Commission of the Ministry of Planning. In most cases overseas firms rely on the services of a local attorney.

▶ **Project financing**

Several infrastructure renovation contracts are funded by grants or loans from the World Bank or other International Development Banks. The Overseas Private Investment Corporation (OPIC) offers financial assistance to small US companies and provides political risk insurance, loans, and investment guarantees. Two World Bank-related institutions, FIAS (Foreign Investments Advisory Service) and MIGA (Multilateral Investment Guarantee Agency), are active in Benin. Potential development financing is also available through the African Development Bank, the West African Bank for Development (BOAD), the European Development Fund (FED), and the International Fund for Economic Development (FIDA).

▶ **Labor**

A largely unskilled workforce is organized in four trade union confederations. Due to high unemployment (no official statistics) there is a substantial surplus of workers. A considerable number of skilled workers also continue to reenter the job market as privatization eliminates jobs in former state enterprises. Foreign firms have also had considerable success with in-house training and the government has established several technical schools. Salaries have not kept pace with the cost of living after devaluation. Labor reforms aiming at greater flexibility are underway.

▶ **Business climate**

There are guarantees against nationalization and the post-Marxist Benin is going out of its way to make the country investor friendly. In disputes between the state and a foreign firm, Benin recognizes the Hague Permanent Arbitration Court as the final authority. It also subscribes to the International Center for Settlement of Investment Disputes, which is part of the World Bank Group. Laws protect against IPR infringements. Benin is a signatory of the OAPI Convention of Yaounde (African Organization for Intellectual Property) and the World Intellectual Property Organization.

Botswana

Once one of the world's poorest countries, Botswana is credited by the World Bank as the country with the greatest rate of economic growth from 1966-1997, averaging an annual rate of 9.2%, well ahead of South Korea at 7.3% and China at 6.7%. It has since settled down to a more modest but respectable 5%. Today an average per capita GDP of $3,100 makes it one of the wealthiest nations on the continent and places it in the World Bank's upper-middle income category. Botswana is the only African country to have obtained a sovereign investment grade rating from the Economist Intelligence Unit. This "miracle" has been attained through judicious utilization of limited resources, good governance and sound macroeconomic policies.

Country profile

The Republic of Botswana is a large, sparsely populated, landlocked country sharing borders with five other countries. Its terrain varies from the arid Kalahari Desert to the lush forests of the Okavango Delta and the dry savannah of the Limpopo Valley. Botswana is constantly in need of rain, hence the national motto, *Pula* or rain.

More than 80% of its 1.5 million citizens are Tswana (plural Batswana, singular Motswana). They speak various dialects of the Sotho language, Setswana. The rest are Herero, Mbukushu, Subia and Fwe, apart from a few whites. Half of the population are Christians and the rest adhere to tribal beliefs.

History

The earliest inhabitants of the area were the San, followed by the Tswana. Bechuanaland, as it was known before independence, had been the cross-roads for missionaries, merchants and migrants before Britain annexed and declared it a protectorate in 1885 In a preemptive strike to prevent the Boers of the Transvaal from taking possession. Independence for Bechuanaland under its new name, Botswana, came in 1966. The first elected president, Sir Seretse Khama, remained in power until his death in 1980. Khama was succeeded by Vice President and later Sir Ketumile Masire who remained in power for seventeen years. When Masire retired in 1998, his vice president—an Oxford-educated economist and former Finance Minister—Festus Mogae, was elected president.

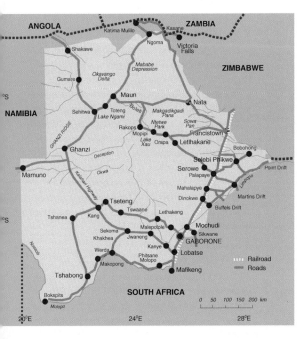

Fast facts

Government

Held out as a model of democracy in Africa, Botswana continues to adhere strictly to its 1966 constitution requiring the election of a president and National Assembly for a period of five years. The President is limited to two terms. The unicameral Assembly is made up of 40 directly elected and four nominated members, a speaker and attorney general. The Botswana Democratic Party, which has been in power since independence, has seen some of its support eroding in recent years.

Economic policy

At independence in 1966, Botswana was one of the 20 poorest nations. The discovery of diamonds in 1971 and sound economic policies enabled it to attain one of the world's highest economic growth rates, averaging 11.3% between 1980 and 1990. Under its Industrial Development Policy the government utilized mineral wealth to develop human resources and infrastructure, communications facilities and utilities. The stock exchange sought new listings to attract business on the foreign capital markets. The 1998 Africa Competitiveness Report of the World Economic Forum placed Botswana third in Africa, behind Mauritius and Tunisia, in terms of overall competitiveness. HIV/AIDS, however, presents a major threat to the country, with some estimates putting the infection rate at 36%—the highest in the world.

Privatization

The government has indicated that with the exception of Debswana (diamond mines) and the Diamond Valuing Agency, all parastatals will be privatized. In some instances, Botswana has resorted to a partial sale of equity to private investors. State enterprises in electricity, telecommunications, transportation, water, real estate, cattle and mining sectors have been "commercialized"—the elimination of government subsidies to enterprises run as private businesses with the state as a shareholder. In some instances Botswana citizens are given first rights to purchasing state enterprises.

Sectors

Diamonds, discovered five years after Botswana became independent, account for most of the country's wealth, followed by cattle farming. Diamonds constitute close to 80% of total export earnings. Botswana also has significant deposits of coal, copper-nickel, soda ash, potash and sodium sulphate. Livestock—especially cattle farming—constitutes 80% of the total agricultural income. Sorghum, maize, millet, beans and other crops are cultivated on a subsistence basis. A developing manufacturing sector entails motor vehicle assembly, and pharmaceuticals, leather and textiles, food processing and furniture. Due to the small size of the domestic market, most of these industries are export-oriented.

Trading

Botswana's largest export market is the European Union (74%) with diamonds (70%) as the main commodity. South Africa is in second place with 21% of the total, purchasing mostly vehicles and beef and supplying 78% of Botswana's imports. Estimates for 1999 show the US supplying a mere $34.2 million of Botswana's total purchases of $2.25 billion, and purchasing $23.5 million of the country's total exports of $2.3 billion. Principal US exports were manufactured goods, including heavy machinery, electrical appliances, data processing machines, radar appliances, communication and electrical equipment. US imports consisted largely of textiles, clothing and handicrafts.

Investment

Foreign direct investment (FDI) forms a major portion of overseas capital flows into Botswana, followed by portfolio investments. The latter have grown considerably since the establishment of the Botswana Stock Exchange in the 1990s. Not surprisingly, mining draws the largest percentage of FDI. Significant foreign capital has also gone into the development of infrastructure and, in recent years, the manufacturing and tourist sectors. Most foreign equity and non-equity investments came from South Africa (80%). The remainder originated largely in the European Union (12.7%), with the U.K. and Luxembourg as major sources. Investments from the US constitute 3.3% of the total and went largely into the service, manufacturing and tourism sectors. The automobile industry remains a priority and vehicle assembly is now the country's second most important industry. By far the largest foreign investor in Botswana is South Africa's Anglo-American Corporation (De Beers), which has a multimillion dollar stake, along with the Government of Botswana, in the country's major diamond mining industry, Debswana.

Financial sector

The central bank—the Bank of Botswana—has an impressive track record managing the commercial banking sector and monetary policies. Foreigners have access to credit at local market rates and often receive preferential treatment over local borrowers. There are four commercial banks and one investment bank, all with correspondent arrangements in the US. Nonresidents are no longer restricted from issuing bonds on the stock market and are able to hold bonds with maturity periods of over one year. This is designed to encourage inward portfolio investments. Dual listings are also permitted on the Botswana Stock Exchange. The establishment of an International Financial Services Center (IFSC) in the wake of progressive economic liberalization, the abolition of exchange controls, high foreign exchange reserves, and the maintenance of a favorable macroeconomic environment present a potentially lucrative business opportunity for US companies interested in operating offshore banking, insurance and accounting facilities in Southern Africa

Taxes and tariffs

Taxes in Botswana are among the lowest in southern Africa. Corporate tax rates are 25%, including a 15% concessional rate for manufacturers and providers of financial services.

Business activity

AGRICULTURE
Sorghum, maize, millet, pulses, groundnuts (peanuts), beans, cowpeas, sunflower seed, livestock.

INDUSTRIES
Diamonds, copper, nicekl, coal, salt, soda ash, potash, livestock processing.

NATURAL RESOURCES
Diamonds, copper, nickel, salt, soda ash, potash, coal, iron ore, silver.

EXPORTS
$1.7 billion (1999 est.): diamonds (76%), nickel (4%), copper, meat.

IMPORTS
$1.98 billion (1999 est.): foodstuffs, vehicles and transport equipment, textiles, petroleum products.

MAJOR TRADING PARTNERS
EU, Southern African Customs Union (SACU), Zimbabwe.

Doing Business with Botswana

▶ **Investment**

There is scope for investment in motor vehicle assembly, photovoltaic manufacturing, financial services and tourism. Investment incentives are offered. The Botswana Export Development and Investment Agency assists investors through all the preliminary stages and provides support services, such as purchasing or leasing of property, obtaining work and residence permits, licenses, and grants. The Botswana Development Corporation seeks out suitable partners for specific projects and the National Development Bank offers long-term loans. Under the Financial Assistance Policy, grants are extended to labor-intensive projects outside the cattle farming and diamond sectors.

▶ **Trade**

State purchase of drugs (particularly to combat HIV/AIDS) and a growing need for computer hardware and software, mining, construction, telecommunications equipment, as well photovoltaic and water supply systems, offer trade opportunities. As a result of frequent droughts, there is often a need for corn, sorghum, wheat, and rice.

▶ **Trade finance**

Short-term finance, including pre-and-post-shipment credit, is available through the local commercial banking system and export credit insurance is offered by domestic insurance companies. Eximbank financing is available to US exporters.

▶ **Selling to the government**

The Central Tender Board (CTB) awards government tenders in an open process. Lobbying of the CTB is strictly prohibited. Occasionally preferential treatment is given to local participants. Firms are encouraged to make contact with the relevant government ministries or parastatals to ensure proper presentation of tenders for major projects.

▶ **Exchange controls**

Botswana has abolished exchange controls but the authorities monitor capital flows for early warning signals of potentially destabilizing activity. Commercial banks require investors to fill out basic forms for outward and inward transactions.

▶ **Partnerships**

Partnership with a local investor has occasionally been an unwritten requirement for winning government tenders. The government, however, does not impose any performance requirements or local participation on foreign enterprises.

▶ **Establishing a presence**

Foreign private entities may freely establish, acquire, and dispose of interests in local business enterprises. The government does not set any conditions regarding location, local content, local equity, import substitution, export targets, or financing. There is no restriction on the repatriation of profits and dividends, debt service, capital gains, returns on intellectual property, royalties, franchise fees and service fees. Upon disinvestment, foreigners are allowed to reclaim all proceeds.

▶ **Project financing**

OPIC finance and insurance programs apply to US operations in Botswana. Botswana is a member of the Multilateral Investment Guarantee Agency and all four major local commercial banks as well as an investment bank offer financing for new businesses. Six separate development financial institutions also offer specialized services. The borrowing provisions for US and other foreign firms are liberal.

▶ **Labor**

With high unemployment, there is no shortage of workers. Due to the low skill base employers may have to undertake significant training, depending on the industry. Only a small portion of the formal sector—mostly mining and banking— is unionized and strikes are rare. An industrial court ensures impartial adjudication in labor disputes.

▶ **Legal rights**

Civil law is based on Roman-Dutch law and the English criminal legal system applies. Botswana is a member of the International Center for the Settlement of Investment Disputes (ICSID) and the Multilateral Investment Guarantee Agency. The Industrial Property Act and recently revamped Copyright Act brought the country in conformity with the WTO's Trade Related Aspects of International property Rights. The Constitution prohibits nationalization of private property.

▶ **Business climate**

Botswana's business and government community tend to be reserved and formal. English is the official language and used extensively in business, but Setswana is widely spoken. It is wise to reconfirm appointments 24 hours ahead. Meetings may start late and are sometimes interrupted by telephone conversations. Neither is an indication of disrespect or lack of interest.

Burkina Faso

Formerly known as Upper Volta, Burkina Faso is the smallest of West Africa's landlocked states. Despite its relatively small population of ten million and limited natural resources, Burkina has managed to attract foreign attention by streamlining its public sector, privatizing, lifting trade barriers and liberalizing prices. Since 1991 it has worked closely with the World Bank and the IMF in a structural adjustment program. Burkina Faso depends on Ghana and Côte d'Ivoire for outlets to the sea and work opportunities for some of its citizens. The foreign business community, especially those involved in mining and minerals, have started to focus on Burkina Faso—"the land of the honorable."

Country profile

The Democratic Republic of Burkina Faso (or Burkina), formerly known as Upper Volta, is the smallest of Western Africa's landlocked states. It spans the headwaters of the Great Volta River. Burkina is rich in historical relics but relatively poor in natural resources. The climate is tropical. The Gur (or Voltaic) peoples, who also inhabit northern parts of Togo, Ghana and Côte d'Ivoire, dominate Burkina. The largest group of Gur-speaking peoples is the Mossi (or

Moore) around Ouagadougou, the nucleus of their ancient kingdom. The Mande-speaking Bobo and Dyula, found in the southwest around the town of Bobo-Dioulasso and the with the Bisa, who live further east, are related to the people of Mali. In the dry north are the pastoral Fulani. About half the population adhere to traditional ethnic faiths and the rest are predominantly Muslim.

History

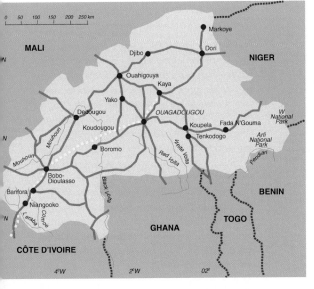

Burkina Faso's orginal inhabitants were the Bobo, Lobi and Gurunsi peoples. The Mosi and Gurma peoples migrated to the region in the 14th Century. From the 15th to the 18th Century the Mossi successfully resisted incorporation into the Mali and Songhai empires as well as Fulani invasions. France conquered the territory between 1895 and 1904. Responding to insurrection in Upper Volta, the French introduced military rule until 1919, when it became a separate colony in the union of French West Africa. Upper Volta received self-government following a referendum in 1958 and full independence in 1960. Shortly after he won the first election, President Maurice Yameogo

169

Fast facts

banned all opposition parties. He was overthrown in 1966 and succeeded by Gen. Sangoule Lamizana, who, as promised, returned the country to civilian rule in 1970 but reverted to authoritarian rule four years later. Until the early 1980s, several further attempts to establish multiparty politics failed. In August 1983 Capt. Thomas Sankara, a 34-year admirer of Libya's Colonel Qaddafi, came to power. He changed the name of Upper Volta to Burkina Faso, a blend of local words meaning "the land of the honorable," and introduced a Libyan-style "Jamahiriya." After several failed attempts, Sankara was assassinated in 1987 and succeeded by Capt. Blaise Compaoré who reversed hardline socialist policies and introduced economic reforms in cooperation with international banks. A new constitution opened the way for elections in 1991, largely boycotted by the opposition parties. Compaoré emerged the winner and was reelected president by an overwhelming margin in 1998.

Government

In November 1998, Compaoré drew 87.5% of the popular vote in his bid for president. His party, the *Congrès pour la Démocratie et le Progrès* (CDP), captured 101 out of the 111 seats in the National Assembly in the general election of May 1997. The main opposition party, the *Parti pour la Démocratie et le Progrès* (PDP), won 6 seats.Executive power is vested in the President, elected by the voters for a 7-year term. The country is divided into 30 provinces, further subdivided into departments, *arrondissements* (wards) and villages.

Economic policy

Once one of the world's poorest countries, Burkina Faso has been implementing a structural adjustment program (SAP) in close cooperation with the World Bank and the IMF. Starting from a mere 0.4% growth rate in 1989, the country averaged 2.3% between 1990 and 1994, reaching a growth rate of 6.1% in 1996. While an increase in agricultural output helped, the government is credited in large part for its diligent enforcement of reforms. Price liberalization and external tariff reduction coupled with banking and financial sector reform, as well as privatization, further enhanced the business environment. In July 2000, the World Bank and IMF announced that Burkina Faso qualified for $700 million in debt relief under the Heavily Indebted Poor Countries Initiative (HIPC).

Privatization

In 1994 parliament approved the restructuring of 42 state-owned enterprises. These included 19 major corporations in banking, brewing, mining, medicine, manufacturing and advertising that have already been restructured. Another 10 have been liquidated and 10 were in the process of being turned over to private control. Further privatization of the state-owned electricity, water and telecommunications utilities is anticipated.

Sectors

Burkina depends in part on foreign aid remittances by its citizens employed in neighboring countries such as Côte d'Ivoire and Ghana. The rural population is largely dependent on subsistence farming and nomadic stock raising. Main food crops are sorghum, millet, yams, maize, rice and beans. Cotton is grown for export. Mining activity is confined to gold, manganese, phosphates, marble and antimony. There are also viable deposits of zinc, silver, limestone, bauxite, nickel and lead. Small scale manufacturing entails flour milling, sugar refining, manufacture of cotton yarn and textiles and the production of consumer goods such as bicycles, footwear and soap.

Trading

Importation of most consumer and other manufactured goods and equipment causes a chronic unfavorable trade balance. The largest trading partner is France but imports from other European countries and the US are growing. Cotton, livestock and gold are principal exports. Abidjan in Côte d'Ivoire is used for bulk imports and exports.

Investment

Mining is the area of greatest interest for foreigners. The authorities have lured foreign mining companies by easing of regulatory laws, reducing taxes, adopting standard investment contracts, and improving the dissemination of geological data. American, Australian and South African corporations have obtained exploration and mining permits in recent times.

Financial sector

The financial and banking sectors have been restructured during the past seven years. Non-performing banks have been liquidated or privatized with the help of foreign partners. Three large commercial banks (with correspondent relationships with New York banks) and four credit institutions provide credit for investment and commercial transactions.

Taxes and tariffs

A value-added tax applies and profits are taxed at rates varying between 5% and 35%. There are three different incentive schedules for investors. The mining investment code provides special customs and fiscal privileges for mining companies during both the exploration and production stages. Only after the existence of extractable mineral deposits is proven may the holder of the exploration license obtain a mining license or concession allowing total exemption from customs fees on raw materials, components, and equipment necessary for production. The license holder also enjoys a seven year exemption from other taxes. Burkina Faso's customs fees are based on goods ad valorem (CIF plus fees and commissions) and include a five percent customs fee, a variable import fiscal duty (DFI) and a variable value-added tax based on the type of goods. Depending on economic conditions, the government may subsidize the importation of certain basic products such as rice and sugar by decreasing custom duties.

Business activity

AGRICULTURE
Peanuts, shea nuts, sesame, cotton, sorghum, millet, corn, rice, livestock.

INDUSTRIES
Cotton lint, beverages, agricultural processing, soap, cigarettes, textiles, gold.

NATURAL RESOURCES
Manganese, limestone, marble, gold, antimony, copper, nickel, bauxite, lead, phosphates, zinc, silver.

EXPORTS
$292 million (1999 est.): cotton, animal products, gold.

IMPORTS
$759 million (1999 est.): machinery, food products, petroleum.

MAJOR TRADING PARTNERS
Côte d'Ivoire, France, Italy, Mali, Togo, Nigeria.

Doing Business with Burkina Faso

▶ **Investment**

Tax exemptions apply to investments in mining and other sectors and an investment code guarantees foreign investors the right to transfer any funds associated with an investment, including dividends, receipts from liquidation, assets, and salaries. Transfers are authorized in the original currency of the investment. Gold mining and diamond exploration are priority areas. Foreign and domestic investors are treated equally. The Ministry of Industry, Commerce, and Mines approves all new investments on the recommendation of the national investment commission.

▶ **Trade**

Telecommunications and computer equipment, pharmaceuticals, and used clothing are areas where US exporters have managed to capture a share of the market. A local agent/distributor is not required by law but can be helpful. There is a market for wheat, yellow corn, semolina, and rice. Most trade restrictions have been removed and tariffs have been steadily reduced.

▶ **Trade finance**

Burkina is eligible for foreign credit insurance assistance through Eximbank programs and is a member of the Multilateral Investment Guarantee Agency.

▶ **Selling to the government**

Road, dam and other construction projects are at times awarded to local companies in partnership with foreign firms. Purchases by state-owned utilities are done on tender.

▶ **Exchange controls**

Transfer of all funds associated with an investment, including dividends, receipts from liquidation, assets, and salaries is allowed without delay.

▶ **Partnerships**

There is a limited number of business people available with the practical experience and financial capacity needed to form a successful partnership There are several Burkinabé joint ventures in the mining sector involving foreign companies.

▶ **Establishing a presence**

Wholly owned foreign ownership in companies is allowed. Proposed foreign businesses operations are, however, subject to a screening process to ensure full compliance with local laws.

▶ **Project financing**

Burkina Faso is eligible for OPIC programs and the potential exists for direct loans and loan guarantees from the World Bank, the European Union and the African Development Bank.

▶ **Labor**

There is a scarcity of skilled workers, mainly in management, and in the engineering and the electrical trades. Burkinabé workers have a reputation for industriousness and loyalty. A code guaranteeing worker's rights is administered by a labor court. There is a well organized trade union movement. Employers must advise workers at least 30 days prior to termination and except in cases of theft or flagrant neglect of duty they have the right to termination benefits.

▶ **Legal rights**

Basic property rights are protected. In a few cases where the government deems expropriation necessary, compensation must be paid in advance. Since 1960, there have only been three cases: In 1968, the electric company (Safelec) was nationalized; in 1970 Comacico-Benin and SECM, film making and distribution companies, were taken over by the state; and in 1980, a manufacturer of ammunition, Carvolt, was expropriated. If an attempt at settlement of a dispute between the government and an investor fails, arbitration is prescribed. Burkina belongs to the African Intellectual Property Organization as well as the World Intellectual Property Organization. A local attorney and/or notary public may be required when securing or closing a contract.

▶ **Business climate**

Business is almost exclusively conducted in French but adequate translation services are available. There is a small but dynamic Chamber of Commerce, which conducts feasibility studies and training, develops business links, and organizes trade shows. It also serves as a bridge between government authorities and business associations. All matters regarding investments and import-export regulations and procedures are handled by the Ministry of Commerce, Industry and Crafts. Most sales and distribution are conducted from the major cities of Ouagadougou and Bobo-Dioulasso. The main commercial banks and insurance companies have, however, branches in secondary urban areas.

Burundi

Like neighboring Rwanda, Burundi has caught the world's attention since the mid-1990s for the wrong reasons. Situated in the scenic Great Lakes region of Africa, this former Belgian colony has been the scene of some of the modern world's worst carnage. The mounting cost in human lives was accompanied by worsening economic conditions. The intensity and extent of repeated episodes of genocide have dismayed onlookers and scared away potential foreign investors. There is still hope that continuing efforts by both eminent Africans and the world community might bring peace to this troubled land and make Burundi safe for foreign business once again.

Country profile

The Republic of Burundi is situated in the high rainfall region bordering Lake Tanganyika. Most of the people are Rundi or Barundi, comprising the Bantu Hutu (Bahutu) peoples (85%) and Nilotic Tutsi (Batutsi) (15%). The Twa (Batwa), descendants of the early Pygmy population, number only in the thousands. The majority of both Tutsi and Hutu are Christians—overwhelmingly Roman Catholic. Kirundi and French are official languages and Swahili is widely spoken.

History

The simple version of history has the Tutsi (Nilotic) cattle breeders arriving in the area from the 15th Century and subjugating the Hutu inhabitants. In reality, the situation is much more complex as boundaries of race and class became less distinct over the years as a result of intermingling. Some put part of the blame for the racial animosity that led to the recent mass-scale killings on the shoulders of German and Belgian colonial rulers who pitched the Hutu against Tutsi for their own gain. When Burundi and neighboring Rwanda were incorporated into German East Africa in 1899, they had been kingdoms for several centuries headed by *mwamis* (kings). After Germany's defeat in World War I these nations were transferred to Belgium under the joint name of Ruanda-Urundi. They were, however, "separated at birth" when they gained their independence in 1962. In 1972, after an abortive coup attempt, between 200,000 and 400,000 Hutus were killed in Burundi and about 200,000 fled the country. Following democratic elections in 1993, a Hutu as-

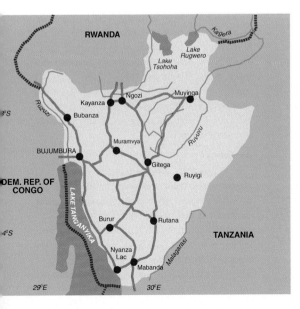

Fast facts

POLITICAL

Head of State	Pres. Pierre Buyoya (1996)
Ruling Party	UPRONA
Main Opposition	FRODEBU
Independence	1 July 1962
National capital	Bujumbura
Official languages	French & Kirundi

PHYSICAL

Total area	10,747 sq. miles 27,830 sq. km. (± Maryland)
Arable land	45% of land area
Coastline	Landlocked

POPULATION

Total	5.73 million
Av. yearly growth	3.54%
Population/sq. mile	563
Urbanized population	8%
Adult literacy	46.0%

ECONOMY[1]

Currency	Burundi franc (FBu)(US$1=821.29)
GDP (real)	$959 million
GDP growth rate	-1.0%
GNP per capita[2]	$140
GDP (ppp)[3]	$4.1 billion
GDP per cap. (ppp)[3]	$740
Inflation rate	17%
Exports	$63 million
Imports	$131 million
Development aid	$125 million
External debt	$1.12 billion
Unemployment	N/A

INFRASTRUCTURE

Railroads	0 km
Paved roads	7%
Motor vehicles	28,000
Air passenger/km	2 million
Telephones/1,000	3
International airport	Bujumbura
Main harbor	Uses Dar es Salaam

1. Statistics are based on World Bank data.
2. Atlas method.
3. See page 151 for an explanation of GDP based on purchasing power parity (ppp).

sumed the presidency for the first time. He was assassinated shortly afterwards by the Tutsi-dominated army. Ultimately in 1995, the ruling Front for Democracy in Burundi (FRODEBU) and the Tutsi-dominated opposition party, the Union for National Progress (UPRONA), formed a coalition government under Hutu President Sylvestre Ntibantunganya, but unrest continued. By mid-1996 an estimated 150,000 had perished. In September 1996, Major Pierre Buyoya, a former Tutsi president, staged a coup and toppled the Hutu-run government and assumed leadership. Conflict continued until July 2001when Buyoya and his adversaries agreed to a transition plan in Arusha, Tanzania, requiring him to step down as president after eighteen months in favor of the Hutu Vice President, Domitien Ndayizeye, who will remain in office for another eighteen months before elections are held.

Government

Burundi has been governed since 1996 by a military government under President Pierre Buyoya. Under pressure of sanctions, a civilian all-party cabinet was appointed in August 1996 and an all-party National Assembly nominated in October.

Economic policy

Before the massacres and instability following the assassination of Burundi's first Hutu president in 1993, the country had already been among the poorest in the world. Since then the economy has been contracting at an alarming rate; by 1996 more than 60% of the population was living in conditions of extreme poverty. The government is constantly preoccupied with crisis management and there is little time left for the restructuring and rehabilitating of the economy. In 2000 the World Bank approved $35 million in credit for an "emergency economic recovery project."

Sectors

Some 90% of the population practice subsistence agriculture. Coffee, tea and cotton are grown for export, while subsistence crops include cassava, bananas, sweet potatoes, pulses, maize, sorghum, yams and peanuts. Cattle rearing and fishing along Lake Tanganyika are also important sources of food. Substantial nickel deposits (about 5% of world reserves) and vanadium are not being mined at present; neither are known reserves of oil, uranium and phosphates. Gold and tungsten are mined on a small scale. Manufacturing involves beer brewing, soft drinks, cigarettes, and the processing of coffee and tea.

Privatization

There were efforts to privatize the deeply indebted water and electricity state enterprises, but these and other restructuring plans are on hold.

Trade

Coffee accounts for 80% of foreign exchange earnings. Other major export items are tea, cotton and hides.

Investment

RTZ and BHP have postponed their nickel exploration while others have suspended activity in gold and vanadium mining.

Financial Sector

International banking transactions can be carried out through the *Banque de la République du Burundi*, the *Banque Commerciale du Burundi* and the *Banque Burundaise pour le Commerce et l'Investissement*. The banking sector suffered mass withdrawals in 1994.

Business activity

AGRICULTURE
Coffee, cotton, tea, corn, sorghum. potatoes, bananas, manioc, beef, milk, hides.

INDUSTRIES
Light consumer goods such as blankets, shoes, soap, components assembly, public works construction, food processing.

NATURAL RESOURCES
Nickel, uranium, rare earth oxides, peat, cobalt, copper, unexploited platinum, vanadium, and gold.

EXPORTS
$63 million (1999 est.): coffee, tea, cotton, hides.

IMPORTS
$131 million (1999 est.): capital goods, petroleum products, foodstuffs, consumer goods.

MAJOR TRADING PARTNERS
UK, Germany, Benelux, Switzerland, France, Japan.

Doing Business with Burundi

▶ **Investment**

Even though minerals such as nickel, vanadium and phosphate have attracted foreign interest, no one is making a serious move until Burundi manages to establish stability and provide security for foreign entrepreneurs.

▶ **Trade**

Foreigners who offer goods are advised to appoint an experienced agent, even though it is not legally required. A sizeable portion of the country's basic needs are handled through purchases by donor countries.

▶ **Selling to the government**

The purchase of petroleum, a major import item, is supervised by the Ministry of Industry and Trade.

▶ **Investment**

Burundi maintains strict control over its supplies of hard currency, all of which are held by the Central Bank. Repatriating profits requires permission from the Central Bank. The conversion of Burundi Francs to dollars often a lengthy and cumbersome undertaking.

▶ **Project finance**

International development assistance is at a virtual halt, apart from humanitarian relief efforts. Financing is not available from OPIC or other known international bodies.

▶ **Project finance**

The majority of the workforce consists of illiterate and semi-literate displaced farmers. Unionized employees, especially in the urban areas, earn somewhat more than the minimum wage which stood at $0.40 per day in the cities of Bujumbura and Gitega and $0.35 in the rest of the country. Many schools have been destroyed in the civil war, leading to lower rates of student enrollment and a limited pool of educated potential employees.

▶ **Business climate**

French and Kirundi are official languages and are widely used in business. Relatively few people speak English.

Cameroon

Cameroon's economy is the most diversified in Central Africa and makes up more than half of the total GNP of the Central African Economic and Monetary Community (CEMAC). Its abundant natural resources, a favorable climate, and well-educated work force make it one of Africa's potentially most competitive economies. Following nearly a decade of economic decline, growth resumed in 1994 after a 50 percent currency devaluation, stabilization of terms of trade, increased external preferential financing and debt relief. New projects funded by the World Bank as well as the African Development Bank will create attractive service and investment opportunities for foreign entrepreneurs. Further renewed foreign investment activity is expected in the wake of a major oil pipeline under construction between Chad and Cameroon.

Country profile

The Republic of Cameroon is situated on a plateau rising to 1,500 m in the Adamawa Mountains. Mount Cameroon is one of a series of volcanoes running southward, into the ocean, and northward, to Bamenda. In the rain forests of the south an equatorial climate prevails while the fertile soil of the western volcanic zone allows cultivation of a variety of tropical crops. There are more than 200 language groups. The largest single group is the Bamileke. Other major peoples include the Fulani, the Chadic, and the Bantu-speaking Fang. The northern Fulani and Chadic are mainly Muslim, while those in the west and south are predominantly Christian, though many still adhere to traditional ethnic beliefs.

History

Cameroon is part of the original home of the Bantu cultural grouping who migrated east and south into the countries now known as the Central African Republic, Gabon and Congo. Little was known about the territory until the arrival of the Portuguese in 1472. Explorer Fernando Po named the Wuri River *Rio dos Camarões* (shrimp or prawn) after large crustaceans found at its mouth. This evolved into the country's present name, Cameroon. During the following three centuries several other European nations and American traders operated

along the Cameroon coast. In 1884, it became the German protectorate of Kamerun, but after the First World War the League of Nations allo-

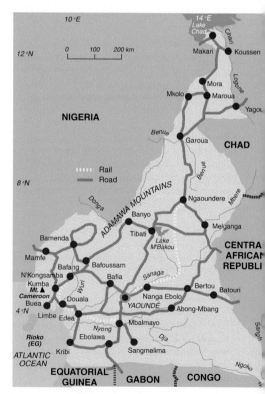

cated 80% of the territory to France (French Cameroun) and the remaining 20%, consisting of two separate areas along the Nigerian border, to the British as Northern and Southern Cameroons. After a protracted insurgency led by the Bamileke, French Cameroun gained its independence in 1960 under President Ahmadou Ahidjo who adopted single-party rule. Parts of the British Cameroons opted to join newly-independent Cameroon while others voted to merge with Nigeria. In 1982 Ahidjo resigned on grounds of ill health and handed power over to Prime Minister Paul Biya. A war of words between the two former allies led to a trial and a death sentence in absentia for Ahidjo, found guilty of subversion. In March 1992 Biya won reelection in disputed multiparty elections, a feat which he repeated in 1997 with a 93% vote after several opponents withdrew.

Government

Cameroon has a strong central government dominated by the President, elected for a seven year term, renewable only once. The president appoints the prime minister and cabinet. The 180-member unicameral National Assembly is elected every five years. Since independence, a single party, the Cameroon People's Democratic Movement (CPDM), has remained in power. The Social Democratic Front (SDF) is the strongest of 150 registered opposition parties.

Economic policy

The IMF, World Bank and Paris Club have instituted programs to help reinvigorate Cameroon's economy. Economic growth continues to be inhibited by a large inefficient parastatal sector, excessive public sector employment, growing defense and internal security expenditures, and by the Government's inability to collect internal revenues effectively, especially in economically important pro-opposition regions. Cameroon has, however, conformed to a triennial economic program and undertaken a number of reforms since 1989 to reduce its own stake in the economy and promote private sector development. Beginning in early 1997, the government initiated meaningful dialogue with the private sector through a series of town meetings.

Sectors

Although agriculture is the dominant sector and employs about three-quarters of the labor

Fast facts

POLITICAL	
Head of State	Pres. Paul Biya (1982)
Ruling Party	CPDM
Main Opposition	SDF
Independence	20 May 1960
National capital	Yaoundé
Official languages	English & French

PHYSICAL	
Total area	475,422 sq. km.
	183,560 sq. miles
	(± California)
Arable land	15% of land area
Coastline	400 km/248 miles

POPULATION	
Total	15.46 million
Av. yearly growth	2.79%
Population/sq. mile	84
Urban population	48%
Adult literacy	74%

ECONOMY[1]	
Currency	CFA franc
	(CFAF)(US$1=752.76)
GDP (real)	$9.23 billion
GDP growth rate	4.4%
GNP per capita[2]	$610
GDP (ppp)[3]	$29.6 billion
GDP per cap. (ppp)[3]	$2,000
Inflation rate	2.5%
Exports	$2.2 billion
Imports	$2.3 billion
Development aid	$527 million
External debt	$8.1 billion
Unemployment	30%

INFRASTRUCTURE	
Railroads	860 km/534 miles
Paved roads	13%
Motor vehicles	169,000
Air passenger/km	436 million
Telephones/1,000	5 (1994)
International airport	Yaoundé
Main harbor	Douala

1. Statistics are based on World Bank data.
2. Atlas method.
3. See page 151 for an explanation of GDP based on purchasing power parity (ppp).

force, Cameroon has one of the few comparatively diversified economies in sub-Saharan Africa. Cocoa is the main cash crop—Cameroon is the world's fifth largest producer—followed by coffee, cotton, tobacco, rubber, palm oil, sugar and bananas. It is the fifth largest producer of petroleum in sub-Sahara Africa. Unexploited mineral wealth includes bauxite, cobalt, chromium, gold, iron, nickel, sapphires, tin, titanium, uranium, and limestone. Cameroon has the largest tropical rain forest after the Democratic Republic of Congo and produces tropical wood (ebony, mahogany, and iroko) both for export and the local industry. During good rainfall years the country is largely self-sufficient in foodstuffs.

Privatization

Cameroon is in the midst of a privatization process that will eliminate all public sector monopolies except for aluminum. Privatized to date are, among others, CAMSUCO (national sugar company), SOCAPALM (the palm oil complex), the CDC (agricultural plantation complex), BICEC (a state-owned bank) and SOCAR (insurance company). Parastatals that are still scheduled for privatization include the national airliner (CAMAIR), the telecommunication companies (CAMTEL and CAMTEL-MOBILE), and the national insurance retirement fund (CNPS).

Trade

Petroleum and gas account for 33% of Cameroon's exports, tropical wood (24%), and aluminum 5.5%. Other exports are coffee, cocoa, cotton, rubber, timber, bananas and pineapples. In 1998 the US supplied 8% of the total imports, making Cameroon its seventh largest customer in Sub-Saharan Africa. US sales include bauxite for an aluminum smelting plant as large local bauxite deposits (the 5th largest worldwide) are too expensive to mine. Other major imports from the US are wheat and flour, petroleum coke and pitch additives for aluminum smelting, used clothing and gross lot discounted and discontinued consumer products.

Investment

France is the leading investor. Construction of the multinational $1.5 billion Chad/Cameroon pipeline should, however, lead to larger US participation. Apart from long-standing investments in oil production, US firms are involved in security services, oral care and hygiene products manufacturing, and fresh fruit production.

Financial sector

There are nine commercial banks under control of the *Banque des Etats de l'Afrique Centrale* (BEAC), a common central bank also serving the five other member countries of the Central African sub-region and regulated by the French government. Cameroon has no securities market or bond market but the Banque Nationale de Paris has been mandated to draw up a model for a small, screen-based securities market for the Central African franc zone. Advisors on the exchange market are the *Société de Bourse de Paris*, Citibank and the International Finance Corporation.

Taxes & tariffs

In 1994 Cameroon implemented a new Regional Reform Program, including tax reform. The new code reduced the number of taxes applied to imports from over seven to four and reduced the overall rate from a overall maximum of 200% to a maximum of 70% on luxury goods and a minimum of 5% on necessities.

Pipeline

A consortium led by ExxonMobil is constructing of a pipeline to carry petroleum from Chad to the Atlantic Ocean by way of Cameroon.

Business activity

AGRICULTURE

Coffee, cocoa, cotton, rubber, bananas, oilseed, grains, root starches, livestock, timber.

INDUSTRIES

Petroleum production and refining, food processing, consumer goods, textiles, timber.

NATURAL RESOURCES

Petroleum, bauxite, iron ore, timber, hydropower.

EXPORTS

$2.2 billion (1999 est.): crude oil and petroleum products, lumber, cocoa beans, aluminum, coffee, cotton.

IMPORTS

$2.3 billion (1999 est.): machines and electrical equipment, fuel, food.

MAJOR TRADING PARTNERS

Italy, US, Spain, France, Netherlands, Germany, Nigeria

Doing Business with Cameroon

▶ **Investment**

A new code simplified foreign investment and introduced financial incentives coupled with minimal eligibility/performance requirements. Equity ownership is subject to limitation only in small and medium size enterprises (SMEs) where a 35% local ownership is required. Privatization in agriculture, reinsurance, banking, telecommunications, water and electrical utilities, rubber production, and transportation has opened up new opportunities. The Industrial Free Zone creates conditions for investors to operate virtually outside the country's established legal and regulatory systems but requires that 80% of the product be sold outside Cameroon.

▶ **Trade**

Cameroon is a favored base for foreign trade with Central Africa. Products with potential include fertilizer, used clothing, heavy machinery and material for forestry, transport and road construction, pipeline construction and related services such as security and communications, computer, electronic equipment, and aircraft parts. Local agents with established links to wholesalers and market knowledge are often the best way into this competitive market. Apart from retail outlets operated by large international oil companies and international car rental companies, franchising is limited.

▶ **Trade finance**

Eximbank finances US goods and services sold to Cameroon. Exporters usually rely on irrevocable, confirmed letters of credit.

▶ **Selling to the government**

Government procurement is handled by the *Direction Générale des Grands Travaux* (DGTC) or Public Works Directorate. Local companies are allowed preferential price margins on all state procurement and development projects. Direct purchases are often made through domestic middlemen who require cash up front on behalf of their foreign clients. Foreign participation in government-subsidized R&D is restricted to programs beyond the technical capability of local firms.

▶ **Exchange controls**

The currency continues to be pegged to the French franc, ensured by the French Treasury, and remains readily convertible. Dividends, return of capital, interest and principal on foreign debt, lease payments, royalties and management fees, and returns on liquidation may all be remitted abroad.

▶ **Partnership**

Foreign firms are free to join with any local entity of their choosing in any form desired. Most foreigners obtain expert local counsel when entering into joint ventures and licensing arrangements.

▶ **Establishing a presence**

The Investment Code Management Unit was established in 1991 to assist foreign and domestic business start-ups. It provides investment authorization and a variety of other services through a network of official correspondents in all the relevant ministries. The law requires at least a 35% local ownership for enterprises under the Small and Medium-Size Enterprise (SME) regime.

▶ **Project finance**

OPIC underwrites viable projects and Cameroon is a member of the Multilateral Investment Guarantee Agency. The World Bank and African Development Bank are further sources of financing.

▶ **Labor**

Even though Cameroon has a high literacy rate and a relatively well-educated labor force most of the unemployed are unskilled and nontechnical laborers. The labor code removed government control over layoffs and firings, and reduced official involvement in labor unions.

▶ **Legal rights**

The IMF and the World Bank, through their structural adjustment oversight, are assisting Cameroon in the reform of its judicial system. Cameroon accepts binding international arbitration of investment disputes and is a member of the International Center for the Settlement of Investment Disputes. It is also the headquarters for the 14-nation West African intellectual Property Organization or *Organisation Africaine de la Propriété Intellectuelle (OAPI)* and is a signatory of the Paris Convention on Industrial Property and the Universal Copyright Convention.

▶ **Business climate**

Cameroon has the largest private sector in French-speaking Central Africa. English is also widely spoken in a business community that does not necessarily conform to western practices. Local business people will first try to "get to know" a potential partner before venturing into concrete discussions. Punctuality is not the norm and patience and persistence are vital.

179

Cape Verde

Cape Verde consists of a group of islands strategically located off Africa's West Coast. It depends largely on income from services to foreign shipping and airlines, remittances from some 700,000 Cape Verdean émigrés and foreign aid. Since opening its economy to the outside world, however, the island group nation has attracted foreign investment in light manufacturing, tourism, fishing, transportation and communications. Foreign firms are beginning to take advantage of Cape Verde's underutilized quotas in the US and European markets by establishing manufacturing and assembly plants in its export free zones.

Country profile

The Republic of Cape Verde consists of ten windswept Atlantic islands about 500 km west of Dakar. The largest is São Tiago (992 sq. km) and the smallest, Santa Lucia (34 sq. km). Mt. Fogo (2,829 m) is an active volcano island that last erupted in 1995. The islands lie in the North Atlantic high pressure belt, are poor in natural resources and prone to droughts and high temperatures. Afro-Europeans make up 71% of the population and the rest are African. Whites account for about 1% of the total. An estimated 700,000 Cape Verdeans are living and working abroad, most of them sending regular remittances to the 400,000 remaining on the islands. Portuguese is the official language, but the vernacular is Crioulo (Creole), derived from Portuguese and West African languages.

History

The islands were uninhabited when Portuguese mariners discovered them during their voyages in search of a sea route around Africa. The first Portuguese governor, appointed in 1462, was based at Ribeira Grande on Sao Tiago, the largest of the islands. A Creole population resulted from intermingling

between the Portuguese and the imported slaves from Western Africa. The Cape Verde islands remained obscure until 1975 when they achieved independence from Portugal under President Aristides Pereira of the African Party for the Independence of Guinea and Cape Verde (PAICV). Pereira turned the islands into a one-party state with a centrally controlled economy. Under pressure from the Movement for the Democracy (MPD) led by Carlos Veiga, Cape Verde was eventually transformed into a

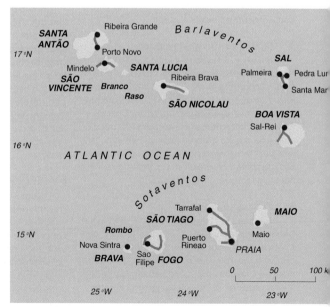

multi-party democracy in 1990. The following year, the MPD won and Veiga took over as prime minister. A former supreme court judge, Antonio Mascarenhas Monteiro, won the presidential election. The MPD was returned to power with a larger majority in the general elections held in December 1995, but in March 2001 Pedro Pires was inaugurated as president after beating his rival, Carlos Veiga, by just 17 votes to succeed Monteiro.

Government

The President, elected for 5 years, has limited powers as real authority rests with the Prime Minister, elected by the 72-member unicameral National Assembly. After the 2001 election, Prime Minister Jose Neves and the *Partido Africano da Independência de Cabo Verde* (PAICV) assumed power with the *Movimento para Democratia* (MPD) in opposition.

Economic policy

After 15 years of state control, the new government in 1991 adopted a development strategy based on market-oriented policies, including an ambitious privatization program. It showed a strong commitment to the implementation of sound macroeconomic and structural reforms and the development of institutions and an infrastructure. Despite slow progress in some sectors, Cape Verde's economic reform policies appear to be paying off, as new businesses are being created, private investment projects are implemented, especially in the tourism sector, construction is booming, and the business community is eager to explore new import markets. Financial and economic legislation has been revised and the government's role in the economy has shifted from a participant in the economy to being a promoter and regulator. Cape Verde's policies have been endorsed and supported by the World Bank, the IMF and many multilateral and bilateral donors, including the US.

Sectors

Fishing (mainly tuna and shellfish) is an important activity in the Atlantic ocean economic zone, 28,350 sq. miles (734,265 sq. km.) assigned exclusively to Cape Verde. With only one third of a potential 50,000 tons of fish products per year exploited due to the lack of adequate technology for deep sea fishing, this sector holds great potential. Agriculture can be

Fast facts

POLITICAL

Head of State	Pres. Pedro Verona Rodrigues Pires (2001)
Prime Minister	José Maria Neves (PAICV) (2001)
Ruling Party	PAICV
Main Opposition	MPD
Independence	5 July 1975
National capital	Praia
Official language	Portuguese

PHYSICAL

Total area	1,557 sq. miles 4,030 sq. km. (± Rhode Island)
Arable land	10% of land area
Coastline	965 km

POPULATION

Total	405,748
Av. yearly growth	1.44%
Population/sq. mile	258
Urban population	50%
Adult literacy	73%

ECONOMY[1]

Currency	Cape Verde escudo (US$1=120.64)
GDP (real)	$460 million
GDP growth rate	8.0%
GNP per capita[2]	$1,060
GDP (ppp)[3]	$581 million
GDP per cap. (ppp)[3]	$1,450
Inflation rate	4.3%
Exports	$135 million
Imports	$292 million
Development aid	$115 million
External debt	$258 million
Unemployment	N/A

INFRASTRUCTURE

Motor vehicles	15,000
Air passenger/km	227 million
Telephones/1,000	47
International airport	Sal
Main harbor	Mindelo

1. *Statistics are based on World Bank data.*
2. *Atlas method.*
3. *See page 151 for an explanation of GDP based on purchasing power parity (ppp)*

practiced on only about one-fifth of the total area and meets about 10% of local consumption needs. Cape Verde emigrant communities in New England and Europe provide a continuous inflow of foreign exchange and other informal assistance to relatives back home. The dry, tropical climate, diverse terrain, warm, clear waters and beautiful, deserted beaches provide ample resources for growing tourism. An international airport on the island of Sal is used as a refueling stop by international air carriers, notably South African Airways which includes this stop on several of its regular flights to and from the US. About 30% of traffic through the airport is cargo moving between Europe and South America. Traffic between the islands is by air and ferry. Mining is confined to pozzolana (a volcanic substance used for cement) and the production of salt, on Sal, through evaporation.

Privatization

In 1997 Cape Verde started privatizing as part of a five-year World Bank-funded program. Several state-owned enterprises have since been privatized, including three hotels, the national telecommunications company, Cabo Verde Telecom, and the oil distribution company, Enacol. Two commercial banks, an insurance company, the state-run power supply company and the Cape Verdean port authority are on the block.

Trade

Cape Verde depends almost completely on imports to meet its basic consumer needs and for industrial inputs. Portugal is Cape Verde's most important trading partner and accounts for almost half of the total trade. In 1998 the US supplied 5.6 % of Cape Verde's imports. Non-factor services to international maritime and air transport top the list of foreign currency earners, followed by bananas, lobster and fresh and frozen fish.

Investment

Since 1993, nearly 109 investment projects totaling $416 million have been licensed. In 1998 alone, a total of $233 million in foreign investment was approved—74% in tourism. Most recent foreign direct investment came from Portugal, Italy, Spain and other European countries, as well as Hong Kong. Recently US and Asian investors have also been targeted by the Cape Verdean foreign investment promotion agency, PROMEX.

Financial sector

The World Bank has been assisting the government of Cape Verde to restructure its financial sector. The first step was to split the Bank of Cape Verde into a central and a commercial bank. The Stock Market of Cape Verde (BVC) was launched in March 1999 with six listed companies. The financial sector includes four commercial banks (two foreign-owned), two insurance companies and a venture capital company created to promote development of the private sector.

Taxes & tariffs

Special tax incentives are extended to firms exporting their entire output from free zones and a 100% tax exemption applies to all dividends earned during the first five years from operations started with foreign capital. Import tariffs have been streamlined.

Expatriates

US-Cape Verdean contacts date from the early 19th Century when the New England whaling industry was at its peak. Today, substantial Cape Verde-American communities live in Massachusetts and Rhode Island.

Business activity

AGRICULTURE
Bananas, corn, beans, sweet potatoes, sugar cane, coffee, peanuts, fish.

INDUSTRIES
Food and beverages, fish processing, shoes and garments, salt mining, ship repair.

NATURAL RESOURCES
Salt, basalt rock, pozzuolana (volcanic ash used to produce hydraulic cement), limestone, kaolin, fish.

EXPORTS
$135 million (1999 est.): shoes, garments, fish, bananas, hides.

IMPORTS
$292 million (1999 est.): foodstuffs, consumer goods, industrial products, transport equipment.

MAJOR TRADING PARTNERS
Portugal, Germany, Spain, France, UK, Malaysia, Netherlands, US.

Doing Business with Cape Verde

▶ **Investment**

A competitive incentive package is offered through the Center for Tourism, Investment and Exports Promotion (PROMEX) which acts as a one-stop shop for foreign investors. While favoring free zone enterprises geared to exports, these incentives also apply in large part to other investments based on infusion of foreign capital. Investors establishing export-driven operations are in many instances assured of generous preferential access to the markets of Europe, West Africa and the United States. Apart from light manufacturing, fishing and tourism offer opportunities.

▶ **Trade**

There is great receptivity for foreign goods, especially items from Portugal which enjoys strong cultural and linguistic links. The smallness of the market and lack of credit have inhibited trade development but the growing need for high-cost items required in the expansion of the country's airports, fishing fleets, telecommunications systems and other infrastructural projects are of special interest to foreign suppliers.

▶ **Trade finance**

The US Department of Agriculture's Commodity Credit Corporation (CCC) administers the Export Credit Guarantee program (GSM-102) providing financing for sales of US agricultural products. Other agencies that provide financing and insurance programs are the International Finance Corporation, the Overseas Private Investment Corporation, Eximbank and the US Small Business Administration.

▶ **Selling to the government**

Government procurement is by tender and typically financed by a multilateral lending institutions such as the World Bank or the African Development Bank. Recent major projects include the building of a longer runway at the international airport of Sal, a new runway at Praia and the modernization of Sao Vicente's airport. Other plans involve harbor improvements and modernization of telecommunications.

▶ **Exchange controls**

Under current law, revenues and profits, capital gains, and loan repayments may be transferred overseas within 60, 90, and 30 days, respectively, after submission of an application to the Bank of Cape Verde (BCV). The BCV pays interest on all transfers where waiting periods exceed 30 days. Transfers are at times delayed when requests involve large sums which might affect Cape Verde's balance of payments. In some instances, the government might opt to make the transfer in installments.

▶ **Establishing a presence**

Joint ventures are allowed and encouraged in fisheries, the airline business and telecommunications. Apart from these partnerships, foreigners have the option of establishing a branch, a limited liability company or a full corporation. Franchising is limited.

▶ **Financing projects**

Multilateral Investment Guarantee Agency and Overseas Private Investment Corporation programs apply. The US Trade and Development Agency, the World Bank and the African Development Bank provide funding for feasibility studies and other investment planning services. Bank credit is available to foreign investors under the same conditions as those for national investors. The private sector has access to credit instruments such as loans, letters of credit and lines of credit. There are clear legal guidelines for accounting but they are not totally consistent with international norms.

▶ **Labor**

With an unemployment rate of about 28% labor is readily available, much of it unskilled. Technical, managerial and professional talent is difficult to find. The recently revised labor code makes work contracts more flexible. There is no set minimum wage and prevailing levels are around $0.70 per hour.

▶ **Legal rights**

Disputes between foreign investors and the government are settled either through a single referee or an arbitration commission. Referees may be foreigners of a different nationality than the parties involved in the dispute. Final appeals can be made to the International Center of Settlement of Investment Disputes (ICSID). There have not been any such disputes in recent years. Since 1990 Cape Verde has had copyright laws and it is a signatory to several treaties providing protection.

▶ **Business climate**

Business practices and customs follow the Portuguese model. While Portuguese is spoken in most business circles, English is gaining wider acceptance and some French is spoken as well.

Central African Republic

The Central African Republic (CAR) is, as its name indicates, at the center of the African continent. It is a sparsely populated country, well endowed with natural resources. Its remoteness from the nearest seaports is a drawback. Plagued in the past by slavery, colonial neglect and brutal tyrants, the CAR has managed to nurture and strengthen the fragile democracy introduced in 1993 when it held its first free elections. Structural reforms have been introduced in conjunction with the World Bank and the government is actively seeking foreign involvement in a variety of minerals to augment its income from diamonds and gold.

Country profile

The Central African Republic is a landlocked and sparsely populated undulating plateau. During the rainy season much of the southeast is impassable as several rivers overflow into the Ubangi, the great tributary of the Congo River. Vast parts of the northern and eastern regions have been set aside for nature conservation. There are two major ethnic groups: the river peoples (Yakoma and Mabaka) and the savannah peoples (such as the Sara). Sango is spoken widely and used in broadcasting. More than two-thirds of the total population are Christians, though many still profess traditional ethnic beliefs.

until 1931. In 1960 CAR achieved independence under the one party rule of President David Dacko. Five years later his cousin, sergeant Jean-Bédel Bokassa, seized power, declared himself president in 1972 and ultimately crowned himself emperor in 1977. In 1979, Bokassa's brutal rule came to an end when French troops reinstated Dacko. Two years later Dacko was once again ousted in a military coup, this time by Gen. André Kolingba. In 1993 internal and international pressures forced Kolingba to hold a multi-parry presidential election which he lost to Ange-Félix Patassé, who once served in

History

The slave trade, especially during the 17th and 18th centuries, had a massive impact on the old kingdoms in this region, decimating their populations. By the turn of the 19th Century the French established themselves at Bangui and founded the colony of Ubangi-Chari (named after two main rivers). Local resistance to excesses by French companies who administered the territory culminated in the Kongo Wara wars from1928

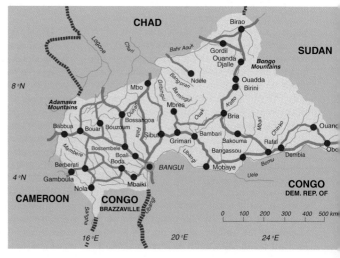

Bokassa's cabinet. Since then African forces and the UN Mission in the Central African Republic (MINURCA) have helped resist destabilizing forces inside the CAR. Patassé was reelected in September 1999, defeating Kolingba and several other candidates.

Government

In terms of the new 1995 constitution the President has executive powers, is elected for a maximum of two 6-year terms and appoints the Prime Minister and Council of Ministers. The bicameral legislature consists of a 109 member National Assembly, elected for 5 years, and a nominated Economic and Regional Council. In 1998 Patasse's Movement for the Liberation of the Central African People (MLPC) won with a plurality of 47 and Kolingba's Central African Democratic Assembly (RDC) came second with 20 seats.

Economic policy

The government has agreed to a framework for economic reform, including the privatization of key parastatals under an IMF-approved Extended Structure Adjustment Facility (ESAF) in 1998. Devaluation of the country's currency had already stimulated exports and the production of cash crops as well as diamond mining and timber. The government is committed to tax reform.

Sectors

The agricultural sector in CAR contributes some 55% of the GDP and employs an estimated 80% of the labor force. Key primary food crops include bananas, cocoa beans, coffee and sugar cane. Meat products range from beef, chicken, goat meat and mutton to pork. The CAR is almost self-sufficient in food and has the potential of becoming a net exporter. Export crops are cotton, coffee, cattle, organic material and tobacco leaves. Mining largely involves alluvial diamonds and gold, together contributing about 4% of the nation's gross domestic product. Key industries are diamond mining, sawmills, breweries, textiles, footwear, and assembly of bicycles and motorcycles.

Privatization

Privatization of state enterprises had just begun when the civil unrest broke out in 1996 and has since been significantly delayed. A 49% share of the national telecommunications operator, Socatel has been sold .

Fast facts

POLITICAL	
Head of State	Pres. Ange-Félix Patassé (1993)
Prime Minister	Anicet Georges Dologuele (1999)
Ruling Party	MLPC
Major Opposition	RDC
Independence	13 August 1960
National capital	Bangui
Official language	French

PHYSICAL	
Total area	241,313 sq. miles 622,980 sq. km. (2 x New Mexico)
Arable land	3% of land area

POPULATION	
Total	3.5 million
Av. yearly growth	2.04%
Population/sq. mile	15
Urban population	39%
Adult literacy	44%

ECONOMY[1]	
Currency	CFA franc (CFAF)(US$1=752.76)
GDP (real)	$1.18 billion
GDP growth rate	3.4%
GNP per capita[2]	$300
GDP (ppp)[3]	$5.5 billion
GDP per cap. (ppp)[3]	$1,640
Inflation rate	2.6%
Exports	$178 million
Imports	$253 million
Development aid	$97 million
External debt	$878 million
Unemployment	6%

INFRASTRUCTURE	
Railroads	0 km
Paved roads	2%
Motor vehicles	15,000
Air passenger/km	227 million
Telephones/1,000	2
International airport	Bangui
Main riverport	Bangui

1. Statistics are based on World Bank data.
2. Atlas method.
3. See page 151 for an explanation of GDP based on purchasing power parity (ppp).

Investment

Foreign direct investment is primarily concentrated in the diamond mining, gold and timber sectors.

Trade

France continues to be the major trade partner, providing about 50% of the CAR's needs, on top of another 14% share by the EU. The US, Japan, and Iran are significant suppliers of products such as wheat flour, other processed foods, pharmaceuticals, consumer goods, industrial products, vehicles, and petroleum products.

Financial sector

Banking in the CAR is under control of the French-controlled *Banque des Etats de l'Afrique Centrale* (BEAC), which regulates five francophone countries in the Central African sub-region.

Taxes and tariffs

General corporate income tax is 40%, with agricultural companies subject to a rate of 25.5%. Agricultural and consumer cooperatives are exempt from income tax.

Business activity

AGRICULTURE

Cotton, coffee, tobacco, manioc, yams, millet, corn, bananas, timber.

INDUSTRIES

Diamond mining, sawmills, breweries, textiles, footwear, bicycles and motorcycles.

NATURAL RESOURCES

Diamonds, uranium, timber, gold, oil.

EXPORTS

$178 million (1998 est.): diamonds, timber, tobacco, coffee, cotton.

IMPORTS

$253 million (1999 est.): food, textiles, petroleum products, machinery, electrical equipment, motor vehicles, chemicals, consumer goods, industrial products.

MAJOR TRADING PARTNERS

Belgium, Luxembourg, Côte d'Ivoire, Spain, Egypt, France, Cameroon, Germany, Japan.

Doing Business with Central African Republic

▶ **Investment**

Several American firms have expressed interest in mechanizing the largely manual diamond sector and getting involved in the mining and exploration of gold, copper, iron ore, tin, uranium and zinc. The mining industry is regulated by the Ministry of Energy, Mines, Geology and Water Resources. The government has invited foreign participation in the underdeveloped telecommunications sector by freeing up value added network services and partially lifting restrictions on cellular services development. The CAR shows good potential for foreign involvement in ecotourism in its rain forest and savanna regions. Tentative steps have been taken by foreign entrepreneurs to develop facilities in areas such as the primeval rain forest, Dzanga-Sangha National Park, in the southwestern region of the country.

▶ **Trade**

Even though there is a strong interest in American goods, US exporters should expect tough competition from France with which the CAR has maintained strong commercial ties. Importers of consumer items and personal vehicles have expressed an interest in US goods, but logistic problems tend to impede sales and distribution.

▶ **Selling to the government**

In selling to the government foreign firms usually concentrate on projects financed by donors.

▶ **Exchange controls**

Capital, profits and dividends can be freely transferred. The transfer of more than CFA 500,000 requires permission from the Ministry of Finance.

▶ **Partnerships**

As tax and customs laws may be more strictly enforced against foreigners, it is useful to have a local partner to negotiate the complex web of regulations required to establish a business.

▶ **Labor**

The workforce is largely unskilled.

▶ **Legal rights**

Foreign investors are assured of equal treatment under law which guarantees freedom from expropriation and nationalization, barring special circumstances, and freedom from political or economic interference.

▶ **Business climate**

Business is mostly conducted in French.

Chad

Landlocked Chad is Africa's fifth largest country and one of its poorest. This, however, is likely to change as it continues to demonstrate macroeconomic stability, capacity building, democratic reform and social progress in addition to a multi-billion dollar oil pipeline will boost income. Once completed this pipeline, built by a an ExxonMobil-led consortium, will carry oil from Chad's Doba basin tothe port of Kribi in Cameroon. Industrial growth is bound to follow, drastically transforming a country that has up to now depended largely on agricultural exports and subsistence crops and livestock. This development is expected to open up new opportunities for foreign investors, not only in petroleum-related industries but in a range of other manufacturing and service areas. The country's substantial deposits of gold, marble and natron have also been under foreign focus in recent years.

Country profile

The landlocked Republic of Chad is the fifth largest country in Africa. Its capital, N'Djamena, is situated near the confluence of the country's only two rivers, the Chari and the Logone, which flow from the south into Lake Chad. There are sharply contrasting climatic zones varying from wet savannah in the south to arid Sahara Desert conditions in the north. Except for scattered Arab-speaking and Chadic groups, most of the peoples are of Nilo-Saharan origin, comprising the Bagirmi and the Sara of the south, the Maba in the Waddai region, and the Kanuri in the Sahara region. The desert peoples also include the Zaghawa along the eastern border, and the Tubu of the Tibesti Mountains. French and Arabic are official languages but some English is spoken, apart from 100 local languages. More than half the country is Muslim and the rest is divided evenly between Christianity and traditional African religions.

History

Artifacts dating back to 5000 BC have been discovered at burial sites in the Sahel and Southern Sahara regions, inhabited by nomadic Negroid people, many of whom turned to the Muslim faith as early as the 10th Century. Towards the end of the 19th Century, converted Christians from the south sided with French troops against the north. In 1910 Chad was incorporated into French Equatorial Africa. In 1957 the Chadians formed their first elected government

187

Fast facts

POLITICAL

Head of State	Pres. Idriss Déby (1990)
Prime Minister.	Nagoum Yamassoum (1999)
Ruling Party	MPS
Major Opposition	URD
Independence	11 August 1960
National capital	N'Djamena
Official languages	French & Arabic

PHYSICAL

Total area	495,752 sq. miles 1,284,000 sq. km. (3 x California)
Arable land	3% of land area

POPULATION

Total	7.5 million
Av. yearly growth	2.65%
Population/sq. mile	17
Urban population	21%
Adult literacy	39%

ECONOMY[1]

Currency	CFA franc (CFAF) (US$1=752.76)
GDP (real)	$1.68 billion
GDP growth rate	-0.7%
GNP per capita[2]	$230
GDP (ppp)[3]	$7.5 billion
GDP per cap. (ppp)[3]	$1,000
Inflation rate	15.0%
Exports	$260 million
Imports	$465 million
Development aid	$236 million
External debt	$944 million
Unemployment	N/A

INFRASTRUCTURE

Railroads	0 km
Paved roads	1%
Motor vehicles	16,000
Air passenger/km	222 million
Telephones/1,000	1
International airport	N'Djamena

1. Statistics are based on World Bank data.
2. Atlas method.
3. See page 151 for an explanation of GDP based on purchasing power parity (ppp).

and a year later voted to become a self-governing member of the French Community. The territory became independent on 11 August 1960 with southerner Francois Tombalbaye as its first president. Two years later, in response to growing internal unrest, he banned the opposition. Muslim opponents formed the Chad Liberation Front (Frolinat) and took control of the north. French assistance to Tombalbaye was countered by Libyan financial and military aid to Frolinat. After the withdrawal of the French military in 1972, Libya laid claim to and annexed the Aozou Strip in northern Chad. Tombalbaye's perished during a military coup in April 1975, setting off a series of destabilizing events that prompted incursions by Libyan, Nigerian and French troops. In 1990, former army chief Idriss Déby finally deposed the French-favored ruler, Hissene Habre, declared himself president and announced his commitment to a multiparty system. In 1994 the International Court of Justice ruled in Chad's favor in the Aozou dispute, forcing Libya to withdraw. Déby emerged as the winner in the presidential election of 1996 and his *Mouvement Patriotique du Salut* (MPS) won a majority in the National Assembly in 1997.

Government

The president is elected by popular vote for a five year term and appoints the prime minister and cabinet. The 125-seat unicameral National Assembly is elected to serve four years. The majority party, supporting Pres. Déby, the *Mouvement patriotique du Salut* (MPS), controls 63 seats in the National Assembly. The strongest opposition party, the *Union pour le renouveau* (URD), a party of the south, is led by Abdelkader Kamougue, and holds 29 seats.

Economic policy

The World Bank, the European Union and France are assisting Chad in its efforts to alleviate poverty and stimulate economic growth under a structural adjustment program adopted in 1994. In recent years there has been steady progress towards democratic government and restoring political stability. The government has begun to disengage itself from key sectors of the economy, has liberalized pricing, and is promoting competition.

Sectors

Growth in some sectors has been constrained

by Chad's lack of outlets to the sea. There are no railways and the roads are inadequate. Agriculture accounts for 80% of the workforce. Cotton is cultivated in the south and livestock in the north. Food crops include sorghum, millet, dry beans, sesame, potatoes, rice and maize. The only minerals extracted in quantity are soda and rock salt but there are known reserves of chromium, tungsten, titanium, iron ore, wolfram, gold, uranium and tin. The imminent exploitation of oil deposits at Doba in the south after the construction of a 1,000-km pipeline across Cameroon to an offshore tanker terminal at the Atlantic port of Kribi is expected to stimulate industrial activity way beyond the current cotton processing and small scale food, textiles, brewing, tobacco, and leather plants.

Privatization

There has been steady progress towards privatization. The Banque Meridien BIAO Tchad (BMBT-BIAT) and l'Office National Hydraulique Pastoral et Villageois (ONHPV) have already been reconstructed. Slated for privatization are, among others, SONASUT (the sugar monopoly), STEE (water and electricity), TIT (international telecommunications), ONPT (post office and telecommunications), Air Chad, and Cotontchad (cotton monopoly).

Investment

Foreign direct investment represents more than half of the total capital in Chadian enterprises. As a result of historical ties, France leads the way with an estimated 50-60% of the total. Other significant investors are the Benelux countries, Italy, Taiwan, US, Japan, Saudi-Arabia, and Libya. In October 2000, ExxonMobil Corporation's affiliate, Esso Chad, started construction in the Doba basin on the Chad-Cameroon pipeline project in partnership with Chevron and Petronas. At a construction cost of $3.5 billion it will produce about 22,500 barrels of oil per day—a total of 1 billion barrels over its 30-year life.

Trade

Cotton is the most important cash crop, accounting for about 90% of export revenues. Gum Arabic, groundnuts, sesame, sugar cane and tobacco are additional cash crops. Livestock is a source of traditional wealth and exported either on the hoof or as frozen meat, hides and skins. Mineral exports include soda and rock salt (mainly to Nigeria) and natron, used in the preservation of meat and in tanning. Once the pipeline project to Cameroon is completed oil is certain to overtake other exports in importance. Major imports include machinery and transportation equipment, industrial goods, petroleum products, consumer goods and foodstuffs.

Financial sector

As a member of Communautè Financiére Africaine (CFA) zone, Chad belongs to the regional central bank, Banque des Etats de l'Afrique Centrale (BEAC), which controls distribution of its money and the transfer of funds. There are five commercial banks in Chad, some with US correspondent relationships.

Taxes and tariffs

The corporate tax rate is 45% and a turnover tax of 15% applies to all services and products. Additional revenues in 1998 are expected from the newly-installed Impot General Liberatoire (IGL), a tax levied on small business and the informal sector. As a member of the Central African Regional Customs Union (UDEAC), Chad has reformed import and value-added taxes.

Business activity

AGRICULTURE
Cotton, sorghum, millet, peanuts, rice, potatoes, manioc, cattle, sheep, goats, camels.

INDUSTRIES
Cotton textiles, meat packing, beer brewing, natron, kaolin (sodium carbonate), soap, cigarettes, construction materials.

NATURAL RESOURCES
Petroleum, uranium, natron, kaolin, fish.

EXPORTS
$260 million (1999 est.): cotton, cattle, textiles.

IMPORTS
$465 million (1999 est.): machinery and transportation equipment, industrial goods, petroleum products, foodstuffs, textiles.

MAJOR TRADING PARTNERS
Portugal, Germany, Thailand, Costa Rica, South Africa, France, Nigeria, Cameroon, India.

Doing Business with Chad

▶ **Investment**

ExxonMobil affiliate, Esso Chad—leading a consortium including Chevron and Petronas—is constructing a 663 miles (1,070 km) oil pipeline from the Doba basin in Chad to Kribi in Cameroon at a cost of $3.5 billion. This massive development opened up significant opportunities for foreign firms in finance, construction, oil-related industries and telecommunications. Chad's mineral reserves, including gold, marble and natron, have also attracted interest from investors. Livestock, still largely unexploited, present opportunities in meat and dairy production, leather, glue, fertilizer and other products. Spirulina (blue-green algae) in Lake Chad, shea trees, sesame seed oil, and a need for solar and wind power are other potential areas of investment. Privatization opens up further areas for foreign private participation. While currently uneconomic as a result of poor infrastructure, deposits of copper, silver, zinc and other metals hold future promise. Tax incentives apply to most investment.

▶ **Trade**

Imports include pharmaceutical products, flour milling products, malt, starchy food gluten, industrial chemicals, organic and non-organic, cellulose acetates, tire tubes, new and used tires for buses and trucks, paper products, grease-proof paper, rags, used and new textiles and shoes, steel, cable and tubes, tools and hardware, compressor parts, pumps, and air conditioners. There is a growing need for electric power systems; construction, mining, and agriculture machinery; telecommunications equipment and services; and food processing and packaging equipment.

▶ **Trade finance**

Eximbank has financed projects for ventures in the past. Short- to medium-term trade financing can also be obtained from the commercial banks and longer term arrangements through multilateral lending institutions such as the World Bank, African Development Bank, the *Fonds Europeen de Developpement* (FED), and the Islamic Development Bank.

▶ **Selling to the government**

Government tenders are published in the local press. The Minister of Finance and Economy together with his staff act as the National Authorization Office (NAO), selecting tenders on behalf of the relevant ministries. Large procurements are usually financed by the multilateral lending institutions.

▶ **Exchange controls**

There are no restrictions on the transfer of funds. As a member of the Central African Regional Customs Union (UDEAC) and the regional monetary union (CEMAC), Chad uses the CFA franc, supported by France at a fixed value.

▶ **Partnerships**

Foreign firms have entered into joint venture opportunities in the textile, agricultural and transportation sectors.

▶ **Establishing a presence**

Structuring can be in terms of a limited liability company (S*ociété à Responsabilité Limitée*— SARL) or a *Corporation Societe Anonyme* (SA) with at least seven shareholders. Both have to be registered with a number of state agencies before authorization is granted by the Ministry of Commerce.

▶ **Financing projects**

Major development projects are funded by multilateral donors such as the World Bank and African Development Bank. Foreign investors might be able to obtain financing on the local market but credit allotments are limited in range and lending criteria are rigid.

▶ **Labor**

Over 80 percent of the workforce is engaged in unpaid subsistence farming, herding and fishing. Unionized labor has no ties to the government and a new labor code has been drawn up in conjunction with the World Bank. Mandatory allowances to workers include transportation, health indemnity, bonuses, and vacation pay.

▶ **Legal rights**

Law is based on the French Napoleonic Code and Chadian customary law. Chad is a member of the Cameroon-based West African Intellectual Property Rights Organization but due to administrative limitations protection against copyright infringements is not guaranteed.

▶ **Business climate**

There is local tendency to take time developing a broad base of understanding and mutual trust during personal contact before proceeding with serious business discussions. When visiting Chad, it is advisable to have corporate and business materials available in French.

Comoros

Consisting of four major and a number of minor islands in the Indian Ocean east of Mozambique, the Comoros archipelago has been struggling to attain political stability and economic growth since its independence in 1975. Comoros suffers from limited natural resources and a population torn by ancient divisions. Since 1997 the Comorian federal state has been threatened with secession by the islands of Anjouan and Mohéli and endured some 20 coups or attempted coups. Efforts continue to stabilize the political situation with the help of the African Union as a successor to the OAU, and other organizations, and to make the islands more attractive for much-needed foreign economic involvement.

Country profile

The four main islands and islets of the Comoros Islamic Federal Republic are scattered like stepping stones across the northern end of the Mozambique Channel, a stretch of Indian Ocean between the African coast and Madagascar. Three of the islands, Grande Comore (Ngazidja), Anjouan (Ndzuani) and Moheli (Mwali), constitute the federal republic, while the fourth, Mayotte (Maore) is a disputed French territory. These islands are the summits of a submerged volcanic ridge. Mount Karthala (2,040 m) on Grande Comore has the largest live crater in the world. The climate on all the islands is tropical, hot and humid, with abundant rainfall in most places. More than 100,000 Comorians live in France. The island population is mainly of Arab, African (Swahili) and Malagasy origin. Arabic and French are the official languages but Kiswahili is the common tongue. Most Comorians are Sunni Muslims.

History

Originally part of an extensive trade network in the northern Indian Ocean, these islands became known as Comoros—a corruption of the name Jazair al-Komr (Islands of the Moon) given by Arab mariners. A thousand years ago Ndzuani (Anjouan) was settled by Arabs and Shirazi (Persian) Muslims, replete with slaves. Since 1912 the Comoros had been administered as a colony by the French from Madagascar. In 1946 it was separated and in 1961 granted limited self-government. In 1974, when Comoros voted for independence, Mayotte with its Christian majority voted against joining the other largely Islamic islands and opted for continued French rule. The first post inde-

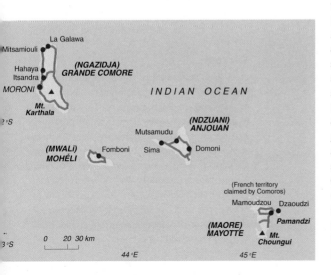

Fast facts

POLITICAL

Head of State	Col. Azaly Assoumani (1999)
Ruling Party	Military rule
Independence	6 July 1975
National capital	Moroni
Official languages	Arabic & French

PHYSICAL

Total area	838 sq. miles
	2,170 sq. km.
	(12 x Washington, DC)
Arable land	35%
Territorial sea	12 nautical miles

POPULATION

Total	562,723
Av. yearly growth	3.11%
Population/sq. mile	838
Urban population	36%
Adult literacy	58%

ECONOMY[1]

Currency	Comoron franc (CF) (US$1=558.10)
GDP (real)	$216 million
GDP growth rate	-1.4%
GNP per capita[2]	$370
GDP (ppp)[3]	$400 million
GDP per cap. (ppp)[3]	$700
Inflation rate	2.5%
Exports	$50 million
Imports	$78 million
Development aid	$30 million
External debt	$210 million
Unemployment	20%

INFRASTRUCTURE

Railroads	0 km
Paved roads	70%
Motor vehicles	5,000
Air passenger/km	3 million
Telephones/1,000	9
International airport	Moroni
Main harbor	Moroni

1. Statistics are based on World Bank data.
2. Atlas method.
3. See page 151 for an explanation of GDP based on purchasing power parity (ppp).

pendence president, Ahmed Abdallah, was ousted after less than a month in office and replaced by a young populist, Ali Solihi. Since then coups, attempted coups and mercenary incursions have been part and parcel of the nation's political life. Elected in 1996, President Mohammed Taki died in November 1998 under suspicious circumstances and was succeeded by the president of the High Court, Tadjidine Ben Said Massoude. He was in turn replaced in 1999 during the latest coup engineered by Col. Azali Assoumani, who reintroduced military rule. The OAU has since demanded that Assoumani return the Comoros to civilian rule. In July 2000 seventy percent of the inhabitants of Mayotte voted for greater autonomy on condition that their island remains part of France.

Government

In terms of the Constitution, the President is elected for 6-year terms, and appoints a Council of Ministers. Provision is made for a 43-member unicameral Federal Assembly elected for 2-year terms. These provisions have been suspended and Comoros is currently under military rule.

Economic policy

In the early nineties Comoros embarked on free market reforms under a structural adjustment program supported by the World Bank and the IMF. The government wage bill was drastically cut, the currency was devalued and some institutions privatized. However, the islands seem likely to depend on outside aid for the foreseeable future as the result of a slump in world prices for their main exports, vanilla and ylang-ylang, during the nineties.

Sectors

Agriculture,—including fishing, hunting, and forestry—is the leading sector, contributing 40% to GDP and employing 80% of the work force. Major food crops are cassava, sweet potatoes, rice, bananas, yams and coconuts. Rice, the main staple food, is imported. The principal cash crops are vanilla, ylang-ylang oil (a perfume base) and cloves, mostly produced on plantations owned by expatriates. Manufacturing involves distillation of essences such as ylang ylang, vanilla processing, extrusion of plant oils, soap, soft drinks, plastics and woodwork. The tourist industry is small but developing.

Privatization

A French company in mid-1997 took over management of the country's ailing electrical utility and other French companies are likely to follow suit as privatization continues. A South African firm has purchased government hotels.

Investment

Efforts by the government to attract foreign investment have been marred by political instability. Sluggish growth in South Africa, considered to be the prime candidate for investment capital, has had a negative effect.

Trade

Vanilla, cloves and ylang-ylang are major exports. Remittances from Comorians living overseas are another a prime source of foreign currency. France, Germany, and the United States are major buyers and France, Pakistan, South Africa, the United Arab Emirates and Kenya are the major suppliers.

Financial sector

Comoros is a member of the *Communauté financière africaine* The *Banque Nationale de Paris Intercontinentale* is the country's only international financial institution.

Taxes and tariffs

The corporate income tax rate is 40%. There is a 15% tax on distributed dividends.

Business activity

AGRICULTURE
Vanilla, cloves, perfume essences, copra, coconuts, bananas, cassava (tapioca).
INDUSTRIES
Tourism, perfume distillation, textiles, furniture, jewelry, construction materials, soft drinks.
EXPORTS
$50 million (1999 est.): ylang-ylang, cloves, perfume oil, copra.
IMPORTS
$78 million (1999 est.): rice and other foodstuffs, consumer goods, petroleum products, cement, transport equipment.
MAJOR TRADING PARTNERS
France, US, Germany, South Africa, Kenya.

Doing Business with Comoros

▶ Investment

The government has encouraged foreign investment by offering a number of special tax and other incentives. Opportunities for profitable trade and investment will, however, remain underutilized until Comoros resolves its deep-seated political problems and follows through with much needed economic reforms. Telecommunications, road construction, fishing and tourism are promising potential future areas for investment once longer term stability is restored.

▶ Trade

The US can be competitive in supplying items such as medical equipment and supplies, cellular telephone systems and solar energy units, once the political and economic climate improves. The Japanese have helped fund a satellite facility for Comoros which should stimulate growth in the communications sector and create a demand for equipment. Current commerce between the United States and Comoros is limited.

▶ Exchange controls

The government allows transfer of capital, profits and dividends.

▶ Labor

Unemployment and underemployment are widespread. The low educational level of the labor force contributes to a subsistence level of economic activity, high unemployment, and a heavy dependence on foreign grants and technical assistance.

▶ Business Climate

French is the language of business and daily life in Comoros, although some Arabic and Swahili are spoken. Comoros is a Muslim country, and visitors should observe conservative norms of dress and behavior.

Congo, Dem. Rep.

As Africa's third largest country, richly endowed with mineral and other natural resources, the Democratic Republic of Congo (DROC) or Congo (Kinshasa) has the potential to become one of its most prosperous nations. However, until peace and stability are restored and effective economic reforms introduced it seems destined to be little more than the renamed ravaged continuation of Mobutu's Zaire. While some foreign investors have already acted in anticipation of future improvement, others are straddling the fence as the international community and African neighbors debate over the best ways to resolve the ongoing struggle in the DROC.

Country profile

The Democratic Republic of Congo (commonly referred to as *Congo Kinshasa* to prevent confusion with the neighboring Republic of Congo or *Congo Brazzaville*) is Africa's third largest country after Sudan and Algeria. The entire Congo Basin is well watered and dense rainforests extend along the Congo River and its tributaries. The eastern border is fringed with mountains overlooking a series of lakes including Albert, Edward, Kivu and Tanganyika. Roughly 80% of the country's inhabitants speak Bantu languages, ranging from the predominant Kongo to the Mongo, the Tumba and Lulua. The remainder, concentrated along the northern border, belong to the Adamawan Ubangian and Sudanic linguistic families. Kiswahili is widely spoken in the eastern parts of the country and in Shaba. More than 75% of the population adhere to Christianity.

History

Some 3,000 years ago the original hunter-gatherer Pygmies in the Congo Basin were joined by land tilling Bantu speaking peoples from the north and northeast. Building on the ex-

plorations of American journalist Henry Morton Stanley in the 1870s, Belgian King Leopold I assembled an international consortium of bankers to exploit the Congo's natural resources. At the Berlin Conference of 1884-1885 the European powers recognized Leopold's claim to this vast region. Following widespread public concern over inhumane labor practices in the Congo, the Belgian government took over the administration of the territory in 1908. In 1960,

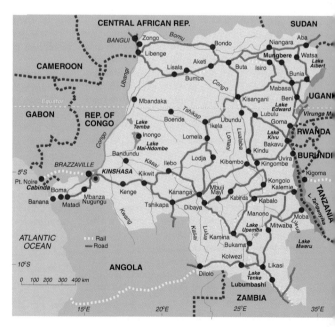

when Belgium granted independence to an ill-prepared colony, a power struggle ensued, fueled in part by the big powers. Joseph Kasavubu, Moise Tshombe and Patrice Lumumba rapidly passed on stage making way for Col. Joseph-Desiré Mobutu who exercised autocratic rule over Zaire, as he called the country, for more than three decades. After a belated failed attempt under severe internal and external pressures to introduce multiparty politics, an ailing Mobutu was ousted by Laurent Desiré Kabila and his Alliance of Democratic Forces for the Liberation of Congo-Zaire (ADFL) in 1997 with the support of the Rwandan and Ugandan governments. Kabila renamed Zaire the Democratic Republic of Congo (DROC) and placed a ban on all political parties and public demonstrations. A new insurrection by disillusioned former compatriots in the northeast backed by Rwanda and Uganda prompted Angolan, Namibian and Zimbabwean troops to come to Kabila's aid. Unrest continues despite the Lusaka Accords of 1999 calling for internal peace and the withdrawal of forces from neighboring African nations.In January 2001, Joseph Kabila became president after his father's assassination by a disgruntled bodyguard. He promised elections.

Government

A new constitution to be drafted by an appointed commission for consideration by a Constituent Assembly and submission to the President has been delayed by renewed fighting in the northeastern region. In the meantime the country is governed by a self-proclaimed President, Joseph Kabila, who succeeded his father Laurent-Desiré Kabila in 2001.

Economic policy

When the Kabila Government took control in May 1997 after 37 years under Mobutu Sese Seko the civil service was dysfunctional, the physical infrastructure in disrepair, and most state industries bankrupt. Cited as priorities were the revitalization of the mining, agricultural and transport sectors in terms of a 3-year, $3 billion recovery plan. The DROC entered into negotiations with donors and creditors in regard to its $15 billion external debt.

Sectors

Arable land is plentiful and inland waters contain abundant supplies of fish. DROC was the world's largest producer of cobalt, the sec-

Fast facts

POLITICAL

Head of State	Pres. Joseph Kabila (2001)
Ruling Party	MPR
Independence	30 June 1960
National capital	Kinshasa
Official language	French

PHYSICAL

Total area	905,568 sq. miles 2,345,410 sq. km. (¼of US)
Arable land	3%
Coastline	37 km/23 miles

POPULATION

Total	50.5 million
Av. yearly growth	2.96%
Population/sq. mile	57
Urban population	29%
Adult literacy	59%

ECONOMY[1]

Currency	Congolese franc (US$1=349.30)
GDP (real)	$6.1 billion
GDP growth rate	8.0%
GNP per capita[2]	$110
GDP (ppp)[3]	$34.9 billion
GDP per cap. (ppp)[3]	$710
Inflation rate	147%
Exports	$1.9 billion
Imports	$1.9 billion
Development aid	$177 million
External debt	$13.35 billion
Unemployment	N/A

INFRASTRUCTURE

Railroads	5,000 km/3,107 miles
Paved roads	2%
Motor vehicles	373,000 (1994)
Air passenger/km	480 million
Telephones/1,000	1
International airport	Kinshasa
Main harbor	Matadi

1. Statistics are based on World Bank data.
2. Atlas method.
3. See page 151 for an explanation of GDP based on purchasing power parity (ppp).

ond largest of industrial diamonds and the fourth largest of copper. Diamonds are largely retrieved from alluvial and kimberlite deposits. Crude oil production is small compared to other Sub-Saharan African oil producers, but output from its small offshore fields remained steady during the 1990s and continues to serve as a reliable source of revenues. Due to extensive smuggling gold production is estimated to be much higher than quantities reflected in official statistics. The country has a hydroelectric potential of 100,000 megawatts (MW) or 13% of the world's total. Manufacturing is concentrated in Kinshasa and the mining centers of Shaba and ranges from brewing, food processing and textiles to vehicle assembly.

Privatization

At the peak of the Mobutu-driven nationalization more than 140 enterprises belonged to the state. Since then, several were liquidated, privatized, or replaced by new ones. Today there are 116 of which 56 are fully publicly owned and 60 with mixed ownership. Kabila has signaled his intention to further privatize.

Investment

In recent years, most investments under the code were in transportation, chemical products and pharmaceuticals, wood, food processing, mining, and services. The largest US investment is in oil with Chevron in the lead. Belgian-owned firms are prominent as minority owners in several major parastatal firms. Lebanese, South Asian and South African business people have a growing economic influence and French interest is reviving. The diamond industry is controlled by the state-owned *Societe Miniere de Bakwanga* (Miba), which markets its diamonds through Sediza, a subsidiary of the international De Beers Central Selling Organization.

Trade

Copper, cobalt, coffee, petroleum, and diamonds account for most of the country's foreign exchange earnings. In the mid-1990s diamonds contributed nearly half of export earnings while copper and cobalt contributed about 20%. The US (22%) is, after the Benelux countries (43%), the biggest buyer of Congolese products. As a supplier of products to the DROC the US ranks fifth behind South Africa, Benelux, China, and the Netherlands.

Financial sector

The banking system comprises the central bank, twelve commercial banks and a development bank—the *Société Financière de developpement* (SOFIDE). There are five other financial intermediaries, a postal checking system and 19 credit cooperatives. Most commercial banks maintain correspondent arrangements with banks operating in the US.

Taxes and tariffs

Corporate tax is 40% of income, capital gains and branch profits. Foreign investments valued between $200,000 and $10 million (local currency equivalent) receive extensive tax concessions on profits and dividends.

Foreign presence

Over the years the country's size, population, economic potential, resources and location have made it attractive to Western business, apart from official strategic considerations during the Cold War. By the mid-nineties, however, relations have become strained as the US and its allies tried to persuade Mobutu to introduce democratic reforms. Many foreign firms withdrew amidst civil disorder and an economic downturn.

Business activity

AGRICULTURE

Coffee, sugar, palm oil, rubber, tea, quinine, cassava, bananas, root crops, corn, fruit, wood products.

INDUSTRIES

Mining, mineral processing, consumer products, cement, diamonds.

NATURAL RESOURCES

Copper, cobalt, cadmium, petroleum, industrial and gem diamonds, gold, silver, zinc, manganese, tin, germanium, uranium, radium, bauxite, iron ore, coal, hydropower potential, timber.

EXPORTS

$1.9 billion (1999 est.): diamonds, copper, coffee, cobalt, crude oil.

IMPORTS

$1.9 billion (1999 est.): consumer goods, foodstuffs, mining and other machinery, transport equipment, fuel.

MAJOR TRADING PARTNERS

Benelux, US, South Africa, France, Germany, Italy, UK, Japan, China, Netherlands.

Doing Business with the Dem. Rep. of Congo

▶ **Investment**

With the exception of the minerals extraction sector, the government neither requires nor seeks participation in foreign investments. There is minimal screening of foreign investment. A bilateral investment treaty (BIT) has been in place with the US since 1989, guaranteeing reciprocal rights and privileges to each country's investors. A *Zone Franche d'Inga* (ZOFI) was established to attract potential investors, especially heavy industry users of energy.

▶ **Trade**

Export opprtunities exist in used clothing, telecommunications and computer equipment, refrigeration and air conditioning equipment, electrical generators and distribution equipment, pharmaceuticals, aircraft and related equipment, cosmetics, four-wheel drive passenger vehicles, commercial trucks, mining, construction, agricultural, and forestry equipment, and food products such as rice, wheat, dried milk products, processed tomato products, canned meat and fish, and poultry. Trained professionals without regular employment offer a range of services from the complex to the mundane, including translating and interpreting, setting up appointments with key officials, following-up with local businesses, arranging accommodation and transportation, and facilitating passage through DROC's notoriously slow airports.

▶ **Trade finance**

Although hard-currency accounts are available at commercial banks, most businesses avoid them because of high maintenance costs. International transfers and transfers between various regions of the country are frequently done by direct agreement between businesses. Local banks sometimes serve as matchmakers.

▶ **Selling to the government**

Due to political unrest and a drop in revenues, government procurement is currently in a state of flux.

▶ **Exchange control**

The transfer of dividends and other funds associated with investments is allowed but licenses are required for all transactions in foreign exchange, including import payments.

▶ **Establishing a presence**

A branch office or sales subsidiary may be a useful method of representation where a large ongoing market exists or frequent contacts are required. Sometimes exporters rely on a group of firms selling complementary items by establishing a jointly owned sales subsidiary. There are five possibilities: *Société Privée à Responsibilité Limitée* (SPRL)— a limited liability company that combines the character of a partnership and a corporation; *Société Privée à Responsabilité Limitée* (SARL) — a joint stock company; *Société Cooperative* (SC)— where each member has a single vote; *Société en Nom Collectif* (SNC)—a simple partnership; and the *Société en Commandité Simple* (SCS)—a limited partnership.

▶ **Financing projects**

DROC is a member of the World Bank's Multilateral Investment Guarantee Agency, which offers insurance to new foreign investments against foreign exchange risk, expropriation and civil unrest.

▶ **Labor**

Even though a large urban population provides a ready pool of available labor—some with high school and university education—skilled industrial labor is in short supply. Minimum wages are set on a regional basis by the government for all workers in private enterprise. Strict labor laws can make termination of employees difficult. Outside the major cities, large companies often become involved in providing infrastructure including roads, schools, and hospitals. As foreign undertakings mature, the government expects the number of expatriates employed to diminish.

▶ **Legal rights**

Although arbitrary seizure of property was a problem during the early months of the Kabila regime, the government has brought the practice under control in recent months. DROC is a member of the World Intellectual Property Organization and the Paris Convention for the Protection of Industrial Property. However, enforcement of IPR regulations has been lax due to bureaucratic disarray. The complexities of DROC law make the hiring of local legal professionals necessary.

▶ **Business Climate**

French is the business language and little English is spoken. European traditions of social etiquette apply. A suit or coat and tie (for men) and a business suit (for women) are appropriate for business appointments or meetings with government officials.

197

Congo, Republic of

The Republic of Congo or Congo (Brazzaville) is sub-Saharan Africa's fourth largest oil producer (after Nigeria, Angola, and Gabon). Most of its estimated proven reserves of 1.5 billion barrels is offshore, making it heavily dependent on foreign expertise and technology. foreign companies are heavily engaged in the exploration and production of oil and gas and as suppliers of equipment and machinery. Serious ethnic rivalry and warfare has not disrupted this vital sector but have caused potential investors in other sectors to put their plans on hold.

Country profile

The Republic of Congo (commonly referred to as *Congo Brazzaville* to distinguish it from the Democratic Republic of Congo or *Congo Kinshasa*) lies within the catchment areas of the Congo and Ubangi rivers. The climate is tropical. The population is Bantu-speaking with the Kongo, Teke and Mboshi forming 85% of the total. About 45% are Christians.

History

Some 600 years ago when the Bantu-speaking people moved into the region it was inhabited by Pygmies. Towards the end of the 15th Century Portuguese merchant mariners established relations with the Kongo kingdom at the mouth of the Congo river and conducted slave trade until it was abolished in the 19th Century. French colonization began in the late 19th Century when Count Savorgnan de Brazza signed a treaty with the chief of the Batekes, Makoko. In 1910 Congo became part of French Equatorial Africa and in 1960 gained its independence under Pres. Fulbert Youlou. After several coups Col. Denis Sassou-Nguesso took control in 1979 and established stability with a one-party regime. In free elections held in 1993, Pascal Lissouba won the presidency but his party failed to obtain an absolute majority and a four month civil war erupted which led to the large-scale destruction of Brazzaville. In 1997 Lissouba's fragile coalition government came to an end when Sassou-Nguesso's supporters, with the help of Angolan forces, took over as president. At the end of 1999 a peace agreement was signed between Sassou-Nguesso, from the north, and the rebels representing the populous south. The truce seems to be holding.

CENTRAL AFRICAN REP.
CAMEROON
Souanke
Dia
Ngabala
Dongou
2°N
EQ. GUINEA
Sembe
Ouesso
Epena
Implondo
Lioesso
Sangha
Likouala aux Herbes
Ubangi
Equator
Likoual
Makoua
Kandeko
Keile
Owando
GABON
Ewo
Kouyou
Oyo
Mossaka
Gamboma
Mbinda
Ngo
Congo
2°S
Bambama
Mpouya
Banda
Djambala
Zanaga
Kibango
Mpe
DEM. REP. OF CONGO
Mayombe Mts.
Sibiti
Odziba
Ngabe
Nzambi
Loubomo
Madingou
Mindouli
BRAZZAVILLE
4°S
Madingo-Kayes
Loango
Boko
Pointe Noire
CABINDA
ATLANTIC OCEAN
2°E
14°E
16°E
18°E
0 50 100 150 200 250 300 km

Government

The present constitution, adopted after a referendum held in March 1992, provides for an executive President and a Prime Minister, who heads the government, and a bicameral legislature comprising the National Assembly and the Senate. Following Lissouba's overthrow on 15 October 1997, an appointed Government of National Unity (GNU) or national Transitional Committee has been assisting Pres. Sassou-Nguesso.

Economic policy

Pres. Denis Sassou-Nguesso promised economic reforms and privatization and renewal of cooperation with international financial institutions. Progress was slowed by the resumption of armed conflict in December 1998. The 1999 peace agreement has kindled new hope.

Sectors

The economy presents a mixture of village agriculture and handicrafts, an industrial sector based largely on oil, support services, and a government characterized by budget problems and overstaffing. The main food crops are maize, cassava, rice and yams; the main cash crops are cocoa, coffee, sugar and palm oil. With its more than 90 bridges and 12 tunnels, the over 500 km stretch of Congo-Ocean Railway, built in the colonial era, is not only an engineering feat but provides a vital link in the transport system of equatorial Africa. The railway starts at Pointe Noire with its modern deep-water harbor, opened in 1939 and still regarded as one of the best equipped in Africa. After Nigeria and Cameroon, Congo is the third largest gas resource base in Sub-Saharan Africa. Pointe Noire, Congo's economic and petroleum capital, has not been directly affected by the insecurity elsewhere in the country.

Privatization

In April 1998, the Congolese government established a new national petroleum company, the *Société Nationale des Pétroles du Congo* (SNPC), to market Congo's crude oil and to assume all upstream functions of the former state-owned company, Hydro-Congo. Privatization of Hydro-Congo's downstream operations has been underway since 1997 with Elf and Shell as major participants. Prior to the 1997 civil war, Congo's national utility, *Société Nationale d'Electricité* (SNE), was one of the several government entities considered for privatization.

Fast facts

POLITICAL

Head State	Pres.Denis Sassou-Nguesso (1997)
Ruled by	National Transitional Council
Independence	15 August 1960
National capital	Brazzaville
Official language	French

PHYSICAL

Total area	132,046 sq. miles 342,000 sq. km. (± Montana)
Arable land	0.5%
Coastline	105 miles/169 km

POPULATION

Total	2.7 million
Av. yearly growth	2.16%
Population/sq. mile	21
Urban population	59%
Adult literacy	78%

ECONOMY[1]

Currency	CFA franc (CFAF)(US$1: 752.76)
GDP (real)	$2.29 billion
GDP growth rate	-3.0%
GNP per capita[2]	$690
GDP (ppp)[3]	$3.9 billion
GDP per cap. (ppp)[3]	$1,500
Inflation rate	5.0%
Exports	$1.7 billion
Imports	$1.6 billion
Development aid	$282 million
External debt	$5.4 billion
Unemployment	N/A

INFRASTRUCTURE

Railroads	497 miles/800 km
Paved roads	10%
Motor vehicles	46,000 (1994)
Air passenger/km	264 million (1994)
Telephones/1,000	8 (1994)
Intl. airports	Brazzaville & Pointe Noire
Main harbor	Pointe Noire

1. Statistics are based on World Bank data.
2. Atlas method.
3. See page 151 for an explanation of GDP based on purchasing power parity (ppp).

Investment

Elf Aquitaine (Elf) holds a dominant position in exploration, production, and refining with Italy's ENI-Agip playing an important secondary role. US firms engaged in offshore exploration and production include Chevron, CMS/Nomeco, and Exxon. In a recent development Elf (51% interest) partnered on the Haute Mer Permit with Chevron (30%), SNPC (15%), and Energy Africa (Engen) (4%).

Trade

Oil accounts for 70% of Congolese government revenue and 85% of Congo's exports. It is the 15th largest supplier of crude to the United States.

Taxes and tariffs

Corporate income tax and capital gains are taxed at 45%, and a 20% tax is levied on dividends. Import duties range from 15% on primary and capital goods to 50% on some consumer goods.

Business activity

AGRICULTURE
Cassava, sugar, rice, corn, peanuts, vegetables, coffee, cocoa, forest products.

INDUSTRIES
Petroleum extraction, cement, lumbering, brewing, sugar milling, palm oil, soap, cigarettes.

NATURAL RESOURCES
Petroleum, timber, potash, lead, zinc, uranium, copper, phosphates, natural gas.

EXPORTS
$1.7 billion (1999 est.): petroleum, lumber, plywood, sugar, cocoa, coffee, diamonds.

IMPORTS
$1.6 billion (1999 est.): capital equipment, construction materials, foodstuffs, petroleum products.

MAJOR TRADING PARTNERS
US, Belgium, Luxembourg, Taiwan, China, France, Italy, UK.

Doing Business with Rep. of Congo

▶ **Investment**

The success of deepwater exploration off the coast of the Congo and neighboring Cabinda (Angola) has sparked renewed interest in these areas. Hydrocarbon legislation enacted in 1994 offers production-sharing agreements (PSAs) to foreign oil companies in partnership with the national oil company, SNPC. Contractors finance all investment and recover their expenditure when the production begins. In 1995, foreign companies were given the option of converting existing exploration and production joint venture contracts to PSAs and since then all major operators in Congo have signed up. Other sectors of interest to foreign investors are forestry, mining, agriculture, pharmaceuticals, and construction.

▶ **Trade**

Major imports by Congo include heavy machinery, vehicles, business equipment, clothing, pharmaceuticals, consumer goods, and foodstuffs. US exports are inhibited in part by high transport costs, a cumbersome local bureaucracy, and lack of established networks between US and Congolese traders. The French, with extensive local knowledge and an on-the-ground presence have the edge.

▶ **Exchange controls**

As a member of the franc zone, the Congo shares the BEAC as a central bank with neighboring central African states.

▶ **Establishing a presence**

A center for business enterprises (known by its French acronym, CFE) assists foreigners who wish to establish themselves in the Congo.

▶ **Financing projects**

The International Finance Corporation was a major lender to the N'Kossa offshore project. Most of the financing for projects in the growing oil and gas sector is, however, arranged by the major oil companies themselves.

▶ **Labor**

A new labor code aims at making the country more investor-friendly.

▶ **Business climate**

Conducting business in the Congo requires a knowledge of French. Business customs conform to the European model as a result of years of French influence in the region.

Côte d'Ivoire

Even though its attempt at democratic multiparty rule was derailed by a coup in December 1999, Côte d'Ivoire has impressed many with its stability and growth. It is considered a key player among the member states of the former French West Africa. Côte d'Ivoire is the world's largest producer of cocoa and also a significant exporter of coffee, forest products, cotton, rubber, bananas, pineapples, and palm oil. A relatively well-developed infrastructure and a sophisticated financial sector have prompted foreign firms to establish their regional headquarters in Côte d'Ivoire.

Country profile

The Republic of Côte d'Ivoire forms a low plateau less than 500 m. above sea level, bordered in the west by the Nimba mountains stretching northwards to the confluence of the Sassandra, the Red and the White Bandama, and the Komoe rivers. Rainfall along the coast averages 2,000 mm. per year and gradually decreases northward, to around 1,000 mm. The Baoule dominates with 23% of the total population, followed by the Bete (18%), the Senoufou (15%), and Malinke (11%). The country has an immigrant and expatriate population of over 2 million. More than 120,000 Lebanese are mostly engaged in business and French expatriates number around 50,000. French is the official language. About 38% of the population are Muslim, especially in the north, and 28% Christian, mainly in the southeast.

History

First settled by the Kru and subsequently the Mande-speaking people (including the Muslim Malinke) and the Kwa, Côte d'Ivoire came into French orbit in the 1840s. Forts were built along the coast to facilitate ivory and slave trade. The colony of Côte d'Ivoire was established in 1893 and French colonists, encouraged by the colonial government, began with cocoa and coffee cultivation on large estates with the help of forced labor. In the 1930s a Baoulé medical officer, Félix Houphouet Boigny, took up the cause of black farmers. The name Boigny, which was added to signify "irresistible force," proved prophetic. In 1960 Houphouet Boigny became the executive President of newly independent Côte d'Ivoire and for the next 30 years exercised one party rule. In the country's first free elections in 1990 he was reelected by a margin of 82%. Houphouet Boigny died on 7 December 1993, at the age of 88 and was succeeded by the speaker of the Na-

Fast facts

POLITICAL	
Head of State	Pres. Laurent Gbagbo (2000)
Ruling Party	FPI
Main opposition	PDCI-RDA
Independence	7 August 1960
National capital	Yamoussoukro[4]
Official language	French

PHYSICAL	
Total area	124,502 sq. miles 322,460 sq. km. (± New Mexico)
Arable land	8%
Coastline	320 miles/515 km

POPULATION	
Total	15.8 million
Av. yearly growth	2.35%
Population/sq. mile	128
Urban population	44%
Adult literacy	44%

ECONOMY[1]	
Currency	CFA franc (CFAF)(US$1=752.76)
GDP (real)	$11.9 billion
GDP growth rate	2.8%
GNP per capita[2]	$700
GDP (ppp)[3]	$24.2 billion
GDP per cap. (ppp)[3]	$1,680
Inflation rate	6.0%
Exports	$4.96 billion
Imports	$4.2 billion
Development aid	$467 million
External debt	$14.8 billion
Unemployment	N/A

INFRASTRUCTURE	
Railroads	660 km
Paved roads	8%
Motor vehicles	246,000
Air passenger/km	282 million
Telephones/1,000	8
International airport	Abidjan
Main harbor	Abidjan

1. Statistics are based on World Bank data.
2. Atlas method.
3. See page 151 for an explanation of GDP based on purchasing power parity (ppp).
4. Abidjan is the administrative capital.

tional Assembly, Henri Konan Bédié. On 24 December 1999, Bédié and his elected government were deposed in a military coup led by former army chief of staff General Robert Guei who promised to stay in power only "to sweep the house clean." Instead he decided to run for president in the October 2000 elections. He was defeated by his main rival, Laurent Gbagbo, leader of the *Front Populaire Ivorienne* (FPI).

Government

The constitution provides for an executive president elected by popular vote for a 5-year term. He appoints a Prime Minister, who in turn selects the Council of Ministers. In the October 2000 presidential election, President Gbagbo received 59.4% against the other major candidate, Gen. Guei's 32.7% . Gbagbo's Front Populaire Ivorienne (FPI) narrowly defeated the *Parti Démocratique de la Côte d'Ivoire* (PDCI-RDA) by gaining 96 seats against 94 in the 175-member National Assembly, with a few smaller parties holding the rest. The *Rassemblement des républicains* (RDR) boycotted the election.

Economic policy

From the outset Pres. Houphouet-Boigny's government followed conservative and pragmatic pro-Western policies, with emphasis on economic growth rather than wealth redistribution. During the first 20 years following independence the economy grew at an average annual rate of 7.5%. A severe drop in the price of cocoa and coffee in the eighties saddled the country with a large external debt and prompted it to take steps to diversify the economy. The government's strategy has four goals, referred to as "the legs of the African elephant": 1) export diversification, 2) encouraging crops other than coffee and cocoa, 3) encouraging extractive industries, and 4) reinforcement of Côte d'Ivoire's already developed services sector.

Sectors

More than 33% of the GDP activity is in agriculture, forestry or fishing. Côte d'Ivoire is the world's leading exporter of cocoa and a significant producer of cotton, coffee, sugar and rubber. In recent years there has been considerable expansion into the cultivation and export of mangoes, cashews, flowers and silk. New mining and petroleum codes were enacted in the mid-nineties to encourage foreign exploration of gold and nickel and offshore oil production. Mining plays a small role in the economy but oil has been extracted from offshore fields since the late 1970s. The country has considerable largely unexploited iron ore, bauxite and manganese deposits. Manufacturing revolves mostly around the processing of agricultural, forestry and petroleum products, and textiles, chemicals and import substitution. Tropical weather and a well-developed infrastructure make tourism a promising sector.

Privatization

Most of the 60 state-owned enterprises earmarked in an ambitious privatization program in the early nineties have been privatized. Projects include restructuring of the telecommunications company, a vegetable-oil producer, the country's leading hotel, an electricity company, the state oil refinery and the national airline.

Investment

Foreign firms have focused largely on mining and oil exploration. Contracts have been concluded with Canadian, Australian and South African mining houses, focusing largely on gold and, in one instance, nickel. Offshore oil and gas exploration and production drew interest from US, Canadian and European firms. France, however, continues to be the most important foreign investor, accounting for more than half of the total. Attracted by Côte d'Ivoire's track record of political stability until 1999, its liberal investment code, and convertible currency, some 50 US companies have invested about $1 billion. Following the liberalization of cocoa and coffee exports, US-based Cargill and other commodity trading multinationals have invested in both local processing and the export of raw cocoa beans.

Trade

Côte d'Ivoire is the world's leading exporter of cocoa beans, contributing over 30% of the world's output. It ranks third in Africa in the export of coffee beans, after Ethiopia and Uganda, and is the leading sugar cane producer in West Africa. The country competes with Mali and Nigeria for first place in West Africa as producer of cotton lint and with Nigeria as a supplier of tobacco leaves. Rice and meat are imported despite significant local production. Imports—primarily from France, Nigeria, the US, Ghana, and Germany—range from industrial inputs to transportation equipment, food and beverages, fuel and lubricants to consumer goods.

Financial sector

Côte d'Ivoire is a member of the *Communauté Financière Africaine* (CFA), a financial grouping of Francophone African countries and belongs to the *Union Economique et Monétaire de l'Afrique de l'Ouest* (UEMOA). The BCEAO, located in Dakar, is the central bank for UEMOA members and the French Treasury guarantees convertibility of its currency. There are 15 commercial banks, regional stock exchange, and over 30 insurance companies. The African Development Bank is headquartered in Abidjan. The World Bank and the International Finance Corporation also maintain regional offices in the city.

Taxes and tariffs

Corporate, capital gains and branch tax rates are 35%. There are several exempt categories for companies developing industrial or agricultural enterprises. The value added tax rate was reduced to 20% from 25% and the weighted average duty rate has been reduced from 43% to 33%. HSBC Equator Bank is among the foreign banks in the country.

Business activity

AGRICULTURE
Coffee, cocoa beans, bananas, palm kernels, corn, rice, manioc, sweet potatoes, sugar, cotton, rubber, timber.

INDUSTRIES
Foodstuffs, beverages, wood products, oil refining, automobile assembly, textiles, fertilizer, construction materials, electricity.

NATURAL RESOURCES
Petroleum, diamonds, manganese, iron ore, cobalt, bauxite, copper.

EXPORTS
$4.96 billion (1999 est.): cocoa, coffee, tropical woods, petroleum, cotton, bananas, pineapples, palm oil, fish.

IMPORTS
$4.2 billion (1999 est.): food, consumer goods, capital goods, fuel, transport equipment.

MAJOR TRADING PARTNERS
Netherlands, France, Germany, US, Italy, Nigeria.

Doing Business with Côte d'Ivoire

▶ **Investment**

Investors who establish themselves in regions outside Abidjan are entitled to an 8-year tax exemption instead of 5 years. Companies seeking priority enterprise status, eligible for these tax holidays and other benefits, might be required to purchase Ivorian products. The *Centre de Promotion des Investissements en Côte d'Ivoire* (CEPICI) serves as a "one-stop-shop" for foreign investors, helping them to find suitable opportunities and serving as a link with the public sector. Investments from outside the Franc Zone must be approved by the external finance and credit office of the Ministry of Economy and Finance. Apart from privatization and the relaxation of state monopolies, a variety of opportunities exists in projects such as waste water and solid waste collection networks in regional cities, the connection of the Mali-Côte d'Ivoire and the Guinea-Côte d'Ivoire electrical grids, and the Abidjan-Ghana expressway, many on a BOT (Build-Own-Transfer) basis.

▶ **Trade**

Opportunities exist in high value food products, paper products, telecommunications, computers and software, consumer electronics and agricultural, irrigation, mining, construction, air-conditioning, refrigeration, medical, security, and power generation equipment, as well as textile, forestry and woodworking machinery, and cosmetics, toiletries, pharmaceutical and health care products. In the past 5 years, several oil and gas projects have come into production creating a need for field equipment.

▶ **Trade finance**

Eximbank financing is available. Competitive credit terms are important considerations in purchasing decisions.

▶ **Selling to the government**

The Ivorian Government periodically issues procurement tenders in local newspapers and sometimes in international media. The *Bureau National d'Etudes Techniques et de Developpement* (BNETD) usually acts on behalf of other ministries in projects financed by the World Bank and the African Development Bank.

▶ **Exchange controls**

By law all exchange transactions relating to foreign countries must be handled by authorized banks. Foreign exchange for import payments must be purchased either on the date of settlement specified in the commercial contract or at the time the required down payment is made. French Franc-based transactions are the easiest and more common.

▶ **Partnerships**

Many foreign firms rely on local partners or agents. An increasing number of Ivorians who trained abroad are available as partners.

▶ **Establishing a presence**

The CEPICI assists foreign firms with formalities such as registration, incorporation, and the modification or dissolution of a local entity. The four most common forms of business are *Association et Participation* (Joint Venture); *Succursale* (Foreign Branch), a *Société à Responsabilité Limitée* (Limited Liability Company); and *Société Anonyme* (Stock Corporation).

▶ **Financing projects**

The Overseas Private Investment Corporation offers loans, loan guarantees and insurance products to US investors. The US Trade and Development Agency finances feasibility studies and the World Bank and the African Development Bank support government procurement. Côte d'Ivoire is a member of the Multilateral Investment Guarantee Agency.

▶ **Labor**

Unskilled labor is readily available but clerical, technical, managerial, and professional talent is more difficult to find. Wage rates are relatively high by regional standards.

▶ **Legal rights**

A new arbitration tribunal has been established under the auspices of the Chamber of Commerce. Côte d'Ivoire is a member of the international center for the settlement of investment disputes (ICSID) and a party to the Paris Convention and the African Intellectual Property Organization (OAPI), which recently adopted revisions to conform to the WTO agreement on trade-related intellectual property issues (TRIPS).

▶ **Business climate**

Business customs in Côte d'Ivoire are decidedly European. French is the official language and prevalent in business. Academic titles and degrees are frequently used by members of the expatriate community or those who received their schooling abroad.

Djibouti

As one of the smallest countries on the African continent and with limited natural resources, Djibouti is largely dependent on its service sector. It provides a rail link from the strategically located Djibouti harbor to Ethiopia's Addis Ababa and telecommunication cable connections between Northern Europe and Asia. A nagging deficit makes it dependent on foreign assistance. The government is actively seeking to redress the problem by encouraging foreign involvement in mining, shipping and services. Djibouti is host to several thousand French military personnel and allows the US naval and air defense access.

Country profile

The Republic of Djibouti is a small country at the juncture of the Red Sea and the Gulf of Aden, slightly larger than Swaziland and The Gambia. It consists mainly of a volcanic rock-strewn desert interrupted by patches of arable land, salt lakes and pans, and has high temperatures, high humidity and a low annual rainfall. Its population consists largely of the Issa Somali clan. There is also a strong Afar minority. Both groups are Muslim Cushitic-speaking peoples with a traditionally nomadic lifestyle. The small but influential Arab element comes mainly from Yemen and the expatriate community is mostly French, some of them refugees from Somalia. More than two thirds of the population live in the port city of Djibouti.

History

Around the 3rd Century B.C. Arabs migrated to what is today Djibouti. Their descendants, the Afars or Danakil people, were joined a century later by the Issas who migrated from southern Ethiopia. Both the Afar and the Issa were nomadic livestock herders who spoke related Cushitic languages and adopted the Muslim faith. Portuguese and Turkish slave traders in the region were eventually followed by the French, British and Italians who competed for control of the sea route through the Red Sea and the Suez Canal. The French prevailed. From 1888, they developed the port of Djibouti on the southern side of the Gulf and in 1917 connected it by means of a 480 mile (780 km) railway to Addis Ababa in Ethiopia. In 1958 the Afar voted to remain a self-governing part of France in a referendum boycotted by most of the Issas. The same happened in 1967 when the French Territory of the Afars and Issas was granted responsible self-government and renamed French Somaliland. The quest for national

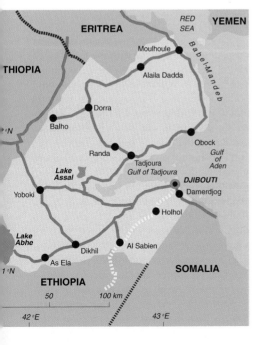

205

Fast facts

unity was, however, stimulated by the territorial claims made on the territory by the independent Somali Republic to the south. In a third referendum in March 1977, the electorate voted overwhelmingly in favor of independence. A senior Issa politician, Hassan Gouled Aptidon, became executive president of the Republic of Djibouti, a single party state. In September 1992 the voters adopted a multiparty constitution and in 1999 Aptidon finally stepped aside opening the door for Ismail Omar Guelleh to be elected president.

Government

The 1992 Constitution provides for a president elected for a maximum of two 6-year terms. It is customary for the prime minister to be appointed from the Afar minority. In the 1999 election the *Rassemblement populaire pour le Progrès* (RPP) captured 54 seats and the Front pour la *Restauration de l'Unité et de la Démocratie* (FRUD) the remainder in the 65-member unicameral Chamber of Deputies. Guelleh is supported by both parties.

Economic policy

Djibouti's economy has been weakened by battles against Afar rebels during the 1990s. In March 2000 they signed a peace accord with the new government. In October 1995 the entire country was declared a free export zone to encourage foreign involvement.

Sectors

The agricultural sector in Djibouti contributes only 3.5% of the GDP but employs an estimated 75% of the people. The service sector constitutes 76.0% of GDP. Djibouti serves as both a transit port for the region and an international transshipment and refueling center. The Djibouti port facility and the railroad that links it to Addis Ababa account for most of the economic activity. The port, the heart of the country's economy, is well equipped. Its container facilities have been greatly expanded but are increasingly being challenged by improved facilities at Saudi Arabia's Jeddah harbor and Ethiopia's Assab port. The country will soon host a state-of-the-art submarine cable link running from Northern Europe to East Asia. At least ten international airlines use the airport at Djibouti as a stopover. An oil refinery was built in 1990. A small fishing industry is being developed. Surveys have indicated the presence of a few minerals such as copper, gypsum and sulfur, but as yet none of them are mined commercially. Manufacturing is limited to small-scale concerns. The principal source of energy is thermal plants. An expatriate community contributes significantly to the economy.

Privatization

Recent attempts at privatization of state enterprises have met with lukewarm response from potential investors.

Investment

Djibouti has had limited success in attracting foreign investment. Although efforts were made to reduce restrictions on foreign investors, recent warfare and harsh environmental conditions in the region have deterred investors.

Trade

Exports consisting of cattle, refined sugar, crude organic material, fish, hides and skins, and coffee are mostly transhipments from Ethiopia. A large portion of Djibouti's imports are destined for Ethiopia, Somalia and other neighboring regions.

Financial sector

There is a sophisticated private banking service in place. With its almost unrestricted commercial and financial sectors, Djibouti is actively courting offshore banking and insurance firms.

Taxes and tariffs

The corporate income, capital gains, and branch tax rates are 20%. There is a 10% withholding tax on dividends for nonresidents. Residents are exempt from the withholding tax on dividends and interest.

Business activity

AGRICULTURE
Fruit, vegetables, goats, sheep, camels.

INDUSTRIES
Limited to a few small-scale enterprises such as dairy products and mineral-water bottling.

NATURAL RESOURCES
Geothermal areas.

EXPORTS
$207 million (1997): hides and skins, coffee (in transit).

IMPORTS
$285 million (1997): food, beverages, transport equipment, chemicals, petroleum products.

MAJOR TRADING PARTNERS
Ethiopia, Somalia, Yemen, Saudi Arabia, France, Italy, Thailand.

Doing Business with Djibouti

▶ **Investment**

Shipping and other port-related activities are seen as prime candidates for investment. The country also shows potential for geothermal and solar energy production. There are small known gold deposits as well as diatomite, geothermal fluids, mineral salts, gypsum, perlite, pumice, and possibly petroleum. Oil interest focuses on the southern region and the offshore area along the Gulf of Aden. Djibouti is trying to lure offshore banking with its liberal economic regime.

▶ **Trade**

Merchandise exports of local origin are insignificant and almost all food requirements and consumer goods have to be imported. Djibouti's well-equipped harbor is a transshipment point for products to and form Ethiopia by rail. It is also used by both French and US naval ships.

▶ **Exchange controls**

The currency, the Djibouti franc, is pegged to the dollar and is freely convertible. There are no foreign exchange restrictions.

▶ **Labor**

An unemployment rate of 40% to 50% continues to be a major problem. Skilled labor is, however, relatively expensive.

▶ **Business climate**

The business practices are Middle Eastern and the language French.

Egypt

As the most populous Arab country, Egypt is both African and Middle Eastern. Some ten million of Egypt's total population of 63 million have developed western consumption patterns and even among the poor majority consumption habits are changing rapidly thus expanding the potential for imported goods. Because of its strategic position in the region, Egypt continues to receive strong donor support, including about $2 billion in annual US economic and military assistance, a good portion translating into orders for American products. Despite infrequent fundamentalist acts of terror, Egypt enjoys political stability and its economy has made great strides integrating into the global market.

Country profile

The Arab Republic of Egypt is today as dependent on the river Nile as it was in the days of the pharaohs. Agriculture centers around the valley of the Nile. Even though they speak Arabic, Egyptians are not Arabs but a mixture of peoples tracing their ancestry back to the Nubians, Berbers, mixed Arab-Berber groups and Europeans. At least 90% are Muslim and 6% Christian Copts, apart from Roman Catholic, Protestant and Jewish minorities.

History

Today Egypt maintains virtually the same borders as those during the time of the pharaohs. First conquered in 332 BC by Alexander the Great it passed on to Roman control in 31 BC. In 639 Muslims from Arabia conquered Egypt and transformed it into an Arabic-speaking Muslim country. Extended Turkish rule, a brief French presence under Napoleon and British caretaker rule led to the recognition of a sovereign, independent state under King Fuad on 28 February 1922. Violent protests against continued British military presence at the Suez Canal in the 1950s led to a bloodless coup. King Farouk was replaced by Colonel Gamal Abdel Nasser who ruled until his death in 1970. He was succeeded in 1970 by his deputy, Anwar Sadat, who signed the Camp David Peace Accords in 1979 and was assassinated two years later by members of the Islamic Jihad organization. Sadat was succeeded by his deputy, General Hosni Mubarak.

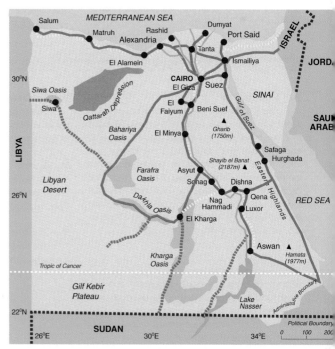

208

Government

The President is elected by a two-thirds majority of the People's Assembly (Majlis) and confirmed by referendum. President Hosni Mubarak was re-elected to a fourth six year term in October 1999. The 444 members of the People's Assembly are directly elected for a five-year term. The National Democratic Party (NDP) has dominated the Assembly since its establishment in 1978. It won 353 seats in the November 2000 election and was joined by 35 independents. Non-partisans form the main opposition.

Economic policy

Egypt maintains a market economy with the state sector accounting for 30 percent of GDP and the private sector 70 percent. In recent years a significant portion of Egypt's infrastructure development has been funded through foreign assistance. An economic stabilization program started in 1991 has led to an improvement in the real GDP growth rate from 2% to 5% and a decrease in inflation from 20% to 3%. During this nine year period foreign currency reserves increased from $7 to $17 billion and the budget deficit decreased from 17 to around 1 percent of GDP. Over the past two years, legislation has been passed to increase private sector activity in Egypt and allow greater foreign participation. Structural reforms, including privatization in key areas such as insurance, banking, and telecommunications are underway.

Privatization

Since January 1996 serious steps have been taken toward selling off state-owned enterprises. The basis has been laid for expanded participation by the private sector and foreign investors in the banking and insurance sectors. Private investment in key infrastructure areas has increased significantly. All future power generation projects will be constructed on a build-own-operate-transfer (BOOT) basis. The government has sold cellular phone concessions and has opened airports, ports, and port services to private investors.

Sectors

Tourism and the Suez Canal account for 32% of GDP and 34.7% of the total earnings from goods and services. The oil and gas sector account for about 6.7% of Egypt's GDP and 33.7% of its exports. Agriculture's share of the GDP has fallen from 20% in 1987 to 17.3% in 1999.

Fast facts

POLITICAL

Head of State	Pres. Hosni Mubarak (1981)
Ruling Party	NDP
Main Opposition	Non-partisans
Independence	1922
National capital	Cairo
Official language	Arabic

PHYSICAL

Total area	386,666 sq. miles 1,001,450 sq. km. (3 x New Mexico)
Arable land	3%
Coastline	1,522 miles/2,450 km

POPULATION

Total	60.3 million
Av. yearly growth	2.2%
Population/sq. mile	177
Urban population	49%
Adult literacy	54%

ECONOMY[1]

Currency	Pound (£E) (US$1=3.92)
GDP (real)	$68.7 billion
GDP growth rate	6.0%
GNP per capita[2]	$1,250
GDP (ppp)[3]	$188 billion
GDP per cap. (ppp)[3]	$2,850
Inflation rate	3.6%
Exports	$14.3 billion
Imports	$21.7 billion
Development aid	$2.05 billion
External debt	$29.95 billion
Unemployment	10%

INFRASTRUCTURE

Railroads	2,983 miles/4,800 km
Paved roads	40%
Motor vehicles	1.7 million (1994)
Air passenger/km	6.3 billion (1994)
Telephones/1,000	43 (1994)
International airport	Cairo
Main harbor	Alexandria

1. Statistics are based on World Bank data.
2. Atlas method.
3. See page 151 for an explanation of GDP based on purchasing power parity (ppp).

Trading

Despite productivity gains since the mid-1980s, Egypt remains one of the world's largest food importers. In 1998 the US supplied 4.2 billion of the 6.0 billion metric tons of imported wheat as well as a substantial percentage of corn, soybean, vegetable oil and high-value agricultural products. It is also a significant importer of oil and gas field machinery, military equipment, automotive parts, construction and medical equipment, telecommunications equipment, packaging and paper material and, more recently, environmental equipment and materials. In 1998 the US sold $3 billion in goods to Egypt and purchased $698 million, amounting to a favorable US trade balance of some $2.3 billion. Petroleum products and cotton are major export items.

Investment

In March 1999, the US Department of Commerce put the total stock of American foreign direct investment (FDI) in Egypt at around $2 billion. Official local statistics put the United States at the top of the list of investing countries. In 1998, according to the General Authority for Investment and Free Zones (GAFI), the US participated in 204 projects totaling $543 million, out of a total of 1,254 worth $3.4 billion by non-Arab investors. GAFI figures, however, do not include investment in the petroleum sector, the chief recipient of US FDI in Egypt. According to company data, US direct investment in the oil and gas sector is in excess of $7 billion.

Financial sector

Banks are supervised by the central bank of Egypt. A total of 69 institutions comprise 9 public sector banks, 29 commercial banks, 33 investment banks and 7 specialized banks. Privatization stimulated foreign interest in the capital markets and in March 1999 there were 26 mutual funds in operation—19 managed in Egypt and 7 offshore. In April 1999, the market capitalization of the Cairo and Alexandria Stock Exchange (CASE) stood at $26.9 billion with a listing of 925 companies. In 1999, Moody's Investors Service assigned a Baa1 rating to the domestic currency government bonds while Standard and Poor's gave Egypt an investment grade rating of BBB-. Several US mutual funds include Egyptian stocks, and 54 local issues are included in the IFC's general index.

Taxes and tariffs

Since 1991, under its economic reform program developed in conjunction with the IMF and the World Bank, Egypt has reduced its tariff rates to a maximum rate of 40%, except in the case of certain automobiles, alcoholic beverages, and luxury items. An Egyptian import ban on textiles is permitted under the WTO's eight year transition period.

US relations

In 1992 the US and Egypt signed a Bilateral Investment Treaty and two years later the US-Egyptian Partnership for Economic Growth and Development placed relations between the two on a special level. An annual aid program of $800 administered by USAID since 1975 promotes infrastructure development and privatization. The US finances most of Egypt's big-ticket defense procurements at a yearly rate of $1.3 billion. On July 1, 1999, Egypt and the US signed the Trade and Investment Framework Agreement (TIFA).

Foreign

Overseas petrochemical giants are heavily involved in Egypt's petroleum industry. Foreign firms are also active in the financial sector and in a wide range of manufacturing industries.

Business activity

AGRICULTURE

Cotton, rice, corn, wheat, beans, fruit, vegetables, cattle, water buffalo, sheep, goats, fish.

INDUSTRIES

Textiles, food processing, tourism, chemicals, petroleum, construction, cement, metals.

NATURAL RESOURCES

Petroleum, natural gas, iron ore, phosphates, manganese, limestone, gypsum, talc, asbestos, lead, zinc.

EXPORTS

$14.3 billion (1999 est.): crude oil and petroleum products, cotton yarn, raw cotton, textiles, metal products, chemicals.

IMPORTS

$21.7 billion (1999 est.): machinery and equipment, food, fertilizers, wood products, durable consumer goods, capital goods,

MAJOR TRADING PARTNERS

EU, US, Japan.

Doing Business with Egypt

▶ **Investment**

As a result of the government's privatization program, the private sector's role has steadily expanded in key sectors such as metals (aluminum, iron, and steel), petrochemicals, cement, automobiles, textiles, consumer electronics, and pharmaceuticals. The government has made development of high technology a priority and seeks to attract export-oriented manufacturing firms. Generous tax and other incentives are offered. Franchising of fast-food restaurants and clothing stores is a growing business in Egypt.

▶ **Trade**

The huge US favorable trade balance with Egypt is ample proof of the possibilities existing beyond the supply of military equipment funded largely by US government grants. Wheat and other agricultural products, medical equipment, computers, construction equipment and a whole range of consumer goods are imported. Foreign firms can sell directly within Egypt as long as they register, but most rely on domestic companies for wholesale and retail distribution.

▶ **Trade finance**

Apart from Eximbank facilities, USDA/FAS operates an Export Credit Guarantee Program for Egyptian private sector importers of US food and agricultural commodities. USAID/Egypt sponsors a Private Sector Commodity Import Program (CIP) that makes dollars available to Egyptian private sector importers through some 22 Egyptian banks.

▶ **Selling to the government**

Egyptian procurement is either done with national budgetary funds or by using aid funds from USAID or other donors. In the case of USAID-funded procurement, project announcements are made in the US "Commerce Business Daily," published in Chicago. US military aid finances most of Egypt's big-ticket defense procurements. Only registered commercial agents can work on tenders. Government employees are judged on their ability to squeeze the final penny from the lowest bidder—a practice commonly referred to in Arabic as "momarsa."

▶ **Exchange controls**

The Foreign Exchange Law of May 1994 allows individuals and legal entities to retain and transfer foreign exchange abroad and entitles banks to conduct foreign exchange transactions.

▶ **Partnerships**

In most sectors foreigners are allowed any measure of shareholding in a partnership, ranging from a few percentage points to close to 100 percent.

▶ **Establishing a presence**

There are several choices, depending on the nature and size of the intended business. Some companies, which intend to conduct market research in scientific, technical or consulting fields, might resort to representative offices funded entirely by remittances from abroad and not subject to Egyptian tax. Oil, construction, and consulting firms often rely on branch offices.

▶ **Project financing**

OPIC and US TDA support US investment. Egypt is currently included in the International Finance Corporation index for emerging markets and there has been an increase in corporate bonds issued by private sector companies.

▶ **Labor**

The abundance of labor has led to low prevailing wages and the use of labor-intensive technologies. Workers may join trade unions but are not required to do so.

▶ **Legal rights**

The government guarantees against nationalization. The US-Egypt Bilateral Investment Treaty also protects against expropriation and provides for nonbinding, third party arbitration in investment disputes. Even though Egypt is a signatory of several international IPR treaties, the US Trade Representative felt obliged to place Egypt on a priority watch list in April 1998—a designation retained through 1999. In the meantime, the US assisted Egyptian authorities in their efforts to increase intellectual property rights (IPR) protection, primarily through USAID programs.

▶ **Business climate**

Egyptians with whom foreigners do business are typically trilingual (English-French-Arabic), well-traveled individuals who pride themselves on seeking out good deals at decent prices. The Egyptian market is a complex and highly competitive one and an Egyptian agent is frequently essential. Be prepared to bargain. Negotiations are bound by an unspoken culture that assumes that there is not any final, best price that cannot be reduced.

Equatorial Guinea

Once largely dependent on cocoa and coffee, Equatorial Guinea has had the world's fastest growing economy since 1997, largely as a result of off-shore oil discoveries and a market-oriented government. Referred to by some as the "Kuwait of Africa" tropical Equatorial Guinea is expected soon to over-take Gabon and the Republic of Congo as the third largest oil producing country in Sub-Saharn Africa. The Economist Intelligence Unit forecasts Equa-torial Guinea to be the only country in the world with an economic growth rater higher than 10 percent in 2001. It offers a convenient entry point to the franc zone countries of Africa.

Country profile

The Republic of Equatorial Guinea covers an area roughly the size of Hawaii, consisting of widely scattered regions—Rio Muni or Mbini on the mainland (which constitutes 92% of the total land area), Bioko island (with 22% of the population and the capital of Malabo), tiny Annobon Island, some 650 km to the south, and the islets of Corsico and Elobey off the main-land estuary. Some 80% of nearly a half million Equato-Guineans live in Mbini—about 150 km wide and extending 200 km inland. Its equatorial climate supports extensive rainforests where mahogany and okoume are grown. Some 125 miles (200 km) from Mbini is Bioko (for-merly known as Fernando Po Island), which forms part of a submerged volcanic mountain range with exposed points as far as Annobon Island to the south and Mt. Cameroon to the north. The Bantu-speaking Fang is the largest group in Mbini while the original inhab-itants of Bioko Island are the Bubi and the Fernandino—the latter descendants of former slaves whose Krio language has become the *lingua franca*. Annobon is inhabited by a fish-ing community of mixed ori-gin. Both French and Spanish are official lan-guages. Most people in the mainland region profess ethnic faiths, but Bioko Island is over-whelmingly Roman Catholic.

History

In the 1470s the Portuguese reached Fernando Po (later renamed Bioko) and three other tropical islands in the Gulf of Guinea. Bubi

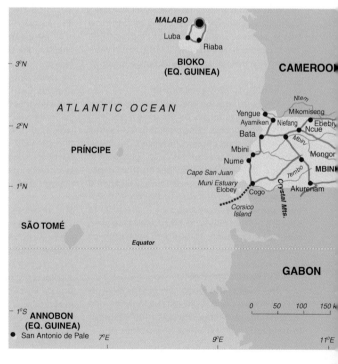

hostility and Bioko's hot, humid climate prompted the Portuguese to concentrate on the deserted islands of Sao Tome, Principe and tiny Annobon further south. In 1778 Portugal bartered Bioko and Annobon to Spain for territory in South America. Until 1858, when the Spanish finally took possession, the British leased Bioko as a naval base for anti-slavery operations. The British developed the port of Clarence, renamed Santa Isabel by the Spanish—today's Malabo, the capital of Equatorial Guinea. Rescued slaves who chose to remain are today known as the Fernandinos. They spoke pidgin English which evolved into Krio. In the 1880s, Spain added a slither of territory on the mainland to its island possessions, named it Rio Muni (today's Mbini) and formed Spanish Guinea. In response to pressures from so-called *emancipados*, the colony was granted independence on 12 October 1968 under Pres. Macias Nguema who led a decade-long campaign of terror resulting in the death of 20,000 people. One-third of the total population of 300,000 sought asylum in neighboring countries. Cubans and North Koreans helped to keep Macias in power and the Soviet Union was allowed to exploit fish resources from a fishing-cum-military base on Bioko Island. In the process Macias drove one of Africa's most prosperous colonies into bankruptcy. On 3 August 1979, the chief of the army, Lt.-Col. Teodoro Obiang Nguema Mbasogo, replaced his uncle by force, took immediate steps to stabilize the country and cultivated relations with Western donor countries and organizations. He was elected unopposed as president for a 7-year term in June 1989 and reaffirmed in the country's first post-independence, multi-party election in 1993.

Government

The present Constitution, endorsed by referendum on 16 November 1991, provides for a multiparty system. The President, vested with executive powers, is elected by the voters for 7-year terms and appoints the Prime Minister who heads the government and appoints the Council of Ministers. The 80-member Chamber of People's Representatives serves a 5 year term. In the most recent presidential election in March 1999, Obiang's *Partido Democratieo de Guinea Ecuatorial* (PDGE) won 75 seats. The main opposition, *Union Popular,* won 4 seats.

Fast facts

POLITICAL

Head of State	Pres. Teodoro Obiang Nguema Mbasogo (1979)
Ruling Party	PDGE
Main Opposition	UP
Independence	12 October 1968
National capital	Malabo
Official languages	Spanish & French

PHYSICAL

Total area	10,830 sq. miles 28,050 sq. km. (± Maryland)
Arable land	5%
Coastline	296 km

POPULATION

Total	465,746
Av. yearly growth	2.55%
Population/sq. mile	44
Urban population	36%
Adult literacy	81%

ECONOMY[1]

Currency	CFA franc (CFAF)(US$1≈752.76)
GDP (real)	$373 million
GDP growth rate	15.1%
GNP per capita[2]	$1,060
GDP (ppp)[3]	$660 million
GDP per cap. (ppp)[3]	$1,500
Inflation rate	6.0%
Exports	$712 million
Imports	$597 million
Development aid	$26 million
External debt	$201 million
Unemployment	30%

INFRASTRUCTURE

Railroads	0 km
Motor vehicles	N/A
Air passenger/km	7 million
Telephones/1,000	7
International airport	Malabo
Main harbor	Malabo, Bata

1. Statistics are based on World Bank data.
2. Atlas method.
3. See page 151 for an explanation of GDP based on purchasing power parity (ppp).

Economic policy

At independence in 1968, Equatorial Guinea's per capita income was one of the highest in Africa, but dropped to one of the lowest after a decade of mismanagement under the Macias regime. The new government is liberalizing the economy and privatizing some state enterprises to create a favorable investment climate. Since 1997 Equatorial Guinea has had the world's fastest growing economy. There are long-term incentives for job creation, training, promotion of non-traditional exports, support of development projects and indigenous capital participation, freedom to repatriate profits, exemption from certain taxes and capital and other benefits.

Sectors

Limited oil production began in 1991 and since the discovery of major additional oil reserves off Bioko Island in 1995 Equatorial Guinea has been referred to by some as the "Kuwait of Africa." It is currently producing approximately 200,000 barrels per day and is expected to overtake Gabon and the Republic of Congo as the third largest oil-producing country in Africa. Other areas with good potential include fishing, timber, tourism, and mining. There are modest deposits of iron ore, lead, zinc, manganese, uranium, tantalum and molybdenum. Good prospects also exist in agriculture with cocoa, coffee, palm oil, bananas and coconuts as major crops. Deep water port facilities serve as convenient outlets for neighboring countries. The small, isolated island of Annobon lies in a 314,000-square kilometer exclusive maritime economic zone amid some of the Atlantic's richest fishing grounds.

Privatization

In 1998, a decision was taken to privatize the distribution of petroleum products in the country. Private investors have been co-opted to increase electrical capacity and parastatals and public enterprises have been earmarked for privatization in the agro-industry (cocoa), transport (airline, shipping and maritime transport), public utilities (electricity, water and telecommunications) and several other sectors.

Investment

The US is a major investor in oil and gas operations in Equatorial Guinea but Spain as the former colonial power maintains a sizeable portion of the holdings in the country.

Trade

Spain, France, Italy, Cameroon, Nigeria and the US are important suppliers of food, petroleum products, automobiles, machinery, and iron and steel. The US, Cameroon and Côte d'Ivoire are major buyers of oil and fuels and the Netherlands, Spain, Germany, France and Italy top the list of purchasers of cocoa, timber and coffee.

Financial sector

Interest rates are set by the regional central bank (BEAC), monitored and regulated by the French Government. There are two commercial banks regulated by the Banking Commission for Central African States (COBAC)— an affiliate of a Cameroonian bank and another affiliate of a French bank.

Taxes and tariffs

A flat tax of 6.25 % applies to all petroleum revenues. Generalized preferential tariffs apply to goods being shipped to other CEMAC countries. The number of taxes applied to imports was reduced from over seven to four and the overall rate from a maximum 47 % to a maximum 12 % on the most heavily taxed imports. Custom's assessments were simplified.

Business activity

AGRICULTURE

Coffee, cocoa, rice, yams, cassava (tapioca), bananas, palm oil nuts, manioc, livestock, timber.

INDUSTRIES

Petroleum, fishing, sawmilling, natural gas.

NATURAL RESOURCES

Timber, petroleum, small unexploited deposits of gold, manganese, uranium.

EXPORTS

$712 million (1999 est.): petroleum, timber cocoa.

IMPORTS

$597 million (1999 est.): petroleum, food, beverages, clothing, machinery.

MAJOR TRADING PARTNERS

US, Japan, Spain, China, Nigeria, Cameroon, France.

Doing Business with Equatorial Guinea

▶ **Investment**

The investment code allows repatriation of profits and offers tax and other incentives for job creation, training, the promotion of non-traditional exports, and the support of development projects. Investments in non-traditional products in rural areas are favored. Foreign investment is not subject to screening and foreign equity ownership is not restricted. The government is offering attractive terms to foreign entrepreneurs willing to explore and exploit the country's mineral wealth. Fisheries, salting, livestock feeds, cocoa paste, palm oil, transportation and communications, water purification and sanitation, and power and energy have been identified as priority areas for investment.

▶ **Trade**

Apart from oil production equipment, airplanes, watercraft, heavy road and logging equipment, construction materials, agricultural inputs such as fertilizers and equipment, foodstuffs, used clothing and shoes offer sales opportunities. Foreign firms are advised to obtain the services of agents with local knowledge. There are few franchise operations in Equatorial Guinea but international oil companies might soon be able to retail petroleum products, currently limited to Total, the government's partner.

▶ **Trade finance**

Importers and exporters use internationally accepted methods of settlement. Foreign firms sometimes grant credits of 180 days for consumer goods and 24 months for small machinery and equipment but an irrevocable, confirmed letter of credit is standard practice.

▶ **Selling to the government**

Programs financed jointly by international financial institutions and the Government are open to unrestricted competition. Privatization of specific industries might in future present opportunities in the transport sector (both the national airline and the national shipping corporation), and in public utilities (water, electricity and telecommunications).

▶ **Exchange controls**

Foreign exchange controls are enforced primarily for statistical purposes and to enable the Ministry of Finance to certify that remittances conform with established regulations. Authorizations for foreign transfers are routinely granted.

▶ **Partnerships**

Partnerships in certain areas are mandatory as local entrepreneurs have exclusive rights in the manufacture of arms, explosives and other weapons, the gathering, treatment and storing of toxic, dangerous and radioactive materials or waste products and the production of alcoholic beverages excluding beer.

▶ **Financing projects**

The World Bank's resident representative in Yaoundé, Cameroon, and its affiliate, the International Finance Corporation 's regional offices in Douala also handles applications from Equatorial Guinea. The African Development Bank Group has been involved in the country and OPIC operates in the country. The International Development Association has on occasion provided loans for projects involving foreigners.

▶ **Labor**

Unemployment is difficult to quantify in a developing economy where so many of the citizens are toiling the land or underemployed in rural areas but the UN Development Program has estimated it to be as high as 88 %. A Spanish company (FTF-First Training and Finance) was contracted by the government to regulate labor supplies, initially for the petroleum industry, but subsequently for other sectors.

▶ **Legal rights**

Foreign and domestic investors are provided with guarantees that comply with international norms. Trademark enforcement is weak as Equatorial Guinea is not a member of the 14-nation West African intellectual property organization, *Organisation Africaine de la Propriété Intellectuelle.* Equatorial Guinea does, however, accept binding international arbitration of investment disputes with foreign investors and is a member of the International Center for the Settlement of Investment Disputes. It is also a signatory to the Convention on the Recognition and Enforcement of Foreign Arbitral Awards.

▶ **Business Climate**

The business community closely follows Spanish customs and the language most often used is Spanish, with some French. Equato-Guineans insist on getting to know a potential partner before starting concrete discussions.

215

Eritrea

Eritrea, Africa's youngest nation, gained its freedom from Ethiopia in 1991 after a 30-year war of liberation and achieved statehood after a referendum in 1993. It triumphed over tremendous odds in a struggle that reduced substantial parts of a once fairly prosperous country to ashes. The rebuilding process has since been interrupted by renewed border conflict with Ethiopia, starting in 1998 and concluded with a peace agreement at the end of 2000. Eritrea has liberalized its economy and with the help of foreign investment made remarkable progress which is expected to be speeded up after the final cessation of hostilities.

Country profile

The State of Eritrea is one of Africa's smaller countries. As an extension of Ethiopia's mountains, the Eritrean highlands form a steep escarpment, overlooking a narrow coastal plain. With an annual rainfall of 500-1,000 mm the escarpment constitutes the most productive agricultural region. The Tekeze river forms part of the border with Ethiopia and drains into the Nile. The Danakil Depression (130 m below sea level) is one of the hottest places on earth. Nomadic livestock herders occupy the coastal plain. Eritrea's economic zone in the Red Sea includes more than 350 islands of various shapes and sizes, fringed by coral reefs, with a total land area of 515 sq. miles (1,335 sq km). Eritrea's people are of Ethio-Semitic, Cushitic and Nilotic origin. The main language is Tigrinya, spoken by the Tigray—the principal Ethio-Semitic group. Cush-itic groups live on both sides of the border with Sudan in the northwest, and the Afar (a.ka. the Adal or Danakil)roam the southern coastal strip. English, taught at schools, is the most widely spoken European language. The Tigray are predominantly Christian, belonging to the Eritrean Orthodox

Church. There are sizeable minorities of other Christian denominations and Muslims.

History

Eritrea used to be part of the ancient Ethiopian empire built around Axum (Aksum). During the 4th Century AD Ethiopia's emperors converted to Christianity and established the Ethiopian Orthodox Church throughout the realm. From about the 8th Century Axum went into decline. When Emperor Menelik II came to

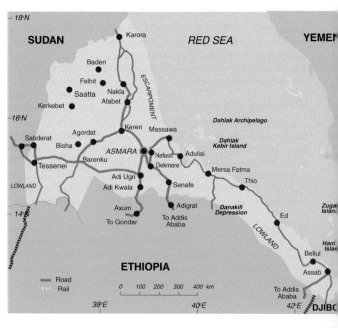

power at the turn of the 19th Century and founded a new capital, Addis Ababa (the new flower) to replace Asmara (the flower), the Tigray in the north revolted. In 1889, Menelik ceded to Italy the northern and northeastern fringes of his empire in the hope of satisfying Rome's territorial ambitions.

The Italian colony of Eritrea—a name derived from Mare Erythraeum, the old Roman designation for the Red Sea—was adopted in 1890. After a humiliating defeat when they tried to expand their influence south into Ethiopia, the Italians concentrated on colonizing Eritrea. In 1936, however, Italy conquered Ethiopia and ruled over both colonies until 1941 when the Allied forces defeated Mussolini's troops and returned Ethiopian emperor Haile Selassie to the thrown. Selassie pressed for the re-incorporation of Eritrea into its "motherland." In 1952 the UN General Assembly decided Eritrea should become an autonomous state federated with Ethiopia.

Barely ten years later, however, Emperor Haile Selassie abrogated the federation, dissolved Eritrea's national assembly and absorbed the country as Ethiopia's 14th province. Various liberation movements became active and eventually the Eritrean People's Liberation Front (EPLF) emerged victorious when Eritrea won its independence in May 1993. The EPLF leader, Isaias Afwerki, became president. Since its independence, Eritrea and Ethiopia have disagreed about the exact demarcation of their borders and in May 1998 border clashes began. They erupted into a war that lasted until the beginning of 2000 that resulted in the loss of tens of thousands of lives on both sides and depleted state coffers. A cease-fire was signed in June 2000 and a peace agreement concluded later in the year. The UN agreed to provide peace-keeping troops to patrol the buffer zone.

Government

A Constitution adopted in May 1997 provides for an executive President elected for a maximum of two 5-year terms. The National Assembly serves for a 5-year term as well and consists of elected members from each of the Regional Assemblies. The Eritrean People's Liberation Front (EPLF), that became the People's Front for Democracy and Justice (PFDJ), has been ruling the country since independence.

Fast facts

POLITICAL

Head of State	Pres. Isaias Afwerki (1993)
Ruling party	PFDJ
Independence	24 May 1993
National capital	Asmara
Working languages[5]	Tigriña, Arabic and English

PHYSICAL

Total area	47,742 sq. miles 124,320 sq. km. (± Pennsyvania)
Arable land	12% of land area
Coastline	1388 miles/2,234 km (incl. Red Sea islands)

POPULATION

Total	3.98 million[4]
Av. yearly growth	3.88%
Population/sq. mile	90
Urban population	17%
Adult literacy	52%

ECONOMY[1]

Currency	Nafka (US$1=10.20)
GDP (real)	$681 million
GDP growth rate	0.8%
GNP per capita[2]	$200
GDP (ppp)[3]	$2.5 billion
GDP per cap. (ppp)[3]	$660
Inflation rate	8.0%
Exports	$66 million
Imports	$509 million
Development aid	$129 million
External debt	$242 million
Unemployment	N/A

INFRASTRUCTURE

Railroads	116 miles/300 km
Paved roads	14%
Motor vehicles	N/A
Telephones/1,000	4
International airport	Asmara
Main harbors	Massawa & Assab

1. Statistics are based on World Bank data.
2. Atlas method.
3. See page 151 for an explanation of GDP based on purchasing power parity (ppp).
4. Not including 0.5 million refugees awaiting repatriation.
5. Eritrea does not have an official language.

Economic policy

The government is actively seeking foreign private investment and partnerships with international donors. In coordination with the World Bank and the IMF it developed a liberal macroeconomic policy with an investment code that offers significant incentives to foreign investors. Until recently, however, the border war with Ethiopia has substantially slowed new investment.

Sectors

Agriculture and fishing account for about half the national product (GDP) and two-thirds of exports. Around 60% of the population is engaged in or dependent on crop cultivation and livestock raising. Main crops are teff, millet, wheat, sesame, sorghum, barley, vegetables, pulses, cotton, fruit and coffee. Fishing waters offer sardine, anchovy, shrimp and lobster in abundance. Eritrea has deposits of salt and other minerals such as basalt, limestone, marble, granite, sands, silicates, gold, silver, copper, nickel, zinc, chrome, sulphur and potash. Prospecting is underway for oil and gas. Manufacturing involves glass, cement, footwear, textiles, beverages and canned food.

Privatization

Privatization is planned for most of Eritrea's 42 state-owned enterprises, industries and hotels. A dozen public enterprises were privatized over the past two years—including a dairy factory, a brewery, and a corrugated iron sheet factory—some in the form of public-private partnerships and others through outright sale to foreign or local investors.

Investment

No precise country breakdown of foreign direct investment statistics is available but the US share was estimated at $100 million in 1999. Other major investors include South Korea, Italy, and China. As of December 31, 1998, the Eritrean investment center has licensed close to 700 projects worth $561 million, approximately half in foreign capital.

Trade

Multilateral lenders who have been impressed with the government's fiscal discipline, despite the recently concluded border war, readily provided financing for imports needed for reconstruction and development. Principal sources for imports consisting largely of construction, farming, telecommunications equipment, agricultural products and raw tobacco) are Italy, Ethiopia (until May 1998), Sudan, Saudi Arabia. The US purchases mostly unfinished raw materials, garments, and textiles.

Financial sector

The Eritrean banking system has been described as "strong but primitive." A housing and commerce bank, an agriculture and industry development bank and the commercial bank of Eritrea operate alongside the central bank of Eritrea. The central bank of Eritrea, though a government entity, operates independently from the ministry of finance. Although Eritrea allows foreign banks to operate in the country, no foreign bank has opened as yet.

Taxes and tariffs

Tariffs ranging from 2% to 50% have been imposed on essential goods such as capital equipment, industrial inputs, pharmaceuticals, school supplies, books, food, livestock, and seed. Customs duties on imports of capital goods, intermediate industrial spare parts, and raw materials have, however, been fixed at a nominal 2%. On luxury goods, liquor, tobacco, prepared foods (particularly those that compete with domestic products), automobiles, and electronic equipment the tariff is between 50% and 200%.

Business activity

AGRICULTURE
Sorghums, lentils, vegetables, maize, cotton, tobacco, coffee, sisal, livestock, fish.

INDUSTRIES
Food processing, beverages, clothing and textiles.

NATURAL RESOURCES
Gold, potash, zinc, copper, salt, potential of oil and natural gas, fish.

EXPORTS
$66 million (1999 est.): livestock, sorghum, textiles, food, small manufactures.

IMPORTS
$509 million (1999 est.): processed goods, machinery, petroleum products.,

MAJOR TRADING PARTNERS
Sudan, US, Italy, Saudi Arabia, Yemen, Egypt.

Doing Business with Eritrea

Investment

Investment policy gives domestic and foreign investors equal access to land, utilities, and other production units in all sectors of the economy except domestic retail and wholesale trade and import agencies. A variety of tax and export incentives are extended to investors, especially those involved in relatively depressed areas. Foreign firms are encouraged to participate in the privatization process where, in some cases, the government has favored partnership agreements over outright sales. Among the target areas for foreign investment are fishing, offshore oil and gas exploration, mining, tourism, the development of alternative energy sources such as thermal, wind, and solar, as well as construction enterprises to repair roads, bridges, airports, and railways, rehabilitate port facilities, improve water and sewage networks, and build houses and office and industrial sites.

Trade

Energy, mining, agribusiness, construction, telecommunications, transportation, tourism, heavy equipment, light industry, and marine resources offer significant opportunities for trade. There is a constant shortage of heavy construction equipment and a demand for agricultural and mining equipment. Suppliers of used equipment may find a ready market in a country with the reputation of being able to keep anything running. (During their war for independence the Eritreans thrived on Soviet style vehicles captured from their Ethiopian opponents). There is an expanding English speaking middle class with an appetite for Western consumer products.

Trade finance

Nearly all import financing is done on a letter of credit basis. There are two banks in Eritrea authorized to issue LCs—the commercial bank of Eritrea and the housing and commerce bank.

Selling to the government

Many government purchases are associated with donor financed projects and are subject to bidding and procurement rules of the donors. There is no central procurement office and each ministry handles its own needs. The tenders are open to public bidding and advertised in the local papers. Major governmental infrastructure projects, including road, airport, harbor and hospital construction, create an ongoing need for foreign equipment, expertise and materials.

Exchange controls

The national bank of Eritrea has adopted a free-floating exchange rate. Foreign investors are allowed to remit profits and dividends, principal and interest on foreign loans, and fees related to technology transfer as well as the proceeds from the sale of liquidation of assets.

Partnerships

The government encourages joint ventures with foreign firms, especially in mining and the privatization of state-owned businesses. Franchising is a relatively new concept but former expatriate Eritreans tend to be good candidates as licensing partners.

Establishing a presence

A business licensing office has been established as a one-stop shop to short-circuit procedures. Private entities, both domestic and foreign, have the right to establish, acquire, own, and dispose of most forms of business enterprise but companies affiliated with the ruling party, the People's Front for Democracy and Justice (PFDJ) enjoy certain advantages over other firms.

Financing projects

The Overseas Private Investment Corporation offers risk insurance and loans to US investors. Eritrea is a member of the Multilateral Investment Guarantee Agency.

Labor

Eritrea has an inexpensive but industrious and disciplined workforce but skilled manpower in certain fields is hard to obtain. All workers in public and private enterprise are members of the national confederation of Eritrean workers.

Legal rights

Foreign investors may choose to submit disputes to local settlement under the laws of Eritrea, in terms of The Hague convention or by presenting its case to the Eritrea investment center. Eritrea also abides by the International Convention on the Settlement of Investment Disputes. There are currently no formal mecanhism to protect intellectual property rights, patents, and copyrights.

Business climate

Business customs are Western and English. Italian and Arabic are widely spoken. Everyone in the business community seems to know each other and considerable value is placed on character.

219

Ethiopia

The land of kings and legends, Ethiopia is the oldest independent country in Africa and the original home of coffee. Political and economic reforms and the conclusion of a costly war against Eritrea should enable it to make economic progress. Ethiopia not only holds the promise of becoming a significant exporter once it has fully utilized its resources but as Africa's third most populous country—after Nigeria and Egypt—it could develop into a major market for foreign products once per capita incomes have risen above current lows. The new government has introduced an economic reform program in conjunction with the World Bank and donor countries.

Country profile

More than half of the Federal Democratic Republic of Ethiopia is at high altitudes. Its highest point, Ras Dashen (4,620 m) is Africa's fourth highest mountain. The national capital, Addis Ababa, is 2,450 m above sea level. The mountainous region is bisected by the Great Rift Valley. South of Addis Ababa a chain of freshwater and salt lakes extends along the valley floor to Lake Turkana at the country's southwestern corner. Numerous large rivers, including the Blue Nile, flow from east to west towards the Nile Basin. The highest rainfall (over 1,000 mm) occurs in the west and southwest. Ethiopian society is a mixture of Caucasoid and Negroid peoples. The three principal groups are the Ethiopian Semites, the Cushites and the Omotic cluster of peoples and tongues, with two subgroups, the Amhara and the Oromo, accounting for 70% of the total population. A much smaller group, the Tigray, speaking Tigrinya, inhabits the far northern highlands and extends across the border into Eritrea. Half the population are Orthodox Christians, 35% are Muslims and the remainder adhere to ethnic beliefs.

History

Early mixing between the Cushitic, Omotic and Nilotic Negroid peoples produced a racially mixed population in ancient Ethiopia. From about 800 BC

there was an influx of Semitic peoples from Saba (now Yemen) across the Red Sea into the highlands of present-day Eritrea and northern Ethiopia. The name Ethiopia (a Greek name meaning "land of dark people") began to apply to the empire centered around the city of Axum. In 333 AD Ethiopian Emperor Ezana was converted to Christianity and, by the 14th and 15th centuries when this territory was surrounded by Muslim regions, tales were told in Europe about the mysterious Christian kingdom of Prester John. Emperor Menelik II came to power

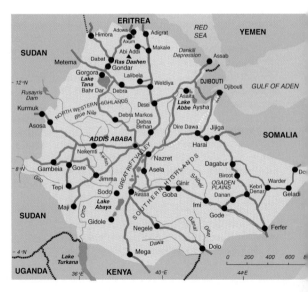

at the turn of the nineteenth century and founded a new capital, Addis Ababa, to replace Asmara as the capital. Shortly after his ascension to the throne in 1889, Emperor Menelik ceded to Italy the northern and northeastern fringes of his empire to placate Rome but the Italians still tried to incorporate Ethiopia, suffering a humiliating defeat. In 1936 Italy extended its rule over Ethiopia as well and in 1941, with Mussolini's defeat by the Allied forces. Emperor Haile Selassie was restored to the throne. At his insistence that Eritrea be rejoined to the "motherland" the UN General Assembly made it an autonomous state within an Ethiopian federation. In 1962 Selassie abrogated the federation and absorbed the country as Ethiopia's 14th province. Setbacks in the ensuing war with Eritrea and internal dissension led to the imprisonment and alleged strangling in jail of Haile Selassie in 1974. Major Mengistu Haile Mariam, who replaced him, introduced a Soviet-style regime—known as the Dergue—which led to the killing of 100,000 opponents or critics. In 1991 the brutal 14-year dictatorship of Mengistu ended when the Tigray-led Ethiopian People's Revolutionary Democratic Front (EPRDF) marched into Addis Ababa. Mengistu fled, making way for Meles Zenawi who was reconfirmed as executive prime minister in Ethiopia's first-ever multiparty elections in 1995 and again in August 2000. Dr. Negaso Gidada is president.

Government

A constitution adopted in 1994 provides for a bicameral parliament consisting of a 117-member upper chamber (Council of the Federation) and 527-member lower chamber (Council of People's Representatives). A non-executive President is elected by both houses for a six-year term. The executive Prime Minister is chosen by the majority party in the Council of People's Representatives. Zenawi's EPRDF—coalition of several major parties—won a landslide victory in August 2000. A total of 28 parties represented in the lower chamber. The Amhara National Democratic Movement (ANDM) forms the main opposition.

Economic policy

The government adopted a Five-Year Development Plan in 1995 to enhance agricultural productivity, improve rural infrastructure, encourage

Fast facts

POLITICAL
Head of State	Pres. Negasso Gidada (1995)
Prime Minister	Meles Zenawi (1995)
Ruling Party	EPRDF
Main opposition	ANDM
Independence	2,000 years
National capital	Addis Ababa
Official language	Amharic

PHYSICAL
Total area	435,184 sq. miles 1,127,127 sq. km. (2 x Texas)
Arable land	12% of land area
Coastline	Landlocked

POPULATION
Total	59.7 million
Av. yearly growth	2.16%
Population/sq. mile	143
Urban population	13%
Adult literacy	36%

ECONOMY[1]
Currency	Birr (BR) (US$1=8.29)
GDP (real)	$6.7 billion
GDP growth rate	6.2%
GNP per capita[2]	$100
GDP (ppp)[3]	$32.9 billion
GDP per cap. (ppp)[3]	$560
Inflation rate	3.9%
Exports	$894 million
Imports	$1.9 billion
Development aid	$669 million
External debt	$9.28 billion
Unemployment	N/A

INFRASTRUCTURE
Railroads	484 miles/780 km
Paved roads	14%
Motor vehicles	60,000
Air passenger/km	1.6 billion
Telephones/1,000	3
International airport	Addis Ababa

1. Statistics are based on World Bank data.
2. Atlas method.
3. See page 151 for an explanation of GDP based on purchasing power parity (ppp).

private investment, promote participation of the private sector in the economy, mobilize external resources, and pursue appropriate macroeconomic and sectoral policies. It also embarked on a program of economic reform and a phased privatization program.

Sectors

Agriculture accounts for more than half of GDP, more than 90% of foreign earnings and over 80% of employment. Coffee, cotton and sugar are major cash crops and food crops include cereals, particularly teff, maize, and sorghum. Ethiopia's cattle population of around 30 million head is by far the largest in Africa, yet commercial slaughtering (2.3 million head annually) is lower than that of South Africa, with a much smaller human and cattle population. Mineral resources include appreciable reserves of natural gas (in the eastern region), gold, copper, zinc, potash and iron ore. Manufacturing is largely in processed foods, consumer goods and textiles for the home market, and hides for export, handicrafts and leather. Tourism is seen as a growth industry in this country with its cultural diversity, mountains, lakes, rivers, ancient cities.

Privatization

From 1995 when the government started selling state-owned enterprises, 180 entities have been privatized, including the Pepsi Cola and Coca-Cola bottling plants. In the agricultural sector most marketing boards have been abolished, enabling farmers to sell their crops to the highest bidder. Coffee marketing has been opened to competition.

Investment

As of 1998 the Ethiopian Investment Authority approved 163 foreign investment projects with total projected capital investment of $1.2 billion—90 wholly foreign-owned and 73 joint ventures. US investors were involved in 11 of the new projects with a total investment of $30 million. Ethiopia's major foreign investors include Saudi Arabia, South Korea, Kuwait, and Italy.

Trade

Primary exports are coffee, hides and skins, sesame seeds, pulses, chat, live animals, honey and beeswax, and fruits and vegetables. Coffee (arabica) is by far the most important export commodity, constituting about two-thirds of exports by value. Main imports are semi-finished goods, crude petroleum and petroleum products, transport and industrial capital goods, medical and pharmaceutical products, motor vehicles, civil and military aircraft, raw materials, and agricultural machinery and equipment.

Financial sector

There are six private banks and seven private insurance companies. The National Bank of Ethiopia (NBE) promotes monetary stability by regulating credit and exchange. Foreign banking is not permitted in Ethiopia but most of the commercial banks have correspondent relations.

Taxes and tariffs

Customs duties have been reduced on a wide range of imports. Tariff rates range from 0% to 50%, with an average of approximately 20%. The government plans to reduce the maximum rate to 30%.

Local time

Ethiopia uses the Julian calendar, which is divided into 12 months of 30 days each and a 13th month of five or six days at the end of the year. The Ethiopian calendar is 7 years and 8 months behind the Gregorian calendar. By anyone's calendar, Ethiopia is the oldest independent country in Africa.

Business activity

AGRICULTURE

Cereals, pulses, coffee, oilseed, sugar cane, potatoes, hides, cattle, sheep, goats.

INDUSTRIES

Food processing, beverages, textiles, chemicals, metals processing, cement.

NATURAL RESOURCES

Small reserves of gold, platinum, copper, potash, natural gas.

EXPORTS

$894 million (1999 est.): coffee, leather products, gold, oilseed.

IMPORTS

$1.9 billion (1999 est.): food and live animals, petroleum and petroleum products, chemicals, machinery, motor vehicles and aircraft.

MAJOR TRADING PARTNERS

Germany, Japan, Italy, UK, Djibouti, Saudi Arabia, US.

Doing Business with Ethiopia

▶ **Investment**

Investors in relatively underdeveloped regions of Ethiopia are eligible for exemption from income tax for up to five years. With the lowest telephone line density in Africa and plans to award a series of contracts to expand services, telecommunications offers good potential. Foreign firms are excluded from the domestic banking, insurance services, high volume air transport or freight services, forwarding and shipping agency services, rail transport services, and non-courier postal services. Foreigners are welcomed to participate in privatization but in some instances the government promotes joint ventures with Ethiopian private concerns rather than outright sales.

▶ **Trade**

The country's main imports include motor vehicles, petroleum products, civil and military aircraft, spare parts, construction equipment, medical and pharmaceutical products, agricultural and industrial chemicals, agricultural machinery, fertilizers, irrigation equipment, and food grains. The government requires that all imports be channeled through Ethiopian nationals registered with the government as official import or distribution agents. Ethiopia maintains restrictions and taxes on the export of coffee and chat and regulates the sale of petroleum products.

▶ **Trade finance**

The Ethiopian government relies on grants and external borrowing on highly concessionary terms to finance the external current account deficit.

▶ **Selling to the government**

Road building, telecommunications development and other infrastructural projects are open for international competitive bidding and are funded by either the Ethiopian government or major international financial institutions such as the International Development Association of the World Bank and the African Development Fund.

▶ **Exchange controls**

All foreign exchange transactions must be carried out through authorized dealers under the control of the National Bank. Foreign investors may freely remit profits and dividends, principal and interest on foreign loans, fees related to technology transfer, proceeds from liquidation of assets or transfer of shares, and funds required for debt service or other international payments.

▶ **Partnerships**

Foreign investors are encouraged to go into joint ventures especially where there is the prospect of technology transfer, improvement of the country's foreign exchange position, utilization and development of natural and human resources and added value in various economic sectors.

▶ **Establishing a presence**

Both foreign and domestic private entities have the right to establish, acquire, own, and dispose of most forms of business enterprises. State-owned enterprises have, however, considerable *de facto* advantages over private firms when it comes to cutting red tape, access to credit and swift customs clearance.

▶ **Financing projects**

The Overseas Private Investment Corporation offers risk insurance and loans to US investors. Ethiopia is also a member of the Multilateral Investment Guarantee Agency. Capital is sometimes available from the International Development Association of the World Bank or the African Development Bank for roads, energy, health and education projects. The International Finance Corporation also offers some equity financing.

▶ **Labor**

Labor is readily available and inexpensive, but skilled manpower is scarce. About 300,000 workers are members of unions and approximately 40% of the urban workforce is unemployed.

▶ **Legal rights**

There has been no expropriation since the transitional government replaced the Mengistu rule. Disputes arising out of foreign investment may be submitted to a competent Ethiopian court or to international arbitration. There are no regulations for the registration of patents and copyrights. Some protection can be secured through registration of trademarks at the Ministry of Trade and Industry and the publication of cautionary notices in local newspapers.

▶ **Business climate**

While Amharic is spoken throughout the country and Oromiffa and Tigrinya also widely used, English is the second official language and understood in most business circles. Ethiopians are universally addressed by first name even in formal situations.

Gabon

Gabon is one of Sub-Saharan Africa's wealthiest countries and a major supplier of oil to the United States. It is also a significant exporter of manganese and timber. Gabon is seen as having the potential of becoming a regional hub for services to other countries in the region. There is an active recruitment of foreign investors and privatization has opened up opportunities in transport, telecommunications and manufacturing. The discovery of a range of strategic minerals has stimulated interest in this sector, as well.

Country profile

The Republic of Gabon is a small equatorial country of rivers, estuaries and lagoons. Most of Gabon lies in the basin of the Ogooue river and its main tributary, the N'Gounie. The Ogooue is navigable from its delta to Booue, some 300 km upstream. The interior plateau rises to 1,300 m at the southern Chaillu Mountains on the Congo border and the northern Crystal Mountains reaching into Equatorial Guinea. Equatorial forest covers three quarters of the land surface. The climate is hot and humid. The majority of the Bantu-speaking peoples are Fang and there are sizeable minorities of Mbeti, Tsogo, Njabi, Shira, Teke, Omyene, Mpongwe Punu. One-tenth of the population are expatriates from neighboring countries and France. The majority is Christian, due in part to the efforts of the famous Dr. Albert Schweitzer who spent most of his adult life in his missionary leper hospital at Lambarene on the Ogooue River. French is the official language.

History

The earliest inhabitants of the Gabonese jungles were small bands of Pygmies or Babinga. Some 600 years ago Bantu-speaking peoples from the north started settling the coastal areas. They moved to the interior from the 16th Century. The Portuguese established contact in 1472 and were followed by Dutch, British and French who traded in slaves, ivory and precious tropical woods with the coastal kingdoms. The French established a fortified settlement on the Gabon estuary which evolved into Libreville, a community for liberated slaves. At the urging of explorer Count Pierre Savorgnan de Brazza, the areas known as Gabon and the Middle Congo were occupied by France in 1886. In 1910 part of Gabon was incorporated into

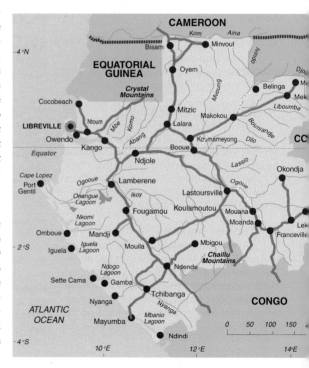

224

French Equatorial Africa but a year later the northern parts of Gabon and Congo Brazzaville were ceded by treaty to German Cameroon. They were returned to the French after World War I and in 1960 a unified Gabon became an independent republic. When its first president, Leon M'Ba, died in 1967 Vice-President El Hadji Omar Bongo took over and continued his predecessor's one-man rule until 1992 when he was obliged to call general elections in response to strong internal student and worker pressures. (After his conversion to Islam in 1973, Bongo changed his given names, Albert Bernard). His *Parti démocratique gabonais* (PDG) won 66 seats against the opposition parties' 64. In 1993 Bongo was elected president in a disputed election. He was re-elected in 1998 for another seven year term.

Government

An executive President is directly elected by the voters for a maximum of two 5-year terms. He appoints the Prime Minister and the Council of Ministers. The bicameral legislature consists of a 91-member Senate and the 120-member National Assembly, both elected for 5-year terms. The majority party in both chambers is President Omar Bongo's *Parti démocratique gabonais* (PDG). The *National Rally of Woodcutters or Bucherons* (RNB) is the largest of a number of opposition parties. The opposition controls several city governments.

Economic policy

Recent reforms in coordination with the World Bank aim to build a stronger and more diversified economy and reduce debt through privatization and diversification. The government has stepped up its efforts to attract foreign skills and technology to assist in the effort. Privatization is underway.

Sectors

The economy is dominated by the oil sector, which accounts for about half of GDP and government revenue, sixty percent of gross investment, and over three quarters of merchandise exports. With an annual production of around 16 million metric tons from both offshore and onshore wells, Gabon is Africa's third largest oil producer. After oil, timber and manganese are major foreign currency earners. The government is encouraging investors to develop value added operations in the timber industry

Fast facts

POLITICAL
Head of State	Pres. El Hadj Omar Bongo (1967)
Ruling Party	PDG
Main Opposition	RNB
Independence	17 August 1960
National capital	Libreville
Official language	French

PHYSICAL
Total area	103,347 sq. miles 267,670 sq. km. (± Colorado)
Arable land	1% of land area
Coastline	550 miles/885 km

POPULATION
Total	1.26 million
Av. yearly growth	1.48%
Population/sq. mile	12
Urban population	50%
Adult literacy	63.2%

ECONOMY[1]
Currency	CFA franc (CFAF)(UD$1: 752.76)
GDP (real)	$5.47 billion
GDP growth rate	-6.2%
GNP per capita[2]	$4,170
GDP (ppp)[3]	$7.7 billion
GDP per cap. (ppp)[3]	$6,400
Inflation rate	1.0%
Exports	$1.96 billion
Imports	$1.7 billion
Development aid	$42 million
External debt	$3.2 billion
Unemployment	21%

INFRASTRUCTURE
Railroads	404 miles/650 km
Paved roads	8%
Motor vehicles	40,000
Air passenger/km	718 million
Telephones/1,000	30
International airport	Libreville
Main harbor	Libreville/Owendo

1. *Statistics are based on World Bank data.*
2. *Atlas method.*
3. *See page 151 for an explanation of GDP based on purchasing power parity (ppp).*

as less than 10% of the logs are currently locally processed. Okoume, a soft mahogany, represents 75% of wood production. The remainder consists of a large variety of exotic hardwoods. Gabon is Africa's second largest producer of manganese after South Africa and the fourth largest uranium source (after Niger, South Africa and Namibia). High-grade iron ore is still largely unexploited and there is scope for small-scale gold mining. Agriculture, livestock and fishing make up a little less than 8% of GDP. The principal food crops are cassava, maize, manioc, fruit and vegetables. Palm oil, cocoa, coffee, sugar cane, cotton and rubber are cultivated for export. Industry, including energy and construction, accounts for only 10% of GDP and consists of the SOGARA oil refinery in Port Gentil, a cement plant, paint factory and the processing of sugar, flour, beer, cigarettes and bread. The telecommunications system is one of the most advanced in Africa.

Privatization

Privatization is underway in various sectors. Targets include the Trans-Gabonese railway (OCTRA), the state electricity and water monopoly (SEEG), and the telecommunications monopoly, *Office des Postes et Télécommunications du Gabon* (OPT). Experienced international consultants have been engaged to help evaluate needs and to manage tenders.

Investment

With the help of their government, French firms manage to maintain an edge over competitors from other countries. US firms are most active in the petroleum sector but in recent years some have started focusing on fisheries, port development, transport, and light industry. Spain, Germany, Italy, and Britain are also significant players.

Trade

Until oil was discovered, tropical timber was the main export item. Today it accounts for only 10% of exports compared with petroleum's 80% share and around 10% for uranium and manganese. The US provides only 10% of Gabon's needs, but buys about two-thirds of its oil (averaging $1.5 billion per year), as well as minerals and timber. US sales to Gabon consist largely of petroleum-related machinery and other heavy equipment.

Financial sector

French banks dominate in a relatively sophisticated system offering full corporate banking services. Gabon is a member of the French franc zone. The BEAC, headquartered in Yaoundé, issues currency and controls liquidity within the zone. There is no stock exchange.

Taxes and tariffs

Although there have been tariff disputes over the importation of exploration equipment in the past, there are few barriers in the crude oil sector where most of US firms are involved. Normally equipment used in the crude oil sector—such as seismic boats and drilling equipment—enters on a duty free basis. Customs duties apply to virtually all other imported goods at rates of up to 30%. An 18% value-added tax is levied on companies with revenues exceeding $400,000.

Foreign presence

Since its independence Gabon has been pro-West and has maintained a strong relationship with the United States and Europe. American manufacturers have been involved in the installation of 13 earth stations for the domestic satellite network and the establishment of a cellular communications system.

Business activity

AGRICULTURE

Cocoa, coffee, sugar, palm oil, rubber, cattle, okoume (tropical softwood), fish.

INDUSTRIES

Food and beverage, textiles, lumbering, plywood, cement, petroleum, extraction and refining, manganese, uranium, gold, chemicals, ship repair.

NATURAL RESOURCES

Petroleum, manganese, uranium.

EXPORTS

$1.96 billion (1999 est.): crude oil, timber, manganese, uranium.

IMPORTS

$1.7 billion (1999 est.): machinery and equipment, foodstuffs, chemicals, petroleum products, construction materials.

MAJOR TRADING PARTNERS

US, China, France, Japan, Cameroon, Netherlands, Côte d'Ivoire.

Doing Business with Gabon

▶ **Investment**

Apart from ongoing opportunities in the petroleum sector, Gabon offers considerable scope in mining of alkaline, niobium, titanium, gold, diamonds and phosphates. Privatization opens up new investment opportunities to foreigners in transport, telecommunications and manufacturing, involving parastatals such as Air Gabon, the Trans-Gabonese railway (OCTRA), the national post and telecommunications authority (OPT), the sugar monopoly (SOSUHO) and the oil refinery (SOGARA). There is also an active recruitment of investment in wood processing, light industries, fisheries and port development.

▶ **Trade**

The largest portion of foreign sales to Gabon relates to petroleum exploration and mining equipment, as well as other heavy machinery. Major local mining operations—manganese (COMILOG), uranium (COMUF) and phosphate (SOMIMO)—maintain large inventories of US cranes, drag lines, trucks and tractors. Foreign manufacturers have also developed a share in the growing market for state-of-the-art equipment in the telecommunications sector. Gabon is a net food importer.

▶ **Trade finance**

Credit is provided through six commercial banks and payment is usually by irrevocable letters of credit. A parastatal funded by the African Development Bank helps finance purchases by small and medium-sized firms owned by Gabonese nationals.

▶ **Selling to the government**

In the past a poor payment record discouraged the Eximbank and other overseas agencies from extending credit to the government. As Gabon gets its house in order and better utilizes its substantial petroleum revenues this is bound to change. For the present, however, firms are advised to ensure that funds have been set aside in the official budget for specific items when they make the deal.

▶ **Exchange controls**

There are no restrictions on foreign capital and funds may be transferred freely for commercial transactions through regular banking channels. Funds can be transferred with minimal formality within the franc zone (including to France) and repatriation of capital is not subject to onerous restrictions.

▶ **Partnerships**

Joint ventures and licensing are limited but will increase as Gabon's proceeds with privatization. Both US and European soft drinks and beers are produced in Gabon under license.

▶ **Establishing a presence**

To open a branch, applications must be filed with the Ministry of Commerce, the Tax Office of the Ministry of Finance, and the Social Security Office (*Caisse Nationale de Sécurité Sociale*—CNSS). The process can take up to three months and local legal assistance is advisable. Gabonese law allows foreign and local firms to operate as branches constituted locally as limited corporations, *Sociétés à Responsabilité Limitée* (SARL), or corporations, *Sociétés Anonymes* (SA).

▶ **Financing projects**

Gabon is a member of the Multilateral Investment Guarantee Agency. OPIC involvement has been minimal.

▶ **Labor**

Some 20% of Gabon's population are alien Africans active in the informal sector as well as in low and high skill jobs in the formal sector. A serious shortage of Gabonese managers compels firms to recruit non-Gabonese Africans and the Department of Labor reluctantly authorizes such employment, mindful of the objective of the National Employment Commission to replace these expatriates with qualified Gabonese citizens. Labor unions and confederations are active.

▶ **Legal rights**

There have been no instances of expropriation or nationalization of foreign firms. In some cases the government has mediated settlements of commercial or labor disputes on terms more favorable to foreign firms than those offered by the courts. Gabon is a member of the African Intellectual Property Office (OAPI) based in Yaoundé, Cameroon, and its courts enforce property rights. Registration is handled by the Ministry of Commerce.

▶ **Business climate**

Experience has shown that to be successful an overseas firm needs tenacious, French-speaking representatives who make repeated visits to potential customers. Personal contact and a knowledge of the territory are important. French is the only language of commerce.

Gambia, The

In 1994, The Gambia exchanged military for civilian rule and liberalized its economy. It launched a socioeconomic development program under the banner "Vision 2020 - The Gambia Incorporated" with the aim of transforming itself into a middle income country by offering a stable investment environment, efficient banking sector, and competitive private sector. As the smallest country on the African continent, this slither of land along the Gambia river jutting into the heart of Senegal has found a niche in tourism and as a trading post between West Africa and the world. Foreign observers have been impressed by its economic program during the past few years. Construction projects and tourism have drawn foreign participants to this former British colony which seems set on a course of sound macroeconomic principles.

Country profile

The Republic of The Gambia meanders for 470 km along the banks of one of Africa's most navigable rivers, the Gambia, into Senegal. The capital and main port of Banjul is built on a small peninsula on the south bank of a large, lake-like estuary. Beautiful beaches and warm coastal waters are the main tourist attractions. The climate is hot and humid. Ethnic groups comprise the Mande, including the rural Mandinka, and the Atlantic peoples, including the Wolof. English is the official language but Wolof is spoken in the towns and Mandinka in rural areas. About 85% of the population are Muslim. There is also a sizeable Christian minority.

History

From the 13th Century the Wolof, Malinke and Fulani peoples settled in the region. Portuguese mariners explored the waters of the Gambia river in the 1450s reaching far into the interior. In 1651, the Duchy of Courland (today's Latvia) took possession of islands in the river and small tracts of land alongside, notably Banjul and St. Andrew (now James Island), starting the first or-

ganized European settlement on the African mainland south of the Sahara. (The Cape of Good Hope was settled by the Dutch in the following year). In 1681 the French founded an enclave at Albredabut and during the 17th Century Gambia was occupied by various English merchant companies. From the 17th to the18th Centuries Gambia was at the center of the slave trade and in 1888 it was declared a British colony. Dawda Jawara, the leader of the People's Progressive Party, led Gambia to independence in 1965. For a few years in the 1980s, Sir Dawda acted as vice-president of Senegambia, an experimental union with surrounding Senegal. After its dissolution he and his party again won elections in 1987 and 1992 but in July 1994 Dawda Jawara was ousted in a bloodless mili-

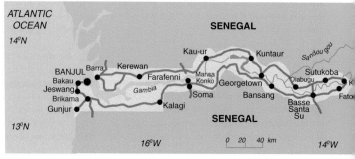

tary coup by Lieut. Yaya Jammeh. In September 1996 Jammeh was elected president over three other candidates. Censorship and a ban on some opposition parties continue and during 2000 violent student protests and a failed coup attempt marred progress.

Government

The National Assembly has 49 members elected for a five year term and 4 appointed members. In January 1997 Jammeh's *Alliance for Patriotic Reorientation and Construction* (APRC) won more than two-thirds of the seats. The main opposition party, the United Democratic Party (UDP) holds 7 seats.

Economic policy

The government launched an economic development program under the banner "Vision 2020—The Gambia Incorporated" to capitalize further on a macroeconomic framework put in place with the help of successive IMF and World Bank structural adjustment programs. After declining in 1994-95, real Gross Domestic Product rebounded, growing by 5% both in 1997 and 1998.

Sectors

Agriculture accounts for 23% of gross domestic product (GDP) and employs 75% of the labor force. Peanuts account for 5.3% of GDP, other crops 8.3%, livestock 4.4%, and fishing 1.8%. Food crops include rice, maize, millet, sorghum, cassava and pulses. Industry contributes 12% of GDP. Manufacturing involves groundnut and fish processing, brewing, footwear, perfume, cement and brick production. Known mineral deposits include kaolin, tin, ihnenite, zircon and rutile. The country has had considerable success in developing its tourist industry, which contributes about 12% of GNP.

Trade

Britain is The Gambia's major export market, accounting for 26% of the total, followed by Senegal with 22% and France with 21%. Britain is also a major supplier, with 14% of The Gambia's total imports, followed by Belgium, the Netherlands and Côte d'Ivoire. The Gambia is an important entrepot for goods distributed to neighboring countries.

Investment

Growth sectors include construction, tourism, transportation, and to a limited degree,

Fast facts

POLITICAL

Head of State	Pres. Yaya A.J.J Jammeh (1994)
Ruling Party	APRC
Main Opposition	UDP
Independence	18 February 1965
National capital	Banjul
Official language	English

PHYSICAL

Total area	4,361 sq. miles 11,295 sq. km. (2 x Delaware)
Arable land	18% of land area
Coastline	50 miles/80 km

POPULATION

Total	1.3 million
Av. yearly growth	3.35%
Population/sq. mile	334
Urban population	29%
Adult literacy	35%

ECONOMY[1]

Currency	Dalasi (D) (US$1=15.77)
GDP (real)	$429 million
GDP growth rate	6.4%
GNP per capita[2]	$340
GDP (ppp)[3]	$1.3 billion
GDP per cap. (ppp)[3]	$1,000
Inflation rate	3.0%
Exports	$199 million
Imports	$262 million
Development aid	$43 million
External debt	$432 million
Unemployment	N/A

INFRASTRUCTURE

Railroads	0 km
Paved roads	35%
Motor vehicles	10,000
Air passenger/km	50 million
Telephones/1,000	17
International airport	Banjul
Main harbor	Banjul

1. Statistics are based on World Bank data.
2. Atlas method.
3. See page 151 for an explanation of GDP based on purchasing power parity (ppp).

Business activity

agriculture crop production and fisheries. Schools, roads, hospitals, a new airport terminal building, a new national television station (the first in The Gambia), and Arch 22, a tourist attraction, have been built since 1994. The tourism sector continues to attract private sector investment.

Financial Sector

Foreign exchange earnings are too small to pay for the country's imports, leaving it heavily dependent on bilateral and multilateral aid to cover the deficit. Foreign aid contributes 80% of the government's revenue.

Taxes & tariffs

The corporate tax rate has been reduced from 50% to 35 % in January 1996 for companies producing properly audited returns. There is a capital gains tax and customs levies on international trade based on the CIF as well as *ad valorem* value of imports. A flat 10% sales tax applies to all goods and services.

Doing Business with The Gambia

▶ Investment

Designated as priority sectors for investment are manufacturing, agriculture, livestock, fisheries, forestry, mining and quarrying, tourism, and support services such as air cargo, transportation, banking and finance. Investments in these sectors qualify for exemption from customs duty and sales tax on imported capital goods and construction materials as well as special land lease arrangements. Investment incentives need to be negotiated up front. A one-stop office simplifies the establishment of foreign enterprises in The Gambia.

▶ Trade

Most trade restrictions in the form of quotas, licensing, or other restrictive instruments of commerce have been removed.

▶ Exchange controls

There are no exchange controls in effect. Profits and dividends from registered nonresident investments can be transferred without any restriction.

▶ Establishing a presence

Under the Companies Act, foreigners may establish public or private companies either unlimited or limited in terms of shares or guarantees. Incorporation simply requires a memorandum and articles of association and registration is swift.

▶ Project finance

The Gambia is a member of the Multilateral Investment Guarantee Agency.

▶ Labor

With a relatively high unemployment rate and less than 40% of the population literate, semi-skilled and unskilled workers are readily available.

▶ Legal rights

There are constitutional safeguards for the payment of adequate compensation in case of property acquisition or nationalization and the right to appeal to the Supreme Court. This generally positive record was marred by a January 1999 state takeover of the Gambia Groundnut Corporation, a subsidiary of the Swiss-based Alimenta group.

▶ Business Climate

The business language is English but French is also spoken as a result of The Gambia's close relationship with Senegal and Côte d'Ivoire.

Ghana

Often cited by the World Bank and the IMF as an African "success story," Ghana has been applying their recipes for growth and poverty alleviation in recent years. Since 1994 it managed to attain an average GDP growth rate of between 4 and 5.5 percent. These economic policies, coupled with relative stability on the political front, have helped Ghana to attract the attention of foreign investors and stimulate renewed growth in agriculture and mining.

Country profile

The Republic of Ghana lies on a low plateau ranging between 500 and 1,000 ft. (150 to 300 m) above sea level. The Volta River feeds off its White and Black tributaries and has been

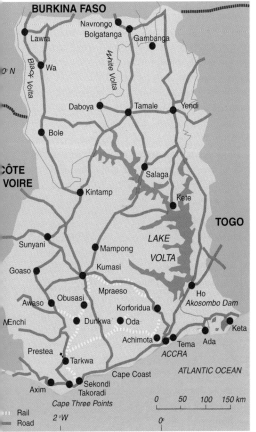

dammed at Akosombo to form the vast Lake Volta stretching 250 miles (400 km) inland and covers 3.5% of the land area. English is the official language, but 75 native languages and dialects are also spoken. The Akan cultural group (consisting of the Asante, Fante, and Brong) forms 40% of the population. About 38% adhere to ethnic beliefs while Christianity (43%) dominates in the south and the Muslim faith (12%) remains strong in the far north.

History

Gold first attracted European exploration along what became known as the Gold Coast. In 1482 the Portuguese built the first fort at Elmina (The Mine). The Dutch, French, British and Germans followed. From the 16th until the 19th Century trade in gold was overshadowed by the slave trade. During this period the Asante people gained dominance and prompted weaker tribes such as the Fante to seek British protection. Britain took control and abolished slavery from the mid-19th Century. The British colony, Gold Coast, together with the former UN trust territory, British Togoland, was granted independence as Ghana in 1957, under the leadership of Kwame Nkrumah. After he was ousted in 1966, Nkrumah's military successors—Generals Joseph Ankrah, Kofi Busia, Ignatius Acheompong and Frederick Akkuffo—perpetuated one party rule. Inflation soared and corruption went unchecked. In 1979 a young Flight Lieutenant, Jerry Rawlings, seized power and installed Hilla Limann as president. In 1981 Rawlings seized power again. As head of the

Fast facts

POLITICAL

Head of State	Pres. John Agyekum Kufuor (2000)
Ruling Party	NPP
Main Opposition	NDC
Independence	6 March 1957
National capital	Accra
Official language	English

PHYSICAL

Total area	92,010 sq. miles
	238,305 sq. km.
	(± Oregon)
Arable land	20% of land area
Coastline	335 miles/539 km

POPULATION

Total	19.4 million
Av. yearly growth	3%
Population/sq. mile	212
Urban population	36%
Adult literacy	69%

ECONOMY[1]

Currency	Cedi
	(US$1=7,275)
GDP (real)	$7.4 billion
GDP growth rate	4.4%
GNP per capita[2]	$390
GDP (ppp)[3]	$33.6 billion
GDP per cap. (ppp)[3]	$1,800
Inflation rate	27.7%
Exports	$2.6 billion
Imports	$3.9 billion
Development aid	$523 million
External debt	$6.29 billion
Unemployment	20%

INFRASTRUCTURE

Railroads	621 miles/1,000 km
Paved roads	25%
Motor vehicles	135,000
Air passenger/km	478 million
Telephones/1,000	3
International airport	Accra
Main harbor	Accra-Tema

1. Statistics are based on World Bank data.
2. Atlas method.
3. See page 151 for an explanation of GDP based on purchasing power parity (ppp).

Provisional National Defense Council (PNDC) he abolished the constitution and jailed Limann. In 1992 a multiparty system was adopted and a presidential election held, which Rawlings won easily. He won reelection in 1996 but in December 2000 his deputy in the New Democratic Party (NDC), John Evans Atta Mills, was defeated in his bid for the presidency by John Agyekum Kufuor of the New Patriotic Party (NPP).

Government

The President holds executive power and legislative power is vested in the 200-member National Assembly, both elected for a four year term. In the December 2000 elections the New Patriotic Party (NPP) defeated the ruling National Democratic Congress (NDC) to form a new government under President John Kufuor.

Economic policy

Ghana embarked on an economic recovery program funded with low-interest loans from the IMF and World Bank affiliates. It required drastic cuts in government expenditure, a balanced budget, currency devaluation, reduction of the state's role in the economy and the encouragement of free enterprise. Despite charges from the left that he betrayed the revolution, Rawlings forged ahead. The state-run Cocoa Board alone laid off 22,000 workers when it ended its monopoly. Tax collection improved and funds were funneled into infrastructure enhancement. The government remains under heavy pressure from international financial institutions and donors to adhere to a policy of fiscal discipline.

Privatization

Barely ten years into the economic reform program 64 state enterprises had been divested, 34 were liquidated and 30 privatized. In a heavily oversubscribed sale of its share in Ashanti Goldfields, the government earned $320 million. The Ghanaian government also sold most of its shares in Standard Chartered Bank (Ghana), Accra Breweries, Equity Insurance, Guinness Ghana, Kumasi Breweries, Pioneer Tobacco and Unilever (Ghana). The government is continuing with this divestiture of state-owned enterprises and reducing its direct role in the economy.

Sectors

Ghana has large deposits of gold, diamonds, bauxite and manganese, as well as sizeable forests and arable land. It has a good potential in hydroelectric power. Agriculture is the most important economic sector. Ghana is among the world's largest exporters of cocoa. Timber is another major foreign currency earner. Crops grown for sale to local agro-industries include sugar, cotton, oil palms and rubber. Subsistence crops are rice, maize, sorghum, millet, groundnuts, yams and fruit. Mining is the second largest earner of foreign exchange. Gold tops the list with diamonds and manganese gaining in importance. Manufacturing remains relatively modest. Apart from a large aluminum smelter, most other industrial activity revolves around agro-business such as the processing of cocoa and beer brewing.

Trading

Ghana's largest traditional trading partner is the United Kingdom, with Nigeria second, and the United States third. The past three years have, however, seen an increase in the US share of Ghana's total imports (from 10 percent to over 18 percent)—a trend that is expected to continue. Ghana is currently the third largest importer of US goods in Sub-Saharan Africa.

Investment

Foreign direct investment is aggressively pursued by the Ghanaian government in an effort to stimulate growth as donor assistance is expected to diminish. Foreign investment in Ghana is mostly in mining and manufacturing. Britain is the largest investor with direct investments exceeding $750 million, much of it attributable to Lonrho's 41% stake in Ashanti Goldfields Corporation. US investments are largely in mining and foods and are expected to rise as there have been expressions of interest by American companies in the acquisition of state-owned communications and manufacturing firms earmarked for divestiture. There are significant investments by other foreign nationals through the government's privatization program. Norwegian investors are part owners of the state's Ghana Cement Works (GHACEM). Ghana Telecom is operated by the state in partnership with Telecom Malaysia. Lately, South African companies have become active in the mining sector.

Financial sector

The Central Bank oversees 11 commercial banks, 5 merchant banks and over 100 rural banks. In recent years, however, several state-owned banks have been privatized. Nonbank financial institutions (NBFIs) include a Stock Exchange, 21 insurance companies, the Social Security and National Insurance Trust (SSNIT), two discount houses, the Home Finance Company, numerous building societies, a venture capital company, a unit trust and 5 leasing companies. HSBC Equator Bank has representation in Ghana.

Taxes and tariffs

The orporate income tax rate is 35%, except for income derived from nontraditional exports (8%) and hotels (25%). A 10-year tax holiday applies to enterprises in the export processing zones. Foreign nationals pay a flat tax of 35%, irrespective of their income level. The US has no double-taxation agreement with Ghana. Generally, import duty rates are 0% for raw materials and capital goods; 10% for intermediate goods; and 25% for consumer goods. A flat tax of 15% is imposed on all imported and locally manufactured commodities.

Business activity

AGRICULTURE
Cocoa, coffee, rice, cassava (tapioca), peanuts, corn, shear nuts, bananas, timber.

INDUSTRIES
Mining, lumbering, light manufacturing, aluminum smelting, food processing.

NATURAL RESOURCES
Gold, timber, industrial diamonds, bauxite, manganese, fish, rubber.

EXPORTS
$2.6 billion (1999 est.): gold, cocoa, timber, tuna, bauxite, aluminum, manganese ore, diamonds.

IMPORTS
$3.9 billion (1999 est.): capital equipment, petroleum, consumer goods, food, intermediate goods.

MAJOR TRADING PARTNERS
UK, Germany, US, Netherlands, Japan, Nigeria.

Doing Business with Ghana

▶ **Investment**

Ghana's telecommunications sector and roads need repair and expansion and deregulation opened up this field for foreign investment. Gold mining remains the focus of growth and exploration by foreign mining companies continues. The Ghana Investment Promotion Center Act of 1994 extends incentives to foreign investors, including tax holidays, accelerated depreciation, locational privileges and other inducements.

▶ **Trade**

Food processing and packaging equipment, telecommunications equipment, secondhand clothing and motor vehicles, mining machinery, construction and earth-moving equipment, computers and peripherals as well as hotel and restaurant equipment offer opportunities for exporters. The channels of distribution available to foreign suppliers of goods and services in Ghana are wholesalers, retail outlets, and agents or distributors.

▶ **Trade finance**

Traditional trade finance instruments such as letters of credit, collections, and funds transfers are available to the exporter. USDA credit guarantee programs provide access to financing for imports of wheat, rice, feed grains, vegetable oil, protein meal, dairy products, as well as agricultural equipment.

▶ **Selling to the government**

The Ghana Supply Commission (GSC) handles procurement on behalf of the government and its agencies. Procurement is typically financed by a multilateral lending institution such as the World Bank, the African Development Bank or the International Finance Corporation.

▶ **Exchange Control**

The government of Ghana has moved away from exchange controls and has permitted the establishment of Foreign Exchange Bureaus. The cedi can now be readily exchanged for foreign currency.

▶ **Partnerships**

The Ghanaian Investment Code provides legislative encouragement for joint venture activities. The government guarantees transfers of capital, profits and dividends.

▶ **Establishing a presence**

Foreigners intending to invest in Ghana should first contact the Ghana Investment Promotion Center (GIPC), a one-stop shop for economic, commercial and investment information. The minimum required equity for foreign investors is $10,000 in joint ventures or $50,000 for enterprises wholly owned by foreign nationals. Trading companies either wholly or partly owned by non-Ghanaians require a minimum foreign equity of $300,000 and employment of at least 10 locals.

▶ **Project financing**

Private sector projects in Ghana might qualify for International Finance Corporation assistance and, in the case of US firms, Overseas Private Investment Corporation loans, loan guarantees and insurance. All the programs of the Eximbank apply. The US Trade and Development Agency finances feasibility studies.

▶ **Labor**

Ghana has a large pool of inexpensive, unskilled labor. Even though there is no legal requirement to involve labor in management deliberations, joint consultative committees involving management and labor are common.

▶ **Legal rights**

Ghana follows British common law and recognizes the right of foreign and domestic private entities to own and operate business enterprises. Ghana is a member of the World Intellectual Property Organization and the English-speaking African Regional Industrial Property Organization (ESARIPO). In 1996, the Ghana Arbitration Center was established to strengthen the legal framework for the protection of commercial and economic interests.

▶ **Business climate**

English is the official language and is used in most business transactions. Normally Ghanaian businessmen wear business suits during working hours and resort to traditional attire for social functions. Often, however, they may also be found in traditional attire during business hours. Businesswomen wear African attire during business hours as well as for social functions.

Guinea

Guinea's economy has been under reconstruction since 1984 when the socialist dictatorship of Sékou Touré came to an end. While the informal sector response to the more liberal economic policies introduced by Touré's successor, General Lasana Conté, has been impressive, international trade, agricultural production, and manufacturing have showed slower progress. Poor physical and institutional infrastructure, an erratic and unpredictable judicial system, and corrupt practices contributed to the weak formal sector response. In July 1996, President Conté appointed a new government, which promised major economic reforms, including financial and judicial reform, reduction of public expenditures, and improved revenue collection. The country is rich in minerals and fertile land and should by all accounts be relatively prosperous. Under the new regime foreigners have begun to show interest.

Country profile

The Republic of Guinea is a kidney-shaped country with a coastline marked by shallow estuaries and mangrove swamps. Apart from French, the official language, several native languages are spoken. The Ful (or Fulani), inhabiting the Futa Jallon Highlands, is the largest single group but collectively the Mande people (comprising the Baga, Nalu, Kisi and Landuma) form the majority. Guinea is largely Muslim with less than 2% Christians, mostly Roman Catholic.

History

Portuguese explorers arrived in the second half of the 15th Century. Though not a major slave trading region, the Los Islands near Conakry were used as slave depots. After the Portuguese came the British and eventually the French, who gained possession of the territory in 1884. Under the leadership of a trade union leader, Sékou Touré, Guinea voted in a 1958 referendum to reject an offer by France of autonomy within the French Community. The French granted Guinea independence and withdrew all assistance and personnel. Touré's socialist dictatorship led to economic decay and the emigration of close to 1 million citizens. After Touré's death in 1984, Gen. Lansana Conté seized power. In 1992 a multi-party system was introduced and Conté retained the presidency in the 1993 election. He was reelected in 1998.

Government

In terms of the new constitution both the president and a 114-seat unicameral National Assembly are elected for

235

Fast facts

POLITICAL

Head of State	Pres. Lansana Conté (1984)
Ruling Party	PUP
Main opposition	RPG
Independence	2 October 1958
National capital	Conakry
Official language	French

PHYSICAL

Total area	94,925 sq. miles 245,857 sq. km. (± Oregon)
Arable land	3% of land area
Coastline	320 km

POPULATION

Total	6.5 million
Av. yearly growth	2.8%
Population/sq. mile	79
Urban population	30%
Adult literacy	36%

ECONOMY[1]

Currency	Guinea franc (GNF)(US$1=1,940)
GDP (real)	$4.2 billion
GDP growth rate	3.2%
GNP per capita[2]	$540
GDP (ppp)[3]	$8.8 billion
GDP per cap. (ppp)[3]	$1,180
Inflation rate	3.5%
Exports	$763 million
Imports	$828 million
Development aid	$401 million
External debt	$3.0 billion
Unemployment	11%

INFRASTRUCTURE

Railroads	646 miles/1,040 km
Paved roads	16%
Motor vehicles	46,000
Air passenger/km	33 million
Telephones/1,000	1
International airport	Conakry
Main harbor	Conakry

1. Statistics are based on World Bank data.
2. Atlas method.
3. See page 151 for an explanation of GDP based on purchasing power parity (ppp).

five year terms. Conté's Party for Unity and Progress (PUP) holds a majority over the Rally of the Guinean People (RPG) and a number of smaller parties.

Economic policy

In 1984 President Conté inherited a country impoverished by his predecessor's socialist-driven policies and launched an ambitious program of reform, aimed at dismantling the 24-year-old centralized, state-run economy. Measures were adopted to create a market economy and open the country to trade and investment from outside. Significant progress has been made in downsizing and improving the performance of the public sector, the regulatory environment, liberalizing the price controls, exchange and trade system, and increasing the efficiency of the tax collection.

Privatization

The government is gradually disengaging from productive and commercial activities. After a modest two year privatization plan concluded in 1997, a new, more comprehensive program has been introduced. Plans are afoot to sell the state's 49 % stake in the country's largest bauxite mining company, Compagnie des Bauxites de Guinee (CBG). Although there were several publicized investment failures in 1996 and 1997 (mainly due to corruption and poor management), reforms and privatization efforts in the energy sector are bound to create opportunities for foreign investment. Water and electricity production grew 8.5% in 1999 and another 15% growth is projected for 2000. This significant increase in energy production is due mainly to the completion of the hydroelectric site at Garafiri. The French and Canadians are primary investors in the energy sector.

Sectors

Even though only 3% of the land is under cultivation, agriculture accounts for about one-third of the GDP and provides work for three-quarters of the labor force. Coffee is the most important export crop. Bananas, cotton, pineapples, palm oil, groundnuts and citrus fruits are also grown. Forestry, while still in its infant stage, shows considerable potential. Mining remains the most dynamic sector and accounts for most of Guinea's export earnings. The country's bauxite reserves, estimated at 20 billion tons, constitute one-third of the world's total. With annual exports of 17.5 million tons, Guinea is the world's third largest supplier of bauxite and aluminum. Apart from aluminum smelting, the manufacturing sector is small and mostly geared to the local market.

Trading

Guinea remains largely dependent on mining exports. In 1996 mining receipts accounted for 75 % of the country's foreign exchange earnings. Guinea imported 138,350 metric tons of consumer goods (29 % of its total imports) in 1999. In spite of the growth of its domestic agriculture, Guinea is still a large importer of agricultural products, tobacco, and alcoholic and non-alcoholic beverages. Flour imports originate largely in France with some Belgian contribution. Principal sugar suppliers include France, Belgium, and Italy.

Investment

Investment has been moderate. According to Guinean officials, foreign investors are awaiting the completion of judicial and economic reforms aimed at promoting private sector development before they act. France is Guinea's strongest traditional economic partner and provides extensive development assistance. French businesses are active in a variety of sectors including banking, insurance, shipping, communications, construction, agricultural export, and manufacturing. Canadians and Belgians also have a strong local presence. In 1996 Malaysians began investing in Guinea in telecommunications and banking. They have also expressed interest in investing in construction, tourism and agriculture. Lebanese traders are involved in real estate, small manufacturing enterprises, and telecommunications, supermarkets, wholesale food, and electronics.

Financial sector

The banking system is being reconstructed with the assistance of the IMF and the World Bank. New regulations are expected to be in place early in the new millennium.

Taxes and tariffs

In 1994, through a variety of income and import tax increases, the burden on international businesses increased significantly. International financial experts in Conakry criticized this step as one that diminished the level of compensation to investors in Guinea's poor infrastructure and difficult work environment. In 1996 an 18% value added tax (VAT) was introduced on all items except exports, international transportation, and certain basic food items. Since 1998, the government has focused on improving tax administration and collection to increase revenues from non-mining sources. Guinea has a flat import tax rate of 33% on most items. Public investment projects and donor organizations are exempted. A surtax of between 20% and 70% is imposed on luxury items, such as vehicles, alcohol and tobacco. In 1996, the government appointed a Swiss company, SGS, to manage customs.

Aid

Guinea received official grants and loans totaling $280 million in 1998. Much of this was in the form of assistance for the development of infrastructure and advisory services and provided in conjunction with Guinea's Public Investment Program (PIP). Priority areas were education, health, agricultural marketing, rural road construction, and rural enterprise development. During the past few years, USAID has supported the construction of over 1,000 km of rural roads in Guinea.

Business activity

AGRICULTURE
Rice, coffee, pineapples, palm kernels, cassava (tapioca), bananas, sweet potatoes, cattle, sheep, goats, timber.

INDUSTRIES
Bauxite, gold, diamonds, alumina refining, light manufacturing, agricultural processing.

NATURAL RESOURCES
Bauxite, iron ore, diamonds, gold.

EXPORTS
$763 million (1999 est.): Bauxite, alumina, diamonds, gold, coffee, fish, agricultural products.

IMPORTS
$828 million (f.o.b 1999 est.): petroleum products, metals, machinery, transport equipment, textiles, grain and other foodstuffs.

MAJOR TRADING PARTNERS
Russia, US, Belgium, Ukraine, Ireland, Spain, France, Côte d'Ivoire, Hong Kong.

Doing Business with Guinea

▶ **Investment**

Privatization in the telecommunications, banking and energy sectors has opened up new areas for foreign investment. Under the auspices of The United Nations Development Program and the United Nations Industrial Development Organization Guinea listed over 100 private and public investment projects, totaling more than $150 million in the agriculture, fishing, industry, and public works sectors. Other targeted sectors include mining, manufacturing, transportation, and energy. Investing is simplified by the the Office of Private Investment Promotion (OPIP), a one-stop business registration office, centralizing the administrative, legal, fiscal, and other formalities.

▶ **Trade**

Apart from agricultural products, good prospects for exports to Guinea are machinery and equipment, petroleum products, construction/semi-finished material, industry/manufacturing, telecommunications and hi-tech equipment (computers, soft/hardware), and consumer goods (canned/dry supermarket goods, textiles, cosmetics, used clothing, alcoholic and other beverages, and tobacco products). Expansion of telecommunication and Internet services should increase the demand for cellular phones, relay towers, and switches.

▶ **Trade finance**

Guinea qualifies for three US Department of Agriculture export promotion programs: the dairy export incentive program, a GSM-102 credit program, and a wheat export enhancement program.

▶ **Selling to the government**

Donor countries and institutions usually stipulate the bidding rules for foreign-financed public investment projects. The AGCP (Guinean Central Procurement Agency) handles projects/contracts over one million dollars. The Public Market (*Marché Publique*) handles projects/contracts under one million dollars.

▶ **Exchange control**

All initial capital investments and earnings generated can be converted and repatriated, but only 50% of Guinean capital can be converted or transferred.

▶ **Partnership and presence**

The US Embassy commercial officer, local Chamber of Commerce, the Employers' Associa-tion, and Guinean Offices of Investment Promotion are all useful points of contact for business people contemplating establishing a presence. No franchises currently exist in Guinea.

▶ **Project financing**

The African Development Bank's private sector window in Abidjan has funding available for development-oriented business projects. The Overseas Private Investment Corporation will also accept applications for investment projects in Guinea. The US Trade and Development Agency assists in the financing of feasibility studies.

▶ **Labor**

Labor is ample but there is a critical shortage of skilled managers and administrators with private sector experience. Employers no longer need to go through the labor office to hire or fire an employee, and there is no obligation to employ only Guineans. The labor code legalizes labor unions and the right to collective bargaining.

▶ **Legal rights**

The legal, regulatory, and accounting systems are based upon French civil law but are not always applied uniformly or transparently. While Guinea's laws are designed to promote free enterprise and competition, senior government officials have publicly acknowledged shortcomings due to corruption and lack of training. The government has committed itself to strengthening the judicial and legal institutions to attract more foreign investment and improve economic conditions. The establishment of an independent Arbitration Court is specifically aimed at protecting foreign business people from corruption within the judicial system. Guinea is a member of the African Intellectual Property Organization comprised of 15 African countries and the World Intellectual Property Organization. The country is in the process of modifying its intellectual property right laws to bring them up to international standards.

▶ **Business climate**

Most Guineans are Muslim, and Islam plays a major role in shaping the customs and habits of the local business culture. Foreigners should be familiar with the basic tenets of Islam to facilitate business dealings. Friendship and trust are very important and it takes time to build a successful working relationship. Patience and face-to-face contact are requirements for successful business.

Guinea Bissau

In the 1980s Guinea-Bissau emerged from a long period of civil unrest to record impressive economic growth. For a decade until the outbreak of renewed fighting in1998 it registered one of the highest growth rates in West Africa and the third highest on the continent. As the world's sixth largest producer it continues to rely heavily on the export of cashew nuts, as well as from other agricultural products such as peanuts, palm kernels and timber. However, nuts and timber might soon be eclipsed by the mining and petroleum sectors if yields live up to expectations raised by recent finds.

Country profile

The Republic of Guinea-Bissau consists mostly of low-lying marshland. The name of its capital, Bissau, is included in its name to distinguish it from its larger neighbor, Guinea. Its coastline is interrupted by meandering rivers, wide estuaries and adjoined by 18 islands known as the Bijagos (Bissagos) Archipelago. The climate is tropical, hot and wet. Rainfall in the north ranges between 1,000 and 2,000 mm. Within a relatively small area, Guinea-Bissau contains an ethnically diverse population consisting of seven significant cultural groups alongside the dominant Balanta. There is a sizable expatriate community of Portuguese, Syrian and Lebanese traders, most of them involved in commerce. The majority of Guinea-Bissau's inhabitants adheres to traditional ethnic beliefs while one-third is Muslim and about ten percent Christian. Portuguese is the official language but several native tongues are spoken as well as French, mostly in business circles.

History

In the 13th Century Guinea-Bissau was part of the Kingdom of Gabu in ancient Mali. During the 15th Century Portugal built forts along the coast and engaged in slave trade with the rulers of the region. Rios de Guine, (as it was called then) was administered by the Portuguese from Cape Verde until 1879 when it became a separate colony. After the abolition of slavery, groundnut cultivation became the mainstay of the eco-nomy. At the Berlin Conference in 1885, Portuguese Guinea was formally recognized by the European powers. By the 1950s the Balanta and other coastal peoples joined with Cape Verdean dissidents to form the *Partido Africano da Indepen-*

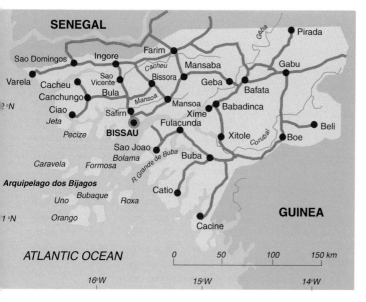

SENEGAL
Pirada
Sao Domingos
Ingore
Farim
Cacheu
Mansaba
Gabu
Varela
Cacheu
Sao Vicente
Bissora
Geba
Canchungo
Bula
Mansoa
Bafata
Ciao
Safirn
Mansoa
Babadinca
Jeta
Xime
Fulacunda
Beli
Pecize
BISSAU
Sao Joao
Xitole
Boe
Bolama
Buba
Caravela
Formosa
R. Grande de Buba
Corubal
Arquipelago dos Bijagos
Catio
Bubaque
Uno
Roxa
GUINEA
1 °N
Orango
Cacine
2 °N

ATLANTIC OCEAN

| 0 | 50 | 100 | 150 km |

16°W   15°W   14°W

Fast facts

1. Statistics are based on World Bank data.
2. Atlas method.
3. See page 151 for an explanation of GDP based on purchasing power parity (ppp).

dência da Guiné é Cabo Verde (PAIGC) and engaged in an armed struggle against the Portuguese rulers. In September 1974 when the Portuguese army overthrew the Caetano dictatorship in Lisbon, Guinea-Bissau was the first of the five Portuguese African territories to achieve independence. Its first ruler, Pres. Luiz Cabral, was deposed by the military veteran prime minister Joao Vieira in 1980. Vieira practiced one-party rule until he was forced by public pressure to hold free elections in July 1994. Viera and his PAIGC remained in power until January 2000 when Kumba Ialá and his Party for Progressive Social Renewal (PRS) won at the polls.

Government

The President is elected by popular vote for 5-year terms, has executive power and appoints the Prime Minister and the Council of Ministers. Members of the 100-member unicameral National Assembly are elected for 4-year terms. President Kumba Ialá and his Partido para a Renovaçao Social (PRS) was installed in January 2000 after they defeated Malam Bacai Sanhá and the PAIGC in the December 1999 elections. The Resistência da Guiné-Bissau-Movimento Bafatá (RGB) emerged as the main opposition.

Economic policy

Guinea-Bissau's structural adjustment program involving trade reform and price liberalization helped it to attain one of the highest growth rates in Sub-Saharan Africa for almost a decade until progress was disrupted by renewed civil strife in 1998. With a return of peace in 1999, there are renewed efforts to restore production, processing and marketing of rice, cashews, fruits, vegetables, fish and forestry products to prewar levels and to exploit potential petroleum resources.

Sectors

Agriculture, fisheries and forestry account for about 90% of employment, an estimated 50% of GDP, and about three-quarters of export revenues. Even though cashew nuts and groundnuts are major export crops, most agriculture consists of subsistence food production and the raising of livestock in the higher-lying areas. Petroleum promises to become a significant foreign exchange earner.

Privatization

A new investment law was adopted to facilitate private participation in all key sectors. A privatization council appointed to oversee the restructuring of state-owned businesses resumed its activity after the restoration of peace.

Investment

Offshore oil was discovered in 1958 near Guinea-Bissau's border with Senegal but it took until the 1980s to obtain funding from the World Bank for an offshore seismic survey. Exploration agreements signed with foreign oil companies were held up by a border dispute with Senegal. In 1995 an agreement was reached which entitled Senegal to 85% of the petroleum and mineral resources in the disputed area.

Trade

At about three quarters of export revenue, cashew nuts are the major foreign exchange earner. The downstream petroleum industry is largely dependent on refined petroleum products imported from neighboring countries.

Financial sector

Guinea-Bissau joined the West African Monetary Union (WAEMU) in 1997 and incorporated its central bank into the Central Bank of West Africa (BCEAO).

Taxes and tariffs

Comprehensive tax reform was adopted in 1997 with the introduction of a generalized sales tax, review of customs tariffs and the reform of excise taxes.

Business activity

AGRICULTURE
Rice, corn, beans, cassava (tapioca), cashew nuts, peanuts, palm kernels, cotton, timber, fish.

INDUSTRIES
Agricultural products processing, beer, soft drinks.

NATURAL RESOURCES
Fish, timber, phosphates, bauxite, unexploited deposists of petroleum.

EXPORTS
$56 million (1999 est.): cashews, fish, peanuts, palm kernels, sawn lumber.

IMPORTS
$96 million (1999 est.): foodstuffs, transport equipment, petroleum products, machinery and equipment.

MAJOR TRADING PARTNERS
Spain, India, Thailand, Italy, Portugal, Netherlands, US.

Doing Business with Guinea-Bissau

▶ Investment

Since 1993 when it reached a settlement in an offshore territorial dispute with Senegal, Guinea Bissau has placed 4 offshore blocks on offer. The government is also actively seeking foreign participation in the development of its underutilized fish and timber sectors. In mining there is also good potential for exploration and exploitation. Guinea-Bissau's considerable hydropower potential is another area that attracts the attention of foreign investors. Railroad repair and other infrastructure projects are in the offing.

▶ Trade

Substantial quantities of rice are being imported. Once further developed, the country's fish and timber resources could be of special interest to foreign importers. Gasoline and kerosene form a significant portion of the country's import needs.

▶ Selling to the government

Future business with the government will most likely be in petroleum equipment, timber and mining machinery, road and rail construction equipment and rolling stock. Procurement, distribution and marketing of fuel products are carried out by the state owned oil company, *Distribudora de Combustiveis e Lubrificantes* (DICOL) together with the Portuguese oil company, Petrogal.

▶ Exchange controls

As a member of the West African Monetary Union (WAMU), Guinea Bissau offers currency convertibility and applies few controls.

▶ Business climate

Although Portuguese is the official language, French is widely used. Customs in the business community are French-European.

Kenya

Kenya has become synonymous with safari travel. Tourism is a major industry. Even though it has had difficulty maintaining the 5.2% average growth rate attained during its first three decades of independence, recent reforms and market deregulation should stimulate greater interest among foreign investors and generate renewed growth. Noticeable in recent years has been the increased foreign participation in Kenya's capital markets after the liberalization of foreign exchange flows.

Country profile

The Republic of Kenya is bisected by the Great Rift Valley extending from Lake Turkana in the north to Lake Natron on the Tanzanian border. There are some 20 national parks, including Masai Mara (adjoining Tanzania's Serengeti park), Amboseli and Tsavo. The equator runs across the foothills of snow-capped Mount Kenya (17,057 ft/5,199 m), Africa's second highest mountain. Three quarters of the population consist of Bantu-speaking peoples (Kikuyu, Luhya and Kamba) while the remainder are Nilotic (Luo, Maasai or Masai, Samburu, Turkana and Kalenjin). Other minority groups include the Indian, Arab and European expatriates. English and Swahili are official languages. About three-quarters of the population is Christian while the rest adhere to ethnic beliefs.

History

The discovery of fossilized remains of humanlike beings and Stone Age relics from archaeological sites in Kenya gave rise to the belief that this region might well be the cradle of humanity. Paleontologists estimate that people may first have inhabited Kenya 2 million years ago. The Nilotic people expanded southward during the beginning of Christian era into western Kenya where they absorbed the Cushitic and Omotic communities. They were joined by the Bantu-speaking peoples and in the 10th Century Muslim merchants began to develop ports and trading stations along the coast. Portuguese explorer Vasco da Gama was the first European to drop anchor at Mombasa in 1498. The region became a British protectorate in 1890 and a

crown colony in 1920. In 1905 Nairobi, strategically located halfway along the newly completed railway to Lake Victoria, became the capital of the British East Africa. To the chagrin of the locals, white settlers had occupied almost all the prime agricultural land by the 1950s. Discontented with the slow progress towards meaningful land reform and political change, the Kikuyu-dominated Mau Mau movement under the leadership of Jomo Kenyatta engaged in a drawn-out, costly struggle. Independence was

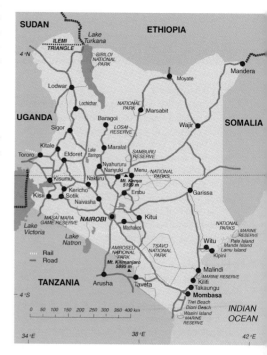

granted by Britain in 1963 and Kenyatta was elected president as leader of the Kenya African national Union (KANU). In 1978 when Kenyatta died, he was succeeded by Vice-President Daniel arap Moi, a member of the minority Kalenjin group, chosen as a compromise candidate by the Kikuyu-dominated KANU to promote unity. From 1964 until 1992, when President Moi under severe pressure called elections, KANU exercised single party control over Kenya. Moi has been reelected twice since for five year terms.

Government

An executive President is elected for a maximum of two 5-year terms. In the National Assembly 210 members are elected by popular vote, 14 members are elected by the speaker and attorney general and 12 seats are allocated to the strongest parties. In the most recent December 1997 election President Moi's Kenya African National Union (KANU) won by a comfortable margin over the Democratic Party (DP), National Democratic Party (NDP), the Forum for the Restoration of Democracy (FORD) and several smaller parties. In a surprising decision, Moi appointed one of his severest critics, Richard Leakey (son of well-known paleontologists Louis and Mary Leakey), to his cabinet.

Economic policy

In the wake of an economic downturn after 30 years of sustained growth, the government embarked on a substantive reform program in the mid-1990s, dismantling foreign exchange controls, allowing a free-floating exchange rate, removing import licensing, and liberalizing marketing and decontrolling prices. Privatization and tax reform are vital ingredients. In July 2000 the World Bank resumed loans to Kenya, ending a three year suspension.

Sectors

Agriculture provides employment to 75% of the workforce and accounts for about 30% of GDP and 50% of merchandise export value. Kenya is among the world's leading exporters of tea and coffee (mostly high-grade arabica). It is the world's largest supplier of pyrethrum, a natural insecticide. It also exports cut flowers, vegetables and fruit, cotton, sugar, pineapples, sisal, hides and skins. The country is self-sufficient in maize, the major staple food. Soda ash is mined and large deposits of tita-

Fast facts

POLITICAL

Head of State	Pres. Daniel Toroitich Arap Moi (1978)
Ruling Party	KANU
Main Opposition	DP
Independence	12 December 1963
National capital	Nairobi
Official languages	English & Swahili

PHYSICAL

Total area	224,960 sq. miles 582,650 sq. km. (2 x Nevada)
Arable land	7% of land area
Coastline	333 miles/536 km

POPULATION

Total	28.8 million
Av. yearly growth	1.59%
Population/sq. mile	135
Urban population	28%
Adult literacy	80%

ECONOMY[1]

Currency	Kenyan shillings (KSh)(US$1=78.66)
GDP (real)	$9.7 billion
GDP growth rate	1.3%
GNP per capita[2]	$350
GDP (ppp)[3]	$43.9 billion
GDP per cap. (ppp)[3]	$1,550
Inflation rate	2.5%
Exports	$2.6 billion
Imports	$3.3 billion
Development aid	$482 million
External debt	$6.89 billion
Unemployment	50%

INFRASTRUCTURE

Railroads	1,268 miles/2,040 km
Paved roads	14%
Motor vehicles	344,000 (1994)
Air passenger/km	1.7 billion (1994)
Telephones/1,000	9 (1994)
International airport	Nairobi
Main harbor	Mombasa

1. Statistics are based on World Bank data.
2. Atlas method.
3. See page 151 for an explanation of GDP based on purchasing power parity (ppp).

nium and zircon have been discovered along the coast. Other minerals include fluorspar, salt, limestone and precious stones. Manufacturing comprises beverages, tobacco, textiles, electric and electronic appliances, metal products, food products, petroleum products, machinery, glass, cement, pulp and paper products, sugar and confectionery. Relying on its ample wildlife and numerous game reserves, tourism has become one of Kenya's major sources of foreign exchange. Regular visits by British royalty and famous personalities, Hollywood productions such as *Mount Kilimanjaro*, *The Macomber Affair* and *Out of Africa* and the writings of Robert Ruark, Ernest Hemingway and others have made this country a premier destination for safari enthusiasts.

Privatization

In the first eight years of a privatization program that started in the early 1990s Kenya divested from 165 public enterprises. A start has been made contracting out the container terminal operations at Mombasa harbor and the airport operations to private enterprise. The Kenya Railways Corporation has commissioned private contractors to provide maintenance and Kenya Airways was partly privatized in 1996.

Investment

More than 200 foreign companies are registered in Kenya—most of them from the United Kingdom, Germany, and the US—and engaged in the manufacturing of products ranging from shoes to pharmaceuticals, petroleum products to beverages, foodstuffs, vehicles and automobiles. About 75 US companies are involved with an estimated $300 million in investment.

Trade

More than 40% of Kenya's exports (especially manufactured products and re-exported petroleum) go to COMESA countries. The European Union (including the UK) is Kenya's main supplier and second largest export market. However, in recent years South Africa has become a major source, while Kenya's exports to South Africa have shown substantial growth. US exports to Kenya include wheat, aircraft, fertilizer, soybean oil, and aircraft parts. Tea exports, Kenya's largest single foreign exchange earner, netted $520 million in 1998. Tourism, catering on an average to 700,000 visitors per year, is second, and coffee third.

Financial sector

Kenya has a well-developed financial sector comprising 48 licensed national and internationally-affiliated banks, 11 non-bank financial institutions, 4 building societies, 2 mortgage finance companies and 48 foreign exchange bureaus. HSBC Equator Bank is among several major foreign banks offering full services. The Capital Markets Authority regulates the stock market and the brokerage firms. More than 60 firms are listed on the Nairobi Stock Exchange (NSE), a fully computerized facility which is in the process of installing an electronic central depository system (CDS). Several foreign banks have a presence.

Taxes and tariffs

The taxation system has been streamlined and modernized and rates were lowered in recent years. The maximum individual marginal tax rate has been reduced from 65% to 32.5% and the company tax rate was cut from 45% to 32.5%. Kenya progressively reduced its number of customs duty bands (including the zero rate) from 8 to 4 and the maximum tariff rate dropped from 45% to 25%. Still, the government adopted a more protectionist tariff regime in 1999.

Business activity

AGRICULTURE
Coffee, tea, corn, wheat, sugar cane, fruit, vegetables, dairy products, beef, pork, poultry, eggs.

INDUSTRIES
Small-scale consumer goods (plastic, furniture, batteries, textiles, soap, cigarettes, flour), agricultural products processing, oil refining, cement, tourism.

NATURAL RESOURCES
Gold, limestone, soda ash, salt barytes, rubies, fluorspar, garnets, wildlife.

EXPORTS
$2.6 billion (1999 est.): tea, coffee, petroleum products.

IMPORTS
$3.3 billion (1999 est.): machinery and transportation equipment, consumer goods, petroleum products.

MAJOR TRADING PARTNERS
Uganda, Tanzania, UK, Germany, Egypt, South Africa.

Doing Business with Kenya

▶ Investment

Investment opportunities exist in tourism, agriculture (including ostrich and crocodile farming), and the manufacturing of electronics, plastics, chemicals, pharmaceuticals and engine parts. Foreign manufacturers are encouraged to use Kenya as a base to access and penetrate the larger East and Central African market. Special incentives are extended to factories in Export Processing Zones. Incentives offered to investors in the manufacturing and hotel sectors include tax breaks on the cost of buildings and capital machinery. The Investment Promotion Center provides a one-stop entry. As privatization proceeds new opportunities are offered in infrastructure development.

▶ Trade

There is a growing need for equipment relating to power generation, telecommunications, road building and food processing. A US firm has been successful in selling solar panels. Since the reduction of duties and VAT on computers, US and other foreign suppliers have been enjoying a healthy growth. US exporters who do not manufacture or assemble locally usually rely on local distributors with a thorough knowledge not only of the Kenyan but the regional market. Other than Coca-Cola, franchising has not been particularly successful.

▶ Trade finance

The US Eximbank is open to short- and medium-term financing for government and private sector entities in Kenya. Several banks and specialized financial institutions finance Kenyan exporters and importers.

▶ Selling to the government

Extensive road and rail repair with funding from the World Bank, African Development Bank, and other multilateral and bilateral sources should provide ample opportunity for foreign construction and engineering firms.

▶ Exchange controls

The Exchange Control Act has been repealed and there are no restrictions on converting or transferring funds associated with an investment or trade.

▶ Partnerships

Unlike franchising, joint ventures and licensing are common as they combine local marketing expertise with foreign manufacturing competence.

▶ Establishing a presence

To establish a presence, foreign firms merely need to register with the Kenyan Registrar of Companies. Incorporation of a company in Kenya as a subsidiary of a foreign entity is more complicated and usually requires the services of a local attorney.

▶ Financing projects

The Overseas Private Investment Corporation provides services to US investors. Kenya is also a member of the Multilateral Investment Guarantee Agency. Apart from the World Bank, IFC and African Development Bank, the Industrial Development Bank (IDB)—a Kenyan government-funded financial institution—provides medium and long term loan finance.

▶ Labor

Women constitute more than 25% of the work force in finance, insurance, and other business services and over 29% in public administration and agriculture. Some textile factories are almost exclusively staffed by women. The informal sector, known as *jua kali*, employs about 64% of all workers and accounts for about 90% of all new jobs outside the agricultural small holdings. Kenyan law provides safeguards and benefits for workers and spells out mechanisms and procedures to address complaints relating to worker rights. Wage scales for 12 different categories of employees are stipulated. Often benefits include housing and transportation.

▶ Legal rights

The Foreign Investment Protection Act protects investors against expropriation. There is also legislation to control monopolies and restrictive trade practices. Patents, trademarks and trade secrets are the responsibility of the Kenya Industrial Property Office in the Ministry of Research, Technical Training and Technology. Copyrights are handled by the Attorney General's office. Kenya is a member of several international and regional intellectual property conventions.

▶ Business Climate

Business executives are relatively informal and open to new ideas. The use of first names at an early stage of a business relationship is acceptable. Friendship and mutual trust are highly valued. English is spoken across the country.

245

Lesotho

The small mountainous Kingdom of Lesotho is entirely surrounded by South Africa on which many of its citizens have traditionally depended for labor, especially in the gold mines. The sale of water to its large neighbor as the massive Lesotho Highlands Project enters its second phase, is expected to compensate in part for an erosion of job opportunities in South Africa's mines. Despite political upheaval, Lesotho averaged a growth rate of about 10% in the 1990s, making it one of the top ten performers in Africa. The emphasis is on manufacturing for export to South Africa and other countries where Lesotho enjoys duty-free privileges.

Country profile

The terrain of the small, mountainous Kingdom of Lesotho has been likened to Switzerland and Andorra. Altitudes in the eastern half exceed 2,440 m and peaks in the northeast and along the Drakensberg mountains go beyond 3,350 m. Thabana Ntlenyana (3,482 m) in this range is the highest point in Southern Africa. Lesotho receives heavy rainfall (averaging 1,900 mm) and winter snow. Water is the country's most valuable natural asset. Lesotho has one of Africa's most homogeneous populations, consisting almost exclusively of Basotho. More than 90% are Christians, of whom about 45% belong to the Roman Catholic Church and the rest to various Protestant denominations. English is the official language but Sesotho is widely spoken.

History

In the 19th Century King Moshoeshoe I brought together a number of splinter groups in this mountainous stronghold, giving birth to the Basotho nation. It was in reality a kingdom made up of refugees from the fierce tribal wars in neighboring regions. Through smart military and diplomatic strategies Moshoeshoe managed to keep his enemies at bay until he was challenged by the Dutch-descended Boers who established their own Orange Free State Republic alongside his kingdom and then started making territorial claims. War

ensued that led to the defeat of the Basotho at Thaba Bosiu. Moshoeshoe was forced to cede some of his best land to the Boers. Fearing further intrusion from the Boer republic the king asked for British protection. It was annexed to the British Cape Colony in 1871 but in 1884 it was restored to direct control by the British Crown. Lesotho functioned as the so-called Basutoland Protectorate until 1966, when it regained its independence. It functioned as a multiparty democ-

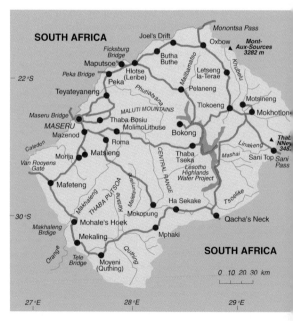

racy until 1986—most of these years under Chief Lebowa Jonathan, a descendant of Moshoeshoe—when a military regime took power. The country returned to an elective political system in 1993 as a constitutional monarchy. Recent years have seen considerable political intrigue, an abortive coup attempt and unrest that necessitated the intervention of South African and Botswana forces to maintain the status quo. These troops left in March 1999 after peace was restored. King Letsie III has ruled since the death of his father, King Moshoeshoe II, in 1996. Prime Minister Pakalitha Mosisili heads the government as leader of the dominant Lesotho Congress for Democracy (LCD).

Government

Lesotho is a constitutional monarchy. Although the King is the head of state his powers are limited and real authority rests with the Prime Minister as the leader of the strongest party. Legislative power is vested in Parliament, consisting of a 65-member National Assembly elected for 5 year terms, and a Senate made up of 33 Principal Chiefs, the descendants of the chiefs originally appointed by King Moshoeshoe I. In 1998, Prime Minister Mosisili's LCD recived 60.7% of the total vote and captured 78 of the seats in the Assembly. The Basotholand Congress Party (BCP) received 24.5% of the popular vote and holds one seat in opposition. The other one remains vacant.

Economic policy

Despite impressive gains in recent years, the government still faces severe and growing unemployment and underemployment in some areas as cutbacks in the South African mining sector continue to eliminate job opportunities for its expatriate workers. Since 1988 reform policies have been aimed at flexibility and efficiency in tax collection, deregulation of the agricultural markets, and privatization of public enterprises.

Sectors

Agriculture employs a quarter of the workforce. Subsistence farming—mainly animal husbandry and maize cultivation—is the predominant activity, with wool and mohair as major exports. Other crops include wheat, sorghum, beans and sunflower oil. The contribution of the industrial sector to GDP has increased from 34 per cent in 1990 to 44 per cent in 1996. It provides employment for a quarter of the workforce. Most of the activity is in labor-intensive small to medium-sized clothing, footwear and textile enterprises. Lim-

Fast facts

POLITICAL

Head of State	King Letsie III (1996)
Prime Minister	Pakalitha Mosisili (1998)
Ruling Party	LCD
Main Opposition	BCP
Independence	4 October 1966
National capital	Maseru
Official languages	English & Sesotho

PHYSICAL

Total area	11,718 sq. miles
	30,350 sq. km.
	(± Maryland)
Arable land	11% of land area
Coastline	Landlocked

POPULATION

Total	2.1 million
Av. yearly growth	1.8%
Population/sq. mile	183
Urban population	23%
Adult literacy	82%

ECONOMY[1]

Currency	Loti
	(US$1=8.23)
GDP (real)	$1.0 billion
GDP growth rate	2.5%
GNP per capita[2]	$570
GDP (ppp)[3]	$5.1 billion
GDP per cap. (ppp)[3]	$1,550
Inflation rate	2.5%
Exports	$222 million
Imports	$891 billion
Development aid	$98 million
External debt	$712 million
Unemployment	50.0%

INFRASTRUCTURE

Railroads	1.2 miles/2 km
Paved roads	18%
Motor vehicles	18,000
Air passenger/km	9 million
Telephones/1,000	9
International airport	Maseru

1. Statistics are based on World Bank data.
2. Atlas method.
3. See page 151 for an explanation of GDP based on purchasing power parity (ppp).

ited mining operations consist largely of artesian digging for diamonds. There are, however, reserves of uranium, iron ore, lead and peat. Tourism is a growing sector. Lesotho's single most important asset is the $5 billion Lesotho Highlands Water Project (LHWP) which is entering its second phase of construction. Water from the highlands has already started to flow to South Africa's thirsty Witwatersrand industrial complex and at full capacity the LHWP is expected to contribute an estimated 5% of GDP. The project is planned to span over five phases, providing ample opportunity for foreign entrepreneurs and jobs for the people of Lesotho.

Privatization

With the assistance and advice of the World Bank, Lesotho planned to spin off at least four parastatals per year. The process has, however, been proceeding at a slower pace. Since 1997 less than 10 of the 31 companies slated for privatization have been sold. One of the first to be spun off was Lesotho Airways and the most recent involved Lesotho Bank, when a private South African bank purchased a 70% share. There is speculation that the Lesotho Telecommunications Corporation (LTC) and the Lesotho Electric Company (LEC) may soon be on the block.

Investment

Lesotho has had considerable success in diversifying its traditional export base by moving into the production of textiles and electrical goods, footwear, radios and television sets with the help of foreign entrepreneurs, mostly from Europe, South Africa, Hong Kong, Singapore and Taiwan. The Lesotho Highlands Water Project (LHWP) represents major involvement by foreign firms from Europe, South Africa, Hong Kong, Singapore and Taiwan, as well as the United States. Two Canadian mining companies, Messina Diamond Corp. and Diamond Works, have taken options on diamond exploration.

Trade

Most of Lesotho's exports go to other SADC countries. Fifty percent of its imports originate from the region, primarily from South Africa. However, 40% of its exports find markets in North America. Export growth has been strong in livestock, leather products, furniture, and garments—the latter produced for the most part by Taiwanese-owned factories.

Financial sector

Lesotho is a member of the South African Common Monetary Area (CMA) and its currency, the Loti (plural Moloti) is at parity with the South African rand. It is therefore easily convertible for business transactions. Three local banking groups have branches throughout the country and two international banks have entered the market. The Lesotho Agricultural Development Bank (LADB) serves the agricultural sector.

Taxes and tariffs

Subsidiaries and branches of foreign companies are taxed at a rate of 35% on profit. Manufacturers are taxed at 15% and entitled to incentive breaks on personnel training and a variety of other items. As a member of the South African Customs Union (SACU), Lesotho's import tariffs and trading regime are determined collectively with other member states. Customs regulations allow temporary importation of raw materials on a duty-free basis.

Foreign presence

Foreign companies handle most of their business with Lesotho from South African-based branches and subsidiaries as they incur no duties on crossborder transactions within the SACU.

Business activity

AGRICULTURE
Corn, wheat, pulses, sorghum, barley, livestock.

INDUSTRIES
Food, beverages, textiles, handicrafts, construction, tourism.

NATURAL RESOURCES
Water, agricultural and grazing land, some diamonds and other minerals.

EXPORTS
$222 million (1999 est.): manufactures (clothing, footwear, road vehicles), wool and mohair, food and live animals.

IMPORTS
$891 million (1999 est.): food, building materials, vehicles, machinery, medicines, petroleum products.

MAJOR TRADING PARTNERS
Southern African Customs Union (SACU), North America, EU, Asia.

Doing Business with Lesotho

▶ Investment

As the principal government investment agency, the Lesotho National Development Corporation (LNDC) assists with loans, serviced sites, training grants and work permits. New factories are allowed duty-free importation of raw materials and components and effective export processing zone status anywhere in the country. A non-repayable skills training grant covers 75% of the wage bill during the initial training period at newly-established manufacturers. Loan finance is provided by the LNDC for projects which can demonstrate long-term economic viability and sometimes it will take equity in new developments considered to be in the national interest. Continuing privatization provides new opportunities.

▶ Trade

Imports include agricultural products, pharmaceuticals, iron tubes and pipes, metalwork and office machinery. As the Lesotho Highlands Water Project (LHWP) enters its second phase there is a continuing need for construction equipment and engineering services. The consumer market is relatively small but several foreign companies have taken advantage of Lesotho's extensive preferential trade privileges in southern Africa, Europe and elsewhere by establishing export-oriented factories and assembly points.

▶ Trade finance

The customary irrevocable letter of credit is supported by a sophisticated private banking system.

▶ Selling to the government

Purchases of heavy equipment and engineering services by the LHWP are handled independently in accordance with internationally-accepted tendering procedures. There are several other government projects where outside donors control tenders. To date, for example, the World Bank assists with projects in agriculture, infrastructure, health, population, education, water, and land management and conservation.

▶ Exchange controls

As a member of the Common Monetary Area (CMA) Lesotho applies the same controls as South Africa, Swaziland and Namibia. Although closely monitored, the transfer of funds for trade and investment purposes and the repatriation of profits and dividends present no serious problem.

▶ Partnerships

The Lesotho-South Africa treaty governing the LHWP stipulates that all foreign companies working on this multi-billion dollar project must enter into joint ventures with local firms. In all other operations foreign investors, have the option of either involving local partners or setting up on their own.

▶ Establishing a presence

The LNDC serves as a one-stop shop for any foreign firm that wishes to establish an office, a branch or a manufacturing plant in the country. The process is relatively uncomplicated and does not take long.

▶ Financing projects

The World Bank, the International Development Association and the International Finance Corporation have been financing projects seen as vital to the national interest. Lesotho is a founding member of the Multilateral Investment Guarantee Agency. The LNDC provides loan finance for up to 15 years.

▶ Labor

The formal sector work force has a high literacy rate and an aptitude for new skills. Training grants are extended to new factories for up to 50% of the payroll. Wages are considerably lower than in neighboring South Africa. While this can be an advantage it also poses the danger of turnover as workers are lured to higher incomes across the border.

▶ Legal rights

Lesotho has no history of expropriation or nationalization of private property. It is a member of the International Center for the Settlement of Disputes. Like South Africa, Lesotho's legal system is based on Roman Dutch law. Intellectual Property rights are protected under laws drafted in cooperation with the World Intellectual property Organization . Lesotho is a signatory to the convention on the settlement of investment disputes between states.

▶ Business climate

The business environment shows a strong British influence and can be likened to that of neighboring South Africa. It is, however, customary to approach serious business at a slow and deliberate pace. English is widely spoken in both business and social circles.

Liberia

Since July 1997 when free elections restored democratic rule after seven years of civil war, Liberia has been at work trying to repair its ravaged economy with the help of the IMF and other donor programs. Despite ample water, mineral resources, forests and a favorable climate for agriculture, the recovery program is expected to take time given the extent of the damage and continuing threats from insurgent groups. Still, some foreign investors that left during the war are returning and there are signs of renewed interest from others in Africa's oldest republic, established more than two centuries ago by freed American slaves.

Country profile

The Republic of Liberia has a hot and humid monsoon climate lasting from April to November. The coastline is straight, with shallow, mangrove-fringed lagoons and no natural harbors. The land rises from the broad coastal plain to a plateau and high mountain ranges on the northern borders. Diamonds are extracted from the river valleys and timber and rubber from the forests. Some 30 indigenous groups belong to three cultural or linguistic groupings—the Mandé and Atlantic Mel in the northern half of the country and the Kru (or Kruan) in the southern half of the country. The Liberians of African-American lineage, who dominated the country's politics from the 1820s to 1980, account for only 5% of the total population and are concentrated around Monrovia and other coastal centers. There are also small groups of Lebanese and Ful (Fulani) in these cities and towns. English is the official language but a Creole version referred to as Merico or Liberian English is the mother tongue of the Americo-Liberians. More than 70% of the population profess ethnic religious beliefs, 20% practice the Muslim faith and 10% are Christians.

History

A thousand years ago the territory now known as Liberia was occupied by the Mandé, Kru and Atlantic Mel-speaking peoples from the north and east and in the mid-15th Century the coastal towns were conducting a flourishing slave trade with European merchants. Modern Liberia (derived from the Latin *liber* or freedom) was the creation of the American Colonization Society (ACS) founded in 1816 to encourage the return of freed slaves to Africa, similar to a program organized by the British in Sierra Leone. Over a preiod of 40 years some 12,000 slaves were voluntarily resettled. The original constitution denied indigenous Liberians equal rights with these American emigrants and their descendants. With

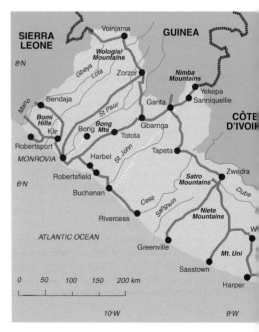

modest assistance from the US government, Monrovia, named after President James Monroe, and other settlements such as Robertsport, Buchanan, Greenville and Harper, were established. On 26 July 1847 Liberia declared itself a sovereign and independent republic. Though the government at Monrovia claimed to rule all the people along the Liberian coast and for some distance inland, effective administration was limited to the coast where the settlers and their descendants lived. It was only since 1920 that real progress was made towards opening up the interior with the help of a 43 mile (69 km) railroad from Monrovia to the Bomi Hills. American influence remained strong. The US dollar was then, and still is, the preferred currency. Firestone rubber company was the first major investor. Some official assistance came from the US as well. President William Tubman, a descendant of the African American settlers, served seven consecutive terms and his successor, William Tolbert, ruled from 1971 to 1980, when he was killed by Master Sergeant Samuel Doe, self-styled leader of the National Democratic Party of Liberia (NDPL). A devastating civil war raged from 1989 until 1996. Order was eventually restored and Charles Taylor's National Patriotic Front of Liberia won free elections in July 1997, coinciding with the 150th anniversary of the oldest independent republic in Africa. Heavy fighting occurred in northern Liberia during 2000 as Pres. Taylor's government troops tried to contain rebel insurgents.

Government

In accordance with the Abuja Accord struck in the Nigerian capital with the backing of the United Nations, the US, the European Union and the Organization of African Unity the warring Liberian factions agreed to participate in presidential and legislative elections during July 1997. In these election, declared fair and free by international observers, Charles Taylor's National Patriotic Party (NPP) (formerly the National Patriotic Front of Liberia) won 49 of the 64 seats in the House of Representatives and 21 of the 26 Senate seats. The main opposition party, the United Party (UP), won 7 seats in the House, followed by the All Liberia Coalition Party (ALCOP) with 3 seats, and a number of smaller parties. Taylor appointed several opposition members to his cabinet. The President, Vice-President, and Representatives all serve six year terms while the Senate serves for nine years.

Fast facts

POLITICAL

Head of State	Pres. Charles Ghankay Taylor (1997)
Ruling Party	NPP
Main Opposition	UP
Independence	26 July 1847
National capital	Monrovia
Official languages	English

PHYSICAL

Total area	43,000 sq. miles 111,370 sq. km. (± Tennessee)
Arable land	4% of land area
Coastline	360 miles/579 km

POPULATION

Total	2.9 million
Av. yearly growth	5.76%
Population/sq. mile	74
Urban population	51%
Adult literacy	51%

ECONOMY[1]

Currency	Liberian dollar (L$) (US$1=1.0)
GDP (real)	$357 million
GDP growth rate	N/A
GNP per capita[2]	$1,000
GDP (ppp)[3]	$2.8 billion
GDP per cap. (ppp)[3]	$1,000
Inflation rate	N/A
Exports	$1.1 billion
Imports	$3.65 billion
Development aid	$101 million
External debt	$2.07 billion
Unemployment	70%

INFRASTRUCTURE

Railroads	305 miles/490 km
Paved roads	6%
Motor vehicles	33,000
Air passenger/km	7 million
Telephones/1,000	2
International airport	Monrovia
Main harbor	Monrovia

1. Statistics are based on World Bank data.
2. Atlas method.
3. See page 151 for an explanation of GDP based on purchasing power parity (ppp).

Economic policy

The new government faces a daunting task. During the long civil strife GDP fell by 10% a year as production halted at mining and rubber installations and the single oil refinery was forced to shut down. Only the registration of foreign merchant vessels under the Liberian flag continued operating smoothly from a small Washington office. The new government has appointed a 18-person public service commission to undertake a comprehensive review of the Liberian civil service, and to combat corruption and waste. Abundant natural resources should make Liberia a good candidate for increased foreign involvement once sufficient progress is made in streamlining the bureaucracy and implementing the economic reform guidelines worked out in conjunction with the IMF.

Sectors

More than two-thirds of Liberia's workforce is dependent on agriculture. Rubber is the principal cash crop and provided 28% of export revenue before the war. Starting with Firestone many years ago, significant rubber plantations are still foreign-owned even though smallholders are today responsible for over half the total production. Coffee and cocoa are grown for export while palm oil is mainly produced for the domestic market. Food crops include rice, cassava and vegetables. Commercial ocean fishing concentrates on shrimp. Iron ore is the premier mining activity and normally accounts for 55% of all exports. In 1994 the value of diamond sales exceeded that of iron ore. There are known deposits of bauxite, manganese, columbite, uranium, tantalite, copper, tin, lead, and zinc. Manufacturing is confined mainly to textiles, food processing, wood products, cement and chemicals. The infrastructure was left devastated by the civil war.

Privatization

Despite public declarations in favor of a free market system the government has recently granted monopolies in rice, gasoline, and cement imports and production.

Trade

Major exports from Liberia include diamonds, iron ore, rubber, timber and coffee, while exports consists of mostly of fuels and lubricants, chemicals, machinery and transport equipment, manufactured goods, and rice and other foodstuffs. During the seven year civil war trade was curtailed and skewed as the fighting factions apportioned assets for their own gain and traded informally in iron ore and diamonds from areas under their control. Rubber exports have since resumed in full and proper channels have been established for trade in diamonds, iron and other minerals.

Investment

In 1925 the US Firestone Rubber Company became a major foreign player in Liberia when it obtained a 99-year lease on 1 million acres of forest near Monrovia. For decades Firestone was the country's largest employer. It branched into a number of other financial and commercial areas, but rubber remained its major export until the 1950s when iron ore production gained dominance.

Financial Sector

Currently, banks in Liberia operate only as a repository for funds. A fee is charged to receive a wire transfer, to make a deposit or withdrawal, or to cash checks. Banks do not pay interest or make loans.

Business activity

AGRICULTURE
Rubber, coffee, cocoa, rice, cassava (tapioca), palm oil, sugar cane, bananas, sheep goats, timber.

INDUSTRIES
Rubber and palm oil processing, diamonds.

NATURAL RESOURCES
Iron ore, timber, diamonds, gold.

EXPORTS
$1.1 billion (1998 est.): diamonds, iron ore, rubber, timber, coffee.

IMPORTS
$3.65 billion (1998 est.): fuel, chemicals, machinery, transportation equipment, manufactured goods, rice and other foodstuffs.

MAJOR TRADING PARTNERS
Belgium, Norway, Ukraine, South Korea, Japan, Italy.

Taxes and tariffs

Duties on imported goods range from 2.5% to 25%. The higher rate applies to luxury items such as electronic equipment, clothes, and alcoholic beverages.

Special ties

Special ties between the US and Liberia date back to its creation in the 1820s. This close relationship continues to be tested by the human rights abuses, corruption and lawlessness during the fierce and drawnout civil war. The US government, however, continues to finance projects through its Agency for International Development (USAID) such as food aid, humanitarian assistance, the demobilization and reintegration of ex-combatants, and the promotion of democracy and good governance.

Doing Business with Liberia

▶ **Investment**

A National Investment Commission was established to grant incentives to foreign investment, some in the form of monopolies in areas such as rice and gasoline importation. This practice has served to stifle further foreign interest. Also still in force is the 1975 "Liberianization" law that prohibits foreign ownership of businesses such as travel agencies, retail gasoline stations, and beer and soft drink distributorships. Investors also have to cope with a myriad of ministries and agencies, conflicting rules and regulations, and bureaucratic red tape. Drastic reforms have been suggested to attract larger foreign involvement in the utilization of Liberia's rich resources.

▶ **Trade**

Relatively cheap products such as used clothing, used cars, and used equipment offer trade prospects. There is also is a demand for US consumer goods such as toiletries, hair products, and other personal care items. It is expected that the market for pesticides and chemical fertilizers should improve as post-conflict Liberia returns to full production in the agricultural sector.

▶ **Selling to the government**

Until current reforms have taken effect and economic conditions improve, the Liberian government is unlikely to be a significant market. Once infrastructural projects commence, foreign supplies and services will no doubt be needed.

▶ **Exchange controls**

There is no difficulty obtaining Liberian currency at the unofficial rate and there are no restrictions on converting or transferring investment funds.

▶ **Establishing a presence**

Foreign firms considering establishing an office are strongly advised to retain the services of a local attorney. They should also take cognizance of a law that mandates that Liberian nationals should be employed at all levels, including upper management.

▶ **Project financing**

Liberia does not participate in OPIC or other investment insurance programs. Foreign investors will also find it difficult obtain credit on the local market.

▶ **Labor**

A considerable number of skilled professionals emigrated during the civil war. There is, however, no shortage of unskilled and semiskilled labor in Liberia. Unofficial unemployment figures are as high as 85%. Current law requires that Liberian nationals should be employed at all levels and the Ministry of Labor has on occasion held up work permits for expatriates and intervened in disputes between investors and their Liberian employees.

▶ **Legal rights**

Liberia's judiciary has at times been subjected to political, social, familial, and financial pressures. Currently several US firms are in litigation over the expropriation of property during the seven-year civil conflict. In past cases the government has been accused of settling such claims at well below market value.

Libya

Top quality oil reserves—the largest on the African continent—coupled with a relatively small population enable Libya to top the rest of the African continent in per capita income. Subjected to UN and US economic sanctions since 1992, the partial lifting of the UN embargo that followed in the wake of Libya's extradition of two suspected terrorists in the Pan Am 103 bombing has brought some Europeans back. In March 2001, the Bush Administration indicated that core unilateral economic sanctions prohibiting US-Libyan busines will remain in place until all the requirements of the UN Security Council have been met. In the meantime, several major American oil companies have signalled their intention to regain their past position in Libya, when permitted.

Country profile

The Great Socialist People's Libyan Arab Jamahiriya sits on a vast plateau. The Tripolitania region, centered around Tripoli has a Mediterranean climate. To the south is the dryer Jefara Plateau and in the east the high escarpment of Cyrenaica, with Benghazi at its hub. Sabha, Kufra and Jofra are clusters of oases, with extensive croplands under irrigation. The predominantly Arab and Muslim population speak Western Arabic dialects. There are various Berber and Tuareg minorities around Tripoli and at oases in the desert.

nance ended in 1942 when the German-Italian Axis was defeated in the Western Desert. The British took Tripolitania and Cyrenaica and the French occupied the Fezzan. In 1951 Libya became independent under King Idris. Wealth followed the discovery of oil in 1960 and led to corruption and discontent. On 1 September 1969, a 28-year-old army captain, Muammar Qaddafi, seized power. Eight years later he formed a monolithic General People's Congress and renamed the country, the *Great Socialist People's Libyan Arab Jamahiriya.*

History

The first inhabitants of Libya were Berber tribes. Ancient Libya was invaded by Phoenicians, Numidians, Greeks, Romans, Vandals and Byzantines, followed in 648 by Arabs and the Turks in 1551. Both Tripolitania and Cyrenaica became part of the Ottoman Empire. Tripolitania became one of the outposts for the Barbary pirates who exacted "tribute" payments from merchant ships in the Mediterranean. This practice led to a four year war between the Pasha of Tripoli and the US ending in a peace treaty in June 1805, exempting US ships from this "tribute." Before World War II Italy took control of the coastal towns while the Turks ruled the interior. After the war, the Italians began to pacify the country. Its domi-

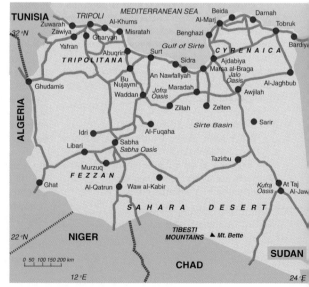

254

Government

Since March 1977 Libya has been ruled according to the tenets of Qaddafi's Third Universal Theory enunciated in his Green Book. The electorate is divided into some 1,500 People's Congresses, each electing 13-member People's Committees (local governments) which in turn send two members each to a General People's Congress (national legislature), which meets briefly once a year. The General People's Congress elects the General Secretariat (the highest executive body) and the General People's Committee (cabinet). In 1977 Muammar Qaddafi was elected Revolutionary Leader and head of state.

Economic policy

Oil revenues and a small population give Libya one of the highest per capita incomes in Africa, but, as in the case of several other oil producers, there is considerable inequality in actual incomes. Non-oil manufacturing and construction sectors have expanded from largely processing agricultural products to include the production of petrochemicals, iron, steel, and aluminum and currently account for about 20% of GDP. Agriculture constitutes only 5% of GDP but employs 18% of the labor force. The Great Manmade River project, designed to move water to the coast from aquifers deep in the Sahara, has absorbed some 10% of Libya's annual public expenditure and is almost completed. Another major plan involves rail links with Egypt and Tunisia.

Privatization

In the late 1980s the centrally planned (socialist) economy began to be opened up for free enterprise in an effort to counter the effect of lower oil prices and sanctions. A few economic and social services formerly performed by the state are now handled by private enterprise.

Sectors

Petroleum production accounts for between 30% and 40% of GDP; construction 11%; public services and administration 12%; transportation and communication 5%; manufacturing 5%; and agriculture 4%. Less than 2% of the country is arable. There are deposits of iron, potassium, magnesium, sulphur, gypsum and phosphate. In the 1970s huge investments were made in import substituting factories and refineries for the liquefaction of natural gas and the processing of other petrochemicals, the manufacture of iron, steel industries and concrete piping and auto assembly.

Fast facts

POLITICAL	
Head of State	Col. Muammar Qaddafi (1969)
Ruling Party	Arab Socialist Union
Independence	24 December 1951
National capital	Tripoli
Official language	Arabic

PHYSICAL	
Total area	679,359 sq. miles 1,759,540 sq. km. (± Alaska)
Arable land	1% of land area
Coastline	1,100 miles/1,770 km

POPULATION	
Total	6.2 million
Av. yearly growth	2.4%
Population/sq. mile	8
Urban population	86%
Adult literacy	78%

ECONOMY[1]	
Currency	Libyan Dinar (LD) (US$1=0.56)
GDP (real)	$23.5 billion (1995)
GDP growth rate	N/A
GNP per capita[2]	N/A
GDP (ppp)[3]	$38 billion
GDP per cap. (ppp)[3]	$6,700
Inflation rate	24.2%
Exports	$6.8 billion
Imports	$6.9 billion
Development aid	$10 million
External debt	N/A
Unemployment	30%

INFRASTRUCTURE	
Paved roads	56%
Motor vehicles	770,000 (1994)
Air passenger/km	425 million
Telephones/1,000	48
International airport	Tripoli
Main harbors	Tripoli, Benghazi

1. Statistics are based on World Bank data.
2. Atlas method.
3. See page 151 for an explanation of GDP based on purchasing power parity (ppp).

Trade

Petroleum exports account for about 95% of Libya's foreign hard currency earnings. The government claims that UN sanctions since 1992 have cost the country more than $24 billion in revenues. The state-owned National Oil Corporation maintains a virtual monopoly over the marketing of all Libyan oil and gas. State enterprises also control most manufacturing, agriculture and trade outside the petroleum sector. Libya imports about 75% of its food requirements. There is the potential for a large increase in Libyan gas exports to Europe. Major trading partners are Italy, Germany, United Kingdom, Spain, South Korea and France.

Investment

Since 1968, Libya's oil industry has been run by the state-owned National Oil Corporation (NOC) along with a number of smaller subsidiary companies. The leading foreign oil producer in Libya is Italy's Agip-ENI, operating in the country since 1959. Two US oil companies—Exxon and Mobil—withdrew from Libya in 1982, following a US trade embargo in 1981. Five other US companies—Amarada Hess, Conoco, Grace Petroleum, Marathon, and Occidental— remained active in Libya until 1986, when the Reagan administration ordered all US firms to cease activities. In 1992 the international community joined the US by imposing sanctions against Libya. These UN mandated sanctions imposed by individual Western countries were lifted in 1999 in response to Libya's extradition of two suspected terrorists for the Lockerbie trial in a Scottish court assembled in The Hague. Apart from a relaxation in restrictions on the trade of a few items—including pharmaceuticals— the US has, however, kept its embargo in place until further review. Since the lifting of UN sanctions against Libya several US oil companies are reported to have traveled to Libya to survey assets which they were forced to abandon and might be able to repossess in the foreseeable future. In recent times, Libya has been actively courting foreign oil companies and issued an official assurance to American companies that they would be allowed to reclaim the fields that they abandoned, once US sanctions are lifted.

Lockerbie

While the US continues to view Libya as a "nation of concern" and the Libyan leader accuses Washington of being an implacable foe of Libyan and Arab interests, the return of American oil interests to this part of the world seems imminent. Relations between Libya and the US and its western partners reached an all-time low following the "Lockerbie Affair" in December 1988 when all 259 passengers aboard Pan Am flight 103 died in an explosion over Lockerbie in Scotland—an event blamed by London and Washington on two Libyan nationals. Qaddafi's refusal to extradite the two suspects led to the imposition of mandatory economic sanctions against Libya by the UN Security Council on 31 March 1992. The US formulated its own sanctions under the Iran and Libya Sanctions Act. The effect of sanctions on the Libyan economy is seen to have forced Qaddafi to seeking a way out of the impasse by extraditing the suspects for trial in The Hague. This led to the lifting of UN sanctions and the reestablishment of economic and diplomatic relations by most nations, excluding the US. Early in 2001, one of the two accused, Abdel Baset Ali Mohmed Al-Megrahi, was convicted and sentenced to twenty years in a Scottish jail. While accepting that Libya has complied with some of the UN Security Council's requirements, London and Washington have insisted that Libya still has to accept responsibility for the actions of the convicted Libyan official and pay appropriate compensation before the matter can be closed.

Business activity

AGRICULTURE

Wheat, barley, olives, dates, citrus, vegetables, peanuts, beef, eggs.

INDUSTRIES

Petroleum, food processing, textiles, handicrafts, cement.

NATURAL RESOURCES

Petroleum, natural gas, gypsum.

EXPORTS

$6.8 billion (1998 est.): Crude oil, refined petroleum products, natural gas.

IMPORTS

$6.9 billion (1998 est.): machinery, transport equipment, manufactured goods.

MAJOR TRADING PARTNERS

Italy, Germany, Spain, France, Turkey, Greece, Egypt, UK, Tunisia, Eastern Europe.

Doing Business with Libya

▶ **Investment**

Since the lifting of UN sanctions the overseas focus has been on the development of several dormant oil exploration and production projects. Continued expansion of gas production remains a high priority in Libya. The National Oil Corporation is offering concessions to foreign partners. Libya has had no railroad in operation since 1965, as all previous systems were dismantled. Current plans are to construct a 890 mile (1,435 km) standard gauge line from the Tunisian frontier to Tripoli and Misratah, continuing inland to Sabha, the center of a mineral-rich area, as well as another that will link Tobruk with As Sallum in Egypt.

▶ **Trade**

Sanctions have caused delays in a number of field development and capital projects in the oil sector. Since the lifting of UN sanctions Libya has resumed purchases of oil industry equipment. Latest trade figures show a growing market in food and live animals, manufactured goods, machinery and equipment and chemicals. Most purchasing is done by the government and foreign currency payments, even in the case of private sector purchases, are state-monitored and controlled. The National Oil Corporation prefers to sell crude to refiners under long-term contracts and very little Libyan oil finds its way onto the spot market.

▶ **Trade finance**

Since April 1999 Libya has been eligible for international export credit guarantees and risk assurance. In the past commodity imports have been purchased by confirmed letters of credit at standard terms. Despite occasional administrative delays, Libya has maintained a good payment record in the past.

▶ **Selling to the government**

Most sales to Libya are in fact to the government. State agencies hold monopolies on a broad range of products. For example, pharmaceuticals—one area where US firms are once again allowed to trade—are purchased at public tender by the Medical Supply Organization. In several other areas the Export-Import Board allocates foreign exchange for the importation of specific products by state or even to private enterprises. Libya is a major purchaser of agricultural products and US producers of wheat, barley and other products are expected to gain largely once sanctions are lifted. There are constant modifications and a local expert is needed to keep potential exporters current.

Equipment for the National Oil Corporation and its subsidiaries is largely sourced through a central purchasing agency in London.

▶ **Exchange controls**

Controls apply. Even though the government has declared the intention to unify the official and parallel market exchange rates, a large differential persists.

▶ **Partnership**

To ensure that overseas interests were not subject to the asset freeze imposed by UN sanctions in the early nineties, Libyan holdings, both outright and in partnership with foreign firms, went out of their way to obfuscate and disguise their partnerships. Since the UN lifting of sanctions, the Libyan authorities have actively sought new partnerships.

▶ **Establishing a presence**

Since the final departure of its oil companies in 1986, the US has not had any formal links with Libya. The imminent return of US business will no doubt be welcomed in a variety of forms.

▶ **Project financing**

Despite occasional instances of administrative delays, Libya has maintained a good payment record on foreign service contracts. Although international financing has become available after the lifting of UN sanctions, Libya is not likely to be a candidate for major loans. The government is expected to continue shying away from long-term debt in its endeavors to maintain a balanced financial position in foreign transactions.

▶ **Labor**

A constraint is imposed on the economy by the shortage of skilled and unskilled labor. The country relies on a large contingent of foreign technicians and about a million migrant manual workers from Egypt and other neighboring countries. Most Libyan workers are absorbed by an extensive state bureaucracy. In 1990, some 70% of all Libyan salaried workers were on the state's payroll.

▶ **Business climate**

Even though Arabic is the official language and often the only one spoken by officials, both English and Italian are widely used in the business community. Local representatives are essential to establish a long-term presence and make inroads.

Madagascar

The world's fourth largest island, Madagascar, is emerging from several years of neglect and beginning to attract the attention of investors with its ample supply of natural resources, labor, and an ecosystem with great potential for tourism. Since the mid-1980s the government, in cooperation with the IMF and World Bank, reduced budget deficits, corrected the overvaluation of the currency and removed trade barriers. Madagascar seems set to take full advantage of a second adjustment program started in 1997. In recent years, foreign investors have been taking a closer look at this Indian Ocean island, said by experts to have formed part of the main African continent in prehistoric times.

Country profile

The Republic of Madagascar (known as the Malagasy Republic from 1959 to 1975 and as the Democratic Republic of Madagascar from 1975 until 1992) is situated 400 miles off the east coast of Africa. It is the world's fourth largest island after Greenland, New Guinea and Borneo, and nearly twice the size of the British Isles, measuring 1,570 km from north to south and 570 km at its widest. The highest point is the volcanic Mt. Tsaratanana (2,876 m) in the far north. The east coast is hot and humid, the central highlands around Antananarivo temperate, and the savanna regions in the southwest, arid. There are 18 ethnic groups of Malay-Polynesian, African and Arab origin. The Merina highlanders are the largest group, followed by the coastal Betsimisisaraka. Later arrivals include French, Comorians, Indians and Chinese. More than half the population follow traditional tribal beliefs brought from Borneo. The remainder are mostly Christians apart from a few Muslims.

History

The Malagasy are of mixed Malayo-Indonesian and African-Arab ancestry. Settled originally around the 10th Century by Borneo mariners who arrived in outrigger canoes, the island was first claimed by the Portuguese early in the 16th Century. They named it Madagascar after a reference to such an island in the writings of Marco Polo. After destroying existing Arab settlements on the island, the Portuguese were displaced by the

French. Towards the end of the 19th Century the island was formally handed over to France by the British in return for a free hand in Egypt and Zanzibar. After several uprisings, a referendum called

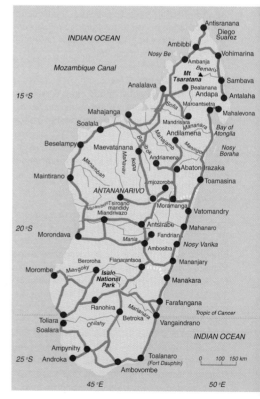

by France in 1958 showed Madagascans over-whelmingly in favor of independence within the French community. In 1959, pro-French Philibert Tsiranana became the first president. He was ousted in May 1973 in an army coup led by Maj. Gen. Gabriel Ramantsoa. Commander Didier Ratsiraka, who was named president in June 1975, nationalized banks, insurance companies, shipping companies, the oil refinery and a leading foreign trading company. In response to riots following his reelection in 1989 under suspicious circum-stances, Pres. Ratsiraka agreed to share power with more democratically-minded Albert Zafy. In the 1993 election Zafy won the presidency only to be impeached by parliament for abusing his constitutional powers during an economic crisis. He was defeated in the 1996 presidential elec-tion by Commander Didier Ratsiraka with a nar-row margin of 50.7% against his 49.3% share of the popular vote.

Government

The executive President serves four-year terms. The Prime Minister and the Council of Min-isters are appointed by the President. A bicam-eral Parliament consists of the Senate, consisting of indirectly elected and appointed members, and the National Assembly whose 150 members are elected on a basis of proportional representation for 4 years. The Association for the Rebirth of Madagascar or *Andry sy Riana Enti-Manavotra an'i Madagasikara* (AREMA) holds a majority over Eco-nomic Liberalism and Democratic Action for Na-tional Recovery (Leader/Fanilo) and several other parties.

Economic policy

The Malagasy government began to imple-ment market-oriented reforms in 1994. It liberal-ized exchange, trade, and price systems; elimi-nated restrictions in key economic sectors, such as petroleum, food, and transportation; and be-gan to tighten fiscal and monetary policies. A broadening of the tax base and strengthening of tax administration achieved a major increase in revenues and a reduction in deficits. Returning confidence boosted domestic financial savings and investment. Real GDP growth of almost 4% in 1998 (an increase of more than 1% of GDP per capita) resulted from increased foreign invest-ment, especially in export zone manufacturing and tourism.

Fast facts

POLITICAL

Head of State	Pres. Didier Ratsiraka (1997)
Prime Minister	Tantely Andrianarivo (1998)
Ruling Party	AREMA
Main Opposition	Leader-Fanilo
Independence	26 June 1960
National capital	Antananarivo
Official languages	Malagasy & French

PHYSICAL

Total area	226,657 sq. miles 587,042 sq. km (2 x Arizona)
Arable land	5% of land area
Coastline	3000 miles/4,828 km

POPULATION

Total	14.87 million
Av. yearly growth	2.8%
Population/sq. mile	68
Urban population	30%
Adult literacy	65%

ECONOMY[1]

Currency	Malagasy franc (FMG) (US$1=6,451)
GDP (real)	$3.4 billion
GDP growth rate	4.7%
GNP per capita[2]	$260
GDP (ppp)[3]	$10.3 billion
GDP per cap. (ppp)[3]	$730
Inflation rate	4.5%
Exports	$921 million
Imports	$1.2 billion
Development aid	$880 million
External debt	$4.35 billion
Unemployment	23%

INFRASTRUCTURE

Railroads	547 miles/880 km
Paved roads	11%
Motor vehicles	80,000
Air passenger/km	567 million
Telephones/1,000	2
International airport	Antananarivo
Main harbor	Toamasina

1. Statistics are based on World Bank data.
2. Atlas method.
3. See page 151 for an explanation of GDP based on purchasing power parity (ppp).

Sectors

Agriculture, including fishing and forestry, is the mainstay of the economy, accounting for 32% of GDP. Major capital-intensive industries are oil refining, fertilizer and cement production, textile manufacturing and the processing of agricultural products. Madagascar is the world's 10th largest chrome producer. Prospecting by US and European companies since the 1970s has led to the discovery of small deposits of oil and gas. Madagascar also has substantial reserves of high quality chrome ore, graphite, mica, bauxite and iron ore as well as small deposits of uranium, quartz, monazite, garnet, amethyst, ilmenite, zircon and titanium. Tourism is a growing sector and expected to become a major foreign exchange earner..

Privatization

In the course of the privatization of the public bank, BFV, its nonperforming loans were transferred to a debt workout unit (SOFIRE), which is responsible for continuing the recovery effort. The second public bank (BTM) was offered for sale in 1998. The petroleum company (SOLIMA) was also put up for sale. Forty other state enterprises will eventually be offered for sale, including the national carrier, Air Madagascar.

Trade

Agriculture, including fishing and forestry, contributes 70% of export earnings. Minerals, with chromium in the lead, form about 5% of exports. Other export items include iron ore, graphite, mica, and bauxite.

Investment

France is the leading foreign investor, followed by Hong Kong, Singapore, Germany and Italy. Some 125 foreign companies are involved in the island's Export Processing Zones (EPZ). Offshore fishing and shrimp farming have also developed into significant foreign exchange earners in recent years, attracting both Japanese and European investors. The discovery of important deposits of sapphires in the north and the south of the country has attracted investors from the United States, Thailand, Indonesia, Israel and Europe. A US firm, Telecel, is involved in the modernization of Madagascar's telecommunications system. The Iridium system is on sale in the country. The local Internet service has grown considerably since 1998 when 10 service providers were licensed.

Financial Sector

The banking system comprises six commercial banks, of which several are under foreign control. Union Commercial Bank (UCB) and State Bank of Mauritius (SBM) are branches of Mauritian parent companies of the same name. The former state bank BFV was purchased by the French bank *Société Générale*, and BTM bank is in the process of privatization. For private banks, financial statements are required that are in compliance with international standards.

Taxes and tariffs

In 1998 the government started to reorganize its tax department and improve coordination between revenue-collecting units on the basis of a plan developed with the assistance of the IMF. Since 1991, Export Processing Zone (EPZ) regulations in Madagascar have allowed foreign or Malagasy investors to qualify for a permanent exemption from taxes, including taxes on imports of primary materials. However, in an effort to cut down on fraudulent production for the local market by EPZ companies, the Government imposed a VAT, refundable upon proof of export.

Business activity

AGRICULTURE

Coffee, vanilla, sugar cane, cloves, cocoa, rice, cassava (tapioca), beans, bananas, peanuts, livestock.

INDUSTRIES

Meat processing, soap, breweries, tanneries, sugar, textiles, glassware, cement, automobile assembly, paper, petroleum, tourism.

NATURAL RESOURCES

Graphite, chromite, coal, bauxite, salt, quartz, tar sands, semiprecious stones, mica, fish.

EXPORTS

$921 million (1999 est.): coffee, vanilla, cloves, shellfish, sugar, petroleum products.

IMPORTS

$1.2 billion (1999 est.): intermediate manufactures, capital goods, petroleum, consumer goods, food.

MAJOR TRADING PARTNERS

France, US, Japan, Germany, Réunion, Iran, South Africa.

Doing Business with Madagascar

▶ **Investment**

A *"guichet unique"* or one-stop office coordinates new investment proposals. In recent years the government has dismantled some of the regulatory and tax constraints impeding foreign investment, especially in the energy, mining, hydrocarbon, telecommunication, and air transportation sectors. Other areas with good investment potential include hotels and other tourist facilities, aquaculture, and apparel manufacturing. An Export Processing Zone (EPZ) is a major area for foreign direct investment.

▶ **Trade**

Manufacturers of telecommunications, mining and petroleum extraction equipment, road-building and repair machinery, automotive spare parts, lubricants, hardware and civil aviation equipment will be able to sell in Madagascar as the country's development and reconstruction programs unfold. A need for wheat, flour and edible oils in a liberalized market offers further potential for exporters. Import licenses are not needed except for a few strategic items. Telecommunications items, however, do require prescreening to ensure compatibility.

▶ **Trade finance**

Eximbank has introduced a new program to assist US trade with Madagascar. Local credit is available to exporters of traditional agricultural products such as vanilla, coffee, cocoa and cloves at relatively high interest rates.

▶ **Selling to the government**

Tenders for government-funded projects are usually announced in official and local journals or on radio and television. Normally these bids are handled in a transparent fashion although on occasion international bids have been awarded to favored local suppliers without explanation. Lack of transparency does not, however, appear to have affected the privatization process where public bidding has generally been open and foreign investors have been welcomed.

▶ **Exchange controls**

Exchange controls were eliminated in 1996 and there are no restrictions on converting or transferring funds associated with a foreign investment, including remittances of investment capital, earnings, loan repayments, and lease payments into foreign currency at a legal market clearing rate.

▶ **Partnership**

Local partners are helpful in finding a way through a bureaucratic maze requiring from investors a series of permits from several government ministries. The Malagasy partner is likely be a minority shareholder.

▶ **Establishing a presence**

In 1996, in a drastic departure from its socialist past, Madagascar adopted laws allowing for the first time not only local private interests but foreigners the freedom to establish, acquire, and dispose of business interests.

▶ **Project finance**

On March 31, 1998, OPIC and Madagascar signed a bilateral Investment Incentive Agreement. Madagascar is a member of the Multilateral Investment Guarantee Agency. The World Bank and the African Development Bank have also financed a variety of infrastructure projects.

▶ **Labor**

There is widespread unemployment and wage rates in the country are among the lowest in the world. Malagasy workers are easily trained and skills are readily available in areas such as textiles, knitting, and clothing assembly.

▶ **Legal rights**

Madagascar is busy restoring foreign trust after the seizure by its socialist government in the 1970s of property owned by foreign oil companies to create SOLIMA, the state oil company. The expropriation claims of some of the affected companies have been settled. Today the government is committed to a system of arbitration for commercial conflicts under a new arbitration law. Madagascar is a member of the World Intellectual Property Organization and has two offices for IPR protection: OMAPI, *Office Malgache de la Propriété industrielle* (Malagasy Office for Industrial Property) and OMDA, *Office Malgache des Droits d'Auteurs* (Malagasy Office for Copyrights).

▶ **Business climate**

Malagasy people are culturally reserved. The concept of sales service and customer support is relatively new to the island and is primarily practiced by distributors of computers and automobiles. Retailers of most consumer goods rarely accept returns. French is the language of business but a substantial number of people also speak English.

Malawi

Landlocked Malawi is one of the most densely populated countries on the African continent. With some of the continent's most fertile soil and ample rainfall, it relies heavily on agricultural products such as tobacco, tea and sugar. Recent reforms aimed at liberalizing and diversifying the economy have led to higher growth rates, reduction of deficits, and lower inflation. Removal of government controls and privatization are expected to attract a higher degree of foreign direct investment and expertise not only in agriculture but also its largely undeveloped mining sector. Privatization has involved several foreign purchases in recent years. Export processing zones offer tariff-free access to neighboring countries and quota privileges to overseas markets.

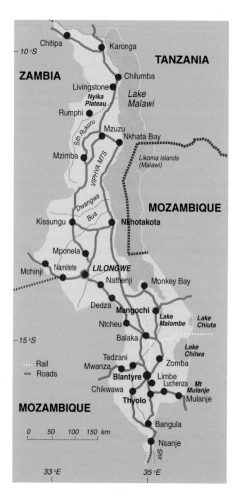

Country profile

The landlocked Republic of Malawi stretches for 840 km along the fertile western and southern sides of Africa's third largest lake—Lake Malawi. The country's width varies between 80 and 160 km. Lake Malawi and the much smaller Malombe, Chiuta and Chilwa lakes take up 20% of the total area. The Shire River, a tributary of the Zambezi, feeds into the Malawi and Malombe lakes while the Shire Highlands, which peak at Mount Mulanje (3,050 m), overlook the country's principal tea-growing region. Further to the north are the Viphya Mountains and the Nyika Plateau. The climate is temperate, with high rainfall and moist savanna woodland vegetation in the high-lying areas and dry savanna along the lakes. The closely related Chewa and Nyanja ethnic groups account for about half of the total population. Other significant groups in the south are the Lomwe, Yao, and Ngoni and in the north the Tumbuka, Tonga and Nkhonde. English and Chichewa are official languages. More than half of the population is Christian with the remainder split evenly between the Muslim faith and their own ethnic beliefs.

History

Lake Malawi was named after the 16th Century Maravi empire that extended to the Indian Ocean and comprised peoples such as the Chewa, Nyanja, Nyasa, Nsenga, Phiri and Zimba, who broke away from the Lunda-Luba kingdom in the southern Congo Basin. There was early contact with Portuguese along the Mozambique coast and Arab traders who settled along the coast of modern-day Tanzania. David Livingstone first visited Lake Malawi in 1859 and was followed by other missionaries and a group of Glasgow businessmen, who set up the African Lakes Company and established Blantyre—named after David Livingstone's Scottish birthplace—that became the territory's largest urban center. In 1891 Malawi (then known as Nyasaland) became a British colony and in 1953 it was incorporated into the Federation of Rhodesia and Nyasaland together with Northern Rhodesia (Zambia) and Southern Rhodesia (Zimbabwe). Dr. Hastings Banda—who qualified as a medical doctor in both the US and Scotland—led the opposition against this federation and ultimately forced the British in 1962 to grant independence to the new state of Malawi. In the 1970s, over objections from the OAU, President Banda established diplomatic relations with apartheid South Africa and accepted considerable financial and technical assistance, including the funding and construction of the new capital at Lilongwe to replace Blantyre. In 1994 an aging and ailing Banda was pressured into holding the first free elections since independence. Banda and his ruling Malawi Congress Party were swept from office. Muslim businessman Bakili Muluzi became president and was reelected in 1999. Banda, the target of criminal court procedures, died in a Johannesburg hospital in 1997.

Government

The executive President and Vice President are elected on one ballot by popular vote for 5-year terms. The 192-member National Assembly is also elected for five year terms. In the 1999 election President Muluzi's and Vice President Malewezi's United Democratic Front (UDF) won 93 seats against 66 for the Malawi Congress Party (MCP) and 29 for the Alliance for Democracy (AFORD) and 4 for independents.

Economic policy

Economic structural adjustment programs have been applied with the help of the World Bank, International Monetary Fund, and other donors since 1981. Programs aimed at diversification, privatization of state enterprises and reduction of deficits and inflationary expenditures have helped to strengthen the economy and attract foreign investors. A wide range of

Fast facts

POLITICAL

Head of State	Pres. Bakili Muluzi (1994)
Vice President	Justin C. Malewezi (1999)
Ruling Party	UDF
Main Opposition	MCP
Independence	6 July 1964
National capital	Lilongwe
Official languages	English & Chichewa

PHYSICAL

Total area	45,745 sq. miles 118,480 sq. km. (± Pennsylvania)
Arable land	18% of land area
Coastline	Landlocked

POPULATION

Total	10 million
Av. yearly growth	1.57%
Population/sq. mile	170
Urban population	15%
Adult literacy	58%

ECONOMY[1]

Currency	Malawian kwacha (MK) (US$1=72.25)
GDP (real)	$1.75 billion
GDP growth rate	4.0%
GNP per capita[2]	$200
GDP (ppp)[3]	$8.9 billion
GDP per cap. (ppp)[3]	$940
Inflation rate	83.4%
Exports	$490 million
Imports	$770 million
Development aid	$366 million
External debt	$2.59 billion
Unemployment	NA

INFRASTRUCTURE

Railroads	485 miles/780 km
Paved roads	20%
Motor vehicles	8,000
Air passenger/km	289 million
Telephones/1,000	3
International airport	Lilongwe
Largest city	Blantyre

1. Statistics based on World Bank data.
2. Atlas method.
3. See page 151 for an explanation of GDP based on purchasing power parity (ppp).

donor-sponsored rural development programs have enabled a number of subsistence farmers to become cash crop producers. From 1964 to 1979 the economy grew at an average annual rate of nearly 6%.

Sectors

Fertile soil and ample rainfall form the basis of a thriving agricultural sector that employs nearly half of the workforce and directly or indirectly supports an estimated 85% of the population. Smallholders grow food crops such as maize, potatoes, groundnuts, cassava and plantains, and keep livestock. Estate farmers account for the bulk of the major export crops such as tobacco, tea and sugar. Both fishing and forestry are being developed and coal is mined on a scale sufficient to supply the country's domestic needs. Limestone is extracted for cement production. Major bauxite deposits at Mount Mulanje are not mined due to prohibitive transportation costs. Manufacturing largely involves agricultural processing and includes tea factories, sugar refineries, cotton gins, tobacco plants, sawmills and plywood manufacturers, oil and grain mills, abattoirs and cold storage plants. Other manufacturing includes textiles, footwear, cement, fertilizer, soap, and matches. Lake Malawi and the various national parks are tourist attractions.

Privatization

Privatization is progressing in all sectors. Recent government privatization initiatives are aimed at improvement of roads and the telecommunication system with the help of overseas investors. Foreigners are allowed to participate in all phases of the privatization program but in some cases nationals are given preferential treatment ranging from discounted share prices to subsidized credits. These concessions are extended to locals on the precondition that the shares or assets be retained for at least two years.

Investment

The Malawi Investment Promotion Agency puts private foreign direct investment at an annual amount of about $10 million over the past four years. Understandably, this level is considered insufficient to complement local private and public sector investment and new investment is aggressively pursued through promotional programs abroad.

Trade

Major overall trading partners are South Africa, Zimbabwe, UK, Japan and Germany. The US, UK, South Africa, Japan, and Germany are the largest purchasers. With a 60% share of the total, tobacco tops the list of exports.

Financial sector

Malawi has a sound banking sector, monitored and regulated by the Reserve Bank of Malawi (RBM). There are five full-service commercial banks of which the largest two—the NBM and CBM—are state-owned. As of June 25, 1999, 1,159.01 million shares with a market capitalization of some $170 million were traded on the Malawi Stock Exchange.

Taxes and tariffs

There are efforts to reduce or eliminate various tariff and non-tariff barriers. In 1998, the Government removed export taxes on tobacco, sugar, tea and coffee. Duties of 10% and 15% on industrial machines, designated raw materials, and intermediate goods were reduced to 5% and 10%, respectively. In July 1999 the maximum import tariff rate was lowered from 30% to 25% and customs duty on aviation fuel was eliminated.

Business activity

AGRICULTURE

Tobacco, sugar cane, cotton, tea, corn, potatoes, cassava (tapioca), sorghum, pulses, cattle, goats.

INDUSTRIES

Tea, tobacco, sugar, sawmill products, cement, consumer goods.

NATURAL RESOURCES

Limestone, uranium, coal, bauxite.

EXPORTS

$490 million (1999 est.): tobacco, tea, sugar, coffee, peanuts, wood products.

IMPORTS

$770 million (1999 est.): food, petroleum products, semimanufactures, consumer goods, transportation equipment.

MAJOR TRADING PARTNERS

US, South Africa, Germany, Japan.

Doing Business with Malawi

Investment

Investment incentives include duty-free importation of raw materials for manufacturing industry, and tax holidays. There are several export processing zones (EPZs) that offer tariff free access into South Africa as well as quota privileges for textiles and sugar in the European Union and the US. Manufacturers also enjoy export advantages to neighboring countries such as Zambia, Tanzania, Congo (Kinshasa). Agriculture is the sector where Malawi competes most successfully internationally and there is a concerted effort to find alternatives to tobacco growing with its uncertain future.

Trade

There is a growing Malawi market for computers, peripherals and software. Used clothing, equipment and vehicles are major imports. Product distribution in Malawi can be problematic as some rural areas become inaccessible during the rainy season from November to April. Infrastructural and community programs sponsored by USAID, the World Bank, and the African Development Bank present opportunities for the sale of materials, equipment, and expertise.

Trade Finance

Overseas purchases are financed primarily through secured letters of credit. Short-term export finance Eximbank insurance is available to US exporters.

Selling to the government

The government issues tender notices for supplies and services in local and international publications 15 to 90 days in advance. Completed bids accompanied by the required deposit are submitted to Malawi Government Central Tender Board (MGCTB) and opened in the presence of bidders or their representatives. As Malawi upgrades its transport and telecommunications systems, major purchases and service contracts are imminent.

Exchange controls

There are no restrictions on remittance of foreign investment funds (including capital, profits, loan repayment and lease repayment) as long as it was originally sourced from abroad and registered with the Reserve Bank of Malawi (RBM).

Partnerships

Joint ventures are allowed under the Partnership Act. The amount and shareholding are not regulated but joint ventures must be licensed by the Registrar General in the Ministry of Justice.

Establishing a presence

Foreign businesses are allowed to establish themselves either through a subsidiary, branch, franchise, joint venture, or licensing relationship. Currently, US subsidiary or affiliate US companies operate in the agro-industry (mostly tobacco), computers and office equipment, and petroleum products. MIPA, as well as organizations such as the Malawi Chamber of Commerce and Industry, the Malawi Development Corporation (MDC), and the Malawi Export Promotion Council (MEPC) all assist foreign firms with registration.

Financing projects

Malawi has had an OPIC investment guarantee agreement since 1967 and is a signatory to the Multilateral Investment Guarantee Agency. The World Bank's International Development Agency, the African Development Bank, and USAID are principal donors.

Labor

Unskilled labor is readily available but skilled staff is scarce. Union membership is still low and there is a general lack of awareness of worker rights and benefits. Only 13% of the formal sector workforce belongs to unions.

Legal rights

The legal system is based on British common law. The courts accept and enforce foreign court judgments that are registered in accordance with established legal procedures. Malawi is a member of the International Center for Settlement of Investment Disputes and accepts international arbitration of investment disputes. Malawi is a member of the World Intellectual Property Organization, the Berne Convention, and the Universal Copyright Convention. The Copyright Society of Malawi (COSOMA) administers the Copyright Act and the Registrar General administers the Patent and Trademarks Act and oversees the protection of industrial intellectual property rights.

Business climate

Malawians are courteous and easygoing in business. Their approach shows the strong influence of the British. It is a small country where most prominent business people know each other well.

Mali

Economic activity in landlocked Mali depends largely on farming and fishing along the Niger river that meanders through the desert. In the nineteenth century explorers braved the difficult route to Timbuktu in search of legendary gold-paved streets that turned out to be a figment of the imagination. Today, however, Mali is Africa's fourth largest gold producer and currently both South African and Canadian mining companies are exploring for more. In 1992 a long period of post-independence autocracy bent on socialism made way for a democratically elected government and economic reform policies supported by international agencies. The country is actively seeking foreign participation to help boost agricultural production and develop mining prospects.

Country profile

Most of landlocked Republic of Mali consists of monotonous plains, less than 500 m above sea level. The more than 4,000 km long Niger river flows northeast from Guinea through the heart of Mali into the Sahara desert. Between the towns of Ségu and Timbuktu it branches into lakes and swamps forming the Masina Delta. Both the Niger and its tributary, the Bani, are vital for transport and irrigation. In the summer moist maritime winds move in from the Gulf of Guinea and in winter the dry *harmattan* blows from the Sahara Desert in the north. The Sahel Belt, bordering the desert, extends from Senegal and Mauritania through Mali. Mandé-speaking peoples, consisting of the Bambara, Malinké (Manding or Mandinka) and Soninké, account for half the population. Other significant groups include the Ful (or Fulani), the Senufo, the Dogon, and the Songhai. The nomadic Tuareg are concentrated around the scattered oases of the Sahara to the north of Timbuktu and Gao and speak Berber. About 80% of the population are Muslim and the rest split between Christianity and ethnic beliefs. French has official status and Bambara is the *lingua franca*.

History

The advent of the camel as a means of transport across the desert some 1,800 years ago stimulated trade between Mediterranean Africa and ancient Mali, a creation of a Mandé group, the Malinké. The Malinké empire ruled regions of Mali from the 12th to the 16th Century while the Songhai empire reigned over the Timbuktu-Gao region in the 15th Century. Originally explorers

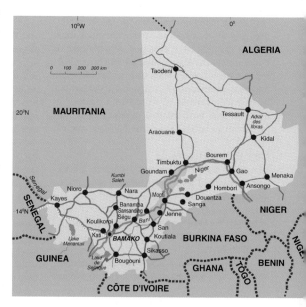

braved the arduous route inland in search of the legendary golden riches of Timbuktu, only to discover that the tales were heavily inflated. Morocco conquered Timbuktu in 1591 and controlled it for two centuries. In the late 19th Century the French set out from their colony in Senegal to establish a colonial empire that would stretch to the Red Sea. With their claims validated at the 1885 Berlin Conference, the French applied a combination of diplomacy and military force to overpower several Sahelian states, including Mali. As French Soudan it was first incorporated into French West Africa and afterwards given joint independence with Senegal in the Federation of Mali. Shortly after independence in 1960, the federation split up and French Soudan became Mali. The first Malian president, Modibo Keita, opted for a one-party state, severed ties with France, introduced socialist policies and sought assistance from the Soviet Union. In 1968 the Keita dictatorship was overthrown by Lieutenant Moussa Traoré who retained one-man rule while adopting some free-market policies. Violent repression of pro-democracy forces prompted Liet.-Col. Amadou Toumani Touré to depose Traoré and facilitate the country's first free elections in 1992. Alpha Oumar Konaré and his ADEMA party emerged victorious and Touré stepped down. Mali's second multiparty elections took place in May 1997 with Konaré easily reelected.

Government

The 1992 constitution provides for an executive President, elected by popular vote for 5-year terms. The President appoints the Prime Minister and the Council of Ministers. The 147-member unicameral legislature also serves for a 5-year term. In 1997 President Alpha Oumar Konaré was returned to power with 95.9% of the total vote. His *Alliance pour la Démocratie en Mali-Parti Pan-Africain pour la Liberté, la Solidarité et la Justice* or Alliance for Democracy in Mali-Pan-African Party for Liberty, Solidarity and Justice (ADEMA) maintained its majority in the legislature with 128 seats. The *Parti pour la Rénaissance Nationale* or Party for National Renewal (PARENA), with 8 seats, forms the main opposition. There are thirteen smaller parties.

Economic policy

Since 1992 the emphasis has been on free trade and private enterprise, promoted in cooperation with the IMF, World Bank, and bilateral

Fast facts

POLITICAL

Head of State	Pres. Alpha Omar Konarê (1992)
Prime Minister	Ibrahim Keita (1994)
Ruling Party	ADEMA
Main Opposition	PARENA
Independence	22 September 1960
National capital	Bamako
Official languages	French

PHYSICAL

Total area	478,764 sq. miles 1.24 million sq. km. (2 x Texas)
Arable land	2% of land area
Coastline	Landlocked

POPULATION

Total	10.4 million
Av. yearly growth	3.01%
Population/sq. mile	22
Urban population	30%
Adult literacy	38%

ECONOMY[1]

Currency	CFA franc (CFAF)(US$1=752.76)
GDP (real)	$2.8 billion
GDP growth rate	5.5%
GNP per capita[2]	$250
GDP (ppp)[3]	$8.0 billion
GDP per cap. (ppp)[3]	$790
Inflation rate	5.0%
Exports	$650 million
Imports	$939 million
Development aid	$478 million
External debt	$3.0 billion
Unemployment	N/A

INFRASTRUCTURE

Railroads	398 miles/640 km
Paved roads	11%
Motor vehicles	30,000
Air passenger/km	215 million
Telephones/1,000	2
International airport	Bamako
Main harbor	Uses Dakar in Senegal

1. Statistics are based on World Bank data.
2. Atlas method.
3. See page 151 for an explanation of GDP based on purchasing power parity (ppp).

donors, including the United States. Pres. Konaré has earned praise for his attempts to stimulate economic growth. Strict adherence to IMF guidelines has stimulated foreign investment and enabled Mali to become the second largest cotton producer in Africa. Export taxes, import duties, and price controls have been reduced or eliminated and a new investment code was adopted.

Sectors

Even though only 3% of the total land area is arable more than 80% of the people make a living in agriculture, accounting for half of Mali's GDP. Mali is Africa's fourth largest and Sub-Saharan Africa's largest producer of cotton. Other cash crops are groundnuts, sugar cane and rice. Food crops include millet, sorghum and maize. Livestock is responsible for half of the agricultural sector's activity. The country is self-sufficient in freshwater fish and a significant exporter. Gold mining has become an important contributor to GDP and has attracted considerable foreign interest, including the leading mining producers in South Africa. Mali also has deposits of bauxite, iron ore and tin. Prospecting is underway for petroleum, copper, lithium and diamonds. Manufacturing is mainly confined to small-scale agricultural processing for domestic consumption and export. Other industries include soft drinks, textiles, soaps, plastics, cigarettes, cement, bricks, and agricultural tools and equipment.

Privatization

Around 90% of all production is still in the hands of state enterprises, but privatization is continuing. A US firm, for example, won an international bid to purchase the state-owned tannery.

Investment

Foreign direct investment in Mali's manufacturing sector is modest but growing. Canadian and South African mining houses have become prominent players in the gold mining sector while the French are dominant in cotton production, food processing, and petroleum retailing—a sector where ExxonMobil has also been a significant player for some time.

Trade

Mali is the largest producer and exporter of cotton in Sub-Saharan Africa. Gold accounts for one third of its foreign exchange earnings. Although the French dominate the automobile and consumer goods market, North American, Asian,

and other African nations are steadily gaining. Côte d'Ivoire and Senegal supply a whole range of essential consumer goods. Exports of US goods to Mali were estimated at $26 million in 1998.

Financial sector

As a member of UEMOA, Mali's banking system is regulated from the regional central bank in Dakar, Senegal. Commercial banks enjoy considerable liquidity but tend to invest in Western capital markets instead of local enterprises. The ongoing privatization program is expected to make the local market more attractive. In 1994, the government started issuing treasury bonds that carry tax advantages for investors. Companies in Mali are expected to list on the UEMOA stock exchange.

Taxes and tariffs

Except for a 3% levy on cotton and gold, taxes on exports were eliminated in 1990. Import duties on some goods were reduced or eliminated in 1994. The tax system remains complicated and in the view of some outsiders needs further overhaul to make it more attractive for foreign investors.

Business activity

AGRICULTURE
Cotton, millet, rice, corn, vegetables, peanuts, cattle, sheep, goats.

INDUSTRIES
Minor local consumer goods production, food processing, construction, phosphate and gold mining.

NATURAL RESOURCES
Gold, phosphates, kaolin, salt, limestone, uranium, bauxite, iron ore, manganese, tin, unexploited copper deposits.

EXPORTS
$630 million (1999 est.): cotton, gold, livestock.

IMPORTS
$939 million (1999 est.): machinery and equipment, construction materials, petroleum, foodstuffs, textiles.

MAJOR TRADING PARTNERS
Thailand, Italy, China, Brazil, Côte d'Ivoire, France, Franc zone, EU.

Investment

The investment code favors investment in export-oriented and labor-intensive businesses. The mining code encourages investments in medium and small mining enterprises and allows two year exploration permits free of charge. The investment, mining, and commercial codes all offer duty-free importation of capital equipment, tax advantages for new ventures in priority industries and repatriation of profits and capital. Foreign investors go through the same one-stop screening process as domestic investors. Criteria for approval include the size of capital investment, the potential for added value, and the level of job creation. Any company that exports at least 80% of its production is entitled to tax-free status.

Trade

Mali imports petroleum products, chemicals, vehicles, machinery, processed foods, pharmaceutical products, used clothing, cosmetics, electronics, telecommunications equipment, mining equipment, and most manufactured items. Most exporters to Mali make use of local agents or distributors.

Trade finance

Payment is usually by irrevocable letters of credit. US investors in Mali enjoy short and medium term Eximbank coverage.

Selling to the government

Significant government purchases usually involve programs sponsored by international agencies and donors such as USAID. These procurement contracts offer opportunities for foreign suppliers of agricultural, construction, irrigation, computer, and telecommunications equipment and services. Bidding rules are normally set by the donors.

Exchange controls

Although there are no restrictions or limits on the repatriation of capital or profits, the regional central bank requires that all remittances be channeled through it, together with supporting commercial documents.

Partnerships

Several overseas investors in the manufacturing and service sector have opted for partnerships or joint ventures. Such arrangements are encouraged but not required by the government. In the case of joint ventures involving the government, its share is limited to 20%.

Establishing a presence

Establishing a presence requires a one-stop procedure (*guichet unique*). Manufacturers apply at the National Directorate of Industries and Trading Companies and at the National Directorate of Economic Affairs. The Chamber of Commerce and Industry assists in the process and registration takes on an average between 30-45 days. Foreign investors are allowed full ownership. They are also permitted to purchase shares in privatized parastatal and other domestic companies.

Financing projects

Mali is eligible for Overseas Private Investment Corporation financing and insurance programs. It is a member of the World Bank's Multilateral Investment Guarantee Agency.

Labor

Skilled workers laid off by the state and college and high school graduates without employment prospects are available in the job market. Workers have the right to belong to unions and although a warning notice is not required, mediation is generally sought before workers resort to striking. Although not mandatory, firms often find it useful to liaise with official labor inspectors—especially when hiring and firing.

Legal rights

In rare instances of expropriation of property the Malian government has done so in accordance with international law. The investment code allows a foreign company which signs an agreement with the government to refer to international arbitration in cases where the local courts are unable to resolve disputes in a satisfactory manner. Mali is a member of the International Center for the Settlement of Investment Disputes and New York Convention of 1958 on the recognition and enforcement of foreign arbitrage awards. The *Direction Nationale des Industries* implements copyright and patent protection. Mali is a signatory to the WTO TRIPS agreement. Intellectual property right infringement has not been a serious problem.

Business climate

Very little English is spoken in the French-oriented business community. Malians place great emphasis on protocol and courtesy and discussions normally start with an extensive exchange of pleasantries. Although most Malians are Muslim and do not drink, smoke, or eat pork, they usually do not object to foreigners doing so.

Mauritania

Making the most of its resources despite large stretches of desert and the world's third lowest population density after Namibia and Mongolia, Mauritania has made notable progress in recent years. A democratically elected government has been pursuing market-oriented policies since 1992 and welcomed foreign participation in key sectors such as mining, fishing and agriculture. There is prospecting for mineral resources, including oil and gold. Privatization is expected to attract larger inflows of capital and spur economic growth and development.

Country profile

Some 70% of the Islamic Republic of Mauritania consists of the Sahara Desert. Both the desert and the Sahel regions rise from monotonous coastal plains in the west to a low plateau eastward and northward, exceeding heights of 500 m above sea level at the iron- bearing hills around Fderik and Zouerate. Only the southernmost strip, along the northern bank of the Senegal River receives sufficient rainfall (up to 800 mm) for intensive crop cultivation. Most Mauritanians are descendants of Berbers and Arab immigrants, but black groups such as the Wolof, Tukulor, and Soninke and the nomadic Tajakant and Regeihat are present in significant numbers. Hassaniya Arabic, which had enjoyed equal status with French since 1967, became the only official language in 1991. The Mandé languages of the Soninké, Fula and Wolof are also recognized as national languages and used in schools. French is still widely spoken in commerce. The Muslim faith prevails.

History

Mauritania was first inhabited by black peoples and Berbers. From the 7th Century, following the advent of the Arabs in Northern Africa, the Berbers in the region were converted to the Islamic faith and they in turn proselytized the Tukulor and other black communities in the Sahel region. As was the case in Morocco, Arab and Berber intermixing led to the emergence of Moors (derived from the Latin *Mauri* or French *Maures*) who viewed themselves as *al-Bidan* (white) as opposed to their *al-Sudan* (black) neighbors. Portuguese slave traders established a base on Arguin Island (Tidra) from 1443. The French took over the region in the 1930s. In 1960, over strenuous opposition from Morocco, which laid claim to the territory, Mauritania became independent under President Moktar Ould Daddah (son-in-law of French president Charles de Gaulle). Ould Daddah's party had won all the seats in a 1959 general election. In 1976 Spain ceded Spanish (Western) Sahara on a

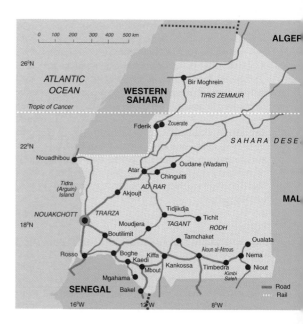

270

50/50 basis to Morocco and Mauritania. The Polisario guerrillas, who sought independence for Western Sahara, attacked targets in Mauritania, drawing it into a protracted and costly war. In 1997, in the midst of growing opposition to this unpopular war, Ould Daddah was ousted by Lt-Col. Khouna Ould Haidalla, who assumed the presidency and appointed Col. Maaouiya Ould Sid'Ahmed Taya as his prime minister. Mauritania dropped its territorial claims, leaving the way clear for Morocco to expand its influence over all of Western Sahara. In 1984 Taya assumed the presidency. He exercised autocratic rule until 1992 when his *Parti Républicain Démocratique et Social* (PRDS), or Social and Democratic Party, won in free elections. Tension between the Moorish and black non-Moorish groups has eased since the restrictions on political parties were lifted after the adoption of a new democratic constitution at a referendum in 1991. Pres. Taya was reelcted by a large margin in 1997.

Government

The 1991 Constitution provides for an executive President elected by popular vote for six year terms. The President appoints the Prime Minister and Council of Ministers. A bicameral parliament or *Barlamane* consists of a 56-member Senate or *Majlis al-Shuyukh*, elected by municipal leaders for six years, and a 79-member National Assembly, (*Al Jamiya al-Wataniyah*) elected by popular vote every five years. With 71 seats in the Assembly the Democratic and Social Republican Party (PRDS) led by President Taya holds an overwhelming majority over the *Action pour Changement* or Action for Change (AC), with a single seat, and six independents. The PRDS holds 52 of the 56 Senate seats.

Economic policy

The government has successfully implemented an IMF and World Bank-sponsored structural adjustment program. Reforms include privatization and restructuring of the banking sector, liberalization of the exchange rate system, and reduction of trade and investment barriers. These reforms resulted in an average increase in real GDP (in local currency) to 5% during the 1993-1998 period from 2% in 1992. But they did not come without a certain measure of political risk. Pres. Taya's restructuring programs have at times provoked protests, the most serious being the so-called bread riots in Nouakchott in 1995.

Fast facts

POLITICAL

Head of State	Pres. Maaouiya Ould Sid'Achmed Taya (1984)
Ruling Party	PRDS
Main Opposition	AC
Independence	28 November 1960
National capital	Nouakchott
Official languages	Hasaniya Arabic

PHYSICAL

Total area	397,964 sq. miles 1,030,700 sq. km. (3 x Arizona)
Arable land	Less than 1%
Coastline	469 miles/754 km

POPULATION

Total	2.58 million
Av. yearly growth	2.99%
Population/sq. mile	7
Urban population	54%
Adult literacy	41% (1994)

ECONOMY[1]

Currency	Ouguiya (UM) (US$1=253.27)
GDP (real)	$1.2 billion
GDP growth rate	4.3%
GNP per capita[2]	$410
GDP (ppp)[3]	$4.7 billion
GDP per cap. (ppp)[3]	$1,890
Inflation rate	4.7%
Exports	$370 million
Imports	$471 million
Development aid	$263 million
External debt	$2.03 billion
Unemployment	23%

INFRASTRUCTURE

Railroads	700 km
Paved roads	22%
Motor vehicles	13,700
Air passenger/km	289 million
Telephones/1,000	4
International airport	Noakchott
Main harbor	Nouadhibou

1. *Statistics are based on World Bank data.*
2. *Atlas method.*
3. *See page 151 for an explanation of GDP based on purchasing power parity (ppp).*

Sectors

The economy depends largely on the mining of iron and copper ore and fishing in the Atlantic. Less than 3% of Mauritania is cultivable and only one-fifth of its food crop requirements is produced locally. Imported cereals supplement the locally-grown food crops consisting mainly of millet, sorghum, maize, rice and vegetables. Livestock (cattle, sheep, goats and camels) account for about 15% of GDP or three-quarters of the total agriculture production. Only 10% of the working-age population is employed in the formal sector of the economy. Marine fishing around Nouadhibou contributes 5% of GDP. Joint-venture companies are responsible for about 95% of output, most of it processed locally. At an estimated 6 billion tons, Mauritania's iron ore reserves are among the largest in the world. Other mineral resources include gold, copper, phosphates, sulphur, gypsum and uranium. Prospecting for petroleum is underway. Development is hampered by large-scale deforestation, over-exploitation of fishing grounds and a chronic water shortage.

Privatization

The telecommunications, electricity, and air transport companies are being privatized.

Investment

Foreign investment dried up during ethnic clashes between 1989 and 1991 but resumed modestly towards the mid-1990s after the government introduced new incentives. US corporations are among a list of foreign investors including firms from France, Saudi Arabia, China, Belgium, Australia and Ireland in areas such as petroleum, mining, food processing, banking, fishing and manufacturing.

Trade

With 58% of the total, iron ore is the country's leading export earner, followed by fishing, which accounts for 38% of the total. Mauritania imports almost all its food, machinery and consumer needs, including foodstuffs, vehicles and spare parts, petroleum products, building materials, mining equipment, telecommunications equipment, electronics, cosmetics and most other manufactured items. French, Spanish and Asian goods dominate the market but there is a growing demand for US-made items. In recent years exports of US goods to Mauritania have ranged between $30 and $50 million annually and consisted mostly of mining equipment.

Financial sector

Financial sector reforms have been introduced with the assistance of the World Bank and the IMF. Banking supervision has been strengthened to encourage development of an interbank market and to ensure solvency. There are five commercial banks and about 30 exchange offices in Mauritania. The Central Bank fixes the exchange rate for the ouguiya through a basket of currencies involving its principal trading partners.

Taxes and tariffs

Recent laws focus on a more efficient and simplified revenue collection system coupled with lower rates. Still, import duties remain relatively heavy as rates vary from 9% to as high as 43%. Value Added Tax (VAT) rates on imported goods are divided into two categories: 5% for essential and 14% for non-essential goods. VAT is not applied to exported goods.

Foreign relations

Despite a temporary break in diplomatic relations during the Gulf War, when Mauritania supported Iraq, relations with the US have been good. Mauritania is a key supporter of the Middle East Peace Process and one of the few Arab League countries to recognize Israel. The US has long been an important provider of equipment to the mining sector.

Business activity

AGRICULTURE
Dates, millet, sorghum, root crops, cattle, sheep, fish products.

INDUSTRIES
Fish processing, mining of iron ore and gypsum.

NATURAL RESOURCES
Copper, iron ore, gypsum, fish, phosphate.

EXPORTS
$370 million (1999 est.): fish and fish products, iron ore, gold.

IMPORTS
$471 million (1999 est.): foodstuffs, consumer goods, petroleum products, capital goods.

MAJOR TRADING PARTNERS
Japan, Italy, France, Algeria, Spain, China, US.

Doing Business with Mauritania

▶ **Investment**

Incentives are offered to investors in small- and medium-sized enterprises and export-oriented manufacturing utilizing local manpower and raw materials in areas outside of Nouakchott and Nouadhibou. Government priorities range from reorganization of the fishing sector to gold and other mineral prospecting, increased water supply and improved irrigation systems to rural road construction and rehabilitation, and telecommunications expansion to increased electricity generation.

▶ **Trade**

Three market segments are considered to be prime prospects for US exporters: foodstuffs (especially wheat, flour, rice, powdered milk, and canned food), mining equipment (machinery and trucks), and telecommunications. Foreign firms have also been successful in supplying fishing gear, wind and solar energy equipment, pharmaceutical and medical products, computers and software, cosmetics, toiletries, and oil and clothing.

▶ **Trade finance**

Most imports are by irrevocable and confirmed letters of credit issued by local banks. Some Mauritanian importers hold bank accounts abroad and pay for imports without involving their local bank. The Foreign Credit Insurance Association (FCIA) insures purchases by the state mining company, SNIM.

▶ **Selling to the government**

Purchases are usually by tenders (*avis d'appel d'offres*) but direct negotiations are common in small transactions involving local suppliers. Major projects are often guaranteed and controlled by international donors. The Central Procurement Board (*Commission Centrale des Marchés*) monitors all government procurement.

▶ **Exchange controls**

The foreign exchange system has been liberalized, and repatriation of dividends and capital as well as payments for overseas goods and services are possible through commercial banks without prior approval from the Central Bank.

▶ **Partnerships**

The government offers a wide range of incentives to encourage partnership arrangements. Current joint ventures are primarily with other Arab countries in the mineral, fishing, and banking subsectors.

▶ **Establishing a presence**

An official investment agency (*Guichet Unique de l'Investissement*) and the Mauritanian Chamber of Commerce and Industry offer assistance and advice to foreigners who wish to establish an office. Even though procedures can be handled without a local lawyer, foreign investors with long-term plans usually retain one to ensure strict compliance from the outset.

▶ **Financing projects**

Mauritania relies for about 85% of its project funding on loans from The African Development Bank, IMF, and European Investment Bank, and the Islamic Bank.

▶ **Labor**

Even though unemployment is high among high school and college graduates, there is a shortage of factory-skilled workers and managerial staff in all sectors, with the possible exception of mining. Workers are free to associate with and establish unions at local and national levels. Work stoppages are rare. Foreign firms are normally at liberty to hire any number of expatriates, except in areas such as industrial fishing where crews are required to have five Mauritanians per vessel.

▶ **Legal rights**

Since Mauritania's independence, there has only been one case of nationalization when in 1974 the government took over a mining company from a majority French partner. It paid a mutually agreed sum in compensation. Disagreements over investment issues are settled in the courts or in terms of arbitration procedures in conformance with the rules of the World Bank. Mauritania is a member of the African Intellectual Property Organization, the Paris, Berne and Hague conventions and the World Intellectual Property Organization.

▶ **Business Climate**

A working knowledge of French or Arabic is an advantage but interpreters are readily available. As a Muslim country, consumption of alcohol and pork is taboo. A handshake is customary when initiating and closing a business meeting but it should be remembered that some conservative Muslim men will not shake a woman's hand.

Mauritius

Mauritius is one of Africa's notable success stories. When it became independent in 1968, this small island country in the Indian Ocean was an underdeveloped single crop community. In the next 30 years it branched out from sugar into several other sectors and averaged a growth of about 6% per year. This raised per capita income to $3,690, the second highest in Africa. Unemployment dropped to 2%, making Mauritius the only African country to have experienced labor shortages in recent years. This was accomplished with few natural resources.

Country profile

The Republic of Mauritius comprises the main island and a much smaller Rodrigues Island, about 500 km northeast, as well as two dependencies, the virtually uninhabited Cargados Carajos (600 km north), and Agalega, with a few hundred inhabitants (1,200 km north). It also lays claim to the uninhabited French island of Tromelin (500 km north) and the British Chagos Islands about halfway to Sri Lanka. The Chagos group includes Diego Garcia, used as an American military communications base. Mauritius itself measures about 58 km by 47 km and has a subtropical climate, beaches, coral reefs and scenery that attract thousands of upscale tourists. Its inhabitants trace their ancestry to three continents—Africa, Asia and Europe. The Indian group (Hindu and Muslim) accounts for 69% while citizens of mixed Afro-European origin (Creoles) constitute 27%. Education levels and health standards are high. About 52 percent of the population is Hindu and 16 percent Muslim.

History

The Dutch first came to this island in 1638 and named it Mauritius (after the Dutch leader, Mauritz of Nassau). They made way for the French in 1715, who renamed it Isle de France, stayed until 1810 and lost it to the British, who reinstated the name Mauritius. Indentured Hindu workers were brought from India to work on sugar estates. Their descendants are in the majority, followed by Creoles (of mixed, predominantly African slave origin), Muslim Indians, Chinese and a few Europeans. The Creole population gave birth

to a language based on the French, Malagasy and African languages, which became the *lingua franca* of the island. Mauritius received its independence under the British crown in 1968 and became a Republic in 1992. Continuous political squabbles, splits and shifting alliances do not seem to have derailed a climate of continuity and stability. Prime Minister Navin Ramgoolam headed an unstable coalition government for five years before being ousted at the polls by an opposition alliance in

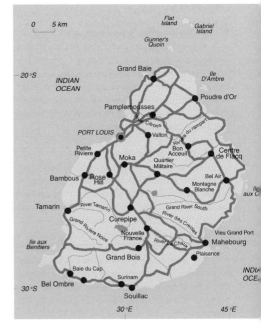

September 2000. Sir Anerood Jugnauth, leader of the *Movement Socialiste Miltant* or Militant Socialist Movement (MSM), will be prime minsiter for three years before handing over to his coalition partner, Paul Berenger, of the *Mouvement Militant Mauricien* (MMM), for the remainder of the five year term. Berenger will be the first non-Hindu to hold office since Mauritius won independence in 1968.

Government

Both the president and the prime minister, who heads the government, are elected for 5 years. Incumbent President Cassam Uteem of the MMM was elected in 1992 and reelected in 1997. The unicameral National Assembly, elected by the voters for 5-year terms, has 62 members plus an additional maximum of eight seats allocated to the "best losers"—the unsuccessful candidates with the largest number of votes. Currently a coalition of the Militant Socialist Movement (MSM) and the Mauritian Militant Movement (MMM) with 54 seats holds a comfortable majority over the opposition coalition grouping of the *Parti Travailiste* or Labor Party (PTr) and the *Parti Mauricien Xavier Duval or Mauritian Party of Xavier Duval* (PMXD) with their 6 seats. The main island is divided into nine districts with municipal councils elected in the urban areas.

Economic policy

Starting with a monocrop, impoverished island nation some 30 years ago, Mauritius has earned the top spot among African countries on the UN Human Development Index. Today it is a diversified economy, relying not only on exports of sugar, but textiles and services such as tourism and financial and offshore business. Mauritius, however, faces new challenges as both sugar and textiles are losing their preferential access to major markets in Europe and the US. The emphasis is on productivity and turning some of its most companies into multinationals. The aim is to make Mauritius a regional trade and financial center.

Privatization

Even though the government's share of GDP is modest it still controls key sectors. The State Trading Corporation regulates imports of rice, flour, petroleum products, and cement, and the Agricultural Marketing Board the importation of potatoes, onions and spices. Slated for privatization are trade monopolies, telecommunications, banking and broadcasting entities.

Fast facts

POLITICAL

Head of State	Pres. Sir Cassam Uteem (1992)
Prime Minister	Sir Anerood Jugnauth (2000)
Ruling Coalition	MMM/MSM
Main Opposition	PTr/PMXD
Independence	12 March 1968
National capital	Port Louis
Official languages	English & French

PHYSICAL

Total area	788 sq. miles 2,040 sq. km. (11 x Washington DC)
Arable land	52% of land area
Coastline	110 miles/177 km

POPULATION

Total	1.2 million (1999e)
Av. yearly growth	1.18%
Population/sq. mile	1,499
Urban population	51%
Adult literacy	84%

ECONOMY[1]

Currency	Mauritian Rupee (MauR) (US$1=29.20)
GDP (real)	$4.6 billion
GDP growth rate	3.4%
GNP per capita[2]	$3,700
GDP (ppp)[3]	$11.7 billion
GDP per cap. (ppp)[3]	$10,000
Inflation rate	6.8%
Exports	$2.7 billion
Imports	$2.9 billion
Development aid	$44 million
External debt	$2.39 billion
Unemployment	2%

INFRASTRUCTURE

Railroads	0 km
Paved roads	93%
Motor vehicles	250,000 (1994)
Air passenger/km	3 billion (1994)
Telephones/1,000	117
International airport	Plaisance
Main harbor	Port Louis

1. *Statistics are based on World Bank data.*
2. *Atlas method.*
3. *See page 151 for an explanation of GDP based on purchasing power parity (ppp).*

275

Sectors

Initially heavily dependent on sugar, Mauritius has developed a strong manufacturing and tourism sector in the past few decades. Agriculture's share of GDP shrank to 9%, while manufacturing's contribution rose to 23%. Sugar, however, remains the basis of the economy. It is grown on about half the total land area and employs 14% of the labor force. Apart from high-value textiles, local manufactures include pharmaceuticals, publishing, software, light engineering, and jewelry. Tourism is the third pillar on which the Mauritian economy rests, accounting for 5% of GDP and providing direct and indirect employment for some 50,000 people.

Trade

Sugar and textiles together with a variety of light manufactures account for most of the country's exports. Other significant exports are tea and cut flowers. Mauritius imports three-quarters of its food, especially rice, a staple food. The US is Mauritius' third largest market but it ranks 13th in terms of exports to Mauritius, well behind South Africa, France, India, and the United Kingdom. The US and Singapore are leading suppliers of computers. Main imported raw materials are textile yarn and fabrics (55%), cotton, wool and synthetic fibers (6%), and chemicals (4%). Caterpillar and John Deere are major suppliers of derocking machinery for sugar farms, followed by a few European manufacturers. The US also leads in supplying pivot irrigation systems for these estates.

Investment

Foreign direct investment fell sharply since the early 1980s when many Hong Kong firms, the leading investors in textile manufacturing, relocated for quota reasons. There are a few US investors in the Export Processing Zone (mostly diamond cutting/polishing and garment manufacturing). Most recent foreign direct investment has gone into information technology, printing and publishing, pharmaceuticals, light engineering, high-quality garments, and jewelry. India, UK, France, Germany and South Africa are leading investors.

Financial sector

A sophisticated banking system comprises 10 commercial banks (seven foreign-owned) and 10 financial intermediaries, including the Development Bank of Mauritius, the State Investment Corporation, the Mauritius Leasing Company (a joint private-public venture), as well as two private leasing companies. There are seven offshore banks and 4,600 non-banking off-shore companies providing insurance, funds management, aircraft leasing, consultancy, and data processing. The Stock Exchange of Mauritius has 45 listed companies (including two foreign) and an over-the-counter market with 60 companies. Capitalization is close to $2 billion. The Bank of Mauritius oversees domestic and offshore banks and implements monetary policies. Much of the country's offshore business involves US investment in India, channeled through Mauritius for tax reasons.

Taxes & Tariffs

Tax incentives allow for a corporate rate of 15% instead of the normal 35%. Companies in the Mauritius Freeport are fully exempted. There is no withholding tax on dividends and no tax on capital gains. Mauritius operates a two-tiered system that allows imports from certain countries, including the US, preferential duties ranging between 0% and 80%. A VAT of 10% percent is payable by importers on the CIF value of their imports.

Business activity

AGRICULTURE
Sugar cane, tea, corn, potatoes, bananas, pulses, cattle, goats, fish.

INDUSTRIES
Food processing (largely sugar milling), textiles, clothing, chemicals, metal products, transport equipment, nonelectrical machinery, tourism.

NATURAL RESOURCES
Arable land, fish.

EXPORTS
$2.7 billion (1999 est.): clothing, textiles, sugar.

IMPORTS
$2.9 billion (1999 est.): manufactured goods, capital equipment, foodstuffs, petroleum products, chemicals.

MAJOR TRADING PARTNERS
UK, France, US, Germany, Italy, South Africa, India.

Doing Business with Mauritius

▶ **Investment**

Tax concessions and other incentives are offered in Export Processing Zones scattered around the island. Textiles and apparel account for 80% of EPZ exports, but there has been diversification into the manufacture of watches, electronic measuring instruments, jewelry, leather goods, toys, and optical goods. The Mauritius Export Development and Investment Authority assists investors and promotes exports. Generous incentives are also available to foreign companies operating from the Mauritius Freeport in transshipment and reexportation, offshore banking and other financial services, light manufacturing, and information technology. The authorities encourage both local and foreign private investment in major infrastructure projects ranging from energy to roads and airport construction.

▶ **Trade**

There is growing interest in foreign technology, especially in telecommunications, computers, software, and farm machinery. Opportunities also exist in restaurant and food-processing equipment and design consulting. The government controls prices and markups on items such as rice, flour, cement, cooking gas, infant milk powder, cheese, fertilizer, frozen fish, iron and steel bars, and petroleum products. Major expansion of both traditional and nontraditional sources of energy such as electricity from bagasse and wind power-created demand for turbo-alternators, boilers, machinery to handle bagasse, coal and ash, and associated electrical equipment. There is an ongoing need for machinery and irrigation systems for sugar estates.

▶ **Trade finance**

Mauritius qualifies for the full range of Eximbank loans extended to US exporters. The government-controlled Development Bank of Mauritius provides loans to large and medium-sized industrial enterprises and manages various concessionary lending schemes for small-scale enterprises.

▶ **Selling to the government**

Infrastructure projects such as airport and port development, energy, telecommunications, health, sewage, road and dam construction, and computerization offer opportunities .

▶ **Exchange controls**

There are no exchange control regulations and dividends and royalties are freely repatriated.

▶ **Partnership**

Joint ventures are rare except in architecture, construction and civil engineering projects. Several Mauritian firms, however, manufacture foreign products under license.

▶ **Establishing a presence**

Foreigners usually opt for a limited company or a branch. It is common procedure to nominate two residents to form the company and transfer the shares to the foreign investor after approval. A foreign investor in export-oriented manufacturing is permitted 100% equity, but the government encourages local participation. Foreign participation may be limited to 49% in investments serving the domestic market, and is generally not encouraged in areas where Mauritius has already mastered the technology.

▶ **Project financing**

Mauritius is eligible for OPIC programs and major infrastructure projects are financed by the World Bank, the African Development Bank, the European Investment Bank/European Development Fund, the Kuwait Fund, and the Arab Bank for Economic Development in Africa.

▶ **Labor**

It is not difficult to recruit workers with basic secondary education and some technical training. There is, however, a shortage of skills in financial services and management, especially human resource management. Labor-management relations are generally good and unions account for less than 25 percent of the workforce.

▶ **Legal rights**

The legal system, based on both the Napoleonic code and British common law, protects property, patents and trademarks. Mauritius is a member of the World Intellectual Property Organization and party to the Paris and Bern Conventions for the Protection of Industrial Property and the Universal Copyright Convention. Its copyright law is in conformity with WTO's Trade Related Aspects of Intellectual Property Rights (TRIPS).

▶ **Business climate**

Business customs are Western. For men, normal business wear is a suit. Lunches and cocktail receptions are common business events. International mail, telephone, fax and e-mail services are reliable. The official language is English but French and Creole are used in everyday life.

⚝ Morocco

As the African country closest to Europe, Morocco's economic fate is closely tied to markets across the Mediterranean sea. Separated from Spain by the 13 kilometer Strait of Gibraltar, most of Morocco's trade is directed towards the European Union but there is a concerted effort to expand business relations with the United States. Despite diversity and the lingering Western Sahara dispute, Morocco is one of the most stable countries in the Arab world, due largely to the efforts of the late King Hassan, a consummate politician. It has the largest phosphate reserves in the world, a thriving agricultural sector, rich fisheries, a sizeable tourist industry, and a growing manufacturing sector. Since the early 1980s Morocco has pursued an IMF- and World Bank-driven economic reform program that has led to rising per capita incomes, lower inflation, and smaller deficits.

Country profile

The Kingdom of Morocco is part of a region dominated by the Atlas Mountains that extends into Algeria and Tunisia. The port city of Ceuta at Morocco's northernmost point is Spanish territory, as is Mellila further east. Mount Toubkal in the High Atlas is 13,670 ft (4,165 m) above sea level and snow-capped during much of the year. The much lower Anti-Atlas mountains stretch into in the desert borderlands with large clusters of oases. Between the Atlantic coast and the mountain ranges is fertile agricultural land. Earthquakes sometimes occur and in 1960 one razed Agadir, causing the death of some 15,000 people. About 60% of the population is of Arab and mixed Arabo-Berber origin and speak Arabic, while the remainder still converse in various Berber dialects. Arabic is the official language but French is widely used in business, government and education. Many people in the far north speak Spanish. Islam is the state religion and but there are about 100,000 Christians, mainly Roman Catholic, and several thousand Jews.

History

When the Phoenicians started trading with the region it was already occupied by people of caucasoid origin. These Africans were called barbarians by the ancient Greeks and Romans and the name Berber is probably derived from *barberoi* (Greek) or *barbari* (Latin). Arab-Muslim conquerors in the course of the 7th Century succeeded in converting many Berbers to Islam. Marriages between Arab warriors and Berber women started a

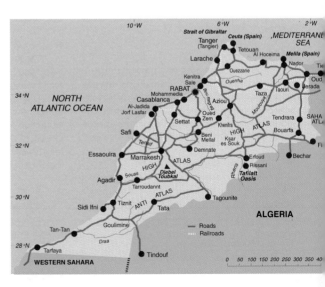

278

process of assimilation. In 1492 the Christians in Spain and Portugal finally overpowered the Moors and caused a considerable migration to Morocco of Muslims and Jews. Following their victory, the Spaniards and Portuguese seized most of the ports along the Maghreb coast. Ceuta and Tanger were already under Portuguese control and Melilla became a Spanish stronghold. In 1684 the city of Tanger, which had been donated to the English by the Portuguese, was reoccupied by the Moroccans. However, Spain held on to Melilla and to Ceuta, which it had acquired from the Portuguese as well. In 1912 France took possession of the larger (central) part of Morocco, with all its important cities, and later that year ceded to Spain two territories to the north and south including Ceuta and Melilla and Rio de Oro (later to become known as the Spanish or Western Sahara). The nationalist opposition in Morocco defeated a combined Franco-Spanish force of over 250,000 in 1926 and forced France to grant it self-government in 1956. Spain had to cede all its possessions except Ceuta, Melilla, Ifni and Spanish Sahara. As the neighboring states (Algeria, Mauritania and Mali) became independent, Morocco claimed, on historic grounds, parts of their territory, as well as the entire Spanish Sahara. King Mohammed V ruled from 1957 until his death in 1961. He was succeeded by his son Mulay Hassan II who ruled until his death in 1999 and was followed to the throne by his heir, King Mohammed VI.

Government

The current constitution, dating back to 1972, combines limited democracy with strong, virtually unlimited royal authority. As head of state, the king may introduce and veto legislation, dissolve the legislature and rule by decree. He appoints the Prime Minister and the cabinet. In 1997 elections the late King Hassan for first time appointed a Prime Minister from the non-royalist grouping in the legislature—74-year old Abderrahmane Youssoufi, leader of the *Union Socialiste des Forces Populaires* or Socialist Union of Popular Forces (USFP). A bicameral parliament consists of a 270-seat *Majlis al-Mustasharin* or Assembly of Counselors elected by local councils, professional organizations, and labor syndicates for nine years, and the *Majlis al-Nuwab*—a 325 seat lower house or Assembly of Representatives elected by popular vote. Both have 5-year terms. The *Rassemblement National des Indé-*

Fast facts

POLITICAL

Head of State	King Mohammed VI (1999)
Prime Minister	Abderrahmane Youssofi (1998)
Ruling Party	USFP
Opposition parties	RNI, UC, MDS
Independence	2 March 1956
National capital	Rabat
Official language	Arabic

PHYSICAL

Total area	172,413 sq. miles 446,550 sq. km. (± California)
Arable land	21% of land area
Coastline	1,140 miles/1,835 km

POPULATION

Total	29.7 million
Av. yearly growth	1.84%
Population/sq. mile	175
Urban population	46%
Adult literacy	47%

ECONOMY[1]

Currency	Moroccan dirham (DH) (US$1=11.66)
GDP (real)	$37.6 billion
GDP growth rate	-0.7%
GNP per capita[2]	$1,260
GDP (ppp)[3]	$107 billion
GDP per cap. (ppp)[3]	$3,200
Inflation rate	3.0%
Exports	$6.6 billion
Imports	$9.7 billion
Development aid	$485 million
External debt	$20.24 billion
Unemployment	19%

INFRASTRUCTURE

Railroads	1,900 km
Paved roads	50%
Motor vehicles	1.2 million
Air passenger/km	4.6 billion
Telephones/1,000	38 (1994)
International airport	Casablanca
Main harbor	Casablanca

1. Statistics are based on World Bank data.
2. Atlas method.
3. See page 151 for an explanation of GDP based on purchasing power parity (ppp).

pendents or National Rally of Independents (RNI) dominates the Chamber of Counsellors with 42 seats, followed by the *Mouvement Démocratique et Social* or Social Democratic Movement (MDS) with 33. In the Assembly of Representatives the USFP holds a majority with 57 seats over the *Union Constitutionelle* or Constitutional Union (UC) with 50, the RNI with 46, and several others.

Economic policy

Since 1983 IMF-style economic reform, including fiscal caution and privatization, has been practiced. Morocco has agreed to the creation by 2010 of a free trade area with the EU which will force Moroccan producers to become more amenable to foreign partnerships. The country has also expressed the desire eventually to become a full member of the EU.

Sectors

Agriculture, fishing and forestry employ about 35% of the working population, account for 15% of GDP and contribute about 25% of the country's export revenues. At 21% a comparatively high proportion of the total area is arable and utilized by large-scale commercial farmers, producing citrus and wine—apart from numerous peasant smallholders. The principal food crops are wheat, barley, maize and vegetables. Sugar cane, sugar beet, olives and cotton are major industrial crops but the principal agricultural exports are citrus, tomatoes, canned fruit, vegetables and wine. The country is self-sufficient in livestock production, mainly sheep. Canned fish and fresh fish, including shellfish, account for around 14% of total exports. Together with Western Sahara, Morocco accounts for 75% of the world's known phosphate reserves and is, after Russia and the US, the world's third largest producer. Other mineral resources include silver, zinc, copper, fluorine, lead, barite, and iron. Coal production is far below domestic demand and output from limited petroleum deposits is negligible. Manufacturing consists largely of textile and clothing. Ancient cities, beach resorts and good weather contribute to a growing tourist industry.

Privatization

Since 1992 when it launched its privatization program, Morocco has sold about half of its 114 state enterprises. Apart from sugar plants, hotels, and banks, the state telecommunications monopoly Maroc Telecom and Royal Air Maroc are scheduled for partial privatization, either through public offerings at the Casablanca Stock Exchange or strategic partnerships.

Investment

Foreign investment has grown considerably since privatization started and the government opened infrastructural projects to private participation, especially in electricity generation and telephone services. US investment is mostly in manufacturing and distribution of petroleum, food, chemicals, industrial machinery and electric and electronic equipment.

Trade

The export of phosphates and derivatives accounts for over a quarter of the total. Morocco is a net exporter of fruits and vegetables, but a net importer of cereals. Textile and clothing comprise 70% of all manufactured exports. The country's industrial exports enjoy virtually free access to the European Union (EU), but many agricultural exports are still limited by tariff and non-tariff barriers. Almost two-thirds of all exports go to the EU, with the US , India and Libya among the other significant purchasers.

Business activity

AGRICULTURE

Barley, wheat, citrus, wine, vegetables, olives, livestock.

INDUSTRIES

Phosphate rock mining and processing, food processing, leather goods, textiles, construction, tourism.

NATURAL RESOURCES

Phosphates, iron ore, zinc, fish, salt, lead, manganese.

EXPORTS

$6.6 billion (1999 est.): food and beverages, semiprocessed goods, consumer goods, phosphates.

IMPORTS

$9.7 billion (1999 est.): semiprocessed goods, capital goods, food and beverages, fuel and lubricants, consumer goods, raw materials.

MAJOR TRADING PARTNERS

EU, Japan, India, US, Libya, Saudi Arabia, Brazil.

Financial sector

Banking is modeled after the French system. There are 12 major banks, five government-owned specialized financial institutions, some 15 credit agencies and 10 leasing companies. Insurance companies, pension funds, and a stock market are the other components of a modern, well developed financial sector. Banks are supervised on a consolidated basis and must provide statements audited by certified public accountants. The Casablanca stock exchange enjoyed a recent revival after new laws made it more efficient and transparent.

Taxes and tariffs

A three-part system consists of a value-added tax, a corporate income tax, and an individual income tax. Even though Morocco gradually reduced barriers to trade over the last decade, the level of protection still remains relatively high. Most imports are subject to customs duties to a maximum of 35%, apart from a surcharge of between 10% and 15%. A value-added tax (TVA) of between 7% and 19% applies to both locally-produced and imported goods.

Western Sahara

At present the territory is administered by Morocco as part of its greater Southern Region but Western Sahara has also been proclaimed the Saharan Arab Democratic Republic (SADR) by a government-in-exile in Algeria, headed by rebel Mohammed Abdal-Aziz. The population of this disputed territory, currently under UN observation, is awaiting a referendum to decide whether they wish to become part of Morocco or establish an independent state.

As Algeria, Mauritania and Mali became independent, Morocco had laid claims on historic grounds to parts of their territory, as well as the entire Spanish Sahara. The latter claim was pursued forcefully by King Hassan. After a proposed UN referendum on the future of the territory failed to materialize, Western Saharan voters were allowed to participate in Moroccan elections in 1993.

Profile

Western Sahara's covers an area of 252,000 km consisting of a low plateau and desert, scattered oases and dry river beds. It shares contested borders with Morocco, Algeria and Mauritania. The climate along the 1,500 km coastline is moderated by the Northern Atlantic Ocean's cold Canaries current. Most of its 220,000 inhabitants (not including thousands of refugees in adjoining lands) are Muslim. They call themselves Saharans or Sadirawi and are of mixed Arabo-Berber origin. The largest group is the northern Tekna, who are preponderantly Berber and related to the inhabitants of southern Morocco. The Regeihat and the Imragen along the coast are nomadic fishermen. Arabic and Berber dialects are widely spoken, apart from a smattering of French and Spanish. More than 80% of the population is concentrated in Al-Aaiun (Laayoune) and settlements along the Saguia al-Hamra Valley in the far north.

Economy

Crop growing, mainly for subsistence, takes place at the numerous oases, and goats, sheep and camels are raised along the coast where the moisture sustains some pasturage. Both the rich offshore fishing waters and vast phosphate deposits at Boukra (Bou Craa) are important economic resources for Morocco. The phosphate rock is transported on a 62 mile (100 km) conveyor belt to the port of Al-Aaiun. The northern region of Western Sahara has greatly benefited from the Moroccan government's large spending on military operations in recent years. In the process, social services, housing and sport facilities, roads, air transport, postal services and telecommunications have been improved. By developing the economy of the region, creating employment opportunities, and improving social services the Moroccan government aims not only at foster goodwill among the locals but also to encourage its own citizens to settle here.

History

At different stages and even as late as the mid-18th Century a vast region—including present-day Western Sahara, southwestern Algeria and much of what is today Mauritania and Mali—was controlled by the successive ruling dynasties in Morocco's Marrakesh, Fes and Meknes areas. The nomadic desert peoples, however, continued to resist the so-called *makhzan* or world of government control. In 1884, during the "scramble" for Africa, Spain grabbed a piece of this desert and declared a protectorate over it. When the territory's international borders were finally established, Spain controlled only the coastlands. The discovery of rich phosphate deposits at Boukra in 1963 intensified the resistance to Spanish domination and stimulated a desire for independence among the indigenous inhabitants. Responding to their appeals, the UN General Assembly adopted several resolutions from 1967 to 1973, condemning the Spanish presence in Western Sahara and affirming the right of the Saharans to self-determination. The *Frente Popular para la Liberacion de Saguia al-Hamray Rio de Oro* (Polisario) was founded in 1973.

Takeover

Under pressure from the Polisario, the UN and Morocco, Spain decided to hold a referendum in Western Sahara on the independence issue. With the referendum still pending, a UN mission reported that the majority of Saharans whom it consulted in the territory were in favor of independence and rejected Morocco's territorial claims. This was interpreted by an infuriated King Hassan as an attempt to influence the outcome of the referendum. Hassan had in the meantime struck a deal with Mauritania to partition Western Sahara between them to counter Algeria in its support of the Polisario. In November 1975 King Hassan responded to the untimely UN interference by mobilizing Moroccans of all political parties and persuasions to stage a massive peaceful march into Western Sahara. In what was known as the Green March, some 350,000 Koran-bearing civilians obliged Spain to capitulate and evacuate, allowing Moroccan troops to move in. A subsequent tripartite agreement between Spain, Morocco and Mauritania paved the way for a formal partitioning of the area between Morocco and Mauritania in 1976. Morocco claimed the phosphate-rich northern two-thirds of the territory and Mauritania the remainder, including the port of Dakhla. In 1997, Mauritania dropped its territorial claims, leaving the way clear for Morocco to expand its influence over all of Western Sahara.

SADR

In defiance the Polisario proclaimed the Saharan Arab Democratic Republic (SADR) and set up a government-in-exile in Algeria, a move that resulted in severance of diplomatic relations between Morocco and Algeria. Thousands of Polisario supporters followed their leaders into exile, settling around the oasis of Tindouf, not far from Algeria's border with Western Sahara. The Polisario subsequently embarked on a guerrilla war against Morocco and Mauritania. In the 1980s it also managed to obtain recognition for its "independent republic" when a majority of OAU member states conferred membership on the SADR over objections and the eventual resignation from the organization by Morocco. Some 70 UN member states recognize the SADR but lately support among African states has begun to erode.

Recent developments

In recent years relations between Morocco and its neighbors have been improving. Algeria joined with Morocco and several others in the Arab Maghreb Union. A cease-fire agreement between Morocco and the Polisario was concluded on 6 September 1991 and a UN Mission for the Organization of the Referendum in the Sahara (Minurso) was established to oversee Western Sahara until the quarrelling parties agree on the details of a long-awaited referendum. In the meantime the integration of Western Sahara into Morocco, continues steadily and it seems increasingly likely that the outcome of the referendum will favor the status quo.

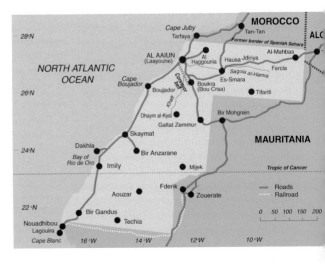

Doing Business with Morocco

▶ Investment

Apart from agricultural land and a few sectors still reserved for the state such as phosphate mining, air and rail transport, and public utilities, foreign participation is strongly encouraged. Under Morocco's privatization program most of these restricted areas are expected to be opened up. A Moroccanization decree limiting foreign ownership in the petroleum refining and distribution sector was repealed and allowed, among others, Mobil Oil to buy back the government's 50 percent share of its local subsidiary. There are no foreign investor performance requirements and incentives apply. In the building of power plants, telephone network expansion and other infrastructure developments the government relies largely on foreign entrepreneurs.

▶ Trade

The favored port of entry is Casablanca and foreign manufacturers and exporters are represented in the market either through their own affiliate branch office or by authorized agent/distributors who import, install and service the equipment. There seems to be ample scope in the fast food sector. Additional franchising opportunities include hotels and motels, automotive parts and services, dry cleaning business equipment and services. Among the top prospects for sales are water distribution equipment, electrical power systems, pollution control, mining, medical and telecommunications equipment, computers and software, and architectural, engineering, tourism and other services. Agricultural needs range from large quantities of wheat to vegetable oil, sugar, and cotton.

▶ Trade finance

Local financing is available for Moroccan investors and importers, but real interest rates are high by overseas standards. Most Moroccan imports are by irrevocable confirmed letters but intense competition at times requires attractive payment terms. The Eximbank provides assistance to US exporters and the US Department of Agriculture extends credit guarantee programs.

▶ Selling to the government

While government purchases are at times directly negotiated, tenders are common. So-called medium and major projects are open to international firms while minor ones are reserved for locals. Major projects are often guaranteed by an international financial entity.

▶ Exchange controls

Foreign exchange is available through the commercial banks upon presentation of documents for the repatriation of dividends and capital by foreign investors, for remittances by foreign residents, and for payments for foreign technical assistance, royalties and licenses.

▶ Partnerships

There is growing local interest joint ventures and at latest count 1,500 have been operating in the manufacturing sector, mostly with French, Spanish and German partners.

▶ Establishing a presence

To form a local company foreigners merely need to file documents with the Secretariat of the Court of First Instance.

▶ Financing projects

In most instances project financing comes from the World Bank, the African Development Bank, the European Investment Bank, the Kuwaiti Fund, the Saudi Fund and the Abu Dhabi Fund.

▶ Labor

Workers are free to form and join unions but only about 6% of Morocco's nine million workers are unionized, mostly in the public sector. Collective bargaining has, however, been a long-standing tradition in some parts of the economy, notably heavy industry.

▶ Legal rights

The law protects and facilitates acquisition and disposition of property rights, including intellectual property rights. Morocco is a member of the World Intellectual Property Organization and party to the Berne copyright, Paris industrial property, and universal copyright conventions. Still dating from the era of French and Spanish protectorates is the requirement that patent and trademark applications to be filed in both Casablanca and Tangier. Morocco is a member of the International Center for the Settlement of Investment Disputes and a party to the 1958 convention on the recognition and enforcement of foreign arbitrary awards.

▶ Business climate

Morocco is a Muslim country and business meetings are best avoided on Friday. Although Arabic is the official language, French is widely used.

Mozambique

Mozambique has accomplished a meteoric rise in fortunes through newfound political stability and sound economic policies that lured foreign investment and trade. Inflation has been slashed from 70% to an average of 8% and real GDP growth has risen by between 7.5 and 11% per year. In an ironic twist Mozambique was hit by devastating floods early in 2000, just after the Economist Intelligence Unit reported it likely to have the highest economic growth rate on the continent for the year. The country is in the process of recovering from this disaster.

Country profile

Much of the Republic of Mozambique consists of a coastal plain and lowland less than 500 m above sea level. The Zambezi River is the largest of 25 rivers in the region. The climate is hot and humid, with temperatures and rainfall rising to the north. Most of the people are Bantu-speaking. The Makua and Lomwe account for 40% of the total. Other inhabitants range from the Yao, Makonde, Sena, Chewa, Shona, to the Tsonga, and Shangaan. Minority groups such as the mestizos (people of mixed descent), Indians and whites—Portuguese and a growing number of South Africans—are prominent in the economy. Portuguese is the official language, but English is widely spoken in business and professional circles.

History

In ancient times northern Mozambique formed part of the trade network in slaves, gold and ivory between Arabs and Persians and the Bantu kingdom of Mwene Mutapa. Intermarriage between these merchants and their African slaves gave rise to a distinct Swahili culture. Portuguese involvement started in 1498 when Vasco da Gama reached Mozambique Island. By 1510 the Portuguese had control of all the former Arab sultanates on the east African coast. Portugal participated in the partitioning of Africa among the European powers in the last two decades of the 19th Century and Mozambique took its present shape on the map in 1890. Mozambique was ruled as an overseas Portuguese

province. In 1964 the *Frente da Libertação de Moçambique* or Liberation Front of Mozambique (Frelimo), led by Dr. Eduardo Mondlane, began an armed revolt against the Portuguese rulers. The struggle was continued after his death in 1969 by Samora Moises Machel. After a military coup in

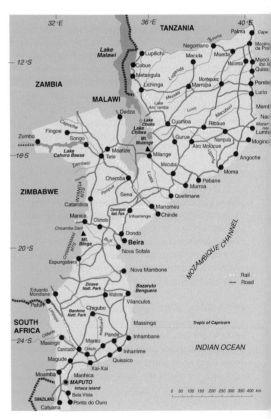

Portugal in 1974, a peace agreement was concluded and on 25 June 1975, 470 years of Portuguese rule ended. Machel became president of an independent Mozambique. Asset-stripping by the fleeing Portuguese, Marxist-Leninist centralization and nationalization, and a paralyzing and costly five year civil war against the *Resistencia Nacional Moçambicana* or Mozambican National Resistance (Renamo), which was aided by white-ruled South Africa and Rhodesia, contributed to the country's rapid economic decay. In October 1986 President Machel was killed when his aircraft crashed close to the South African-Mozambican border. Following the collapse of the Soviet Union, Machel's successor, President Joaquim Alberto Chissano, turned to the West and post-apartheid South Africa to jump start the economy. A general peace agreement between Frelimo and Renamo led to the adoption of a new democratic constitution in 1994. In November 1995, Mozambique was the first non-former-British colony to become a member of the Commonwealth.

Government

Under the new constitution, both the president and the 250-member unicameral Assembly, or the *Assembleia da República,* are elected for 5-year terms. President Joaquim Chissano, who served as president in his capacity as leader of Frelimo, was reconfirmed as head of state in open elections in 1994 and 1999. In the most recent election he defeated his Renamo rival, Afonso Marceta Macacho Dhlakama, by 52.2% against 47.7% of the popular vote. With 133 seats Frelimo maintains a majority in the Assembly over Renamo with its 117 seats, and a few minor parties.

Economic policy

In the 1990s the failed Marxist policies were abandoned in favor of free market practices. Preisdent Chissano's disciplined economic plans drew favorable response from abroad. Mozambique's creditors decided to write off most of its debt and investors took notice. Inflation was brought down from 70% in 1994 to 6% in 1997 and 1998 growth in excess of 11% was attained, placing it among the top performers worldwide. In 1999 relinary figures show a growth rate of 7.3%. Both the IMF and World Bank are involved in the process and privatization is proceeding well. Outside investors are reacting positively to the improved climate in Mozambique. Early in 2000,

Fast facts

POLITICAL

Head of State	Pres. Joaquim Alberto Chissano (1986)
Ruling Party	Frelimo
Main Opposition	Renamo
Independence	25 June 1975
National capital	Maputo
Official language	Portuguese

PHYSICAL

Total area	302,737 sq. miles 784,090 sq. km. (±2 x California)
Arable land	4% of land area
Coastline	1,535 miles/2,470 km

POPULATION

Total	19.1 million
Av. yearly growth	2.54%
Population/sq. mile	19
Urban population	30%
Adult literacy	42%

ECONOMY[1]

Currency	Metical (Mt) (US$1=21,050)
GDP (real)	$3.19 billion
GDP growth rate	7.3%
GNP per capita[2]	$210
GDP (ppp)[3]	$16.8 billion
GDP per cap. (ppp)[3]	$900
Inflation rate	-1.3%
Exports	$465 million
Imports	$1.5 billion
Development aid	$1 billion
External debt	$6.3 billion
Unemployment	N/A

INFRASTRUCTURE

Railroads	1,945 miles/3,130 km
Paved roads	18%
Motor vehicles	111,000
Air passenger/km	443 million
Telephones/1,000	4
International airport	Maputo
Main harbors	Maputo, Beira

1. Statistics are based on World Bank data.
2. Atlas method.
3. See page 151 for an explanation of GDP based on purchasing power parity (ppp).

Mozambique experienced a severe setback as devastating floods not only took a heavy toll in human lives but washed away much of its impressive economic gains.

Sectors

Agriculture is the mainstay of the economy, employing up to 60% of the workforce, mainly in subsistence farming. Principal cash crops are cashew nuts, tea, sugar, sisal, cotton, copra and oil seeds. Maize is the main subsistence crop, but cassava, millet, sorghum, groundnuts, beans and rice are also grown. The country has a rich variety of minerals including large deposits of iron and bauxite ore and coal, tantalite (used in the electronics industry and for special steels) and pegmatite (a source of tantalite), beryl, mica, bismuth and semiprecious stones. Along the coast are also titanium-bearing beach sands. Plans are underway to develop the large natural gas fields at Pande, west of Inhambane, and in the Buzi swamps, near Beira. Manufacturing includes food processing and industrial crops, fertilizer, agricultural implements, cement, textiles, beverages, ceramics, wood processing, tires, and radios. Pristine beaches and national wildlife parks are important tourism assets. Once extensive civil war damage is repaired, Cahora Bassa Dam on the Zambezi—Africa's largest hydropower station in after Aswan High in Egypt—will be capable of supplying not only the needs of Mozambique but those of its neighbors.

Privatization

Over 900 state-owned enterprises have been sold including a cement plant, flour mills, breweries, commercial agriculture operations, cashew processing plants, and fishing and trading companies. The management of coal, sugar, citrus, and container terminals at ports has been entrusted to private consortia. In most of these transactions, there was substantial foreign participation. As a final step to privatizing the financial sector, two of the country's largest state-owned banks have been sold.

Investment

Just under $4 billion in foreign direct investment has been registered during the past five years. South Africa surpassed Britain and Portugal as the most important source of investment after its Industrial Development Corporation (IDC) became an active participant in large projects such as the Mozal plant. Several major US firms have also become involved. These projects, along with the toll road under construction from South Africa and the upgrading of the port of Maputo should provide the impetus for further investment along what has been dubbed the Maputo Development Corridor.

Trade

Exports consist largely of cashews, sugar, cotton, and other agricultural commodities, textiles, seafood, and minerals. In the foreseeable future sales of electric power, natural gas and related products, as well as tourism, is expected to cure the chronic negative current account balance.

Financial sector

Nowhere is the dramatic effect of recent reforms more apparent than in the banking system. The Banco de Mozambique, which acted as both the central bank and the major commercial bank in the past has been replaced by a separate central bank and a number of private banks. HSBC Equator Bank provides services.

Taxes and tariffs

The corporate income, capital gains and branch tax rates in Mozambique are 35% for agricultural companies, 40% for industrial companies, and 45% for all others. A withholding tax of 18% applies to dividends, and 5% to interest.

Business activity

AGRICULTURE

Cotton, cashew nuts, sugar cane, tea, cassava (tapioca), corn, rice, tropical fruit, beef, poultry.

INDUSTRIES

Food, beverages, chemicals (fertilizer, soap, paints), petroleum products, textiles, cement, glass, asbestos, tobacco.

NATURAL RESOURCES

Coal, titanium, natural gas.

EXPORTS

$465 million (1999 est.): shrimp, cashews, cotton, sugar, copra, citrus.

IMPORTS

$1.5 billion (1999 est.): food, clothing, farm equipment, petroleum.

MAJOR TRADING PARTNERS

Spain, South Africa, Portugal, US, Japan, Malawi, India, Zimbabwe, Saudi Arabia.

Doing Business with Mozambique

▶ **Investment**

The Investment Promotion Center (CPI) offers a variety of tax incentives according to regions and the type of investment. Specific performance requirements are built into mining concessions and management contracts and sometimes into the sale of state-owned entities. Approval for investment follows automatically in 10 days if no objections are voiced by the relevant ministries, provincial governor (for investments under $100,000), or the Minister of Planning and Finance (in the case of investments under $100 million). The Council of Ministers must review investments over $100 million as well as those involving large tracts of land. Legislation supports the creation of "Industrial Free Zones." There are good opportunities in energy, mining, fishing, timber, tourism, agriculture and manufacturing of inexpensive goods.

▶ **Trade**

Trade opportunities exist in the energy, mining, fishing, timber, tourism, and agriculture (cashews, cotton, and sugar) sectors. There is a growing demand for construction, telecommunications, agricultural, plastic, food processing and packaging and fishing equipment. Planned new projects such as an aluminum smelter, natural gas pipelines, a direct reduced iron and steel plant, and new mineral sands processing are bound to increase the demand for engineering and construction equipment and expertise. Wheat, rice, and edible oils are imported in reasonably large quantities.

▶ **Trade finance**

Eximbank provides short-, medium-, and long-term financing to US exporters. The US Trade and Development Agency assists with feasibility studies and reverse trade missions.

▶ **Selling to the government**

Major government purchases might be subject to the procurement rules set by international donors as Mozambique often relies on outside financial support. It is, however, necessary for bidders to establish personal contacts within the government and to keep abreast of frequent changes in the procurement process.

▶ **Exchange controls**

Repatriation of profits and repayment of offshore loans have become routine. Investment laws guarantee foreign investors the right to remit loan repayments, dividends, profits and invested capital abroad.

▶ **Partnerships**

Joint ventures are encouraged by the government and can help ease potential problems with regulatory issues and red tape. The government itself favors partnerships with foreign firms in privatization deals.

▶ **Establishing a presence**

The official Investment Promotion Center (CPI) has developed a package of services to assist foreign investors with this process.

▶ **Financing projects**

OPIC has an Investment Incentive Agreement in place. Mozambique is also a member of the Multilateral Investment Guarantee Agency. Some major projects are financed by the World Bank, the African Development Bank, and donor agencies such as USAID. The International Finance Corporation and the Commonwealth Development Corporation provide medium-term loans and equity finance in Mozambique. The US government-sponsored $100 million Southern African Enterprise Development Fund (SAEDF) assists Mozambican entrepreneurs out of its Johannesburg offices.

▶ **Labor**

Most working Mozambicans derive income from more than one activity, and grow corn and vegetables on small parcels of land for personal consumption. Labor unions, created during the socialist years, are gradually asserting their independence from the ruling Frelimo Party.

▶ **Legal rights**

The government grants land-use concessions for periods of up to 50 years with options to renew. Foreign investors have recourse to arbitration through the UNCITRAL (United Nations Commission on International Trade Law) model. The government has also acceded to the New York Convention on the Recognition and Enforcement of Foreign Arbitral Awards. Mozambique has signed the Bern Convention on International Copyrights, as well as the New York and Paris Conventions. Intellectual property right infringement is not considered a significant problem.

▶ **Business climate**

Portuguese is widely spoken but the use of English is growing in business circles. The business community in Maputo is small enough for most to know each other.

Namibia

Despite its sparse population and lack of rainfall, Namibia seems poised to become a convenient gateway to the growing Southern African regional market. Good infrastructure and an efficient, deep-water port at Walvis Bay, coupled with a strong mining and agricultural base, make Namibia a good candidate for investment and future trade. In its effort to bring previously-disadvantaged Namibians into the economic mainstream via private sector commercial development, the Namibian government is actively courting foreign investors. Since independence, personal and corporate tax rates have been cut to improve the business climate.

Country profile

The Republic of Namibia consists of three regions running from north to south: the Namib Desert along the coast, the great escarpment which reaches its highest elevation at the Auas mountains near Windhoek, and the semi-arid Kalahari Basin continuing into Botswana and South Africa. Average annual rainfall for the country is only 270 mm—about 70% of the land is classified as arid and 22% as desert. Underground water sources sustain large herds of cattle on the northern savanna pastures and sheep, including karakul, on the desert scrub in the south. Wildlife abounds and is protected in a number of nature reserves and wilderness areas. The three Bantu-speaking groups—the Ovambo, Kavango and Herero—account for about two-thirds of the population. Whites comprise about 5 percent of the total. Even though English is the official language, Afrikaans is widely spoken, as well as some German. More than 90% of the population is Christian.

History

The San and Nama or Khoikhoi peoples were already in the region 500 years ago when Ovambo and Kavango groups migrated south from present-day Angola. In the 19th Century German merchants settled in the territory around the British possession of Walvis Bay. German forces moved inland to claim what became known as German West Africa, almost annihilating the Herero and the Nama in the process. During the First World War South Africa defeated the Germans in the territory and in 1919 the League of Nations confirmed its control over the mandate of South West Africa (SWA). South African attempts after the Second World War to incorporate the territory instead of submitting it to the control of the newly-formed UN Trusteeship Coun-

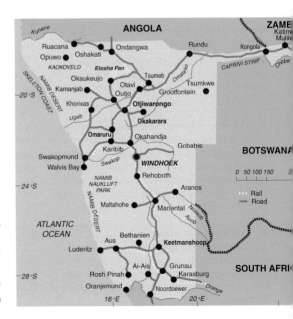

cil led to a lengthy political struggle in the UN. The South West African Peoples Organization (SWAPO), under leadership of Sam Daniel Shafiishuna Nujoma, resorted to arms in 1966 after the International Court of Justice gave a ruling favorable to the South African government. In 1988, a US-inspired peace agreement ended hostilities on the northern border where South Africa was engaged in a protracted battle with Cuban and Angolan MPLA troops, assisted by SWAPO commandos. SWAPO emerged as the victor in an election held in 1989 under supervision of a UN Transitional Assistance Group (UNTAG) and on 21 March 1990, Nujoma was sworn in as president of independent Namibia. He has been re-elected twice since.

Government

The executive President is elected for a 5-year term. He appoints the Prime Minister and other cabinet ministers. The 78-member National Assembly is also elected for 5 years on a party-list proportional basis, while the 26-member National Council—elected every six years by the Regional Councils—serves as an upper house. Nujoma's Swapo has maintained more than a two-thirds majority since independence. In December 1999 Nujoma was reelected president with 76.8% of the total vote against the 10.5% of his nearest rival, Ben Ulenga of the Congress of Democrats (CoD). Swapo captured 55 seats in the National Assembly against the CoD's and the Democratic Turnhalle Alliance's (DTA) 7 seats each. There are also a few smaller parties represented.

Economic policy

There is considerable state involvement in sectors such as postal services, telecommunications, development banking, electricity and water supply, transport, and agricultural commodity marketing. The government has advocated an interventionist role in major infrastructure projects or "high risk ventures" where the private sector is reluctant to participate. At the same time, it has adopted a free market-based investment code with wide-ranging incentives to encourage foreign and local private sector involvement. The goal is to diversify the economy away from heavy dependence on diamonds, uranium, and base metals. Outstanding external debt is among the lowest in Africa, helped by South African President Nelson Mandela's decision in 1995 to write off $200 million owed to South Africa.

Fast facts

POLITICAL

Head of State	Pres. Sam Daniel Shafiishuna Nujoma (1990)
Ruling Party	Swapo
Main Opposition	CoD & DTA
Independence	21 March 1990
National capital	Windhoek
Official language	English

PHYSICAL

Total area	318,694 sq. miles 825,418 sq. km. (½ x Alaska)
Arable land	1% of land area
Coastline	977 miles/1,572 km

POPULATION

Total	1.65 million
Av. yearly growth	1.57%
Population/sq. mile	6
Urban population	36%
Adult literacy	71%

ECONOMY[1]

Currency	Namibian dollar (N$) (US$1=8.23)
GDP (real)	$3.54 billion
GDP growth rate	3.1%
GNP per capita[2]	$1,940
GDP (ppp)[3]	$6.6 billion
GDP per cap. (ppp)[3]	$4,100
Inflation rate	7.0%
Exports	$1.6 billion
Imports	$1.95 billion
Development aid	$174 million
External debt	$178 million
Unemployment	30%

INFRASTRUCTURE

Railroads	1,479 miles/2,380 km
Paved roads	8%
Air passenger/km	751 million
Telephones/1,000	45
International airport	Windhoek
Main harbor	Walvis Bay

1. Statistics are based on World Bank data.
2. Atlas method.
3. See page 151 for an explanation of GDP based on purchasing power parity (ppp).

Sectors

Namibia ranks among the top 20 mining countries in the world. It is a major producer of uranium, pyrites, cadmium, arsenic, gold, silver, fluorspar, and semi-precious stones, but gem quality diamonds are the country's largest generator of foreign exchange. Large offshore natural gas reserves have been discovered. Even though the agricultural sector forms only 11.7% of Namibia's GDP, 70% of the population depend on it. Cattle raising is predominant in the central and northern regions, while karakul sheep, goat, and ostrich are raised in the south. Pilchard, hake, horse mackerel, anchovy and rock lobster are the main catches off the Namibian coast, rated among the world's richest fishing grounds. The primary industrial activity in the country (excluding mining) is meat and fish processing. The tourism industry, currently at 7% of GDP, is expected to grow rapidly.

Privatization

Even though the state continues to control key economic sectors such as electricity, telephones, water, the national airline and the railway, it is moving towards private sector-led growth, Despite strong union opposition, it is proceeding with privatization of select state-owned companies, with minority shares reserved for black empowerment groups.

Investment

The five major foreign investor countries in Namibia are South Africa, Germany, Britain, the US and Malaysia. Namibia obtained a stake in the diamond industry previously monopolized by De Beers in 1994 when it struck an agreement with the company that gave the state a 50 percent share of the new entity, NAMDEB. Diamond output was boosted further through offshore mining by the UK-based Namibian Minerals Corporation. Other mining opportunities such as the Australian owned Haib copper prospect in the far south are among recent areas of focus. Shell has identified a promising gas field offshore that could make the country a significant energy exporter in the next century.

Trade

Exports consist largely of gem-quality diamonds, uranium, base metals, cattle, karakul hides and fish. Namibia's export earnings exceed 50% of the GDP. Imports are similarly high. Around 85% of Namibia's imports originate in or transit through South Africa.

Financial sector

The Bank of Namibia has formal authority over the country's foreign exchange dealings. Namibia enjoys good creditworthiness in international financial circles, and is eligible to draw on the resources of the IMF, the World Bank, and the African Development Bank. Commercial banks provide comprehensive domestic and international services. ABSA is a large service provider in the banking sector. The Namibian Stock Exchange (NSE), which relies in part on double listings of major South African firms, is the second largest African stock market in terms of value of shares listed.

Taxes and tariffs

The corporate tax rate in Namibia is 35% but special breaks are offered as incentives to manufacturers establishing themselves in designated regions where development and job creation are needed. A general sales tax of 8% is levied at the point of final sale. This tax is applied to all products, including those imported through the SACU. Most imports coming in from non-SACU states are dutiable.

Business activity

AGRICULTURE
Millet, sorghum, peanuts, livestock, fish.

INDUSTRIES
Meat packing, fish processing, dairy products, mining (diamond, lead, zinc, tin, silver, tungsten, uranium, copper).

NATURAL RESOURCES
Diamonds, copper, uranium, gold, lead, tin, lithium, cadmium, zinc, salt, vanadium, natural gas, fish, suspected deposits of oil, coal, iron ore.

EXPORTS
$1.6 billion (1999 est.): diamonds, copper, gold, zinc, lead, uranium, cattle, processed fish, karakul skins.

IMPORTS
$1.95 billion (1999 est.): foodstuffs, petroleum products and fuel, machinery and equipment, chemicals.

MAJOR TRADING PARTNERS
UK, South Africa, US, Spain, Japan, Germany.

Doing Business with Namibia

▶ **Investment**

An Investment Center within the Ministry of Trade and Industry assists foreign investors. Investment and tax incentives are available for new and existing manufacturing firms, and an Export Processing Zone (EPZ) has been set up at the port of Walvis Bay. A well-developed infrastructure in Namibia is a good asset for prospective foreign investors looking at Namibia as a gateway to the Southern Africa region. The fishing, tourism, manufacturing, mining, water and energy sectors offer prospects for development and expansion by foreign entrepreneurs.

▶ **Trade**

Namibia, with its solid managerial and physical infrastructure, provides a useful springboard to the central and southern African markets. Useful areas for exporters are agricultural equipment and chemicals, consumer food products, and telecommunications equipment. South African and German-linked concerns dominate the marketing and distribution networks and many of the product line markets.

▶ **Trade finance**

The Eximbank provides insurance and guarantees for US exporters to Namibia. The US Department of Agriculture provides credit guarantees for up to three years for qualifying exports.

▶ **Selling to the government**

Government purchases are usually by tender. Often Namibian government needs are too modest to interest the larger US supplier, but there are notable exceptions. In an effort to diversify sources of supply, the government contracted in late 1996 with Detroit-based Barden International to supply more than 800 General Motors vehicles to its motor pool. Barden invested about $15 million in right-hand drive conversion at a plant in Windhoek.

▶ **Exchange controls**

Under the CMA Agreement, the South African rand is also legal tender and exchange controls are similar to those applied in South Africa.

▶ **Partnerships**

The government sometimes allocates business rights to Namibian companies on more favorable terms. For example, in the fishing sector joint ventures with Namibian concession holders are obiviously the best route for foreigners.

▶ **Establishing a presence**

A presence may be in the form of a public or private company, branch of a foreign company, partnership, joint venture, or as a sole trader. A branch of a foreign company must register within 21 days of establishing itself in Namibia. Namibian accountants and auditors should be engaged to ensure strict adherence to local tax and labor laws.

▶ **Financing projects**

The Overseas Private Investment Corporation provides funding and political risk insurance to qualified US investors. Namibia is also a member of the Multilateral Investment Guarantee Agency. Local commercial banks provide project financing in agriculture, commercial fishing, tourism, housing, minerals and mining.

▶ **Labor**

There is a large pool of qualified workers in varying professions but a shortage of highly skilled personnel. A special tax deduction of up to 25% is extended to manufacturing companies that provide technical training. The government will also reimburse companies for costs directly related to employee training under approved conditions. Most workers belong to trade unions. The NUNW, an affiliate of the ruling SWAPO party, represents the workers of seven affiliated trade unions. Wage rates of $200 per month and a 45 hour work week are common. Overtime pay plus annual and maternity leave are standard.

▶ **Legal rights**

Namibia's legal system is based on Roman-Dutch law. The Foreign Investment Act protects investors against expropriation and stipulates steps for the settlement of disputes by international arbitration. The local court system provides an effective means to enforce property and contractual rights. An independent, transparent legal system protects and facilitates acquisition and disposition of property rights. The issue of intellectual property is understood and generally respected by most companies operating in Namibia and, unlike some other developing countries, IPR infringement is not a major problem.

▶ **Business climate**

Business customs are similar to those practiced in neighboring South Africa. Most business with foreigners is conducted in English but among the locals Afrikaans and German are also spoken.

Niger

The Niger river flowing through Sahel terrain is as much of a lifeline for Niger as the Nile is for Sudan and Egypt, both as a source of water and a means of transport. A drastic drop in world demand for uranium has severely damaged this landlocked country's economy. The current emphasis is on exploration and development of alternative mineral resources and the expansion of its agricultural base with the help of foreign investors. Foreign firms have been focusing on gold, coal and oil. Drastic economic reforms have been introduced to make the country more investor-friendly.

Country profile

The Republic of Niger covers a plateau less than 500 m (1,640 ft) high reaching northwards into the Sahara Desert. In the central region the partly volcanic Air Mountains rise to 1,800 m (6,000 ft) above sea level. The perennial Niger River meanders for about 500 km (310 miles) through the southwestern tip of the country. During the flood season from July to September it is navigable by smaller boat and provides irrigation along its banks. The Hausa people extending across the Nigerian border form the largest cultural group, accounting for more than half of Niger's population. The closely related Songhai and Zarma (or Djerma), concentrated along the Niger River, account for about a quarter of the population. These groups and the smaller Kanuri, Daza and Teda factions speak Nilo-Saharan languages. About 10% of the population are Fulani (or Ful) and 3% Tuareg. Over 85% of the population are Muslims, but among some ethnic faiths still prevail.

History

The nomadic Tuaregs were the first inhabitants of this Sahara region. They were followed by the Hausa (14th Century), the Zerma (17th Century), the Goboir (18th Century) and the Fulani. About 1,000 years ago, Arab traders first made contact with the Hausa in the Sahel region and introduced them to the Muslim faith.

The Hausa were subjugated by Songhai around 1500 but regained their independence in 1591. In 1806 Mungo Park, the first European to reach this remote region, encountered Hausa, Songhai, Fulani and Tuareg. In 1903 the French created colonies in the Sahel and southern Sahara, extending from Senegal through French Sudan (Mali) and Upper Volta (Burkina Faso) to Niger. Due to stiff resistance from the Tuareg and Kanuri peoples, France's conquest of Niger was not finalized until 1922. Niger was granted independence in 1960 under Hamani Diori who drove out Marxist rivals headed by his cousin Djibo Bakary. In 1974, Diori was overthrown by Col. Seyni Kountché who invited back Bakary and oth-

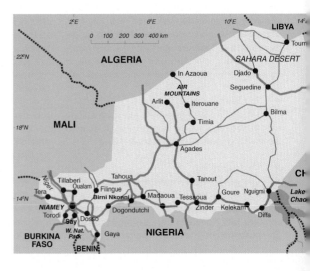

ers and included them in a new government of national unity. When Kountché died in 1987 he was succeeded by Colonel Ali Saibou who solidified one-party rule under the *Mouvement National de la Société de Devéloppement* or National Movement for the Development Society (MNSD). He in turn lost to Mahamane Ousmane and the *Alliance des Forces du Changement* (AFC) in free elections in 1993. Ousmane was ousted in a coup by Ibrahim Baré Mainassara in 1996. Baré, considered corrupt and ineffective as a leader, was assassinated in April 1999 and succeeded by Pres. Mamadou Tandja, who was subsequently reaffirmed in his post in free elections in November 1999. There is a ceasefire in effect between Tuareg rebel movements and the government but these nomadic, impoverished descendants of the Berbers and Arabs maintain a fiercely insular culture and shows little affinity for the black African majority in Niger.

Government

The 1996 Constitution calls for a president to be elected for a 5-year term and a bicameral National Assembly with one 83-seat chamber elected by popular vote for five years and the other yet to be determined. In the 1999 election President Mamadou Tandja and his MNSD won both the presidency and a pluraility in the legislature with 38 seats. The *Convention démocratique et sociale* or Democratic Social Convention (CDS) came second with 17 seats and the *Parti Nigerien pour la Democratie et le Socialisme* or Niger Partry for Democracy and Socialism (PNDS) was a close third with 16 seats. The other seats are shared by smaller parties. The MNSD rules in a coalition with the CDS.

Economic policy

The government is committed to reform of the economy by implementing of a structural adjustment program (SAP) together with the World Bank and IMF. Since the uranium-led boom of the seventies ended, the economy stagnated and new investment practically dried up. Current efforts are to encourage foreign investors to explore alternative mineral sources, including gold and oil.

Sectors

The economy is largely based on subsistence farming and uranium mining. Over 80% of the economically active people depend on subsistence crop growing. Less than 3% of the land is arable, including the irrigated areas along the

Fast facts

POLITICAL	
Head of State	Pres. Mamadou Tandja (1999)
Ruling Parties	MNSD & CDS (Coalition)
Main Opposition	PNDS
Independence	3 August 1960
National capital	Niamey
Official language	French

PHYSICAL	
Total area	489,189 sq. miles 1,267,000 sq. km. (2 x Texas)
Arable land	3% of land area
Coastline	Landlocked

POPULATION	
Total	9.9 million
Av. yearly growth	2.95%
Population/sq. mile	21
Urban population	17%
Adult literacy	15%

ECONOMY[1]	
Currency	CFA Franc (CFAF)(US$1=752.76)
GDP (real)	$2.18 billion
GDP growth rate	-0.6%
GNP per capita[2]	$190
GDP (ppp)[3]	$9.4 billion
GDP per cap. (ppp)[3]	$970
Inflation rate	4.8%
Exports	$322 million
Imports	$452 million
Development aid	$358 million
External debt	$1.64 billion
Unemployment	N/A

INFRASTRUCTURE	
Railroads	0 km
Paved roads	8%
Motor vehicles	34,000
Air passenger/km	215 million
Telephones/1,000	3 (1994)
International airport	Niamey
Main harbor	Landlocked

1. Statistics are based on World Bank data.
2. Atlas method.
3. See page 151 for an explanation of GDP based on purchasing power parity (ppp).

Niger River, where food and cash crops such as millet, sorghum, cassava, rice and cowpeas are grown. Livestock (mainly cattle) are sold to neighboring countries, and hides and skins overseas. Niger has, after South Africa, the largest uranium reserves in Africa. A decline in demand for uranium has, however, slashed foreign exchange earnings by one half since prices peaked in 1983. Other minerals include tin-bearing casserite ore, phosphates, molybdenum, coal and salt. Foreign firms are involved in exploration for gold along the border with Burkina Faso and oil in the Lake Chad region. Manufacturing comprises sugar refining, brewing, cotton ginning, tanning, rice milling, and small-scale production of cement, metals, textiles, plastics, soft drinks and construction materials.

Privatization

Although the government has shown a receptiveness to foreign acquisition of privatized parastatals, the process has been slow.

Investment

The uranium bust of the early 1980s has led to the withdrawal of French and several other European firms. In the eighties ExxonMobil (in partnership with Elf-Aquitaine) discovered oil in southeastern Niger near Lake Chad while Hunt Oil Company concentrated on the northeastern Djado plateau. Other US firms have shown an interest in gold mining and telecommunications. Still, most of the current investment in Niger is French. Coal mining is another area where foreign involvement is on the increase.

Trade

Uranium which contributed around 40% of the export revenue in the boom years, today accounts for merely 8%. Devaluation of the CFA franc has helped to boost exports of livestock, cowpeas, onions, and cotton. There is also an effort to fill the void with any of a range of proven and still to be explored gold, oil, phosphates, molybdenum, coal and salt reserves. Even though Niger currently shows deficits on its trade balance, the long-term outlook is for a modest surplus. Main trading partners are China, Japan, EU countries, Côte d'Ivoire, Ghana, and Benin.

Financial sector

There is one large international bank, the Meridien-BIAO, which serves as a regional institution and has close connections with the French banking system. Smaller banks include the Banque Commerciale du Niger (BCN), jointly owned by the governments of Niger and Libya. All these banks offer an array of financial instruments including letters of credit and short- and long-term loans.

Taxes and tariffs

Despite continuing efforts to make the tax laws more transparent, investors find it prudent to spell out such details beforehand in contractual arrangements with the government. Import duties go as high as 66%. Also levied is a statistical tax of 4.5%. Valaue added taxes of between 10 and 24% and a 4% tax on profits apply.

Assistance

While France remains a major donor, aid has also been coming from the US and other sources. In the eighties when an estimated 2 million people were in danger of starvation in Niger, 200,000 tons of imported food (largely from the US) helped avert the famine. The USAID has been involved in a number of programs aimed at promoting political and democratic reform while the US Department of Defense has extended assistance with military training. ExxonMobil has been active in oil exploration projects.

Business activity

AGRICULTURE

Cowpeas, cotton, peanuts, millet, sorghum, cassava (tapioca), rice, cattle, sheeps, goats, camels, donkeys, horses, poultry.

INDUSTRIES

Cement, brick, textiles, food processing, chemicals, slaughterhouses, light industries, uranium mining.

NATURAL RESOURCES

Uranium, coal, iron ore, tin, phosphates, gold, petroleum.

EXPORTS

$322 million (1999 est.): uranium ore, livestock products, cowpeas, onions.

IMPORTS

$452 million (1999 est.): consumer goods, primary materials, machinery, vehicles and parts, petroleum, cereals.

MAJOR TRADING PARTNERS

Greece, Canada, US, France, Nigeria, Côte d'Ivoire, Belgium, Luxembourg.

Doing Business with Niger

▶ **Investment**

Incentives offered to investors include tax holidays, duty-free importing, subsidized energy and assistance in setting up industrial sites. There are no screening or local ownership requirements but a clear preference for labor-intensive operations exists. The government is actively seeking investment in energy production, mineral exploration and mining, agriculture, food processing, forestry, fishing, low-cost housing, construction, handicrafts, hotels, schools, health centers and transportation. Gold, coal and oil are three mining sectors where US companies have been noticeable in recent years. The planned modernization of the telecommunications system is expected to become an area of keen competition between US and other firms with know-how and equipment.

▶ **Trade**

Overseas suppliers usually approach Niger as part of a larger West African market and supply goods and services via neighboring states. Among the proven markets for US goods are computers and related products, telecommunications equipment, vehicles (especially four-wheel drive), machinery, office equipment, pharmaceuticals (particularly generic drugs), heavy construction and earth-moving equipment, and coal-fired electrical generating equipment.

▶ **Trade finance**

The cost of local credit is high and the most common form of payment remains irrevocable letters of credit. Eximbank extends financing to US exporters.

▶ **Selling to the government**

Aside from donor-financed development projects requiring engineering consulting services, technical assistance, agricultural planning, and specialized equipment, recent government purchases ranged from generic drugs to four-wheel drive vehicles. A local agent may be helpful in the process.

▶ **Exchange controls**

Niger is a member of the Franc zone and its currency is fully convertible into French francs. Investment capital and earnings on invested capital—dividends, interest, loan and lease payments, royalties, and fees—are usually transferred to and from Niger through French banks. There are no restrictions on payments and transfers.

▶ **Establishing a presence**

Private entities can freely establish, acquire, and dispose of interests in business enterprises. Attempts have been made to cut red tape and authorization for investment is guaranteed within three months of the date of application. For those unfamiliar with French law, on which Niger bases its own system, the advice of a local attorney is recommended.

▶ **Financing projects**

The OPIC investment guarantee program has applied since 1962 but there has been little activity on this front.

▶ **Labor**

There is a shortage of professionals as more than half of the 65,000 salaried, formal sector workers are employed in the public sector. Even though wages are low the government considers organized labor a key "social" partner in running and developing the country. Labor-management relations are generally good but there have been instances where the National Federation of Labor Unions (USTN) has practically shut down the country with general strikes as part of politically-inspired protests.

▶ **Legal rights**

Niger has an independent court system which respects and protects property and commercial rights. The investment code guarantees against acts of nationalization or expropriation except when deemed to be in the public interest. There is provision for the settlement of disputes and indemnification either by local arbitration or through the International Center for Settlement of Disputes on Investments. Niger is a member of the West African Intellectual Property Organization (OAPI) and a signatory to the Paris Convention for the Protection of Industrial Property. It is also a member of World Intellectual Property Organization and a signatory to the Universal Copyright Convention.

Business climate

The culture is largely Muslim and business is conducted in a calm and deliberate fashion. Rushing the deal is not only considered unseemly but is often self-defeating The official language is French and the services of an interpreter might be necessary to prevent misunderstandings.

It is a bridge that is enduring and sturdy.

TOGETHER, WE HAVE BUILT A BRIDGE.

Its foundations are mutual respect and lasting

relationships. Its cornerstone is our commitment

to operate in a socially responsible manner.

Now and in the future, ideas and expertise

freely flow back and forth across the bridge.

Chevron stands committed to Africa's economic

development. As a bridge stands, for all to see.

Chevron

The symbol of partnership.

www.chevron.com

Nigeria

With 110 million people, Nigeria is Africa's most populous nation. Its economy is second in size only to South Africa's. It is the continent's major oil producer and the fifth largest supplier of crude to the United States. Under its new rulers there are concerted efforts to have Nigeria's riches trickle down to the broader population and rectify the inequities of past dictatorships. The country offers investors a low-cost labor pool, abundant natural resources, and by far the largest domestic market on the continent. Nigeria's return to democracy in 1999 reopened one of Africa's major markets for overseas business and American, European and Asian investors have not been slow in taking advantage. If the new government is able to overcome years of mismanagement and redirect the country's energies by good governance, the rewards will indeed be impressive.

Country profile

Nigeria is the largest of several West African countries on the Gulf of Guinea. The Niger and Benue rivers flow through a Y-shaped delta into the Gulf of Guinea. The Hausa-Fulani, mostly Muslim, dominate in the north while the Ibo are in the majority in the southwestern part of the country. Major cities, apart from Lagos with a population of 9 million, are Abuja (the capital), Kano, Port Harcourt, and Kaduna. About 50% of Nigeria's population is Muslim, 40% Christian and the rest adhere to ethnic religions.

History

Old kingdoms were flourishing when Portuguese mariners first visited the shores of Nigeria in 1472. In 1914 they were united in one British colony and on 1 October 1960 Nigeria gained its independence. The 40 years since were marred by a series of coups and a major civil war. The Biafra War broke out in May 1967 when the Ibo-controlled Eastern Regional legislature proclaimed an "independent" republic and took up arms to defend itself. Hundreds of thousands of people were killed in a struggle which, despite support from some African and Western countries, ended in defeat for Biafra in January 1970. Following an-

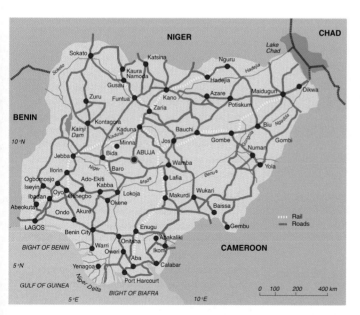

Fast facts

1. Statistics are based on World Bank data.
2. Atlas method.
3. See page 151 for an explanation of GDP based on purchasing power parity (ppp).

other abortive attempt at installing a democratically-elected government in 1993, General Sani Abacha took charge. In 1995 the execution by the Abacha regime of nine political prisoners, including the renowned writer Ken Saro-Wiwa, led to Nigeria's temporary suspension from the Commonwealth and the imposition of sanctions. Following Abacha's death in 1998, four separate elections culminated in the establishment of local, state and federal governments and the swearing in of Olusegun Obasanjo as president in May 1999.

Government

The 1999 constitution introduced a western decentralized form of government. The President is elected by popular vote for a maximum of two 4-year terms and appoints the cabinet or Federal Executive Council. On a federal basis a 109-member Senate and a 360-seat House of Representatives are elected to serve for 4 year terms. Each of the country's 36 states elects its own legislature and a governor. President Obasanju's People's Democratic Party (PDP) won the presidential race against Samuel Falae, supported by the Alliance for Democracy and the All People's Party (AD/APP). The PDP captured 206 of the House seats and 59 Senate seats against the APP's 74 and 29, and the AD's 68 and 20, respectively.

Economic policy

The new government introduced key measures to improve the country's economy and make it more investor-friendly. Concerted efforts have been made to root out corruption, improve the dilapidated infrastructure, privatize state-run industries and promote export-led growth. With oil prices likely to remain high in the foreseeable future, Nigeria should have the means to solve some of the vexing problems inherited from years of mismanagement. After Nigeria's return to democratic rule in 1999, the US and other major industrial nations rapidly reinvigorated relations that had chilled during the Abacha era. OPIC and Eximbank resumed financing of investment in and trade with Nigeria.

Privatization

In 1999 the National Council on Privatization (NCP) announced a three-phase plan to privatize most of Nigeria's state-owned companies. First, 13 banks, cement companies and oil marketing companies, already listed on the Nigerian Stock Exchange, will be sold off. In the second phase, all the state's interest in hotels, automotive plants and similar industries will be sold. In the third stage, likely to occur in 2002, the Nigeria Electric Production Authority (NEPA), Nigeria Telecommunications Limited (NITEL), oil refineries, and the state-owned National Fertilizer Company of Nigeria (NAFCON) will be privatized. The state's most lucrative asset, Nigerian National Petroleum Company (NNPC), is likely to be on the auction block as well.

Sectors

Some 70 percent of the population is engaged in agriculture. In the south, rubber trees, oil palm and cocoa are cultivated for export and in the north groundnuts, cotton and cattle. Currently the agricultural sector accounts for 40 percent of the GDP. Nigeria has, however, slipped in recent years from being a net exporter to becoming a major importer of agricultural products. Petroleum continues to power the Nigerian economy, accounting for almost all of the country's foreign exchange earnings. Manufacturing consists mostly of import-substituting products. Other activities include iron and steel and fertilizer production, automobile assembly and oil refining.

Trading

Nigeria is currently the fifth largest importer of US wheat. In 1998, its oil export revenues accounted for 95 percent of total exports with the US purchasing 49 percent of the total. In 1998 the US recorded a trade deficit of $5.7 billion with Nigeria even though exports, led by oil equipment and wheat, showed a modest 9% increase. Still, in 1998/99 Nigeria was the sixth largest world market for wheat and accounted for 70% of all US shipments to Sub-Saharan Africa. Other substantial American exports to Nigeria included computers and software, medical equipment, automotive parts, cosmetics, textiles and fabrics. In 1998 Nigeria was the fifth largest supplier of crude to the US (behind Saudi Arabia, Canada, Venezuela and Mexico).

Investment

Since 1999, foreign companies, particularly in the oil and gas sector, have been looking at new or expanded investments in Nigeria. Abundant oil reserves have kept the economy afloat and once again hold the key to the future. Total US foreign direct investment in Nigeria is estimated at around $4 billion, largely in the petroleum secor. A newly planned Export Processing Zone (EPZ) at Port Harcourt aims at attracting foreign investments in the manufacturing sector. Incentives have also been approved to encourage investment in downstream oil and gas processing and marketing. The privatization of state-owned properties is expected to diversify and intensify foreign investment.

Financial sector

The Central Bank of Nigeria (CBN) monitors the banking system to ensure compliance with monetary, credit, and foreign exchange guidelines. There are 89 commercial and merchant banks, 67 of them classified as healthy. There are also a number of finance houses and mortgage and community banks throughout the country. Some 200 companies are listed on the Lagos (formerly Nigerian) Stock Exchange, in operation since 1961.

Taxes and tariffs

Nigeria's corporate tax is a flat 30%. In the case of certain small-scale enterprises involved in agricultural production, mining and manufacturing, a rate of 20% applies. Import taxes range from 5% to 60%.

Business activity

AGRICULTURE

Cocoa, peanuts, palm oil, corn, rice, sorghum, millet, cassava (tapioca), yams, rubber, cattle, sheep, goats, pigs, timber, fish.

INDUSTRIES

Crude oil, coal, tin, columbite, palm oil, peanuts, cotton, rubber, wood, hides and skins, textiles, cement and other construction materials, food products, footwear, chemicals, fertilizer, printing, ceramics, steel.

NATURAL RESOURCES

Petroleum, tin, columbite, iron ore, coal, limestone, lead, zinc, natural gas.

EXPORTS

$12.8 billion (1999 est.): petroleum and petroleum products, cocoa, rubber.

IMPORTS

$14.8 billion (1999 est.): machinery, chemicals, transportation equpment, manufactured goods, food and animals.

MAJOR TRADING PARTNERS

US, Spain, Italy, France, UK, Germany, Netherlands.

Doing Business with Nigeria

▶ **Investment**

The new government in 1999 signaled its intention to make Nigeria investor-friendly and to encourage foreign participation. Its privatization program should present foreign investors with new opportunities in oil exploration, banking, hotels, and automotive parts manufacturing. Plans to install 3 million telephone lines per year will require foreign private sector participation will be required.

▶ **Trade**

Oil and gasfield machinery will continue to be prime import items. There is a growing market for computers, cellular phone sets, transmission and switching and other telecommunications equipment. Other prime items include medical supplies, pharmaceuticals, textiles, and wheat and used cars and buses. The demand for earthmoving and roadbuilding machinery will increase as road reconstruction begins.

▶ **Trade finance**

In July 1999 Eximbank returned to Nigeria with a $100 million pilot program, once again making medium-term financing available to US exporters. The Nigerian Export-Import Bank (NEXIM) was established in 1991 to assist banks to provide pre- and post-shipment financing in local currency to support non-oil exports.

▶ **Selling to the government**

Nigeria buys products and services through a "tender board" composed of senior government officials, sometimes together with local consultants or foreign firms represented in Nigeria. *The Central Bank of Nigeria (CBN) does not buy products and services for the government or its agencies and purported inquiries and business proposals emanating from the CBN on behalf of the Nigerian government or any of its agencies should be disregarded as scams.*

▶ **Exchange controls**

Foreign exchange control applies. All applications must be channeled through selected banks to the Central Bank of Nigeria (CBN).

▶ **Partnerships**

Establishment of a joint venture is in itself not sufficient to constitute a legal entity. A foreign firm may, however, participate as a shareholder in a local company incorporated as a joint venture.

▶ **Establishing a presence**

Foreign firms are not allowed to operate through a branch office but obliged to establish a place of business and incorporate to conduct business in Nigeria. A local presence can also be established on the basis of equity participation, joint ventures, an arrangement for the provision of technical services to a Nigerian company, or the purchase of securities in existing Nigerian companies. All foreign companies must register with the NIPC to obtain a business permit.

Project financing

Overseas Private Investment Corporation programs are available to US ventures in Nigeria. The US Trade and Development Agency extends funding for feasibility studies. Financing can also be obtained through any of the local commercial, merchant or industrial banks and, to a limited extent, from insurance companies, building and property development companies, pension funds and institutional investors.

▶ **Labor**

Nigeria has a large, English-speaking workforce, generally better educated and skilled than elsewhere on the continent. Any nonagricultural firm with more than 50 workers must recognize trade unions and deduct dues for union members. Collective bargaining is common.

▶ **Legal rights**

The legal system is fashioned after English Common law. Nigeria is a signatory to the major world agreements on Intellectual Property Protection and a member of the World Intellectual Property Organization. The government's Patents and Design Decree of 1970 and Trademark Act of 1965 regulate the registration of patents and trademarks.

▶ **Business climate**

English is widely spoken. Visitors should make their contacts well before departure for Nigeria. *A fraudulent practice that has received wide publicity is known as "419." It involves an offer to transfer large sums of money with promises of commissions after up-front payments are made by the potential victim. While remaining on their guard against such practices, foreign citizens should also be aware that these scams do not represent the Nigerian business community at large. Scam attempts should be reported to the nearest Nigerian embassy.*

R Rwanda

The 1994 genocide decimated Rwanda, damaged its fragile economic base, severely impoverished the remaining population, and eroded the country's ability to attract private and external investment. This tragic setback came on the heels of an economic downturn in the 1980s as the world price of coffee plunged. Since peace was restored Rwanda has, however, made significant progress in stabilizing and rehabilitating its economy—GDP has rebounded, and inflation has been curbed. Currently, the emphasis is on diversification away from coffee and tea towards mining and tourism.

Country profile

In the west the Republic of Rwanda borders on Lake Kivu. On its eastern border with Tanzania it shares marshy lakes along the Kagera River. The climate is tropical with rainfall ranging between 800 and 1,400 mm (32 and 55 inches). Much of the terrain is covered with lush vegetation. Conservation regions include well-known game parks such as Akagera National Park and Parc National des Volcans where the mountain gorilla and other endangered species are found. Most inhabitants are Banyarwanda, of whom 80% are Hutu and the rest Tutsi. They speak Kinyarwanda which, together with French and English, is an official language. Most Rwandans are Christians.

History

The original inhabitants of Rwanda were the Pygmies or Twa, today numbering barely 1% of the total popualtion. The simple version of history has the Tutsi (Nilotic) cattle breeders arriving in the area from the 15th Century and subjugating the Hutu inhabitants. In reality, the situation is much more complex as boundaries of race and class became less distinct over the years as a result of intermingling. Some put part of the blame for the racial animosity that led to the recent mass-scale killings on the shoulders of German and Belgian colonial rulers who pitched the Hutu against Tutsi for their own gain. When Burundi and neighboring Rwanda were incorporated into German East Africa in 1899, they had been kingdoms for several centuries headed by *mwamis* (kings). After Germany's defeat in World War I these nations were transferred to Belgium under the joint name of Ruanda-Urundi. They were, however, "separated at birth" when they gained their independence in 1962. After periodic outbursts of violence, conciliation between Hutu and Tutsi leaders finally seemed to be in the making when Pres. Juvenal Habyarimana, under international and domestic pressure, began reforms in 1994. The reform process was, however, short-lived as Habyarimana perished in an aircraft

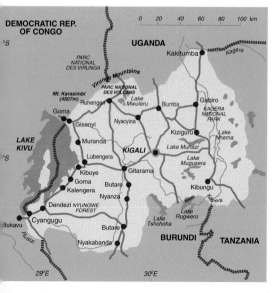

Fast facts

POLITICAL

Head of State	Pres. Paul Kagame (2000)
Prime Minister	Bernard Makuza (2000)
Majority party	FPR
Other parties	MDR, PSD & PDC, PDI
Independence	1 July 1962
National capital	Kigali
Off. languages	Kinyarwanda, French & English

PHYSICAL

Total area	10,170 sq. miles 26,340 sq. km. (± Maryland)
Arable land	35% of land area
Coastline	Landlocked

POPULATION

Total	8.15 million
Av. yearly growth	2.43%
Population/sq. mile	711
Urban population	7%
Adult literacy	64%

ECONOMY[1]

Currency	Rwandan franc (RF)(US$1=432.23)
GDP (real)	$1.8 billion
GDP growth rate	6.1%
GNP per capita[2]	$230
GDP (ppp)[3]	$5.5 billion
GDP per cap. (ppp)[3]	$690
Inflation rate	10%
Exports	$109 million
Imports	$414 million
Development aid	$621 million
External debt	$1.25 billion
Unemployment	N/A

INFRASTRUCTURE

Paved roads	8%
Motor vehicles	10,000
Air passenger/km	1 billion
Telephones/1,000	2
International airport	Kigali
Main harbor	Landlocked

1. Statistics are based on World Bank data.
2. Atlas method.
3. See page 151 for an explanation of GDP based on purchasing power parity (ppp).

downed by a rocket near Kigali on 6 April 1994, along with the president of neighboring Burundi. The next day, the Rwandan government mobilized the country's ethnic Hutu majority in a genocide against the Tutsi and moderate Hutus, a campaign that claimed over 500,000 lives in under one hundred days. Maj. Gen. Paul Kagame and his Tutsi-dominated *multi-ethnic Front Patriotique Rwandais* or Rwanda Patriotic Front (FPR) invaded from Uganda and defeated the Rwanda regime in July 1994. Shortly afterwards, Kagame was appointed Vice President and Defense Minister, and in March 2000 he was sworn in as President. The FPR formed a coalition government similar to the one established by Habyarimana, with Paul Kagame as a Tutsi serving as president and Bernard Makuza, leader of the Hutu-dominated *Mouvement Démocratique Républicain* or Republican Democratic Movement (MDR), appointed prime minister. Although much of the country is now at peace, members of the former regime continue their efforts to destabilize the northwest area of the country through low-intensity insurgency.

Government

The president is appointed by the 70-member Assemblée National du Transition or Transitional National Assembly. Seats in this unicameral chamber are assigned. Kagame's Tutsi-dominated FPR holds 19 seats, Makuza's MDR and two other Hutu-dominated parties—*Parti Libéral* or Liberal Party (PL) and *Parti Social-Démocrate* or Social Democratic Party (PSD)—13 each. The remainder of the seats are split between four other smaller parties, including the *Parti Démocratique Islamique (PDI)* (Islamic Democratic Party).

Economic policy

The government has implemented with the help of the IMF structural reforms, focusing on improving the civil service, privatization, reducing tariffs, and the restructuring of banks.

Sectors

Agriculture is the mainstay of the economy and the largest employer, with coffee and tea as major cash crops. Other export crops are pyrethrum and quinquina. The fishing potential of the lakes is underutilized and forestation programs have come to a standstill. Casserite (tin), wolfram, beryl, colombo-tantalite and gold are mined on a small scale. Large deposits of methane gas under Lake Kivu remain underexploited.

Privatization

In association with the World Bank, privatization started in the late 1990s. About half of the 46 enterprises earmarked have been restructured and another 18 were ceded to the private sector.

Investment

Foreign investment is in commercial establishments, tea, coffee, and tourism. Private investment since the 1994 genocide has dwindled.

Trade

Coffee and tea account for about 85% of total export revenues. Most consumer products come from neighboring countries and Europe.

Financial sector

International transactions can be carried out by the National Bank of Rwanda and four others.

Taxes and tariffs

Since the establishment of the Rwandan Revenue Authority (RRA) in 1998, tax collection has improved and customs duties have been simplified and lowered.

Business activity

AGRICULTURE

Coffee, tea, pyrethrum , bananas, beans, sorghum, potatoes, livestock.

INDUSTRIES

Cement, agricultural processing, beverages, soap, furniture, shoes, plastic goods, textiles, cigarettes.

NATURAL RESOURCES

Gold, casseterite (tin ore), wolframite (tungsten ore), natural gas, hydropower.

EXPORTS

$109 million (1999 est.): coffee, tea, hides, tin ore.

IMPORTS

$414 million (1999 est.): foodstuffs, machinery and equipment, steel, petroleum products, construction material.

MAJOR TRADING PARTNERS

Brazil, Germany, US, Netherlands, UK, Italy, Kenya, Tanzania, Belgium, Luxembourg.

Doing Business with Rwanda

▶ **Investment**

With the passage of an investment code and creation of a one-stop investment promotion agency, Rwanda hopes to attract foreign direct investment. Tax breaks are offered to new firms as well as expatriate employees. While the tea and coffee sectors remain prime targets for investment, privatization will also open up the telecommunications, energy and water supply sectors for foreign participation.

▶ **Trade**

There is also a growing demand for used clothing, 4-wheel drive vehicles, trucks, communications and computer equipment, cosmetics, and consultant services.

▶ **Trade finance**

Unless orders are placed by international agencies, irrevocable letters of credit are the standard mode of payment.

▶ **Selling to the government**

A tender board handles procurement and sets guidelines and policies. It is involved in purchases by all government departments and international donors.

▶ **Exchange controls**

Controls have been relaxed and commercial banks are able to assist in the transfer of overseas payments of profits and dividends.

▶ **Financing projects**

In 1996, humanitarian relief began to shift to reconstruction and development assistance. Rehabilitation and expansion of road, water, health and educational facilities and agricultural projects involve overseas funding. The World Bank, the UN Development Program, the European Development Fund and various countries provide aid.

▶ **Labor**

Four prewar independent trade unions are back in operation. The largest union, CESTRAR, was created in the early nineties as a government institution but has since become fully independent. Minimum wage and social security regulations are in force.

▶ **Business Climate**

Business in Rwanda is conducted in both English and French. There is a strong desire to expand relations with US firms and in sophisticated circles a taste for American goods.

São Tomé & Príncipe

Comprising two small former Portuguese islands off the West African coast, the state of São Tomé and Principé was among the first to ride on a wave of reform towards full democracy. Recent economic changes aim at making the islands less dependent on a single cash crop, cocoa, and to broaden its international business involvement beyond Portugal. Expansion of fishing and crop diversification are underway with the help of international agencies and a growing number of foreign investors.

Country profile

The island country of São Tomé and Príncipe comprises two extinct volcanic islands and four rocky islets about 300 km off the coast of Gabon. The larger island, São Tomé, located on the equator, rises at its peak to over 2,000 m (6,500 ft). The eastern slopes are covered with cocoa plantations and smallholdings cut out of dense rainforest. To the north, Princípe rises to 948 m (3,100 ft) above the sea. The climate of both islands is equatorial Annual rainfall decreases from 5,000 mm (197 inches) on the southwestern slopes of the islands to 1,000 mm (39 inches) on their northeastern sides. Society on both islands is fairly homogeneous, consisting largely of native-born descendants of the early Portuguese settlers and African slaves. There are also a number of Chinese, Cape Verdeans, Mozambicans and Angolans. Portuguese is the official language, but the more common *lingua franca* is Portuguese Crioulo (Creole). Most are Roman Catholic.

History

The island of São Tomé was discovered by Portuguese mariners in 1478 and granted to Portugal's crown prince, together with its sister island, Príncipe (Prince). After the prince's accession to the throne as Joao II, he encouraged settlement of the uninhabited islands to expand the Portuguese presence in this region

and promote trade with Africa. The settlers imported slaves from the mainland and a mixed Afro-European population emerged who spoke a creole language based on Portuguese and various African languages. In the face of fierce competition from Brazil, sugar was replaced by cocoa as the main crop. In 1975 the *Movimiento de Libertaçao de São Tomé e Príncipe* or Movement for the Liberation of São Tomé and Príncipe (MLSTP) under the leadership of Manuel Pinto da Costa, led the islands to independence. Facing economic ruin and under pressure from foreign donors in the late 1980s, the MLSTP government

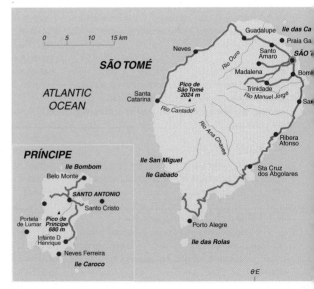

began to liberalize the economy and removed the ban on opposition parties. It was voted out of office in 1990 only to return victorious in 1994 as the interim government failed to cope with economic problems. Miguel Trovoada, who returned from exile to win the presidency in 1991, was reelected in 1996. In1999, Manuel Pinto da Costa, who was Trovoada's strongest opponent in 1996, became prime minister as leader of the MLSTP. São Tomé and Principé is the first African country where, since the introduction of democracy, free political competition not only brought a change of government, but where a former dictatorial ruling party was eventually returned to office.

Government

An executive President is elected for a maximum of two 5-year terms and appoints the leader of the strongest party as Prime Minister. The 55-member unicameral *Assembleia Nacional* (National Assembly) is elected for 4-year terms. In the November 1998 elections the MLSTP won 31 seats with Trovaoda's *Acçao Democrática Independente* or Independent Democratic Action (ADI) a distant second with 16 seats.

Economic policy

After a long period of economic decline and chronic economic and financial imbalances, São Tomé and Príncipe, together with the IMF, implemented vigorous adjustment measures. As a result, a budget deficit of 2.2% of GDP in 1997 was turned into a surplus of 0.7% of GDP in 1998, inflation was reduced from more than 80% to about 21%, and real GDP growth increased from 1.5% to 2.5%.

Sectors

Since the 1800s, the economy of São Tomé and Principé has been based on plantation agriculture—first sugar and later cocoa. At the time of independence, Portuguese-owned plantations occupied 90% of the cultivated area. After independence, control of these cocoa plantations passed to various state-owned agricultural enterprises. The second-largest export crop is coffee, followed by copra, palm kernels, cinnamon, pepper and breadfruit. The principal food crops are taro, cassava, breadfruit and maize. Fishing, which employs 10% of the economically active population, is seen as a vital source of food as well as a valuable future earner of foreign exchange. Efforts are also being made to exploit the country's timber resources. Manufacturing is limited to the

Fast facts

POLITICAL

Head of State	Pres. Miguel dos Anjos da Costa Lisboa Trovoada (1991)
Prime Minister	Manuel Pinto da Costa(1999)
Ruling Party	MLSTP
Main Opposition	ADI
Independence	12 July 1975
National capital	São Tomé
Official language	Portuguese

PHYSICAL

Total area	386 sq. miles 1,000 sq. km. (5 x Washington DC)
Arable land	2% of land area
Coastline	209 km

POPULATION

Total	154,878
Av. yearly growth	3.14%
Population/sq. mile	432
Urbanpopulation	47%
Adult literacy	73%

ECONOMY[1]

Currency	Dobra (Db) (US$1=8,162.48)
GDP (real)	$48 million
GDP growth rate	2.5%
GNP per capita[2]	$270
GDP (ppp)[3]	$164 million
GDP per cap. (ppp)[3]	$1,100
Inflation rate	21%
Exports	$16 million
Imports	$40 million
Development aid	$35 million
External debt	$296 million
Unemployment	50%

INFRASTRUCTURE

Paved roads	68%
Motor vehicles	3,000 (1994)
Air passenger/km	8 million (1994)
Telephones/1,000	20 (1994)
International airport	São Tomé
Main harbor	São Tomé

1. *Statistics are based on World Bank data.*
2. *Atlas method.*
3. *See page 151 for an explanation of GDP based on purchasing power parity (ppp).*

Business activity

production of items such as soap, soft drinks, palm oil, bricks and textiles as well as timber processing. The island's beaches and tropical environment offer good tourism potential.

Privatization

The government has been turning over management of the parastatals, as well as the agricultural, commercial, banking, and tourism sectors, to the private sector. Since 1991 the focus has been on restructuring of the state-run agricultural and industrial sectors. Agricultural privatization involving several cocoa estates has met with mixed success due to a lack of domestic capital. In some cases state-owned plantations have been placed under local and foreign private management to increase efficiency and increase production levels.

Investment

Private investment is expected to grow from 18.4% of GDP in 1998 to 45% of GDP in 2002. Two American oil companies, ExxonMobil and Environmental Remediation Holding Corporation, have begun oil exploration activities in São Tomé's recently delineated exclusive economic deep water zone.

Trade

The dominant crop on São Tomé is cocoa, representing about 98% of exports. Other export crops include copra, palm kernels, and coffee. Portugal is one of the major trading partners.

Financial sector

The authorities have set a relatively high reserve requirement ratio of 22% and the government's counterpart funds were transferred to the central bank, enhancing liquidity in the banking system. The collection of proceeds from privatization and the sale of oil exploration concessions contributed to government liquidity.

Doing Business with São Tomé & Príncipe

▶ Investment

An aggressive pursuit of potential foreign investors has met with limited success. The task is complicated by the small size and relative isolation of the islands, remaining foreign exchange controls, and low productivity and human resource development. There are attempts to stimulate interest abroad not only in tropical agriculture, but in areas such as tourism, industrial fishing, and manufacturing in a regional free trade zone. There is hope that São Tomé and Principé might strike petroleum in reasonable quantity and join other nations in the region who built new economies on such bonanzas. In 1993, the government announced plans to designate a free trade zone to attract offshore investors and stimulate development of the country's shipping and manufacturing sectors.

▶ Trade

Even though priority is given to the development of food crops in an effort to reduce the large food import bill, the islands are still heavily reliant on foreign sources. In the 1990s foodstuffs accounted on average for about 35% of total imports.

▶ Financing projects

The government relies on foreign assistance from various donors. The UN Development Program, the World Bank, the European Union, and the African Development Bank have all at different stages financed projects.

▶ Labor

The local workforce is largely involved in agricultural activity. Lack of employment has led to an exodus of workseekers abroad.

Senegal

Historically Senegal and its capital, Dakar, served as the gateway to West Africa. Although its industrial and commercial base is smaller than that of rival Côte d'Ivoire, it is equipped with one of Africa's most efficient and modern infrastructures and populated by a sophisticated people with an international, distinctly French, outlook. In the late 1990s Senegal met all IMF benchmarks in its macroeconomic program. A decent supply of minerals coupled with a cosmopolitan environment have attracted many European and—more recently— an increasing number of American entrepreneurs.

Country profile

The Republic of Senegal consists largely of a low plateau between 100-200 m above sea level. Three perennial rivers flow through the region— the Senegal, Gambia and Casamance. All three open up in large deltas or estuaries, replete with expansive beaches, national parks and tourist resorts. The Senegalese Peninsula with its ample rainfall was appropriately named Cape Verde or Green Cape. The Wolof in the northwest are the largest ethnic group and account for about 40% of the total population. Their language is a *lingua franca* in Senegal along with French, the official tongue. Other significant groups include the Serer,

Tukulor, Ful (or Fulani), Mandé and a large Mauritanian (Moorish) community. More than 90% adhere to the Muslim faith but there is a small Christian minority in Dakar. Ethnic beliefs survive.

History

The earliest evidence of civilization in this region are mysterious circles of huge stone columns (megaliths) in the vicinity of the Gambia and Saloum rivers. The inhabitants of modern Senegal and The Gambia are descendants of Negroid peoples who settled some 1,400 years ago. From 1445 Portuguese mariners traded with the Wolof and Serer kingdoms but in 1588 they were driven out by the Dutch. Ultimately the French gained dominance from their settlement on St. Louis Island in the estuary of the Senegal, capturing Rufisque and Gorée Island, which served as slave trading posts until the abolition of this trade in the first half of the 19th Century. Millions of Africans were shipped from Gorée to the New World during the 1700s. Eventually these coastal centers and Dakar became integral parts of France, electing their own deputies to the National Assembly. France not only annexed Senegal, but used the colony as a base for further expan-

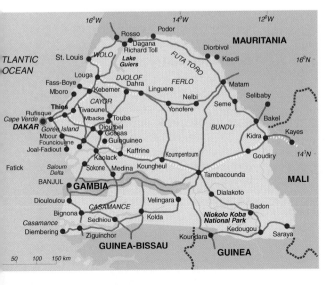

Fast facts

POLITICAL

Head of State	Pres. Abdoulaye Wade (2000)
Ruling Party	SOPI (Coalition)
Main Opposition	APF & PSS
Independence	4 April 1960
National capital	Dakar
Official language	French

PHYSICAL

Total area	75,749 sq. miles 196,190 sq. km. (± South Dakota)
Arable land	12% of land area
Coastline	531 km

POPULATION

Total	10.05 million
Av. yearly growth	3.32%
Population/sq. mile	131
Urban population	41%
Adult literacy	35%

ECONOMY[1]

Currency	CFA franc (CFAF)(US$1=752.76)
GDP (real)	$5.2 billion
GDP growth rate	5.1%
GNP per capita[2]	$530
GDP (ppp)[3]	$15.6 billion
GDP per cap. (ppp)[3]	$1,600
Inflation rate	1.8%
Exports	$1.5 billion
Imports	$1.8 billion
Development aid	$449 million
External debt	$3.13 billion
Unemployment	N/A

INFRASTRUCTURE

Railroads	761 miles/1,225 km
Paved roads	29%
Motor vehicles	90,000
Air passenger/km	224 million
Telephones/1,000	9
International airport	Dakar
Main harbor	Dakar

1. Statistics are based on World Bank data.
2. Atlas method.
3. See page 151 for an explanation of GDP based on purchasing power parity (ppp).

sion eastward. A Catholic poet-politician, Léopold Sedar Senghor, led Senegal to independence in 1960 and exercised virtual one-man rule until his voluntary retirement in 1981 when he stepped down in favor of his prime minister, Abdou Diouf. During his term as president, Diouf witnessed the creation in 1982 together with The Gambia of the Confederation of Senegambia and its breakup in 1989. In the free and open presidential election of March 2000, Diouf, as leader of the *Parti Socialiste du Sénégal* or Socialist Party of Senegal (PSS), was defeated at the polls and succeeded as president by Abdoulaye Wade, representing the *Parti Démocratique Sénégalais* or Senegalese Democratic Party (PDS). Wade inherited an on-going problem posed by the *secessionist Mouvement des forces democratiques de Casamance* (MFDC), led by the Rev. Augustin Diamacoune in southern Senegal.

Government

The present constitution dates from 1963 but has been revised as recently as February 1998 to make provision for a Senate. The executive President is directly elected by the voters for a term of seven years, renewable once. He appoints the Prime Minister who forms the cabinet. The bicameral legislature consists of a 120-member National Assembly *(Assemblée Nationale)* and a 60-member Senate *(Sénat)*, both elected for five-year terms. In the April 2001 election the SOPI Coalition comprising President Wade's PDS and a half dozen smaller parties captured 89 seats in the Assembly. A woman, Mme. Madior Boye, was appointed prime minister. The PSS won 10 seats and a number of smaller parties the remainder. In the Senate, elected in January 1999, Diouf's PSS still holds all 45 elected seats.

Economic policy

Senegal has met all IMF benchmarks and macroeconomic indicators show a respectable performance with an annual GDP growth rate of 6% in the late 1990s, and inflation down to below 3%. There has been an increasing emphasis on measures to attract private sector investment after completion of the first phase of economic liberalization.

Sectors

The economy remains heavily dependent on agriculture which employs about 75% of the working population and accounts for over one-fifth of GDP. Groundnuts, cotton and sugar are major cash crops. Staple foods are millet, sorghum, maize and rice. Livestock is raised across the country. Fresh and canned marine fish is the principal export and involves some 10% of the working population. Even though the mining sector accounts for less than 2% of GDP, exports of phosphate rock, phosphate acid and fertilizers contribute more than 25% of foreign earnings. There are large unexploited iron ore and limited gold reserves. Titanium, zirconium and rutile are mined south of the Cape Verde Peninsula. Natural gas from offshore wells fuel a power station near Dakar and modest oil deposits off the Casamance coast are still to be exploited. Food processing, textiles, chemicals and petroleum products, plastics, paint, soap and pharmaceuticals are manufactured.

Privatization

Privatization is considered as key to attracting foreign investment. In the 1990s 18 enterprises were earmarked for restructuring, including the state-owned telecommunications company, a peanut oil processor, the national power utility, the railroad company and several hotels. There is a desire on the part of the government to continue influencing the direction of these large entities by retaining a stake. For example, a subsidiary of France Telecom was allowed to purchase a one-third share in SONATEL and the government insists on retaining 51% control over the power utility SENELEC.

Investment

Among the US firms involved in Senegal are GTI (in a build, own, operate and transfer—BOOT—power project), Motorola (developing paging systems), and Senelec (a factory for fuel-efficient lights and refrigerators). As privatization offers new opportunities, US and other firms are expected to challenge the historic dominance of the French in the industrial sector. Irish and Canadian companies are involved in gas exploration while South African and Australian firms have become involved in gold and other mining operations.

Trade

Fresh and canned marine fish is the principal export, contributing over 30% of export revenue. Senegal is the largest exporter of groundnuts on the continent and the fifth largest exporter of phosphates. Major imports include crude and refined petroleum products, machinery, electrical appli-

ances, rice, grain, lubricants, and dairy products. France remains Senegal's largest trading partner, followed by India, Germany, Nigeria, and the US. Principal exports from the US, which maintains a surplus, are rice, wheat, and other agricultural commodities, as well as petroleum products, computer equipment, used clothing, and cosmetics. Tourism is also a major foreign exchange earner .

Financial sector

Senegal shares the *Banque Central Des Etats de L'Afrique de L'Ouest* (BCEAO), or Central Bank of West African States, with other members of the CFA franc zone. In the wake of a serious banking crisis in the 1980s, significant reforms were introduced with the assistance of the World Bank. Five stronger banks emerged with greater liquidity, tighter controls and a full range of services.

Taxes and tariffs

Corporate income tax is levied at 33.33%. Payroll taxes are 3% for national salaries and 6% for expatriate salaries. A value-added tax (VAT) of 20% is charged for most goods. Some services (such as the rental of a furnished room or telephone service) are taxed at a reduced rate of 12.5% and luxury items at a 50% rate.

Business activity

AGRICULTURE
Peanuts, millet, corn, sorghum, rice, cotton, tomatoes, green vegetables, cattle, poultry, pigs, fish.

INDUSTRIES
Agricultural and fish processing, phosphate mining, fertilizer production, petroleum refining, construction materials.

NATURAL RESOURCES
Fish, phosphate, iron ore.

EXPORTS
$1.5 billion (1999 est.): fish, groundnuts (peanuts), petroleum products, phosphates, cotton.

IMPORTS
$1.8 billion (1999 est.): food and beverages, consumer goods, capital goods, petroleum products.

MAJOR TRADING PARTNERS
France, EU, India, Côte d'Ivoire, Mali, Nigeria, Cameroon, Algeria, US, China, Japan.

Doing Business with Senegal

▶ **Investment**

The Dakar Industrial Free Zone (DIFZ) is an industrial park dedicated primarily to export-oriented and labor-intensive manufacturing. Investors in the DIFZ and other designated areas enjoy tax-free status and duty-free entry of raw materials and components. Foreign investors need to register at a central one-stop facility to qualify for these and other incentives. The emphasis is on investment outside the Dakar region, small- and medium-sized enterprises and sectors such as agriculture, fishing, manufacturing, mineral extraction, and tourism. US investors are engaged in hotel renovation programs on the historic slave site, Goree Island, off the coast of Dakar. Majority Senegalese ownership is a requirement in food production and fishing projects and most enterprises are obliged to employ a certain number of local workers.

▶ **Trade**

Although Senegal has until now offered a relatively limited market for US products, the liberalization of the economy, freer access for imports, and new developments in power generation and in telecommunications are expected to broaden the scope. Best deals in the past were in agricultural commodities, mining, tourism, information technology, and used clothing. There is a strong growth in the computer market and products ranging from air conditioners to cosmetics. US and other importers have concentrated on groundnuts and phosphates from Senegal. Distribution is mostly through large French-owned or Lebanese firms.

▶ **Trade finance**

Irrevocable letters of credit are the preferred form of payment. Local financing is tight.

Selling to the government

Both in privatization deals and major government purchases foreign firms are invited to present bids. Procurement of goods and services with the help of multilateral funds is in accordance with international rules for competitive bidding. In recent years, major government contracts involved telecommunications, energy and water projects.

▶ **Exchange controls**

Senegal's currency, the CFA Franc, is freely convertible into French francs at a fixed rate. Foreign investors are guaranteed repatriation of profits and capital. Transactions are channeled through authorized banks, the postal administration, or the regional central bank, the BCEAO.

▶ **Partnerships**

In major privatization deals involving telecommunications, energy projects and the like, the government insists on being a partner with foreign private investors. It is also actively promoting joint ventures between foreign and domestic entrepreneurs in certain sectors of the economy.

▶ **Establishing a presence**

There is provision for several types of companies, including general partnerships, limited liability companies (LLC), public limited companies (PLC), and joint venture enterprises. Incorporation costs are moderate. Copies of all agency agreements between foreign principals and local distributors or agents must be submitted to the Department of Internal Trade and Prices for final approval.

▶ **Financing projects**

The Overseas Private Investment Corporation provides insurance and assistance to US investors. Several international agencies are involved in major projects.

▶ **Labor**

There is a reasonable availability of unskilled and semi-skilled labor but investors with a need for specialized skills need to factor in expenditure for training purposes.

▶ **Legal rights**

Property rights are protected and there are no known cases of expropriation involving US or other overseas firms. Senegal is a member of the Cameroon-based African Intellectual Property Organization or *Office African et Malagache de la Propiété Industrielle* (OAMPI), which safeguards trademarks, patents, and industrial designs among its members. It is also a member of the Paris Convention for the Protection of Industrial Property and the Berne Convention for the Protection of Literary and Artistic Works.. Trademarks are filed through the Central Office and granted protection by OAMPI for 20 years, renewable indefinitely.

▶ **Business climate**

The business culture has a decidedly French flavor. Still, usage of English is growing as efforts intensify to lure larger investment from the United States, Britain and countries such as South Africa and Australia.

Seychelles

Income from tourism has helped Africa's smallest state, Seychelles, to rank first in terms of GNP per capita. Already a crossroad for sea and air travellers and freight shipping, the multi-island nation is now intent on becoming a major offshore banking and insurance center by offering facilities comparable to places like the Bahamas. Recent investor-friendly reforms and privatization have lured investment in fishing and manufacturing from the US and Europe. A tuna processing plant partly owned and operated by a US firm is the biggest single employer on the islands.

Country profile

The Republic of Seychelles comprises 115 small islands scattered over an area of about 1.3 million sq. km (0.5 million sq. miles) in the Indian Ocean, just south of the equator some 1,600 km (1,000 miles) east of Mombasa. The main island, Mahe, about 27 km (17 miles) long and 8 km (5 miles) at its widest, is the largest of 40 non-volcanic Inner Islands formed by granite rock, renowned for their unique flora and fauna. The outlying islands consist of nine archipelagos, including coralline atolls and groups of volcanic islands. The Aldabra, Farquhar and Desroches island groups are all included in the Republic of Seychelles. Most Seychellians are of mixed descent, primarily African and European. French-Kreol is the lingua franca and an official language, together with English. The population is predominantly Christian.

History

The Seychelles were uninhabited when the Britsih east India Company discovered the archipelago in 1609. It soon became a haven for pirates. The islands were claimed by the French in 1756 and administered as part of the colony of Mauritius. In the Peace Treaty of Paris in 1814 the French signed over Séchelles to the British who anglisized the name to its current spelling. The Seychelles islands gained independence in 1976 under a coalition government headed by Sir James Mancham, leader of the Seychelles Democratic Party (DP), as president, and Marxist nationalist, France Albert René of the *Front Progressiste du Peuple Seychellois* or Progressive Front of the Seychelles People (FPPS) as prime minister. In 1977 while Mancham was abroad, René overthrew him and set up a one-party pro-Soviet state. (The American space agency's radar station which paid a substantial rent, was allowed to stay). In 1992, in the wake of Soviet Union's demise, René lifted restrictions on opposition parties and won handsomely

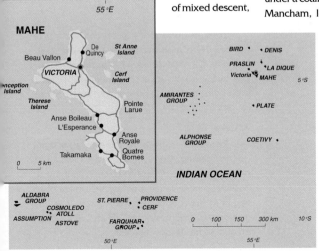

Fast facts

at the polls. He was reelected with two-thirds of the vote in 1998. Mancham was a distant third.

Government

An executive President is elected by popular vote for a 5-year term and appoints a Council of Ministers. A unicameral 35-seat National Assembly, or Assemblée Nationale, consists of 25 elected seats and 10 appointed on a proportional basis to parties that won 9% or more of the popular vote. In the 1998 election, René's FPPS gained 30 seats against 3 for the Opposition Unie or United Opposition (OU) and 1 for Mancham's DP.

Economic policy

Despite reforms to attract foreign investors, the government still plays a large role in the economy and accounts for 40% of GDP. Seychelles has, however, undertaken an intensive review of its policies in support of its application for membership of the World Trade Organization.

Sectors

Tourism and fishing are major sectors apart from some agriculture and small-scale manufacturing. A fully equipped international airport on Mahe island not only handles an inward tourist flow but serves as a stopover on international routes. Victoria has the deepest port in the Indian Ocean and serves as a major fish and freight transshipment point. There are plans to enlarge port facilities to cater to oil and gas products.

Privatization

Privatization has created new investment opportunities. A celebrated case is the partial purchase several years ago by a subsidiary of US-based Heinz of a state-owned tuna plant.

Investment

Foreign investment in recent years was largely in telecommunications, tourism and manufacturing. Recent expansion has turned the tuna-processing plant owned and operated by Heinz in partnership with the government into the largest employer on the islands.

Trade

Leading foreign exchange earners are tourism and fishing, largely geared to exporting of canned tuna, fish, and frozen shrimp and prawns. Recently several varieties of Seychellian tea have begun to break into overseas markets. The import market is dominated by Indian, French, British and South African suppliers.

Financial sector

Four international banks maintain branches in the Seychelles. Corporate tax, withholding tax on dividends and interests, wealth tax, capital gains tax, customs duties, stamp duty, and exchange controls have been waived for offshore investors. The Insurance Act, modeled on similar legislation in Singapore, makes provision for the licensing of offshore insurance companies.

Taxes and tariffs

Investors are exempted from withholding tax on dividends, personal income tax, wealth tax and the like. Some trade regulations, however, are still restrictive and at variance with WTO standards. Imports usually require government approval in one form or another and price controls apply to imports. Import permits for "essential" goods, including raw materials, are automatically approved while nonessentials are subject to quotas. Capital goods can, however, be imported without restriction.

Business activity

AGRICULTURE

Coconuts, cinnamon, vanilla, sweet potatoes, cassava (tapioca), bananas, broiler chickens, tuna fish.

INDUSTRIES

Fishing, tourism, processing of coconuts and vanilla, coir (coconut fiber),rope, boat building, printing, furniture, beverages.

EXPORTS

$386 million (1999 est.): fish, cinnamon, bark, copra, petroleum products (reexports).

IMPORTS

$483 million (1999 est.): manufactured goods, food, petroleum products, tobacco, beverages, machinery and transportation equipment.

MAJOR TRADING PARTNERS

France, UK, China, Germany, Japan, Singapore, South Africa.

Doing Business with Seychelles

▶ **Investment**

Several government organizations have been established to assist potential foreign investors. A one-stop shop, the Seychelles International Business Authority (SIBA), is largely preoccupied with the registration of offshore companies and promoting the Seychelles as a hub in the Indian Ocean region while the Seychelles International Trade Zone concentrates on tax-exempt, export-oriented operations in the zone. The greatest potential for US investors is in tourism, fisheries, light manufacturing and infrastructure. There is growing foreign interest in newly created opportunities for secure and confidential offshore banking and insurance facilities.

▶ **Trade**

Marketing of products is inhibited by a lack of adequate foreign exchange and the government policy of restricting non-essential imports.

▶ **Trade finance**

The foreign exchange shortage is one of the main obstacles to doing business in the Seychelles.

▶ **Selling to the government**

The state-owned Seychelles Marketing Board has a monopoly on the importation of essential products such as rice, sugar and dairy products.

▶ **Financing projects**

Major infrastructure investments are typically financed by bilateral donors such as France, Kuwait and China and multilateral agencies such as the World Bank, the European Development Bank and the African Development Bank.

▶ **Legal rights**

By its own admission, the Seychelles is not sufficiently equipped by law to provide intellectual property protection. Steps are underway to tighten the laws and improve monitoring.

▶ **Labor**

The local workforce is easily adaptable to manufacturing and service sector tasks. In the fishing sector, there is a wealth of talent.

▶ **Culture**

Business is conducted at a an easy pace in either English, French or Creole. Seychellians are quite informal and casual dress is the norm even at the senior government and company levels.

Sierra Leone

In recent years, this promising former British protectorate suffered heavily as rival forces engaged in fierce fighting. Substantial mineral, agricultural and fishing resources in Sierra Leone remain underutilized as potential foreign investors steer clear. Interruption in the mining of diamonds, bauxite and rutile has practically dried up the flow of foreign currency and the mass exodus of professionals from Sierra Leone is continuing. Hopes are that this country will regain its equilibrium in the foreseeable future and start back on the road of recovery.

Country profile

The Republic of Sierra Leone is a country of many rivers perched on a mountainous peninsula. From the coast the land rises gradually to the Loma and Tingi mountains near the northern border. As the capital of a country with an average rainfall of between 79 and 197 inches (2,000 and 5,000 mm) per year, Freetown is one of the world's wettest cities. Rainforest covers much of the terrain. The Temne and Mende are major groups, There are substantial Creole (or Krio) and Lebanese minorities. English is the official language, but Krio, an English-based Creole language, is the *lingua franca*.

History

The Bulom people were the first to settle in the region, followed by the Mende and the Temme in the 15th Century and the Fulani. In the middle of the 15th Century, Portuguese mariners began to sail up the broad mouth of the Sierra Leone River in search of fresh water. They named the mountainous peninsula, Serra Lyoa and traded in gold, ivory and slaves. During the last half of the 16th Century a Mende warrior people invaded the region and subjugated the local communities. Towards the end of the 18th Century liberated slaves from North America sponsored by private British patrons found a province in Sierra Leone. In 1808 Britain turned the capital, Freetown, into a naval base to enforce the abolition of slavery and in 1896 declared a protectorate

over the interior to prevent it from falling into French hands. After the discovery of gold, diamonds, iron ore, bauxite and rutile, the colony experienced considerable economic growth. Since Dr. Milton Margai and his Sierra Leone People's Party (SLPP) led Sierra Leone to independence in 1961, the colony has experienced more than its fair share of coups and counter-coups. On 25 May 1997, the democratically-elected government of President Ahmad Tejan Kabbah was overthrown by a disgruntled coalition of personnel of the Armed Forces Revolu-

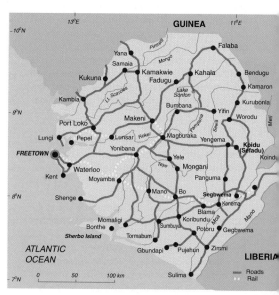

tionary Council (AFRC) and the Revolutionary United Front (RUF) under the command of Major Johnny Paul Koroma. In 1998 Kabbah was reinstated by the Economic Community of West African States Cease-Fire Monitoring Group (ECOMOG). Since January 1999, when renewed fighting broke out between the AFRC/RUF and ECOMOG troops, commerce has been at a standstill and hundreds of thousands of people have been driven from their homes.

Government

The current constitution provides for an executive President, directly elected for a maximum of two 4-year terms. The 80-member House of Representatives serves for 5-year terms and consists of 68 seats decided by general election on a proportional basis and 12 reserved seats for representatives of the traditional chiefs. The Sierra Leone People's Party (SLPP) and its alliance partners hold a majority over the United National People's Party (UNPP). Pres. Kabbah won nearly 60% of the popular vote in 1996.

Economic policy

The IMF introduced an enhanced structural adjustment facility in 1994 and the World Bank's commercial lending arm, The International Finance Corporation, assisted with financing. Through far-reaching structural reforms, including trade and exchange rate liberalization and strengthened fiscal management, inflation was brought down from 100% in 1990/91 to 6% in 1996 and the budget deficit reduced from 12% in 1989/90 to 6% in 1996. There have, however, been drastic reverses as a result of the recent outbreak of violence.

Sectors

Agriculture, mostly on smallholdings, provides a livelihood for about 70% of the population. Rice is grown by most farmers, but despite government efforts to promote self-sufficiency, increasing quantities have to be imported. Other food crops include maize, cassava, sweet potatoes and sorghum. The major export crops are coffee, cocoa, palm kernels and ginger. Fishing is a growing industry with oysters and shrimp as major products. Diamonds are mined in alluvial fields around the eastern towns of Koidu-Sefadu and Kenema by numerous individual diggers and a government-controlled corporation. Rutile (titanium dioxide) mined in the sands on Sherbro Island has overtaken diamonds as the principal export. Sierra Leone is currently the world's sec-

Fast facts

POLITICAL	
Head of State	Pres. Ahmad Tejan Kabbah (1996)
Ruling Party	SLPP
Main Opposition	UNPP
Independence	27 April 1961
Capital	Freetown
Official languages	English

PHYSICAL	
Total area	27,698 sq. miles 71,740 sq. km. (± South Carolina)
Arable land	7% of land area
Coastline	402 km

POPULATION	
Total	5.3 million
Av. yearly growth	4.34%
Population/sq. mile	187
Urban population	35%
Adult literacy	31.4%

ECONOMY[1]	
Currency	Leone (Le) (US$1=1,830.80)
GDP (real)	$731 million
GDP growth rate	-8.1%
GNP per capita[2]	$140
GDP (ppp)[3]	$2.7 billion
GDP per cap. (ppp)[3]	$530
Inflation rate	37.4%
Exports	$93 million
Imports	$135 million
Development aid	$137 million
External debt	$1.26 billion
Unemployment	N/A

INFRASTRUCTURE	
Railroads	85 km
Paved roads	11%
Motor vehicles	48,000
Air passenger/km	66 million
Telephones/1,000	3
Main intl.airport	Freetown
Main port	Freetown

1. Statistics are based on World Bank data.
2. Atlas method.
3. See page 151 for an explanation of GDP based on purchasing power parity (ppp).

ond largest producer of this mineral, an essential ingredient in paints. Also, bauxite ore has overtaken diamond mining in importance.

Investment

Foreign investment, mostly British, is largely concentrated in the mining sector. Output in diamond mining is expected to increase once stability returns.

Trade

Diamonds have for many years been the principal export, but in recent years rutile accounted for over 40% of export earnings, followed by bauxite ore and diamonds.

Financial sector

Private foreign exchange bureaus operate freely, bank accounts in foreign currencies are available, and interest rates fairly reflect market conditions. Banking and tax laws are being reformed.

Business activity

AGRICULTURE

Rice, coffee, cocoa, palm kernels, palm oil, peanuts, poultry, cattle, sheep, pigs, fish.

INDUSTRIES

Mining (diamonds), small-scale manufacturing (beverages, textiles, cigarettes, footwear), petroleum refining.

NATURAL RESOURCES

Diamonds, bauxite, iron ore.

EXPORTS

$93 million (1999 est.): diamonds, rutile, cocoa, coffee, fish.

IMPORTS

$135 million (1999 est.): foodstuffs, machinery and equipment, fuel and lubricants.

MAJOR TRADING PARTNERS

Belgium, Spain, US, UK, Côte d'Ivoire, Belgium, Luxembourg.

Doing Business with Sierra Leone

▶ **Investment**

For security reasons most foreigners pass on the considerable potential in this troubled country as rebels continue to operate in the mineral-rich northern and eastern portions of the country. While fighting has caused suspension of most mineral operations, foreign entrepreneurs are expected back as soon as stability can be restored. In the past the mineral industry accounted for 20% of the nation's gross domestic product, 80% to 90% of export earnings, and employed almost 15% of the total workforce, primarily in rural areas. There are opportunities in the mining of bauxite, cassiterite, clays, columbite, diamonds, gold, iron ore, kaolin, lignite, platinum, dimension stone, and tantalite.

▶ **Trade**

Reconstruction and repair of roads, schools, hospitals, airports and telecommunications connections, largely with the help of donor funding, are areas where foreigners are bound to play a meaningful role in the future. Some projects have already been initiated with the help of funding from international donor agencies. Sales of food, clothing and other supplies at this time are mostly to humanitarian and specialized agencies that will in-

sist on giveaway pricing to augment donations. Once Sierra Leone has regained its equilibrium it should again become a small but vibrant market for a wide range of consumer goods.

▶ **Exchange controls**

The foreign exchange rate is market-determined. Private foreign exchange bureaus operate freely and bank accounts in foreign currencies are allowed.

▶ **Financing projects**

Sierra Leone has been a MIGA member since 1996 and has pending applications with the institution for projects in agribusiness, mining and telecommunications. World Bank activities have focused on sectoral programs and projects in the agriculture, education, infrastructure, and health sectors. The IFC's portfolio as of July 31, 1998 totalled $5.2 million (in Sierra Rutile).

★ Somalia

Foreign business with Somalia remains on hold as the struggle between the fighting factions continues. Economic progress has stalled in most parts of the country in the wake of the unrest and instability that followed the fall of the military regime in 1991. After failed attempts by US and UN military forces to impose a settlement while overseeing the distribution of international food and other humanitarian aid, Somalia has been left largely to its own devices since the mid-1990s. A transitional government installed in 2000 faces strong opposition from rival factions. In the northwestern region, clans in former British Somaliland have established their own independent Republic of Somaliland and in the central region other clans have formed the Puntland State of Somalia.

Country profile

The largely inoperative Somali Democratic Republic has a rhino-horn shaped coastline of more than 3,000 km (1,684 miles)—the longest in Africa—which earned it the designation, Horn of Africa. The Ras Hafun peninsula, to the south of Cape Guardafui at the Horn's tip, is the African continent's most easterly point. Ethiopia cuts into

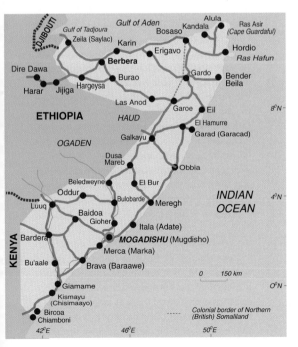

Somalia, virtually dividing it into northern Somalia (the former British Somaliland) and southern Somalia (formerly Italian Somaliland). In the north a steep escarpment rises inland from a narrow coastline towards Ethiopia. The south consists largely of monotonous plains below 500 m (1,650 ft) and the region adjoining the Juba and Shibeli rivers provides grazing for livestock. About half of the largely homogenous population is nomadic and the other half evenly divided between settled farming regions of Juba-Shebeh and the towns. Islam is the prevailing faith and most Somalians speak Somali, which, together with Arabic, is an official language. English and Italian are the main European languages.

History

While early civilizations were flourishing in the lower Nile Valley several thousand years ago, there was a migration southward into this region. Most of these early settlers were Cushites of caucasoid origin such as the Berbers and the ancient Egyptians and Nubians. About 1,500 years ago Negroid peoples arrived from the west and in the course of time extensive intermixing occurred. Arab and Persian merchant mariners founded the port of Mogadishu in the

Fast facts

10th Century and subsequently Merca, Brava, Kismayu, Lamu, Kilwa and other settlements further to the south. First the Hawiya Cushite clan near Mogadishu and in the ensuing years most others adopted the Muslim faith. In the 16th Century the area bordering the Gulf of Aden was part of the Turkish Ottoman empire. The Portuguese controlled the coastal centers in the south but were driven out early in the 18th Century by the Omani Arabs who gained control of the coast from Zanzibar and Mombasa to Mogadishu. Through all this activity the Somali peoples remained divided. At the height of the colonial era at turn of the 19th Century the Somalis were ruled by three European powers—France, Britain and Italy—and Ethiopia, in five separate regions. By mutual agreement, Italian and British Somaliland were united and given their independence as the united Republic of Somalia in 1960, while French Somaliland became the independent Republic of Djibouti in 1977. Somalis continue to live in Kenya's North-West Frontier province and in Ethiopia's Ogaden desert. After a brief period of democracy, the Republic of Somalia fell under the power of General Mohammed Siad Barre, who nationalized the economy as part of his economically disastrous policy of "scientific socialism."

Recent developments

In 1977 Barre attempted to distract attention from his domestic failures by sending army units to help Somali rebels trying to take over Ethiopia's Ogaden. The Ethiopians enlisted Cuban help and dealt the Somali troops heavy losses. An estimated one million ethnic Somalis sought refuge in Somalia from war and droughts. In 1991 the Majerteen and Hawiye clans formed the United Somali Congress (USC) and forced Barre to flee. Once in control of Mogadishu, the USC found itself split between supporters of Ali Mahdi Mohammed and Mohammed Farah Aydeed, triggering another internal battle. Intervention by US and UN troops to enforce a peace and oversee the delivery of international food and medical supplies to refugees saved numerous lives but ended in political failure. The fighting between the factions resumed in 1995 after the foreign forces evacuated. In what had been British Somaliland, Mohammed Ibrahim Egal was named president of the self-styled Somaliland Republic and managed to keep the area largely out of the troubles in the rest of the country. In recent years there has been an influx of Somalis from

Mogadishu into this northwest region, trying to escape the brutal fighting and enjoy relative peace.

Government

Since 1991 Somalia has been without a central government or sovereign economic authority. In August 2000 a parliament convened in neighboring Djibouti and elected a new president, Abdulkassim Salat Hassan. Ali Khalif Galaid was appointed prime minister. Despite recognition of this transitional government by several neighboring countries, Somali warlords in Mogdishu and the breakaway regions of Somaliland and Puntland have not.

Economic policy

The continuing power struggle in and around the former capital, Mogadishu, and along the routes of communication has all but halted economic activity or planning in southern Somalia. In northwest Somalia, however, where Ibrahim Egal has been installed as President of a separate Republic of Somaliland, the picture appears less bleak. Economic planning and activity in this region focuses largely on rebuilding of roads, and telecommunication lines.

Sectors

Agriculture accounts for about two-thirds of GDP with livestock raising as the main activity. The major cash crop, bananas, is cultivated along the Juba and Shibeli rivers for export, mostly to Italy. Also grown for cash in this region are cotton and sugar cane while food crops include sorghum and maize. Northern Somalia is the world's largest source of incense and myrrh. Even though Somalia has the longest coastline in Africa, its fishing industry is still relatively undeveloped. Mining is confined to the commercial extraction of salt and gypsum but there are reserves of iron ore, uranium, beryl and columbite. With an estimated 7 million tons, Somalia has the world's largest reserves of gypsum hydrite but extraction has been limited. Manufacturing is largely in agricultural and food processing.

Business activity

AGRICULTURE
Bananas, sorghum, corn, sugar cane, mangoes, sesame seeds, beans, cattle, sheep, goats, fish.

INDUSTRIES
Small industries, including sugar refining, textiles , petroleum refining (shut down).

NATURAL RESOURCES
Uranium.

EXPORTS
$123 million (1995 est.): livestock, bananas, hides, fish.

IMPORTS
$60 million (1995 est.): manufactures, petroleum products, foodstuffs, construction materials.

MAJOR TRADING PARTNERS
Saudi Arabia, Yemen, Italy, Egypt, US, Kenya, Djibouti, Brazil, Pakistan.

Doing Business with Somalia

▶ **Investment**

Once peace is restored, foreign activity in oil exploration and mining is bound to follow. A large number of minerals have been discovered, including gold, gypsum, iron ore, kynite, lead barite, limestone piezo-quartz, tin, sepiolite titaniferous sand, and uranium. To date, only limestone and gypsum deposits have been exploited commercially. The recovery of gas reserves in the Ogaden region of Ethiopia and oil across the Red Sea in North and South Yemen spurred interest in Somalia on the part of Chevron, Conoco, Exxon Mobil and others. Since the disintegration of Somalia most of this activity ceased but the self-proclaimed Somaliland Republic has recently indicated that oil prospecting contracts signed by the former government of united Somalia in its region would be honored. Telecommunications and fishing are future prospects.

▶ **Trade**

The only potential sales to most of Somalia at this stage are in food and other supplies to UN and other agencies involved in relief programs.

▶ **Financing**

Most of Somalia's international financing consist of humanitarian assistance and disaster relief with UN agencies and some NGO programs involved.

Our influence in the world of fine paper has spread across the globe.

Sappi is a global pulp and paper company that is proud of its South African roots. Today we are the world's largest producer of the coated woodfree paper used for everything from wine labels to art books to quality magazines as well as the dissolving pulp used to produce viscose fabrics. We manufacture on three continents and export to over a hundred and fifty countries. As a focused and growing global enterprise we are in a position to offer our customers better service, more innovative products and a wider choice of the world's leading brands of fine paper wherever they may be.

sappi

The word for fine paper

www.sappi.com

South Africa

Rated by the UN as one of the world's 26 industrialized nations and by the US Commerce Department as one of a few select Big Emerging Markets (BEMs), South Africa offers great potential for exporters and investors with the right products, resources and commitment. South Africa has a substantial and sophisticated market with significant growth potential, well-developed financial institutions and capital markets, first-rate communication and transport links and readily available, inexpensive electrical power and raw materials. It offers easy access not only to neighboring markets but elsewhere in Africa. In areas such as mining, information technology and paper production South African companies have become major international players.

Country profile

The Republic of South Africa at the southern tip of the African continent comprises 1,219,090 sq. km. or 470,893 sq. miles (including two island possessions more than 1,920 km/1,193 miles southeast of Cape Town—Prince Edward and Marion. The country is within the subtropical high pressure belt and wide expanses of ocean have a moderating influence on the climate. More than 76% of the population is of black African heritage; some 12.7% whites; 8.5% Colored; and 2.5% East Indian. Two-thirds of black Africa belongs to the Nguni group and speak Xhosa, Zulu, Swati and Ndebele. The rest belongs to the South, North and West Sotho (Tswana), the Tsonga, and the Venda. The Coloreds are a mixed race and Indians are the descendants of indentured laborers brought to Natal by Britain in the 1860s to work on sugar plantations. Forebears of the Afrikaners and English-speaking whites came from the Netherlands, France and Britain in the 17th and early 19th centuries, and, more recently, Germany, Portugal, Italy, Greece and other European countries. There is also a sizeable Chinese community. Next to English and Afrikaans, nine major Bantu languages enjoy official status. South African society is predominantly Christian but there are also sizeable minorities of Muslims, Jews and Hindu.

History

The region is said to have been occupied by small nomadic groups of San or Bushmen hunter-gatherers 100,000 years ago. Some 2,000 years

Map legend:
- Rail
- Highways

ZIMBABWE
MOZAMBIQUE
BOTSWANA
NAMIBIA
SWAZILAND
LESOTHO

Messina
Louis Trichardt
Palaborwa
Pietersburg
Kruger National Park
PRETORIA
Skukuza
Mafikeng
Nelspruit
Vereeniging
Johannesburg
Klerksdorp
Kroonstad
Sishen
Hluluwe Park
Upington
Welkom
Kalahari Gemsbok Park
Kimberley
Ladysmith
Richards Bay
Alexander Bay
BLOEMFONTEIN
Pietermaritzburg
Port Nolloth
Kenhardt
De Aar
Aliwal North
Durban
Springbok
Victoria West
Middelburg
Port Shepstone
ATLANTIC OCEAN
Calvinia
Umtata
Port St. Johns
Vanrhynsdorp
Cradock
Bisho
Saldanha
Beaufort West
Graaff Reinet
East London
Worcester
CAPE TOWN
Port Elizabeth
Cape Point
Mossel Bay
Knysna
Cape Agulhas
Bredasdorp
INDIAN OCEAN

0 — 480 Kilometers
0 — 300 Miles

24°S

20°E   24°E   28°E   32°E

321

Fast facts

ago they were gradually displaced by the pastoral Khoi or Hottentot and 1,500 years ago migrant Bantu entered the region from the north-central part of the continent. Portuguese explorer Bartholomeu Dias was the first European to set foot on South African soil in August 1487. It was, however, only on 6 April 1652 that a small group of Dutch under command of Jan van Riebeeck of the Dutch East India Company settled at the Cape. In 1689 they were joined by French Huguenots who developed the settlement into a notable wine producer. Britain took control of the Cape in 1806. The new British settlers aligned themselves with the Dutch frontiersmen. However, relations between the British authorities and the Boers (farmers)—as these descendants of the original Dutch and French settlers called themselves—were strained. The Boers trekked north and established their own independent Republics of the Transvaal and the Orange Free State. After their defeat by Britain in the Anglo-Boer War of 1899-1902 both Boer Republics were ruled from Westminster for eight years until 31 May 1910 when, together with the Cape and Natal colonies, they received independence as part of the Union of South Africa. Until 1994 the country was ruled by a succession of white governments applying segregation in one form or another. Beginning in 1912 the African National Congress (ANC) represented much of the disenfranchised black majority. In 1960s, the ANC abandoned its non-violent stance at the insistence of leaders such as Nelson Mandela, Walter Sisulu and Govan Mbeki. With most of these leaders later convicted and jailed at Robben Island, the ANC continued its struggle from abroad. The decision in 1990 by President F.W. de Klerk to scrap apartheid and negotiate a new South Africa with Mandela and his comrades led to the first free elections on 24 April 1994. The ANC won and Nelson Mandela became president. After his retirement in 1999, Deputy President Thabo Mbeki led the ANC to its second major victory and assumed the presidency.

Government

Parliament consists of a National Assembly with 400 members elected on a proportional basis, and a National Council of Provinces (NCOP), consisting of 54 permanent members and 36 special delegates representing provincial interests. The President, formally elected by the National Assembly, is both the Head of State and leads the Cabinet. Each of the nine provinces has its own legislature consisting of between 30 and 80 members and is headed by a premier representing the majority party. Since the 1999 election the ANC has held a two-thirds majority in the national parliament with 266 seats against 38 for the largely white Democratic Party led by Tony Leon and 34 for the Inkatha Freedom Party (IFP) headed by Zulu Chief Mangosuthu Buthelezi. The IFP is in coalition with the ANC while the DP has formed the Democratic Alliance together with the New National Party (NNP) with its 28 seats and the Federal Alliance (FA) with its 2 seats. The other nine smaller parties include the white right-wing Vryheidsfront (Freedom Front) and the black left-wing Pan African Congress of Azania (PAC). The ANC also governs in all the provinces except two—the Western Cape, where the Democratic Alliance rules, and Kwazulu/Natal, where the IFP governs.

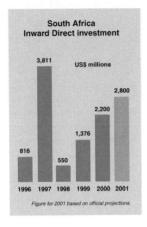

South Africa Inward Direct investment

US$ millions

816 — 1996
3,811 — 1997
550 — 1998
1,376 — 1999
2,200 — 2000
2,800 — 2001

Figure for 2001 based on official projections.

Economic policy

The South African government sees its broad goals as the creation of a strong, dynamic and balanced economy; the elimination of poverty; meeting the basic needs of every South African; development of human resources; protection against racial or gender discrimination in hiring, promotion or training; the development of a prosperous and balanced regional economy in southern Africa; and integration into the world economy. Rolled out in July 1996, its Growth, Employment and Redistribution (GEAR) macroeconomic strategy set specific goals in all spheres of economic activity, ranging from gross domestic product growth to budget deficits, interest rates, inflation and job creation. Even though the country has fallen short in terms of GDP growth and job creation, it held its own on inflation and deficit targets. The government continues to receive good ratings from Moody's, Standard & Poors, Fitch and other rating agencies.

Sectors

South Africa has a modern, well-diversified economy. Agriculture contributes about 4.5% of the gross domestic product (GDP) and accounts for 13% of the total employment. Mining and min-eral processing—even though they have been outstripped by manufacturing in recent years—remain vital to the economy. They still make an 8% direct contribution to GDP and employ more than half a million. South Africa's mineral wealth is found in diverse geological formations. The Witwatersrand Basin around Johannesburg yields 98% of South Africa's gold output while the Bushveld Complex, spanning the North-West and Mpumalanga provinces, contains the world's largest reserves of platinum group minerals (PGMs), chromium, vanadium, nickel, fluorspar and andalusite, apart from substantial supplies of antimony, asbestos, diamonds, coal, fluorspar, phosphates, iron ore, lead, zinc, uranium, vermiculite and zirconium. Both South Africa's fishing and forestry industries have developed into key economic players on the domestic scene and important currency earners. The sophistication of its manufacturing industry places South Africa in the company of the world's thirty top industrial nations. Nearly 32% of GDP is derived from secondary industry and policy-makers are devoting particular attention to sound, accelerated development of this sector. South Africa manufactures a wide range of consumer goods, including food products, textiles, footwear and clothing, metal and chemical products, and paper and paper products. The production of capital goods such as machinery, transport and electrical equipment is also expanding. In 1997, manufacturing, electricity, gas, water and construction contributed almost a third of the nation's total GDP, compared to agriculture's 4.5% and mining's 7.8%. South Africa's modern and extensive transport system places it in the company of top industrialized nations. A number of countries in southern Africa use this network to move their imports and exports. In the past the government has assisted strategic undertakings with subsidies and preferential treatment, including ADE (diesel engines), SASOL (synthetic fuels and petrochemicals), IDC (Industrial Development Corporation), CSIR (Scientific and Industrial Research), Mossgas, the Strategic Fuel Fund, and Soekor (oil and gas exploration). Since 1994, however, the trend has been to privatize.

South Africa's Major Trading Partners				
Country	Exports		Imports	
	2000 Total R Billion³	%¹	2000 Total R billion³	%¹
US	18.5	12.11	16.0	11.77
Germany	11.8	7.78	18.0	13.24
UK	15.2	8.95	11.6	8.57
Japan	12.1	7.98	10.7	7.9
Italy	4.3	2.79	4.5	3.32
France	2.9	1.87	5.7	4.2
Total Trade²	136.0	100	152.8	100

1. Percentage of total South African imports and exports.
2. Total trade, including all others.
3. Rand billion, constant 1995 prices.

Source: SA Department of Trade & Industry

Privatization

In 1995, under a "National Framework Agreement" (NFA), government, business, and labor agreed to a substantial program of restructuring and privatization of state assets. Partially or fully privatized so far are the Airports Company, six radio stations of the state-owned SA Broadcasting Corporation, Telkom (the national telecommunications company), and South African Airways (SAA). The two biggest deals to date are the sale in 1997 of 30% percent of Telkom SA to a consortium of SBC Communications of the US and Telekom Malaysia for $1,261 million and the sale in 1999 of 20% of SAA to Swissair for $230 million. Deals in the offing involve an additional stake in Telkom and the restructuring of Denel (a defense contractor), Eskom (a power utility), and Transnet (the country's major transport group). Earnings from privatization over the next four years are expected to exceed $5.6 billion. So far the government has managed to overcome opposition from the trade unions and the South African Communist Party.

Investment

The US tops the list of foreign investors between 1994 and 1998 with a total of R14.3 billion, followed by Malaysia with R6.7 billion, Britain (R6.2 billion), Germany (R2.6 billion) and Japan with R1.8 billion. From 1994 until mid-1999, SBC Communications was a close second on the FDI list to Malaysia's Petronas. Dow Chemicals, Coca-Cola, IBM, Salem, Goodyear, Duracell, Ford and McDonalds are other big US investors. Main sectors for investment were telecommunications, energy and oil, automobile manufacturing, food

and beverages, chemicals and plastics and mining. Dow Chemical's takeover of Sentrachem for $850 million in 1998 is the largest single outright purchase of a South African private company in recent years. During the past six years, however, direct investment abroad by South African multinational firms has outpaced FDI inflows. South Africa has also become the largest source of investment not only in neighboring SADC nations but much of the rest of Africa.

Trade

In 2000, the US topped the list of nations trading with South Africa. Other significant trading partners were Germany, the United Kingdom, Japan, Italy and France. In February 1999, the U.S. and South Africa signed a Trade and Investment Framework Agreement (TIFA)—the first in Sub-Saharan Africa. The US is a major supplier of wheat and rice to South Africa and in 1999 accounted for 11% of the country's total agricultural imports. The US also has a significant share of the growing market for high technology equipment, computers and software, and machinery. As a result of the liberalization of its economy, South Africa's ratio of trade in goods and services to gross domestic product increased from 53.6% in 1994 to 64.8% in 1997.

Financial sector

The South African Reserve Bank (SARB) oversees a world-class banking system comprising 56 fully licensed institutions and 60 representative offices of foreign banks. The JSE Securities Exchange is Africa's largest and one of the world's top twenty exchanges. As of July 1999, the total capitalization value of the more than 600 firms listed on the JSE firms exceeded R1.3 trillion—approximately $216 billion. In 1995 the JSE began permitting banks and foreign firms to join its registry. Foreign trade accounts for a sizeable portion of the daily volume. Among the significant foreign banks that have expanded into South Africa to assist investors and traders is HSBC Equator Bank. This bank also has operations in Angola, Côte d'Ivoire, Ghana, Mozambique and Uganda.

Sophistication

The level of sophistication of South Africa can best be judged by looking at the size of the top one hundred companies and tracing the success that its private sector has had in capturing

Before you invest
in African soil,
choose a partner that knows
the lie of the land.

Introducing the IDC.

Our mission is to contribute to the generation of balanced, sustainable economic growth in Southern Africa and beyond, through promoting entrepreneurship and building competitive industries and enterprises based on sound business principles. We do this by providing capital in the form of straight loans, equity, and quasi-equity, to both new and existing private sector enterprises in the tourism, agro-industry, mining and manufacturing sectors. But we are much more than a loan capital resource. In our 60 years of providing competitive loans and equity to Southern Africa's entrepreneurs, we have developed a sound understanding of what delivers long-term business success.

Before finance is approved, ventures are thoroughly researched by an expert team, so that when we invest, we do so with total confidence and commitment to long-term involvement. In short, we help make viable ideas happen – matching the vision of international investors with our own. Because we believe it takes vision to see vision.

IDC

TOGETHER, WE CAN TURN BIG IDEAS INTO BIG BUSINESS.

For more information, contact the IDC. Tel: +2711 269 3000; Fax: +2711 269 3116; E-mail: callcentre@idc.co.za; Website: www.idc.co.za

world market share not only in mining and minerals but manufacturing and information technology. Notable among these are Sappi, which leads the world in the production of fine coated paper with a market share of 25% in the US and in Western Europe, and more than 60% in Africa; South African Breweries which ranks fifth worldwide and operates breweries in Africa and Europe; Anglo American and Billiton with mining interests spanning the globe; and Datatec and Didata that have become world players in information technology after acquisitions in Japan, Europe and North America. Sappi today has manufacturing operations in eight countries on three continents and sells in more than a hundred countries. Barloworld, the country's major industrial brand management company, has a significant presence not only in other African countries but around the world, including the United States, the UK and Europe. It is the world's largest independent lift truck dealer, a leading provider of comprehensive transport solutions, a vendor of cement, lime, paints and coatings, and steel tube, as well as a provider of financial services and leasing. Its brand name portfolio includes such familiar names as Caterpillar, Mercedes Benz, BMW, Toyota and Hyster. The shares of Sappi and Barloworld and other major South African firms trade not only on the JSE Securities Exchange but on foreign exchanges as well. Both Barloworld and Sappi have a considerable foreign shareholding—more than 60% of Sappi's stock was foreign-owned in April 2001.

Key partners

The Development Bank of Southern Africa (DBSA) works with donors and partners at international, national and regional levels on targeted infrastructural and strategic developments. It is playing an increasingly important role in the Southern African Development Community (SADC). Its investment portfolio has grown rapidly, with approved cumulative loans increasing from R10.3 billion in March 1996 to R21.1 billion by March 2000. Another key component in the South African arsenal to attract and assist foreign participation in the country and on a regional basis is the Industrial Development Corporation of South Africa Limited (IDC). The IDC provides financial and technical assistance for the development of value-adding greenfield expansion or rehabilitation projects in Africa. Its field of interest ranges from manufacturing to energy, mining, minerals beneficiation, agriculture, agro-process-

ing, tourism, information technology, telecommunications and selective franchising. The IDC provides loan finance for a period of between five and ten years for sustainable, worthwhile projects—up to 50% in the SADC region and 25% elsewhere on the continent. It also provides medium- to long-term credit for importers of South African capital goods and services. By June 2001 the IDC's portfolio of African projects under implementation or investigation comprised 17 in 13 countries, excluding South Africa. The IDC has the largest centralized, multi-disciplinary project evaluation group in Southern Africa.

Taxes & tariffs

With the exception of mining companies which are subject to special rates, the corporate tax rate is 30%. A secondary tax on companies (STC) is imposed at a rate of 12.5% on the net dividends and withholding taxes are levied on interest and royalties paid to non-residents. A 14% value-added tax (VAT) applies. Exports are zero-rated, and no VAT is payable on imported capital goods. In keeping with its WTO commitments, the government has sought to reform a complex tariff structure of the past.

Business activity

AGRICULTURE

Corn, wheat, sugar cane, fruit, vegetables, beef, poultry, mutton, wool, diary products.

INDUSTRIES

Mining (world's largest producer of platinum, gold, chromium), automobile assembly, metalworking, machinery, textiles, iron and steel, chemicals, fertilizer, foodstuffs.

NATURAL RESOURCES

Gold, diamonds, platinum, uranium, coal, iron ore, phosphates, manganese.

EXPORTS

$33.3 billion (1999 est.): gold, other minerals and metals, food, chemicals, manufactured goods.

IMPORTS

$30 billion (1999 est.): machinery, transport equipment, chemicals, petroleum products, textiles, scientific instruments.

MAJOR TRADING PARTNERS

US, UK, Germany, Italy, Japan, France.

Doing Business with South Africa

▶ **Investment**

Since 1994 steps have been taken to make South Africa more attractive to foreign investment by reducing import tariffs and subsidies to local firms; eliminating discriminatory non-resident shareholders tax; removing remaining limits on hard currency repatriation; reducing by half secondary tax on corporate dividends; lowering the corporate tax rate on earnings to 30 percent; and allowing foreign investors 100 percent ownership. Foreign investors are not screened or subjected to performance or other special requirements. The government, however, encourages investments that will strengthen, expand, or enhance technology in various industries. Foreign firms are entitled to the same export incentive programs, tax allowances and other trade regulations applicable to domestic enterprises. As the Government pushes ahead with plans to attract strategic equity partners for its large parastatal organizations, there is an increased sensitivity to the concerns of foreign investors.

Incentives and assistance are also available to both locals and foreigners under the Small/Medium Manufacturing Development Program (SMMDP). Since 1994 major areas for investment have been in telecommunications, energy and oil, motor and components, food and beverages, chemicals and plastics, mining, manufacturing and hotels. A Government program of Spatial Development Initiatives (SDIs) has enhanced investment opportunities outside the major industrial centers. An official agency, Investment South Africa (ISA), provides information and assistance to prospective investors, helps identify opportunities, and assists them in finding joint venture partners and obtaining technology and capital. Franchising is an established practice. The Department of Trade and Industry must approve manufacturing royalties.

▶ **Trade**

Rapid development and expansion of telecommunications, large new pollution and waste management systems, increased use of computers and high technology devices, modernization of airports, the introduction of managed health care and a growing market for security systems are only a few areas where American products have found ready acceptance in recent years. The US remains a major exporter of agricultural products and current estimates indicate that for the medium term South Africa will continue to rely in part on imports to meet its food needs. Principal imports for the year 2000 include wheat (600,000 tons), corn (700,000 tons), rice (550,000 tons), vegetable oils (60,000 tons) and a variety of consumer-oriented food products. Most prospective exporters to South Africa find that this country replicates on a smaller scale their domestic market, both in product preference and marketing methods.

At the same time, US importers have been able to purchase sophisticated local manufactures and sold them back into the US market at handsome profits. Lately the rapidly growing tourism sector has provided a market for US suppliers of information systems, marketing, design, architecture, finance and management planning. E-commerce is expected to play a significant role in future business. South Africa is an extremely competitive marketplace and it is essential that exporters provide adequate servicing, spare parts, and components, as well as qualified personnel capable of handling inquiries. It is common to appoint a single agent or distributor capable of providing national coverage either through a single office or a network of branch offices and outlets. South Africa is an ideal springboard for trading with the 13 other countries of the Southern African Development Community (SADC) and the neighboring members of the South African Customs Union (SACU).

▶ **Trade finance**

All Eximbank programs are available to US exporters of goods and services to South Africa. South Africa's sophisticated financial sector provides overdraft facilities and short- to long-term credit. Key areas of business for foreign banks include trade finance, letters of credit, foreign exchange activities and services to offshore investors.

▶ **Selling to the government**

Not only the central government but nine provincial governments and hundreds of local authorities present a market for overseas suppliers of sophisticated goods and services. Government purchasing is done through competitive bidding on tenders published in the State Tender Bulletin and some of the leading newspapers. A local agent is needed to act on behalf of foreign bidders. When selling to the government, consideration should be given to the government's goal to expand black participation in the economy. Even though there are no set rules pressure is growing to include "set-asides" for black businesses. In some large-scale infrastructure projects, such as a recent tender for a third cellular license, including a Black Economic Empowerment (BEE) partner was mandatory. The government's Industrial Participation Program (IPP) mandates a countertrade/offset package for all state and parastatal purchases of goods, services, and lease contracts above $10 million. Under this program, bidders on governmental and parastatal contracts must submit an industrial participation package worth 30 percent of the imported content value. The bidder has seven years to fulfill this obligation.

▶ **Exchange controls**

Exchange controls are administered by the South African Reserve Bank's (SARB) Exchange Control Department through commercial banks that are authorized to deal in foreign currency. In March 1997, the Finance Ministry started to relax foreign exchange controls. Royalties, software license fees, and certain other remittances to non-residents still require the approval of the SARB.

▶ **Legal rights**

An independent judiciary allows full recourse without political interference in disputes over property or any other facet of business. Patents may be registered for 20 years and trademarks for 10 years, renewable for an additional 10 years. While South African IPR laws and regulations are largely TRIPS-compliant, there is still concern over copyright piracy and trademark counterfeiting and the US is working with the government to find ways of reducing infractions.

▶ **Partnerships**

In looking for partners, foreign firms have a range of choices between sophisticated large, medium-sized and smaller entities. Often the choice is determined by prevailing politics which favor black enterprise participation in government contracts. The government has leaned towards Private Public Partnerships (PPPs) in some projects, inviting foreign firms to enter in a joint venture with the authorities. It also makes good sense for foreigners with designs on the regional SADC market and other areas of Africa to join forces with South African firms with extensive local knowledge.

▶ **Establishing a presence**

South Africa's Companies Act provides for clear, transparent regulations concerning the establishment and operation of businesses. Foreign investments are organized under the same rules and regulations as domestic firms with one exception: overseas companies may opt to operate as "external companies" which do not pay tax on undistributed profits. Share capital duty is based

instead on the shares of the parent firm. Foreigners may normally buy into local firms without limitation, either by acquiring shares or assets. There is no record of any expropriation or nationalization of American or any other foreign investment in South Africa.

▶ **Financing projects**

The Development Bank of Southern Africa and the Industrial Development Corporation assist in the financing of projects involving local partners. The Overseas Private Investment Corporation backs and insures US projects in South Africa. The US Trade and Development Agency funds feasibility studies, consultancies, training programs, and other project planning services in the area. Under current exchange controls foreigners need special permission to borrow locally as part of an effort to prevent excessive "gearing" through local financing. The World Bank's International Finance Corporation has established the Africa Enterprise Fund (AEF) to finance projects ranging from $100,000 to $1.5 million at market interest rates.

▶ **Labor**

The government has promised to review labor legislation in response to complaints that the South African labor market is over-regulated. There are 2.2 million unemployed people in South Africa—23% of the economically active population. Unemployment rates are highest among black South Africans (29%), followed by Coloreds (16%), Indian (10%), and Whites (4%). Nearly 35% of the workers belong to unions . The strongest among them, the 1.8 million member Congress of South African Trade Unions (COSATU), is a full partner in the ANC governing alliance. Even though strike activity has declined sharply under the ANC-led government, COSATU and others have not been slow at using mass stayaways for political purposes.

▶ **Business climate**

Business customs in South Africa are similar to those in the US and Western Europe. South African business people tend to dress conservatively and those of the old school make every effort to be on time for appointments. Even though English dominates, business ignores Afrikaans at its own peril, especially if it is consumer-oriented. There is a level of language sensitivity among Afrikaners that prompts most local firms and many foreign entities to advertise and print their literature in both languages.

Sudan

The mineral and agricultural potential in Africa's largest country, Sudan, remains largely untapped as foreign investors await a resolution to the ongoing costly battle between its Muslim north and non-Muslim south. As long as it remains at war with itself, Sudan will have to defer its dreams of becoming the breadbasket of Africa and the Middle East through large scale irrigation of fertile land along the Nile and its tributaries.There has, however, been recent foreign activity in oil and minerals.

Country profile

The Republic of Sudan spans more than 2,000 km from north to south along the Sahel Belt on the fringe of the Sahara Desert. The Arabs named the territory the territory *bilad al-sudan*— land of the blacks. Except for a few peaks such as Mount Kinyeti (3,187 m/10,456 ft) on the Ugandan border and Mount Marra (3,070 m/10,072 ft)) on its border with Chad, Sudan consists largely of plains below 1,000 m/3,280 ft). The White and Blue Nile tributaries join in Sudan to form the world's longest waterway as it flows north into Egypt. All three of the continent's major linguistic supergroupings—Afroasiatic, Nilo-Saharan and Niger-Congo—are present. More than 70% of the population is Muslim, mostly in the north. There are substantial numbers of Christians in the south. Arabic is the official language.

History

In ancient times the stretch of desert along the Nile drew Negroid people from the south and Caucasoids from the north. Based at Meroe, Nubian civilization reached its zenith in the third and second centuries BC. Sudan became an Anglo-Egyptian condominium in 1899 and gained its independence in 1956. It has since been plagued by ethnic and religious strife between the Arab Muslim north and largely black southern region. Temporary peace followed the granting of wide regional autonomy to southern Sudan in the 1970s but the battle resumed when Khartoum tightened its control once again in the 1980s. In 1996, Gen. Omar Hassan Ahmed al-Bashir, who came to power by military coup in 1989, was elected president over forty other candidates. He was reelected in 2000. A fragmented Sudan People's Liberation Movement/Army (SPLM/A) under Pagan Amum continues to fight for secession of the south. There have been attempts on the part of Libya and Egypt to bring the warring parties to the negotiation table.

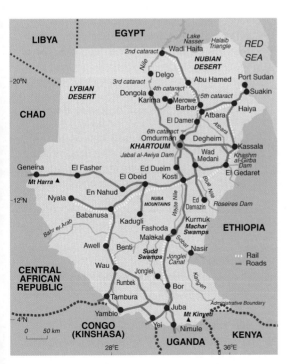

Fast facts

1. Economic statistics are for 1998 and based on World Bank data.
2. Atlas method.
3. See page 151 for an explanation of GDP based on purchasing power parity (ppp).

Government

A nonparty system that evolved from military rule allows for an elected executive President, serving 5-year terms. He appoints vice presidents and the Council of Ministers. The 400-member National Assembly serves 4-year terms—275 members are elected and 125 seats filled by presidential appointees. As war prevented elections in the south, President Omar al-Bashir appointed its representatives. In 1999 he disbanded parliament and declared a state of emergency. Elections were held again in December 2000 but boycotted by most opposition parties. The ruling National Congress Party (NCP) won 355 of the 400 seats.

Economic policy

Sudan reached agreement with the IMF in 1999 on a reform program aimed at streamlining investment procedures, promoting privatization, eliminating most of the non-targeted consumer subsidies, and liberalizing the foreign trade and exchange regimes. Real GDP growth accelerated to an average of 6% in 1998 and inflation declined from 133% in 1996 to 17%.

Sectors

Two-thirds the population depend on crop farming or grazing. With the help of several major water projects, Sudan accounts for 16% of Africa's total irrigated land. Food crops include sorghum, wheat, peanuts, dates, yams, sugar cane, and a variety of fruits and vegetables. Cotton for export is grown in the region between the Blue and White Niles. Sudan accounts for about four-fifths of the world's supply of gum Arabic and is the largest producer of sesame seeds. It has, after Ethiopia, Africa's largest cattle herd. There is fishing along the rivers and the coast. A recently-completed pipeline carries oil for export to Port Sudan. Small amounts of chromium, manganese, and mica are produced. Other minerals with potential include gold, magnesite, and salt. Manufacturing involves processing of agricultural products, textile, paper mills, sugar and petroleum refineries and consumer goods.

Privatization

The government has mapped out a privatization strategy and partnered with foreign oil companies in the development of oil resources.

Investment

Foreign investment focuses largely on oil exploration and exploitation in the southern region. In February 1984 Chevron suspended operations following attacks by the SPLA and in March 1990 sold its interest in the Abu Jarra field and left, leaving the field to Swedish, Malaysian, Dutch, Canadian, Saudi, Iranian and Chinese suitors, and Sudan's Sudapet. There is some US involvement in sugar cane and cotton growing.

Trade

Until recently more than 50% of Sudan's export revenues came from cotton lint and cottonseed. Other major exports are gum Arabic, sorghum, peanuts, and sesame seeds. This is bound to change as oil exports increase. Main trading partners are Saudi Arabia, Italy, Germany, Britain, Thailand, Japan, and China.

Financial sector

Sudan has prohibited the establishment of foreign banks since 1985. The application of Islamic law to banking practices in 1991 put an end to the charging of interest in official transactions.

Business activity

AGRICULTURE
Cotton, groundnuts (peanuts), sorghum, millet, wheat, gum arabic, sesame, sheep.

INDUSTRIES
Cotton ginning, textiles, cement, edible oils, sugar, soap distilling, shoes, petroleum.

NATURAL RESOURCES
Crude oil, some iron ore, copper, chrome, industrial metals, gold, uranium.

EXPORTS
$594 million (1997 est.): cotton, sesame, livestock, meat, gum arabic.

IMPORTS
$1.4 billion (1997 est.): foodstuffs, petroleum products, manufactured goods, machinery and equipment, chemicals, textiles.

MAJOR TRADING PARTNERS
Saudi Arabia, UK, China, Italy, South Korea, Germany, Egypt.

Doing Business with Sudan

▶ **Investment**

In February 2000, as reports piled up of government atrocities against the local population around the newly built pipeline to Port Sudan, the US Treasury imposed sanctions on the Greater Nile Oil Project, the consortium set up to exploit the oil. Khartoum is reportedly planning a second pipeline that will bypass eastern regions, where the first pipeline is under frequent attack from opposition forces. This new pipeline is expected to double Sudan's production. US investment in oil exploration in the past is estimated at $1 billion. More than 80% of all available concessions in oil exploration has been allotted to international companies. There is an ongoing effort to involve foreign firms in iron ore, manganese, magnesite, silver, gold, chromium ore, gypsum, mica, zinc, tungsten, copper and uranium mining. High grade deposits of gold have, however, been discovered in the Red Sea Hills, with reserves estimated at 100 tons. The expansion of Sudan's hydroelectric station at Roseires on the Blue Nile and a projected new station the 4th cataract are planned in conjunction with foreign partners.

▶ **Trade**

Sudan offers opportunities to exporters of machinery, transportation equipment, metal goods, and textiles.

▶ **Selling to the government**

The $400 million Roseires dam extension project and a hydroelectric project, the Al Hamdab hydroelectric dam, provided construction contracts with foreign loan funding.

▶ **Financing projects**

There has been some progress toward normalizing Sudan's relations with international and regional financial institutions.

▶ **Labor**

Most of the work force is engaged in agricultural or pastoral occupations. Some 1.75 million workers belonged to the principal trade union federation, the Sudan Workers Trade Unions Federation, until it was banned after the 1989 coup.

▶ **Legal rights**

Sudan's judicial system comprises a civil branch that handles most cases and an Islamic branch dealing exclusively with personal and family matters.

▶ **Business Climate**

The government enforces strict adherence to the Muslim faith and the business environment conforms.

Swaziland

The Kingdom of Swaziland—the smallest country on the African mainland after The Gambia—has enjoyed steady economic growth through free market policies that attracted sizeable foreign investment from neighboring South Africa and abroad. The monarchy has been under considerable pressure from within and outside to unban political parties and allow true democracy. While progress on the political front might be slow, Swaziland continues to stay among the leaders on the continent as far as economic reforms are concerned. This, together with a good measure of stability, present an environment conducive to investment and free trade.

Country profile

The Kingdom of Swaziland is a stamp-sized country squeezed between the Drakensberg and Lebombo mountains and bordered by South Africa and Mozambique. Rainfall is highest in the elevated region (more than 1,000 mm/39 inches) and lowest in its so-called lowveld (less than 750 mm/30 inches). Four large rivers flowing from South Africa—the Komati, Mbuluzi, Great Usutu and Ngwavuma—provide irrigation. Several nature reserves and game sanctuaries combined with a temperate climate, spectacular scenery and Swazi cultural life, attract visitors. More than 80% of the population are Swazi belonging to the Nguni-speaking peoples. Most are Christians and English and siSwati are official languages.

History

Late in the 16th Century the Embo-Nguni people moved into southern Africa and settled in what is today southern Mozambique. Towards the middle of the 18th Century, King Ngwane III led the Dlamini and related clans across the Lebombo Mountains into Swaziland. Culminating with the rule of King Mswati the Dlamini clan extended their power over an area much larger than modern Swaziland and became known as the amaSwati or Swazi. In 1846 white migrants from the Cape Colony laid claim to a large portion, insisting that Mswati II had ceded it to them by treaty. Swazi denials were fruitless and the kingdom continued to shrink. In 1895 Swaziland passed under the administrative control of President Paul Kruger's Transvaal Republic. The Anglo-Boer War of 1899-1902 brought this arrangement to an end and in 1903 Britain took over the administration of Swaziland. In 1968 Swaziland's independence was restored under King Sobhuza who ruled as an absolute monarch until his death in 1982. Several of Sobhuza's 67 sons from marriages to 100 wives engaged in a

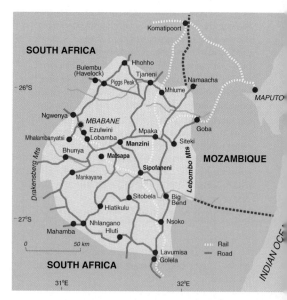

power struggle which was eventually resolved when King Mswati III took to the throne in 1986. Since then he has ruled as Africa's only remaining absolute monarch. King Mswati has reintroduced Swaziland's old, non-party political system of *Tinkhundlas*—a collection of chiefdoms serving as constituencies.

Government

Swaziland is a modified traditional monarchy ruled by King Mswati III together with an appointed prime minister. An advisory 5-year term Parliament or *Libandla* consists of 30-seat Senate (10 members elected by the House of Assembly and 20 appointed) and the 65-seat House of Assembly (10 appointed by the monarch and 55 elected by popular vote). Balloting is done on a nonparty basis and candidates are nominated by the local council of each constituency. The king can veto any law passed by the legislature and at times rules by decree.

Economic policy

With a modern infrastructure, Swaziland has attained one of the largest per capita manufacturing sectors in Africa. The government aims at further development of a modern export-oriented sector producing side-by-side with a traditional subsistence sector producing for local consumption. Swaziland's economy compares favorably with most of Africa but even though the government has taken the right steps to encourage further investment it has been, in the view of some critics, slow in responding to international pressures to introduce labor reforms. Privatization of some sectors previously dominated by the state is underway. King Mswati has taken the lead in facing up to the dangers of HIV/AIDS, which has become a major threat to the nation. Apart from active campaigns to promote awareness and to co-opt foreign assistance, the king has ordered his subjects to follow his own example and that of his seven wives by undergoing routine AIDS tests.

Sectors

More than 10% of the population is directly dependent on the sugar industry— the country's single largest employer and leading exporter. Other important crops are cotton, maize, tobacco, rice, vegetables, citrus fruits and pineapples. Swaziland has Africa's largest manmade forest covering 7% of the country's total land area and earning valuable foreign currency through the sale

Fast facts

POLITICAL

Head of State	King Mswati III (1986)
Prime Minister	Barnabas Sibusiso Dlamini (1996)
Ruling Party	Elections on a non-party basis
Independence	6 September 1968
National capital	Mbabane
Official languages	English & siSwati

PHYSICAL

Total area	6,703 sq. miles 17,360 sq. km. (± New Jersey)
Arable land	11% of land area
Coastline	Landlocked

POPULATION

Total	985,330
Av. yearly growth	1.91%
Population/sq. mile	162
Urban population	28%
Adult literacy	78%

ECONOMY[1]

Currency	Lilangeni (E) (US$1=8.23)
GDP (real)	$1.4 billion
GDP growth rate	2.0%
GNP per capita[2]	$1,400
GDP (ppp)[3]	$4 billion
GDP per cap. (ppp)[3]	$4,200
Inflation rate	8.0%
Exports	$1.3 billion
Imports	$1.2 billion
Development aid	$30 million
External debt	$437 million
Unemployment	22.0%

INFRASTRUCTURE

Railroads	186 miles/300 km
Paved roads	28%
Motor vehicles	38,000
Air passenger/km	48 million
Telephones/1,000	21
International airport	Manzini

1. Statistics are based on World Bank data.
2. Atlas method.
3. See page 151 for an explanation of GDP based on purchasing power parity (ppp).

of wood and pulp. Iron ore, asbestos, industrial-quality diamonds and coal are being exploited. Until the late 1980s when diversification spawned textiles, footwear, beverages, sweets and beer processing, four-fifths of the industrial sector depended largely on the processing of agricultural and forestry products, sugar, cotton and meat. Tourism plays an important role in the economy.

Privatization

The Swazi Post and Telecommunications Corporation (SPTC) is among the key state enterprises earmarked for privatization. Joint venture partners are sought for Royal Swazi National Airways Corporation and the construction of a new terminal at Matsapa International Airport.

Investment

Foreign direct investment has long been a vital element in an economy favorably disposed towards outsiders. During years of sanctions against the apartheid regime in South Africa, foreign firms found a convenient escape across the border in Swaziland. With sanctions something of the past, Swaziland has continued to lure foreign entrepreneurs, among them leading South African beer, and paper and pulp conglomerates. The Central Bank does not track foreign direct investment (FDI) by sector or country but statistics indicate a preponderance of South African firms, accounting on average for 45% of the total annual inflow. British firms are second followed by the Taiwanese. There have also been modest inflows from the US, Denmark, the Netherlands, and Germany. Coca-Cola's syrup concentrate plant (also known as CONCO) is a leading exporter.

Trade

South Africa—a fellow member of the South African Customs Union—accounts for 80% of Swaziland's imports and 50% of its exports. Sugar is a major export item but there has in recent years been a strong growth in the export of electronic appliances, textiles, and processed food. Swaziland experiences a large trade deficit with South Africa and has been trying to compensate for this by expanding its trade with the rest of the world where it has managed a comfortable surplus in recent years. It is likely that trade liberalization measures within the SACU and the Southern African Development Community (SADC) will lessen Swaziland's heavy dependence on South Africa.

Financial sector

There are four commercial banks monitored by the Central Bank of Swaziland. The government-owned Swaziland Development and Savings Bank was liquidated in June 1995 and is being restructured. An exchange was established in July 1990 by Sibusiso Dlamini, a former World Bank executive who became Swaziland's prime minister, to enable ordinary Swazis to become stakeholders in their economy. It remains closely tied to the South African market and operates under similar conditions.

Taxes and tariffs

Companies are taxed at 37.5% rate on profits derived from a Swaziland source. Three provisional tax payments are made and the balance is payable or refundable at the close of the tax year. Dividends are exempt from company tax but subject to a non-resident shareholders tax of 12.5% to 15%. Sales tax at 12% or 20% is charged on certain transactions, imported goods, and the sale of locally-manufactured goods and services. Interest on borrowings abroad (subject to prior approval of the Central Bank) may be remitted subject to provision for a non-resident tax on interest of 10%.

Business activity

AGRICULTURE

Sugar cane, cotton, maize, tobacco, rice, citrus, pineapples, corn, sorghum, peanuts cattle, goats, sheep.

INDUSTRIES

Mining (coal and asbestos), wood pulp, sugar, soft drink concentrates.

NATURAL RESOURCES

Diamonds, asbestos.

EXPORTS

$1.3 billion (1999 est.): soft drink concentrates, sugar, wood pulp, cotton yarn, citrus and canned fruit.

IMPORTS

$1.2 billion (1999 est.): motor vehicles, machinery, transport equipment, foodstuffs, petroleum products, chemicals.

MAJOR TRADING PARTNERS

South Africa, EU, Mozambique, North Korea, Japan, UK, Singapore.

Doing Business with Swaziland

Investment

Four industrial areas have been set aside for special development. The principal estate is at Matsapha between Mbabane and Manzini, offering easy rail and road access to the ports of Durban and Port Richards in South Africa and Maputo in Mozambique. Incentives include tax allowances for new and existing businesses and, in the case of pioneering enterprises that bring unique operations and skills, a tax holiday of five years. Far from discriminating against foreigners, the government has been accused at times of favoring expatriate business over local entrepreneurs. In some instances overseas entrepreneurs have been able to avail themselves of government-financed research programs. Opportunities exist in sugar, wood pulp, timber, citrus, canned fruit and the manufacturing of textiles, electrical and electronic goods.

Trade

Many foreign firms opt for assembly and distribution points in South Africa to sell computers and software, telecommunications equipment, and a range of consumer goods in Swaziland and other smaller markets in the SACU. The sugar, wood pulp, and fruit industries have in the past offered good markets for US sales of harvesting, loading, weeding, fertilizing, and irrigation equipment. The upgrading of the infrastructure continues to create demands for air traffic control and other airport equipment, road building machinery, and rolling stock for the railroads and trucks.

Trade finance

Export financing is available through Eximbank. Irrevocable letters of credit are common practice.

Selling to the government

Sometimes the government gives preferential treatment to local tenders. A large proportion of government contracts are filled by South African and other southern African companies. Privatization of the fixed line system, hydroelectric projects, low- and middle-income housing and railroad construction are projects where foreign participation is actively sought.

Exchange controls

As a member of the Common Monetary Area, Swaziland permits repatriation of profits and dividends (after a withholding tax of 15%) upon application to the Central Bank. There are no exchange regulations affecting transactions within the CMA.

Partnerships

US firms are noticeable in the franchising of fast food restaurants and retail stores, usually established as an extension of their South African network. In recent years, however, Swazi entrepreneurs have been insisting on cutting their own deals directly with US firms instead of going through South Africa.

Establishing a presence

Registration of either a wholly-owned foreign enterprise or a joint venture takes approximately two weeks and is usually carried out by local attorneys and accounting firms. Business sites for industrial operations are available from the Ministry of Enterprise and Employment and the Swaziland Industrial Development Corporation (SIDC).

Financing projects

The Overseas Private Investment Corporation, the US Trade and Development Guarantee Agency, and the Multilateral International Guarantee Agency are active in Swaziland. Project financing for infrastructure development is available through the World Bank and African Development Bank.

Labor

An estimated 10% of the work force is employed in South Africa. Relations between organized labor and government have been strained over political issues in the past few years. After the banning of political parties, labor unions have taken on the role of activists.

Legal rights

Although a dual legal system comprising Roman-Dutch and customary law is a source of confusion to some foreigners, it is generally administered in a fair and reasonably swift manner. There are also traditional royal courts where the king as supreme authority adjudicates in disputes. Swaziland is in the process of tightening its patent and copyright legislation. Under new legislation, the government relies on technical assistance from the African Regional Industrial Property Organization in Harare and coverage has been extended to pharmaceutical and agricultural chemical products. An updated Copyright Act is styled after that of the World Intellectual Property Rights Organization .

Business climate

The business culture shows a strong British and South African influence.

 # Tanzania

Although renowned for its political stability, Tanzania suffered severely from three decades of decay under a centralized socialist economy. It proceeded on the road to recovery with the election of a capitalist-minded democratic government in 1995. Considering the degree to which this potentially prosperous nation was allowed to slip during the socialist one-party regime of the late President Jules Nyerere, the challenge is quite formidable. Encouraging progress in infrastructure rebuilding and privatization with the help of foreign capital and expertise have, however, placed Tanzania among the bright prospects on the continent.

Country profile

The United Republic of Tanzania is a land of lakes and offshore islands. It includes the southern half of Lake Victoria, most of the eastern half of Lake Tanganyika [at depths of 1,433 m (4,700 ft) the world's deepest after Russia's Lake Baikal] and borders on Lake Malawi in the south. Its offshore areas include the densely populated spice islands of Zanzibar and Pemba and the fishing resort, Mafia Island. In the north is Africa's highest mountain, snow-capped Mount Kilimanjaro (5,896 m/19,344 ft). Rainfall inland averages 750 mm (29.5 inches). The coastal region and the islands of Zanzibar and Pemba share a humid tropical climate. The savanna plains of mainland Tanzania support a rich and diverse wildlife in at least 12 national parks, 10 game reserves and various other conservation areas. There are 120 Bantu-speaking groups, none of them large enough to dominate the rest. There are also a number of non-Bantu groups speaking Maasai, Cushitic and Khoisan languages. Influential Arab and Indian minorities reside in the coastal centers and on Zanzibar and Pemba. The 60% who do not adhere to ethnic beliefs are evenly split between Christianity and Islam. Swahili and English are official languages.

History

The discovery of the remains of the *Australopithecus hominid* family in Tanzania's Olduvai Gorge supports claims that this region gave birth to humanity. About 3,000 years ago Khoisan peoples entered the region, followed by caucasoid Cushites and Negroid Nilotes from the north. As long as 2000 years ago traders from Egypt (Greeks and Romans), Axum (Ethiopians), Arabia, the Persian Gulf, India and Indonesia visited the shores and around 500 AD the

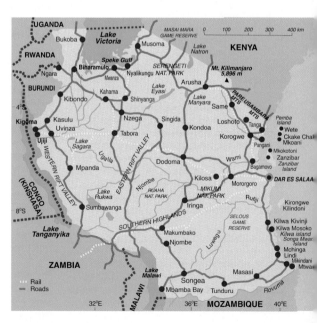

336

Bantu-speaking peoples moved in from the great lakes. Portuguese explorers reached the coastal regions in 1500 and held some control until the 17th Century. Most strongholds established by the Portuguese had fallen into Arab hands by the early 19th Century. In 1840 Sayyid Said, the Imam of Muscat (Oman), took up residence on Zanzibar Island and established a sultanate that spanned over the entire coastal belt and associated islands of present-day Tanzania and Kenya. Homegrown spices, slaves, and ivory from the mainland were traded in Zanzibar, which eventually became a base from where the likes of Livingstone and Stanley explored. In 1871 American journalist Henry Stanley went from Zanzibar to look for Livingstone and found him at the slave depot of Ujiji (close to Kigoma) on Lake Tanganyika, using the memorable phrase, "Dr Livingstone, I presume?" A German East African Protectorate formed in 1891 included Tanganyika and its coastal belt (formerly part of the Zanzibar Sultanate), as well as the kingdoms of Ruanda and Rundi. After Germany's defeat in World War I, Tanganyika was handed over to Britain and Ruanda-Urundi to Belgium. The Zanzibar Protectorate remained a separate sultanate under British rule. Julius Nyerere and his Tanganyika African National Union (TANU) gained independence for Tanganyika in 1961. Three years later it joined with Zanzibar in the United Republic of Tanzania and Zanzibar, with the island retaining a certain measure of independence. Over the next 30 years Nyerere's well-intentioned socialist communes (ujaama) led to economic disaster. In 1984 he was succeeded by his vice president, Ali Hassan Mwinyi, who introduced some changes and in 1995 newly-elected President Benjamin Mkapa set Tanzania firmly on the road to reform. In October 2000 Mkapa was reelected by a comfortable 74.9% of the popular vote over his nearest rival, Ibrahim Lipumba.

Government

The executive President and the Vice President of the Republic of Tanzania are directly elected by the voters for a 5-year term. Zanzibar elects its own president to handle internal affairs on the island. The unicameral 274-seat National Assembly or Bunge also serves for 5 years—232 members are elected by popular vote, 37 seats allocated to women nominated by the president, and five seats reserved for representatives of the Zanzibar House of Representatives. In the 2000

Fast facts

POLITICAL

Head of State	Pres. Benjamin William Mkapa (1995)
Ruling Party	CCM
Main Opposition	CUF
Independence	26 April 1964
National capital	Dar es Salaam/ Dodoma[4]
Official languages	English & Swahili

PHYSICAL

Total area	364,900 sq. miles 945,090 sq. km. (2 x California)
Arable land	3% of land area
Coastline	885 miles/1,424 km

POPULATION

Total	31.3 million
Av. yearly growth	2.14%
Population/sq. mile	97
Urban population	25%
Adult literacy	74%

ECONOMY[1]

Currency	Tanzanian shilling (TSh) (U$1=886)
GDP (real)	$5.5 billion
GDP growth rate	4.7%
GNP per capita[2]	$210
GDP (ppp)[3]	$22.1 billion
GDP per cap. (ppp)[3]	$730
Inflation rate	13.5%
Exports	$1.2 billion
Imports	$2.45 billion
Development aid	$1 billion
External debt	$6.38 billion
Unemployment	N/A

INFRASTRUCTURE

Railroads	2,218 miles/3,570 km
Paved roads	4%
Motor vehicles	104,000
Air passenger/km	165 million
Telephones/1,000	3
International airport	Dar es Salaam
Main harbor	Dar es Salaam

1. Statistics are based on World Bank data.
2. Atlas method.
3. See page 151 for an explanation of GDP based on purchasing power parity (ppp).

election Pres. Mkapa's *Chama Cha Mapinduzi Party* or Revolutionary State Party (CCM) captured 244 seats against the 15 won by its main rival, Ibrahim Lipumba's Civic United Front (CUF). A few smaller parties are represented as well.

Economic policy

Since 1995 Tanzania has been consolidating and strengthening the tentative steps taken since 1985 to reverse the disastrous socialist policies of the past. With the assistance of the IMF, economic reforms were implemented, including cuts in state expenditure, reduction of the civil service, devaluation of the currency, privatization of state corporations and removal of price controls. In recent years growth rates rose to 3.5% and inflation was drastically reduced.

Sectors

Agriculture employs about three quarters of the working population and together with fishing and forestry contributes around 55% of GDP. The principal cash crops on the mainland are coffee and cotton, followed by cashew nuts, tobacco, tea and sisal. On the islands of Zanzibar and Pemba, cloves, copra, tobacco, vanilla, peppermint, rubber and seaweed are produced. Maize, millet, sorghum, cassava, rice and bananas are the main food crops. Fishing involves marine activity around the islands and freshwater catches in Lake Victoria and Lake Tanganyika. The cattle population of over 13 million head is the fourth largest in Africa. Added recently to well-established supplies of gemstones such as diamonds, rubies, sapphires and a variety of semiprecious stones are recent discoveries of gold, nickel, copper and cobalt. There are also confirmed reserves of phosphates, graphite, uranium, niobium, titanium, vanadium and natural gas. Tourism is a major industry.

Privatization

Most of the 150 state properties privatized are medium-sized manufacturing enterprises and trading companies. The government is, however, committed to restructuring major public utilities in telecommunications, power, water and sewerage and transport.

Investment

Since Tanzania established its Investment Promotion Center in 1990, it has approved more than a thousand projects worth some $3 billion involving investors from Britain, Germany, Italy, Thailand, India, Canada, South Africa and the US. Sectors that have attracted most of the foreign capital are manufacturing, tourism, agriculture, fisheries and mining.

Trade

Coffee, cotton and tourism are major foreign exchange earners together with diamonds and a variety of other minerals. The US share of Tanzania's imports is modest but growing.

Financial sector

After nearly 25 years of government monopoly, legislation was passed in August 1991 to allow private banks back into Tanzania.

Taxes and tariffs

Steps are underway to harmonize differing tariff rates on the mainland and in Zanzibar. In 1995, the government introduced a uniform tax of 5% on imported capital goods, thereby rationalizing (and encouraging) investment across the board.

Business activity

AGRICULTURE

Coffee, sisal, tea, cotton, pyrethrum (insecticide made from chrysanthemums), cashew nuts, tobacco, cloves (Zanzibar), corn, wheat, cassava (tapioca), bananas, fruit, vegetables, cattle, sheep, goats.

INDUSTRIES

Primarily agricultural processing (sugar, beer, cigarettes, sisal twine), diamond and gold mining, oil refining, shoes, cement, textiles, wood products, fertilizer, salt, tourism.

NATURAL RESOURCES

Hydroelectric potential, phosphates, iron and coal.

EXPORTS

$1.2 billion (1999 est.): coffee, manufactured goods, cotton, cashew nuts, minerals, tobacco, sisal.

IMPORTS

$2.45 billion (1999 est.): consumer goods, machinery and transportation equipment, industrial raw materials.

MAJOR TRADING PARTNERS

India, Germany, Japan, Malaysia, Rwanda, Netherlands, South Africa, Kenya, UK, Saudi Arabia, China.

Doing Business with Tanzania

▶ **Investment**

The Tanzania Investment Center (TIC) seeks out, directs and assists foreign investment. In designated priority areas investors are entitled to generous incentives. Opportunities range from large infrastructural projects to smaller industrial developments. Through foreign participation, internal air charter services have increased from five to more than twenty. Road reconstruction and tourism are other areas targeted by foreign investors. Foreign firms have teamed up with locals in the mining of gemstones, gold, ferrous metals and petroleum and gas exploration.

▶ **Trade**

Trade opportunities exist in industrial equipment, textiles and used clothing, telecommunication equipment, aircraft and parts, computers and software, corn, and soy bean and wheat, much of the latter destined for refugees from the troubled Great Lakes area who spilled across the border into Tanzania. There are a number of bonded warehouses in Dar es Salaam which serve as transit points for shipments to Uganda, Rwanda, Burundi, the Democratic Republic of Congo, Zambia, and Malawi.

▶ **Trade finance**

An irrevocable letter of credit confirmed by an outside bank is normal practice. Local financing is available, usually at high interest rates, while a parastatal insurance company provides cover against loss, damage and destruction.

▶ **Selling to the government**

Procurement is by tender boards although in certain unspecified instances the government purchases on a direct basis. Tenders are usually issued at the beginning of each calendar year. Sometimes international donor agencies help set the requirements and the rules.

▶ **Exchange controls**

Although Tanzania continues to be plagued by intermittent shortages of foreign exchange, the advent of exchange bureaus has made it easier to transfer profits, dividends and other investment returns.

▶ **Partnerships**

Several local firms rely on franchising arrangements with US firms, an arrangement that is expected to grow in popularity as Tanzania progresses into a free enterprise environment. Privatization also presents increased opportunities for joint ventures and licensing arrangements. The use of local legal advice might be necessary to ensure that both parties in such arrangements are on the same page as misunderstandings sometimes arise due to cultural differences.

▶ **Establishing a presence**

In establishing a presence, foreign firms have the choice of entering into a joint venture with a local firm or creating a wholly-owned subsidiary. Both are reasonably easy to set up, especially with local legal advice and the assistance of the TIC.

▶ **Financing projects**

The Overseas Private Investment Corporation supports US investors. Project financing is also available from institutions such as the World Bank, Tanzania Development Finance Co. Ltd, Tanzania Investment Bank, Tanzania Venture Capital Fund, East African Development Bank, African Development Bank and the International Finance Corporation.

▶ **Labor**

Although labor is plentiful in Tanzania, it is largely unskilled. The few jobless but highly educated Tanzanians often lack managerial experience and need further training.

▶ **Legal rights**

While property rights, including intellectual property, are protected by law, enforcement might be lacking in some instances. The establishment of commercial courts is expected to expedite cases involving commercial disputes. Still, many of the antiquated provisions dating from the colonial and post-independence socialist era still need to be revised. After a long history of expropriation which culminated in 1973 with the nationalization of several European firms, Tanzania has in recent times maintained a clean record on this score. Tanzania is a member of both the International Center for Settlement of Investment Disputes and Multilateral Investment Guarantee Agency.

▶ **Business Climate**

Strong traces of European influences in the business community and a fluency in English might be deceptive. Americans are advised to ensure complete understanding on important issues when entering into agreements. In most cases it does help to engage a local legal adviser with past experience in international business negotiations.

Togo

Togo's capital, Lomé, was once the hub of a regional economy but in recent years it has been seriously challenged by political and economic difficulties and developments in neighboring states. In efforts to regain its prominence, Togo is relying on a superior port and airport, high quality telecommunications, one of the most liberal trade regimes in the region, and an experienced, vibrant business community. Largely a country known for its coffee, cotton and cocoa, as well as large supplies of phosphate, Togo offers ample opportunity for entrepreneurs interested in manufacturing for export.

Country profile

The Republic of Togo extends about 540 km (335 miles) inland from a narrow, 56 km (35 mile) coastline along the Bight of Benin in the Gulf of Guinea. Sandy barrier beaches separate a chain of lagoons and lakes, including Lake Togo, from the sea. Most of the land lies below 500 m (1640 ft). The southern two-thirds of the country is drained by the Mono River, flowing from the Atakora Mountains. Vegetation varies from moist savanna, oil palm plantations and patches of dense forest in the south, to dry savanna in the northern lower rainfall areas. The Ewe, including the Mina and other related groups, account for about 45% of the total population. The Kabre (Kabye), Fulani, Mande and the Gurma make up the rest. Both Ewe and Kabre have the status of national languages and are taught in the schools. The voodoo (vodun) religion is prevalent in the coastal regions of Togo and Benin from where it spread during the slave trade era to the Caribbean and the Americas. Christians and Muslims number less than half of the population.

History

The Voltaic peoples and the Kwa were the earliest known inhabitants. Unlike its neighbors, ancient Togo was not an area of kingdoms but settled by refugees from the strong neighboring military states. When European traders visited these shores towards the end of the 15th Century the Ewe and the Mina were already entrenched on the coastlands and the Kabre established in the north. In the late 1880s, while the British and

the French were focusing on other parts of the so-called Slave Coast, the Germans took the land of the Ewe and the Kabre by treaty. Togoland's borders were finally fixed in 1897. Although their rule was as authoritarian as that of other colonial governments, Germany turned Togoland into a model colony with good roads and railways and a well-equipped harbor at Lomé. After Germany's defeat in World War I, Togo was split into two parts. The western section was placed under British administration and the larger eastern part given to the French. A UN referendum in the mid-forties in both territories—largely boycotted by the Ewe—decided against reunification and when the Gold Coast be-

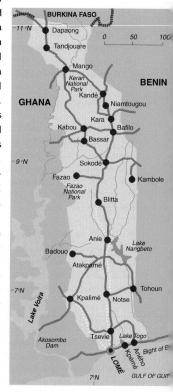

came the independent state of Ghana in March 1957 it included British Togoland. French Togoland became the independent Republic of Togo in 1960. In 1967 the government led by the Polish-descended Nicolas Grunitzky was overthrown in a bloodless coup by Kabre army colonel Etienne Eyadema. After a few months of interim rule by a newly constituted National Reconciliation Committee Eyadema, took over as president. The first decade of Gnassingbé (a name he adopted to promote national unity) Eyadema's autocratic rule was marked by rapid economic growth while the 1980s were fraught with decay. Internal pressures and a threat by France to withhold much-needed economic assistance persuaded Eyadema to lift the restrictions on opposition parties in April 1991. More than 70 parties emerged but a politically astute Eyadema managed to win the election in 1993. He was reelected to the presidency in 1998.

Government

The Constitution adopted after the 1992 referendum provides for an executive President directly elected for a term of five years, renewable once. The President appoints the Prime Minister from the majority party in the 81-member National Assembly, also elected for 5-year terms. In the March 1999 election Pres. Eyadema's *Rassemblement du Peuple Togolais,* or Rally of the Togolese People (RPT), won 79 seats in the legislature after the opposition boycotted the elections. The main opposition, the *Coordination des Forces Nouvelles,* or Coordination of New Forces (CFN), holds no seats. Two seats are held by independents.

Economic policy

Current World Bank and IMF structural adjustment programs stress privatization and liquidation of state-owned enterprises, withdrawal of the government from commodity marketing and agricultural inputs, the streamlining of government operations, and promotion of both administrative and judicial transparency. Near term prospects are for modest economic growth and restrained inflation.

Sectors

Agriculture employs about 80% of the working population and contributes 35% of the GDP. The main export crop is cotton, followed by coffee, cocoa, palm kernels and shea nuts. Sugar cane and groundnuts are also grown. The country is largely self-sufficient with food crops such as rice,

Fast facts

POLITICAL

Head/State	Pres. Gnassingbé Eyadema (1967)
Ruling Party	RPT
Main Opposition	CFN (no seats)[4]
Independence	27 April 1960
National capital	Lomé
Official languages	French

PHYSICAL

Total area	21,926 sq. miles 56,790 sq. km. (± West Virginia)
Arable land	38% of land area
Coastline	35 miles/56 km

POPULATION

Total	5 million
Av. yearly growth	3.51%
Population/sq. mile	229
Urban population	30%
Adult literacy	55%

ECONOMY[1]

Currency	CFA franc (CFAF) (U$1: 752.76)
GDP (real)	$1.48 billion
GDP growth rate	2.1%
GNP per capita[2]	$330
GDP (ppp)[3]	$8.2 billion
GDP per cap. (ppp)[3]	$1,670
Inflation rate	7.2%
Exports	$425 million
Imports	$563 million
Development aid	$130 million
External debt	$1.38 billion
Unemployment	N/A

INFRASTRUCTURE

Railroads	326 miles/525 km
Paved roads	32%
Motor vehicles	41,000
Air passenger/km	215 million
Telephones/1,000	5
International airport	Lomé
Main harbor	Lomé

1. Statistics are based on World Bank data.
2. Atlas method.
3. See page 151 for an explanation of GDP based on purchasing power parity (ppp).
4. The CFN did not capture seats. There are only two independents in the Assembly.

sorghum, millet, yams, cassava, vegetables and tropical fruit. Livestock is important in the northern savanna regions. There is small-scale marine fishing and limited forestry. Mining activity concentrates on phosphates which account for more than a third of export earnings. Limestone, marble and salt are extracted and there are known reserves of iron ore, bauxite, dolomite and chromite. Manufacturing involves beverages, footwear, textiles and plastics. Togo has a flow of tourists from Europe.

Privatization

The government has been working with the World Bank setting as future benchmarks the privatization of phosphate mining and telecommunications. The ginning of cotton has already been opened to private firms competing with SOTOCO, a restructured parastatal, and the agricultural commodity marketing monopoly was liquidated. Some 20 private firms have been granted marketing licenses for coffee and cocoa. The state pharmaceutical sales company lost its monopoly, allowing private competitors to enter the market with a wide range of generic drugs.

Investment

Both privatization and the establishment of export promotion zones (EPZs) have drawn foreign direct investors. In recent years foreign firms have purchased from the government an oil refinery, dairy, cement plant, brewery, spaghetti factory, flour mill, and an edible oil refinery. Toward the end of 1999 there were more than 30 firms from the US, Denmark, Germany, Norway, and Hong Kong active in Togo's EPZs, manufacturing, assembling and distributing cement, textiles, leather goods, automobiles, and petroleum products.

Trade

Togo's major agricultural export crops are coffee, cocoa, and cotton but phosphates tops the list in terms of total foreign exchange earnings. Primary customers are France, Canada, South Africa, and the Philippines, followed by Greece, Poland, Brazil, and the US. The well-established modern harbor of Lomé serves as a convenient entry point for trade with the surrounding region. It is estimated that much more than the 30% of imports officially designated for re-export cross the border in informal trade.

Financial sector

Over the years Togo developed an efficient, modern banking system to support its role as regional trading center. After the economic and political crisis years a review of the financial sector—undertaken together with the World Bank—has led to restructuring and recapitalization. However, Togo still has some way to go before it regains its reputation or position as a regional banking center. All major banks maintain correspondent relationships with US banks.

Taxes and tariffs

Good progress was made towards simplifying and streamlining the tax system. The value-added tax has been unified at 18%. Import tariffs are to be set in accordance with an external tariff regime for WAEMU members. Togo has one of the most liberal tariff regimes in the CFA zone.

Business activity

AGRICULTURE
Coffee, cocoa, cotton, yams, cassava (tapioca), corn, beans, rice, millet, sorghum, livestock, fish.

INDUSTRIES
Phosphate mining, agricultural processing, cement, handicrafts, textiles, beverages.

NATURAL RESOURCES
Marble, phosphate, limestone.

EXPORTS
$425 million (1999 est.): cotton, phosphates, coffee, cocoa.

IMPORTS
$563 million (1999 est.): machinery and equipment, consumer goods, petroleum products.

MAJOR TRADING PARTNERS
Canada, Taiwan, Nigeria, South Africa, Ghana, France, China, Cameroon.

Doing Business with Togo

▶ **Investment**

The recently resumed privatization process is expected to attract foreign direct investment in energy, telecommunications, banking, and hotels. Togo has distinguished itself throughout the 1980s as an investor-friendly, western-oriented country but foreign interest waned during the period of political unrest. The government is trying to restore the investment levels of the past in areas such as agriculture, manufacturing, mining, and tourism. Applications are evaluated by the Planning Ministry in consultation with the National Investment Commission, which sets conditions once approved. The process takes about a month. Investors can obtain EPZ status in two designated zones entitling them to a less restrictive labor code, foreign currency-denominated accounts and tax advantages.

▶ **Trade**

Togo offers a limited domestic market but a good potential in its traditional role as a transshipment point to neighboring countries. Imports include used clothing and shoes, computer equipment, cosmetic products, and wheat and meat, but as privatization proceeds the need for telecommunications and power generation equipment is expected to grow. Togo operates a free port .

▶ **Trade finance**

Normally irrevocable letters of credit are used. Eximbank facilitates trade. Some of the larger trade prospects involve development projects funded by the World Bank, the West African Development Bank, and the African Development Bank.

▶ **Selling to the government**

Plans to develop self-reliance in power generation and improve telecommunication will require large-scale purchases of services and equipment. Tenders will most likely be handled by the international and invididual country donor agencies.

▶ **Exchange controls**

There are no restrictions on the transfer of funds to other West African franc zone countries or to France but the transfer of funds elsewhere requires Finance Ministry approval.

▶ **Partnerships**

Even though Togolese business people eagerly pursue partnerships with American and other foreign firms, most of them offer local expertise and management instead of funding. The government encourages joint ventures. Although a few US firms, including Coca-Cola, rely on licensing agreements, franchising is limited.

▶ **Establishing a presence**

Establishing an office in Togo is in theory relatively simple, but administrative obstacles and delays are common. If there are expatriate managers they must obtain residence permits. The authorization to open an office comes from the Ministry of Commerce. Companies also need to register with the Commercial Court and the Togolese Chamber of Commerce at a minimal fee. The final step is the purchasing of an importer's card from the Ministry of Commerce, at about $150 per year.

▶ **Financing projects**

Multilateral institutions involved in funding projects in Togo include the African Development Bank, the ECOWAS fund, the West African Development Bank, and the World Bank.

▶ **Labor**

There is a large pool of qualified university graduates and unskilled workers but a shortage of workers with technical skills and practical experience. Separate wage scales are negotiated by employers, workers, and the government for industry, construction, public works, commerce, and banking. Although several labor confederations have combined forces to negotiate more effectively with the government and business, they have had limited impact.

▶ **Legal rights**

The investment code provides for the resolution of investment disputes involving foreigners under bilateral agreements with various governments or prearranged conciliation and arbitration procedures between the interested parties. Togo is a member of the International Center for the Settlement of Investment Disputes. Lack of transparency and predictability of the judiciary in the enforcement of property rights is being addressed in conjunction with the World Bank.

▶ **Business Climate**

French is the language of business and so is the culture itself. While foreigners without a working knowledge of French might have problems conversing, deal-making should not be a problem for those who have operated in the European market. There is no shortage of professional interpreters.

Tunisia

Tunisia—Africa's northernmost country—has enjoyed modernization, stability and relative prosperity over a long period and is arguably the most cohesive and progressive society in the Maghreb region. Women have been liberated in what is the oldest Muslim stronghold on the continent. Metro railways run across the sites of ancient cities. Its former socialist government spawned a market-orientated economy. This middle-income country offers a good potential for foreign entrepreneurs not only as a market in itself but to serve as a convenient springboard to the EU with which Tunisia has a free trade agreement. Tunisia is expected to lift all remaining trade barriers with the EU in 2007.

Country profile

The Republic of Tunisia, on the western side of the great Gulf of Sirte, is the smallest country in North Africa with the largest proportion of arable land. Its northern portion enjoys a Mediterranean climate with winter rainfall varying from at least 400 to over 1,000 mm (16 to 39 inches). The country's only perennial river is the Medjerda, opening into wide coastal plains around the city of Tunis. Apart from a small Berber presence, Tunisians are largely descendants of migrants who in Carthaginian times made this crossroads region their home. Their culture is predominantly Arab and the Muslim faith prevails. French is widely spoken and taught in schools.

History

More than 3,000 years ago the Phoenicians established trading posts in the region and, according to legend, in 814 BC a group of exiles under the leadership of Princess Dido fled from Tyre (in present-day Lebanon) and founded Carthage (the New City). Carthaginian colonizers in Sicily and Spain encountered Roman opposition and became embroiled in a protracted struggle known as the Punic Wars which lasted from 264 until 146 BC when Carthage was finally defeated and razed. The Romans called their conquered territory Africa, a name probably derived from Afrig (Arab: Ifriqiya), the name also given to the Berber group living to south of Carthage.

Carthage was rebuilt by Julius Caesar and became an important center for Christianity in the Roman empire. Except for an interval of Vandal rule from

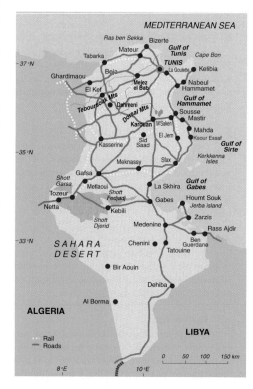

344

439-533, Carthage remained part of the Roman Empire until 669 when the Arabs invaded. After the Arabs took control of the region which they called the Maghreb, they virtually annihilated Carthage and founded the new city of Tunis. In Tunisia, as elsewhere in the Mahgreb region, Berbers assimilated with the Arab rulers and adopted their faith. Tunisia became part of the Ottoman Empire in 1570. France invaded Tunisia in 1881 and ruled it as a protectorate until 1956 when a freedom movement under Habib Bourguiba finally forced it to grant independence. First as prime minister and afterwards as president-for-life, Bourguiba stayed in office until the age of 84 in 1989 when he was declared physically and mentally unfit to govern by a panel of medical doctors. The life-presidency was subsequently abolished and an age limit of 70 years introduced. He was succeeded as president by Zine El Abidine Ben Ali who has since been re-elected for two successive terms of 5 years. In the October 1999 election he gained 99.4% of the total vote against two rivals.

Government

The executive President is elected for a maximum of two 5-year terms, appoints the Prime Minister and heads the Cabinet. President Ben Ali was hardly challenged in the most recent presidential election. His party, the *Rassemblement Constitutionelle et Démocratique,* or Constitutional Democratic Rally (RCD), won 148 of the 182 seats in the unicameral Chamber of Deputies or *Majlis al-Nuwaab.* The *Mouvement des démocrates socialistes,* or Movement of Socialist Democrats (MDS), captured 13 seats and the remaining 21 were split among four smaller parties.

Economic policy

Since 1986 Tunisia has implemented two structural adjustment programs (SAPs) together, with the IMF and managed, after a long period of post-independence socialist economic stagnation, to boost GDP growth to 4.5% per annum, cutting inflation to 5% and increasing exports by more than 6.0%. Privatization has, however, proceeded slowly and involved mostly smaller enterprises.

Sectors

Despite its modest natural resources, Tunisia has made impressive economic strides. Agriculture, fishing and forestry provide employment to a third of the workforce. With one-third of the cultivated land under olive trees, Tunisia is one of

Fast facts

POLITICAL

Head/State	Pres. Zine El Abidine Ben Ali (1987)
Head of Govt.	PM Hamed Karoui (1989)
Ruling Party	RCD
Main Opposition	MDS
Independence	20 March 1956
National capital	Tunis
Official languages	Arabic

PHYSICAL

Total area	63,170 sq. miles 163,610 sq. km. (± Georgia)
Arable land	19% of land area
Coastline	713 miles/1,148 km

POPULATION

Total	9.5 million
Av. yearly growth	1.39%
Population/sq. mile	152
Urban population	57%
Adult literacy	69%

ECONOMY[1]

Currency	Tunisian dinar (TD) (U$1=1.44)
GDP (real)	$21.3 billion
GDP growth rate	6.2%
GNP per capita[2]	$2,150
GDP (ppp)[3]	$49 billion
GDP per cap.(ppp)[3]	$5,200
Inflation rate	3.3%
Exports	$8.7 billion
Imports	$9.2 billion
Development aid	$204 million
External debt	$11.8 billion
Unemployment	15.6%

INFRASTRUCTURE

Railroads	1,404 miles/2,260 km
Paved roads	76%
Motor vehicles	547,000
Air passenger/km	2 billion
Telephones/1,000	54
International airport	Tunis
Main harbors	Tunis & Sfax

1. Statistics are based on World Bank data.
2. Atlas method.
3. See page 151 for an explanation of GDP based on purchasing power parity (ppp).

the largest producers and exporters of olive oil in the world. Tunisia is, after Morocco, the largest producer of phosphates in North Africa but the quality of the rock is poor and extraction is largely geared towards the production of fertilizer. Tunisia is one Africa's smaller oil producers, managing a modest export after supplying its domestic needs. The recent discovery of the Miskar gasfield in the Gulf of Gabes will make the country self-sufficient in natural gas. Iron ore, zinc, lead, aluminium fluoride and salt are mined. Textiles and leather goods account for about 85% of manufactured exports, with mechanical and electrical goods and chemicals growing industries. Some four million tourists (mainly from Germany and other European countries) visit the beaches, oases and historic sites each year.

Privatization

So far only the smaller among 189 public enterprises identified for privatization have been sold. Mindful of labor opposition, the government has been moving slowly. In 1995 a 20% share was sold in Tunis Air and in 1998 two cement plants and several semi-public firms were privatized through offerings on the stock exchange and direct sales. The most significant recent step in the privatization program was the awarding of an international tender for the first private build-own-operate (BOO) power generation to an American-led international consortium.

Investment

As much as 75% of foreign direct investment (FDI) has been in the energy sector, largely in petroleum exploration and development. There is, however, a growing interest in manufacturing and official statistics list some 1,600 companies fully or partially owned by foreigners. Foreign investment in agriculture is valued at $140 million and involves around 80 joint ventures ranging from aquaculture to flower production. France is the largest single source of foreign investment, followed by Italy, Germany, Belgium, Switzerland and the United Kingdom. Over the past five years, however, the US has been the third-largest source of FDI and recent developments in the energy industry are expected to bolster that position further.

Trade

Textiles and tourism are major foreign currency earners, followed by hydrocarbons, agricultural products, phosphates and chemicals. The European Union represents 80% of total trade. The US accounts for 1% of Tunisian exports and 5% of its imports.

Financial sector

The banking system is a mixture of private and state-owned institutions comprising 13 commercial banks, eight development banks, one savings bank, five portfolio management institutions, eight leasing companies, eight offshore banks, and two merchant banks. The government is still a controlling shareholder in most of these banks which are regulated by the Central Bank of Tunisia. The financial markets, consisting of a semi-privatized stock exchange and a number of bond and stock funds, showed impressive growth through the first half of 1999. To encourage firms to list on the exchange, the government introduced tax incentives in late 1998, reducing the corporate tax rate from 35 to 20 percent for companies with at least 30 percent of their shares traded on the exchange.

Taxes and tariffs

In 2007 Tunisia will form a free trade area with the EU and lift remaining protective barriers. The first phase of tariff reduction and elimination of quantitative import restrictions envisaged in the EU agreement was completed in 1996.

Business activity

AGRICULTURE
Olives, dates, oranges, almonds, grain, sugar beets, grapes, poultry, beef, dairy products.

INDUSTRIES
Petroleum, mining (particularly phosphate and iron ore), tourism, textiles, footwear, food, beverages.

NATURAL RESOURCES
Petroleum, phosphate, iron ore.

EXPORTS
$8.7 billion (1999 est.): hydrocarbons, textiles, agricultural products, phosphates, chemicals.

IMPORTS
$9.2 billion (1999 est.): industrial goods and equipment, hydrocarbons, food, consumer goods.

MAJOR TRADING PARTNERS
EU, North African countries, US.

Doing Business with Tunisia

▶ **Investment**

A broad range of incentives for foreign investors includes tax relief, reduced tariffs on imported capital goods, and depreciation schedules for production equipment. Companies exporting at least 80% of their production enjoy a ten-year tax holiday. Additional incentives are available to attract investment in designated depressed areas and in sectors such as health, education, training, transportation, environmental protection, waste treatment, and research and development in technological fields. The best investment opportunities are in the infrastructure improvement (hydrocarbons, power generation, transportation, telecommunications) or in offshore, export-oriented, labor-intensive industries such as textiles and light manufacturing. Tunisia has two free trade zones—one at Bizerte and the other at Zarzis—offering tax and customs duty exemptions to manufacturers.

▶ **Trade**

The best prospects for exporters are in agricultural products such as wheat, barley, livestock and meat, agricultural equipment, and luxury and durable goods. It is customary to rely on local agents and distributors. Exclusive distribution contracts are, however, forbidden by law.

▶ **Trade finance**

Most transactions are by irrevocable letters of credit. Reputable importers usually have no problem in obtaining the necessary financing from local bank. For US exporters Eximbank financing and insurance are available.

▶ **Selling to the government**

Government purchases are usually by tender published in the local media and sometimes in selected foreign journals. Factors that might influence the selection of bids are their contribution to the local economy and employment, the level of transfer of skills or technology, and impact on the balance of trade. US bidders have typically been stronger on price and technology while European firms have offered better financing packages and links to the local economy. Depending on the size and complexity of the project, the decision-making procedure can take several months. Decisions on major projects might even require the approval of the Chamber of Deputies, which goes into session for only about half of the year. Performance bonds of between one and ten percent are common on government contracts.

▶ **Exchange controls**

Central bank authorization is needed for some foreign exchange transactions.

▶ **Partnerships**

Even though there are examples of successful US joint ventures, many businesses are family-owned and often resist outside management. The government has blocked several proposed partnerships in department stores and restaurants.

▶ **Establishing a presence**

Registering an office of a foreign company in Tunisia is relatively simple. The Foreign Investment Promotion Agency (FIPA) offers a one-stop shop to investors and it generally takes about two weeks to complete the process. When it involves fisheries, tourism, transportation, communications, and other specified sectors it might take longer as government approval is needed. Foreign investors are permitted to purchase up to 49% of the shares in resident firms.

▶ **Financing projects**

OPIC provides political risk insurance and other services while the World Bank and African Development Bank support projects relating to the environment, privatization, road construction, dams and irrigation.

▶ **Labor**

About 15% of the workforce belongs to the national labor confederation, the General Union of Tunisian Workers (UGTT). Working conditions are established through triennial collective bargaining agreements between the UGTT and the National Employers Association (UTICA). Tunisian law limits the number of expatriate employees per company.

▶ **Legal rights**

To ensure enforcement, foreign firms must register their trademarks and industrial designs with the Tunisian Institute for Standardization and Intellectual Property (INNORPI). Tunisia is a member of the World Intellectual Property Organization, and has signed the agreement on the protection of patents and trademarks.

▶ **Business climate**

Tunisia is a relatively open society that sees itself as a bridge between the European and Arab worlds. Although the official language is Arabic, French is widely spoken.

Uganda

Emerging under new rule in 1987 from a long period of mismanagement and political upheaval, Uganda has undergone an impressive turnaround in recent years. Through diligent application of sound macroeconomic policies, it has averaged a growth rate of 7%, posting the highest continuous economic growth in Africa. The Ugandan government has shown a singular commitment to economic reform in line with IMF suggestions and a determination to attract foreign investors and traders through privatization and other incentives.

Country profile

The Republic of Uganda is situated north of Lake Victoria and consists largely of prime agricultural land. The equator cuts across the northern shores of this lake. The Victoria Nile links Lake Victoria with Lake Kyoga and Lake Albert. Much of the country is covered by moist woodland savanna, with large tracts of equatorial forest. There are 10 national parks and a number of other game and forest reserves. The largest population groups are of Nilotic origin. The Bantu-speaking people account for 20%. English is the official language, but, as elsewhere in Eastern Africa, Swahili is the *lingua franca*. Some 75% of the population are Christians, with Roman Catholics in the majority. Many people, mostly in the north, have ethnic beliefs.

History

About 500 BC Bantu-speaking peoples migrated to the area now known as Uganda. By the 14th Century there were three dominant kingdoms in the region— the Buganda, Bunyoro and Ankole. In the 19th Century explorers such as Richard Burton and Robert Livingstone found Uganda settled by the Nilotic peoples in the north and Bantu in the south, including the Baganda, from whom the country derived its name. In the 1890s Britain in a deal with Germany took possession of Uganda and Kenya while Germany apportioned Tanganyika (Tanzania) for itself. Independence from Britain in 1962 was fol-

lowed by several decades of turmoil. Milton Obote seized power with the help of the second-in-command of the army, Colonel Idi Amin, and took Uganda down the road of nationalization before he was ousted in 1971 by Amin. Considered by many as one of Africa's most brutal leaders ever, Amin expelled the large Asian (mainly Indian) community and carried out massive purges resulting in the death of thousands. After exiled Ugandans with the help of neighboring Tanzania toppled Amin, Obote bounced back by winning a presidential election in 1980. This time he pur-

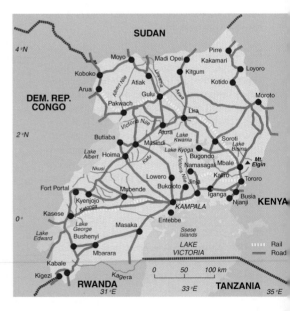

sued liberal IMF-style economic policies to obtain aid from western donors and the economy perked up slightly until another coup in 1985 led to further instability. In 1986 a rebel army led by Yoweri Museveni, leader of the National Resistance Movement (NRM), took control. President. Museveni banned rallies by other political groups and invited his opponents to join the NRM. In the process he brought peace and a measure of prosperity. He was reelected in 1996 and 2001. In the most recent election Museveni received 69.3% of the vote over his main rival, Kizza Besigye, who got 27.8%.

Government

A new 1995 constitution provided for a strong executive President, to be elected every five years, but with significant requirements for parliamentary approval of presidential actions. The National Parliament of 276 consists of 214 directly-elected representatives from geographical constituencies and special indirectly elected seats for representatives of women (39), youth (5), disabled (5), labor (3), and the army (10). Under the transitional provisions of the new Constitution, the nonparty system of government, including explicit restrictions on the activities of political parties, was to continue for five years, with a referendum in the fourth year to determine whether Uganda should adopt a multiparty system. The referendum took place in 2000 and voters opted to continue under non-party rule. Uganda is one of few African countries that maintains an electoral democracy while political parties are either banned or prohibited from contesting elections.

Economic policy

Museveni has had remarkable success in lifting Uganda out of the ruins left by Amin and Obote. In 1987 Uganda signed a three-year loan program with the IMF and implemented reforms. Since then it attained growth rates averaging 7% per year, lowered the budget deficit and inflation, and dismantled price controls and state monopolies. The civil service payroll has shrunk by more than 100,000. Growth in sectors such as manufacturing, mining, transport, communications, and construction has led to a doubling of the size of the economy. Still, Uganda remains one of the poorest countries in the world (ranking 141 out of 162 nations in the UNDP's 2001 Human Development Index) and needs considerable further input. Uganda has taken among African nations

Fast facts

POLITICAL

Head of State	Pres. Yoweri Kaguta Museveni (1986)
Ruling Party	Elections on a non-party basis
Independence	9 October 1962
National capital	Kampala
Official language	English

PHYSICAL

Total area	93,065 sq. miles 241,038 sq. km. (± Oregon)
Arable land	34% of land area
Coastline	Landlocked

POPULATION

Total	22.8 million
Av. yearly growth	2.83%
Population/sq. mile	255
Urban population	14%
Adult literacy	65%

ECONOMY[1]

Currency	Ugandan shilling (Ush) (US$1=1,700)
GDP (real)	$6.9 billion
GDP growth rate	7.4%
GNP per capita[2]	$310
GDP (ppp)[3]	$22.7 billion
GDP per cap. (ppp)[3]	$1,020
Inflation rate	2.6%
Exports	$726 million
Imports	$1.5 billion
Development aid	$883 million
External debt	$3.48 billion
Unemployment	N/A

INFRASTRUCTURE

Railroads	770 miles/1,240 km
Paved roads	8%
Motor vehicles	43,000
Air passenger/km	52 million
Telephones/1,000	2
International airport	Kampala
Main harbor	Kampala (Lake Victoria)

1. Statistics are based on World Bank data.
2. Atlas method.
3. See page 151 for an explanation of GDP based on purchasing power parity (ppp).

the fight against HIV/AIDS by reducing the rate of new infections through an intensive public health campaign.

Sectors

Agriculture and fishing are the mainstay of the economy, employing more than 80% of the working population and contributing about 44% of GDP. The country has long been famous for its robusta coffee, grown around Mount Elgon and in the foothills of the Ruwenzori Mountains. Other cash crops are cotton, tea, tobacco and sugar cane. The main food crops are plantains, cassava, millet, maize, rice, beans and groundnuts. Commercial cattle and dairy farming is undertaken in the southwest. Freshwater fish from the country's many lakes meets a high proportion of the population's protein needs and is also exported. Mining has been neglected for some time, but a revival is underway. There are extensive copper and iron ore reserves and hitherto less viable deposits of tungsten, tin, phosphates, columbo-tantalite, beryl, bismuth and limestone. Manufacturing revolves largely around food processing and import-substituting items such as textiles, cement, soap, plastics and metal products. Tourism has become a growth industry in recent years.

Privatization

The government has committed itself to privatization but the program has been marred by several failed deals, a lack of transparency, and rampant asset stripping. Latest on the list of entities to be privatized is the Uganda Electricity Board (UEB).

Trade

Agricultural production, with coffee as a major component, represents the major portion of Uganda's export earnings. Other agricultural exports include flowers, vanilla, silk, cotton, tobacco and tea.

Investment

Most investors in Uganda involve companies and individuals with experience in the country or elsewhere in Africa. Prominent among them are British and Indian firms, as well as growing numbers of Kenyan and South African entities. There has been significant foreign investment in the past two years in the beverage industry by Coca-Cola, Pepsi, South African Breweries and Guinness.

Financial sector

The Bank of Uganda (BOU) monitors 18 commercial banks and two development banks. A deposit insurance fund with contributions from the government and banks is in place to protect depositors. A stock exchange was established on 6 June 1997 by the Uganda Securities Exchange (USE) Ltd.—a company formed by eight licensed broker/dealers and investment advisers. HSBC Equator Bank provides services to US and other foreign customers and most local banks maintain correspondent relationships.

Taxes & Tariffs

Resident companies and foreign branches of companies are taxed at a 30% rate. Dividends are subject to withholding tax at a 20% rate for residents and 15% for nonresidents. Management fees, dividends, royalties and interest paid to nonresidents may be remitted to non-resident shareholders with the approval of the Bank of Uganda and are subject to a 15% withholding tax. Businesses with annual revenues of more than $35,000 are subject to a 17% VAT. To reduce costs and increase competitiveness, all 30% import duties have been reduced to 15%. Excise surcharges are set at 10%.

Business activity

AGRICULTURE

Coffee, tea, cotton, tobacco, cassava (tapioca), potatoes, corn, millet, pulses, beef, goat meat, milk, poultry.

INDUSTRIES

Sugar, brewing, tobacco, cotton, textiles, cement.

NATURAL RESOURCES

Copper, gold, cobalt, limestone, salt.

EXPORTS

$726 million (1999 est.): coffee, gold, fish and fish products, cotton, tea, corn.

IMPORTS

$1.5 billion (1999 est.): transportation equipment, petroleum, medical supplies, iron and steel.

MAJOR TRADING PARTNERS

Spain, Germany, Netherlands, France, Italy, Kenya, UK, Japan, India, South Africa.

Doing Business with Uganda

▶ **Investment**

Food processing, livestock, tourism, infrastructure, and transportation, import substitution, light manufacturing, mining, and telecommunications offer prospects for foreign investment. In an effort to revive mining, the government is encouraging foreigners to exploit deposits of copper, cobalt, gold, tin, tungsten, and oil. Accelerated depreciation incentives are offered. Acquisition, takeovers and greenfield investments are permitted.

▶ **Trade**

A small but growing middle class offers a ready market for quality consumer goods but new products often have to compete with used goods, especially in automobiles and clothing. The Uganda Manufacturers Association (UMA) and the Ugandan National Chamber of Commerce and Industry offer assistance to local agents and distributors.

▶ **Trade finance**

Eximbank provides short- to medium-term loans for US exporters. The Bank of Uganda supports export credit guarantees by commercial banks. Letters of credit and other standard instruments are also used. Sellers are advised to collect as much as possible of the price in cash and to collateralize all loans in cases where buyers are unknown.

▶ **Selling to the government**

The Central Tender Board controls tenders and advertises in the newspapers or send s invitations to organizations in Kampala. SWIPCO, a US-based company, is responsible for auditing all procurement of $50,000 and above by Ugandan ministries and parastatals.

▶ **Foreign exchange**

Foreign exchange, based on a market-determined exchange rate, can be freely purchased. The Investment Code of 1991 allows foreign exchange remittances with respect to transfer of foreign technologies. There are no foreign exchange controls affecting legitimate trade.

▶ **Partnership**

There are no restrictions on foreign ventures with local investors.

▶ **Establishing a presence**

The Uganda Investment Authority (UIA) offers advice on registry, licensing, immigration, tax, and customs matters, and sublicenses and permits. For-eign investors may form wholly-owned companies or joint ventures with local investors. There is no minimum equity capital requirement for companies. A branch of a foreign company may operate in Uganda if it registers with the Registrar of Companies and delivers to the Registrar a certified copy of the Memorandum and Articles of Association.

▶ **Project financing**

Most development projects are funded by outside donors who often give preference to purchases from companies based in their own country. In March 1998, Uganda signed an agreement allowing OPIC to broaden the scope of its activities. Local banks are generally weak and hesitant lenders.

▶ **Labor**

The private sector resorts to on-the-job training of unskilled and semiskilled workers to compensate for a shortage of skilled workers. Unions are relatively weak and labor unrest is rare. Employers must contribute an amount equal to 10% of the employee's gross salary to the National Social Security Fund (NSSF). Monthly salaries range from $60 to $140 for unskilled labor, $160 to $270 for skilled labor, and $350 to $670 for a junior manager.

▶ **Legal rights**

The law allows expropriation for public purposes through a transparent process and investors are guaranteed fair market value compensation within 12 months. The leadership has repeatedly reaffirmed Uganda's resolve that private property will never again be arbitrarily expropriated as it was in the dreaded Amin era. Instead, Uganda is in the process of returning land expropriated at the time, mostly from the Indian population. Commercial laws are based on the British mode. The Registrar of Patents awards patents for an initial period of 15 years, with a possible five-year extension. Uganda is a member of the International Center for the Settlement of Investment Disputes and opened a commercial court in August 1996.

▶ **Business climate**

Business decisions are often made by consensus. Initial business meetings are focused more on people's backgrounds and families than the business on hand. It is not uncommon for Ugandans to arrive late and for meetings to run over their scheduled time. Most business is conducted in English.

Zambia

Transition to multiparty democracy in 1991 enabled landlocked Zambia to change its fortunes through drastic economic reforms and a privatization program that could well serve as a model for others. While persisting depressed mineral prices inhibited growth, liberalization and diversification of its economy helped set Zambia on a firm road to recovery. Zambia, however, remains largely dependent on copper, cobalt, zinc and lead and hopes remain that a rise in prices might soon materialize. Privatization of state-owned mines has increased foreign holdings and overseas interest in a variety of other sectors is growing.

Country profile

The landlocked Republic of Zambia shares boundaries with eight other countries. It is part of the high African plateau averaging more than 1,000 m (3,280 ft) and rising towards the northeastern Muchinga Mountains. Most of the country consists of savanna terrain. The Bantu-speaking population comprises more than 70 ethnic groups with the Bemba dominant in the northeastern Copperbelt region, the Nyanja in the east and around Lusaka, the Tonga in the south and the Lozi in the west. English is the official language. About two-thirds of the people are Christians and the rest profess traditional ethnic beliefs.

History

Paleontologists claim that humans inhabited the region between one and two million years ago. During the 15th Century the Luba, Lunda (Kazembe), Bemba (Chitimukulu) and Lozi (Barotse) kingdoms flourished in the region stretching from Shaba (in Congo Kinshasa) to Zambia. They were joined in 1840 by fugitives from upheavals in the Zulu kingdom in South Africa. By the 1880s, driven by his dream of a British Empire from the Cape to Cairo, Cecil John Rhodes and his British South Africa Company (BSA) claimed the region. In 1924 Northern

Rhodesia, as it was known, was transferred to the British government and in the late 1920s the discovery of vast copper reserves lured mining moguls from Britain, South Africa and America and thousands of white settlers. In 1953 Northern Rhodesia (over strong objections from its inhabitants) was linked together with Nyasaland (later Malawi) and Southern Rhodesia in a white-ruled Federation of Rhodesia and Nyasaland. Agitation by Northern Rhodesia's Kenneth Kaunda and his United National Independence Party (UNIP) and

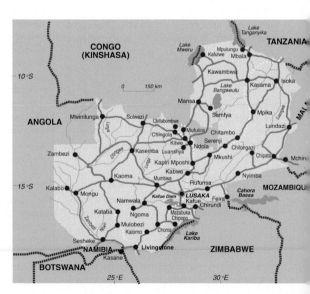

352

Dr Hastings Banda of Nyasaland led to the dissolution of the Federation in 1963. In October 1964 President Kaunda led Zambia to independence. In the ensuing years he consolidated his rule by banning the opposition and nationalizing the copper mines and other assets. In 1991, the relaxation of the ban propelled trade union leader and head of the Movement for Multiparty Democracy (MMD), Frederick Chiluba, to victory against Kaunda at the polls. He restored democracy and instituted drastic economic reforms. Despite an abortive coup attempt and some political unrest, Pres. Chiluba has managed to maintain stability since. He was reelected in November 1996, defeating his closest rival, Dean Mungomba, by 70.2% of the vote against 12.1%.

Government

Under the constitution an executive President is elected by popular vote for a maximum of two 5-year terms. He presides over a cabinet appointed by the majority party in the 159-seat National Assembly, also elected for 5 years. In 1996 President Chiluba MMD captured 127 of the seats against 5 for the strongest opposition party, the National Party (NP).

Economic policy

Since 1991 Zambia has moved aggressively towards a freer investor-friendly economy by removing price controls, reducing tariffs and privatizing. Tight fiscal and monetary policies coupled with democratic governance have resulted in renewed balance of payments (BOP) support from bilateral and multilateral donors and helped restore foreign investor confidence. In 1998 the government and IMF reached agreement on a second Enhanced Structural Adjustment Facility. In 1999 a slump in world copper prices adversely affected Zambia as this mineral provides 80% of the country's export earnings.

Sectors

Zambia has six times as much agricultural land as Zimbabwe but only 20% of it is cultivated. Currently agriculture employs about 40% of the workforce, largely on a subsistence basis. Cash crops include tobacco, seed cotton, coffee, fresh flowers and groundnuts. The main food crops are maize, rice, sorghum, millet, soy beans and wheat. Livestock farming is largely under control of small-scale farmers in the southern and western provinces. There is a reasonably large fresh fishing sector and half of the land area is forest, provid-

Fast facts

POLITICAL

Head/State	Pres. Frederick Jacob Titus Chiluba (1991)
Ruling Party	MMD
Main Opposition	NP
Independence	24 October 1964
National capital	Lusaka
Official languages	English

PHYSICAL

Total area	290,583 sq. miles 752,610 sq. km. (± Texas)
Arable land	7% of land area
Coastline	Landlocked

POPULATION

Total	9.7 million
Av. yearly growth	2.12%
Population/sq. mile	33
Urban population	43%
Adult literacy	76%

ECONOMY[1]

Currency	Zambian kwacha (ZK) (US$1=3,630)
GDP (real)	$3.7 billion
GDP growth rate	2.4%
GNP per capita[2]	$330
GDP (ppp)[3]	$8.3 billion
GDP per cap. (ppp)[3]	$880
Inflation rate	43.9%
Exports	$701 million
Imports	$1.3 billion
Development aid	$650 million
External debt	$6.7 billion
Unemployment	22%

INFRASTRUCTURE

Railroads	1,345 miles/2,164 km
Paved roads	17%
Motor vehicles	164,000
Air passenger/km	428 million
Telephones/1,000	9
International airport	Lusaka

1. Statistics are based on World Bank data.
2. Atlas method.
3. See page 151 for an explanation of GDP based on purchasing power parity (ppp).

ing fuel wood and timber for mining and industrial use. The economy depends primarily on the copper industry which was nationalized by former Preisdent Kaunda to boost government income. The country fell into heavy debt as copper prices plunged in the 1970s and 1980s. Zambia is the second largest producer after Congo (Kinshasa) of cobalt and also exports lead and zinc. Its gemstones, especially emeralds, remain largely unexploited. Over one-third of its manufacturing output consists of processed food and beverages. Other major products include textiles, chemicals and metal products. Zambia has a promising tourist potential and shares with Zimbabwe popular attractions such as Victoria Falls and Lake Kariba.

Privatization

Most of Zambia's 330 parastatal companies have been privatized since 1991, including a major brewery, bakery, farms, several hotels, a mill and the copper mining conglomerate Zambia Consolidated Copper Mines (ZCCM). Among the other state enterprises slated for privatization in the next few years are the telecommunications parastatal (ZAMTEL), Nitrogen Chemical of Zambia (NCZ), Zambia State Insurance Corporation (ZSIC), Zambia Postal Services Corporation (ZAMPOST), Zambia Electricity Supply Corporation (ZESCO) and Zambia Railways (ZR). Heavily indebted Zambia Airways could not find a buyer and was closed down in 1994.

Investment

Large-scale privatization and the freeing up of sectors previously reserved for government monopoly has boosted foreign direct investment over the past ten years. Among the megadeals were the selling of the large state copper mining giant ZCCM to South Africa's Anglo American. Manufacturing operations have sprung up, involving several American investors.

Trade

Zambia derives about 80% of its export earnings and about half of its government tax revenue from copper. The mining and marketing of copper, cobalt, lead and zinc are handled by the recently privatized Zambia Consolidated Copper Mines (ZCCM). Diversification efforts are underway to help expand the export share of tourism, agricultural products and manufactured goods.

Financial sector

The financial sector experienced rapid growth since 1992 as a result of the liberalization of banking, insurance, the removal of controls on interest rates, and the easing (and eventual elimination) of capital controls. Today there are 15 banks—6 of them foreign-owned subsidiaries, 7 belonging to local investors, 1 to the government and 1 under joint ownership of the Zambian and Indian governments. HSBC Equator Bank is prominent among foreign providers of corporate banking services. The banking sector is supervised by the central bank, the Bank of Zambia, which reports to the Ministry of Finance and Economic Development. The Lusaka Stock Exchange (LSE) trades shares of a few major companies.

Taxes and tariffs

Responding to complaints from domestic businesses over the liberalized trade regime, the government introduced some tariff protection in 1999. Among the goods that may still be imported duty-free are mining and agricultural machinery, medicines, pharmaceuticals, veterinary and medical equipment, chemicals in bulk, fertilizers, and seeds. Most other goods fall into one of three tariff bands: 5% on selected raw materials and capital equipment, 15% on intermediate goods, and 25% on final products.

Business activity

AGRICULTURE

Corn, sorghum, rice, peanuts, sunflower seed, tobacco, cotton, sugarcane, cassva (tapioca), cattle, goats, pigs, poultry, beef, pork.

INDUSTRIES

Copper mining and processing, construction, foodstuffs, beverages, chemicals, textiles, fertilizer.

NATURAL RESOURCES

Copper, zinc, lead, cobalt, coal.

EXPORTS

$701 million (1999 est.): copper, cobalt, zinc, lead, tobacco.

IMPORTS

$1.3 billion (1999 est.): machinery, transportation equipment, foodstuffs, fuel, petroleum products, electricity, fertilizer.

MAJOR TRADING PARTNERS

Japan, South Africa, US, Saudi Arabia, India, Thailand, Malaysia, UK, Zimbabwe.

Doing Business with Zambia

▶ **Investment**

The Zambian Investment Center (ZIC) seeks and an investment board screens foreign direct investments. The privatization process is open to foreign bidders and there are no requirements relating to local content, equity, financing, employment or technology transfer. Incentives are offered in regard to investments in rural enterprises, farming, and the manufacturing of non-mineral exports. Companies listed on the Lusaka Stock Exchange qualify for reduced corporate income tax. Mining, tourism, insurance, telecommunications and energy are prime areas of investment.

▶ **Trade**

Horticultural inputs, veterinary medicines, wheat and corn are siginificant import items. There is also a growing demand for heavy machinery and construction equipment as Zambia introduces major new infrastructure rehabilitation projects. Franchising is expanding in printing, fast food, postal services, computer/office supplies, telecommunications, education, and business services.

▶ **Trade finance**

Short-term local borrowing is expensive. Many buyers either undertake their own financing or seek funding outside the country. An irrevocable letter of credit is the most common method of payment. Eximbank programs are available.

▶ **Selling to the government**

The government has an ongoing need for products and services relating to rehabilitation of the country's railway and road networks, hydroelectric power, mining, and telecommunications. Many of these projects are funded by multilateral lending institutions and bilateral donors and subject in part to their tender requirements. All government purchases are channeled through the National Tender Board.

▶ **Exchange controls**

There are no controls on the movement of capital in or out of Zambia. Bank accounts may be held in local or foreign currency, and funds are easily transferred or allowed to be held offshore.

▶ **Partnerships**

In the few instances where franchising arrangements have been made they were done on the basis of British law. Joint ventures and licensing are inhibited by a shortage of local capital.

▶ **Establishing a presence**

To establish itself in Zambia a foreign firm must register with the Registrar of Companies at the Ministry of Commerce, Trade and Industry. Payment of a fee and submission of the company's charter are required. The minimum nominal capital required is approximately $200 and a registration fee of 2.5% of this startup capital is charged. Certificates of Incorporation are usually issued within 24 hours.

▶ **Financing projects**

Apart from bilateral and multilateral government agencies, commercial banks and venture capital funds are playing an increasing role in the financing of projects. The Overseas Private Investment Corporation , the International Finance Corporation and the Commonwealth Development Corporation also offer project financing, political risk insurance, and investor services.

▶ **Labor**

Labor is readily available although companies often have to invest in training to make up for a lack of skills. While the government stipulates preference for locals in positions where qualified, foreign firms are allowed automatic allowed work and residence permits for five expatriate workers when they invest, and more when justified later.

▶ **Legal rights**

The investment code allows for international arbitration should internal attempts at settlement of a commercial dispute fail. US companies have been successful in getting court rulings enforcing their contracts, even against parastatal companies. Trademark protection is considered adequate and there are fines for revealing business proprietary information. Copyright protection is limited and does not yet cover computer software. Zambia is a signatory to a number of international agreements on patents and intellectual property, including the Paris and Bern Convention and the African Regional Industrial Property Organization (ARIPO), and is a member of the World Intellectual Property Organization.

▶ **Business climate**

Business customs were shaped and influenced by the British (and Americans) since the end of the 19th century. Visitors who have conducted business in any of Southern Africa's English-speaking countries will find the environment in Zambia quite familiar.

355

Zimbabwe

As one of Africa's most sophisticated countries, Zimbabwe's economic performance has been a disappointment in recent years. International observers blame its failure to live up to expectations—despite ample mineral and agricultural resources, a well-developed infrastructure, advanced financial services and solid manufacturing sector—on misguided official policies. As internal pressures for political and economic reform continue, foreign investors are holding back and many promising opportunities for investment and trade expansion are left untouched. With recent impressive opposition gains, expectations are that the country's fortunes might turn around in the short term.

Country profile

The Republic of Zimbabwe is situated on an extension of the South African Highveld Plateau. The Zambezi and Limpopo rivers run along the country's northern and southern borders. At Victoria Falls the Zambezi plunges for 100 m (328 ft) over a width of 1.5 km (1 mile) into a narrow ravine, sending up a spray that earned it the indigenous name of *Mosi-oa-Tunya*—the "smoke that thunders." Downstream is Kariba Dam, the second largest human-made lake in Africa after Lake Volta in Ghana. Hwange National Park is one of several national parks. Rainfall in the highveld region averages 800 mm (31.5 inches) and along the lower regions less than 400 mm (15.7 inches). More than three-quarters of the population are Shona or Mashona. The second largest group is the Ndebele or Matabele, accounting for about 15% of the total. The white population number some 80,000 and Asians around 15,000. English is the official language. Well over half of the population is Christian and the rest adhere to traditional beliefs.

History

The remains of humans dating back 500,000 years have been discovered in the region. The country traces its history back to about 500 when the city of Great

Zimbabwe (house of stone) was developed by the ancestors of the Shona. Around the middle of the 19th Century, the territory was invaded by Ndebele or Matabele migrants from the south. In 1890 Cecil John Rhodes' British South Africa Company (BSA) started a white settlement at Salisbury (today's Harare, the capital of Zimbabwe). The territory was named Rhodesia, after Rhodes, and in 1923 white settlers were given the choice of joining South Africa or becoming a self-governing colony within the British Empire. They opted for

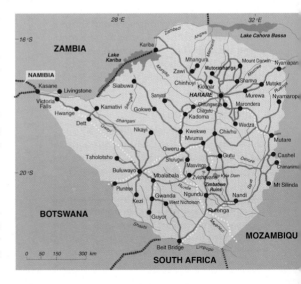

the latter. By law the best cropland was reserved for a rapidly-growing white settlement, restricting blacks to grazing areas. Joshua Mqabuko Nkomo's Zimbabwe African Peoples Union (ZAPU) and Robert Gabriel Mugabe's Zimbabwe African National Union (ZANU) led the black protest against this inequity. They resorted to arms in 1965 when Prime Minister Ian Smith and his ruling Rhodesian Front issued a unilateral declaration of independence (UDI). UN-imposed sanctions and a protracted guerilla war on two fronts involving ZAPU and ZANU forced Smith to the negotiating table and in April 1980 Zimbabwe gained independence under Prime Minister (later President) Robert Mugabe. A quota of 20 seats was temporarily reserved for whites. Mugabe soon nullified Nkomo's role and his newly formed ZANU-Patriotic Front won 116 of the 120 parliamentary seats in 1990, which gave him virtual one-man-one-party rule. Land resettlement has been at the center of an ongoing political battle. One-third of the country's arable land is owned by 4,000 white farmers. Mugabe's support for forceful occupation of white farmland by displaced "war veterans" has placed him at the center of a storm that led to near victory for the opposition Movement for Democratic Change (MDC) in the June 2000 elections. Mugabe was last reelected president in 1996 for a six year term. He has continued expressing support for the land seizures despite a majority vote against it in a referendum held in February 2000.

Government

The 1980 independence constitution was changed in 1987 to eliminate the 20 seats reserved for representatives of white voters and replace the post of prime minister with that of executive President, directly elected by the voters for 6-year terms. In the most recent presidential election, in March 1996, Pres Mugabe was re-elected but in the parliamentary elections of June 2000, the Movement for a Democratic Change (MDC) won a record 57 of the contested seats against the ruling Zanu-PDF's 62. One seat is held by the Zimbabwe African National Union-Ndonga (ZANU-N). Chiefs hold 10 of the seats as ex-officio members and the president appoints another 20.

Economic policy

In 1998 the government launched the Zimbabwe Program for Economic and Social Trans-

Fast facts

POLITICAL

Head of State	Pres. Robert Gabriel Mugabe (1980)
Ruling Party	ZANU-PF
Main Opposition	MDC
Independence	18 April 1980
National capital	Harare
Official language	English

PHYSICAL

Total area	150,803 sq. miles 390,580 sq. km. (± Montana)
Arable land	7% of land area
Coastline	Landlocked

POPULATION

Total	11 million
Av. yearly growth	1.02%
Population/sq. mile	75
Urban population	32%
Adult literacy	87%

ECONOMY[1]

Currency	Zimbabwean dollar (Z$) (U$1=54.95)
GDP (real)	$8 billion
GDP growth rate	0.1%
GNP per capita[2]	$610
GDP (ppp)[3]	$26.2 billion
GDP per cap. (ppp)[3]	$2,400
Inflation rate	32.0%
Exports	$2.5 billion
Imports	$2.6 billion
Development aid	$344 million
External debt	$4.56 billion
Unemployment	45%

INFRASTRUCTURE

Railroads	1,715 miles/2,760 km
Paved roads	17%
Motor vehicles	400,000
Air passenger/km	666 million
Telephones/1,000	12
International airport	Harare

1. Statistics are based on World Bank data.
2. Atlas method.
3. See page 151 for an explanation of GDP based on purchasing power parity (ppp).

formation (ZIMPREST) as the second phase of its Economic Structural Adjustment Program (ESAP) with the focus on unemployment and poverty, inflation and interest rate reduction, public and private savings, economic empowerment, and human resource development. Progress was hampered, however, by price controls, state interference in several sectors and the recent politically-motivated and state-supported violence and invasion of farms. Mugabe's support for the squatters has led to foreign sanctions.

Sectors

The agricultural sector contributes 20% of GNP and employs about 70% of the total labor force. Approximately 4,400 large commercial farms, covering 29% of the total land area, account for some 80% of marketed agricultural output. Maize, wheat, barley, cassava, soy beans, bananas and oranges are food crops. There is also a substantial production of cotton, sugar, coffee and beef but tobacco is by far the most important cash crop. Zimbabwe accounts for 17% of the world's total. Mining of gold, chrome, nickel and asbestos provides employment to some 60 000 workers. Other important minerals are coal, copper, iron ore, tin, silver, platinum, phosphate, limestone, cobalt and lithium. The manufacturing sector contributes a quarter of GNP and is dominated by engineering, chemicals, metals, textiles, chemicals and food and minerals processing. The tourist infrastructure is reasonably well developed.

Privatization

Even though privatization might present attractive investment opportunities for US foreign investment, the government has signaled its intention to limit foreign ownership. Progress has been slow.

Investment

A survey conducted by the Confederation of Zimbabwe Industries (CZI) in the late 1980s indicated that 25% of all industrial concerns have some foreign ownership. As these include mostly large companies, foreign investment accounts for 40% to 50% of the country's industrial output. The latest estimates put the total value of foreign investment at $5 billion, mostly held by British and South African interests.

Trade

Tobacco is by far the most important cash crop, earning more than 25% of export revenue.

Mining of gold, chrome, nickel and asbestos accounts for about 40% of total export earnings. Zimbabwe's largest trading partner is South Africa, followed by Britain, Germany and the US.

Financial sector

The financial sector is Sub-Saharan Africa's largest and most sophisticated after South Africa. Two major international and a number of domestic commercial banks operate 194 branches. South Africa's ABSA provides full services from Harare. There are also a number of merchant banks, finance houses, and building societies. The Reserve Bank of Zimbabwe (RBZ) is responsible for oversight, setting monetary controls and advising government fiscal policies. More than 60 companies are listed on Zimbabwe's stock market but trading is thin and most small companies are closely held.

Taxes and tariffs

The corporate profits tax rate for both foreign and domestic companies is 37.5% but a variety of deductions are allowed for depreciation, training, research, and investment in growth points. There is also a refund of a 15% sales tax on capital goods purchased in Zimbabwe and intended for use in priority projects or investment in growth points.

Business activity

AGRICULTURE

Corn, cotton, tobacco, wheat, coffee, sugar cane, peanuts, cattle, sheep, goats, pigs.

INDUSTRIES

Mining (coal, clay, numerous metallic and non-metallic ores), copper, steel, nickel, tin, wood products, cement, chemicals, fertilizer, clothing and footwear, foodstuffs, beverages.

NATURAL RESOURCES

Gold, copper, chrome, nickel, tin, asbestos.

EXPORTS

$2.5 billion (1999 est.): tobacco, chromium, gold, ferro alloys, cotton.

IMPORTS

$2.6 billion (1999 est.): machinery and transport equipment, other manufactures, chemicals, fuels.

MAJOR TRADING PARTNERS

South Africa, UK, Germany, Japan, US.

Doing Business with Zimbabwe

▶ **Investment**

The Zimbabwe Investment Center (ZIC) was created as one-stop shop for potential investors. Incentives for investors include allowances on the purchase of industrial and commercial buildings, implements and machinery, and for training, as well as special mining leases. The government, however, still prefers majority Zimbabwean participation in new investment projects and the degree of local ownership remains an important criterion in the evaluation of investment proposals. Its privatization program announced in late 1998 limits foreign ownership to between 15 and 20%, down from previous levels of 30 to 35%. There are a number of sectors reserved for domestic investors such as horticulture, game, wildlife ranching, forestry, fishing, freight and passenger transport (excluding airlines), and tobacco products. Investing in export processing zones entitles foreigners to a five-year tax holiday and duty-free importation of raw materials and capital equipment.

▶ **Trade**

There is a market for transportation equipment and parts, construction and farm machinery, computers and peripherals, chemicals and plastics, textile machinery telecommunications equipment and food products. Exports include ferrochrome, nickel, tobacco, gold, sugar, and clothing.

▶ **Trade finance**

Eximbank offers facilities to US exporters and financing is also available from local banks at relatively high interest rates.

▶ **Selling to the government**

There is an increasing demand for equipment related to telecommunications, power generation and road building and repair. Purchases are through tender and sometimes involve multilateral and bilateral financing.

▶ **Exchange controls**

Foreign investors are allowed to remit all their after-tax profits. The government monitors all capital outflows relating to prospective outward investment and dividend remittances.

▶ **Partnerships**

Partnership is the preferred form of foreign investment, especially if it advances black economic empowerment. Several US firms have entered the market through franchising agreements relating to consumer goods and services.

▶ **Establishing a presence**

Approval from the Zimbabwean Investment Center is required in all cases where a new business is established, an existing one expanded, or part or all of a business acquired.

▶ **Financing projects**

There are investment agreements in place with the Overseas Private Investment Corporation and the World Bank's Multilateral Investment Guarantee Agency. Project financing is also available from two Zimbabwean development banks and a venture capital company.

▶ **Labor**

Unskilled and semi-skilled labor is readily available but there is a growing shortage of technical skills. The 1985 Labor Relations Act sets strict standards for occupational health and safety, working hours and minimum wage. The Zimbabwe Congress of Trade Unions (ZCTU), the country's umbrella labor organization, consisting of 35 member unions and about 300,000 members, is a powerful advocate for workers.

▶ **Legal rights**

Zimbabwe's judiciary has a reputation for fairness and independence. The country is a member of the World Intellectual Property Organization but efforts to honor intellectual property ownership and rights are sometimes hampered by ineffective means of enforcement. Recently, remittances for royalties, technical services and management fees have been suspended in some instances due to the severe hard currency shortage. Government buyouts of both foreign investors and commercial farmers since independence have generally been on a mutually agreed basis. Recently, however, the government sanctioned white commercial farmland invasions by "war veterans" without proper compensation, causing a serious dent in foreign investor confidence. Once investors have exhausted local remedies, appeal to private arbitration is allowed in accordance with the rules and procedures of the UN Commission on International Trade Law.

▶ **Business climate**

Business customs generally follow the British model and are fairly formal. Despite bureaucratic red tape and a lack of transparency in some instances, patient and persistent companies with experienced local representation manage to develop profitable businesses.

IT IS NOT ONLY WHAT YOU HAVE TO SAY BUT HOW YOU SAY IT

WE HAVE HELPED OTHERS
RISE TO THE OCCASION IN
PRINT.

TRY US WITH YOUR
CORPORATE
NEEDS IN
COMPANY
BROCHURES,
ANNUAL
REPORTS,
PROPOSALS,
PRESENTATIONS,
AND OTHER
PUBLICATIONS.

WE DO NOT ONLY
PUBLISH OUR OWN
BOOKS. WE SHARE OUR
WRITERS AND DESIGNERS
WITH COMPANIES INTERESTED
IN SOARING TO NEW HEIGHTS.

GIVE US YOUR
RAW DATA AND
WE WILL
DO THE
REST.

BUSINESS BOOKS INTL - NEW CANAAN - CT 06840 - USA
TEL: 203-966-9645 FAX: 203-966-6018
WEB: WWW.BUSINESSBOOKSUSA.COM EMAIL: EDITOR@BUSINESSBOOKSUSA.COM

Chapter 8

Key Players in Africa

The African Renaissance will not become a reality through either borrowing or begging. It will only be accomplished by entrepreneurship within Africa and private capital from outside. The new leadership on the continent has shown clear intent to create a more attractive environment for foreign investment and to pursue trade and tourism more aggressively.

The economic future and stability of Africa rests largely on the shoulders of innovative and enterprising Africans and foreigners who build and prosper together on a continent with vast untapped natural and human resources.

The advertisers who helped to make this book possible are all key players in Africa. In the following pages they tell in their own words about their involvement in a continent which they believe likely to be one of the success stories of the 21st Century.

African Travel, Inc.

African Travel, Inc. has been a leading provider of group and individual travel to Africa for more than a quarter century. It caters for both business and leisure travelers and has been involved in air and land arrangements for major groups as well as individuals. Its team of specialists in California relies on a network of representatives on the continent to take care of every detail of client's needs. It forms part of one of the world's largest travel companies, Far & Wide.

1. Is African Travel, Inc. insured?

As an active member of the United States Tour Operators Association (USTOA) African Travel, Inc. is required to post $1 million with USTOA to reimburse, in accordance with the terms and conditions of the USTOA consumer protection plan, the advance payments of African Travel, Inc. customers in the unlikely event of a bankruptcy or insolvency.

2. What destinations do you operate your tours to in Africa?

Most of our tours cover Eastern Africa (Kenya, Tanzania & Seychelles) and Southern Africa (South Africa, Botswana, Zimbabwe, Namibia, Zambia), as well as Egypt.

3. What type of programs do you offer?

Our programs include scheduled tours that are locally hosted (a guide from each city or area the client is visiting) and independent tours that can be designed based on the travelers needs. Our brochure tours are guaranteed to operate with a minimum of two passengers. The average group size is 10 passengers.

4. What is the major difference between African Travel, Inc. and the other major wholesalers who sell travel to Southern and Eastern Africa?

We have a very dedicated, experienced staff – with over 375 combined years of travel expertise who have an in-depth knowledge of the destinations included in our tours. All of our tour programs are designed to be flexible to accommodate changes that the traveler might want to incorporate. Our staff of safari experts will be happy to custom-design a program to any of the areas in Southern and Eastern Africa plus Egypt. We have enduring and successful relationships with our vendors, giving us the opportunity to offer competitive prices.

5. Does African Travel, Inc. offer any travel insurance that passengers can purchase before departing from home? If so, does it cover medical or emergency evacuation from remote areas?

African Travel, Inc. offers a passenger travel protection program through Insure America. This insurance includes trip cancellation/trip interruption, travel delay, medical protection, baggage protection, travel accident protection and worldwide emergency assistance. For any pre-existing medical conditions the exclusion will be waived if insurance is purchased within 24 hours of initial deposit payment.

A detailed policy outlining the coverage and emergency contact information, is given to all clients upon receipt of deposit. African Travel, Inc. programs to remote areas also provide "Flying doctors" insurance as a supplement. This insurance provides emergency medical evacuation.

8. How physically demanding are your programs, especially the game drives and game viewing activities?

Generally, the tour programs are not physically demanding, and are enjoyed by anyone who is reasonably fit. The only physical activity on safari is a game walk, but usually they are not strenuous. Participation in these activities are at the discretion of tour participants.

AFRICAN TRAVEL INC.
1100 E. Broadway
Glendale, CA 91205
Tel: (818) 507-7893
Fax: (818) 507-5802
Toll free: 1-800-421-8907
E-mail: ati@africantravelinc.com
Website: www.africantravelinc.com

"When you choose to travel to Africa, you are making a decision that will change your life. Africa is more than a destination. It's an experience.

Why do both leisure and business travelers select African Travel to make their arrangements? Even though we are headquartered in Glendale, California, Africa is our home and our passion. And we have resident representatives on call for 24-hours a day in most parts of the continent.

Our team of business travel advisors and safari specialists have a track record that spans over decades of serving the needs of business executives, leisure travelers and eco-tourists—both as individuals and in small, medium and large groups.

Dave Herbert
President

www.africantravelinc.com

363

Barloworld
Leading brands

Barloworld Limited is an international industrial brand management company, which operates in 32 countries, and sells products and services in more than 90. With headquarters in Johannesburg, it is one of South Africa's most global companies, with more than 60 percent of its earnings derived offshore. Its portfolio of managed brands are among the most familiar anywhere – Caterpillar, Hyster, Mercedes Benz, BMW, Toyota, Freightliner, Plascon, PPC. The list is endless.

The company was established in South Africa nearly 100 years ago, and over the past 40 years has evolved into one of the biggest and most respected industrial companies at home, and a global player of note. It employs around 24,000 people.

Last year, the company introduced a new corporate identity and changed its name to Barloworld, with a logo incorporating a world icon and words "Leading brands," to promote a cohesive global image more in keeping with its transnationality into the new millenium.

THE COMPANY'S BUSINESS LINES INCLUDE:

Equipment—Barloworld is one of the leading Caterpillar dealers with operations in South Africa, Spain, Andora, Angola, Botswana, Bulgaria, Lesotho, Malawi, Mozambique, Namibia, Portugal, Sao Tome and Principe, central Siberia, Swaziland and Zambia. It also represents Perkins diesel engines, Ingersoll Rand drilling rigs and Dezzi articulated dump trucks in South Africa.

Industrial Distribution— Barloworld is the world's largest independent lift truck dealer. It distributes the leading brand, Hyster, in the southeast United States, United Kingdom, Belgium and southern Africa. It also distributes Freightliner trucks and Ditch Witch trenching equipment in certain states in the United States, and manufactures Lamson vacuum conveyance systems in the United Kingdom.

Motor and Logistics—The company is a leading provider of comprehensive transport solutions in southern Africa with 56 dealerships representing the leading vehicle brands in South Africa, Botswana and Namibia. It also has an emerging logistics operation and a growing motor dealership network in Australia.

Cement and Lime—Cement, metallurgical grade lime and allied products are manufactured and distributed in South Africa, Zimbabwe and Botswana.

Scientific—Laboratory equipment, manufactured under the Bibby Sterilin brand, in the UK and exported worldwide. Barloworld Melles Griot, a household name in the field of photonic, lasers and optomechanical instruments, sold worldwide from manufacturing operations in the UK, US and Japan.

Coatings—Decorative coatings in a range of branded paints, coatings and related products and the market leader in South Africa with the Plascon range, and number two in Australia with the Taubmans and Bristol brands. Market leader in speciality niches in the UK with the International brand.

Steel Tube—Market leader in South Africa for the manufacture of small bore steel tube and pipe and related products.

PERFORMANCE

Two years ago, the company adopted Value Based Management (VBM), which is based largely on simultaneously creating wealth for shareholders, value for customers and value for employees, as the yardstick of its success. It was this principle, says Barloworld Chief Executive Tony Phillips, which was the main driver behind the recent excellent results produced by the company.

For the latest published period, the half year to 31 March 2001, worldwide revenues grew 28 percent to R13.4-billion (US$1.66-billion) and operating profit by 47 percent to R719-million (US$89 million). Earnings per share before exceptional items increased by 31 percent to 193 cents (US cents 24).

LISTING INFORMATION

Barloworld's primary listing is on the JSE Securities Exchange South Africa, with secondary listings on the London, Brussels, Antwerp, Frankfurt, Zurich and Namibian stock exchanges. The shareholder register reveals a broad cross-section of institutional and private investors, primarily based in South Africa, the UK and United States. The share is highly liquid and this contributes to its attractiveness for international investors. The share code is BAW.

WHERE TO FIND US

For further information contact:

Mark Drewell
Head of Corporate Communication
Barloworld
Tel: 27 11 445-1204
Email: *mdrewell@barloworld.com*
WEBSITE: *www.barloworld.com*

"We are focused on building an international industrial brand management company that delivers world-class performance and profitability. We create stakeholder value by building powerful industrial brands and long-term relationships"

Tony Phillips, Chief Executive

In October 2000, acquisition of US-based Barton Freightliner not only added more than $285 million to Barloworld's revenues, but gave it a major foothold in the US truck market. The deal will more than double Barloworld's revenues from its North American operations, most of which comes from its Hyster materials handling dealerships, which operate across eight states in the South east. Other US operations include laser and photonics (Melles Griot); laboratory equipment (Dynalab) and trenching and directional boring equipment (Ditch Witch).

365

A commitment in word.
And in deeds.

Throughout the long history of the global search for oil, it would be hard to identify more resilient business partnerships than those forged between Chevron and many African nations. Chevron is one of the largest US investors in Africa. It is involved in exploration, production, shipping, delivery, and trading. Caltex, a Chevron-Texaco joint venture in Africa since the 1930's, refines and markets petroleum products. With such diverse resources, Chevron brings the breadth of its international experience to its African operations.

But Chevron brings more than experience. One of its greatest strengths is its cutting-edge technology. It uses this technology to improve oil and natural gas exploration and production while lowering costs.

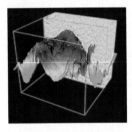

Its success, however, should not only be measured in financial strength and technical expertise but also in opportunities for employment, training and career development for Africans. Over the years, Chevron has provided jobs, training and management opportunities for thousands of Africans. Today, 85% of the work force in its African operations are national employees.

Sensitivity

Chevron also believes that economic progress must be accompanied by a sensitivity to the health and well-being of communities and the environment. So, it invests in a variety of community development and environmental projects. Helping to create sustainable economic climates fosters local business opportunities and further underscores Chevron's commitment to the community.

And, Chevron continues to expand its role in the economic development of Africa. For instance, deep-water exploration is in progress offshore Angola, and in 1999, Chevron became the country's first deep-water oil producer with the start-up of the Kuito Field. It expects to boost investment in Africa over the next 10 years in order to significantly increase oil production.

In other words, Chevron embraces opportunities that the future holds and stands committed to Africa's economic development.

Investing in partnerships
Investing in Africa

Chevron has been partnering with African nations for more than 60 years to develop, refine and market energy resources. This long-term commitment has built strong partnerships and a strong foundation for the future. Today, Chevron's operations in Africa account for more than 900,000 barrels of crude oil per day, with 85% of its African work force comprising national employees.

Angola — Chevron is the largest oil producer in Angola with about 500,000 barrels per day, accounting for approximately two-thirds of the crude oil produced there. With 32 major fields, Chevron is Angola's first deepwater oil producer through its Kuito Field, which began producing just two and a half years after first discovery.

Nigeria — Chevron has been doing business in Nigeria for about 40 years since it first discovered oil in shallow water near the Escravos River. Today, fields operated by Chevron, in partnership with the Nigerian National Petroleum Corp., encompass 2.2 million acres and account for about a fifth of the nation's total crude output. Total average production at the end of 2000 was 430,000 barrels of oil per day.

Additional gas-related projects under way include: the Escravos Gas Project, to gather and process gas; the Escravos Gas to Liquids Plant, converting natural gas into premium, clean-burning fuels in partnership with Sasol Synfuels International; and the West African Gas Pipeline, to supply Nigerian natural gas to Benin, Ghana and Togo.

Democratic Republic of Congo — Chevron has been active in the Democratic Republic of Congo since 1959. Through a 50% joint venture, Chevron produces nearly 70% of the country's oil from eight offshore platforms, averaging more than 17,000 barrels of oil per day.

Republic of Congo — With total investment of more than $1 billion, Chevron is the largest U.S. investor in the Congo with interests in two currently producing fields, Nkossa and Kitina. Combined production from both was over 90,000 barrels of oil per day by the end of 2000.

Equatorial Guinea — In 2000 Chevron signed a five-year production-sharing agreement with the government of Equatorial Guinea to explore offshore acreage (4,250 square kilometers) in the Rio Muni Basin. Chevron has opened its first office in Equatorial Guinea and plans to begin exploration in 2001.

Chad and Cameroon — In 2000, Chevron acquired a 25% interest in an international consortium to develop the Doba oil fields in Southern Chad and transport, via a 1000-kilometer pipeline, about 225,000 barrels per day through Cameroon. The fields are expected to produce about 1 billion barrels of oil over the life of the project.

Caltex, a Chevron and Texaco joint venture, has been operating in Southern and Eastern Africa since the 1930s. Today, Caltex has more than 4,600 worldwide retail outlets as well as interests in refineries, lube-oil blending plants, terminals, and marine and aviation services.

Chevron

The symbol of partnership.

Cohen and Woods International, Inc.

Optimistic about Africa's future

Upon retirement from the United States government in 1994, we resolved to stay actively involved in international and especially African affairs; our common interests and rewarding previous experience working together led us to establish "COHEN AND WOODS INTERNATIONAL." Our efforts are devoted primarily to the provision of advisory services on Africa. We serve both private and official organizations, businesses and agencies, and African governments seeking strategic advice and counsel.

Africa's highest priority is economic growth and development, and we are contributing to this endeavor. Essential ingredients include increased business investment, political stability and security, a positive international image, and a favorable environment for the private sector.

Experience

Our combined 80 years of experience as diplomats and government executives – specializing in African affairs – assure that we can be of practical assistance to international firms seeking new opportunities in Africa and to African governments seeking to better understand and adjust to the dynamics of the post-Cold War world.

Above all, we believe there is absolutely no reason why Africa cannot achieve the same levels of growth and poverty reduction enjoyed by other areas of the world.

Our personal experience with Africa's political, economic and security requirements have given us insights of substantial value to international business firms seeking to better understand mid- and long-term investment risks and opportunities in Africa.

Opportunities

At the same time, our many African friends know that we always speak to them frankly about their interests and their options as they seek to enhance their opportunities for more fruitful external relations, and to increase the flow of private investments. We are especially convinced that new opportunities for expanded relations with the United States are available to those African governments that are ready to reach out in a constructive manner.

Contribution

We look forward to working with our partners, public and private, in contributing to greater prosperity, security and growth for the people and nations of Africa.

We anticipate that our most valuable contributions will continue to be in the sphere of strategic advice and counsel, but we also provide representational services as desired. We also offer our services in the planning and implementation of particular projects, whether in the public or private sectors, spanning the full range of stability, security, investment, and developmental activities.

THE PRINCIPALS

HERMAN J. COHEN

Ambassador Herman J. (Hank) Cohen served with the United States Department of State from 1955 to 1993, attaining the rank of Career Ambassador.

His career was dedicated to African affairs, culminating in service as Assistant Secretary of State for African Affairs from 1989 to 1993.

During his career, Ambassador Cohen served as Ambassador to The Gambia and Senegal, and held other overseas postings in Zaire, Zambia, Zimbabwe (then Rhodesia), Uganda, and Paris.

Ambassador Cohen also served in the White House as Special Assistant to the President and Senior Director for Africa, National Security Council.

Prior to joining the Foreign Service, Mr. Cohen served as an Infantry Officer in Germany. Ambassador Cohen is the recipient of the Presidential Distinguished Rank Award, as well as the French Legion of Honor and the Belgian Order of Leopold II. The American Academy of Diplomacy gave him their award for writing the most distinguished book on diplomacy in 2000.

JAMES L. WOODS

James L (Jim) Woods served with the United States Department of Defense from 1960 to 1994, with principal duties in International Security Affairs.

His assignments have included several tours with the Defense Security Assistance Agency and the Defense Advanced Research Projects Agency.

During the first half of his career, Mr. Woods focused mainly on East and Southeast Asia, but from 1978 to his retirement he worked exclusively on African issues, culminating in service as Deputy Assistant Secretary for African Affairs from 1986 to 1994.

Prior to joining the Office of the Secretary of Defense, Mr. Woods served as an Armor Officer in Germany.

Mr. Woods is the recipient of the Presidential Meritorious Rank Award, two Secretary of Defense's Meritorious Rank Awards, and the Department of Defense Distinguished Civilian Service Medal. He is also a Distinguished Graduate of the U.S. Armed Forces Industrial College.

CONTACT US:

Cohen and Woods International, Inc.
1621 N. Kent Street, Suite 1619
Arlington, VA 22209   USA
Tel:(703) 516-9510 Fax:(703) 516-4547
Email:cohenandwoods@cohenandwoods.com

Development Bank of Southern Africa

The Development Bank of Southern Africa (DBSA) is a development finance institution wholly owned by the South African government. It is a leading development finance institution that supports economic and human development, growth and institutional capacity building in southern Africa, primarily through infrastructure investments.

It is one of five national development finance institutions tasked with promoting development. The organization supplements the flow of private and public funds by forming partnerships with the public and private sectors for infrastructure development projects. The DBSA works with donors and its other partners at international, national and provincial levels to build relationships with all key role players in development and to promote the best possible use of resources in order to reach the goals of development initiatives.

Three principles form the foundation for the DBSA's operations. These are: maximizing its development impact, being additional to other funding sources and maintaining sound banking principles.

DBSA's support to development in southern Africa (R21.1 billion loan funding to date) revolves mainly around loan and equity funding for municipal, bulk and connector infrastructure (86%) and entrepreneurial support and social and institutional infrastructure. It actively supports developments through cofunding and technical assistance.

Co-funding: Co-financing arrangements more than doubled the project value of the DBSA's contribution. The cumulative leverage ratio to date is 1:1.1.

Technical assistance: With a focus on institutional capacity building, policy and planning is provided by way of technical assistance grants or loans, as well as the provision of technical expertise from the organization's pool of highly qualified and experienced development experts. In addition, the DBSA provides policy analysis and support through a continuous service of development publications, advice and support to clients and a development information database which is accessible to all.

The DBSA operates in all the provinces of South Africa and in the 14 countries of the Southern African Development Community (SADC). It provides the following products and services:

Products: Loans, guarantees, quasi-equity, grants, technical assistance grants, equity investments.

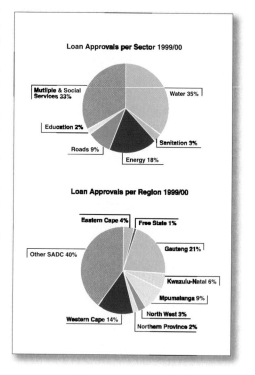

Loan Approvals per Sector 1999/00

Mutliple & Social Services 33%
Water 35%
Education 2%
Sanitation 3%
Roads 9%
Energy 18%

Loan Approvals per Region 1999/00

Eastern Cape 4%
Free State 1%
Other SADC 40%
Gauteng 21%
Kwazulu-Natal 6%
Mpumalanga 9%
North West 3%
Northern Province 2%
Western Cape 14%

Services: Training, agency services, advisory services, development information, development strategies, capacity building.

1999/2000 highlights include:

- ☑ The DBSA approved investment loans totaling R2,008 million for projects with a total capital value of R6 365 million—64 per cent of this amount was for infrastructure development in South Africa and 36 per cent was invested in SADC countries
- ☑ The South African projects funded or co-funded by the DBSA benefited 1.1 million households and 5.5 million individuals. Some 502,000 households were connected to water, 51,000 to sanitation and 252,000 to electricity and 368,000 received multiple services.
- ☑ DBSA funding is estimated to have created 33,700 person-years of employment.
- ☑ The Bank was awarded an investment grade Baa3 rating by Moody's, the international credit rating agency.
- ☑ The Bank's risk management policy and procedures were benchmarked by international experts and found to be sound.
- ☑ The Bank leveraged funding from other sources at a rate of R2.17 for every R1 it invested.
- ☑ The DBSA introduced the concept of a development fund to provide grant funding for capacity building in clients that are not currently creditworthy.
- ☑ The Bank established a public development information centre and provided policy and capacity support to stakeholders such as the office of the President, the Department of Finance and the Worldwide Fund for Nature.
- ☑ The National Productivity Institute of South Africa presented the Bank with a Gold Award for productivity improvements.

For further information contact:

Zaid Nordien (zaidn@dbsa.org)
Manager
Corporate Communications and Marketing
Development Bank of Southern Africa
PO Box 1234
Halfway House, 1685
South Africa
Tel: 27 11-313-3116
Fax: 27 11-313-3628

OUR MISSION

To fulfill its catalytic role, the DBSA:

✓ helps to mobilise additional investment by co-financing public- and private-sector investments

✓ promotes public and private partnerships for infrastructure

✓ provides technical assistance focused on strengthening policy, institutional capacity and environmental management in support of Bank projects and programmes

✓ shares skills and knowledge with institutions and clients to maximise the development impact and quality of specific project interventions

✓ provides professional and administrative resources for managing special infrastructure development initiatives on behalf of government and/or development institutions.

Website: www.dbsa.org

Respect the Community. Protect the Future.

The history of ExxonMobil in Africa is one marked with success. Yet success is nothing without the respect and protection of both the environment and its individuals. To that end, ExxonMobil has undertaken a wide array of initiatives in Africa which are designed to improve the communities in which we live and operate, including:

- Support for education, including scholarships and provision of facilities and teaching aids
- Libraries and language centers for local children
- Infrastructure development, such as bridge construction, electrical power and civic planning
- Partnerships with Non-Government Organizations (NGOs) on community improvement programs
- Civic activities including support for orphans and elderly people

Several public health programs have received special attention in recent years with grants totaling millions of dollars. Malaria, a major cause of death in Africa, is the target of three programs — the Harvard Malaria Initiative, Medicines for Malaria Venture, and Roll Back Malaria — that receive ExxonMobil financial support.

Programs to fight other diseases that are prevalent in Africa, such as HIV/AIDS and Maternal & Neonatal Tetanus, also are receiving ExxonMobil funding. Additional health-related programs include construction of clinics and installation of water lines to bring fresh water to villages.

In June of this year, ExxonMobil was a leading sponsor of the Dakar conference on the phase-out of leaded gasoline in sub-Saharan Africa. The elimination of leaded gasoline is an important step toward bringing cleaner air to African cities and reducing health care costs.

The safety of our employees, contractors, customers and neighboring communities is also of critical importance to ExxonMobil. We are currently working hard to ensure that all hauliers of ExxonMobil petroleum products in Africa comply with stringent internal safety requirements. The problem of road safety in Africa is a serious one; six African countries top the list of nations with the highest road fatalities. ExxonMobil is committed to enhancing the safe and reliable transport of its products across the continent.

In addition to its community programs, ExxonMobil provides significant economic benefits to African communities by providing jobs for hundreds of employees and contract workers.

World-Class Operations for Africa.

As nations around the world work to improve their economies and the lives of their citizens, the need for increased supplies of oil and gas is critical. In the worldwide search to find those supplies, Exxon Mobil Corporation has focused growing attention on the resource potential of Africa.

On a continent where its Esso and Mobil branded petroleum products have been marketed for many decades, ExxonMobil is making multi-billion-dollar investments in new oil and gas exploration and development that will provide significant production for decades to come.

Countries receiving direct benefit from these investments are Algeria, Angola, Cameroon, Chad, Egypt, Equatorial Guinea, Niger, Nigeria, Republic of the Congo, and Sao Tome & Principe.

Key ExxonMobil assets include significant production in Nigeria and Equatorial Guinea, major new developments underway in Angola, Chad and Nigeria, and a pre-eminent acreage position in the high-potential deepwater province of West Africa.

In Nigeria, ExxonMobil is the largest non-government net liquid producer. In Angola, ExxonMobil and its co-venturers have announced 22 discoveries since 1996 that represent world-class development opportunities. In Chad, construction is underway on the Doba project, including the 1000 km pipeline through Cameroon to the Atlantic coast.

In addition to significant investments in exploration and production projects, ExxonMobil has an extensive marketing presence in Africa. ExxonMobil is the continent's third-leading fuels marketer and Africa's premier marketer of lubricants and petroleum products, with Esso and Mobil branded service stations in 29 countries across the continent.

ExxonMobil also owns an interest in four refining facilities in Senegal, Ivory Coast, Cameroon and Gabon.

ExxonMobil is enthusiastic about the long-term growth prospects for Africa.

HSBC Equator

Member HSBC Group

HSBC Equator was founded in 1975 as a merchant bank to pursue trade finance opportunities in sub-Saharan Africa. As Africa has remained its sole market, HSBC Equator has developed a unqiue understanding of how to do business on the continent. Guided by its philosophy of "working in partnership with Africa", HSBC Equator has developed strong relationships with both the private and public sectors.

Led by a culturally diverse and experienced group of professionals and support staff, HSBC Equator offers innovative and customised solutions to meet its clients' changing needs. This broad range of products and services are provided through five major business units:

Institutional Banking

This division primarily focuses on the marketing and delivery of a wide range of correspondent banking products, capitalising on the HSBC Group's global reach through over 6,500 offices in 79 countries and territories.

Investments, Fund and Wealth Management

This division manages equity funds, such as the Africa Growth Fund and the Kenya Equity Fund, as well as offers world-class wealth management services, combining a local presence with the HSBC Group's investment products.

Structured Trade Finance

This division supports inter and intra Africa trading activity. Through innovative and customised financial structures, this division arranges over US $1 billion in trade related financing for its African public and private sector

clients every year. Principal services and products offered include import finance, pre and post export finance, loan syndications and working capital finance.

Investment Banking

This division offers a full range of project, structured finance and advisory services with specific industry and country expertise. In addition to its vast privatisation and mergers and acquisitions expertise, this division's industry expertise includes aviation, agro-industry, manufacturing, mining, telecommunications and tourism.

Commercial Solutions

This division specialises in the supply of commercial goods, including capital equipment, and services to businesses across sub-Saharan Africa, primarily in the transportation, telecommunications, construction, mining and manufacturing sectors.

Africa network

A network of strategically located offices in sub-Saharan Africa provides HSBC Equator with essential insight into the needs of its clients and the ability to offer them timely and efficient service.

Contact:

HSBC Equator's African offices are complemented by teams of professionals in its offices in London, Washington DC, Connecticut and the Bahamas. HSBC Equator is also supported by the global network of its shareholders, being 60% owned by the HSBC Group, one of the largest financial services organisations in the world and 40% owned by Nedcor, one of the largest banking groups in South Africa.

For further information about HSBC Equator's full range of services in Africa, contact:

Mr. Kofi O. Sekyere
HSBC Equator Bank plc
South Africa Representative Office
4th Floor, Block F, Nedcor Sandton
135 Rivonia Road, Sandown 2146
South Africa
Tel: +27 11 294 5000;
Fax: +27 11 295 5000
E-Mail: kosekyere@usa.net.
Website: www.equator-africa.com

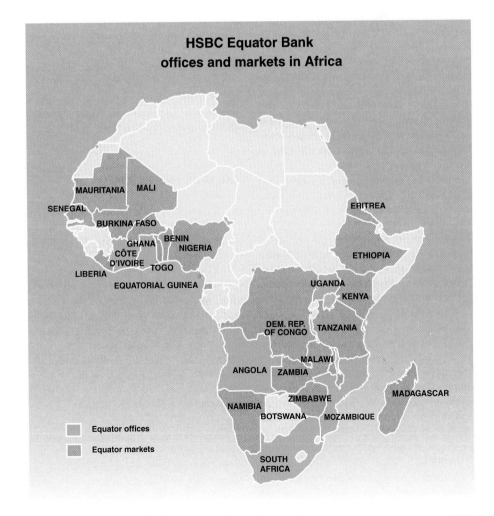

HSBC Equator Bank offices and markets in Africa

The Industrial Development Corporation of South Africa Limited (IDC)

A catalyst for development on the African Continent

Perceptions of Africa as an investment destination are rapidly changing, for international investors are no longer falling prey to gross generalizations or stereotyping. That is, regional or even national characteristics and advantages throughout the African continent are at long last being evaluated on their individual merits. There are indeed encouraging signs that numerous African countries will succeed in attaining exponential growth in foreign direct investment inflows, as the international investor community takes a more differentiated look at the continent, identifying and/or examining opportunities on a country-by-country, industry-by-industry basis.

Increased investment in viable infrastructure and business opportunities is a key focus of the *Millennium Africa Recovery Programme* (MAP). The programme envisages both continent-wide and regional initiatives to reposition Africa in the global economic arena and place African countries, both individually and collectively, on a sustainable growth path. Economic development initiatives, such as infrastructure development and economic integration, are to be managed at regional or sub-regional levels.

As a long-term objective, economic integration is of critical importance to the member states of the Southern African Development Community (SADC), and indeed for Africa as a whole, for it not only carries the politically-beneficial element of co-operation between neighboring countries and a louder voice in global forums, but also many potential economic benefits for the individual economies.

Regional integration presents numerous opportunities for profitable cross-border investments targeting the individual countries' natural resource endowments and comparative advantages, as well as for the augmentation of intra-regional trade on the back of preferential access to a substantially wider potential export market. It also enhances the visibility of individual countries as potential markets, as suppliers of goods and services and as global investment destinations.

Economic integration within the SADC will thus facilitate trade and investment flows and will

be conducive to the generation of higher rates of fixed investment; the diversification and enhancement of national production bases and export baskets; the realisation of economies of scale; technology and skills transfer; efficiency and productivity gains; employment creation and, amongst others, an improved access to financial resources and information.

The IDC's role in Africa

Established in 1940, the Industrial Development Corporation of South Africa Limited (the IDC) is a self-funding development finance institution wholly owned by the South African Government.

As a key driver of the regional integration process and a leading promoter of the MAP, the South African Government views the IDC as a catalyst for sustainable industrial development in the Southern African Development Community in particular, and Africa in general. Hence the expansion of the IDC's geographical mandate beyond South Africa's borders – to the entire SADC region since 1997 and, very recently, to the remainder of the African continent.

In an effort to contribute meaningfully to the regional integration process and the promotion of sustainable development, the IDC has progressively intensified its involvement in Africa by:

- ❏ Acting as a catalyst for investments in productive capacity;
- ❏ Identifying sound investment opportunities and promoting inward investment;
- ❏ Providing extended credit facilities to African buyers of South African capital goods and related services;
- ❏ Supporting regional development initiatives;
- ❏ Providing inputs into economic policy formulation; and
- ❏ Providing consultancy services.

Project development

The IDC provides financial and technical assistance for the development of value-adding greenfield, expansion or rehabilitation projects in Africa. Its sectoral focus includes manufacturing in its widest sense, energy, mining, minerals beneficiation, agriculture and agro-processing, tourism, information technology, telecommunications and selective franchising. The IDC's basket of financial instruments, in turn, comprises equity financing, quasi-equity, commercial loans, export financing, wholesale finance, guarantees and venture capital funding.

The project for which finance is required must be sizeable and sustainable, showing prospects of an acceptable level of profitability within a reasonable time frame. An operating partner is absolutely essential, since the IDC does not participate in the day-to-day management of an enterprise. The overall IDC contribution must not exceed 50% of the total funding requirements for projects in the SADC region (a maximum of 25% for projects elsewhere in Africa) and the IDC prefers that its exposure does not exceed that of the project's shareholders, members or owners.

Loan finance is normally provided for a period of 5 to 10 years, depending on the purpose for which the finance is required as well as the ability of the undertaking to repay the facility, and IDC funding is tailored to suit the project's cash flow requirements. The IDC may require security, the form and nature of which will relate to the applicant's specific circumstances. IDC equity participation, if required, should be within a 20% to 30% range.

The project's developmental impact is of critical importance, particularly with respect to job creation, export earnings, value addition, the expansion of a country's production base and, among others, poverty reduction. Each proposal is, however, considered on its own particular merit.

The IDC's portfolio of African projects under implementation or investigation comprised some 37 projects in 13 countries (excluding South Africa) by June 2001.

Export financing

The provision of medium- to long-term credit to importers of South African capital goods and services is a further instrument of IDC support to Africa's development. These facilities are available in South African rands, US dollars or euros, and may finance up to 85% of the contract amount, as long as a South African content of at least 70% is achieved.

Through the provision of export finance, the IDC thus facilitates the growing participation of South African industry in African projects and thereby permits the attainment of a more balanced industrial development within the continent. Facilities exceeding the $400 million mark have been authorised over the past five years in support of South African exports to SADC member states, for activities as diverse as aluminium smelting, a coal mine rehabilitation, copper mining, a brewery, rose growing facilities, fishing activities and oil rigging.

Your preferred business partner

The Industrial Development Corporation of South Africa is the largest centralised, multi-disciplinary, project evaluation group in Southern Africa. It has a broad experience base and an exemplary track record in industrial development spanning six decades; and the IDC possesses the human and financial resources to help realise Africa's enviable potential in a determined, responsible and pro-active manner.

Contact details

The IDC
19 Fredman Drive, Sandton 2196
South Africa
Tel +27 11 269 3000
Fax +27 11 269 3116
E-mail callcentre@idc.co.za
Website www.idc.co.za

PAN AFRICAN COMMUNICATIONS NETWORK LIMITED

The World Trade Organization (WTO) has been encouraging African countries to liberalize their telecommunications systems so that they can participate in a universal service. However, there has always been a fear in Africa that this will only benefit Western companies. There is no doubt that Africans deserve an affordable service, much like that enjoyed by developed markets. Effective and cheap communication holds great benefit to any society, be it in the field of education, health, trade or better relations. Pan African Communication Network (PACONET), a Mauritius company, is bridging the divide by bringing low cost communication to the African continent.

PACONET has in AIG African Infrastructure Fund both a financial and strategic investor. Emerging Markets Partnership is the principal adviser to the fund and the American International Group (AIG) is the principal sponsor. His Excellency Nelson R. Mandela is the Chairman of the Fund's Advisory Board. The major investors in the Fund are the International Finance Corporation (IFC), the African Development Bank (AfDB), and Sheikh Mohammed Hussain Al-Amoudi.

Growth

Some African countries have the highest projected economic growth in the world. This growth, coupled with recent advances in telecommunications on the continent, resulted in an enormous expansion in both teledensity and subscribers to the Internet. Africa continues to deregulate its telecommunication markets while recent advances in technology, in particular Packet Switched technologies and the Internet, have resulted in new, faster and cheaper methods of transmitting information. All of this has opened the door for private investment on the continent. One of the major obstacles to Internet growth has been the lack of telecommunication infrastructure as well as the cost barrier. Telephone calls and Internet access in Africa still ranks as some of the most expensive in the world.

PACONET's presence in various African countries allows it to interconnect directly from one country to another, a system often called

meshing. Previously, many countries relied on North American or European switches to route their data traffic—even destined for a neighboring country. It is PACONET's goal to mesh as much of the African continent as possible, thus allowing for cheaper regional traffic at lower costs to the users.

Licences

PACONET has obtained the necessary licenses in a number of African countries allowing it to install the infrastructure to provide bandwidth, voice and data services. Management continues to interact with the various communication authorities in an effort to expand the company's network into new territories, allowing everyone to participate in this first truly African network. The goal to provide all countries seamless connectivity with each other without having to route via another continent is fast becoming a reality as PACONET adds new countries to its network.

Outsourcing

PACONET follows a policy of outsourcing to local companies wherever possible. It supports the notion that Information and Communications Technologies (ICT) are enablers of the economy, social development and skill development. The rapid deployment of satellite-based packet switched communications networks that support the integration of voice, data, Internet and Multimedia services will provide the most cost effective short term solution to the vast imbalances across the continent, within countries and between Africa and the rest of the world.

378

PACONET uses the latest satellite, broadband wireless local loop and packet switched technologies to provide integrated communications services because it believes that these technologies offer the most cost-effective and speedy way to address Africa's immediate needs. It believes that Africa cannot afford to wait for traditional terrestrial based solutions to be deployed, even though in the long run these technologies may well challenge the effectiveness of satellite technologies. These satellite based solutions, correctly deployed in niche market areas, provide communications solutions easier, cheaper and quicker than any other solution available today.

Network

PACONET's network is based on the provision of intra-continental connectivity bandwidth utilizing satellite capacity leased from Geostationary satellite operators. Building or utilizing existing land earth stations at the two ends of the circuit accesses the satellite bandwidth. PACONET's satellite network utilizes a combined point-to-point and point-to-multipoint architecture to deploy a combined "star" and "mesh" configuration. It allows PACONET to customize its offerings in individual African countries. The VoIP switch is based on frame-relay architectures, supporting recognized frame relay protocols for optimum performance.

PACONET's network is fully managed via a Remote Management System (RMS) to ensure optimal network performance. PACONET also provides for a billing platform, capable of "off-switch" billing and traffic flow analysis. The satellite earth stations typically consist of 3.8-meter VSAT antennae equipped

Diagram 1

Diagram 2

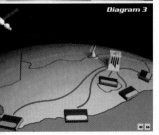

Diagram 3

for C-band reception. This choice is based on the availability of satellite bandwidth across the continent in one contiguous satellite footprint to ensure that economies of scale are achieved in the best utilization of leased satellite bandwidth. PACONET makes use of Single Carrier Per Channel (SCPC) and Multiple Carrier Per Channel (MCPC)—Dedicated and Demand Assigned Multiple Access (DAMA) services deployed cost-effectively to provide thin route services on a point to point basis for carrier inter-connectivity.

[The three network diagrams provide a high level overview of PACONET's Network].

PACONET's MISSION

PACONET is committed to its social responsibility in the following ways:

☑ Training young Africans in the latest technology;

☑ Supplying bandwidth and infrastructure for educational needs, with emphasis on distance learning and literacy projects;

☑ Applying World Bank environmental standards to all its projects;

☑ Providing access to communication and Internet facilities to disadvantaged communities through the implementation of Telephone and Internet Centres/Kiosks;

☑ Enhancing government communication requirements in each of the countries where PACONET obtains an operating license;

☑ Providing universities and other learning institutions with instant access to the latest information and cross-cultural exchanges; and

☑ Creating employment.

Contact Details

Ike Hasson, CEO
PACONET International
4th Floor, Design Centre
179 Loop St, Cape Town
South Africa, 8001
Tel: 27 21-424-7227
Fax: 27 21-424-6843
E-mail: PACONET@hotmail.com
Website: www.PACONET.net

sappi

Sappi Limited is the world's leading producer of coated fine paper, used in high quality publications such as annual reports, catalogues, brochures and magazines—with a market share of approximately 25% in the United States and in Western Europe, and more than 60% in Africa.

The company also produces commodity products such as packaging papers and newsprint and pulp, including paper pulp and dissolving pulp. With a market share of approximately 16% Sappi is the leading producer of dissolving pulp in the world—typically used in the manufacture of viscose textiles.

A decade ago, Sappi set out to become a global company by the millennium. This South African company first purchased the market leader in Germany in 1992, then the market leader in North America in 1994, and finally the European market leader in 1997. In five years, Sappi developed from a South African forest products company, with some foreign investments, to the world's leading producer of coated fine paper. Today the company has manufacturing operations in eight countries on three continents and sells into more than a hundred countries. More than 80% of its sales are outside southern Africa. Sappi

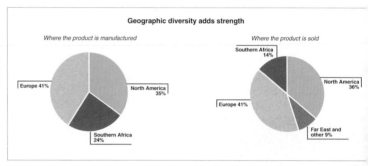

Geographic diversity adds strength

Where the product is manufactured

Europe 41% · North America 35% · Southern Africa 24%

Where the product is sold

Southern Africa 14% · North America 36% · Europe 41% · Far East and other 9%

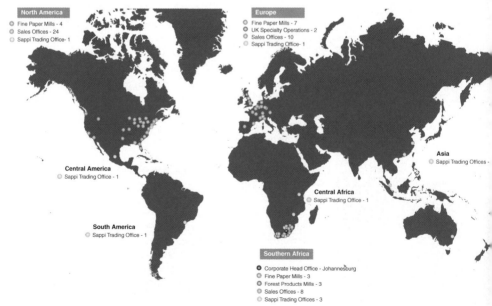

Sappi has manufacturing operations on 3 continents and in 8 countries and customers in over 100 countries.

North America
- Fine Paper Mills - 4
- Sales Offices - 24
- Sappi Trading Office- 1

Europe
- Fine Paper Mills - 7
- UK Specialty Operations - 2
- Sales Offices - 10
- Sappi Trading Office- 1

Central America
- Sappi Trading Office - 1

South America
- Sappi Trading Office - 1

Central Africa
- Sappi Trading Office - 1

Asia
- Sappi Trading Offices -

Southern Africa
- Corporate Head Office - Johannesburg
- Fine Paper Mills - 3
- Forest Products Mills - 3
- Sales Offices - 8
- Sappi Trading Offices - 3

produces five million tons of paper annually, 80% of it fine paper. The company is approximately 90% pulp integrated. Sappi employs 19,300 people worldwide.

Performance

Its operating performance, margins, return on capital and on equity are at the top end of the sector and compare favorably with market norms by any standard. In his latest annual report Sappi's executive chairman, Eugene van As, announced 23.5% after-tax return on equity and an 18% pre-interest and tax return on capital employed.

Environment

Sappi takes its environmental responsibility seriously. The key to this responsibility is information, education and a willingness to research, develop and implement cleaner, better methods of production. Sappi's global environmental policy entrenches the key principles of sustainable development—economic, social and environmental. Sappi strives for continual improvement in the management of its impact on the environment through its chosen environmental management system, ISO 14001.

During October 2000 the World Wide Fund For Nature (WWF) International honored Sappi for its Sappi/WWF Forests and Wetlands five year initiative, as a "Gift of the Earth." WWF acclaimed this eco-tourism initiative, in unique indigenous forests and wetlands, for giving rural communities a stake in conserving some of South Africa's most threatened natural areas.

Listing

Sappi is listed on the Johannesburg, New York, London and Frankfurt Stock Exchanges.

Corporate Affairs Manager
Sappi Limited
48 Ameshoff Street
Braamfontein, Johannesburg 2017
Tel: 27-11-407 8111
Fax: 27-11-403-8236
Email: corporateaffairs@za.sappi.com
www.sappi.com

"We have secured an enviable leadership position in Europe, North America and Africa and we will build on that in the future. We will strengthen our existing market shares through the development of new products and use technology, which has always played a major role in our past success, to deliver value-added products to our customers. We have a wide spread of shareholders. There has been a strong foreign buying of Sappi shares and the spread of our shareholders is now wider than ever. When we listed on the New York Stock Exchange, we stated that our target was to attain 65% foreign shareholding in the company to reflect more or less the spread of our assets. At the end of April 2001 the foreign shareholding had risen to about 61%."

Eugene van As
Executive Chairman
Sappi Limited

Sappi's shareholders
April 2001

Pie chart: North American Investors 40%; European Investors 21%; South African Investors 39%.

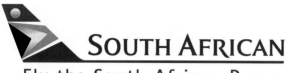

SOUTH AFRICAN

Fly the South African Dream

As Africa's premier airline for almost 70 years, South African Airways is the only nonstop carrier between the US and South Africa with daily B747-400 service from Atlanta and New York to Johannesburg and Cape Town. In addition, it operates the only nonstop service from the US (from JFK) to Lagos, Nigeria, with three departures weekly.

With the growth of its vast international network and global alliances – such as a partnership with Delta – and dedicated customer service programs, it is set to reach even greater heights in the years to come.

The Plane Truth

With its striking livery inspired by the colors of the South African flag, its fleet is one of the youngest and most modern in the sky; a reputation further substantiated by being the first airline to purchase and operate the highly advanced Boeing 737-800. Moreover, its on-time performance record can be consistently and favorably compared to the best American and European carriers—be it for domestic, within Africa or international services.

Class, Class, Class

Superb service, comfort and hospitality are the hallmarks of SAA's award-winning in-flight service in each of the three classes on international and long-haul flights. In fact, the readers of Condé Nast Traveler have voted South African Airways one of the world's top airlines three years in a row. South African Airways was recently ranked in the top 10 international airlines in Zagat's 2001 International Airline Survey.

Its Business Class provides personal attention to the needs of the executive traveler. The spacious seats are equipped with moveable headrests and extendible leg rests, plus individual entertainment systems. Menus feature a choice of freshly prepared cuisines, served on fine china and accompanied by an extensive wine selection.

First class service simply redefines luxury. Before boarding, passengers can relax in any of our First Class lounges around the world. All flights feature fully-reclining sleeper seats and exquisite 'round-the-clock' service. Each passenger receives an onboard amenity kit, individual video screen and a full sized linen covered duvet for added comfort. This includes several a la carte meal options, preceded by caviar and champagne. A wheeling salad bar buffet also allows discerning passengers additional healthier options.

A Global Network

With the establishment of a codeshare relationship with Delta Air Lines, SAA now offers passengers access to a global network which connects over 503 cities around the globe. The partnership affords easy connections from over 29 cities throughout North America, while SAA's domestic routes, including SA Express and SA Airlink, offer convenient same-day transfers and direct flights to over 22 major African cities, such as Harare, Windhoek, Dar-es-Salaam and Nairobi.

South African Airways takes the business and leisure traveler to Africa and beyond, with

convenient routes to key gateways in the Middle East, Asia and Australia. All on Africa's most modern fleet. All with impeccable inflight service. All of which makes it just a little more worldly than other carriers.

Voyager's other partners include over 45 of the world's leading names in airlines, hotels, car rentals, financial services and telecommunications.

Allow South African Airways to welcome you aboard soon and find what you've been missing. You'll discover the flight just flies by. For more information or reservations call 1-800-722-9675 or visit www.flyssa.com

Frequently First Choice

South African Airways' Voyager, already acknowledged to be one of the worlds outstanding frequent flyer programs, has been further enhanced by its partnership with Delta. Now frequent flyers can accumulate miles on both carriers, earning and redeeming them in the Voyager or Delta SkyMiles programs. Voyager members receive additional benefits through an agreement with American Express Membership Rewards Program, which allows Amex card members to redeem travel certificates for airline tickets.

Tips, Tools and Trivia

Travel Tips

These travel tips are mere general guidelines and travelers are advised to check with authoritative sources at embassies, their own respective government departments, travel agencies and airlines before they start on their journey. Arriving without the proper documentation can lead to embarrassing and costly experiences. Insufficiently documented visitors are liable to be held at the port of entry and sent back at their own expense.

ACCOMMODATION

Major international hotel chains such as Marriott, Intercontinental, Hilton and Le Meridien have established themselves in cities across Africa. There are also a number of homegrown hotel groups that offer economy to luxury services. Some countries grade hotels according to the quality and extent of their services on a scale of one to five stars.

AIR TRAVEL

As Africa's premier airline, South African Airways provides convenient non-stop services from North America to South Africa, Nigeria and several other key points on the continent—as well as extensive intracontinental services. It has frequent flights from the Far East and Europe. Several major European and some Far Eastern, Middle Eastern and a few US carriers also provide connections to Africa. Although most other African nations have their own national airlines, few serve intercontinental routes.

BUSINESS HOURS

Across the continent the variation in business hours is minimal. North African countries usually go for longer lunch breaks and later closings. Foreigners should not interpret lack of punctuality in some cultures as a sign of disrespect or disinterest. Keep in mind that there are Africans who find the Western obsession with speed and immediacy in conducting business not only strange but downright rude. Not much can be gained by insisting on fast decisions in a societies where ample group discussion and consensus are prerequisites.

CREDIT CARDS

While major credit cards are widely used and accepted in the larger cities across the continent and even in remote parts in some countries, it is prudent to enquire beforehand whether this form of payment is accepted in any specific part of Africa. In a few countries, travelers are cautioned against widespread credit card fraud and might be advised to rely on travelers checks or cash payments instead.

CAR RENTAL

Multinational car rental firms all have a presence in some but not all African countries—mostly on a franchise basis. It plugs visitors into an easy reservations network and ensures familiar standards. There are also domestic services but for those who are just passing through and do not know the country well enough to judge their reliability, the familiar names might be a better option. Keep in mind that outside urban areas roads and driving conditions can present quite a challenge and chauffeur-driven vehicles or public transport should be considered. For obvious reasons, foreigners—unless they are adventurous and amply equipped with water and other supplies—are dissuaded from taking long trips into the desert or African hinterland. Driving in most of the former British colonies is on the left-hand side of the road and in the former French, Spanish, Italian and Portuguese possessions on the right-hand side. There are exceptions, such as former British-ruled Ghana, where driving is on the right.

CLIMATE

Hollywood's Africa conjures up images of people in khaki and pith helmets braving steamy jungles and forbidding deserts. Most visitors will do neither. Safari-goers usually find themselves in savanna terrain where most of the animals live. While the weather in some West African countries might be summed up in terms of hot and humid, most areas present a much more complex weather profile. During summer in South Africa, for instance, travelers find themselves moving between Mediterranean-type weather at the southern coast to subtropical and humid weather on the east coast and dry heat inland. Countries such as Egypt, Algeria, Libya and Tunisia offer pleasant Mediterranean climates on their coast in contrast to searing hot days in the inland desert, followed by cold nights. For a description of climate and weather patterns in individual African countries visit *www.worldtravelguide.net/navigate/region/afr.asp.* and for a daily updated weather forecast in major African cities visit *www.usatoday.com/weather.*

CLOTHES

While locals in North African and West African countries wear sensible traditional dress to cope with hot weather, foreigners are often obliged to wear suit and tie to business meetings. Even though the trend is towards greater informality in some countries, this formal dress code largely prevails. Travelers who plan to go on safari outings are usually advised to bring along a separate smaller bag for travel to any of the remote parks and game reserves. The feeder aircraft that serve these routes maintain strict baggage limits, requiring travelers to leave the bulk of their baggage in safekeeping at their hotel or the airport.

EMAIL

Business travelers who rely on email to communicate will find an increasing number of major hotels in the larger African cities offering not only cable and other data transmission connections for laptop carriers but also business centers, replete with computers. Another growth industry in Africa is Internet cafés. The continent still has some way to go but the pace is picking up towards full connection to the information highway. As elsewhere, email is bound to replace snail mail and faxes as the preferred mode of communication on the continent.

ELECTRICITY

Consider Africa 220 volts AC 50Hz territory— and at a few places power might surge up to 380 volts. There is a whole array of power connections in use, ranging from two and three-prong round to bayonet type plugs. Remote areas and some game parks rely on their own power generation and some have no electricity at all.

FOOD

Expect on a continent with hundreds of cultures and customs to find a wide choice of local dishes. Middle Eastern fare dominates in North Africa and down south traditional tribal dishes are mixed in with colonial and other imported cullinary delights from India, Malaysia and Indonesia. For centuries Zanzibar has been an important source for spices. When served uncooked or unprocessed food, such as salads and fruit, call for the same caution as applies in the case of drinking water.

HEALTH

In most African countries a valid yellow fever vaccination certificate is required for travellers over one year of age. Even though most do not require proof of cholera vaccination as an entry condition, it remains a serious risk in some regions and travelers opt for it purely on a precautionary basis. Although largely contained and eradicated in the urban and developed areas of the continent, malaria remains a risk, especially for those touring game park regions. Mefloquine or other medication should be taken on a prophylactic basis and, in potentially infected areas, mosquito nets and repellents are used at night. The experts caution against swimming and paddling in fresh water in some outlying areas as *Bilharzia* (schistosomiasis) might be present. *Hepatitis A, B* and *E* are present and *meningococcal meningitis* may occur. *Leishmaniasis* and human *trypanosomiasis* (sleeping sickness) are present in a few isolated areas. Avoid tick bites which spread African tick typhus. Wear shoes to avoid soil-borne parasites. *While all or most of these warnings might seem inappropriate when visiting city centers, it is better to take precautions. When in doubt, call your physician or neighborhood health department for advice.*

MEDIA

In this modern day and age where CNN and other 24-hour news channels are piped into hotel rooms all over the continent, travelers are able to stay on top of the news without understanding the local language. Being conversant in both French and English will, however, enable a visitor to read local papers from Cape to Cairo and understand most of the local TV and radio news broadcasts. Those who have access to the Internet and wish to stay abreast of daily news developments across the continent should visit *www.allafrica.com.*

MEDICAL SERVICES

Medical facilities across the continent run the gamut from poor to fair and excellent. At the one end of the spectrum is war-torn Sierra Leone where medical facilities are extremely limited and continuing to decline and at the other South Africa where hospitals are modern and medical staff well trained. (It is in Cape Town where the world's first heart transplant was performed.) Health insurance is recommended and travelers are advised to take an ample supply of their own personal medication along. Insurance is available that provides accident protection and emergency assistance in Africa. Programs for remote areas also include *Flying Doctors* insurance which facilitates emergency medical evacuation.

MONEY MATTERS

In most African countries the US$ is the preferred currency but in former French and British colonies franc and pounds are widely used. Sometimes additional exchange rate charges can be avoided by using travelers checks. However enticing, black market exchange of foreign into local currency is always a risk and official bureaus at airports, banks or hotels should be used instead. In the Democratic Republic of Congo, locals in possession of US dollars are liable to be charged with treason. *[For past and current exchange rates see page 389 and for real-time exchange rates visit the following website: www.xe.com].*

PHOTOGRAPHY

Safarigoers who intend to take first-class pictures of animals will need telephoto lenses. Even in private game reserves where visitors are afforded the opportunity to see lions, leopards, elephants and others closer up, a safe distance is maintained for obvious reasons. Africa also presents a treasure house of scenery, cultures and creations where ordinary photographic equipment can produce outstanding results. Photographic stores in major cities stock the products of leading manufacturers and undertake repairs while film supplies are available at hotels and remote areas frequented by tourists. It is prudent, however, to bring along spare custom batteries and other maintenance items.

PUBLIC HOLIDAYS

In North Africa Muslim holidays are observed and in the southern region mostly Christian holidays. In several West African countries where both faiths are practised extensively, both Muslim and Christian holidays are observed. Add in national days, workers' days and a number of other specials and some African countries may have 14 public holidays per year. Others have as few as four. As Muslim festivals are timed according to local sightings of various phases of the moon, there are no fixed dates. Ethiopia and Eritrea still use the Julian calendar, divided into 12 months of 30 days each, and a 13th month of five or six days at the end of the year, resulting on Christmas Day 2001 falling on January 7. The Julian calendar is seven years and eight months behind that of the rest of the world. (For an up-to-date listing of national public holidays in specific African countries visit *www.worldtravelguide.net/navigate/region/afr.asp)*

PUBLIC TRANSPORT

Most major cities are served by reasonably well-run and reliable taxis. While public transport offers a cheaper way of getting around, buses and trains—with few exceptions—tend to be overcrowded and in some instances downright chaotic.

SECURITY

Seasoned travelers know the potential pitfalls when leaving valuables unattended or strolling down dark and lonely alleys in cities anywhere in the world. While some might marvel at the great sense of decency that prevails in Africa at large, it is advisable to apply the same caution and alertness that one would in large cities anywhere. Hotels have minisafes in bedrooms for personal valuables or alternatively provide safekeeping at the front desk. It should be noted that even though South Africa, for example, ranks alarmingly high on the world's crime charts, comparatively few visitors have been personally affected. In a few isolated regions of Africa, the problem of crime pales in comparison to the brutality and dangers of fierce civil upheaval and war. The US State Department *(www.state.gov)* provides online travel advisory updates to African and other countries which it considers to be high-risk destinations.

SHOPPING

Africa markets itself as the continent of curios. Wood carvings of people, animals and masks come in all sizes, some in dimensions that necessitate shipping. In the latter case it is obviously advisable to purchase from reputable dealers instead of street vendors. Other items include ivory, gold and silver objects and jewelry, beadwork and weaving. Vendors of animal skins will provide treatment certificates and other documentation required by customs in the US and other countries. There

☎ CALLING AFRICA - COUNTRY CODES

COUNTRY	TO[1]	FROM[2]	COUNTRY	TO	FROM
Algeria	213	00	Morocco	212	00
Angola	244	00	Mozambique	258	00
Benin	229	00	Namibia	264	09
Botswana	267	00	Niger	227	00
Burkina Faso	226	00	Nigeria	234	009
Burundi	257	90	Rwanda	250	00
Cameroon	237	00	São Tomé and Principe	239	00
Cape Verde Islands	238	0	Senegal	221	00
Central African Republic	236	19	Seychelles	248	00
Chad	235	15	Sierra Leone	232	00
Comoros	269	10	Somalia	252	19
Congo (Brazzaville)	242	00	South Africa	27	09
Congo (Kinshasa)	243	00	Sudan	249	00
Côte d'Ivoire	225	00	Swaziland	268	00
Djibouti	253	00	Tanzania & Zanzibar	255	000
Egypt	20	00	Togo	228	00
Equatorial Guinea	240	00	Tunisia	216	00
Eritrea	291	00	Uganda	256	000
Ethiopia	251	00	Zambia	260	00
Gabon	241	00	Zimbabwe	263	00
Gambia	220	00			
Ghana	233	00	**OTHER TERRITORIES**		
Guinea-Bissau	245	00	Diego Garcia	246	00
Guinea	224	00	Mayotte Island	269	10
Kenya	254	000	Réunion Island	262	00
Lesotho	266	00	St. Helena	290	01
Liberia	231	00			
Libya	218	00			
Madagascar	261	00			
Malawi	265	101			
Mali	223	00			
Mauritania	222	00			
Mauritius	230	00			

Source: AT&T

1. The country code to be used when making international calls to a particular African country before dialing the city area code and number. 2. The access code needed to make an outgoing international call from a specific African country or territory before dialing another country and city code and telephone number.

⏰ CITIES

Abidjan—GMT, Accra—GMT, Addis Ababa—GMT+3, Algiers—GMT+1, Antananarivo—GMT+3, Asmara—GMT+3, Bamako—GMT, Bangui—GMT+1, Banjul—GMT, Bissau—GMT, Brazzaville—GMT+1, Bujumbura—GMT+3, Cairo—GMT+2, Casablanca—GMT, Conakry—GMT, Dakar—GMT, Dar es Salaam—GMT+3, Djibouti—GMT+3, Freetown—GMT, Gaborone—GMT+2, Harare—GMT+2, Johannesburg—GMT+2, Kampala—GMT+3, Khartoum—GMT+3, Kigali—GMT+3, Kinshasa—GMT+1, Lagos—GMT+1, Libreville—GMT+1, Lilongwe—GMT+2, Lomé—GMT+1, Luanda—GMT+1, Lusaka—GMT+2, Malabo—GMT+1, Maputo—GMT+2, Maseru—GMT+2, Mbabane—GMT+2, Mogadishu—GMT+3, Monrovia GMT, Moroni—GMT+3, Nairobi—GMT+3, N'Djamena—GMT+1, Niamey—GMT+1, Nouakchott—GMT, Ouagadougou—GMT, Port Louis—GMT+4, Porto Novo—GMT+1, Praia—GMT, São Tomé—GMT, Tripoli—GMT+2, Tunis—GMT+1, Victoria—GMT+4, Windhoek—GMT+1, Yaoundé—GMT+1.

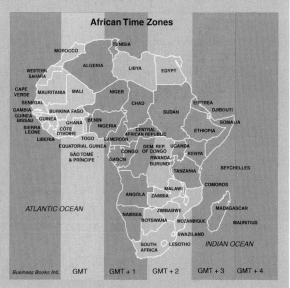

African Time Zones

Business Books Intl. GMT GMT + 1 GMT + 2 GMT + 3 GMT + 4

Trivia

What's in a Name?

In the section on Libya we refer to the leader of that country as Col. Muammar Qaddafi. We could have picked any of some forty alternative spellings but this one seemed to be the most commonly used. It places us in league with *National Geographic* but brings us in conflict with other notable media such as *Associated Press* (Moammar Ghadafi), *Le Monde* (Mouammar Kadhafi) and *Time Magazine* (Muammar Ghaddafi). It is not only Colonel Qaddafi (or al-Qaddafi) who manages to play havoc with the English language. That legendary place in Mali that was once thought to be the ultimate El Dorado was alternatively referred to in writings over the years as Timbuctou, Timbuctu, and Timbuctoo before the majority seemed to have settled for Timbuktu. The spelling of the names of several other African personalities and places remains in dispute.

Africans

What do UN Secretary General Kofi Annan from Ghana and one of his predecessors, Boutros Boutros-Ghali of Egypt, South African Nobel peace prize laureates Nelson Mandela, F.W. de Klerk, Desmond Tutu and the late Albert Luthuli, Nobel literature prize winners Nadime Gordimer of South Africa and Wole Soyinka of Nigeria, basketball stars Dikembe Mutombo of the DR of Congo and Akeem Olajuwon of Nigeria, Olympic marathon champions Josia Thugwane of South Africa (1996) and Gezaghne Abera of Ethiopia (2000), supergolfers Gary Player, Ernie Els and Retief Goosen of South Africa and Nick Price of Zimbabwe, South African actress Charlize Theron and pop star Dave Matthews have in common? They are all Africans.

is a ban on the importation of ivory in several countries. Do not expect to get diamonds or gold items at bargain prices in Africa. Outside the risky black market, prices are controlled. African artists, however, add a special local flavor and charm to their jewelry designs that attract foreign buyers.

TELECOMMUNICATIONS

European visitors who are on GSM integrate seamlessly with their own equipment into cellphone networks in several major African countries. US and other visitors who operate on a different mobile system will find convenient stalls and stores at some airports and in major cities where they can rent phones. Cellphone communication has grown at a faster pace in the African continent than anywhere else in the world. Calls from hotels are usually subject to a heavy surcharge. Most hotels offer facsimile services.

TRAINS

Train buffs looking for the unusual will find it in several parts of the continent. Kenya's Nairobi to Mombasa train and South Africa's renowned state-of-the -art luxury Blue Train and exquisite Rovos Rail are favorites. Sadly, however, in many parts of the continent railroads have fallen into disrepair.

VISAS

Citizens of the United States, United Kingdom and other European countries, as well as Japan need visas (obtainable at fees ranging from $20 to $100) for travel to most African countries. Exceptions are Botswana, Lesotho, Mauritius, Morocco, Namibia, Senegal, Seychelles, and South Africa, where no visas are required. In Zambia, US and Japanese citizens are not exempted and in Zimbabwe only the British and Canadians are exempted. *[Regulations change and travelers are advised to contact the respective embassies or consulates before embarking on their trip].*

WATER

Even though drinking water in some African countries poses no danger, it is better to err on the safe side. While South Africans, for example, might find it peculiar to see anyone resort to bottled water unless they prefer the taste and don't mind paying extra, drinking water out of the faucet in many other countries borders on being reckless. There may be the risk of *diarrhoeal diseases,* the *dysenteries* and various *parasitic worm infections* in both water and uncooked vegetables or fruit washed in contaminated water. Where there are no signs posted in bathrooms, the rule of thumb is not to drink water from any faucet anywhere before asking the question: "Is the water safe?' While this question might irritate and even offend some of the locals, most will understand.

African currencies and exchange rates

	Currency	Symbol	Regime[1]	1997[2]	1998[2]	1999[2]	2000[3]	2001[4]
Algeria	Dinar	DA	composite	57.7	58.7	66.6	74.25	75.12
Angola	New Kwanza	Nkz	m.float	0.2	0.4	2.8	13.36	20.17
Benin	CFA Franc	CFAF	Fr. Franc (100.0)	583.7	590	615.7	701.56	752.76
Botswana	Pula	P	composite	3.7	4.2	4.6	5.37	5.69
Burkina Faso	CFA Franc	CFAF	Fr. Franc (100.0)	583.7	590	615.7	701.56	752.76
Burundi	Burundi Franc	FBu	composite	352.4	447.8	563.6	785.73	821.29
Cameroon	CFA Franc	CFAF	Fr. Franc (100.0)	583.7	590	615.7	701.56	752.76
Cape Verde	Escudo	C.V. Esc.	composite	93.2	98.2	102.7	118.8	120.64
Cent. Afr. Rep.	CFA Franc	CFAF	Fr. Franc (100.0)	583.7	590	615.7	701.56	752.76
Chad	CFA Franc	CFAF	Fr. Franc (100.0)	583.7	590	615.7	701.56	752.76
Comoros	Com. Franc	CF	Fr. Franc (75.0)	383.7	442.5	461.8	527.49	558.10
Congo, DR of	Cong. Franc	CDF	US-$ (2.50)	1.3	1.6	140,286	NA	349.30
Congo, Rep.	CFA Franc	CFAF	Fr. Franc (100.0)	583.7	590	615.7	701.56	752.76
Côte d'Ivoire	CFA Franc	CFAF	Fr. Franc (100.0)	583.7	590	615.7	701.56	752.76
Djibouti	Djib. Franc	DF	US-$ (177.72)	177.7	177.7	177.7	NA	175.00
Egypt	Eg. Pound	£E	m.float	3.4	3.4	3.4	3.86	3.92
Eq. Guinea	CFA Franc	CFAF	Fr. Franc (100.0)	583.7	590	615.7	701.56	752.76
Eritrea	Nafka	Nfa	----	7.2	7.4	..	9.5	10.20
Ethiopia	Birr	Br	float	6.7	7.1	7.9	8.25	8.29
Gabon	CFA Franc	CFAF	Fr. Franc (100.0)	583.7	590	615.7	701.56	752.76
Gambia, The	Dalasi	D	float	10.2	10.6	11.4	13.48	15.77
Ghana	Cedi	¢	float	2,050	2,314	2,647	7,102	7,275
Guinea	Guinea Franc	GNF	m.float	1,095	1,236	..	1,821	1,940
Guinea-Bissau	CFA Franc	CFAF	Fr. Franc (100.0)	583.7	590	615.7	701.56	752.76
Kenya	Shilling	KSh	float	58.7	60.4	70.3	78.37	78.66
Lesotho	Loti	L	SA Rand (1.0)	4.6	5.5	6.1	7.58	8.23
Liberia	Liberian dollar	L$	US-$ (1.0)	1	41.5	41.9	1	1
Libya	Libyan Dinar	LD	SDR (8.5085)	0.4	0.4	0.5	0.53	0.56
Madagascar	Franc	FMG	float	5,090	5,441	6,283	6,791	6,451
Malawi	Kwacha	MK	float	16.4	31.1	44.1	78.43	72.25
Mali	CFA Franc	CFAF	Fr. Franc (100.0)	583.7	590	615.7	701.56	752.76
Mauritania	Ouguiyas	UM	composite	151.9	188.5	209.5	252.39	253.27
Mauritius	Rupee	MauR	composite	21.1	24	25.2	27.77	29.20
Morocco	Dirham	DH	composite	9.5	9.6	9.8	10.57	11.66
Mozambique	Metical	Mt	float	11,543	11,874	12,775	15,870	21,050
Namibia	Namib.dollar	N$	SA Rand (1.0)	4.6	5.5	6.1	701.56	752.76
Niger	CFA Franc	CFAF	Fr. Franc (100.0)	583.7	590	615.7	701.56	752.76
Nigeria	Naira	N	US-$ ((82.0))	21.9	21.9	92.3	110.32	111.80
Rwanda	Rw. Franc	RF	SDR (201.8)	301.5	312.3	333.9	417.84	432.23
São Tomé & P.	Dobra	Db	m.float	4,552.50	6,883.20	7,119.00	2,417.04	8,162.48
Senegal	CFA Franc	CFAF	Fr. Franc (100.0)	583.7	590	615.7	701.56	752.76
Seychelles	Rupee	SR	SDR (7.2345)	5	5.3	5.3	6.28	5.62
Sierra Leone	Leones	Le	float	981.5	1,563.60	1,804.20	2,088.77	1,830.80
Somalia	Shilling	SoSh	float	..	..	..	2,616.41	2,606.90
South Africa	Rand	ZAR	float	4.6	5.5	6.1	7.58	8.23
Sudan	Dinar	SDD	m.float	157.6	200.8	252.6	258.85	257.41
Swaziland	Lilangeni	SZL	SA rand (1.0)	4.6	5.5	6.1	7.58	8.23
Tanzania	Shilling	TSh	float	612.1	664.7	744.8	805	886
Togo	CFA Franc	CFAF	Fr. Franc (100.0)	583.7	590	615.7	701.56	752.76
Tunisia	Dinar	TD	m.float (1.0)	1.1	1.1	1.2	1.38	1.44
Uganda	Shilling	USh	float	1,083	1,240	1,454	1,820	1,700
Zambia	Kwacha	ZK	float	1,314.50	1,862	2,388	4,499	3,630
Zimbabwe	Zimb. Dollar	Z$	float	12.1	23.7	38.3	55.11	54.95

1. Regimes: float=floating exchange rate; m.float=managed float; if a currency is named, the country pegs its currency to the named currency, and the parity is shown in parenthesis, for example, US-$ (2.7) indicates that a currency is pegged to the U.S. dollar at a parity of 2.7 currency units per US-$. 2. Average for the year; 3. Exchange rate on December 29, 2000; 4. Exchange rate on July 22, 2001.

Sources: World Bank, Canadian Bank, http://www.xe.com/ucc/full.shtml

Super sevens

SEVEN BIGGEST ISLANDS

	Sq. miles	Sq. km.
Greenland	839,000	2,175,597
New Guinea	316,515	820,033
Borneo	286,914	743,107
Madagascar	226,657	476,068
Baffin (Canada)	183,810	476,068
Honshu (Japan)	88,925	230,316
Great Britain	88,758	229,883

THE SEVEN LONGEST RIVERS

	Miles	Km
Nile (Africa)	4,180	6,690
Amazon (South America)	3.912	6,296
Mississippi (USA)	3,170	5.970
Yangtze Kiang (China)	3,602	5,797
Ob (Russia)	3,459	5,567
Huang Ho (China)	2.900	4,667
Yenisei (Russia)	2,800	4,506

THE SEVEN SUMMITS[1]

	Feet	Meters
Mt. Everest (Asia)	29,035	8,850
Mt. Aconcagua (Sth.Am.)	22,834	6,960
Mt. McKinley (Nth. Am.)	20,320	6,194
Mt Kilimanjaro (Africa)[2]	19,340	5,895
Mt. Elbrus (Europe)	18,510	5,642
Vinson Massif (Antarctica)	16,066	4,897
Kosciusko (Australia)	7,316	2,230

1. Highest peaks on each of the 7 continents.
2. The world's highest "free standing" mountain.

THE SEVEN BIGGEST LAKES

	Sq. miles	Sq. km
Caspian Sea (Russia etc)[1]	152,239	394,299
Superior (US-Canada)	31,820	82,414
Victoria (Tanz.-Uganda)	26,828	69,485
Huron (US-Canada)	23,010	59,596
Michigan (USA)	22,400	58,016
Aral (Kazakhstn-Uzbeki.)	13,000	33,800
Tanganyika (Tanz.-Congo)	12,700	32,893

1. Considered landlocked lake even though Romans
called Mare Caspian a sea because of its saltiness.

THE SEVEN CONTINENTS

	Sq. miles	Sq. km
Asia[1]	17,212,041	44,579,000
Africa	11,065,000	30,065,000
North America	9,465,290	24,256,000
South America[2]	6,879,952	17,819,000
Antarctica	5,100,021	13,209,000
Europe[3]	3,837,082	9,938,000
Australia[4]	2,967,966	7,687,000

1. Includes the Middle East.
2. Includes Central America and the Caribbean.
3. Includes the recently-independent states of the former Soviet Union.
4. Includes Oceania.

THE SEVEN LARGEST DESERTS[1]

	Sq. miles	Sq. km
Sahara (Africa)[2]	3,500,000	9,065,000
Arabian (M. East)	1,000,000	2,590,000
Kalahari (Africa)[3]	220,000	569,800
Gt.Victoria (Australia)	250,000	647,500
Gt. Sandy (Australia)[4]	150,000	388,500
Gibson (Australia)	120,000	310,800
Simpson (Australia)	56,000	145,040

1. Subtropical deserts are the hottest, consisting of parched terrain with rapid evaporation. The Namib in Namibia (13,000 sq. miles/33,600 sq. km) is a cool coastal desert region).
2. Covers parts of Algeria, Chad, Egypt, Eritrea, Ethiopia, Libya, Mali, Mauritania, Morocco & Western.Sahara, Niger, Somalia and Tunisia.
3. Spans parts of Botswana, Namibia and South Africa.
4. Also known as The Outback.

Source: Time Almanac, 2001

Recent events in Africa

Following is a summary of significant events in Africa over the past eighteen months, compiled by allafrica.com, the premier Internet-based Africa news source:

January 2000

3. Senegal's President Diouf pardons 200 prisoners detained in connection with Casamance separatist movement; U.S. suspends bilateral aid to Côte d'Ivoire following a coup in December by Gen. Robert Guei. Former President Henri Konan Bedie leaves Togo for France. **4.** Mozambique's opposition party, Renamo, rejects a high court ruling on the validity of the December elections but President Chissano is sworn in ten days later; Sudanese Islamic leader, Hassan Al-Turabi, claims Uganda is conspiring with President Omar Bashir's Khartoum government to reduce his powers. **13.** Nigeria agrees to maintain its troops in the West African peacekeeping force for an additional 90 days and Ecomog redeploys in the north two days later. **14.** Djibouti proposes a transitional government for Somalia; Presidents Museveni (Uganda), Buyoya (Burundi), Mkapa (Tanzania) begin two days of talks on situation in Burundi. **15.** Cape Coast University in Ghana closes down as students continue to boycott lectures to protest a new grading system. **16.** Nelson Mandela starts work as Burundi peace mediator. **21.** Kumba Yala wins Guinea Bissau's election after second round. **22.** Serious flooding in Mozambique. **23.** Algerian military launches major offensive against Islamic militants. **24.** Special session on the conflict in Democratic Republic of the Congo at UN Security Council in New York.

February 2000

15. In a referendum Zimbabweans give a resounding 'no' to a draft constitution, which the opposition says would have allowed the president to retain extensive powers while removing the obligation to pay compensation to white farmers in return for taking their land. **20.** Flooding worsens in Mozambique. **21.** Hundreds die during religious violence in Kaduna, northern Nigeria, triggered by Christian fears that Islamic Sharia law may be imposed. **23.** Second Lusaka Summit on the DR Congo conflict held with the original signatories of the 1999 Agreement; Floods continue to devastate Mozambique after heavy rains are compounded by Hurricane Eline. President Chissano appeals for more aid.

March 2000

8. Arusha talks on Burundi begin with over 100 Burundian political representatives and a host of other regional leaders. **17.** Separatist Casamance rebels launch new wave of attacks in Senegal. **18.** Five hundred followers of a Ugandan cult found burnt to death in a church in Kanungu, Uganda. An investigation leads to the discovery of hundreds more dead in mass graves around the country. **20.** Abdoulaye Wade wins presidential election in Senegal after second round run off, ending nearly 20 years of Abdou Diouf's rule. **23.** Rwandan president Bizimungu quits office. **27.** Nelson Mandela opens new round of Burundi peace talks. **31.** Landmark privatization of Zambia's copper mines.

April 2000

US resumes military assistance to Nigeria. **3.** Europe-Africa summit opens in Cairo, attended by heads of state. **6.** Tunisia's first president Habib Bourguiba dies at 96 years. **8.** All sides in the DR Congo conflict agree to a new ceasefire to start on 14 April. **11.** New clashes in Ogoniland, Nigeria; South African cricket captain Hansie Cronje fired following a match-fixing scandal in which he reportedly sold game information to a bookie. **17.** Paul Kagame becomes Rwanda's new president. **22.** Daily News offices in Zimbabwe bombed. **24.** Kofi Annan begins 5-nation African tour.

May 2000

2. RUF rebels kidnap UN peacekeepers in Sierra Leone, indirectly leading to the deployment of British troops later in the month; Somali Reconciliation talks start in Djibouti. **5.** Ugandan and Rwandan forces clash in Kisangani, a rebel-held town in eastern DRC. The former allies initially try to work out their differences, but a diplomatic war of words continues after the fighting between the two armies stops. **6.** Sudan's president, Omar al-Bashir sacks his former Islamic ally, Hassan al-Turabi, as secretary general of the ruling party. **12.** US President Bill Clinton issues executive order to make it easier for African countries to get HIV/AIDS drugs. **14.** RUF in Sierra Leone frees 139 UN hostages. **17.** RUF leader Foday Sankoh captured in Freetown, Sierra Leone. **23.** Major battles between Ethiopia and Eritrea after Algiers talks falter, ending ten months of relative calm; 30,000 refugees stream into Sudan. **24.** Zimbabwean President Robert Mugabe signs a constitutional amendment to allow his govern-

ment to forcibly acquire white-owned land. **28.** Rest of the 500 UN hostages released by RUF in Sierra Leone. **29.** ECOWAS endorses the deployment of 3,000 additional troops to Sierra Leone to shore up the faltering peace process. **31.** Ethiopian Prime Minister Meles Zenawi declares war with Eritrea over.

June 2000

1. Nigerian government raises price of fuel by 50 per cent, causing the country to grind to a halt and provoking a major quarrel with unions and pressure groups about the lack of consultation before the decision was made. **2.** Oil and gas finds in Namibia estimated to be sufficient to meet the nation's needs for the next 1000 years. **5.** As election nears, Zimbabwe Teachers Association claims 200 schools have been attacked amid intensifying political violence against the MDC-led opposition by supporters of Zanu-PF government. **6.** World Bank approves oil pipeline from Chad to Cameroon to be constructed by consortium led by ExxonMobil. **13.** Unions and pressure groups reach compromise agreement with Nigerian government over fuel price rise. **15.** Rwandan Bishop Misago acquitted of genocide charges. **18.** Cessation of hostilities' signed in Algeria between Ethiopia and Eritrea, and agreement to work towards full peace accord. **20.** Sierra Leone President Tejan Kabbah asks the UN to arrange for the trial of RUF rebel leader Foday Sankoh on war crimes charges. **22.** Cotonou Accord between Europe and African, Caribbean and Pacific states replaces Lome Agreement. **23.** Cape Town faces environmental disaster after oil spill from a shipwrecked tanker starts threatening beaches and wildlife. **27.** Robert Mugabe's ruling party Zanu-PF wins hotly contested general election in Zimbabwe with 62 parliamentary seats against 57 for the opposition MDC party. **28.** Conference on conflict diamonds is held in London. **29.** Referendum on Uganda's political system held. President Museveni's Movementists win despite fierce opposition from multi-partyists.

July 2000

4. The ex-President of Chad, Hissen Habre, cleared of torture charges in Senegalese court. **6.** FIFA gives World Cup 2006 to Germany, not South Africa as widely expected amid charges of foul play. **8.** Opposition forces launch invasion of northern Liberia. **9.** International AIDS conference opens in Durban, South Africa, drawing close scrutiny because of President Mbeki's reported doubts over the link between HIV and AIDS. The meeting hears strong calls for cheaper or free anti-AIDS drugs for Africa. **10.** 36th summit of the Organization of African Unity opens in Lomé, Togo, where leaders agree to establish an African Union. The plan is said to have originated with Libyan President Ghadafi. **19.** Burundi peace talks begin in Arusha, Tanzania. **20.** G8 meets with Obasanjo, Bouteflika, and Mbeki in Okinawa to discuss what the world's richest nations might be prepared to do for the world's poorest. **23.** Referendum in Côte d'Ivoire to decide to who is an Ivorian and who can run for office. **28.** IMF financial support for Kenya resumes after three year suspension. **31.** Liberia is threatened with sanctions by Washington and London for supporting RUF rebels in Sierra Leone.

August 2000

1. Katsina and Jigawa in Nigeria introduce Sharia, bringing to a total of six the states that adopted Islamic law. **4.** FIFA agrees to rotate future World Cup finals between their six continental confederations from the year 2010. The first rotation would go to Africa; Floods damage thirty percent of the houses in Cameroon's financial capital, Douala, following three days of severe torrential rains. **8.** Nigeria's Senate President Dr. Chuba Okadigbo is impeached. **11.** Cape Town bomb blast kills four in one of a series of explosions attributed to Pagad. **13.** New parliament sworn in at Mogadishu—Somalia's first for ten years. **14.** The UN Security Council unanimously adopts a resolution requesting that Secretary General Annan urge the Sierra Leone government to create a special court for war crimes; Southern African leaders meet in Lusaka for one-day summit to resuscitate the peace process in the DR Congo. **16.** Côte d'Ivoire's military ruler Robert Guei says he will participate in presidential elections after previously denying any interest in political power. **18.** Six African countries involved in the civil war of the DR Congo (DRC) agree to appoint a new facilitator for the DRC's internal political dialogue. **20.** Swazi King takes AIDS test and urges the rest of the country to follow his example. **19.** Senegal and Guinea Bissau sign military and economic pacts. **21.** Sierra Leone's rebel RUF chooses a new leader, General Isa Sesay. **24.** American Priest, Father Kaiser, is found dead in Kenya after having worked there for 36 years. **26.** Somalis meeting for reconciliation talks in Arta, Djibouti, choose Abdiqassim Salat Hassan to be their country's first president, after ten years without a government; Comoran head of state, Col. Azali Assoumani, and Anjouan separatist leader, Lt. Col. Said Abeid, sign a joint declaration to end the crisis in the islands. **25.** President Clinton starts out on his second visit to Africa, with the first stop in Nigeria. **28.** Burundi peace accord signed in Arusha, Tanzania in the presence of US president Bill Clinton and mediator Nelson

Mandela but key elements on both Hutu and Tutsi sides refuse to participate. **30.** Tens of thousands of people come out to greet the newly appointed Somali president as he enters Mogadishu. **4.** Military authorities in Côte d'Ivoire claim to have defeated a coup attempt.

September 2000
6. Three-day UN Millennium Summit opens with Namibian President Sam Nujoma co-chairing. Peace-keeping in Africa is high on the agenda. **11.** Mauritius opposition scores landslide victory in elections. **20.** Burundi peace meeting ends in failure in Kenya. **21.** India announces pullout of its troops in the UN peacekeeping force in Sierra Leone after tensions over leadership of the mission. **29.** Anti-corruption commission is set up in Nigeria. **30.** Cameroon's national soccer team, the Indomitable Lions win Olympic gold in Sydney 2000 Olympics; African runners win three gold, three silver and two bronze medals;

October 2000
1. Nigeria's 40th anniversary of independence is celebrated and debated. **3.** US President Clinton promises that the Africa Growth and Opportunity Act, AGOA, will benefit 34 African countries by liberalizing import restrictions. **7.** The Ivorian Supreme Court bans veteran politician and economist Alassane Ouattara from standing in forthcoming elections; military ruler Robert Guei and five others are approved; Abdulsalami Abubakar, Yakubu Gowon, Muhammadu Buhari and Ibrahim Babangida—all former military leaders—and Ernest Shonekan, head of the interim national government in 1993 attend a meeting with President Obasanjo over the future of Nigeria. **14.** President Hassan returns to Somalia to lead transitional governme nt. **15-21.** Battles in Lagos between Hausa traders and a Yoruba vigilante group, the OPC, leave at least 8 dead. The riots spread, eventually requiring intervention by President Obasanjo. **18.** The Zimbabwean capital, Harare, is engulfed by food riots after a steep rise in bread prices. **19.** Deaths from the Ebola epidemic in Uganda reach 41. The government increases calls for international help as domestic medical supplies run out. Before the virus could be contained, 173 died. **22.** Front Populaire Ivoirien leader Laurent Gbagbo takes an early lead in the presidential election in Côte D'Ivoire. **23.** Robert Guei declares himself winner of Ivorian elections despite widespread charges that he actually lost. His soldiers occupy the Electoral Commission's offices. **24.** Nigeria's Human Rights Violations Investigations Commission, the 'Oputa Panel' begins hearings. **24-25.** Protestors in Ivorian capital, Abidjan, take to streets

and forcibly oust Guei; Laurent Gbagbo claims victory, Guei flees. **29.** Tanzania's multiparty elections are marred by violence on islands of Zanzibar and Pemba. **30.** Ethiopia-Eritrea negotiations for a full peace agreement break down.

November 2000
5. The remains of Emperor Haile Selassie are reburied in the Ethiopian capital, Addis Ababa, amidst pomp and celebrations. **6.** Botswana President Festus Mogae says his people must accept the probability that half, if not more of the country's natural deaths are caused by HIV/AIDS. **9.** Opposition party Renamo and police clash in Mozambique. The conflict continues over the weekend leading to more than forty fatalities; In Zanzibar, 18 opposition supporters are released after three years of detention without trial. **11.** The Sierra Leonean government signs a cease fire with RUF rebels after talks in Abuja. **17.** The Zanzibar opposition calls for new polls in light of election violence. **19.** There are fresh reports of a cholera outbreak in Madagascar, a disease that caused 860 deaths between December 1999 and April 2000. **20.** Chief Gen. Ansumane Mane declares himself the supreme commander of the armed forces in Guinea Bissau. **22.** Journalist Carlos Cardoso is murdered in Mozambique. **23.** Sudan's former prime minister, Sadiq el Mahdi, returns from Egypt after four years of exile; The Guinea Bissau government claims that loyal army units have neutralized troops backing renegade former army chief, Gen. Ansumane Mane. **27.** Angolan parliament endorses President dos Santos' Amnesty offer to all who lay down their arms.

December 2000
3. More than 1,500 delegates gather in Addis Ababa to attend the African Development Forum 2000 focusing on HIV/AIDS. **7.** Ghana holds elections. Long time ruler Jerry Rawlings is barred by the Constitution from seeking another term. The race pits main opposition leader John Kufuor against Vice President John Atta Mills. **11.** Thousands flee fighting in southern Guinea. **12.** The Algiers peace accord is finally signed by leaders of Eritrea and Ethiopia, bringing to an end two years of war over boundary disputes. **16.** Casamance peace talks in Senegal fail again. **17.** Ghanaian soccer club Hearts of Oak win CAF final in Ghanaian city of Accra. Teargas is used to subdue the crowd. **21.** The UN study of sanctions against Angola charges that Burkina Faso and Togo have helped the Angolan rebel movement, Unita, to import illegal arms from Europe. **23.** Incumbent President Omar al Bashir wins Sudan's national elections, after a polling that lasted 10 days. **28.** Run-off in Ghana's presiden-

tial elections; NPP's John Agyekum Kufuor is declared the winner after defeating the NDC's John Atta Mills.

January 2001

1. Mozambique's Zambezia Province once again succumbs to torrential rains reminiscent of the previous year's devastating floods; Cameroon Lions are named African soccer team of 2000; Hassan al-Turabi is detained in Sudan; The UNHCR agrees to help repatriate Sierra Leonean refugees stranded in southern Guinea amid heavy fighting. **7.** Senegal votes in a referendum on independence for Casamance, while neighboring Guinea Bissau reinforces its borders. A total of 94% vote to remain part of Senegal. **9.** Last reported case of Ebola fever in the epidemic that began in Uganda on October 8 claimed 173 lives. **10.** Morocco hosts 34th conference of the International Human Rights Federation. **12.** Liberia's President Charles Taylor says his country is 'disengaging' from Sierra Leone peace process—interpreted as a promise to end support for the RUF rebels. **15.**New and revitalised East African Community launched in Arusha, Tanzania. **16.** DR Congo President Laurent Kabila assassinated in Kinshasa by a bodyguard; Kinshasa placed under curfew.**17.** Seventeen African leaders participate at the 17-19 January, France- Africa Summit in Yaoundé, Cameroon. **17.** Joseph Kabila, son of assassinated Laurent Kabila, assumes DR Congo presidency and is eventually sworn in on January 6; Zimbabwe decides that troops will stay in DRC and support the younger Kabila; Burundi agreement implementation committee meets. **19.** Teenage mother in Nigeria whipped under Sharia law for having had sex outside marriage, provoking strong international disapproval. She claimed she had been raped by three men and became pregnant. **26.** Tanzanian police shoot two while raiding the offices of the opposition Civic United Front in Zanzibar; riots follow, ultimately resulting in 31 deaths. **27.** The president of Médecins sans Frontières describes the refugee crisis in Guinea as the "worst case scenario" with hundreds of thousands of Sierra Leonean and Liberian refugees remaining stranded between fighting groups.**28.** Daily News offices bombed in Harare, Zimbabwe and fingers are pointed at the security forces. **30.** South African President Thabo Mbeki presents African Renaissance Plan to the World Economic Forum in Davos. **31.** The Lockerbie trial over the bombing of Pan Am returns a guilty verdict. Libya vows to appeal; Sierra Leone postpones presidential and parliamentary elections for six months because of a lack of security.

February 2001

1. Rebel Unita forces attack northern city of Uige in Angola. **5.** Four men go on trial in New York charged with involvement in the bombing of the US embassies in Nairobi and Dar es Salaam in 1998. **9.** The Polisario Front, the Western Sahara's independence movement, declares the 10-year ceasefire null and void in frustration over lack of UN action.**10.** African Super Cup final in the Ghanaian city of Kumasi between Ghana's Hearts of Oak and Egypt's Zamalek. Hearts win 2-0. **12.** Ethiopia begins troop withdrawal from Eritrea. **16.** Peace conference on DR Congo begins, Rwanda boycotts. **17.** Comoros government and Anjouan secessionist leaders agree to try and reunite the country.
19. Scientists announce that Africa will be hardest hit by global warming. **20.** Hassan Al-Turabi arrested by Sudanese security forces on suspicion of conspiracy against the Bashir government. **22.** Parties in the DR Congo conflict agree to a new timetable for withdrawal of troops. **24.** Fespaco 2001, Burkina Faso's international film festival, opens in Ouagadougou; Ghana removes fuels subsidies, and gas price rises by 60 percent, causing energy crisis; Rebels launch major attack on suburbs of the Burundian capital, Bujumbura. **25.** Half of Malawi's districts declared disaster areas due to flooding; the whole of Southern Africa is badly affected, with Zambia and Mozambique hardest hit. **26.** Burundi peace talks in the Tanzanian town of Arusha end in failure.

March 2001

1. OAU's Sirte II summit in Libya; 28 Heads of State attend, the African Union will now be proclaimed in May. 3 Abdoulaye Wade dismisses his Prime Minister, Moustapha Niasse, and appoints a woman, Mme. Mame Madior Boye to take his place. **7.** UN imposes sanctions on Liberia, to come into effect in two months, in response to evidence of Monrovia's involvement in arms and diamonds trafficking with Sierra Leonean rebels. **9.** Walter Kansteiner selected by US Secretary of State, Colin Powell, to be Assistant Secretary of State for African Affairs; Nigerian Senate begins a public sitting on fuel deregulation in an effort to stem the fuel shortages which have crippled road transport. **10.** Army reasserts its authority in Burundi's capital, Bujumbura, after 2 weeks of fighting with rebels. **12.** Besigye loses to Museveni in Uganda presidential elections, held over from earlier in the month.**17.** President Abdoulaye Wade of Senegal describes the peace agreement with the Casamance rebel group, MFDC, as a decisive step towards peace in the troubled southern region of Zinguinchor. **19-20.** Liberia expels ambassadors from Guinea and Sierra Leone and Guinea closes borders in retaliation. **22** . Namibia's Swapo government says it will no longer place advertising in the Namibian newspaper because of its anti-government stance; Benin's second round presidential elections held. President Mathieu Kerekou re-elected. **23.** Somali warlords with Ethiopian support announce their intention to form a joint government to oppose the transitional one. **29.** Major split opens in President Meles Zenawi's TPLF government in Ethiopia after 12 ministers quit the cabinet and set up a new political grouping.

April 2001
2. Zimbabwe troops begin withdrawal from DR Congo. **9.** Two school students face 67 counts of murder, following the Kyanguli School dormitory blaze in Kenya on March 26. **11.** Forty-three people crushed to death in a stampede at a major soccer match at Ellis Park Stadium in Johannesburg. **12.** Burkina Faso announces that more than 1,300 have died from meningitis since beginning of year. **14.** Congo-Brazzaville's peace conference ends with a new constitution and plans for a referendum by the end of the year.**18.**South African Foreign Affairs Minister Nkosazana Dlamini-Zuma and U.S. Secretary of State Colin Powell initiate a comprehensive review of US-South African relations. **19.** Thirty-nine leading pharmaceutical companies drop their court challenge to prevent the South African government from importing, manufacturing or licensing cheap copies of their patented medicines—including anti-AIDS drugs.**22.** Clashes between police and Berbers in Kabylie region of Algeria. **25.** WHO announces a new malaria drug, Malorone, on first ever Africa Malaria Day. **27.** 'War Veterans' in Zimbabwe threaten to attack the embassies of countries they suspect of funding the opposition MDC. The move followed several other attacks on businesses and public institutions. **29.** Uganda promises to pull its troops out of DR Congo; Parliamentary polls in Senegal. Abdoulaye Wade's coalition wins 90 seats out of 120.

May 2001
4. Zambian President Chiluba bows to widespread opposition and abandons his attempt to win re-election in an unconstitutional third term. **5.** Unita rebels attack Angolan town of Caxito. **6.** Shell Oil company blames oil spill in Ogoniland on sabotage. **7.** DR Congo's Bunia-based rebel movement, the Congolese Rally for Democracy Kisangani (RCD-K), said it has unseated its leader, Professor Wamba dia Wamba. **9.** Over 130 soccer fans crushed to death at the Accra Sports Stadium after police fired teargas into the crowd of fans watching a big clash between top Ghanaian rivals, Hearts of Oak and Asante Kotoko. **10.** Libyan leader Muammar Al-Gaddafi meets with Sudan's Omar al-Bashir in Khartoum after a similar meeting with Uganda's Museveni. The talks are aimed at re-establishing relations between the two countries which have been strained since 1994. **11.** US President George Bush and his Nigerian counterpart, Olusegun Obasanjo, meet in Washington to discuss debt, democracy, HIV/AIDS, regional stability and defence; Opposition arrests in Ethiopia reach over 140. **16.** Announcement that US Sub-Saharan African Trade and Economic Cooperation Forum is being established, and foreign, finance, and trade ministers from 35 African nations will meet in Washington in October to launch it. **17.** DR Congo President Joseph Kabila lifts ban on political activity. **20.** Chad holds presidential elections and Idriss Déby wins. Opposition contests results. **22.** US Secretary of State, Colin Powell, begins four nation African tour—to Mali, South Africa, Kenya and Uganda. **26.** Official Declaration of the African Union. **28.** South African panel begins investigation into largest alleged arms scandal in 7 years involving British, French, German, Italian, Swedish and SA firms. **29.** Four found guilty in New York of 1998 bombing of US embassies in Dar es Salaam and Nairobi. **30.** Two and a half million deaths in Congo reported since start of conflict in February 1998. **31.** Somaliland referendum held and the vote is over 97.9% in favor of independence from Somalia; Uganda begins Congo withdrawal process in accordance with Lusaka.

June 2001
17. Travel ban imposed on President Charles Taylor by the UN as part of sanctions imposed because of Liberia's role in handling conflict diamonds. **11.** Four Rwandans found guilty of war crimes committed during the 1994 genocide and sentenced to terms of imprisonment ranging from 12 to 20 years by Belgium's Crown Court. **13.** Sudan Peace Act passed in Congress requiring companies wishing to raise US capital for operations in Sudan to disclose how those operations relate to violations of religious freedoms and other human rights. **18.** South African, Retief Goosen, wins the US Open golf title. **19.** Bill and Melinda Gates Foundation announces that it will commit $100 million to the Global Fund for AIDS and Health. **21.**Total eclipse of sun seen across southern Africa. **27.** South African president Mbeki on state visit to Washington promotes his Millennium African Recovery Plan (MAP). **28.** United Nations Special Session on AIDS in New York. **29.** Kofi Annan wins second term as UN Secretary General.

Diplomatic addresses

African Embassies in the US

ALGERIA
Embassy of the Republic of Algeria
2118 Kalorama Road NW
Washington, DC, 20008
Tel: 202-265-2800 Fax: 202-667-2174

ANGOLA
Embassy of the Republic of Angola
1615 M Street NW, Suite 900
Washington, DC, 20036
Tel: 202-785-1156 Fax: 202-785-1258

BENIN
Embassy of the Republic of Benin
2737 Cathedral Avenue NW
Washington, DC, 20008
Tel: 202-232-6656 Fax: 202-265-1996

BOTSWANA
Embassy of the Republic of Botswana
1533 New Hampshire Ave NW
Washington, DC, 20036
Tel: 202-244-4990 Fax: 202-244-4164

BURKINA FASO
Embassy of Burkina Faso
2340 Massachusetts Avenue NW
Washington, DC, 20008
Tel: 202-332-5577 Fax: 202-667-1882

BURUNDI
Embassy of the Republic of Burundi
2233 Wisconsin Avenue NW, Suite 212
Washington, DC, 20007
Tel: 202-342-2574 Fax: 202-342-2578

CAMEROON
Embassy of the Republic of Cameroon
2349 Massachusetts Ave NW
Washington, DC, 20008
Tel: 202-265-8790 Fax: 202-387-3826

CAPE VERDE
Embassy of the Republic of Cape Verde
3415 Massachusetts Avenue NW
Washington, DC, 20007
Tel: 202-965-6820 Fax: 202-965-1207

CENTRAL AFRICAN REPUBLIC
Embassy of Central African Republic
1618 22nd Street NW
Washington, DC, 20008
Tel: 202-483-7800 Fax: 202-332-9893

CHAD
Embassy of the Republic of Chad
2002 R Street NW
Washington, DC, 20009
Tel: 202-462-4009 Fax: 202-265-1937

COMOROS
Embassy of the Republic of Comoros
420 E. 50th St.
New York, NY, 10022
Tel: 212-972-8010 Fax: 212-983-4712

CONGO [KINSHASA]
Embassy of the Dem. Republic of Congo
1800 New Hampshire Ave NW
Washington, DC, 20009
Tel: 202-234-7690 Fax: 202-234-2609

CONGO [BRAZZAVILLE]
Embassy of the Republic of the Congo
4891 Colorado Avenue NW
Washington, DC, 20011
Tel: 202-726-0825 Fax: 202-726-1860

CÔTE D'IVOIRE
Embassy of the Republic of Cote d'Ivoire
3421 Massachusetts Avenue NW
Washington, DC, 20008
Tel: 202-797-0300 Fax:202-462-9444

DJIBOUTI
Embassy of the Republic of Djibouti
1156 15th Street NW, Suite 515
Washington, DC, 20005
Tel: 202-331-0270 Fax: 202-331-0302

EGYPT
Embassy of the Arab Republic of Egypt
3521 International Court NW
Washington, DC, 20008
Tel: 202-895-5400 Fax: 202-244-5131

EQUATORIAL GUINEA
Embassy of the Republic of Equatorial Guinea
2020 16th Street NW
Washington, DC, 20009
Tel: 202-518-5700 Fax: 202-518-5252

ERITREA
Embassy of the State of Eritrea
1708 New Hampshire Ave NW
Washington, DC, 20009
Tel: 202-319-1991 Fax: 202-319-1304

ETHIOPIA
Embassy of the Fed. Dem. Rep. of Ethiopia
2134 Kalorama Road NW
Washington, DC, 20008
Tel: 202-364-1200 Fax: 202-686-9857

GABON
Embassy of the Gabonese Republic
2034 20th Street NW, Suite 200
Washington, DC, 20009
Tel: 202-797-1000 Fax: 202-332-0668

GAMBIA
Embassy of The Gambia
1155 15th Street NW, Suite 1000
Washington, DC, 20005
Tel: 202-785-1399 Fax: 202-785-1430

GHANA
Embassy of the Republic of Ghana
3512 International Drive NW
Washington, DC, 20008
Tel: 202-686-4520 Fax: 202- 686-4527

GUINEA
Embassy of the Republic of Guinea
2112 Leroy Place NW
Washington, DC, 20008
Tel: 202-483-9420 Fax: 202-483-8688

GUINEA-BISSAU
Embassy of the Republic of Guinea-Bissau
15929 Yukon Lane
Rockville, MD, 20855
Tel: 301-947-3958 Fax: 301-947-3958

KENYA
Embassy of the Republic of Kenya
2249 R Street NW
Washington, DC, 20008
Tel:202-387-6101 Fax:202-462-3829

LESOTHO
Embassy of the Kingdom of Lesotho
2511 Massachusetts Ave NW
Washington, DC, 20008.
Tel: 202-797-5533 Fax: 202-234-6815

LIBERIA
Embassy of the Republic of Liberia
5303 Colorado Avenue NW
Washington, DC, 20011
Tel: 202-723-0437 Fax: 202-723-0436

LIBYA
Libyan Permanent Representative to the UN
309-315 East 48th St
New York, NY, 10017
Tel: 212-752-5775 Fax: 212-593-4787

MADAGASCAR
Embassy of the Republic of Madagascar
2374 Massachusetts Avenue NW
Washington, DC, 20008
Tel: 202-265-5525 Fax: 202-265-3034

MALAWI
Embassy of the Republic of Malawi
2408 Massachusetts Avenue NW
Washington, DC, 20008
Tel: 202-797-1007 Fax:202-265-0976

MALI
Embassy of the Republic of Mali
2130 R Street NW
Washington, DC, 20008
Tel: 202-332-2249 Fax: 202-332-6603

MAURITANIA
Embassy of the Islamic Rep. of Mauritania
2129 Leroy Place NW
Washington, DC, 20008
Tel: 202-232-5700 Fax: 202-319-2623

MAURITIUS
Embassy of Republic of Mauritius
4301 Connecticut Ave NW
Washington, DC, 20008
Tel: 202-244-1491 Fax: 202-966-0983

MOROCCO
Embassy of the Kingdom of Morocco
1601 21st Street NW
Washington, DC, 20009
Tel:202-462-7979 Fax:202-265-0161

MOZAMBIQUE
Embassy of the Republic of Mozambique
1990 M Street NW, Suite 570
Washington, DC, 20036
Tel: 202-293-7146 Fax: 202-835-0245

NAMIBIA
Embassy of the Republic of Namibia
1605 New Hampshire Ave NW
Washington, DC, 20009
Tel: 202-986-0540 Fax: 202-986-0443

NIGER
Embassy of the Republic of Niger
C2204 R Street NW
Washington, DC, 20008
Tel: 202-483-4224

NIGERIA
Embassy of the Federal Rep. of Nigeria
1333 16th Street NW
Washington, DC, 20036
Tel: 202-986-8400 Fax: 202-986-8449

RWANDA
Embassy of the Republic of Rwanda
1714 New Hampshire Ave NW
Washington, DC, 20009
Tel: 202-232-2882 Fax: 202-232-4544

SÃO TOMÉ & PRÍNCIPE
UN Mission of São Tomé & Príncipe
400 Park Ave, 17th Floor
New York, NY, 10022
Tel:212-317-0533 Fax: 212-317-0580

SENEGAL
Embassy of the Republic of Senegal
2112 Wyoming Ave NW
Washington, DC, 20008
Tel: 202-234-0540 Fax: 202-332-6315

SEYCHELLES
UN Mission of the Republic of Seychelles
820 Second Avenue, Suite 900F
New York, NY, 10017
Tel: 212-687-9766 Fax: 212-922-9177

SIERRA LEONE
Embassy of the Republic of Sierra Leone
1701 19th Street NW
Washington, DC, 20009
Tel: 202-939-9261 Fax: 202-483-1793

SOUTH AFRICA
Embassy of the Republic of South Africa
3051 Massachusetts Ave NW
Washington, DC, 20008
Tel: 202-232-4400 Fax: 202-265-1607

SUDAN
Embassy of the Republic of the Sudan
2210 Massachusetts Ave NW
Washington, DC, 20008
Tel: 202-338-8565 Fax: 202-667-2406

SWAZILAND
Embassy of the Kingdom of Swaziland
3400 International Drive NW
Washington, DC, 20008
Tel: 202-234-5002 Fax: 202-234-8254

TANZANIA
Embassy of the United Republic of Tanzania
2139 R Street NW
Washington, DC, 20008
Tel: 202-939-6125 Fax: 202-797-7408

TOGO
Embassy of the Republic of Togo
2208 Massachusetts Avenue NW
Washington, DC, 20008
Tel: 202-234-4212 Fax: 202-232-3190

TUNISIA
Embassy of the Republic of Tunisia
1515 Massachusetts Ave NW
Washington, DC, 20005
Tel: 202-862-1850 Fax: 202-862-1858

UGANDA
Embassy of the Republic of Uganda
5911 16th Street NW
Washington, DC, 20011
Tel: 202-726-7100 Fax: 202-726-1727

ZAMBIA
Embassy of the Republic of Zambia
2419 Massachusetts Ave NW
Washington, DC, 20008
Tel: 202-265-9717 Fax: 202-332-0826

ZIMBABWE
Embassy of the Republic of Zimbabwe
1608 New Hampshire Ave NW
Washington, DC, 20009
Tel: 202-332-7100 Fax: 202-483-9326

US Embassies in Africa

ALGERIA
4 Chemin Cheikh Bachir El-Ibrahimi, Algiers 16000
Tel: [213] (2) 69-12-55 Fax: 69-39-79
Web: us-embassy.eldjazair.net.dz.

ANGOLA
Rua Houari Boumedienne No. 32, Luanda
Tel: [244] (2) 347-028/345-481 Fax: 346-924

BENIN
rue Caporal Bernard Anani, Cotonou 2012
Tel: [229] 30-06-50 Fax: 30-14-39
Web: amemb.coo@intnet.bj.

BOTSWANA
P.O. Box 90, Gaborone
Tel: [267] 353-982 Fax: 356-947
E-mail: usembgab@global.co.za

BURKINA FASO
602 Avenue Raoul Follerau, Ouagadougou 01 B.P. 35
Tel: (226) 30-67-23 Fax: (226) 30-38-90
Web: amembouaga@ouagadougb.us-state.gov/

BURUNDI
Avenue Des Etas-Unis , Bujumbura B.P. 1720
Tel: [257] 22-34-54 Fax: 22-29-26
E-mail: @bujumburab.us-state.gov.

CAMEROON
rue Nachtigal, Yaounde B.P. 817
Tel: (237) 23-40-14 Fax: 23-07-53
Web: yaounde@youndeb.us-state.gov.

CAPE VERDE
Rua Abilio Macedo 81, Praia, C.P. 201
Tel: [238] 61-56-16 Fax: 61-13-55

CENTRAL AFRICAN REPUBLIC
Avenue David Dacko, Bangui B.P. 924
Tel: [236] 61-02-00 Fax: 61-44-94

CHAD
Ave. Felix Eboue, N'Djamena B.P. 413
Tel: [235] (51) 70-09 Fax: 51-56-54
Web: paschallrc@ndjamenab.us-state.gov.

DEM. REPUBLIC OF THE CONGO
310 Avenue des Aviateurs, Kinshasa
Tel: [243] (12) 21804 Fax: (88) 43805

REPUBLIC OF THE CONGO
The Brazzaville Embassy Office
is co-located in Kinshasa
Tel: [243] (88) 43608 Fax: (88) 41036

COTE D'IVOIRE
5 rue Jesse Owens, Abidjan 01 B.P. 1712
Tel: [225] 20-21-09-79 Fax: 20-22-32-59

DJIBOUTI
Plateau du Serpent, Blvd, Djibouti B.P. 185
Tel: [253] 35-39-95 Fax: 35-39-40

EGYPT
8 Kamal el-Din Salah St., Garden City Cairo
Tel: [20] (2) 355-7371 Fax: 357-3200

ERITREA
Franklin D. Roosevelt St, Asmara
Tel: [291] (1) 120004 Fax: 127584

ETHIOPIA
Entoto St. P.O. Box 1014, Addis Ababa
Tel: [251] (1) 550-666 Fax: 551-328
Email: usembassy@telecom.net.et.

GABON
Blvd. de la Mer, Libreville B.P. 4000
Tel: [241] 762-003/4 Fax: 745-507

THE GAMBIA
Fajara, Kairaba Ave, Banjul P.M.B. 19
Tel: (220) 392-856 Fax: 392-475

GHANA
Ring Road East - P.O. Box 194, Accra
Tel: [233] (21) 775-348 Fax: 776-008
Web: http:www.usembassy.org.gh.

GUINEA
rue KA 038, Conakry B.P. 603
Tel: [224] 41-15-20 Fax: 41-15-22
Web: www.eti-bull.net/usembassy

KENYA
Mombasa Road
Nairobi
Tel: [254] (2) 537-800 Fax: 537-810

LESOTHO
P.O. Box 333 , Maseru 100
Tel: [266] 312-666
310-116 Fax: E-mail: amles@lesoff.co.za.

LIBERIA
111 United Nations Dr., Mamba Point Monrovia
Tel: [231] 226-370-380 Fax: 226-148

MADAGASCAR
14 & 16, rue Rainitovo Antsahavola, Antananarivo 101
Tel: [261] (20) 22 21257 Fax: (20) 22 34539

MALAWI
P.O. Box 30016, Lilongwe 3
Tel: [265] 783-166 Fax: 780-471

MALI
rue Rochester NY
Bamako B.P. 34
Tel: [223] 22-54-70 Fax: 223712
Web: ipc@usa.org.ml.

MAURITANIA
rue Abdallaye, Nouakchott B.P. 222
Tel: (222) 25-26-60 Fax: 25-15-92
Web: aemnouak@opt.mr.

MAURITIUS
(Also COMOROS & SEYCHELLES)
Rogers House (4th Fl.) John Kennedy St, Port Louis
Tel: [230] 208-2347 Fax: 208-9534

MOROCCO
2 Ave. de Marrakech , Rabat PSC 74
Tel: [212] (7) 76-22-65 Fax: 76-56-61
Web: http://www.usembassy-morocco.org.ma.

MOZAMBIQUE
Avenida Kenneth Kaunda 193, Maputo
Tel: [258] (1) 49-27-97 Fax: 49-01-14
Web: usacomm@mail.tropical.co.mz

NAMIBIA
Ausplan Building 14 Lossen St. , Windhoek
Tel: [264] (61) 221-601 Fax: 229-792
Web: www.usemb.org.na.

NIGER
rue Des Ambassades, Niamey B.P. 11201
Tel: [227] 72-26-61 Fax: 73-31-67
Email: usemb@intnet.ne.

NIGERIA
2 Walter Carrington Crescent, Victoria Island, Lagos
Tel: [234] (1) 261-0050 Fax: 261-9856

RWANDA
Blvd. de la Revolution, Kigali B.P. 28
Tel: (250) 75601/2/3 Fax: 419-710-9346
Email: amembkigali@hotmail.com.

SIERRA LEONE
Walpole and Siaka Stevens Sts, Freetown
Tel: [232] (22) 226-481 Fax: 225-471

SOUTH AFRICA
877 Pretorius St., Arcadia Pretoria 0083
Tel: [27] (12) 342-1048 Fax: 342-2244

SUDAN
Sharia Ali Abdul Latif, Khartoum
Tel: [249] (11) 774611 Fax: [249] (11) 774137

TANZANIA
140 Msese Road, Kinondoni District, Dar Es Salaam
Tel: [255] (51) 666010-5 Fax: 666701
Web: usembassy-dar2@cats-net.com.

TOGO
rue Pelletier Caventou & rue Vauban, Lome B.P. 852
Tel: [228] 21-29-91 Fax: 21-79-52
Web: ustogo1#caf•.tg.

TUNISIA
144 Ave. de la Liberte, Tunis-Belvedere 1002
Tel: [216] (1) 782-566 Fax: 789-719

UGANDA
Parliament Ave, Kampala
Tel: [256] (41) 259792/3/5 Fax: 259794

ZAMBIA
Independence & United Nations Aves, Lusaka
Tel: [260] (1) 250-955 Fax: 252-225

ZIMBABWE
172 Herbert Chitepo Ave, Harare
Tel: [263] (4) 250-593 Fax: 796487
Email: amembzim@africaonline.co.zw.